AMERICAN COMMUNITY BEHAVIOR

Jessie Bernard

AMERICAN COMMUNITY BEHAVIOR

••••••••••••••••

REVISED EDITION

HOLT, RINEHART
AND WINSTON · NEW YORK

Library of Congress Catalog Card Number: 62-15691
20883-0112
Printed in the United States of America

Preface

There is, we are told by those responsible for our defense, a technological revolution every three to five years. The rate of revolution may not be this rapid in our way of thinking about how societies function, but it is rapid enough to make a difference between a sociology book published in 1949, as the first edition of this book was, and one published in 1962, as this one is. The theory of organization, the theory of conflict, the processes of industrialization, the nature of third generations, the nature of power structures, the nature of underdeveloped areas, the nature of direct action—these are only a few of the areas that have come under scrutiny and analysis in the last decade and a half. Despite the rapid increase in our knowledge, however, I have still found the underlying structure of the original edition of this book a useful one.

In the 1940's, when the first edition was in gestation, I was concerned that in a world in which war, strikes, revolutions, rebellions, riots, alarms, and counteralarms were endemic, most sociology curricula gave little recognition to their existence. It was usually not until a student reached upper-level courses that theoretical analyses of such phenomena were offered to him. Introductory textbooks were giving a declining emphasis to conflict and competition. Having myself cut my sociological eyeteeth on that great classic *Introduction to the Science of Sociology* by Park and Burgess—which devoted more than a fourth of its space to competition, conflict, accommodation, and assimilation—this seemed to me distinctly a disservice to students. The first edition of this book was an outcome of my concern.

I still find the most realistic approach to an understanding of modern life in the image of man actively engaged with the problems engendered by competition and conflict, no sooner reducing them to manageable proportions by harnessing them institutionally than new ones emerge. Action, behavior, process, interaction are the keywords.

Many questions had to be answered in designing the book. In what context should the data be presented? After much deliberation the solution selected was a community approach. The book is designed not as a professional how-to-do-it manual for social-work specialists in community organization nor for intergroup specialists nor for planners. It is designed for anyone who is going to have anything to do with community life. It seems to me to include a bare minimum of what participants in community programs ought to know.

Any course that is more than merely factual and descriptive will be a problems course. The problems may be theoretical, they may be political, they may be technical. In this book the problems are problems in the sense of being "issues."

The approach is also institutional, not in the static sense of merely describing substantive areas of community life but in the more dynamic sense. That is, this edition attempts to show how institutional norms—laws as well as customs and mores—influence, if not determine, human interrelationships in the several substantive areas.

As in the first edition there is a minimum of borrowing of psychological interpretations and explanations. The student comes to the study of sociological phenomena with a bias in the direction of such interpretations; he has been subjected to them in the mass media as well as in other academic courses. He tends to find psychological interpretations simpler and often more appealing than sociological ones. The minimization of psychological frames of reference is not intended as a derogation of the contribution of psychology but as an upgrading of sociological points of view.

As in the first edition also, the concrete materials used to illustrate sociological processes are considered intrinsically important in and of themselves. I feel that the student should know not only the processes at work but also the results that they produce in the contemporary world.

Every author of a sociological textbook must face the agonizing decision of what to emphasize and what to exclude among literally dozens of points of view, all of which seem to him indispensable for an adequate presentation of the subject. Equally effective presentations may emphasize theory on the one hand or substantive, factual data on the other. I believe that a text based primarily on theory gives sociology a hothouse, unrealistic atmosphere. Without substantive material the student does not know what the theory is supposed to explain or interpret. An emphasis primarily on subsantive data, however, confuses the student into thinking that sociology is a hodgepodge of scarcely related material. The problem for the author is to find the right "mix." I am convinced that although the sociological framework should always be visible and emphatic, so that the student never loses sight of the fact that he is studying the way societies function, the concrete descriptive, substantive data should never be skimped. The student of sociology should learn how his own society operates; substantive data about specific institutions—enacted as well as crescive—are important.

As in the first edition, the absence of a chapter "defining" sociology—and pointing out how it fits into a logical system of human knowledge, how it differs from other cognate sciences, and its unique and special characteristics—is deliberate. If the instructor feels that such an *apologia* is necessary, he can easily supply it when he has time. But within the restrictions of space imposed upon a book, rigorous selection of contents has to be made. Some textbook writers apply a criterion of selection that reflects a conviction that the discipline itself is the important thing; the author aims to introduce the student to sociology as such. The aim is, if not to make sociologists of all the students, at least to make them aware of sociology itself. Others apply criteria that reflect tradition or convention. This has always been the contents of a conventional text for a college course with a conventional title. No one supposes that there is anything sacred or revealed in these traditional or conventional patterns; it is just that they are more comfortable and unchallenging. The criterion I have used is not in opposition to either of these, but the emphasis is different. It has seemed to me less important to "sell" the science of sociology—now that it is securely established in most curricula—than to "sell" its specific contribution to the student's general education. This emphasis, it seems to me, is in line with current thinking about the presentation of knowledge at the college level. Rather than a formal methodological definition of sociology, then, the student is, in effect, offered here a sample of what sociology concerns itself with, an idea of how the sociologist, as compared with the economist, psychologist, or political scientist, approaches the same subject matter, and a notion of areas that the sociologist alone cultivates. Not what the book could do for sociology but what it could do for the student was uppermost in my mind. I have included what I consider to be the minimum contribution that sociology can make to help understand the community in which he is going to live. This edition is not about sociology, but its sociological framework is, I hope, obvious.

In this edition the concept of community dissociation has been more firmly crystallized. With the help of many generations of students I have given names—"façade" and "parallel dissociation"—to the two types that originally were merely numbered. The several forms that community disorganization may take—functional, normative, schismatic—have been more clearly focused. Violence has been clearly distinguished from conflict as such and has been given more attention than is usual; but the extraordinary importance of this phenomenon has seemed to demand sociological consideration. The theoretical chapters have been expanded somewhat to take into account the great advances of the last decade and a half. For the rest, changes in this edition are primarily in the nature of updating materials; there are also some changes of emphasis.

A final word about value orientation. It was once considered necessary to explain why people live together. Some theorists invoked a gregarious instinct, others a social contract. It is no longer felt that group and community life have to be explained. They are accepted as given, as data. For, as noted in Part I, community life is far older than man. What does have to be explained is not that people live in communities, but how they live in communities. For even a very cursory examination of history—or, indeed, of the current world scene—reveals the bewildering variety of "designs for living" that human beings have evolved for themselves. All are successful to at least the extent that they have survived.

My own values are revealed in this book. My concern is how people live together in democratic regimes—in regimes, that is, that permit freedom for individuals and strive, with whatever success, for equality of opportunity. How do they manage to retain community under these difficult restraints? How do they institutionalize disintegrative forces? How do they maintain community? I believe that it is important to seek answers to these questions. Some of the implications of my value orientation have troubled me. In the first edition of this book, for example, I had no doubts whatever about the undemocratic effects of quotas of any kind. A decade of observation of the processes of desegregation at work, however, has left me much less sure. The concept of "benign quotas," so called, has won my—grudging—acceptance. Other examples might be cited, but this, I believe, is enough.

J. B.

Washington, D. C.
May, 1962

Contents

Part I

Communities and People

COMMUNITY LIFE is older than group life; group life is older than social life; and social life is older than man. The fact that community life is very old, in fact, primordial, does not imply that it is characteristic of all animal forms. Some animals are "solitary"; that is, they do not live in communities or in groups. Some live in groups but do not form communities. And it certainly cannot be maintained that animals who live in communities are higher or lower in the evolutionary scale than those who do not.[1]

Biologists speak of plant and animal communities in forests or in ponds. One-celled animals form "groups" of two to conjugate and the "mateship," temporary or permanent, is one of the most primordial of groups. A primitive kind of social life is characteristic of certain insect communities, as a fairly complex kind is of communities of mammals. Like primates today, our ancestors lived in communities, in groups, and had a fairly developed social life even, no doubt, before they became human.[2]

[1] For an excellent discussion of community, group, and social life among animals, see N. Tinbergen, *Social Behavior in Animals* (London: Methuen, 1953).

[2] Marshall D. Sahlins, "The Social Life of Monkeys, Apes and Primitive Men," in Morton H. Fried, *Readings in Anthropology*, Vol. II: *Cultural Anthropology* (New York: Crowell, 1959), pp. 186-199.

But human communities are not the same as plant or even animal communities; they are *sui generis.* From an ecological point of view, to be sure, man does belong to the animal "community," along with insects, mammals, and other species. (Indeed, ecologists often remind him of the upsetting—it has been called cancerous—effect he and his techniques have on this planet, which we must all share.) Man, however, unlike other animals, lives not only in territorially defined communities, but also in a world of shared and collective values imbedded in institutions (Chapter 1). And it is this world of institutionalized values that distinguishes human communities from all others. This book will deal for the most part with the effect such institutionalized values have on the behavior that goes on in communities.

The relationships between and among men are profoundly influenced by the nature of the communities they live in (Chapter 2). Our concern in this book will be primarily with the behavior that takes place in modern, for the most part urban, communities, but a brief glance at historical trends is offered to place the discussion in perspective.

1

The Nature of Community

As ordinarily used the term "community" connotes territoriality. It refers to people who have living space, and hence many shared interests, in common. The locale may be narrow, as in a small hamlet; or it may be broad, as when the whole United States or even the entire earth is thought of as a single community. The essential point is that many living forms share a common locale, however restricted or extensive. That is, we usually mean a local, spatially, or geographically, defined, community when we use the term.

But territoriality, important as it is, is not the only or even a necessary criterion of community among human beings. Community is also conceived of social-psychologically rather than territorially. We speak thus of a "quest for community" and we speak of the opposite of community in this sense as "alienation," even if the people who are "alienated" share the same living space. Both dimensions—spatial and social-psychological—must be considered in any discussion of community.

The Significance of Territoriality

Territoriality is a basic fact even among animals far below man in the evolutionary scale. Among birds, for example, boundary lines have been called invisible cages. And among gibbons territorial "rights" are vigorously defended against trespass. As a result, each group is locked in its own territory by surrounding groups and any migratory movements are blocked according to the strength of the groups resisting at these boundaries. Analogous and similar territorial phenomena are reported for other animals also.[1]

The significance of territoriality for community lies in the fact that propinquity in and of itself has great influence on the way people relate to one another; it affects the way they accommodate differences, the way they

[1] N. Tinbergen, *Social Behavior in Animals* (London: Methuen, 1953). See also C. R. Carpenter, "Territoriality: A Review of Concepts and Problems," in Anne Roe and G. G. Simpson, eds., *Behavior and Evolution* (New Haven: Yale University, 1958).

work together. The mere fact of propinquity tells nothing, of course, about the nature of the relationships between and among the people involved. It may be warm and intimate or it may be cold and formal. It may be co-operative, it may be divisive. But the fact of propinquity has great implications for the nature of the interaction between or among the social units which share a common area. As it will be emphasized in this book, a shared locale is basic to many forms of conflict. If or when it is possible for one of the parties in a conflict situation to leave or be removed from a locale, the conflict may be obviated. It is precisely because this is so often impossible that conflict occurs. It is the hard fact of having to share a common locale that renders conflict inevitable. Locale is also intimately related to competition, in ways to be discussed in later chapters.

Boundaries and Margins

Territoriality implies boundaries—and boundaries constitute an interesting kind of phenomenon in and of themselves. We have referred to boundaries among animals. Among human beings boundaries often become sore spots in the relationships between groups and communities. Boundary disputes and border incidents have provoked wars between groups from time immemorial, from gang wars on city streets to international wars on all continents. The drawing of boundaries after major wars has been a fundamental problem for peace negotiators. Sometimes wrong boundaries have been sources of much friction, as in the case of many in modern Africa.

It is not only external boundaries, vague or precise, that are significant in intergroup relations; boundaries within the community are also important. As with external boundaries, some of these are "natural" as in the case of ghettoes, Black Belts, and immigrant settlements; others are formally decided upon and may be political—as in the case of voting or police precincts and wards—or functional as in the case of zoning ordinances. Sometimes the formal boundaries are manipulated so as to control group relationships, as when the city of Tuskegee redefined its boundaries to exclude almost all of the Negroes.

Not all intracommunity boundaries, to be sure, are territorial in nature. Some are lines circumscribing not physical space but social relationships. Groups are said to "draw the line" at admitting certain people. These boundary lines, however, real as they are, are not our concern at this point.

Margins differ from boundaries in that they cover a wider area on each side. They are significant because it is at the margins that interaction between members of different groups is more likely to occur. People at the margin are exposed to more conflicting types of stimuli; they are less protected. Many kinds of relationships are different at the margin from those farther toward the center. Marginal areas are likely to be in transition. The term "marginal man" was coined to describe the person who shares two communities, often at home in neither.[2]

The Determination of Boundaries

Because of their importance in affecting intergroup relations, boundaries have to be understood by all concerned. The boundaries of a community may be either political or "natural" or both. Political boundary lines are legal, fairly clear-cut—at least in theory—and deliberate, the result of decisions. They are important to administrators, since administration is spatially limited. But for purposes of understanding community behavior and action, they are often irrelevant.

Natural community boundary lines are crescive, that is, they just grow up. They are discovered rather than, like political boundary lines, decided upon. Sometimes political and natural community limits coincide; more often perhaps, they do not. Indeed, one of the major problems of administering modern communities is the lack of conformity of political boundaries to natural ones.

If they are not based on decision, how can the natural boundaries of communities be discovered? The answer depends, of course, on what criteria are being used to define the community. These may be very simple, such as community identification, or very abstract, such as common planetary interests.

For rural communities one may simply ask people which community they belong to. It is assumed that the limits extend as far as there are people who feel they belong to it. Or one may ask leading citizens to locate the centers and boundaries within the community.[3] More sophisticated is the technique developed many years ago based on market behavior or social participation. The addresses of all farmers who patronized certain local centers for trading or other purposes were plotted on a map. A line was then drawn around these points, thus delimiting the natural open-country community.[4]

Such simple techniques do not suffice, however, for large and complex communities with far-flung boundaries, like modern cities. One criterion for determining boundaries of such communities has been based on the

[2] E. V. Stonequist, *The Marginal Man* (New York: Scribner's, 1937). The concept was first formulated by Robert E. Park.

[3] Linden S. Dodson and Jane Wooley, *Community Organization in Charles County, Maryland*, Bulletin No. A 21, University of Maryland Agricultural Experiment Station, 1943. In this instance the community center coincided with the places where the high schools were located.

[4] C. J. Galpin, *The Social Anatomy of an Agricultural Community,* Agricultural Experiment Station of the University of Wisconsin, Research Bulletin No. 34, Madison, Wisconsin, 1915. Community in the sense that it is delineated in this way is not always unequivocal. People may trade in one center, but attend church in another and send their children to school in still another.

influence exerted by the city. It has been assumed that the influence of a city extends, albeit with diminishing intensity, as far as its newspapers circulate; the radius of the urban community is then measured by the circulation of its daily newspapers.

In recent years, as we shall see, cities are tending to grow together, forming enormous megolopolises, with far-flung boundaries. It is not easy to determine on the basis of any single criterion where one ends and the other begins. The tremendous changes in process at the present time render the old criteria and techniques for delineating even rural community boundaries anachronistic, let alone urban ones.

Boundaries and Common Interests

A more abstract criterion for determining community boundaries is one based on common interests. Boundaries so defined are relative. Sometimes the common interests are fairly obvious. Residents in a city share such important interests as traffic control, schools, streets, sewers, and police, fire, and health protection. For other purposes the metropolitan district becomes the community. If the factories close down in a large city, for example, it is not only residents of the city itself who suffer; thousands of people in surrounding towns and villages who serve that city's inhabitants suffer also. For still other purposes the so-called megolopolis becomes the community; loss of transatlantic shipping business to the Great Lakes megolopolis affects people in the Atlantic megolopolis. States, artificial as their boundaries are, become communities when we consider the common interests of the inhabitants. The people of Massachusetts have common interests as opposed to those, let us say, of the people of South Carolina. The several regions of the nation, too, have many common interests. Indeed, much of American history has been interpreted in terms of the relationship among these large regional communities; historians often speak of the agricultural South and West as contrasted with the industrialized Northeast, intimating the community of interests in these several regions. The nation itself is the locale of a community when we consider its role in international affairs. There is now evolving in Europe a supernational community, the Common Market area consisting of Belgium, the Netherlands, Luxembourg, West Germany, France, Italy, and Great Britain. The boundaries are based on decisions with respect to common economic interests and are not natural in the crescive sense of having just grown up; but they are presumed to be natural in a functional or logical sense. In a certain sense the Communist bloc is a community, as is the rather amorphous unit called the West.

Do all the peoples of the world have enough common interests in the form of common enemies—insects, germs, weather, poverty, ignorance, fallout—to constitute a true community? In 1959 the Rockefeller Report stated that the goal of American foreign policy should be "a community of diverse peoples, cemented by a recognition of law, resting upon a wide range of regional and international institutions." And students of strategic conflict conclude that the logic of modern warfare is such that nations have more in common than in conflict.[5] The locale of such a community is, then, the entire globe.

Community and Conflicting Interests

Community, as bounded by shared values and common interests, is easy to conceive, however far-flung the physical or territorial boundaries may be. But community as bounded by conflicting interests is more difficult to conceive. It is only in recent years, in fact, that we have been made aware of community as related to conflicting interests. We now recognize that individuals or groups are sometimes held in a kind of vise such that the success or failure, wisdom or folly, effectiveness or ineffectiveness of any decision or policy of one individual or group depends on the decisions or policies of others. The community inheres in the interdependent nature of their decisions.

There was a time when conflicting interests could destroy community. Dissident elements seceded or withdrew or were extruded from the locale and community no longer existed between or among the former elements. This is no longer always possible. Thus in international relations, for example, isolation is no longer a feasible policy. No great nation can withdraw from the world community. They are bound to one another not only by common interests but also by conflicting interests. All policies have to be evaluated in terms of the effect they will have on opposing nations. Whenever the decisions of one group must be made with the knowledge that they will influence the decisions of another group, community of this kind exists. The boundaries must be drawn to include opponents as well as those who share our interests.

Community in this sense, in brief, may be based on a common interest which is not at all a result of common values. One recent conflict theorist states the situation as follows:

> . . . in referring to a "common interest," I do not mean that they must have what is usually referred to as a similarity in their value systems. They may just be in the same boat together. They may even be there only because one of them perceived it a strategic advantage to get in that position—to couple their interests in not tipping the boat. If being overturned together in the same boat is a potential outcome, given the array of alternatives available to both parties, they have a "common interest" . . . "Potential common interest" might seem more descriptive.[6]

[5] Thomas C. Schelling, *The Strategy of Conflict* (Cambridge, Mass.: Harvard, 1960), Chapter 1.

[6] Schelling, *op. cit.*, pp. 11-12.

This conception of community—so far removed from the traditional one which tended to have sentimental overtones—is not very congenial to people who like to equate community with warm and loving human relationships; but it has thrust itself upon us with remorseless urgency. The only alternative to community is isolation or destruction of one party.

The Attenuation of Territoriality As a Dimension of Community

We have been emphasizing the territorial aspect of community because it has a profound effect on the relationships of people. But when, as we saw above, the boundaries of communities become world-wide, the strictly territorial dimension has become so attenuated as to be almost meaningless.

Community among human beings is possible without territoriality, as evidenced, for example, by gypsies and by Jews in the Diaspora. It was primarily with the advent of agriculture that territoriality came to acquire its fundamental importance in community.

In an agricultural society an almost mystical relationship is felt to exist between a people and their land. They are felt to belong together. Enemies may destroy people but they cannot take the land. It cannot be alienated. People develop passionate attachments to the soil, to their homeland. They love its rocks and rills, its templed hills. Community is thus deeply rooted in place.

Industrialization has had a profoundly revolutionary effect on the territorial aspect of community. Arnold Toynbee has suggested, in fact, that territoriality as the basis of community, which was so intrinsically a part of agricultural societies, is in modern times becoming anachronistic. Local communities, he suggests, may become merely housekeeping units designed to look after utilities and other services; and the passionate attachments that used to be associated with locale, he predicts, will pass away. The communities we will feel we really belong to, he thinks, will be those people with whom we share a common religion, no matter where they may live.[7] Locale, in brief, will be psychologically unimportant. Even within local communities today the concept "communality" has been proposed for "an interest-circle characterized by the social nearness of members whose places of residence may be widely separated . . . , its members . . . [belonging] not because they share a place of common residence or are identified with the same community, but simply because they share like interests . . ."[8] We hear also of the community of scientists, or of lawyers, or of physicians; or of the financial community or the community of believers.

Increasingly, then, with industrialization the locality or territoriality aspect of community becomes, as Toynbee suggests, attenuated and the

[7] *Issues,* September, 1960. Present reference, *Time,* Sept. 19, 1960, p. 68.

[8] Bessie McClenahan, "The Communality, the Urban Substitute for the Traditional Community," *Sociology and Social Research,* 30 (March-April, 1946), p. 267.

essential benchmark of community comes to be common interests quite independent of territorial boundaries. The implications of this change in the nature of community are profound, although we shall not explore them all in any depth. But the behavior we are to discuss in this volume occurs in any kind of community, whether defined in terms of territoriality or in terms of common interests.

Community As People and As Place: Springdale

It is certainly true that as far as the individual is concerned locale is no longer the fundamental fact it used to be. An industrialized society does not have the same relationship to the land as that characteristic of an agricultural society, and the attitudes and values of the individual reflect this change. Still, communities do exist in space; people do live on land, wherever their interests may lie. And communities in the physical sense have an existence of their own, no matter how people feel about them. They maintain their identity quite apart from any specific generation of people living in them at any given time. Generations of people, in fact, sweep through communities, alter them, but leave them with identities of their own.

Here, for example, is Springdale:

> During the decade of the Thirties . . . while city cousins returned to the township to live off the land or double-up in the old homestead, some of their own cousins left for the city in search of better prospects. Some farmers moved to the village while villagers moved to the farms. Strangers and outsiders bought up small plots of land over the countryside and built shacks to live in. The shack people became a social element in the town. Some were villagers who went into the country and squatted on untended land. Others were descendants of old and once proud "farm families" who never left the land; the old homestead had become a shack through a slow and gradual process of economic poverty and social decline. . . .
>
> World War II opened up a new era of prosperous agriculture. . . . Regional industries were expanding. . . . To the ranks of a small group of village industrial workers was added the labor pool left over from the Thirties. . . . Industrial workers moved into the township in search for places to live. . . .
>
> The social life of the community took on new dimensions and was revitalized. "Newcomers" with new ideas, many of whom worked in other places, sat side by side with newcomers of a generation ago and descendants of original settlers. Polish sons had married Yankee daughters. Farmers and industrial workers and socially outcast shack people were neighbors side by side. . . . New as well as old Springdalers were living through a new world of experiences in an environment whose social past is documented by abandoned country graveyards and one-room schoolhouses.[9]

The people ebbed and flowed; but the community of Springdale itself

[9] Arthur J. Vidich, and Joseph Bensman, *Small Town in Mass Society*. Anchor Books (New York, Doubleday, 1960), pp. 13-15.

remained as an entity in its own right. In a similar way people come and go in New York, Chicago, San Francisco, but the communities themselves, whether loved or hated, continue with identities of their own. Whatever the nature of the allegiance the people feel, the physical community itself persists.

Any alumnus visiting his Alma Mater five years after graduation can document the same processes. There are new buildings. There are new faculty members. There is a wholly different college generation. Even if there are no new buildings or faculty members, things are different. A new generation "owns" the campus now. Each generation sweeps through the college, changing it while being changed by it. But the college retains its own identity.

The Collective Value Dimension of Community

Territoriality is common to both human and animal communities. But only human communities are characterized by values. Any study of community behavior must begin with them.

Values—individual or collective—are considered good or right and therefore to be desired and bad or wrong and therefore to be rejected. They are always quantitative in the sense that some are more or less desired than others or all are equally desired. They reflect, that is, a scale of preference.

Collective values are more than the sum, even the weighted sum, of individual values. Like territorially defined communities or like language —which they resemble in many ways—values seem to have an existence of their own, quite independent of the specific individuals who share them. They have spatial distributions, just as physical phenomena do. Slavery or ethnic values or nationalism, for example, may have clear-cut boundaries. Collective values have life-histories also; they arise, spread, compete, conflict, change, and die out, almost as though they were entities in themselves.

People seem to "inhabit" collective values, as they inhabit spatial areas. They may even leave the physical area characterized by certain collective values, as we shall show presently, and still "inhabit" the collective values. Or, figuratively, the boundaries of the collective values stretch to retain them as they move.

Collective values are taken for granted; they are trite, soporific. They may be explicit or implicit. If they are explicit they may be deduced from a study of professed creeds, ideals, and standards, often stated in official documents. Ideals differ from creeds primarily in that they are stated as goals rather than as *faits accomplis.* (Creeds and ideals are sometimes labeled myths; this does not mean that they are not real. They are as real as anything can be. But they are impervious to objective evidence. People who hold them do so quite independently of what they observe about them.) Sometimes values become embodied in standards, which may be defined as ideals stated quantitatively or formulated in scientific terms. Now instead of a belief in a high standard of living, we have standards of nutrition, housing, sanitation; instead of a belief in equal opportunity, we have standards of education. We have standards for working conditions, health care, and business practices. Sometimes we embody these standards in laws. Sometimes they remain outside of the law, but firmly embedded in community customs. Some are national in scope, others are purely local. In either case standards differ from myths in that they can be dealt with operationally. We can determine whether or not we conform to standards.

Implicit values do not appear in public documents or statements. They may never even be put into words; they are implied in behavior. They are operative nevertheless. They can be delineated only by studying the actual behavior of people. What are their goals as revealed in what they do? What do they reward? Competition, as we shall see later, is one way a community registers its values. The way funds are allocated to competing demands in a tax budget reveals a community's values, as, indeed, the budget of organizations and individuals reveals theirs. Values are revealed in the choices communities make among competing alternatives: for example, closed schools rather than desegregated schools; inadequate schools rather than indebtedness by bonds; lynchings rather than court trials; the family system rather than equality of opportunity.

Explicit and implicit values do not necessarily coincide. They may, in fact, be quite different, as our discussion of community dissociation in Chapter 27 will point out. But the fact that there is often a wide gap between explicit and implicit values does not mean that explicit values may not exert a compelling influence. Sometimes whatever individuals may feel, when a time comes that requires them to stand up and be counted they find they cannot renege on the ideal.

Each individual who shares a collective value acts on the assumption that others will act in accordance with the collective value. Behavior is based on such shared expectations that others will feel, think, and behave in certain ways. People who have shared collective values in this sense build their lives on the premise that they can depend on others to judge people and events according to collective values, whether they approve of these values or not. From this fact flows the ability of collective values to coordinate behavior.[10]

THE COORDINATING FUNCTION OF COLLECTIVE VALUES

A major function served by collective values is precisely one of coordinating the behavior of many people, whether or not they are in direct communication with one another. "Everybody" behaves in a certain way because "everybody" expects "everybody" to do so.

[10] Schelling, *op. cit.*, pp. 67, 89, 92 ff., 135, 172, 283 ff., 289, 294 ff.

The coordination game probably lies behind the stability of institutions and traditions and perhaps the phenomenon of leadership itself. Among the possible sets of rules that might govern a conflict, tradition points to the particular set that everyone can expect everyone else to be conscious of as a conspicuous candidate for adoption; it wins by default over those that cannot readily be identified by tacit consent. The force of many rules of etiquette and social restraint, including some (like the rule against ending a sentence with a preposition) that have been divested of their relevance or authority, seems to depend on their having become "solutions" to a coordination game: everyone expects everyone to expect everyone to expect observance, so that nonobservance carries the pain of conspicuousness. Clothing styles and motorcar fads may also reflect a game in which people do not wish to be left out of any majority that forms and are not organized to keep majorities from forming. The concept of *role* in sociology, which explicitly involves the expectations that others have about one's behavior, as well as one's expectations about how others will behave toward him, can in part be interpreted in terms of the stability of "convergent expectations," of the same type that are involved in the coordination game. One is trapped in a particular role, or by another's role, because it is the only role that in the circumstances can be identified by a process of tacit consent.

A good example might be the *esprit de corps,* or lack of it, of an army unit or naval vessel, or the value system of a particular college or fraternity [or community, such as Springdale referred to above]. These are social organisms that are subject to a substantial rate of replacement, but that maintain their own peculiar identities to an extent that does not seem to be accounted for entirely by selective or biased recruitment. The individual character of one of these units seems to be largely a matter of convergent expectations—everyone's expectation of what everyone expects of everyone—with the new arrivals' expectations being molded in time to help mold the expectations of subsequent arrivals. There is a sense of "social contract," the particular terms of which are sensed and accepted by each incoming generation.

It should be emphasized that coordination is not a matter of guessing what the "average man" will do. One is not, in tacit coordination, trying to guess what another will do in an objective situation; one is trying to guess what the other will guess oneself to guess the other to guess, and so on ad infinitum. The reasoning becomes disconnected from the objective situation, except insofar as the objective situation may provide some clue for a concerted choice. The analogy is not just trying to vote with the majority, but trying to vote with a majority when everyone wants to be in a majority and everyone knows it.[11]

So smooth is such coordination on the basis of collective values that it is often difficult to distinguish behavior resulting from it from organized conspiracy. The organization which goes under the name of "Mafia," for example, depends on such collective values to a large extent; it does not therefore need much formal organization in order to act in a concerted way. The behavior of its members is coordinated by their collective values. It is a case of "everybody" knowing what "everybody" is going to do in a pinch and acting accordingly. The so-called "clannish" behavior of ethnic groups illustrates the same thing. Much of the criticism directed against conformity

[11] *Ibid.,* pp. 91-94.

implies that individuals are being coerced into certain actions; in fact, they may be acting as they do because they really share the collective values which coordinate group or community behavior. For ordinarily collective and individual values do coincide. People accept the values of their community without even thinking about them.

But sometimes they do not. And nothing illustrates better the nature of collective values than these negative cases. Such cases illuminate the power of collective values to coerce individuals.

A southern girl, for example, describes her experience at a party in a northern city at which Negroes were present, as follows:

> I found it not at all difficult to accept them socially, much to my surprise. In that atmosphere it seemed very natural. I talked to them and felt no discomfort at all. Then a girl I had known at (a Southern) college showed up. Everything changed the minute I saw her. Somehow or other we infected one another with prejudice. We became self-conscious about the Negroes and couldn't talk to them as social equals again.

A collective value—racism in this case—not even shared by the two young women themselves re-instated the southern pattern in their relationship with Negroes.

Another illustration, this time from a Jewish boy: "I never felt self-conscious about ordering ham when I was with non-Jews; but when Jews were present, even emancipated Jews like myself, I felt self-conscious about it and hesitated to do it."

One woman reports: "When my former husband and I wanted a divorce we had to leave our home community. We just couldn't have faced our friends; they didn't accept divorce. Everyone would have felt terribly ill-at-ease." Members of ethnic groups have similar experiences. If there are only one or two in a community they may behave as other members of the community do. But when the number reaches a "critical mass" the ethnic values assert themselves and an ethnic community emerges in which individuals are coerced to conform to ethnic norms. Communists, it is stated, understand the coercive nature of collective values and thus always arrange it so that those who are to be exposed to outside values are accompanied by fellow-Communists.

Collective values, then, may be coercive, often even over-riding individual values in the sense of making it costly to defy them. People do things they would prefer not to do and would not do in another setting. Actually, however, the likelihood is that collective values are accepted by the individuals whose behavior is shaped by them, that they are approved of as well as consented to.

Values As an Explanatory Concept

Values help explain behavior. Psychological concepts like motivation, drive, tension tell us what the mechanisms are that activate individuals.

But they do not tell us the direction this activity will take. The psychological and physiological equipment for action of one individual is set into operation by the promise of money; the same equipment in another individual is left unmoved by money, but goes into operation immediately at the promise of fame. The sociologist takes it for granted that the individual has certain psychological equipment, that is, he can be motivated, he will be active. What the sociologist is interested in, however, is the organization and channeling of this motivation. With the same psychological and physiological equipment, some peoples are motivated to reject pork as part of their diet, others accept it. One could study inherited reflexes or other individual mechanisms of motivation and learning forever and never understand asceticism, martyrdom, or other valued forms of behavior. For understanding behavior—both rational and nonrational—the concept of value is invoked.

This leaves the nature of values themselves to be explained. Why are some things preferred to others? Geographic, climatic, technological, economic, political, and social factors have all been invoked to answer this question. None alone is completely adequate. We accept them as given, as data, appealing where necessary to historical explanations to account for them.

The history of the West records the life story of scores of collective values. For thousands of people they were supreme values, the most-to-be-desired thing of all.[12]

Values are of major significance because they find expression in institutions, and as such, channel and direct behavior. They serve to select certain stimuli out of the welter of confusing stimuli that impinge upon us and thus to define situations for us. They help create the image of the world we live in so that people who have differing values interpret identical phenomena differently.

VALUES IN AMERICAN COMMUNITY LIFE

Over a period of 150 years, we are told, several thousand foreign commentators attempted to distil the essence of American values.[13] Scores of social scientists spend their lives researching and interpreting them.[14] And

[12] Racism, feminism, ethnocentrism, Pan-Arabism, Buddhism, Protestantism, humanism, idealism, materialism, totalitarianism, Fascism, Nazism, capitalism . . . The use of "ism" implies an almost cultist value. The list could be vastly extended but these are probably enough to indicate the number and variety that characterize the values of human communities.

[13] Henry Steele Commager, ed., *America in Perspective* (Mentor), p. x.

[14] Robin M. Williams, Jr., *American Society* (New York: Knopf, 1951), pp. 350 ff.; Margaret Mead, *And Keep Your Powder Dry* (New York: Morrow, 1942); *American People* (New York: Norton, 1948); and Clyde Kluckhohn, *Mirror for Man* (New York: McGraw-Hill, 1949); John A. Beery, *Current Conceptions of Democracy* (New York: Teachers College, 1943).

community leaders often try their hand at formulating them also.[15] The results do not always agree, although, as one foreign observer noted, despite the heterogeneity of values of different ethnic and racial, occupational and class groups in our society, there is "a strong unity . . . and a basic homogeneity and stability in its valuations." The seeming chaos of American life fell into order for him when he viewed it in the light of a common creed.[16]

> Americans of all national origins, classes, regions, creeds, and colors have something in common: a social *ethos,* a political creed. It is difficult to avoid the judgment that this "American Creed" is the cement in the structure of this great and disparate nation. . . . There is no doubt that these ideals . . . of the essential dignity of the individual human being, of the fundamental equality of all men, and of certain inalienable rights to freedom, justice, and a fair opportunity . . . are active realities. . . .[17]

Unless one has actually scrutinized the literature on American society it is difficult to realize the tremendous preoccupation revealed in it with the conditions of freedom and equality.[18]

So much, then, for the two dimensions of community—territoriality and shared and collective values. There are other aspects which are of fundamental significance also. They have to do with the nature of the relationships among people in communities and the effect they have on personality. It is to a consideration of these aspects, then, that we now turn our attention.

[15] David Lilienthal, quoted in *American Community Behavior* (New York: Dryden, 1947), p. 72; ACTION (American Committee to Improve Our Neighborhoods), "You—and Urban Renewal," *New York Times,* Oct. 11, 1959, Section 10, p. 18; and, most recently, a committee selected by President Eisenhower, which published *Goals for America* in 1960.

[16] Gunnar Myrdal, *An American Dilemma* (New York: Harper, 1944), pp. 1.

[17] *Ibid.,* pp. 23-24.

[18] For an analysis of American institutions in terms of freedom and equality, see Jessie Bernard, "The United States" in Arnold M. Rose, ed., *The Institutions of Advanced Societies* (Minneapolis: University of Minnesota, 1958), pp. 592-676. The concern of sociologists is not with freedom but with the constraints on freedom; not with equality but on the limitations on equality. The sociologist is preoccupied with all the forms which nonfreedom may take, such as the lack of freedom which goes with close group ties, the lack of freedom which the very existence of institutions implies, the lack of freedom which community imposes on individuals. Similarly the sociologist is concerned with all the forms which inequalities may take—in opportunity, in rewards, in position. The sociologist, in brief, studies the vast system of controls which operate to limit the freedom of human beings and the processes which differentiate and stratify them, resulting in superiorities and inferiorities rather than equalities. In these preoccupations, it should be noted, he shows how greatly he himself is a product of the values of his community.

2

The New World

This world of ours is a new world, in which the unity of knowledge, the nature of human communities, the order of society, the order of ideas, the very notions of society and culture have changed, and will not return to what they have been in the past. What is new is new not because it has never been there before, but because it has changed in quality. One thing that is new is the prevalence of newness, the changing scale and scope of change itself, so that the world alters as we walk in it, so that the years of man's life measure not some small growth or rearrangement or moderation of what he learned in childhood, but a great upheaval.[1]

What Industrialization Has Done to Community Relationships

Primitive communities had kinship ties as well as living space in common. They shared a common blood bond. They had the same ancestors. This common biological heritage, bolstered by magic—the totem—made for especially close and, in fact, indissoluble, ties.

Few if any modern communities in industrialized societies are so closely integrated. The nearest approach would be in fairly isolated religious communities or in certain peasant communities where modern technologies have not yet been introduced. For the most part, however, industrialization and urbanization wipe out, or at least reduce, tribal bonds and substitute altogether different kinds of relationships among people. Industrialization releases people from the engulfing ties that keep them rooted in their native communities; it attenuates territoriality, as we saw in Chapter 1, and renders mobility possible; it destroys ancient limitations to individual movement.

Auguste Comte, who invented the term sociology, was one of the first to report the changes taking place in European society. Carlyle spoke of the disintegration of old relationships and the substitution of what he called the cash nexus between and among men. Karl Marx used the same terminology, pointing out that the bourgeoisie had destroyed feudal ties

[1] J. Robert Oppenheimer, "Prospects in the Arts and Sciences," reported in the *New York Times*, Dec. 27, 1954.

and left "no other nexus between man and man than naked self-interest, than callous 'cash payment.' "[2]

A German sociologist, Ferdinand Tönnies, contrasted the old kind of social relationship on the basis of what he called *Gemeinschaft* (community) with the new kind of relationship which he called *Gesellschaft* (society). Sir Henry Maine, student of the history of law, pointed out that whereas in the past men had been related to one another on the basis of status, they were now related on the basis of contract. Other social observers, such as Frédéric LePlay and Émile Durkheim, reiterated the same refrain. Community in the old sense was being supplanted by a new kind of relationship.[3] There was general agreement among these observers that a tremendous revolution was taking place in the relationships among men. But there was a difference of opinion with respect to its value.

Freedom!

Some analysts viewed the changes as liberating to the individual; he was now free from the old kinship and status bonds that had held him down, immobilizing him; he could now move freely from place to place and also up—as well, of course, as down—the social ladder. Individual, change, progress, reason, and freedom were key concepts in their thinking.[4]

> All of these words reflected a temper of mind that found the essence of society to lie in the solid fact of the discrete individual—autonomous, self-sufficing, and stable—and the essence of history to lie in the progressive emancipation of the individual from the tyrannous and irrational statuses handed down from the past. Competition, individuation, dislocation of status and customs, impersonality, and moral anonymity were hailed by the rationalist because these were the forces that would be most instrumental in emancipating man from the dead hand of the past and because through them the naturally stable and rational individual would be given an environment in which he could develop illimitably his inherent potentialities. Man was the primary and solid fact; relationships were purely derivative. All that was necessary was a scene cleared of the debris of the past. Industrialization would perform this task.[4]

As it was organized in the nineteenth century industrialization demanded that individuals function as individuals; they had to be able to move about. They had to be independent; they had to be self-reliant; they had to have initiative. Individuals sewed tightly into a web of community relationships could not have performed the innovating functions of entrepreneurship demanded by industrialization. The liberation of the individual was therefore glorified.

[2] *Communist Manifesto,* Section 1.

[3] For an illuminating analysis of the process here referred to, see Robert A. Nisbet, *The Quest for Community, A Study in the Ethics of Order and Freedom* (New York: Oxford, 1953).

[4] *Ibid.*, p. 4.

Freedom?

On the part of others, however, there were misgivings. Auguste Comte viewed the breakdown of old social structures with concern and advocated the development of a new religion based on science to reweave broken social bonds; he wanted to reconstruct the old community but on a—to him—firmer base. He felt—as Toynbee does still—that religion was the only way to reorganize community, so he projected a new version of a Catholic church based on science rather than on revelation. On the part of some there was a glorification of the "folk" and they looked back nostalgically to the warmth and security of the old pre-industrialized communities of the past.[5] They viewed the changes brought about with industrialization as isolating of the individual, as destructive of the bonds of community, as exposing the individual to many hazards without the protection of community support. "It is impossible to overlook, in modern lexicons, the importance of such words as disorganization, disintegration, decline, insecurity, breakdown, instability, and the like."[6] The end result of the dissolution of old community ties is described as alienation; men today are viewed as a lonely crowd attempting to escape from freedom in a quest for community.

Alienation

The concept of alienation is not a new one. It can be found in the works of Plato, Seneca, and Augustine.[7] It is in some ways a counterpart to the Christian concept of being "lost" or "unredeemed" or cut off from God. It implies an estrangement from one's fellows. Adjectives like unattached, marginal, lonely, or isolated are often used to describe alienated persons. If alienation is an old phenomenon, however, in its present form and alleged extent it is—historically speaking—new. It has become one of the commonest characterizing epithets applied to modern man.

Karl Marx popularized the term and used it to describe what had happened to the industrial worker when he became, in effect, merely a cog in the industrial process. Since that time "alienation" has come to be used by many other people to refer to any kind of malaise they find in modern man resulting from the destruction of pre-industrial community. It has been used, for example, to refer to feelings of powerlessness, of meaninglessness, of the necessity of unapproved behavior, of isolation, and of self-

[5] The fallacy of this image of community is discussed in George M. Foster, "Interpersonal Relations in Peasant Society," *Human Organization*, 19 (Winter, 1960-1961), pp. 174-178.

[6] Nisbet, *op. cit.*, p. 7.

[7] *Ibid.*, p. 46.

estrangement.[8] A word that, in effect, "covers the waterfront" seems to have little scientific value. While recognizing that "alienation" does, indeed, refer to a complex phenomenon of modern life, we shall not rest much of our analyses or interpretations on it. The preoccupation of commentators and observers of the current scene with the concept of alienation is almost as important as the concept itself.

The Quest for Community: Togetherness, the Lonely Crowd, Escape from Freedom

The term "togetherness" gained much popularity in the 1950's; it reflected a widespread wish to restore some of the warmth and security which, it was believed, went with community in the past. The "lonely crowd" is a term used to refer to individuals, freed from the old kinship and local ties of the past, who now seek a new way of relating to one another. They are not governed in their behavior by tradition, as were members of preindustrialized communities; nor are they directed by early internalized norms, as were the rugged individualists of the nineteenth century; they are, rather, directed by their peers.

Another response to the circumstances of community breakdown has been called an escape from freedom.[9] It is argued that human beings cannot bear the isolation, alienation, and anxiety that accompany individuation. They seek to overcome the loneliness of atomization either in the embrace of totalitarian organizations or in compulsive conformity. The enormous appeal of fascistic movements, of Nazism, and even of Communism, has been interpreted in terms of the profound satisfactions they offer to people who long for the community bonds which modern society denies them.

Where there is widespread conviction that community has been lost, there will be a conscious quest for community in the form of association that seems to prom-

[8] As a feeling of powerlessness, alienation refers to the expectancy or probability held by an individual that his own behavior cannot determine the occurrence of the outcomes he seeks. "There's nothing I can do about it" is the way it looks to the person alienated in this sense. The seat of power seems far away; the individual feels he can have little influence on the course of events, even those that affect him closely. As meaninglessness, alienation refers to the lack of clarity in what one ought to believe; the alienated individual has no established and stable expectancies on which to predict the outcomes of behavior. Alienation in the third sense is based on the feeling that socially unapproved behavior is required to achieve given goals. As isolation, alienation refers to the acceptance of values out of accord with those of a given society. Those who are alienated in this sense are the people who are not comfortable or at ease in their own community. They have different values, values which are not appreciated by those about them. Alienation as self-estrangement refers to the loss of intrinsic meaning or pride in work, as in the case of the worker who works only for his pay check or the housewife who cooks just to get it over with. See Melvin Seeman, "On the Meaning of Alienation," *Amer. Sociol. Rev.*, 24 (December, 1959), pp. 783-791. This analysis is based on the three concepts of reward value, behavior, and expectancy.

[9] Erich Fromm, *Escape from Freedom* (New York: Holt, Rinehart and Winston, 1941).

ise the greatest moral refuge. . . . It is the image of community contained in the promise of the absolute, communal State that seems to have the greatest evocative power.[10]

It can scarcely be denied that the above analyses are correct. There has, indeed, been a revolutionary change in the nature of human relationships as a result of the changes brought about in community or social bonds by industrialization. And as viewed through the sophisticated eyes of social scientists the implications have been widely ramifying.

As viewed through the eyes of the man on the street, however, the implications have been somewhat different. Here the focus of interest is not in great historical trends and their repercussions but rather in contrasts between contemporary rural-urban types. A great nostalgia for what has seemed like an idyllic rural past has haunted people until well into the twentieth century.

The Great Nostalgia

Most of the human species still live in rural communities. But in the West this is no longer true. In the United States, for example, the proportion of the population who lived in rural areas fell below one-half in the census of 1920 and by 1960 the proportion was down roughly to about one fourth.[11] (If only farm population is included, the proportion would be less than one eighth.) But for a long time after 1920 rural values persisted and remained the standards by which all community life was judged. Urban ways seemed somehow wrong or bad.

Human beings, as we have just noted, have not been living in urban communities very long. Cities are therefore still an issue; people are either for or against them. Those who like cities find their influence to be good; those who dislike them find their influence, on the contrary, to be bad. Until recently the latter seemed to outnumber the former. We are only now learning to recognize the fact that pre-industrial communities were not the idyllic havens of our nostalgic dreams. The security, belongingness, and sympathetic rapport which we have imputed to them were no more characteristic of them than of life today.

Since we cannot make on-the-scene studies of pre-industrial communities of the past, we must depend on studies of rural communities today. One anthropologist brings together studies of peasant communities in Mexico, India, Peru, Italy, Slovenia, Egypt, and China. Far from peaceful idylls these reports reveal: feelings of personal insecurity, brittleness in interpersonal relations, fickleness and undependability, suspicion, distrust, intragroup tension and hostility, friends viewed as luxuries that the people

[10] Nisbet, *op. cit.*, p. 33.

[11] Donald J. Bogue, *The Population of the United States* (New York: Free Press, 1959), p. 29.

cannot afford, malicious criticism, endless squabbles passed down from generation to generation, and fierce quarrels.[12]

Nor does a comparison of rural and urban communities in our own society today suggest that one is better suited to human needs than the other. To many people the term "rural community" connotes a community made up of family farms in a rich agricultural area—say, Ohio, Wisconsin, or Iowa—just enough mechanized to eliminate the worst drudgery but not mechanized enough to transform the farm into an agricultural factory. There are pleasant chores, rewarding work, fragrant odors in the kitchen, cooperative programs with neighbors—a wholly entrancing picture. The city, on the other hand, is a depressing, smoke-ridden, treeless slum with only an occasional beauty spot to relieve the otherwise unbearable gloom.

Those who decried the changes which accompanied urbanization were not, like the analysts referred to above, concerned with alienation but rather with the deterioration of personality that cities represented to them. Cities were called "consumers of population" because their birth rates did not satisfy the requirements for reproducing them; city people were full of guile, slick; they were not stable and hence could not be trusted with power.

As a matter of fact, it is impossible to contrast "rural" and "urban" personality types. There are so many kinds of rural communities and so many kinds of urban communities that one generalization can scarcely cover them all. The kinds of forces that shape the personality of a child on a prosperous Iowa farm are probably more like those in certain cities than they are like those which shape the personality of a child on a cotton plantation or in a factory farm in California or Arizona. The Iowa child goes to a well-equipped consolidated school which is equal to an urban school. He has access to an active church. His clothes are like those of city children. He reads the same books and magazines; he listens to the same radio programs and records, views the same television shows. The plantation and the factory-farm child may never have a chance to attend Sunday school. Poverty, isolation, and deprivation stunt personality development. How, then, can we lump all these children together as "rural" and get meaningful results?

Cities, similarly, differ greatly. A child who is reared in, say, Glendale, California, or Winnetka, Illinois, has an environment quite different from that of a child raised in New Bedford, Massachusetts, or Gary, Indiana. New York is very different from Omaha, Nebraska. Within the city itself, an "urban environment" can mean a wealthy suburb or an industrial slum.

For all these reasons most generalizations about rural-urban differences have circumscribed validity. It takes a very sweeping generalization to show statistically significant differences between a group which on the one hand must include sharecroppers, plantation workers, migratory workers, owners of thousand-acre factory farms, as well as ranchers, dairy farmers, sub-

[12] Foster, *op. cit.*, pp. 175-177.

sistence farmers, fruit growers, and gentlemen farmers, and on the other hand must include automobile workers in Detroit, independent businessmen in Memphis, bankers anywhere, carpenters, day laborers, and schoolteachers.

Some of the differences commonly attributed to rural-urban groups turn out to be occupational. For example, the "individualism" which is said to characterize the farmer is probably no different from the same individualism of the independent businessman in the city. The farmer is said to be fatalistic because he is at the mercy of forces over which he has no control, such as the weather. City people may just as well be characterized as fatalistic because they too are at the mercy of forces over which they have no control, such as recessions, inflations, and other man-made calamities which may be just as devastating as natural calamities. (Indeed, it was precisely man's feeling of helplessness or powerlessness in an industrial setting that characterized Marx's conception of alienation.) If we wish to isolate the factor of "ruralness," we must hold constant other factors. We should compare the big-business farmer with the big-business city man; we should compare the migratory worker with the unskilled city worker; we should compare the small, independent farmer with the small, independent businessman in the city. Such factors as age, race, and region would also have to be equated. Then, and only then, can we separate the factor of rural-urban differences *per se,* uncomplicated by occupational factors.

As we have become accustomed to cities and as the proportion of people living in urban communities has increased, many of the old generalizations about rural-urban differences have been challenged. With respect to mental health, for example, the data are by no means as clear-cut as we once supposed. Thus schizophrenia, supposed to characterize those possessing few and loose ties with their fellows—allegedly an urban condition—has been found to be commoner in rural communities than we had supposed, and commoner there than other psychoses. For all kinds of insanity, it has in the past been found that institutional commitments were higher for urban than for rural communities.[13] Yet a study of persons admitted to hospitals during 1940 in Ohio showed that the rate of admission was highest for the thirteen predominantly rural counties.[14] The Selective Service System, furthermore, reported higher rejection rates for farmers than for nonfarmers in World War II.

The urban personality is sometimes characterized as callous. It is certainly true that callous behavior does occur in cities. Newspapers often report incidents such as this: in a New York subway one night, two thieves systematically robbed an intoxicated man while other passengers looked

[13] *Patients in Hospitals for Mental Disease: 1933* (Washington, D. C.: Government Printing Office, 1935).

[14] *Health and Human Resources in Rural Ohio* (mimeographed, Columbia, Ohio, 1944), p. 10. Present citation, Melvin Seeman, *loc. cit.*

on, doing nothing by way of protest; or, an elderly woman slipped down the stairs of an elevated station, falling all the way down, where she lay stunned and gasping while people stared at her without moving to help her.

But the rural personality can also be callous to human suffering. The harshness toward migratory workers in California has been documented before a Senate committee. When farmers made up their minds to break a strike, they did it "in good style, with rubber hose and fan belts," and felt very pleased with themselves.[15] Lynchers, often rural, are callous to human suffering too.

As a matter of fact, callousness to suffering in both urban and rural people is a very old phenomenon indeed. It is probably characteristic of the primitive community's reaction to the stranger. It was common enough in Jesus' day to call forth his parable of the Good Samaritan. What we have, essentially, is repudiation of the stranger or member of the out-group by members of the in-group. In land-anchored communities this sort of behavior was simple and clear-cut, for geographic and psychological propinquity coincided. One lived with his in-group and the outsider was literally as well as figuratively on the outside. In a modern city, on the other hand, and sometimes in a rural community, this relationship is blurred. Members of the in-group still tend to retain their hostility to the outsider. But the outsider lives next door to them. The citizen in a modern urban community may live in the midst of strangers—people who do not belong to his in-group. The kind of thing we described above may result. When outsiders become entangled with an in-group in a rural community, the same sort of thing may happen. It is not necessarily a rural-urban contrast; it is an ingroup-outgroup contrast.

In some rural communities the warmth and hospitality we associate with in-group relationships remain intact, if not in the idyllic form of the nostalgic dream. Church picnics, socials, and gatherings of all kinds often reveal the unaffected kindness and spontaneous generosity which we like to consider typical of rural life. But city people respond generously to appeals to their sympathies also. When a child in St. Louis required hundreds of skin grafts to keep him alive until his own skin could be used to repair a damage produced by burns, the response of men willing to give their own skins to save this little boy was more than adequate. And these were representative of the "urban" type of personality.

In view of these conflicting points of view, it is not surprising to find one study reporting that the personality traits of rural people are not notably different from those of city people.[16]

[15] Paul S. Taylor, *Adrift on the Land* (Public Affairs Pamphlet, No. 42, 1940), p. 24.

[16] William H. Sewell and Eleanor E. Amend, "The Influence of Size of Home Community on Attitudes and Personality Traits," *Rural Sociology,* 8 (April, 1943), pp. 180-184.

Despite the convergence in attitudes between rural and urban persons, the old stereotypes persist. And what is more, they find expression in practical policies. In many states across the nation, cities are underrepresented in legislative bodies, and rural areas are overrepresented. There is great reluctance to redistribute representation in legislatures as urban populations increase, a reluctance rationalized on the basis that farmers are more stable and counteract the radical tendencies of cities. It is true that if we analyze rural-urban differences in voting, we find that city people tend to favor "liberal" legislation more than rural people do. They favor better working conditions, labor unions, more equitable distribution of income and wealth, and better school systems. It is not, however, that the rural community makes one conservative; it is simply that the interests of city dwellers demand a good deal of "radical" legislation which seems to be contrary to the interests of the farmer, who feels he will have to pay for it. We know from even a cursory examination of our own history, however, that when farmers have felt legislation to be necessary for their own interests, they have been just as "radical," if not more so, than the city dweller. The contrast between rural and urban personalities so far as political conservatism is concerned is therefore illusory. The farmer is politically conservative when his interests seem to demand it; he is radical under the same circumstances.

Compromise? The Suburban Explosion

One of the most spectacular trends in the evolution of communities is the recent growth of suburbs. In many cases they resemble pre-industrial communities in their ethnic homogeneity. In addition, they tend to be demographically homogeneous; that is, they are likely to be similar in age, education, and class. They are thus antipodal to the heterogeneous city.

Suburbs have been interpreted by one observer of the current scene as "a tacit revolt against the industrial order," as a retreat "from the great problems of the metropolis, and perhaps of the nation, to the more manageable ones of the periphery," and as an effort to have "the best of both worlds."[17] And yet, "having put industrialism and many of its drives behind them, people are still unhappy . . ." and they "look for spurs when life no longer automatically provides them."[18] The suburb is, in brief, no answer to the great "loneliness" or "alienation" of modern man. Despite a homogeneity that "probably tends to maximize interaction on a neighborhood basis, . . . 'kaffeeklatsches,' and almost frantic 'socializing' of the residents of the newer suburban areas"[19] the suburban community does not

[17] David Reisman, "The Surban Sadness," in William Dobriner, ed., *The Suburban Community* (New York: Putnam, 1958), pp. 375, 379, 383, 385, *passim*.

[18] *Ibid.*, pp. 391, 392.

[19] Walter T. Martin, "The Structuring of Social Relationships Engendered by Suburban Residence," *Ibid.*, p. 104.

achieve the fulfillment of the nostalgic dream—a community where everyone is secure, loved, and cherished. The chances are that the dream itself is only an illusion.

COMMENT

In this chapter we have attempted to trace the revolutionary changes which have occurred in the nature of community ties with industrialization, changes which have freed men from status bonds—kinship and territorial—and given them more scope. Undoubtedly the individual has had to pay a price for this. He has had to accept the disadvantages that went with the new forms of human relationships along with the advantages. This he has been reluctant to do. He has harbored a nostalgic dream of an idyllic past, not at all in conformity with the probable facts, and has attempted, in the suburban community, to achieve the "best of both worlds."

Actually industrialization has vastly increased productivity and, hence, wealth. It has thus made it possible for men to be more generous, less mean. Industrialization increases the size of the pie; increases in one person's share do not have to be at the expense of another's share. People can be more open, more candid; they do not have to hide from one another. Abundance reduces the tension; the relationships in the pre-industrial community were probably a good deal more intense than in modern communities—but it is doubtful that they were any more pleasant.

Whatever the relative merits of pre-industrial and modern communities as matrices for human relationships, one thing is certain: the modern community—rural, suburban, urban—is now our home. We have to make the best of it.

Part II

Organization in the Community

A SEARCHING examination of the concept organization can lead into the profoundest reaches of theology and philosophy. Problems of purpose become involved. The oak tree creates shade; ferns flourish in it. Plants use the carbon dioxide given off by animals. The so-called "web of life" is exquisitely organized. The parts are neatly related. This is organization of a fundamental kind. Is there design here? purpose? plan? Theologians in the nineteenth century were convinced that there was. Indeed, the study of such "harmonies" in nature was a fashionable discipline among the clergy, resulting in numerous tracts and treatises on evidences of Christianity designed to prove the existence of Deity. This is a theological approach to the problems of organization. It is of great import; but it is not germane to our interests here.

Nor are the philosophical problems inherent in organization our concern. Does the organization exist "out there" or is it a product of our way of seeing things? Neither the fern nor the oak has any awareness of the relationship between them. Each can be studied independently. Each can exist away from the other. Where, then, does the relationship exist? Is it true, as Immanuel Kant said, that the mind gives form to nature? To pursue such metaphysical problems, interesting as they are, would take us far afield.

The study of organization in one form or another is a preoccupation of many sciences as well as of theology and philosophy. Physics studies the organization of matter; biology studies the organization of cells and tissues; and psychology studies the organization of thought and personality. The social sciences study the organization of political, economic, and sociological phenomena. The study of social organization has, indeed, been said to be the pre-eminent task of sociology.

There are many appropriate approaches to the study of social organization. In a great classic many years ago, an outstanding sociologist, C. H. Cooley, distinguished four aspects of social organization, namely: groups, publics, classes, and institutions.[1] These categories are not really cognate; the first three refer to people, the fourth does not. In human societies, furthermore, the first three exist within a framework of institutions and can scarcely be conceived of independently of the institutional matrix within which they function. Institutions influence, if they do not actually determine, how people group themselves, how publics operate, and how classes are perpetuated. Social organization may also be approached by way of role systems.[2]

Our interest in organization here is limited to an examination of the nature of social organization only as it reveals itself in community life. The approach in Part Two is by way of community structures and systems (Chapter 3) and of order and institutions (in Chapter 4).

[1] *Social Organization* (New York: Scribner's, 1909).

[2] See Jessie Bernard, *Social Problems at Midcentury* (New York: Holt, Rinehart and Winston, 1957).

3

Structures and Systems

Communities Are Structured

Communities are not chaotic, not hit-or-miss, not mere masses, aggregations, or agglomerations of population in a given locale. They are, rather, structured entities. The term structure refers to the underlying "anatomy" of the community, to the more or less stable, that is, slow-changing "mutual relations of the constituent facts or elements of . . . [the] whole as determining its peculiar nature or character," to invoke the dictionary definition. There are several kinds of such "constituent facts or elements" in communities whose mutual relations determine their "peculiar nature or character." They are physical, demographic, and institutional in form and they are basic to any conceptualization of the community. The physical structure has to do with buildings, streets, roads; the demographic structure has to do with the composition of the population; and the institutional structure has to do with the occupations, the industries, and the power, status, and class relationships in the community. All three of these kinds of structure are reflected in the so-called ecological structure or, preferably, the functional structure of the community in terms of land use. Different parts of the community are used for different functions—industrial, commercial, residential—and the resulting pattern has an enormous impact on the relationships among the people themselves.

PHYSICAL STRUCTURE

In the case of a plant community one can map the location of different species and relate this spatial distribution to the nature of the soil, the contour of the land, and other geographic factors. The physical structure of an insect community may consist of underground tunnels, compartments, and corridors, or of surface colonies made up of houses or anthills. The physical structure of a nonliterate human community may consist of thatched huts arranged in some order or of adobe buildings or of tepees or cliff dwellings.

The physical structure of a community is of sociological importance both because it reflects the social relationships which give rise to it, and because it in turn influences and even limits the social relationships which exist within it.

The physical structure of a community reflects the social system within which it arises. Thus

> . . . the medieval borough around market and cathedral, urban counterpart of the manorial village, expressed the high Middle Ages; the baroque capital of parade avenues, palaces, and *places d'armes* mirrored the absolutist national state; the sooty tangle of factory and slum and the residential segregations of the withdrawn squires on the hill in mill towns and mill cities matched the industrial and railroad age. Each community form . . . was unique, just as the age . . . was unique.[1]

Upon this broad base of social relationships, different physical structures may arise, reflecting the industrial specialization of the community. The physical structure of mining communities, for example, is different from that of oil towns; that of mill towns differs from that of sea or mountain resorts or fishing centers.

> The western mining town was rarely well planned, with the result that shaft houses, tunnel entrances, mine dumps, business structures, the shacks of miners, and other constructions are intermingled. Often trees, clear streams, and green meadows are carelessly destroyed; mining towns set amid scenes of great natural beauty are notorious for their nondescript appearance. . . .
>
> The needs for storing and shipment of the varied products from farms give different characteristics to farm marketing centers. On the Great Plains the towering grain elevators that are visible for many miles across the flat country indicate the locating of a wheat shipping station along the railroad. In contrast, in an apple shipping city there are tightly built cold-storage warehouses and low packing houses, from which long trains of refrigerator cars are loaded. Dairy market towns are characterized by milk processing plants, butter and cheese factories, cooperative feed stores, and business houses that stock milk cans, milking machines, and other equipment. Stockyards for loading railroad cars with cattle and sheep for distant markets may be the principal structure in some lonely livestock shipping station in the western range. Potato storage cellars in southern Idaho and Aroostook County, Maine; big sugarbeet factories with feeding yards nearby for fattening lambs and steers, at many points in southern Idaho and Nebraska along the Union Pacific Railroad. . . .
>
> The appearance of a sawmill town is characteristic. The iron stacks of the mill and the big silo-like refuse burner dominate the settlement. Beside the mill is the pond in which the logs are stored, and extending in long rows are the stacks of sawed lumber convenient to the railroad sidings or ocean docks. The town itself is predominantly built of wood and is apt to have a new and somewhat temporary look. . . .[2]

[1] Conrad M. Arensberg, "American Communities," in Morton H. Fried, ed., *Readings in Anthropology,* Vol. II. *Cultural Anthropology* (New York: Crowell, 1959), p. 353. Original paper, *Amer. Anthrop.*, 57, 1143-1162.

[2] Otis W. Freeman, "Natural Resources and Urban Development," *Annals Amer. Acad. Pol. and Soc. Sci.*, 242 (November, 1945), pp. 30-45.

In a similar way the physical structures of college towns, county seats and state capitals, and resort towns show characteristic patterning.

A modern city has an enormously complex physical structure, consisting not only of the many kinds of specialized buildings, of streets, avenues, and boulevards, and parks but also of a vast underground network of sewer pipes, water conduits, cables, subways, parking facilities, and even bomb shelters.

We have emphasized the physical structure of communities as an expression or reflection of social relationships and industrial activities. But it may be a more positive factor itself; it may, that is, itself influence, if not determine, the social relationships within the community.

Different groups and classes, for example, have different orbits within which they move.[3] The physical structure may thus isolate leaders from the problems of the community, as so vividly described by a student of Regional City:

> The location of the men of power in Regional City tends to isolate them from the mass of people in that community. Consequently they are isolated from many of the problems which affect the average citizen. They daily shuttle by automobile between their homes, their work, and their meeting places. The streets over which they travel pass through many "blighted areas," but the sights of poverty are hidden from view, along most of the routes, by relatively new store fronts, neon signs, and the gleaming chromium of the new cars on display along "automobile row". . . . Location *tends* to isolate the men of power from the mass of citizens less powerful than themselves and from community problems.
>
> The professional men . . . take different routes from home to work. Their way runs through an industrial and warehouse area. The store fronts are painted in sombre colors which are smoke-faded, giving the impression of dominant browns and grays. . . . It is true that the professional men turn into pleasanter suburban streets at the end of their homeward journey, but most of the route is depressing to anyone sensitive to social disorder. The smoke pall, grassless yards, unwashed children rolling abandoned automobile tires as hoops, gray dogs, and the bargain clothing emporiums are constant reminders of decisions which press for attention on the leaders and their executors of power in the community. . . .[4]

Physical structure may influence social relationships in another way also. A physical structure, for example, that was functional at one period may, with the passage of time, become dysfunctional. Streets become too narrow for modern traffic; factories built two or three stories high cannot serve modern production methods that require one-story buildings covering a great deal of land; surface transportation gets clogged up. Similarly prisons and hospitals and schools built to embody one set of values and

[3] Evelyn Aaron, Nancy Hoffman, and David Raphael, "Urban Orbits," unpublished manuscript, based on a study of the daily movements of a sample of residents in Altoona, Pennsylvania.

[4] Floyd Hunter, *Community Power Structure, A Study of Decision Makers* (Chapel Hill, N. C.: University of North Carolina, 1953), pp. 21-22.

ideologies survive long after new points of view have arisen and prevent rather than facilitate the implementation of new programs. A good deal of modern urban redevelopment and planning is devoted to ways and means of redesigning the physical structure of cities, not only to render them suitable for modern living but also to influence group relationships. It is argued, for example, by some students of the city that neighborhoods should be designed for all income classes rather than segregating different income classes in different neighborhoods. There is widespread criticism also of the one-class suburb. The argument is that the physical structure of the community should facilitate group relations rather than encourage segregation on class or ethnic lines.

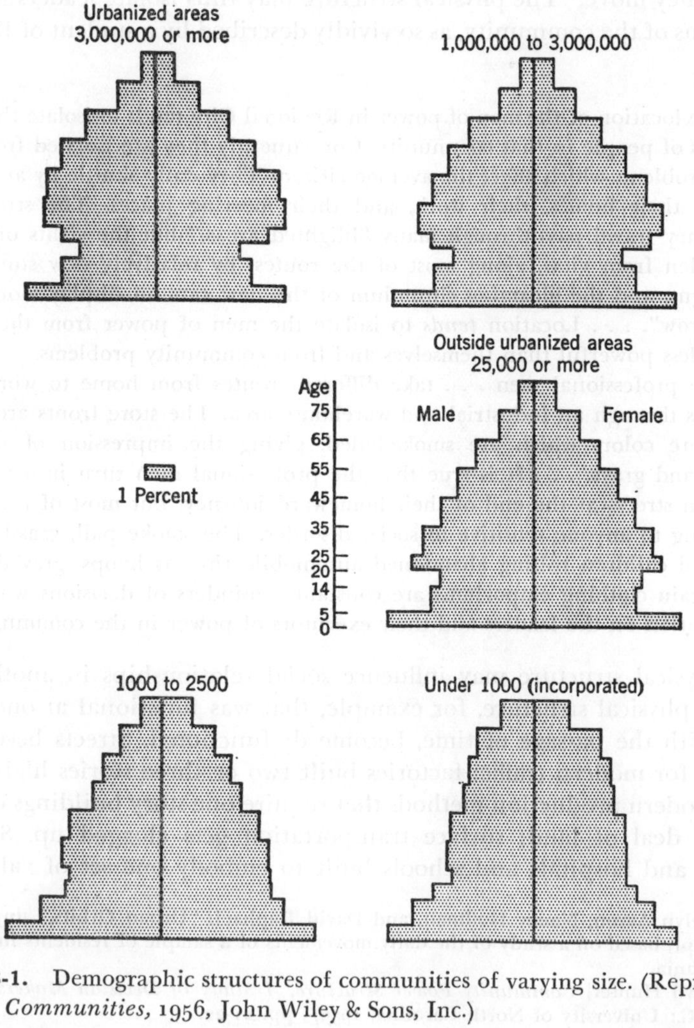

FIG. 3-1. Demographic structures of communities of varying size. (Reprinted with per *Rural Communities,* 1956, John Wiley & Sons, Inc.)

DEMOGRAPHIC STRUCTURE

A community, whether a hamlet or a nation, has a *demographic* structure also. This consists primarily of the age and sex, as shown in Figure 3-1, and also the racial composition of the population. It is usually depicted in the form of a pyramid. Within such a general demographic structure there might well also be substructures of one or more different ethnic or racial components of the community's population. Other elements in the demographic structure have to do with marital status and education.

One can tell a great deal about a community from an examination of its demographic structure. The social consequences of the age structure, for example, are far-reaching. A city or nation with many small children has

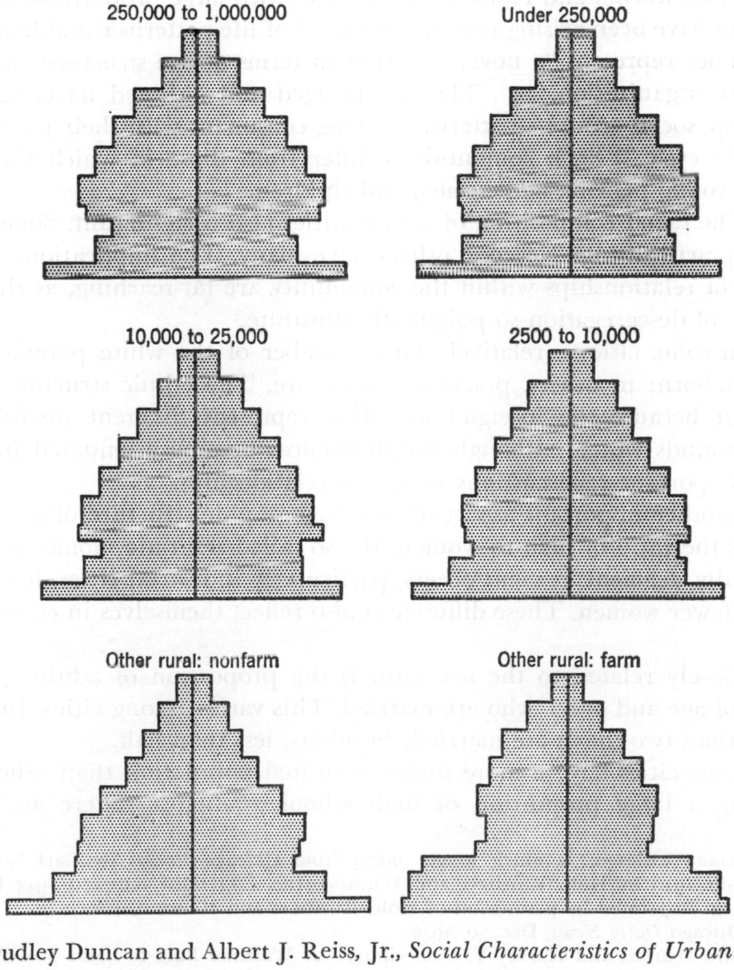

on from Otis Dudley Duncan and Albert J. Reiss, Jr., *Social Characteristics of Urban and*

different problems from those of a city or nation with many elderly people. In a city like Chicago, which Carl Sandburg once described as

> Strong, husky, brawling,
> City of the big shoulders . . .
> Laughing the stormy husky brawling laughter of youth. . . .[5]

the aging of its population has, it is alleged, transformed its personality, so that it was later described as

> Sedate, sedentary, complacent,
> City of the big waistline,
> That is Chicago today.[6]

In California and Florida communities with large proportions of older persons have been arising to create the kind of life-patterns suitable to their age. They represent "a novel situation in terms of age structure and community organization. . . . The middle-aged and old-aged have, and can develop, social groups—patterns of living consonant with their position in the life cycle."[7] Such communities differ from those in which there are many young persons, adolescents, and children.

The racial composition of communities also is significant. Some cities have practically no Negroes, others have many. The implications for all kinds of relationships within the community are far-reaching, as the difficulties of desegregation so poignantly illustrate.

In some cities a relatively large number of the white population is foreign-born; in others, practically none are. The ethnic structure is important because the foreign-born often represent different institutional backgrounds which, although the differences become attenuated in time, have important repercussions in group relationships.

Another important aspect of the demographic structure of a community is the ratio of men to women, the so-called sex ratio. Some cities are markedly deficient in men; others, particularly industrial cities, have relatively fewer women. These differences also reflect themselves in community life.

Closely related to the sex ratio is the proportion of adults (fifteen years of age and over) who are married. This varies among cities. In some, more than two-thirds are married; in others, less than half.

Some cities have a more highly educated population than others, including a large proportion of high school graduates. There are some,

[5] From "Chicago," a much longer poem from *Chicago Poems* by Carl Sandburg. Copyright 1916 by Holt, Rinehart and Winston, Inc. Copyright renewed 1944 by Carl Sandburg. Reprinted by permission of Holt, Rinehart and Winston, Inc.

[6] Chicago *Daily News,* Dec. 30, 1946.

[7] Otto Dahlke, and Harvey V. Stonecipher, "A Wartime Back-to-Land Movement of Old Age Groups," *Rural Sociology,* 11 (June, 1946), pp. 149-152.

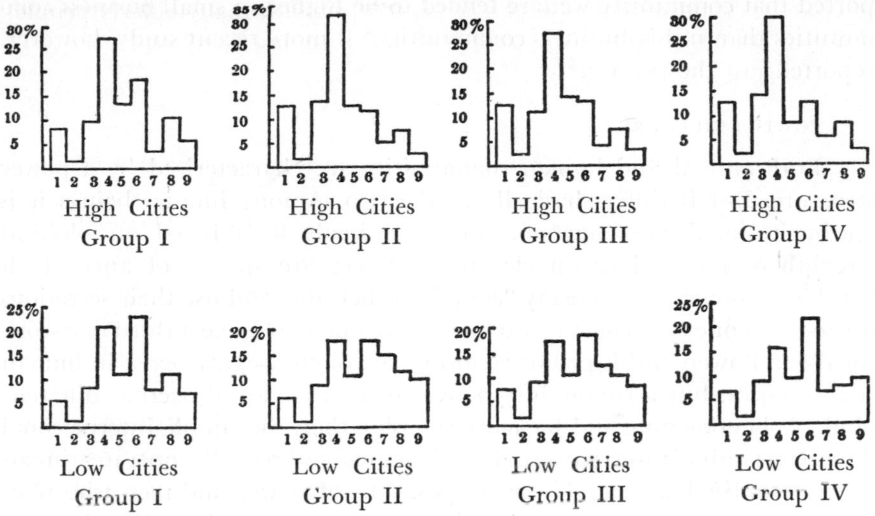

FIG. 3-2. The occupational structure of eight communities. 1. Professional. 2. Semiprofessional. 3. Proprietors. 4. Clerical. 5. Crafts. 6. Operatives. 7. Domestic Service. 8. Service. 9. Laborers. (In the original source "High" and "Low" cities referred to quality of community life, that is to goodness of living conditions; "high cities" had low death rates, good schools, and so forth.) (Reprinted with permission from Paul Bates Gillen, *The Distribution of Occupations as a City Yardstick,* Kings Crown Press, 1951.)

contrariwise, with a large proportion with less than grade-school education. Such variations among communities are as significant as they are among individuals.

INSTITUTIONAL STRUCTURE

Occupational. The occupational structure of communities is a reflection of the way they make their living. In some communities there are many blue-collar workers, in others, conversely, many white-collar workers. Figure 3-2 illustrates the varying kinds of occupational profiles that existed in different cities in the 1940's. Closely related to the nature of the work itself is its organizational setting. In some cities, for example, almost everyone is working for someone else, whether in private industry, as in Gary, Flint, or Birmingham, or in government service, as in Washington. There are marked contrasts also among cities in the proportion of those who are employers of others and those who work for themselves.

Industrial. Both the occupational and the organizational setting of the community are included in the industrial structure. It refers primarily to the size and power of the industrial units. Some communities are characterized by the presence of many small or only moderately large business firms; others are the sites of very large units. One study in the 1940's reported that community welfare tended to be higher in small-business communities than in big-business communities.[8] A more recent study, however, reported just the reverse.[9]

POWER STRUCTURE

Both animal and human communities are characterized by a power structure. But it differs basically in the two. Among human beings it is an institutional phenomenon. Among animals it is based on physical strength or on skill or on cleverness. There are species of ants which "enslave"—some observers say "adopt"—other ants and use their secretions for food. In one experiment, two cats learned how to make a third one work for them. Power in this primitive form may, of course, also exist in human communities; but a community power structure is an altogether different kind of phenomenon, and far more complex than the simple interpersonal dominance-submission pattern found among animals. It operates in an institutionalized setting. There are positions of power and men who wish to exert power must somehow or other come to occupy them. The locus of power in a community may lie in many places—the government, industry, church, union, or any other agency or group. The relationships between and among these concentrations of power constitute a power structure. The people who occupy positions where power is concentrated are sometimes referred to as a power elite.[10]

STATUS STRUCTURE

A structure implies different positions within a general framework. In social structures these different positions are primarily relational in nature and only incidentally spatial. Psychologists have familiarized us with the so-called "peck order" among fowl, which they view as a status structure. In a human community the status structure is variegated; indeed, there are many status structures. Some are based on such criteria as skill, accomplishment, talent. In such status structures, high position is achievable competi-

[8] C. Wright Mills and Melville J. Ulmer, *Small Business and Civic Welfare*. Report of the Special Committee to Study Problems of American Small Business, US Senate, 79th Congress, 2nd Session, No. 135 (Washington, D. C.: Government Printing Office, 1946).

[9] Irving A. Fowler, "Local Industrial Structures, Economic Power, and Community Welfare," *Social Problems*, 6 (Summer, 1958), pp. 41-51.

[10] There is some difference of opinion among students of power structures as to their exact nature. One school of thought views the people-with-power as a single power élite, that is, as fairly tightly integrated, as operating more or less as a single-minded unit, as enjoying a fair degree of solidarity. Marx attributed a high degree of class consciousness also. There are others, however, who feel that there are many power structures and that there is no necessary solidarity among the top people in all of them. One study designed to test this second hypothesis was made in El Paso, Texas. It found that although there was more solidarity in El Paso than in the city of Juarez, across the Rio Grande, the data did "not support a simple model of community power structure in the decision-making process. The responses of the business and political influentials were by no means identical." (William H. Form and William V. D'Antonio, "Integration and Cleavage among Community Influentials in Two Border Cities," *Amer. Sociol. Rev.*, 24 [December, 1959], p. 814.)

tively. But some status structures are based on criteria over which we have no control, such as family or lineage, age, sex, race. Forms of status based on such criteria are said to be ascribed. The kinds of status that are important in human communities—those, for example, based on family, wealth, power—often go together. But they need not always. The poor immigrant may achieve wealth and power also. The status relationships among the several components of a community at any one time are sometimes called the status quo.

CLASS STRUCTURE

There are several criteria of status so closely related as to constitute a *class structure*. Animal communities do not have a class structure in the human sense. It is true, as we have just seen, that animals may stratify themselves into higher and lower status levels as measured by personal dominance or by peck order. But these positions are achieved by each individual; they are not enforced by collective sanctions. There are no lines of succession, no conception of lineage, hence no inheritance of position. The offspring of the dominant male in the jungle does not inherit the position of his father; he has to fight or compete for it. In human societies children are born into certain positions, some higher than others, as we shall see in a later chapter. Even if they rise, the fact that they were born at different levels profoundly influences the rate of ascent. It is the institutionalization of status that is characteristic of social classes in human communities.

The structure of an animal community reflects and embodies individual differences among the members. The class structure of a human community reflects the way it makes its living. For example, a feudal society based on land had one kind of class structure; an industrial society has another. And an automated society will have still another.

The class structure of a community is independent of the specific people who occupy it. The strata which constitute the class structure have relatively great stability; they may last much longer than one generation. It is true that there is, over a period of time, a kind of "circulation of the elite," in the sense that talented people are always working their way up and replacing those at the top; that there is, in effect, a constant stream of people moving through the upper levels of the class structure. But the structure itself, regardless of who occupies it or how they are selected for their positions is fairly stable. Thus for any one generation the positions available in the different levels of the structure are relatively fixed. This means that competition for top positions is restricted by the class one is born into. Life chances are better for some than for others.[11]

[11] A century ago people understood the nature of these social structures without benefit of college courses in sociology. They spoke of their "station" in life. They sought "positions" or "situations" rather than jobs. (Some newspapers still advertise "situations.") They recognized their betters; they knew their place. They knew where they belonged in the social structure as well as they knew where their homes were in the geographic structure of the community.

Community Systems

The concept system has almost as many meanings as the concept community, if not more. In its static aspect it refers to a set of criteria for classification, such as the Dewey system for classifying books in a library or an alphabetical system for filing notes. In its dynamic aspect a system implies movement; it refers to the action and interaction that take place within a structure or between or among structures. Systems may be classified in several ways. One is in terms of the structure within which they operate; thus we would have political, economic, industrial, kinship, ecclesiastical, educational, and the like, systems. (Ethical and moral systems have no specialized structures, but pervade all the structures of a community.) Another classification of systems is in terms of the units involved, such as personality, societal, and cultural systems. Still another classification is in terms of the nature of the controls which guide the activity in a structure. One kind of system may be called a free-flowing system, the other, a system of checks-and-balance.

FREE-FLOWING SYSTEMS

The first type of system may be thought of as the flow of activity through a structure. It is a kind of "flow chart" which guides and directs action. The free-flowing system is channelized behavior. Any particular structure may have several possible channels through which behavior may flow. The system is like a force of traffic police who stand at the several nodal points in the structure and direct some people to go this way and others that way. The school system, for example, provides that children of a certain age, sex, and, in some communities, race, should attend school A. They progress through six or seven years and then are directed to any one of several other schools. At graduation from high school they are again directed either out of the system entirely or on to any one of several institutions of higher learning. The so-called factory system of production channels productive activity one way; the old domestic system channeled it another way. A class system channels upward and downward mobility; if the class structure is rigid and impermeable, we have a closed class system, but if the structure is permeable, so that there are many channels for mobility up or down in the structure, we have an open class system. In extreme form, a closed class system is called a caste system; there is no flow through the structure at all except in the sense that generations may be said to flow through a structure.

CHECKS-AND-BALANCE SYSTEMS

Ecologists sometimes speak of the relationship among organisms in a natural habitat as in a state of balance. If left undisturbed an optimum adjustment between organisms and environment takes place. Whenever anything occurs to upset it, natural forces go into operation to redress the balance.

The classic ideal of our economic system—the so-called "private profit" system—was also one of automatic checks and balances. The theory was that supply and demand would automatically regulate it. If too much productive activity went into making goods the consumer did not want the price would fall, profits would disappear, and the factors of production would be withdrawn from that product; conversely, if not enough productive activity was going into the making of goods the consumer wanted, the price would rise, profits would grow and attract new investment until the product became abundant, and the price would fall. An analysis of American capitalism has pointed out that, quite aside from formal controls, a system of checks and balances does seem to characterize it—not in the market sense of the classic ideal, however, but rather in the control of power. If too much power accumulates anywhere—in government, in unions, in corporations, or even in churches—countervailing power tends to emerge to share, and hence to dilute, the concentrated power.[12] International relations have long been characterized by a system of so-called balance of power or, more recently, of terror. Alliances and coalitions were formed and re-formed in a systematic way to keep any one country from acquiring too much power.

There appears to be something very appealing to many people in this checks-and-balance, or equilibrium, type of system. They like to feel that there are automatic checks at work to keep relationships stable. They want to feel that the status quo is protected from drastic change. They like to feel that there is a fixed or normal way for things to be and that even if for a while something goes wrong, in time everything will be restored to its original state. Most people tend to feel that the world as they knew it in their youth is, somehow or other, the normal way for things to be; the world they see around them is a more or less temporary aberration. After a while things will get back to "normalcy." They like to think in terms of built-in correctives.

"SYSTEMS OF CHANGE"

Neither free-flowing nor checks-and-balance theories provide for change. The function of checks is to restore balance; the original equilibrium returns. Free-flowing systems remain within the channels provided for in the structure. Systems of change are sets of relationships which, though they may check and balance one another, do not lead back to the original equilibrium, but to a different one. So-called philosophies of history often describe such systems. The most famous was Karl Marx's, which stated that every system created or generated the forces which were destined

[12] John Kenneth Galbraith, *American Capitalism* (Boston: Houghton-Mifflin, 1952).

to change it. Industrialization requires educated people; educating people makes them less docile. Ultimately, according to Marx, a stable and fixed system would result; but the heart of his theory for the nineteenth and twentieth centuries was one of constantly emerging change. History was, in effect, a braid made up of different strands, now one was on top, now another; but always there was movement, not fixity.

Most systems in American community life seem to be systems of change. The checks operate not to restore the community to old relationships but to new ones. Groups interact with one another always in the direction of new patterns. There is no fixed or stable "normalcy"; there is only an on-going process. The "good old days" are gone forever.

Implications of Systems for Community Behavior

The implications of the existence of systems are profound. It is extremely difficult, for example, to behave contrary to the system. Systems imply a great deal of functional inter-relationship among parts. There is little room for maneuver outside the system. No matter how much Tolstoi, for example, bemoaned the feudal system in old Russia, no matter how much any single landowner might wish to behave in a more generous way, he could hardly do so by himself. One has to change the structure before he can change the system; they are inextricably related. Sometimes systems provide for the orderly change of structures; but sometimes structures can be changed only by destroying them.

Communities As Social Systems and As Parts of Larger Systems

We referred above to such functional systems as political, economic, industrial, legal, and other kinds of systems. But the term *social* system may cut across any of these. Thus a bank may be part of an economic system; but the bank as a social system is something else again. As a social system it consists of the relationships between or among tellers, janitors, auditors, presidents, customers, and other role performers. A library may be part of a library system, but as a social system it consists again of the relationships between or among cataloguers, accession personnel, reference librarians, borrowers, and so on.

The local community is itself also sometimes conceived as a social system. As such it is thought of as consisting of a set of subsystems—including local government, an economy, an educational system, a recreational system, and so on—which are functionally related to one another, all interacting in such ways that "if one part behaves in a certain way, then other parts will be affected in a specified, predictable manner."[13] This principle

[13] Irwin T. Sanders, *The Community, An Introduction to a Social System* (New York: Ronald, 1958), p. 186.

will be used in explaining and interpreting one form of community disorganization in Chapter 23.

The local community itself, in turn, is part of a larger system—economic, political, religious, or other. For communities are not self-sufficient, autonomous entities, independent and unrelated to other communities. They are integral parts of a larger national community[14]—which, in turn, is itself part of an international community. As a result they are at the mercy of great outside forces that often leave them quite helpless. Here, for example, are people going about their business in a quite satisfactory and satisfying manner. For no reason that they can give, through no fault of their own, the community is disorganized by a catastrophe—natural or man-made—a strike or a new invention that robs its citizens of their jobs. Things happen to communities, as to individuals, that are wholly beyond their control.

The existence of systems operating in structured communities results in order. Even among animals this order can be called a social order. But only among human beings can we speak of this social order as also *normative*. It is at this point that human communities part company with all others. For social order in human communities is institutionalized. Both structures and systems operate within an institutional framework. We turn, therefore, to a more detailed consideration of order and institutions.

[14] O. Dudley Duncan and Albert J. Reiss, Jr., in their volume *Social Characteristics of Urban and Rural Communities 1950* (New York: Wiley, 1956), document in detail the functional relationships among communities.

4

Social Order and Institutions

Social Order

A normative social order, as the term indicates, is an order regulated by norms. That is, it is based on conceptions of right and wrong, proper and improper, acceptable and unacceptable, moral and immoral, legal and illegal, legitimate and illegitimate, conventional and unconventional, tolerable and intolerable, suitable or unsuitable, according to usage, custom, and tradition, or contrary to them. It thus reflects a set of values.

Animal communities do not establish or institute order in their social life; what order there is—and there is a considerable amount of order among animals—results from individual drives, prowess, habits, or species heredity.[1] Collective sanctions are not involved. It is quite conceivable that the same was true for man in his earliest years. And his social life was probably at least as orderly then as that of other primates.

[1] See N. Tinbergen, *Social Behavior in Animals,* (London: Methuen, 1953). The author describes the ways in which various species organize reproductive, parental, group, and fighting behavior, all of which he labels cooperative. He distinguishes two processes by which animal communities arise: one he calls differentiation, because it is essentially an elaboration of the mother-egg relationship; the other he calls construction or integration, since it results from the coming together of independent individuals. "The two processes, differentiation and integration, move in opposite directions; in the former, total dependence of one of the partners develops into a state of mutual cooperation; in the latter, mutual co-operation takes the place of total independence" (p. 104). In general, Tinbergen explains social behavior in terms of "releasers," that is, stimuli highly specialized to release certain correspondingly highly specialized responses in certain animals. Despite his emphasis on "releasers" he does not ignore the fact that "many changes in social structure occur as a consequence of learning processes" (p. 108) which give rise to highly personalized relationships among animals. Clarence R. Carpenter's monograph on the social and community life of the gibbon (*A Field Study in Siam of the Behavior and Social Relations of the Gibbon (Hylobates Lar),* Comparative Psychology Monographs, Vol. 16, 1940, is another illustration of the orderly community life of which primates are capable even without institutions. Reference to pre-human community life is not for the purpose of suggesting that human community life can be interpreted in terms of pre-human factors but, precisely, the reverse. Human community behavior is not determined by biological (which in some cases are chemical) forces; nor even by group forces, as among primates. Social order does exist among pre-human animals; there may even be a large learned component in it; but it is not institutionalized. When sociologists scrutinize such pre-human communities, it is only to determine how much is possible without the distinctive human gift of verbal language and the institutions which it makes possible.

At some time or other in his history man discovered the social order in his own communities, and this discovery was the first step in the process of rendering it normative. With verbal language it could be objectified; it could become abstract; it could acquire a reality above and beyond individual habit. Moral as well as physical controls to maintain it were possible. The young could be socialized not only by physical techniques but also by moral ones; they could be told that a certain thing was wrong in advance, rather than be punished after they had done it. These controls could be established within the young so that the parent did not even have to control its behavior; it controlled itself. The powerful young man did not displace the old king, which he could easily have done, but remained subservient; the old king who could not have fought back with physical force was supported by a complex and tough pattern of collective norms that gave him more than mere physical power.

A social order is a remarkable thing. It has never ceased to produce awe and wonder in those who have observed and studied it. The authors of the oldest written documents in the world looked about them and saw men and women behaving in regular, expectable ways, working, mating, rearing children, respecting authority. They could explain such order only as a divine creation; and, interestingly enough, they discerned the importance of verbal language in this connection.

> It is quite clear that ordered society and organized government had made a great impression on these early thinkers. "Station" or rank and official position and "functions" of government, by which human society maintains itself, were thought to have been ordained by the supreme intelligence and called into being by his word. The practical operations of every-day living, in work and craftsmanship, were in accord with the mandate "which the heart thinks and which has come forth from the tongue."[2]

By this time men could observe their own community behavior. More important, they could judge it.

The highly normative nature of the social order even in early times can be illustrated by such sayings as this one attributed to Confucius: "Extravagance leads to insubordination, and parsimony to meanness. [But] it is better to be mean [and orderly] than insubordinate [and disorderly]." The enormous value which the Jews have traditionally placed on the Law, as prescribed by the Torah or Pentateuch and interpreted in the Talmud, reflects the importance attached to order as a protection against barbarism.

Institutions

A normative social order operates through a complex network of institutions. This statement is a tautology since an institution may itself be

[2] James Henry Breasted, *The Dawn of Conscience* (New York: Scribner, 1933), p. 38.

defined as a complex integration (not an assemblage or aggregation) of norms of behavior, embodying values and regulating the performance of certain functions.[3] The four key words are integration, norms, values, and functions.[4] Leaving the first characteristic to the end, we shall discuss these elements in order.

The elements out of which institutions are built are such norms as: customs, mores, conventions, political rules, laws, charters, constitutions, by-laws, traditions, and the like—to be discussed in greater length below. The values which they embody may, as we pointed out in Chapter 1, vary widely from one community to another; in general they specify what the community considers right or wrong, the thing to do or the thing not to do. They represent human intervention in natural (physical, biological, psychological, and also social—since they are as natural as any other—) processes, themselves value-neutral. The functions which institutions regulate have been classified in many ways; we shall classify them as (1) socialization, (2) selection and/or ordering, (3) accommodation of differences, and (4) norm-violation, all to be discussed in more detail below. The norms which constitute the elements of institutions are not separate and distinct, not "separable entities, but rather phases of a common and at least partly homogeneous body of thought. . . . and it is only by abstraction that we can regard them as things by themselves."[5] They fit one another and "strain for consistency."

It should be pointed out that the intervention of man in natural processes is itself completely natural. It is as natural, that is, for man to attempt

[3] The term "institution" is sometimes used to refer to the physical equipment through which it operates; we thus speak of institutions of learning, penal institutions, and so forth. The term is sometimes used to refer to individual personalities; we say so-and-so has become an institution on this campus or in this community. Social anthropologists do not distinguish between groups or associations and institutions, thus one anthropologist defines an institution as "a group of people who meet together in isolation often enough, regularly enough, and long enough each time, to do something together intensely enough and emotionally enough so that as a separate entity the group builds up its own set of rules, its own internal equilibrium, and its own structure" (Carelton Coons, *Reader in General Anthropology* [New York: Holt, Rinehart and Winston, 1948], p. 604). Sociologists, however, tend to find the distinction between institutions, as sets of norms, and groups or associations a useful and important one. MacIver and Page illustrate the distinction as follows: A state is an association, its constitution, legal codes, forms of government are its characteristic institutions; a church is an association, its creed, forms of worship, and communion are its characteristic institutions; the family is an association, marriage, rules of inheritance are its characteristic institutions; and so on. (MacIver and Page, *Society* [New York: Holt, Rinehart and Winston, 1949], pp. 15-18.)

[4] The concept of need is often embodied in definitions of institutions. Thus Joyce Hertzler speaks of them as satisfying individual wants as well as social needs (*Social Institutions* [Lincoln, Neb.: University of Nebraska, 1946], p. 4). If such a concept is included in the definition, it is important to make clear that the wants and/or needs are those created by institutions themselves. Survival needs were all being satisfied before institutions developed. Related primates survive quite well without institutions. Verbal language made institutions possible; technology made them inevitable. Together they generate all the other needs which institutions now satisfy.

[5] C. H. Cooley, *Social Organization* (New York: Scribner, 1909), p. 314.

to control his physical, biological, psychological, and social world as it is for meteorologic phenomena to produce the weather.[6] Given the kind of creature man is, institutions are not an intrusion on nature.

The Classification of Institutions

The elements out of which institutions are built may be classified according to any one of several criteria. They may be classified in terms of their importance as primary, or pivotal, and secondary, or derivative. They may be classified in terms of the kinds of behavior they deal with as overt (telling us how to behave), and inner, or covert (telling us how to feel or think).[7] They may be classified in terms of the people whose behavior they regulate. They may be classified in terms of whether or not they have formal administrative machinery for enforcement. Or whether they are implicit or explicit, formulated or unformulated. Or in terms of geographical distribution, as American, Russian, and so forth; or in terms of class distribution, as lower, middle, upper. Or in terms of the functions they are designed to regulate, such as reproductive, industrial, political, religious, educational. Each kind of classification has its special value. The major criterion of classification we shall use is in terms of the processes which give rise to them, namely: enacted, crescive, and quasi-crescive.

The Functions of Institutions As Institutions

The functions performed by the existence of institutions may be examined from the point of view both of the individual and of the community. From the point of view of the individual:

> . . . the existence of institutions minimizes the necessity of making choices or solving problems. Cooley has emphasized the saving which they effect for personality by eliminating the strain of too many choices. Many a woman, according to an old illustration, has reconciled herself to an initially unsatisfactory marriage and achieved serenity and calmness because her religion said there was nothing

[6] Some thinkers make a sharp distinction between what they term "natural" and what they term "cultural," or institutional. That the development of institutions introduced a totally new dimension into human life and thus into the biological order is undeniable. But the point here emphasized is that this new dimension is itself wholly natural. The existence of states is as natural as the existence of beehives.

[7] Although specific associations—churches, unions, clubs—often consider it important to standardize the way their members feel and think, such standardization is no longer demanded by communities in democratic societies. Indeed, freedom of thought is one of the fundamental values of such societies. In the Middle Ages, however—and in some totalitarian states even today—communities felt they could not exist if there were heretics or nonbelievers in their midst. The same was true of theocratic New England in the seventeenth century. Most American communities today have learned to live with creedal differences. Even today, however, we do find oaths of loyalty demanded from teachers and others in strategic positions. The institutionalization of inner behavior still seems important to some people.

else for her to do—having no choice she could have no conflict about it. Conversely, not a few women have worn themselves out by divorce and remarriage, seeking a satisfactory relationship which perhaps meant a non-institutionalized one, simply because they were free to do so. If we did not have . . . conventional and customary standards and rules, we would dash ourselves to pieces under the strain of the conflict resulting from constant choice. [The existence] of institutions rests the personality by obviating the necessity for thought or choice or new responses. The girl who has been conventionally reared to the rule that she must never have premarital sexual relations has much less difficulty in meeting the advances of men than the girl raised in an atmosphere less institutionalized in this respect.

The human organism, furthermore, is not always in top form physically. When it is low or depressed or in the down cycle of energy, it needs the support that fixed institutional patterns provide. On the other hand, when it is on the upswing, exuberant, energetic, it also needs the discipline of institutions to prevent it from rash behavior. Therefore, from the point of view of the individual, the institution (1) rests the personality by obviating choice, (2) supports it when it is not in a condition to make fresh responses to its problems, and (3) disciplines it when it is in danger of making foolish ones.[8]

In addition, the existence of institutions makes it possible for each individual to profit from or take advantage of the experience of others.

From the point of view of the community, one function of institutions is that of storing the past, of accumulating experience from the past, as serving, in effect, as banks of past experience; they make man a "time-binding" animal. Institutions also serve such strategic functions as enforcing commitments, both threats and promises, and, most especially, since they embody collective values, they serve a coordinating function, as pointed out in Chapter 1. They make possible the substitution of strategy for violence.

With respect to institutions at least three kinds of questions may be asked, namely: (1) what are the processes which give rise to them; (2) who are the subjects, that is, to whom do the norms apply; and (3) what are the objects of institutionalization, that is, the kinds of behavior for which the norms are designed.

The Processes of Institutionalization

The processes of institutionalization may be viewed from two angles, the collective and the individual. The first point of view emphasizes the processes by which norms of behavior arise in the first place, how they are "instituted," and the second emphasizes how, once instituted, they are built into individuals or how consensus is achieved. Instituting implies innovation; institutionalizing implies securing consent. Institutionalizing is a matter of degree; it may take time. There are no accepted standards for determining when a norm has become institutionalized. The social psychologist

[8] Jessie Bernard, *American Family Behavior* (New York: Harper, 1942), pp. 13-14.

F. H. Allport suggests that at least half of the people involved must conform before a conformity situation may be said to exist. The degree to which a norm is self-enforcing, taken for granted, or conformed to unconsciously is a measure of how well institutionalized it is.

With respect to established norms, to those into which the individual is born, the individual aspects of institutionalization, that is, the process of institutionalizing the behavior of individuals to make it conform to the norms of the community, are usually subsumed under the rubric "socialization." The nature of this process and the problems involved are discussed in Chapter 25. Many agencies are enlisted in the process—family, school, church, police. With respect to newly instituted norms—new laws and statutes—the processes of institutionalizing behavior is more difficult; it involves the "engineering of consent." This will be dealt with in Part Six. Our major concern here, therefore, is with the processes by which norms are instituted, as in the case of enacted norms, or discovered, as in the case of crescive norms, or formulated, as in the case of quasi-crescive norms.

It is quite clear who institutes enacted norms, and the processes have been studied in great detail. Legislatures, kings, councils, committees, commissions, administrative agencies may enact or institute norms. They may take the form of edicts, ukases, proclamations, or of statutes hammered out by representatives of the people. In democratic societies they are usually the result of compromise of some kind or other. Conflicting points of view or factions or groups settle for the best they can get under the circumstances. The result is a norm or statute which attempts to institutionalize behavior in a decided upon way. Such enacted norms are highly purposive. Most bills introduced into our own Congress, for example, like the Constitution itself, contain preambles setting forth in some detail the goals they are designed to achieve. They are forward-looking, guarantors of future behavior.

Not all norms, however, and perhaps not even most of them, are the result of legislative processes. Some just grow up; they are discovered rather than enacted. Although there is some experimental laboratory research on the way sophisticated individual subjects arrive at norms under controlled conditions,[9] we do not know the exact process by which such so-called

[9] Thomas C. Schelling summarizes the work of Muzafer Sherif as follows: "He finds that when no norms exist for a laboratory judgment, they are created by the subjects; and when norms are created for two parties in the same process, each player's developing norm influences the other's. There is a process of genuine learning with respect to values; each side adapts its own system of values to the other's, in forming its own. When the supply of available 'objective' criteria is incapable of yielding a complete set of rules . . . norms of some sort must be developed, mutually perceived, and accepted; patterns of action and response have to be legitimized. In an almost unconsciously cooperative way, adversaries must reach a mutually recognized definition of what constitutes an innovation, a challenging or assertive move, or a cooperative gesture, and they must develop some common norm regarding the kind of retaliation that fits the crime when a breach of the rules occurs" (*The Strategy of Conflict* [Cambridge, Mass.: Harvard, 1960], pp. 168-169).

crescive norms arise and become established in natural communities since they are already old by the time they are discovered.[10] Such consensually created norms are called crescive because they are the result of growth; the term itself has the same root as increase or crescendo. They are backward-looking, conservative, stabilizing. They do, of course, change; but often the change has already taken place before it is recognized.

The first human institutions were probably tacit recognition or normative statements of the relationships human beings found themselves already enmeshed in. The story is told of an African who became the informant for an anthropological linguist studying his language. The African was amazed and delighted to discover that his language had a grammar. He had been speaking it all his life but had never realized the regularity, the organization, the rationale, the structure it had. The same kind of experience characterizes all crescive institutions. We live according to the "grammar" of our community, usually quite unaware of its regularity, organization, rationale, and structure.

[10] Sociologists are not greatly concerned with the origin of crescive norms; they have turned their attention rather to the nature of consensus which is, basically, the bedrock on which crescive norms rest. Early sociologists, however, did feel that some general theory was necessary to explain the emergence of crescive norms, and they turned to some form of natural selection. W. G. Sumner believed the process was "that of trial and failure, which produces repeated pain, loss, and disappointments. Nevertheless, it is a method of rude experiment and selection. . . . The ability to distinguish between pleasure and pain is the only psychical power which is to be assumed. Thus ways of doing things were selected, which were expedient. They answered the purpose better than other ways, or with less toil and pain. Along the course on which efforts were compelled to go, habit, routine, and skill were developed. The struggle to maintain existence was carried on, not individually, but in groups. Each profited by the other's experience, hence there was concurrence towards that which proved to be most expedient. All at last adopted the same way for the same purpose; hence the ways turned into customs and became mass phenomena. . . . In this way folkways arise" (*Folkways* [Boston: Ginn, 1906], p. 2. C. H. Cooley proposed what he called the "tentative process" to explain the origin of crescive norms. He said: "This is no other than what is vaguely known to popular thought as the process of evolutionary selection, or the survival of the fittest, and is also described as the method of trial and error. . . . It is a process of experiment which is not necessarily conscious. That is, the trial of various activities and the guidance of behavior by the result of the trial may require no understanding of what is taking place" (*Social Process* [New York: Scribner, 1918], p. 8) . The fallacy in this line of thinking has been pointed out by many critics. The existence of dysfunctional norms suggests that Sumner's expedience or Cooley's successful experiments were not universally valid. There is no assurance that the trial which succeeded and which was, therefore, accepted was necessarily the best alternative that might have been tried. Sumner himself once pointed out the economic waste of the tabu against cannibalism. And Charles Lamb's story of the origin of roast pig, however apocryphal, illustrates the way wasteful norms might be accepted. The experience of western technologists in underdeveloped areas documents the dysfunctionality of many institutional norms. Efforts to improve the food supply in India, for example, are thwarted by norms which protect the sacred cow; efforts to get rid of malaria are thwarted by religious opposition to the killing even of mosquitoes; efforts to increase the efficiency of getting water by the use of hand pumps are thwarted because of the belief that leather would contaminate the water. Even in our own society customary ways of doing things are not necessarily the best—that is, "the fittest"—ways, as the county agent learns when he tries to substitute contour plowing for the customary way, or as the home economist learns when she tries to improve the customary dietary of people.

Behavior patterns which had become habitual in many individual members of the community as a common reaction of fairly standardized individuals to common situations were discovered and rendered normative. The first social function to be institutionalized may well have been communication. The institutionalization of communication in verbal language then revolutionized all social interaction, adding words to gestures, and making possible the storing of past experience.

Instituted or enacted norms are the creation of individuals and groups; crescive norms are the creation of the "folk." But some norms combine features of both; they are quasi-crescive and there is an interplay between "folk" and individual personalities, so that neither alone may be said to create them; they are joint products. A decision on the part of some human personality is involved.

For illustrative purposes we may imagine a small primitive community of, say, some hundred people. Day in and day out they go about their tasks in a businesslike and matter-of-fact manner, not too different perhaps from gibbons or other primates except that the behavior is now regulated by consensual norms. An outsider might marvel to find strong men submitting to disabilities, a fragile old man exercising great power. With a slight blow, one of the younger men could easily dispossess the older one. Yet he does not. It does not occur to him to do such a thing. For the most part this small community lives and functions peaceably. There is an institutional solution for every contingency. There is not much occasion for discretion or decision or choice, a situation which is the very hallmark of a crescive or consensual situation.

But, being human, the members of this community are different from one another. And these differences may lead to differences in the interpretation of customary rights and duties. On such occasions there is—institutionally created—need, so to speak, for an official grammarian, an official interpreter of the rules. Someone must state what they are. This function is performed by some decision maker.[11]

Two models suggest themselves. In one everybody wants to conform to the norm but a question arises with respect to precisely what constitutes conformity. Zigor, to invent a hypothetical example, wants to marry Chessa, but Lorwa reminds him that Chessa is only the adopted daughter of Saisor, not his blood daughter. There never was any doubt in anyone's mind about the marriage rules in this society until now. Everyone knew exactly who was supposed to marry in which moity; no one ever thought of marry-

[11] In the case of law, this function is performed by a judge. "The Judge . . . [performs] a function not merely subsidiary to the operation of law, but inherent in its very nature. Law exists in order to be applied; and it must be applied through some human agency. If all men apprehended rules in precisely the same manner, if all men were at one about their rights and duties, there would be no need for legal exposition, and indeed, little need at all for "law," as that term is usually understood. But since unanimity is impossible, there arises very early in the development of law the necessity for analysis and application through the medium of the skilled, impartial interpreter. . . ." (Carleton Kemp Allen, *Law in the Making* [New York: Oxford, 1930], p. 73).

ing into a wrong group. But now there is a question. Can Zigor marry Chessa or not? If she were a natural daughter of Saisor there would be no doubt at all. But since she is not, can he? Just what is the rule that covers this specific case? For occasions such as this there must be someone who can interpret the custom, someone who is learned in the customary grammar of this group. In this particular crisis the customs become crystallized. People become aware of them. There is some hitch in observing them and unless provision is made for dealing with the situation there will be great uncertainty and anxiety. It is to perform this function of interpreting the customs, of specifying exactly what they are and how they apply, that, presumably, the profession of judge arose. The judge in preliterate society is someone who remembers way back, someone who has stored precedents in his mind, or someone who knows how to communicate with the gods or spirits for guidance, if necessary, in determining what the rule or law is.

A second model in which personality must inject itself into the operation of rules or norms consists of situations in which there is deliberate deviation or violation of a rule. Until now no one has ever planted yams in the plot beyond the tulip trees; it has remained uncultivated from time immemorial. Now Nessa has dug holes and is planting her yam shoots there. Gorsula challenges Nessa. She cannot do this. It has never been done. Is such a thing right? Is it permissible? Can she get away with this? All of a sudden the group becomes aware of the custom which has kept this land untilled up to now. Who is right? If the group is not to be broken up into divisive partisans there must be someone who can decide whether or not there is a custom regulating the use of this plot of land and whether or not Nessa is violating it. Here again this function of establishing whether there is a custom at all and if so, if it is being violated, is filled by the profession of judge. Whatever he says goes. He is, in effect, a lawmaker. On a more superficial level the same processes are evident in the work of compilers of books of etiquette. Emily Post and Amy Vanderbilt do for convention what the codifier of custom did for law. Authors of dictionaries and grammar books perform an analogous function for language. However performed, or by whom, the function of quasi-crescive processes is to re-interpret the past for the present.

The Products of Institutionalization

It would not be facetious to define institutions as the products of institutionalizing processes. Since we are going to refer to scores of statutes in the course of our discussion of American community behavior, at this point we limit our discussion to three products of crescive processes, namely: custom, mores, and convention. *Custom* is the broadest category; it refers to any norm coming down from the past that regulates fairly fundamental forms of behavior, such as the sexual or racial division of labor, the timing of life rhythms, the use of ceremony or ritual, and the like. *Mores* (singular *mos*) represent a special kind of custom, one that has especially strong sanctions behind it, with a great deal of emotion associated with it, feelings of right and wrong, moral and immoral. Violating the mores is more shocking than is behavior which is merely not customary. Eating human flesh, for example, or nudism, or infanticide. *Convention* is used in two ways. In one way, it refers to norms regulating the amenities, in another, to permitted violation of the mores.

CUSTOM

Customs are so much a part of our lives that we are usually almost oblivious to them. We are so used to them, we accept them so completely that we cannot even see them. They are as omnipresent as the air. They do, indeed, constitute a kind of social atmosphere. And we are as dependent on this atmosphere as we are on air.

Although customs live and express themselves only through human beings, they appear to have life cycles of their own. They arise, spread, reach a peak of power, then subside and fade out. They die and are replaced by new customs. Some live a long time; some are relatively short-lived. Men create and modify them, but they also modify men. Some people are so overcome by the molding power of custom that they become fatalistic. Others realize that men can change customs, and they are more optimistic about controlled change. But it must be admitted that the newcomer is absorbed by the community custom. He may question or challenge it; but if he stays, he assimilates it—or it assimilates him, however one may wish to look at it.

Custom has great inertia. This is well illustrated when a community attempts daylight saving. We are used to waking up at 7:30. We wake up at 7:30 by the clock although by standard time it is 6:30. Once the new plan is put into operation, there is less disturbance psychologically than there would be if we tried to change our schedules, leaving the clock alone.

MORES

Violation of mores seems sacrilegious; they have a sacred kind of sanction. The taboo against cannibalism or infanticide or polygamy or slavery or incest is obviously so fundamental that anyone in any community would be shocked and horrified by a violation of it. The Ten Commandments are a codification of certain of our mores. Family institutions consist very largely of mores. The mores constitute a large part of the institutions of private property.

Mores, like customs, vary from place to place. The Army during World War II felt it necessary to brief soldiers in preparation for exposure to strange ways. They were warned, for example, against trying to date women in North Africa: "Should a respectable woman be found conversing with a man not of the family, scandal would result," they were told. The Army considered it as important to train soldiers to make their way through these foreign ways as through foreign jungles. They needed guides almost as much as pilots needed navigation data about the physical atmosphere into which they were flying.

Even within our own society mores vary from community to community. The sale of alcohol is forbidden in some. In some communities very great exposure of the body is a matter of course; in others, the same exposure would be considered indecent. In some communities it is still against the mores to address a Negro as "Mr." or "Mrs." The play *Tobacco Road* had long runs in some cities, but it was banned in Tulsa, Chicago, Detroit, St. Paul, Albuquerque, and Newark on the grounds of immorality. One of the most dramatic themes in fiction and drama centers about the clash of moral standards in people from different community backgrounds.

Even within a single community mores vary from class to class. Kissing, nudism, petting have quite different moral significance in the several classes.

CONVENTION

The amenities—in clothing, house furnishings, ornaments, entertaining, dress, speech, "social life," the arts—these are, par excellence, the area of convention. This does not mean that convention is unimportant or superficial. It reflects the very ethos of a group, that is, the relative position assigned to one individual in relation to another. In some cultures, for example, there is no virtue in self-effacement. Display and ostentation are encouraged. The Indians of the Pacific Northwest had a so-called "potlatch" ceremony, the purpose of which was primarily to offer an opportunity to show off by giving away property and destroying wealth. The Hopi Indians, on the other hand, carried self-depreciation to a degree which we should consider absurd. In American communities we frown upon self-display and yet under certain circumstances we permit it. When it is permitted, we require that it be hemmed in with restrictions which give it an air of humility. The dress may be ever so expensive, but we must wave off all compliments with a somewhat deprecating smile, lest we appear to be gloating over our sartorial superiority. The party may be ever so costly, but we must act as though it were nothing at all.

We ask about the other person's health, but would be very much surprised if he replied truthfully that he feels terrible. The unformulated rule is: control your aggressions and hostilities, don't invade the other person's personality, and keep interpersonal friction at a minimum. No one is fooled by such conventions. Everyone understands. The conventions act as dikes for holding aggressions in check.

The nineteenth-century Japanese carried the conversational conventions just mentioned even further. For example, two men would meet in the street, take off their hats, and bow very low:

"A: I have not had the pleasure of hanging myself in your honorable eyes for a long time.

B: I was exceedingly rude the last time I saw you.

A: No; it was surely I who was rude. Please excuse me.

B: How is your august health?

A: Very good, thanks to your kind assistance.

B: Is the august lady, your honorable wife, well?

A: Yes, thank you; the lazy old woman is quite well.

B: And how are your princely children?

A: A thousand thanks for your kind interest. The noisy, dirty little brats are well, too.

B: I am now living on a little back street, and my house is awfully small and dirty; but if you can endure it, please honor me by a visit.

A: I am overcome with thanks, and will early ascend to your honorable residence, and impose my uninteresting self upon your hospitality."[12]

Conventional politeness and manners are most important where conflict is most likely to occur. Diplomatic "gobbledygook" is notorious. One Secretary of State made headline news when he signed his letters "Very truly yours" instead of using the conventional "I have the honor to be, sir, your obedient servant." He was in a position to change conventions. When a businessman tried, however, to change the conventional language of business letters—to drop the "dear," for example—although he struck a responsive chord in the hearts of many other businessmen who responded warmly to his suggestion, he had little success.

Where people have no ill feeling, are secure with one another, trust one another, they may dispense with many conventional rules and rely on their faith in the good will of those about them. They can "speak freely" or "talk right out." They do not have to hide behind protective devices.

There are other conventions dealing with propriety in speech, slang, forbidden words. In some languages, including our own, there are two sets of words for sex objects and behavior, one proper and one obscene. It is bad form to use the obscene words in polite society. Curses and oaths are considered improper, but conventions are relaxing in this area and a well-bred woman may even swear on occasion in public. Other words are still taboo. Many humorous situations depend for their humor on unwitting violation of conventions. The piquant French girl who intersperses her conversation with profane or obscene terms, or the outsider who says and does the wrong thing arouses our mirth partly, the psychologists tell us, because these violations make us feel superior and partly because of the unexpectedness and incongruity of such behavior.

Although conventions are not felt to be so strongly tied up with the

[12] R. B. Perry, *The Gist of Japan,* (Westwood, N. J.: Revell, 1897), pp. 87-88.

welfare of the community as are the mores, and their violation is not felt as an equal problem, they are considered binding by most people. In some circles, indeed, conventions are more compelling than the mores. A man may prefer to be seen intoxicated rather than to appear with the wrong kind of tie at a formal gathering. Some criminals are notoriously circumspect with regard to conventional behavior. But conventions are several rungs lower than laws, mores, or even customs in their assessed seriousness. The unconventional person who does not break the law or behave immorally may even be affectionately tolerated.

Conventions, like customs and mores, vary greatly from community to community and, within any given community, among social classes. They also vary among ethnic groups, accounting for some of the dislike felt by native-born Americans for "foreigners," and vice versa. There is admittedly no moral inferiority in the despised group; but the gap created by the differences in conventions is sometimes unbridgeable by conventional members of either group.

It is the second conception of convention—as an institutionalized way of permitting violation of norms—which is of greatest interest to us here. "Conventionalization creates a set of conditions under which a thing may be tolerated which should otherwise be disapproved and tabood."[13] Thus the language and imagery of Shakespeare and of the Bible, as well as the exposure of the body in bathing suits and on the ballroom floor, are covered by conventions which excuse their violation of current mores and thus render them acceptable.

We shall have a great deal more to say about ways in which violation of norms becomes institutionalized, indeed Chapter 27 is devoted to this topic, but it is introduced here only as one function of conventions.

All three kinds of crescive norms may deal with the same kinds of behavior. Thus the mores require us to wear clothes; custom prescribes skirts for women and trousers for men; convention assigns different kinds of dress for different social situations. The mores forbid us to eat certain kinds of food—human flesh, rodents, insects, dogs, cats—and custom regulates how the food we eat is prepared, combined, seasoned; custom also regulates the timing of food intake, the number and spacing of meals. Convention specifies the kinds of food suitable for different occasions; thus there is a conventional menu for teas, for dinners, for picnics. The mores regulate who may sleep with whom and custom fixes the times when people sleep; convention tells what kind of clothing, both for people and for beds, is proper. Sometimes behavior is considered so important that it is regulated by both enacted and crescive norms; mores and statute coincide. Thus it is both against the mores and against the law to murder. But sometimes crescive norms contradict enacted ones, or vice versa. Statutory law may make no distinction in privileges, but custom may. The statute book may state that

[13] Sumner, *op. cit.*, p. 68.

everyone is entitled to equal protection of the law; but custom may deny it to Negroes.

The Subjects of Norms: To Whom Do They Apply?

The second question we raised above with respect to institutions was: to whom do they apply? The answer is that some norms apply to everyone in the community; no one is exempt. No one in our society, for example, is permitted to eat human flesh or practice nudism in public or have more than one spouse at a time. Such norms have been called *universals* by anthropologists.

But some norms apply to only certain elements in the community, to women, let us say, but not to men; to children, but not to adults; to preachers, but not to brick layers; and so on. Thus women may cry; men are not supposed to. Adults may stay up late; children are not permitted to. Clergymen are held to stricter standards of behavior than truck drivers. Such norms, which apply to only certain persons, are called *specialties*. They define roles and status. Many of the norms institutionalizing race relations in the South are specialties in the anthropological sense; they apply to one race but not to the other.

There are some norms about which the subjects have a choice. There are many equally customary ways, for example, to spend a vacation. There are many conventional ways to entertain. A young wife may work after marriage or not; there are no norms proscribing such work as there once were. Such norms which permit of choices are called *alternatives*.

The Objects of Institutionalization

It has been stated that "every kind of activity known to human beings has its rules, the right way and the wrong way."[14] There was a time when such collective phenomena as crowd and mob behavior were, by definition, outside the field of institutionalized behavior. Rioting, fads, crazes, popular manias or hysterias, and panics, for example, have traditionally not been thought of as institutionalized behavior.

But there is some rethinking now in order with respect to the nature of much collective behavior in our day. The kinds of hysterias and manias that used to characterize the ignorant masses of the Middle Ages seem to have subsided with increasing education and literacy. But crowd behavior itself in our day seems to be in the process of becoming institutionalized; leaders in totalitarian societies appear to be able to turn crowds on and off with great precision. "The Street" in the Middle East has become a force to be reckoned with. During a political campaign in our own society the assembling and management of crowds is a basic technique which party

[14] Coons, *op. cit.*, p. 602.

managers know well how to control. A lynch mob behaves according to well-understood norms, conformity to which results from well-understood sanctions. Rioting is relatively rare in civilized societies; most communities see that gatherings likely to erupt in rioting are well policed. In order to prevent panic resulting from disasters and catastrophes, civil defense agencies attempt to institutionalize collective behavior. The indifferent success they have achieved is beside the point here; the important point is that efforts are made to institutionalize even reaction to disaster.

It is only, therefore, such relatively insignificant forms of behavior as flagpole sitting, swallowing gold fish, crowding into telephone booths, raiding college women's dormitories that illustrate the mild nature of crazes and fads in our society. They are not institutionalized—yet. Also, by definition, accidental behavior is not institutionalized behavior. It is, in fact, one of the functions of institutions to prevent accidents.

What, then, do communities attempt to institutionalize? Just about everything. Any function that has to be performed to maintain the community is certain to become institutionalized. It is not that these functions could not be performed without institutions; primates below man, as we have already seen, survive quite well without institutions. But these functions can be so much better performed when they become institutionalized. And once communities came to depend on institutions, survival without them was impossible.

There are many ways of classifying the functions that have to be performed by communities and which are, therefore, the objects of institutionalizing. One is in terms of the specific behavior involved; we speak of reproductive institutions, government institutions, productive institutions, and the like. This is a common approach to the study of communities. For our purposes, however, a more fundamental classification of functions has seemed more suitable. We have selected for study four basic functions: (1) the socializing function which involves the institutionalization of individual behavior; (2) the function of selecting and/or ordering entities, which involves the institutionalization of competition; (3) the function of accommodating incompatible differences, or the institutionalization of conflict; and (4) the seemingly anomalous function of norm violation, or the institutionalization of nonconformity. These are all fundamental; they are all objects of institutionalization. They are the subject matter of our discussions throughout this book.

Functions of Institutionalization

SOCIALIZATION: THE INSTITUTIONALIZATION OF INDIVIDUAL BEHAVIOR

What resources in terms of individual equipment are available for institutionalization? Or, conversely, is there any individual behavior which is not susceptible to institutionalization?

There are certain *autonomic functions* that have not yet been institutionalized, such as pupil dilation and contraction, and bleeding. Others, of course, have, such as sexual behavior, voiding, expulsion of gas, and excretion. Even when autonomic behavior is not immediately institutionalized, the reaction to it may nevertheless be. Thus, according to institutional patterns, animals may sweat, men may perspire, but ladies only glow. In the nineteenth century it was common for ladies to faint; blushing was part of good manners; lacrimation is still called for on certain occasions. Fire-walking in India involves control of many autonomic functions. Soviet psychologists are hard at work now researching problems associated with the conditioning of such functions and it is not inconceivable that the time may come when many autonomic functions now left uninstitutionalized may be. Until the time comes when such conditioning becomes feasible, however, it is likely that most autonomic functions will not be subject to the socialization process.

Only a step away from autonomic functions are such phenomena as *feelings and emotions,* the expression of which is subject to institutionalization. Beliefs and attitudes are, of course, major elements of institutions. *Appearance*—the very size and shape of women's bodies, for example—stance, carriage, gait, posture, are all objects for institutionalization.

The *bonds between and among individuals,* that is, the ties that hold them together in cohesive relationships may also be institutionalized. We sometimes contrast spontaneous relationships with institutional ones. But even the spontaneous ones tend to arise within institutional settings. Institutionalized ties may be based on kinship or on contract; they may be sanctioned or enforced by law, custom, mores, tradition, or other kinds of norms. Noninstitutionalized ties may be based on love or common goals or interests or on mutual aid in achieving separate goals or interests. But noninstitutionalized ties may become institutionalized, as when lovers marry or a neighborhood improvement association incorporates itself. Now the relationship can be enforced even if spontaneous ties are severed.

SELECTING AND/OR ORDERING: THREE FORMS OF COMPETITION

A major function that has to be performed somehow or other throughout all living forms is one of selection. Among lower living forms the function is performed by nature. That is, to use the nineteenth century expression used by Charles Darwin, "natural selection" determines which forms will survive and which will not. The fauna and flora which can breed best under the given circumstances win out over those which cannot breed so successfully. We may say that plants and animals are *in competition* with other plants and animals, although they do not deliberately compete with them.

Among human beings, in addition to this state of being *in competition* with others, there is active and purposive competition. Not only are human beings in competition but they also actively compete with one another, as individuals, as groups, as communities. That is, when they discover that they are in a competitive situation where they or others are to be selected, they do something about it. They try to outdo the others in whatever it is they are doing. This, in its individual form, is sometimes called rivalry. It differs from simply being in competition in that the people involved are aware of the situation and each takes the other's achievement as a target to be outdone.

There is a third form which the process of selecting a winner or survivor may take. Another individual or group of individuals judges the entities and decides which one is to be selected. The winner or survivor is selected on the basis of a judge's decision. For this reason we call this form of competition judgmental competition.

All three of these processes of competition perform the function of selection. Among plants and animals only the first kind prevails. But human beings are not likely long to permit this process to operate without institutionalization. As a result there is scarcely any competitive situation which human beings do not attempt to subject to institutional control.

ACCOMMODATING INCOMPATIBLE DIFFERENCES: THE INSTITUTIONALIZATION OF CONFLICT

The existence of differences is a fundamental fact of life. No two leaves, blades of grass, or other living forms are identical. It is on the basis of such differences that all division of labor or function rests. In addition to inherent differences, there are also acquired differences which result from life experience.

Differences may be compatible, indeed complementary or supplementary in nature, so that they enhance one another. Such compatible differences enrich the whole of which they are part. But some differences are not compatible; indeed, quite the reverse. How to deal with such differences is a basic problem for any community.

At least three approaches are conceivable. One way is to change one or more of the differing entities so that they are no longer incompatible. This may take the form of conversion, brainwashing, persuasion, or any other form of modification of one or more differing entities which renders them similar rather than different. Assimilation is the result.

Another way to deal with incompatible differences is to get rid of one or more of the differing entities. This may take the form of destroying one of the parties. It may take the form of expelling or extruding or ejecting one of the parties. It may take the form of withdrawal or self-isolation. In such cases the incompatible differences have been eliminated by destroying community.

In between these two extremes the incompatible differences must somehow or other accommodate to one another so long as they remain part of the same community. Accommodation may range from a situation in which one of the parties must make most of the concessions—an exploitative situation—through a situation in which the parties bargain out concessions—an equilibration situation—to a situation in which concessions are no longer important because differences are no longer so incompatible—a coalescent situation.

The function of conflict is to arrive at the most feasible accommodation of incompatible differences. Among animals there is no conception of justice involved. But among human beings the process of dealing with incompatible differences is everywhere subjected to institutional controls.

Part III

Competition and Conflict

The world is so full of a number of things,
I'm sure we should all be as happy as kings.

IT IS PRECISELY because the world *is* so full of a number of things that we are not all as happy as kings. Choices have to be made. Selection is inevitable. Everything, everyone cannot win. Everything costs something.

A basic function in any community—plant or animal—is one of selecting winners; and among human beings, ordering the remaining entities along a scale according to some criterion is added. Among animals the poetic conception of Nature as the selecting mechanism led to the very unpoetic conception of natural selection. Among human beings, this function is one of the most highly institutionalized areas of human life. Law, mores, custom, convention weave a powerful web of constraints. Competition is one, but only one, way to select winners and to order the remaining entities. And even where it is permitted, it is itself highly institutionalized. Chapter 5 presents the nature of the selecting and ordering function and the alternatives to competition as a method of performing these functions.

The "number of things" which keep us from being as happy as kings are different among themselves. There are several ways that things can differ among themselves. One way is compatibly and one way is incompatibly. Compatible differences are basic to any division of labor. They make complex organization possible. But incompatible differences are something else again. They may be of many kinds, but the fact that they are incompatible means that the existence of one constitutes a threat to the existence of the other. What to do about such differences is the question answered by conflict; it is the function of conflict to supply the answer.[1]

The kinds of differences which give rise to competition are essentially quantitative; they occur in basically similar entities. A function of competition is to test which of the entities has in greater degree some characteristic or quality, which varies from situation to situation. The end result is the selecting a winner and/or ranking the entities according to the degree to which they have the characteristic or quality being tested. Competition may or may not be social; that is, interaction between or among the entities may or may not occur. The situation is, figuratively speaking, a triangular one in which the entities in the competitive situation or the competing entities are oriented to some goal rather than toward one another.

The kinds of differences which give rise to conflict are qualitative differences which are incompatible with one another. The function of conflict is to find some solution for the situation. Three possibilities present themselves: one set of incompatible entities may be eliminated from the community; the differences may be erased or changed so that they are no longer incompatible; or, finally, a balance or equilibrium of some kind may be worked out in such a way that concessions are maximized for one party and minimized for the other, or optimized for both. Unlike competition, conflict is always characterized by interaction, although in some models—the so-called zero-sum model—the interaction is minimized and takes the form of protecting oneself from the behavior of the opponent.

Part III analyzes the nature of competition and conflict, preparatory to illustrating their operation in American communities in Parts IV and V.

[1] Many other functions of conflict have been delineated in the literature. They are summarized by Raymond Mack and Richard Snyder in "The Analysis of Social Conflict —toward an Overview and Synthesis," *Conflict Resolution,* (June, 1957), pp. 227-229. See also Lewis A. Coser, *The Functions of Conflict* (New York: Free Press, 1956).

5

Selecting and Ordering: Competition

The Conditions of Competition

The conditions which give rise to competition are, first, individual differences or inequalities in qualitatively similar entities and, second, scarcity of some kind. When these two conditions prevail a selection must be made. Competition is one way to make the selection.

INEQUALITIES

If all the entities in a competitive situation or all the competing entities—the distinction is important—were identical or equal, the selection could and probably would be made on a basis of chance. It would make no difference which one were selected. In actual life, however, there are such differences and it does make a difference which one is selected.

The differences are quantitative. That is, they involve inequalities, more or less of something or other. The essential difference is the degree to which one surpasses the other in ability to do something or other, an ability which may be anything at all, varying according to the situation. Let us here simply call it *x*. The function of competition is to determine which entity has more of *x*, whatever it may be in that particular situation—skill, talent, humility, ability to please, to deceive, and so forth.

Among plants and lower animals this *x*-factor is usually ability to breed successfully. The winning entity is the species which can make the best use of the resources available. Among human beings the situation is far more complex. The *x*-factor is by no means self-evident.

Inequalities, then, in the form of quantitative individual differences of some kind or other constitute a basic—and universal—condition of competition.

SCARCITY

The second condition of competition may take several forms. In one form the supply is expandible. In another so-called zero-sum form, the supply is not expandible; it is fixed and no amount of effort can increase it. One has to choose between alternatives, only one of which can be had, a specific CBS television program and a specific NBC program, for example; one cannot increase the amount of time or watch both at the same time. One has to choose between a Republican and a Democrat for president; one cannot elect both. In all these cases differing but similar entities —programs, clothes, potential spouses, candidates—are in competition or are competing for our choice; the scarcity inheres in the fact that there is time or place for only one and neither time nor place can be increased.

COMPETITIVENESS AS A PERSONALITY TRAIT

Sometimes competition is explained or interpreted in terms of competitiveness as a personality trait. As a matter of fact, competitiveness arises where competition is the institutionalized way of dealing with situations of scarcity. As a personality trait competitiveness is much stronger in some people than in others. Some people are highly responsive to competitive challenges. They want very much to win, to surpass, to outdo. Others are not so oriented; they are content to remain in the ranks. The almost universal tendency for people to mitigate the effects of competition suggests that competition is not the result of competitiveness as such.

Dimensions of Competition

Given, then, the basic conditions of inequalities and scarcity, competition will occur unless other institutional alternatives are available.

There are several dimensions which competition may take. It may, for example, be autonomous or judgmental; crescive or contingent; interactional and personal or noninteractional and impersonal; offensive or defensive.[1]

AUTONOMOUS AND JUDGMENTAL COMPETITION

In autonomous competition the process itself selects the winner; in judgmental, someone decides who the winner is. In a race no one has to decide who the winner is; the fastest runner wins. But a committee of judges has to decide who the winner of a beauty contest is. In an auction no one has to decide who gets the object; the highest bidder gets it. In seeking admission to a college, an admissions officer decides who wins. Winners in autonomous competition in effect select themselves; there is no one at the other end of the competitive situation who is deciding who the winner should be. Judgmental competition involves a decision-maker.

If the property being judged is measurable, judgmental competition may be reduced to autonomous competition; and this is a desideratum

[1] I am indebted to James Coleman for suggestions with respect to the dimensions of competition and for terms to apply to them.

often sought. The judge or decision-maker has only to measure the competitors with respect to the criterion in order to choose a winner; judgment is minimized. The contestant with most coups, points, highest grades, best record, or whatever, wins. But if the criterion is qualitative and not yet measurable, or if it is complex, the problem becomes more difficult. It may even happen that there are several criteria that may be applied and they are themselves competitive. The college wants bright students, but it also wants students with a certain cultural background. The employer wants a competent worker, but he also wants him to be white. The fraternity wants good athletes, but it also wants rich boys. The decision problems for the person selecting among competing entities are: what is really wanted? how can this be measured or tested? which of the competing entities has most?

Autonomous competition is usually seen from the point of view of the competing entities; but judgmental competition may be viewed from the point of view of both the competing entities and the judge: from the point of view of the board selecting the successor to the manager, as well as from that of the men being considered for the post; of the executive deciding upon his assistant, as well as of the candidates, and so on.

As culture removes a society farther and farther from brute nature, interposing more and more protection against catastrophe, competition moves increasingly in the direction of judgmental situations. In a crisis, however, the tendency is back toward autonomous competition. It is said that it takes about a year after the beginning of a war to locate the most competent generals and to get rid of those whose position resulted from judgmental rather than autonomous competition. The men who found a competitive organization are at the top as a result of autonomous competition; but their lieutenants and second-men, and even, often, their successors, get their positions as a result of judgmental competition. The process is different in the two situations.

In autonomous competition the competing entity does not have to worry about pleasing a judge; if he is good, the competitive process will prove it. The person engaged in judgmental competition, on the other hand, has to learn how to win the judge or decision-maker rather than how to win the game. As competition becomes judgmental, under the surveillance of boards, commissions, committees, and other decision-makers, a change comes over the process. The criterion of success tends to become ability to please the judge or decision-maker. The students study how to please the teacher rather than how to master the material.

CRESCIVE AND CONTINGENT COMPETITION

Crescive competition has to do with differential rates of growth in a zero-sum, or nonexpandible, area and, hence, survival. The archetypical form is the competitive situation subsumed under the rubric natural selection; ecological competition among plants and animals is crescive in nature. So also is the competition among animal populations, including human ones. One outbreeds the other. It may occur among industries, as when automobiles grow faster than carriages, or oil than coal, or synthetic fabrics than natural ones.[2]

Contingent competition is sometimes called rivalry. It is exemplified by an auction, an arms race, or by keeping ahead of the Joneses. Each competitor attempts to outdo the others. If Mrs. A. serves pie at the club luncheon, Mrs. B. will serve pie with ice cream; Mrs. C. will add whipped cream; Mrs. D. will add nuts. Now Mrs. A. must add fruit. It is called contingent because what each does is contingent on what the others do.

This dimension of competition has come under mathematical analysis as applied to an arms race.[3] The basic condition is that the rate at which one competitor increases his output—of anything—is a function of the rate at which the others increase theirs; in addition, it is a function of the cost of the effort involved. To satisfy those with a psychological slant, the mathematical model also includes personal feelings; in the case of war it is "permanent grievances." The final mathematical model takes the form of two equations which state that the rates of increase will depend positively on the level of the rival's increase, negatively on one's own cost or expenditure, and positively on some other psychological or feeling component.[4]

In both crescive and contingent competition, growth or increase in something or other is taking place; but the relationship among the competing entities is quite different in the two forms.

INTERACTIONAL AND NONINTERACTIONAL COMPETITION

Competition is not always a social process; it certainly is not among plants, and even among human beings interaction between or among the entities is not always present. Sometimes neither of the competing entities is even aware that a competitive situation exists. They are "in competition" with one another without even knowing about it. Reisman's inner-directed man in the nineteenth century, for example, did the best he could, ran his smithy according to his standards of craftsmanship, and did not know that he was in competition with, let us say, the mechanic who could fix the horseless carriage. The competitors in this kind of situation may be said to be in a parallel relationship with one another; each is oriented toward a certain goal toward which he moves, with a minimum of interaction or even relationship between him and others.

Sometimes one competitor but not another sees the competition, as when American workers in the nineteenth century viewed immigrant or

[2] This form of competition can be expressed mathematically in a system of equations. See Anatol Rapoport, *Fights, Games, and Debates* (Ann Arbor, Mich.: Michigan, 1960), pp. 74-84.

[3] L. F. Richardson, "Generalized Foreign Policy," *British Journal of Psychology* Monograph Supplements, 23 (1939). Anatol Rapoport has presented an analysis of Richardson's work in *Journal of Conflict Resolution*, 1 (September, 1957) and *Ibid.*, Chapter 1.

[4] Rapoport, *op. cit.*, pp. 20-21.

Oriental workers as competitors, or as when the leaders in one population see another population as competitors. The union views the nonmember as a potential competitor; the so-called right to work laws view the nonmember as just an individual striving to do the best he can.

To those in a competitive situation who have not yet recognized the fact, it looks as though they were just struggling along, doing the best they know how, not trying to horn in. It may even come as a complete surprise to learn that they are competitors.

Even when competition is interactional, it may be either personal or impersonal. Competition for the use of land in a city, for example, may be interactional, but it is also often quite impersonal.

OFFENSIVE AND DEFENSIVE COMPETITION

Sometimes people are forced to compete in self-defense, much as they would prefer not to. The United States was not originally interested in competing with the USSR in space or missiles or rate of economic growth. But when it was challenged by the USSR it was forced to. A challenger forces a change in the value structure of others and thus forces them to enter his system. They must now accept his values or suffer the consequences. He adds a new alternative to choose from, so much worse than any of the others that they are forced to select his challenge. The blacksmith who loved his craft at the turn of the century did not want to compete with the mechanic who tinkered with the new-fangled contraption, the horseless carriage. But as horses became scarcer and scarcer and horseless carriages commoner and commoner, he was forced to compete with him. Many young women do not want to marry at the age of nineteen or twenty; but the challenge of those who do forces them to enter the competitive race for husbands; they fear that if they do not the eligible men will all be committed.

Who Competes for What?

The competing entities may be anything and the objects competed for may be anything. Plant species are in competition with one another for space, access to soil, foods, sunshine. Animal species, similarly, are in competition, and for the same sorts of things. Theories, ideas, goals, works of art, machines, artifacts, culture traits, philosophies may be in competition with one another.

Human beings compete as individuals with one another for such things as jobs, honors, mates, customers; as members of communities and groups, with other communities and groups for such things as markets, natural resources, industries, adherents; and even as a species, with other species—with insects, for example—for survival.

Competition registers the values of a community which are achievable; obviously one cannot compete for a status which one cannot achieve but which must be the result of ascription, such as race or sex or lineage. With this limitation, people compete for anything that the community or some segment of it will reward them for. Among human beings perhaps the object most universally competed for is appreciative recognition. Competition in all fields—economic, political, educational, family, social life, sports—may be interpreted as illustrating competition for appreciative recognition. The concrete or specific thing which brings appreciative recognition varies widely not only among communities but within special sectors of specific communities. In a Hopi community, for example, girls compete in humility, a trait highly prized among them and therefore one which calls for appreciative recognition.[5] In American communities, for example, businessmen compete for wealth and power; women for social position; students for grades. The person who wins gains appreciative recognition. If ribbons are the badges of achievement, people compete for ribbons. They will compete for whatever gains appreciative recognition in their community. Thus, although we may speak of economic, social, and political competition, in all cases competition for recognition is present.

Although the conditions of competition are universal, it is nowhere left without institutional regulation. Custom and the mores determine who may compete with whom and what may be competed for. In our own society, as we shall illustrate in great detail, there is a vast body of statutory law which intervenes in the competitive process. And in some cases competition is not permitted at all. Alternatives are institutionalized.

Alternatives to Competition

Competition is only one way to meet the problem of inequalities and scarcity. It is the sole method among plants and animals. But human beings

[5] The following conversation between two Hopi girls illustrates competition in humility:

Delphina: Yesterday I did the bummest job for the bahana [white man].

Frances: You did quite well.

Delphina: You didn't see it.

Frances: You should have seen what I did; I couldn't do anything.

The following observations from the researcher's notebook also illustrate the same point: "July 15. Helena and Julia came to our house this afternoon. We played ball with them. Helena was much the more skillful of the two. When I asked both, 'Who plays better?' Julia promptly answered, 'Helena,' while Helena looked slightly embarrassed and said, 'I don't know.'" Cited by Gardner Murphy, Lois Barclay Murphy, and Theodore Newcomb, *Experimental Social Psychology* (New York: Harper, 1937), p. 443. Compare this with the values reflected in the following advertisement in which aggression is sought:

"Tiger Wanted. No less need apply. The man we're looking for has sharpened his claws and toned up his muscles, even though he may be only in his early thirties. He's a lean and hungry guy who has matched wits with some of the smartest marketing men in the field. He's probably done some competitive selling and has spent a few years in an advertising agency. He has an appetite for tough marketing and merchandising problems, particularly in the food field, and he knows it takes IDEAS to solve such problems—HIS ideas. If you're that kind of a tiger, come at us fighting. We've got what you want. . . ." (Advertisement in the *New York Times,* Jan. 24, 1960.)

have evolved other methods in addition. One can, for example, handle the problem of an inadequate supply by attempting to change those who want it or by attempting to increase the supply.

DECREASING OR REGULATING THE DEMAND

One can decrease the demand for scarce things by several methods. One can teach people not to want things that are scarce. Since fame, fortune, and honor, for example, are hard to achieve, one can teach people to reconcile themselves to not obtaining them. In fact, one can make a virtue of renouncing them, a common Oriental, particularly Hindu, approach. Renunciation, asceticism, withdrawal are honored. This is a solution that American communities are not likely to adopt with enthusiasm. Although the mental hygiene movement teaches people to trim their sails, most Americans still seem to feel that the person who is not ambitious, who is not out to win, who plays just for the fun of it, who is satisfied with what he has, is not quite up to standard. Our relatively open-class system stimulates the desire to improve our position. Everywhere our wants are stimulated rather than discouraged. We do not take easily to a philosophy of renunciation.

Also renunciatory in nature is the Christian doctrine of self-sacrifice. It is one of the most effective ways of controlling demand whenever it can be enforced. The Christian theory is that if there is not enough for all, the Christian gives up his share. Manners may be said to reflect the Christian ethic of self-sacrifice. Among the well-mannered, there is never any competition for the last cookie on the plate. Everyone may want it but everyone declines, so that the cookie is left on the plate.

A third way to institutionalize the allocation of scarce goods is to segregate the members of a community into noncompeting groups on the basis of age, sex, race, lineage, or any other convenient categorical criterion, and then assign them arbitrary priorities. Some people get the scarce goods or services because they are old or women or sick or white or native born or veterans or officials. If there is not enough room for everyone in the lifeboat of a sinking ship, the rule is: women and children first. In 1955 when there was a shortage of polio vaccine, it was urged that children under fourteen should have priority. Negroes may not compete with whites, or women with men, for certain kinds of jobs. Caste and class privileges in the community have as one of their functions, although not, of course, a professed one, the limiting of competition as a method of distributing scarce goods. The supply is enough for only a few; the lower orders are not even permitted to know about the existence of certain scarce things, so that they may be prevented from developing a taste for them.

Similar to this priority principle in allocating scarce goods and services is the seniority principle. "First come, first served" is the rule. In the case of public vehicles this seniority principle is coming to take the place of the categorical priority principle; the man who gets there first keeps his seat even after a woman enters. Many unions have incorporated the seniority principle into their contracts. Railroad workers have specified it for allocating desirable jobs. The best runs and the best hours are distributed on a seniority basis. If there are not enough jobs, the men with the longest records get what jobs there are. Unions, as we shall see in Chapter 10, oppose competition among workers on principle.

Another noncompetitive method for allocating scarce goods or services is to distribute them equally. Rationing illustrates this procedure. All share and share alike. The USSR, although far from the communistic goal, is allegedly aiming at realization of this principle. Americans tolerate this solution in times of emergency, but black-market scandals show that they are not likely to take to it as a permanent one, at least not with our present ideology.

One can decrease "effective" demand for wanted things by increasing the price or effort involved in getting them. The formerly wanted things no longer seem to be worth the effort. They are priced out of the market. If, for example, the student is told that in order to get an A he must do an original piece of research, write ten book reports, and pass a dozen tests with a grade of 95 or more, he is likely to conclude that A's are not worth the effort; he stops competing for them.

Demand, finally, may also be regulated on the agreed-upon basis of chance. The scarce goods or services are assigned on the basis of tossing a coin or drawing slips from a bowl. This method is usually resorted to when the competing entities seem so nearly equal with respect to qualifications that testing would not be able to select a winner.

INCREASING THE SUPPLY

As far as Americans are concerned, the ideal solution to the problem of scarcity is, of course, to increase the supply and create abundance. In the eighteenth century, John Millar defined civilization as "that politeness of *mores* which is the natural consequence of abundance and security."[6] And our own Simon Patten, many years ago, tried to teach the importance of this approach. He told us that we no longer needed to live in an economy of scarcity; we could live in a society of abundance. More recently the economist John Kenneth Galbraith has traced the implications of abundance for social life.[7]

Where there is abundance competition is mitigated or eliminated. We do not require people to compete for a grammar school education. Abun-

[6] *Observations Concerning the Distinction of Ranks in Society,* 2nd ed. (London: J. Murray, 1773).

[7] *The Affluent Society* (Boston: Houghton-Mifflin, 1958). Jessie Bernard, *Social Problems at Midcentury* (New York: Holt, Rinehart and Winston, 1957), has also elaborated the effects of abundance on social and societal relationships.

dant facilities have been the goal if not the rule. Interested citizens are called in to a community meeting where the shortage of school facilities is being discussed. How shall it be met? They suggest part-time schools, the use of churches if necessary, and urging retired teachers to come back or married women to return to teaching. No one suggests that since there are not enough facilities for all, the children should compete for what there are: let only the brightest ones go to school, or the wealthiest. No one dreams of excluding a child from elementary schooling just because there are not enough buildings and teachers. We take it for granted that it is our job to provide enough of them. Public parks and playgrounds are also coming slowly to be thought of as in this category. And the time may come when we shall feel the same way about other things, such as medical and dental care.

We sometimes temper the rigors of competition in more personal areas by increasing the number of prizes, rewards, or other competed-for objects. This is likewise in the direction of abundance.

We are, in brief, learning little by little the important lesson that scarcity need not always be inevitable, that abundance is at least technologically possible. And when there is plenty, competition can be less severe. Absolute abundance is, of course, out of the question as long as man's wants are infinitely expansible. But even relative abundance reduces the rigors of competition.

In spite of these alternatives, however, competition remains a standard method for distributing scarce goods in American communities. It behooves us, therefore, to examine its functioning carefully and to evaluate its results.

Competition As a Test: The Concept of Fairness

Competition is a testing process. It is a method for determining which entity has most *X*. Not all tests are competitive, but all competition is essentially a testing process. A competitive test may take the highly regulated, conscious, purposive form of a civil service examination or, at the other extreme, it may be the almost blind, impersonal competition for use of land (industrial, residential, or commercial) in a city.

As a test, competition may be evaluated like any other test in terms of validity, that is, in terms of the extent to which it measures what it is supposed to test. If it succeeds, it is fair. But if, for whatever reason, it does not measure what it is supposed to test or what we want it to test, it is not valid, not fair.

In noncompetitive testing a basic standard of validity is demanded. A test in the psychological or sociological field is said to be valid if it tests what it purports to test. If a test sets out to measure intelligence, for example, but correlates very poorly with other known measures of intelligence, it is said to have low validity. In competitive tests we are not accustomed to speaking of validity. We speak, rather, of fairness. Basically, as applied to tests, fairness and validity are identical concepts. Perhaps it would be better to discard the term "fair competition" altogether and substitute the term "valid competition." The emotional connotations which cluster about the term "fair" might then be obviated and we could view competitive tests with greater detachment. The reader who wishes to substitute the word "valid" for the word "fair" in our discussions throughout the present volume can do so with good logic. Whichever term we use, however, the difficulties involved in validity or fairness are legion; and they are often even greater in competitive than in technical tests.

In the competition which takes place among plants and lower animals, the ability to survive under given conditions is the only trait being tested. By definition, then, such competition must be judged "fair"—that is, a valid test of ability to survive. We might personify the natural forces and suppose Nature to be experimenting with countless variations on certain persistent themes. Some of the variations may have been very beautiful, graceful, elegant. But those traits were not being tested. If species did not, in addition, have the ability to breed prolifically or some other quality making for survival, they were eliminated, regardless of human evaluation.

Among human beings we usually want, or at least profess to want, merit of some kind to be tested or proved, such as efficiency, quality, service, or fitness for office, for marriage, or for responsibility. We set up laws which say that businessmen or politicians may not do certain things which would give them unfair advantage over their competitors for business or office. If they did, something other than merit would be tested. Competition would not, under such circumstances, be a valid test of merit. In other words, we attempt to institutionalize competitive conditions by law or by mores and customs enjoining certain kinds of behavior and prescribing others in order to weed out undesired qualities and to retain desirable ones. If we are successful, we have valid tests or proofs of the qualities we want; we have, that is, "fair competition."

Difficulties in Achieving Fair Competition

Unfortunately, from the point of view of technical efficiency, although we may strive to achieve these goals, it is not always possible to render competition a valid test. The difficulties are enormous. Three are particularly noteworthy. First, we do not always have clear-cut consensus about what we really want to test. When a technician invents a noncompetitive test he usually knows what he is trying to measure. This may or may not be true of a competitive test. In athletic competition we usually do know what we want to test—namely, skill or speed. We set up the rules and conditions of competition in such a way that the best performer wins, and the competitive test is valid or fair. If the institutionalized conditions do not permit the best performer to win, we say they are unfair. What we mean is that they do not permit a valid test of performance. Students sometimes complain that tests are not fair; what they mean is that the tests are not valid measures of what they know.

We do not always agree on what should be measured by a competitive test, however. What, for example, do we want business competition to test? Consumers may want businessmen to compete in low prices; businessmen themselves often speak as though price competition were beneath their dignity. They feel that they ought to compete on some other level. What do we want political competition to test? Theoretically, fitness for office. Actually, perhaps, we want something quite different. Ability to please constituents, for example. It is clear that fairness or validity cannot be expected when we do not know what to test.

A second difficulty in validating competitive tests lies in the fact that even if we know what we want to measure, it is often impossible to determine exactly what is actually being measured. This same difficulty may occur in technical tests, too, but it is exaggerated in competitive tests, especially in community behavior. The test technician may have no particular desire to know what he is testing. In factor analysis, for example, he may speak simply of an *x*-factor, not caring much what name it has provided that it behaves and can be treated as a unitary function. But usually the test constructor can tell pretty well what he is measuring by referring to the results of earlier tests or by checking associated behavior. In competitive tests in community behavior, on the other hand, it is often extremely difficult to determine what it is that is being measured. We may think we are measuring one thing, but actually we may be measuring something altogether different. Sometimes we can only work backwards and, by studying the winners or survivors, determine what the competition was testing.

We may illustrate this difficulty by reference to the nineteenth-century attitude toward free and unregulated competition in the market. Proponents of this policy argued that under such a regime the most efficient businessman in the community would drive the inefficient businessman out of business and thus raise the general level of productive efficiency. The assumption was that the quality being tested competitively was efficiency. Actually, as we now know, efficiency was not always the decisive factor in success. As often as not, the businessman who won out did so by lowering prices at the expense of working conditions for his employees. Not efficiency but ruthlessness or dishonesty was often being tested. In the Darwinian natural-selection theory, the trait allegedly being tested was called fitness to survive. Survival of the fittest was a mouth-filling expression that seemed to have a moral connotation. It was comforting for the rich and well-born to believe that they were the fittest and that their privileges were the just reward of merit, as demonstrated by the great competitive struggle for existence. But what, actually, did this struggle for existence test? Not moral traits, but rather breeding ability. Among animals the struggle for existence, as we have seen, is demographic, or crescive, a test of adaptability as shown in breeding ability and viability. Among human beings, the groups which survive are likewise the groups that leave the most offspring. In school examinations the thing tested is ostensibly the amount of information or knowledge, and grades are presumably distributed according to knowledge displayed. But we know that what is actually tested is too often mere ability to please the examiner. In games of skill it is the skill of the player which is being tested, yet morale, drive, and the will to win are also involved. The fastest runner does not always win. It will be seen, then, that not only is it difficult to make competition test what we think we want it to test, but it is even difficult to determine what it is actually testing.

A third difficulty in validating competitive tests of community behavior lies in the fact that despite our efforts to institutionalize the process we often have relatively little control over it. The test constructor in the laboratory controls his entire operation. He sets it up, creates the conditions, and is master of the situation. For a great deal of competitive behavior in the community no such mastery is possible, at least not in American communities. We are born into a competitive setup, have little to do with the institutionalized conditions, and often do not even become aware that we are being tested without rather advanced social-science training. Under such conditions it is very difficult to keep competition fair—that is, to render it a valid test of traits we want. It may, in fact, select and reward traits that we deplore.

The time may come when noncompetitive tests are set up in community behavior. It is conceivable that technical tests for efficiency, quality, and service may be devised for businesses and that those who fall below certain standards on such tests, even if they are able to market their wares by exploiting customers, may be forced out of business by some superplanning or engineering commission. Similar tests may be set up in other areas of competition. They could be demonstrably valid or fair. They are hardly likely to capture the allegiance of American communities, however, for reasons which we shall presently examine.

We shall have a good deal to say about fair competition when we discuss specific forms of competitive behavior in the several fields of community life. The only point which should be made here is that the concept of fair competition is not necessarily an ethical one. It is identical with the technical concept of validity as applied to the construction of any test. A competitive test is fair in exactly the same sense that a technical test is valid. Given a quality to be tested—and this may be an ethical matter—competition may be judged fair or unfair, valid or invalid, according to how well it selects winners who have this quality.

DO WE REALLY WANT FAIR COMPETITION?

It may be argued that a perfectly valid testing process could conceivably have worse repercussions on personality, especially for mediocre persons, than one in which chance or favoritism or privilege played a part. If competition were always perfectly fair, we would have no excuses for our failures. We would have to face the fact of our own inferiorities. Where the conditions of competition are not kept rigorously fair, those who lose can always blame someone else or luck or circumstances for their failures. Those who could not have won anyway can exonerate themselves and at least retain an illusion of superiority. It has long been recognized that human beings want justice tempered by mercy.

THE INTEGRATING FUNCTION OF COMPETITION

The disintegrative effects of competition are often emphasized almost to the exclusion of any recognition of its integrating effects. But at least in the contingent form it does perform an integrating function also. The fact that entities are competing for the same thing means that they belong to the same public or group. They are "in." Those who refuse to enter the competition are expressing a rejection of the values being competed for; they are "out." The families that do not try to keep up with the Joneses are not in the Joneses' set. In brief, submitting to competition is one way of indicating affiliation, acceptance of common values. To remain out of the competitive race, conversely, is to express contempt or lack of homage for the values of others. Competition thus creates conformity.

An Evaluation of Competition

Our society is often characterized as a competitive one. Whether it is more or less so than other societies in actual fact would have to be determined by empirical study, but it is certainly true that we exalt individual competition and express a belief in its virtues more than most societies, however much we intervene in its actual operation.

What are the pros and cons with respect to competition as a general principle to be applied in allocating limited supplies, in selecting winners, or in ordering entities?

THE PROS

In favor of autonomous competition in American community life is its complete congeniality to American principles; it is consistent, that is, with our strong emphasis on the individual. It is, in fact, an overt expression of the belief in rugged individualism. "A fair field and may the best man win," or, "A fair field and let the devil take the hindmost," expresses a fundamental value of our society.

As a corollary to the exaltation of individual competition in our society is the fact that if the conditions can be kept scrupulously fair, autonomous competition has the great advantage of minimizing any tendency toward bias, nepotism, personal favoritism, or prejudice. There is no one with power to make decisions about qualifications. In this sense it is self-administering. We may attack the umpire if we think he has misapplied the rules, but if the rules have been adhered to, we must accept the results without complaint. This is a particularly appealing phase of autonomous competitive tests as far as citizens in American communities are concerned. The same advantage does not, of course, inhere in judgmental competition.

In favor of contingent or rivalrous and judgmental competition is the fact that it serves as a tremendous dynamo. It stimulates effort. Laboratory studies have shown that the volume, if not always the quality, of work done under competitive circumstances is much greater than the volume under noncompetitive circumstances. The experience of both the USSR and China has shown that although one may eliminate competition among businessmen, nevertheless, if one wants to whip up production, one has to use it among workers, communes, and factories. Even if the only thing competed for is a banner, a ribbon, or a badge, there is no doubt that competition keeps human beings on their toes. When competition is fair and a truly valid test, it also makes for quality in the trait being tested. It selects the best. It makes for speed in the athlete, efficiency in the producer, quality in the product, hard work in the student—at least in some of them.

How, then, can there be any doubt about the merits of competition in selecting winners or ordering entities? The answer is that although it may solve some problems for the community, it raises many more.

THE CONS

It is almost impossible to keep competition going on. For although competition is a universal and perennial process, it is extremely difficult to keep most human beings competing for any length of time in any specific situation. Animals may compete among themselves indefinitely. They cannot understand the implications of their behavior. But human beings cannot be long blinded to the advantages of organization and cooperation. This is true in almost every field where competition is keen. Businessmen within their own communities and on a national scale enter—legally or illegally—into agreements not to compete. Internationally, economic competition is replaced by the cartel. Politicians make deals and divide the jobs. Wage earners form unions to prevent cutthroat competition for jobs. Pacemakers in the factory are punished for setting too severe a standard. Students develop the concept of the "gentleman's grade" and ostracize the "greasy grind." Human beings enjoy a little competition as the spice of life, even creating it artificially if it does not exist. But as a steady diet they evade it. It is too hard to be "bested"—or to avoid being bested—all the time. This is why cooperation is the almost inevitable end result of contingent and judgmental competition. We want everyone else to compete, but we want to be spared the rigors of competition ourselves.

A third difficulty is our ambivalence with respect to competition. The normal thing is for each competitive situation to run its course and come to some conclusion. One species outbreeds another and survives, its competitors being eliminated. One competitor annihilates another and prevails. One reaches the goal and the contest is over. New competitive situations continually arise, to be sure, but each normally reaches a decision and ends. American communities do not approve of competition of this type in business, for it ends in monopoly. Theoretically we believe in what we call fair competition; but there is no such thing in nature as fair competition in the sense in which the term is used here. The essence of competition is the elimination of all but one of the competitors. That is what it means in the form of the "survival of the fittest." American communities do not, however, want this in the economic realm. We create many rules to institutionalize competition and often these prevent its arriving at a normal conclusion. We do not want one competitor to eliminate the others even if he is superior. We protect inefficient competitors just to keep the competition going, as we shall see in Chapter 7; but the traits thus tested cease to represent efficiency, and the consumer often suffers.

The fourth problem related to competition has engaged the attention of thoughtful people for millennia. Competition, we have said, is fair or just when it tests what it sets out to test. If rewards are to be on the basis of speed, then fair competition is competition which tests speed and only speed. It is unfair if anything other than speed determines success. If the quality tested is information, then information alone should determine the winner. That is why we try by institutional rules to prevent cheating, bribery, pull, handicaps, and privileges.

From another angle, however, competition presents a far more difficult problem in justice. We usually concentrate so much on the winners that we forget about the much larger body of losers. Of course in conscious, voluntary, deliberate competition, as in sports and games, we need not worry about the losers. But in the great competition for jobs and status the question is different. Here the losers did not choose to enter the competitive struggle. They were born into it. Suppose they do not have the traits which we test competitively in our society? Suppose they are weak, dull, ugly? Theoretically they should then be eliminated by the struggle for existence, as we call this great competitive process. But our mores do not permit us to kill them. What should the community do with them? What is justice here? If we decide grimly that they should not be helped, on the assumption that they are inherently inferior, they may drag down the entire community. Furthermore, their inferiority may be a result rather than the cause of their low position. We cannot always tell. On the other hand, if we nurse them along, we may, as the Social Darwinian would argue, actually be adding to our burdens and encouraging the survival of unfit strains. Just where justice lies is a hard question. Christianity preaches the tempering of justice with mercy. The Nazi ideology, on the other hand, believed in ruthlessness and looked upon mercy as weakness. (Actually, of course, only the strong and secure can afford to indulge in mercy.)

A final problem posed by competition is its effects on character and personality. Emphasis on winning makes the desire to win assume overwhelming importance. Trophies, titles, and grades become ends in themselves. The technique used to stimulate effort—competition—overshadows the goals sought. Because stakes are high there is a constant temptation to cheat. Profit rather than production of goods is sought, and throat-cutting, unfair practices, and shoddy workmanship are constant temptations. Businessmen often complain that they dislike to do certain things which they are "forced to do" under the pressure of defensive competition. They condemn themselves for doing what they feel they have to do.

By placing too great a premium on success, competition condemns most competitors to a sense of failure, for competition means that most people are bound to lose most of the time.[8] The scarcer the rewards the more people there are who will lose. Is this desirable? Does the benefit derived from stimulating effort overbalance the hurt of frustration suffered by losing? There are, we know, great individual differences in frustration-tolerance. Some people are "good losers"; they take failure in their stride. For others, losing is very hard to take. Some people enjoy competition and do their best under its spur: others are at their worst. Under such circumstances do we do well to subject everyone to it?

Competition may have a warping effect on personality. It generates hostility; others are viewed as rivals or, even, sometimes, as enemies. Along with the feelings of inferiority, fear of failure, and insecurity, this hostility contributes to the development of neuroses.[9]

Where the scarcity which gives rise to competitive behavior is beyond human control, we have little choice but to accept it. But the question is sometimes raised, need we stimulate it? Here is an answer from the point of view of the mental hygienist and psychiatrist:

> Some of our mental breakdowns are caused by the kind of a society in which we live—a highly competitive society in which there are few winners and many losers. The drive for success puts an added strain on living, and some can't survive

[8] Erving Goffman has made acutely perceptive analyses of the ways in which we try to reconcile losers to their failures. See "On Cooling the Mark Out: Some Aspects of Adaptation to Failure," *Psychiatry: Journal for the Study of Interpersonal Relations,* 15 (November, 1952), pp. 451-463.

[9] George Thorman, *Toward Mental Health* (Public Affairs Pamphlet No. 120, 1946), p. 20.

the struggle. Everyone is in competition with everyone else—not only for economic gain, but for esteem, love, respect, and recognition.[10]

The problems raised in community life by competition are, then, as great as the benefits derived from it. How to secure the maximum benefits from it with a minimum of human cost is one of the most vexing problems facing American communities in the twentieth century.

10 *Ibid.*, p. 19

6

The Nature of Conflict

The third great function that has to be institutionalized in any community, as we pointed out in Chapter 4, is that of dealing with incompatible differences. The processes involved are those of conflict. At this point, therefore, we introduce a brief overview of the nature of this function and the ways in which it may be performed. First, however, conflict and competition should be briefly compared and contrasted since they have some elements in common.

Competition and Conflict

When Nikita Khrushchev in the 1950's proposed that a policy of competitive coexistence between the USSR and the United States be substituted for one of conflict, he was using a fundamental distinction between competition and conflict, even when both expressed opposition. The fact that they were, in effect, viewed as interchangeable ways of achieving a given goal highlighted also a fundamental similarity between them.

The close relationship between them is further illustrated by the fact that in some cases the same theoretical or mathematical model can be applied to both. The equations which explain contingent competition, for example, also explain the course which a conflict may take. One student of conflict, in fact, applies the term "fight" to the situation which this model fits.[1] Parameters g and h are included in the equations to take care of the subjective feelings involved. If they stand for hostility or hatred or revengefulness or feelings of grievance, then the model explains the snowballing effect of a community conflict, as well as of competition. Adding a little g to one side has the effect of adding a little more h to the other. Each side stimulates the other to more and more hostile behavior; they are, in reality, "competing" in hostility.

Another common element in competition and conflict is the fact that a scarcity, or zero-sum, situation may be present in both. What one wins

[1] See Anatol Rapoport, *Fights, Games, and Debates* (Ann Arbor, Mich.: Michigan, 1960), Chapter 1.

the other loses. In both, also, there are, however, circumstances which result in common as well as in conflicting interests—in competition the so-called Pareto point, and in conflict a nonzero-sum situation.

Both competition and conflict, furthermore, may be said to vary along a continuum. Both, that is, may vary from destruction to assimilation of an opponent.

As a result of these similarities, it is not always easy to draw a clear-cut distinction between the two processes. Is a prize fight, for instance, a case of competition or of conflict? And a debate? The answer lies in the functions performed or the objectives sought. If the function is to decide which is the better boxer, it is competition. Each is trying to prove to the judges or to the audience that he is better. If the fighters are seeking a championship or a prize, and the opponent is only incidental, the contest, again, is competitive. But when, or if, it makes a difference who the opponent is, so that he is fighting not to prove he is the better boxer or to win a title or prize, but to defeat the opponent, it is conflict.

The distinction may not be important in a prize fight, but it is extremely important in community life. The ability, for example, to permit the succession of power to be decided on the basis of an election or even a more restricted form of competition is characteristic of sophisticated societies, even if primitive. If the succession of power must be decided on the basis of a fight, the situation is quite different; it is no longer a matter of testing or proving the candidates but of destroying opposition. It makes a difference if the USSR "buries" us under superior goods or under the rubble of war.

Despite the similarities and common characteristics of the two processes, therefore, the distinction between them is worth preserving. In their archetypical forms they are quite different. In general it may be said that in contingent competition the relationships involved are triangular; the competitors are oriented toward some goal or judge. In conflict the critical relationship is between or among the parties themselves. In competitive coexistence, for example, the USSR and the United States try to outdo one another in aid to underdeveloped countries, in planes of living or scientific achievement at home; the idea is that the best system wins. The "uncommitted nations" are the judges. In conflict, on the other hand, there is a confrontation between the antagonists. The result may be thermonuclear war in one case (conflict), but vast scientific achievement in the other (competition).

Social-Psychological and Sociological Conflict

Even within the area of conflict itself, furthermore, a distinction must be made at the outset between two related but theoretically distinct kinds of conflict. One includes such phenomena as hatred, prejudice, hostile or negative stereotypes, frustrations, resentments, "tensions," and the like which express themselves in bickering, quarreling, aggression, brawling, fist-fighting, and similar behavior. These are phenomena with which social psychologists, both individual and collective, have concerned themselves. There need be no issues involved in this kind of conflict.[2] There are, of course, "causes" for the feelings and reactions—which may require a professional analyst to lay bare—but not necessarily reasons for them. The people hate first and then find reasons for their hatred. There is no clear-cut goal being sought. The emotion is an end in itself. The function of this kind of conflict may be to make the person himself feel better—"catharsis"—rather than to contribute to any goal. When, for example, it was pointed out to an eight-year-old child that it did no good to beat up her little brother, since he remained just as obnoxious to her as ever, she replied, with the candor and insight of childhood, "But it makes me feel better." There is, in brief, no necessary relationship between the hostility and the achievement of a goal. In this sense it is nonrational.

The second kind of conflict is more goal-oriented; it may be highly purposive and even rational. It deals with incompatible differences in goals or aims or objectives. Issues are involved. Hatred may or may not be present. Indeed, conflict of this kind may exist between or among people who love one another dearly. The only essential characteristic is the existence, at least to some degree, of incompatible differences in goals or objectives. Conflict in this sense is the process by which a feasible accommodation is arrived at. It is this second kind of conflict which shall concern us here.

Parties to Conflict

Conflict may also be classified in terms of the nature of the parties involved. If the "parties" are within the individual—incompatible wishes, goals, aims competing for his choice—we have intra-individual, or psychological conflict, ranging from Burden's ass, immobilized in his tracks because he cannot decide which to eat, the carrot or the hay, all the way to the saintly hermit wrestling with temptation in the desert. Or the conscientious woman torn between satisfying the demands of her role as daughter and her role as wife. Interesting and important as this form of conflict is, we disregard it here. In its extreme form this kind of conflict may lead to multiple personality or personality dissociation, a condition in which incompatible integrations of behavior patterns accommodate the conflict by taking turns, so to speak, in using the body. As in the case of social-psychological conflict, it has been explored in great depth by psychologists, psychiatrists, and psychoanalysts, and a rich literature is available on it.

If the parties to the conflict are individuals, the resulting situation may

[2] This is the kind of conflict which Anatol Rapoport labels "fight" in contrast to "games" and "debates." (*Ibid.*)

or may not be important for the community. A tavern brawl or a feud between two householders may not warrant community concern. But conflicts between or among individuals representing groups or collectivities will almost certainly involve the whole community. And conflicts between or among such groups and collectivities themselves, from street gangs to warring nations, concern everyone.

More fundamental is the classification of conflict in terms of the *number* of parties involved. If there are only two parties—individuals, factions, groups, and so forth, the structure of the conflict is fairly simple. But the addition of a third party, the so-called *tertius gaudens,* immediately changes the situation. The phenomena of coalitions enter the picture. The third party, though weaker than either of the other two, may, by siding with one or the other, have definitive power in the situation. He thus introduces competition into the situation also since each of the original parties may now compete for his adherence, each trying to outbid the other.

In the major conflicts we shall consider, this third party may be the public or it may be the government. It is often a matter of major concern whether the public or the government enters a coalition with one side or the other. According to how it behaves it may add greatly to the strategic armory of one side or, contrariwise, may greatly weaken it.

Although both the understanding and the prosecution of any conflict require knowing who the parties involved are, it is not always obvious who they are. This is especially true when, as in the case of Communists, the seeming parties are really fronts for others. Nor is it always easy to see who the "mastermind" is back of a criminal organization. Our enemies, that is, are not always easy to pinpoint, as Macbeth and Iago so poignantly show.

And just as sometimes we fail to discern who our enemies are, so also we sometimes make a wrong judgment in the opposite direction: we see enemies where none may exist. The behavior of others looks conspiratorial to us. For it sometimes happens, as we saw in Chapter 1, that people behave in a concerted or coordinated way without having to communicate with one another. The coordination is the result of more than common or shared interests. It is the result, in addition, of collective values with the resulting ability to read one another's mind, so that they know what to expect of others and hence what to do themselves to implement their common or shared interests.[3] Outsiders, especially opponents, find such coordination impossible to understand without imputing clear-cut and recognized cooperation or conspiracy. One example is the so-called power elite. Is there a single group of men who constitute a self-conscious power elite, manipulating us against our best interests? Or are there many centers of power operating sometimes together and sometimes at cross purposes? If we ask the men involved we get a vehement No! Of course they do not

[3] Thomas C. Schelling, *The Strategy of Conflict* (Cambridge, Mass.: Harvard, 1960), pp. 92 ff.

constitute a single, self-conscious power elite. But to a confirmed Marxist they are clearly a conspiratorial "ruling class," exploiting the rest of us in a self-conscious way. The "Wall Street" that Communists inveigh against is, to them, also a self-conscious conspiratorial group, enemy to the rest of us.

One final point with respect to parties. In a free and complex society there will be many issues and conflicts. When this is the case, they tend to cancel one another. For people who line up against one another on one issue may line up together on another. The presence of many conflicts means that people often have as much in common as they have in conflict. The people in a community may be viewed as cards in a deck. In one deal they line up against one another. Reshuffled for another deal, they line up together against another hand. Many conflicts thus tend to neutralize one another. Where people line up against one another on one issue only and have no issue to reshuffle them, the cleavage may become very deep. Indeed, if each of the parties to a conflict had racial, economic, religious, cultural, and class interests in common, and if each had no interests in common with the opposing side, conflict might well assume the proportions of civil war.

Issues

Just as an understanding of who the parties in a conflict are is basic to its successful prosecution, so also is an understanding of the issues involved. We speak of issues rather than of "causes" in conflict because causes are almost impossible to determine.[4] The causes of conflict always exist; they are intrinsic in social life since incompatible differences are inevitable. The problem is one of how they are dealt with and why.

In psychological or emotional conflict, as we just saw, there is no issue at all. People dislike or hate or suspect or resent one another and that's that. But in sociological conflict an issue is involved. It may vary in specific cases and range all the way from the care of property, the behavior of children, noise, garbage collection, fluoridation of the water supply, zoning, building laws, the schools—especially the schools—all the way up to the fundamental, if abstract, issue of how competition should be institutionalized.

Issues in community conflict may be classified according to such substantive criteria as economic, social, and political. But a more fundamental classification is in terms of the relationship between the parties and the relationship to the status quo. Issues may thus be classified as "schismatic" if they tend to pull the parties involved in opposite directions and hence to destroy community, or "pressuring" if they push the parties against one

[4] For a discussion of the whole problem of social causation, see R. M. MacIver, *Social Causation* (Boston: Ginn, 1942).

another. One may be pictured as a tug-of-war type of issue, with the parties pulling against one another, so: ⟵ ⟶. The other may be pictured as an Indian-wrestling type of issue, with one party pushing against the other, so: ⟶ ⟵. Examples of schismatic issues are those which produce civil wars, secessions, sects, or the breakdown of social systems. Examples of pressuring issues are those which produce step-by-step advance and retreat, "nibbling away," resistance movements, toe-in-the-door, precedents, for example. So long as slavery was accepted by both North and South it was a pressuring-type issue, the South pushing to extend it legally and territorially and the North resisting its extension. Secession, however, was a schismatic issue; the South was pulling in one direction and the North in another. The existence of labor unions was a schismatic issue; but, once they were accepted, the issues between them and management became pressuring issues, unions pushing for more and more and management resisting. Desegregation is originally a schismatic issue; but once it is settled, it becomes a pressuring issue, the Negroes pushing for more and more privileges, white citizens' councils resisting the push.

Schismatic issues are likely to be categorical in nature: slavery or no slavery, state aid to church schools or no state aid to them. Pressuring issues can be reduced to points on a continuum. The union demands ten cents, the company offers seven cents. When the issue is a pressuring one the problem of strategic limits arises. People often "take a stand" on an issue not because of the intrinsic merits of the case but because if they do not, there is no stopping point.

> [A pressuring-type issue] often makes small concessions less likely than large ones; it often means that the focal point is more persuasive as an *exact* expected outcome than as an approximation. If a bargainer has persistently been unsuccessfully demanding 50 percent, compromise at 47 percent is unlikely; the small concession may be a sign of collapse. Qualitative principles are hard to compromise, and focal points generally depend on qualitative principles. One cannot expect to satisfy an aggressor by letting him have a few square miles on this side of a boundary; he knows that we both know that we both expect our side to retreat until we find some persuasive new boundary that can be rationalized.
>
> In fact, a focal point for agreement often owes its focal character to the fact that small encroachments would lead to more and larger ones. One draws a line at some conspicuous boundary or rests his case on some conspicuous principle that is supported mainly by the rhetorical question, "If not here, where?" The more it is clear that concession is collapse, the more convincing the focal point is.[5]

Some kinds of issues characterize certain kinds of conflict; others, different ones. The issues in buyer-seller conflict, for example, are almost always of the pressuring type; but those between racial and ethnic groups are often schismatic. Schismatic issues are more likely to destroy community than are pressuring issues.

[5] Schelling, *op. cit.*, pp. 111-112.

Three Ways to Deal with Incompatible Differences

The sociological phenomena subsumed under the rubric "conflict" are so variegated and complex that no one theoretical framework will suffice for all. A theory that explains or interprets one kind will not serve the same function for other kinds. At least three theoretical approaches are called for, each dealing with a different way of handling incompatible differences, as indicated in the Introduction to Part III.

One way to deal with incompatible differences is to get rid of one of the parties, either by destroying it, by expelling it from the community, or by withdrawing oneself from the community. Conflict is ended, if not resolved, by destroying community. We call this the schism model.

A second way to deal with incompatible differences is to change one or both or all of the parties involved. This can be done either by converting them, convincing them, persuading them, or by brainwashing them. Whatever technique is used, the end result is to get rid of the differences; the parties are now similar or assimilated. We call this the image-changing model.

Between these two extremes lies a way which does not get rid of differences but tries to find some way to accommodate them. This we shall call the "strategic game" model.

These ways of dealing with incompatible differences may be thought of as lying along a continuum as well as constituting separate and categorical phenomena. Figure 6-1 presents such a continuum in the form of an inverted V, and Figure 6-2 suggests the corresponding degree of schism. The distance between the lines in Figure 6-1 represents the relative strength of common and conflicting interests. At the bottom of Figure 6-1, just over the threshold of destruction of community is the zone of zero-sum conflict, where common interests are at a minimum. Above this is the zone of conflict in which common interests enter the picture. As common interests come to overshadow conflicting interests—however this is brought about—the interests of both parties may coalesce. And, finally, the conflicting interests, and hence the conflict itself, may disappear entirely.

Theory of Schism

A community is made up of groups and classes of people interacting with one another or reacting to one another. A particular status quo is the relationship among them at any given time. If we think of any particular status quo in a community as a coalition of "players," or parties, or as a system of systems, it is theoretically possible for it to move either in the direction of complete schism, or falling apart, or in the direction of complete assimilation. In the first case, community is destroyed; in the second, the differences disappear. If the differences between or among the parties are, or seem to be, so incompatible that they can no longer share the same living space or interact in any way, the social system breaks down. The schism may take the form of divorce, secession, separatism, emigration, isolation, withdrawal; or ostracism, excommunication, banishment, transportation, exile, expulsion. Whether one of the parties withdraws or is forced out by the other, the result is the same. Community is destroyed; the elements in the original social system separate. The conflict cannot be said to be resolved, but it is avoided.

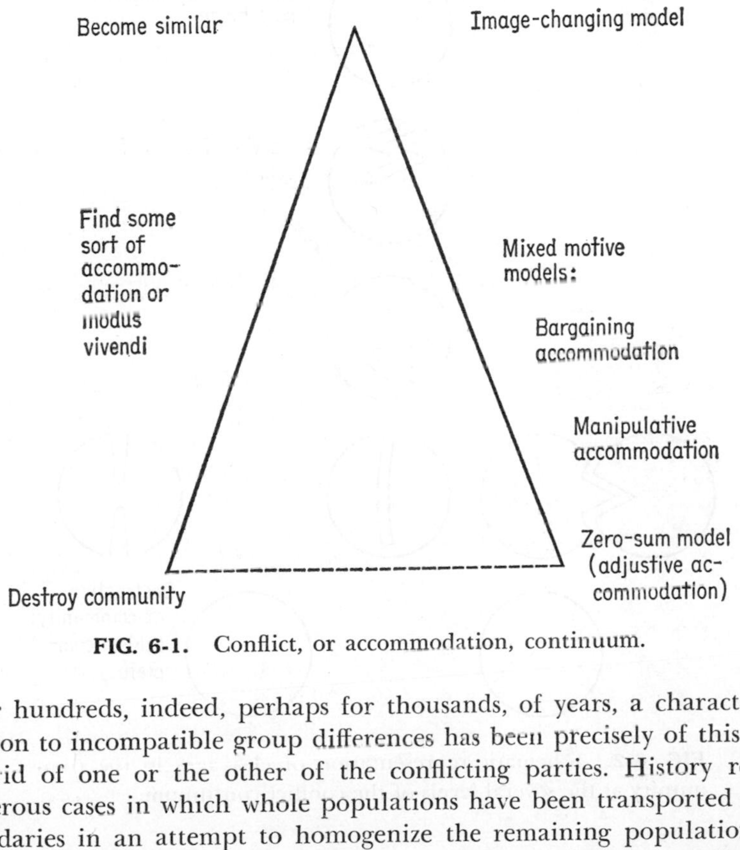

FIG. 6-1. Conflict, or accommodation, continuum.

For hundreds, indeed, perhaps for thousands, of years, a characteristic reaction to incompatible group differences has been precisely of this kind. Get rid of one or the other of the conflicting parties. History records numerous cases in which whole populations have been transported across boundaries in an attempt to homogenize the remaining populations; or secessions, sect formations, emigrations, treks, of one kind or another—including the movements of religious communities out to the wilderness—to protect the homogeneity of the departing populations. The English dissenters who left Holland to come to America when they saw their children in danger of losing their differences are a classic illustration of the obviating of conflict by destroying community. The withdrawal of South Africa from the British Commonwealth is another. Where it was not possible to export populations, the development of enclaves of one sort or another—ghettos or pales—voluntary and crescive at first but involuntary and enacted later on—have not been rare. Sociological barriers have been developed to protect separatism or apartheid and thus prevent assimilation. It has been suggested that Jewish dietary laws may have performed this separating function, preventing Jews from eating with non-Jews. Or political and economic barriers may be erected; isolation was a national policy in our country until well into the twentieth century.

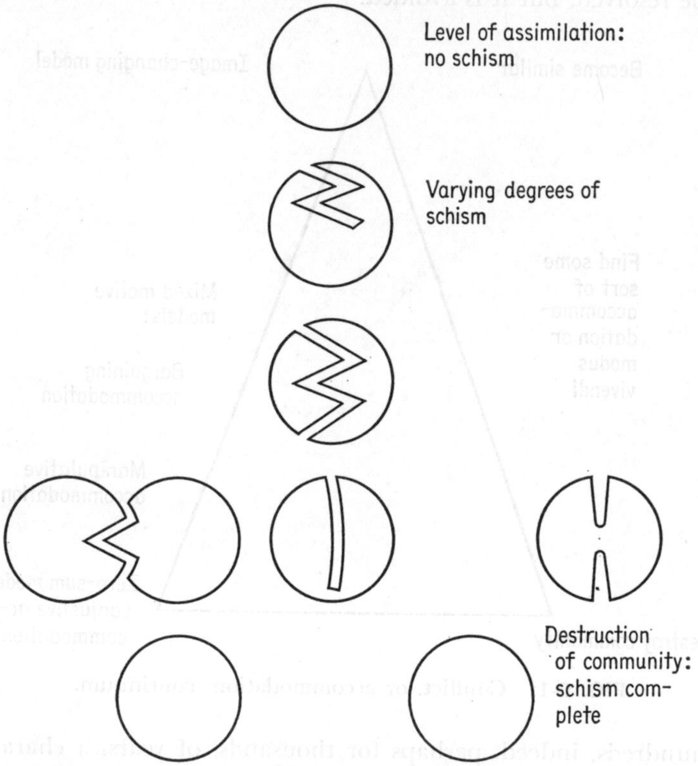

FIG. 6-2. Schematic representation of cleavages in the community at the several levels of the conflict continuum.

If neither form of destroying community was possible, the cognate form of getting rid of differences by getting rid of the people themselves—blood baths, purges, liquidations, massacres, genocides, and slaughter—has also occurred in many forms. In either form, the underlying principle is the same: you get rid of the conflict by destroying community.

Theories of schism attempt to explain how social systems thus fall apart. One such theory is stated in terms of the relative costs to a group of remaining in the system and of withdrawing.[6] It posits a discrepancy between the goal-attainment of a subsystem and the goal-attainment of the supersystem. "If this discrepancy is small . . . it will be advantageous for both systems to 'ally.' . . . In such a case the relationship between the two systems will be a fairly stable one."[7] But sometimes two systems suffer more disadvantages than advantages from maintaining their alliance or coalition. If it is unilateral, that is, if one system bears all the disadvantages, either the disadvantages are removed through bargaining and compromise, or schism results. Even if the sacrifice or cost between the systems is equal, the cost of the alliance or coalition to both may be too great. The theory of schism is stated as follows:

> . . . the increased attainment of a given end entails increased utility to the system up to a certain point, though with decreasing increments of utility as that point is approached. Beyond that point, at first with small decrements but with progressively increasing decrements as the given end is further pursued, utility decreases.

When the parameters for all the systems are the same, all gain by remaining together. But when or if there is a discrepancy between the end-attainment and consequent utility of the systems, there will be a tendency in the direction of schism.

> In alliances of this kind there will surely develop schismatic processes . . . continued coalition between two such systems would become less and less advantageous. . . . In extreme cases the very possibility of a durable liaison between two systems is ruled out by the nature of environmental resistances. Only when those resistances are changed may the utility curves be brought into some sort of rapprochement and the possibility of an alliance between the two systems be recreated.[8]

In other words, when the disadvantages of remaining in the system or community outweigh the advantages—on whatever scale of value they are measured—schism is a likely outcome.

Schism might also be viewed as an illustration of competition; two policies compete. One leads to remaining in the community (or permitting an opponent to remain) and the other to leaving the community (or ejecting the opponent). The policy which yields the greater reward or exacts the lesser cost will be the one selected.

Whichever theory one accepts, it is certainly true that the dissolution of social systems as a way of dealing with incompatible differences becomes more problematic as the world as a whole becomes more integrated and as the areas of community widen. It remains, but it no longer seems to be

[6] Walter Firey, "Informal Organization and the Theory of Schism," *Amer. Sociol. Rev.*, 13 (February, 1948), pp. 15-24.

[7] *Ibid.*, p. 20.

[8] *Ibid.*, pp. 21-22.

necessarily the best or even a good way to handle incompatible differences. In the United States the concept of the so-called pluralistic society has evolved which deprecates schismatic solutions to community relations.

Theory of Assimilation

The theory of schism explains why social systems, or communities, fall apart. The same theories, in reverse, may explain how social systems are built up. They would simply emphasize the advantages, rather than the costs, of belonging to systems. Other theories attempt to explain how certain groups incorporate or swallow up other groups. Political scientists, for example, have expounded the so-called conquest theory of the origin of states, which holds that they arise by conquering neighboring groups and integrating their inhabitants, usually on an exploitative basis.

But our concern here is more than mere integration, for integration may occur at any level of the conflict continuum. We are interested, rather, in the processes by which the units in a system become similar, or assimilated. "An accommodation of a conflict . . . may take place with rapidity. The more intimate and subtle changes involved in assimilation are more gradual. . . . The unity thus achieved is not necessarily or even normally like-mindedness; it is rather a unity of experience and of orientation, out of which may develop a community of purpose and action."[9] Now the incompatible differences are reduced or even eliminated by the changing of one or the other or both of the parties. The emergence of a common enemy often has this effect; the conflicting parties now have more in common—defeating the enemy—than they have in conflict, so that their interests now coalesce.

Ordinarily assimilation is a slow and even unconscious process. But sometimes a deliberate effort is made to change opponents, to change their goals so that they are no longer incompatible; it is an attempt to get rid of the conflict but not of the people involved. How to achieve this end? If we were dealing with rational phenomena, the answer would be to use argument, to marshal facts, to show logical consequences. But changing people's values is not a rational matter. In an argument points are made when one party is caught in a logical inconsistency, in ignorance, in error of fact, or in a misinterpretation. But no amount of piling up of such points will necessarily change an opponent; more is required. Situations must be redefined or, as one commentator says, images must be changed.[10]

Three techniques for changing images have been distinguished; namely: brainwashing, based on the theory of conditioned response; explaining the image away, based on Freudian theory; and removing the threats felt to be associated with alternative images, based on Carl Rogers'

[9] Park and Burgess, *An Introduction to the Science of Sociology* (Chicago: University of Chicago, 1924), pp. 736-737.

[10] Rapoport, *op. cit.*, p. 273.

theory of understanding and permissiveness. Debate, as distinguished from argument, is suggested as a suitable vehicle for such image-changing. By proving to an opponent that you understand his point of view you open him up to a willingness to listen to yours. Debate is thus an effort to persuade or convince an opponent to accept your own image and hence goals.[11] Whatever the technique used, one party is "reborn" or "re-educated," so that he now embraces the goals of his former opponent.

Theory of Strategic Games

Between the two extremes of schism or separation and assimilation lies the area of accommodation. The incompatible differences remain but somehow or other a *modus vivendi* is worked out. It is a situation which the American sociologist W. G. Sumner once called "antagonistic cooperation."[12] Neither party can or even wants to get rid of the other; they must, or even want to, remain in the same community. They have this much in common. Nor can either party win the other over to its side; they have this much in conflict. The resulting outcome depends on the way the relationship between or among the parties is institutionalized, upon the relative strength of the parties, upon the way the relationship is structured, and upon the skill with which the parties use their assets.

The theory of strategic games has been found to apply to such situations. It refers not to situations governed by chance, in which skill is not involved, nor yet to those governed by skill, in which chance is not involved. It refers, rather, to situations in which both skill, of a certain kind, and chance, or risk or uncertainty, are involved. It assumes two players—Ego and Alter, let us call them—with conflicting goals. Both have a set of alternative ways of acting. These they can control. But it assumes also that neither can control the other's way of acting. The situation has been called one of interdependent decision, referred to in Chapter 1, since the success or failure, effectiveness or lack of effectiveness, correctness or incorrectness of any decision on the part of Ego—which he can control—depends on the decisions of Alter—which Ego cannot control. And, of course, vice versa. Each player is trying to win. Win in this case does not necessarily mean overcoming an opponent; it means doing the best possible under the circumstances, even if only to cut one's losses.

In its simplest form there are, let us say, only two players, A and B, and each has two alternative courses of action, *X* and *Y* for A and *x* and *y* for B. There are, then, four possible outcomes or combinations of courses of action: *xX*, *xY*, *yX*, and *yY*. These four outcomes are not determined by the players; they are inherent in the situation. If A follows policy *x* and B follows policy *y*, the result will be *xy*. Now each player has to evaluate each of the four outcomes; how much is each worth to him? The value

[11] *Ibid.*, pp. 273 ff.

[12] *Folkways* (Boston: Ginn, 1906), pp. 16-18, 49, 346.

will, of course, have to be weighted by the relative probability of each, a bird in the hand, presumably, being worth two in the bush.

Although in real life, conflict situations do not come neatly analyzed for us, for theoretical purposes conflicts are usually presented in the form of paradigms or charts or matrices like this:

CONFLICT MATRIX

Ego's alternatives	Alter's alternatives	
	x	y
X	Xx	Xy
Y	Yx	Yy

Or, more simply:

Xx	Xy
Yx	Yy

The combination of letters stands for outcomes, not for combinations of acts. Thus xX might mean: if Alter insists on an aggressive policy (*x*) and Ego insists on a repressive policy (*X*), the result (*Xx*) will be bloodshed, closed schools, a strike. If Alter takes a submissive policy (*y*) and Ego takes on a repressive policy (*Y*), the outcome will be (*yY*), frustration, hostility, and resentment on Alter's part but no violence and Ego will have privileges, although at the price of possible sabotage and much police protection. If Alter insists on an aggressive policy (*x*) and Ego takes an appeasing policy (*X*), Alter achieves integrated schools or housing perhaps and Ego loses some of his privileges (*xX*). If Alter adopts a submissive policy (*y*) and Ego an appeasing one (*X*), Alter does not get what he might have gotten and/or Ego gives up more than he need have given up (*yX*).

The theory of games of strategy is presented in terms of the "utility" of each outcome to the players. The concept of utility is a complex one and by no means consensually fixed. In no case is it assumed that the utilities of the separate players are comparable. That is, the utility or value which an object has for one player cannot be compared with the value which it has for another. However the utilities or values which different objects have for the same player are comparable. In fact, the theory rests on the basic assumption that each player does have a scale of preference for each set of outcomes; he prefers some to others. Not only this, but he prefers one four or ten or *x* times more than he prefers the others. One situation, for example, may have the following form:

4	9
0	5

By convention the values are presented as they look to Ego, and in a zero-sum game the values for Alter are identical but negative, or reversed. Outcome *Xx,* for example is worth 4 to Ego and —4 to Alter; *yX* is worth 9 to Ego, —9 to Alter; *xY* is worth nothing to either one; and *yY* is worth 5 to Ego, —5 to Alter. It is because in such a situation what one player wins the other loses that it is called a "zero-sum" game.

But sometimes this is not the case. Outcomes may have different values to the two players. Such games are presented with two sets of values in each cell, one in the upper righthand corner referring to Alter, in the lower lefthand corner, to Ego, thus:

	4		0			8		0
10		0		or	5		6	
	0		8			4		5
9		3			0		8	

Now *xX* has a value of 10 or 5 for Ego, but 4 or 8 for Alter, and so on. Such situations are not zero-sum because gains and losses do not necessarily cancel out.

Games of strategy have been classified in many ways; according to: the number of players involved, the number of strategies or alternatives involved, or according to whether it was a tacit game of maneuver—of moves, but not talk—or explicit, in which talk was involved; or according to technical characteristics of interest only to mathematicians. One classification, in addition to zero-sum and nonzero-sum games breaks the second kind down into mixed-motive games, common-interest games, and coordinating games.

For our purposes here we shall restate the criteria and distinguish two forms of conflict to which the theory of games of strategy is relevant, namely, adjustive and manipulative.

Adjustive forms of conflict are those in which there is only conflict in the relationship or, at best, only the barest minimum of common interest. It represents the zero-sum situation. The parties minimize the interaction between or among themselves. They behave in such a way as to reduce communication. It is just short of the total destruction of community because they must still make all their decisions in terms of what their opponents can or may do. But secrecy is often important; barriers are high.

The parties are not attempting to control the behavior of their opponents. They adjust to it. They try to "read" one another's mind, to anticipate how they will behave. They then act in such a way that no matter what the opponent does they will achieve at least a minimum success. This is sometimes called the minimax or maxmin principle. In effect each party reduces his opponent to a thing, so far as interaction is concerned. He figures out what the opponent is likely to do and then adjusts his own behavior so that he gets as much as he can, assuming the worst. This is an adjustive situation in the sense that neither party can influence the other;

each accepts the other's position and decides his own course of action in such a way as to minimize his losses and maximize his gains. Each adjusts to the situation as it is.

Sometimes it makes no difference if the opponent knows what one is going to do.[13] Often, however, it does. If so, there is great secrecy involved so as not to let the opponent know one's weaknesses; surprise is a great element, in order to catch the other party off-guard. One tries to confuse his opponent by mixing his actions, the relative frequency of one or the other being determined on the basis of certain ratios. There may be bluffing and feinting to mislead the opponent, but no effort to change him or change his range of choices.

Manipulative forms of conflict take us into the realm of day-by-day power and control relationships, of coercion and deterrence. For they represent the so-called mixed-motive[14] game situation in which the players may have a good many common as well as conflicting interests. The practical implications of this are great. For instead of adjusting to an opponent, the players in a mixed-motive situation try to influence or control him. Not by force or by violence but rather by psychological means, by strategy. And since neither player can directly control the alternatives of his opponent he does it indirectly by his own behavior. He acts in such a way as to influence his opponent's choices. He makes all the opponent's alternatives except the one he himself prefers less desirable. By making an opponent do something Ego wants him to do that the opponent does not want to do—or did not want to do before Ego made any other alternative less preferable—Ego coerces him or, in the same way, deters him. Ego "forces the hand" of Alter, making him do things against his own interest in order to avoid consequences even worse. Interaction is at a maximum in this kind of situation; it depends very largely on knowing one's opponent so well that one knows just what kinds of strategies will be most effective in forcing him to do what one wants. It is control or manipulation by way of change in the value structure of an opponent.

Bargaining is a special form of the mixed-motive game. Buyer and seller may be in conflict about the price of an article, but they have in common an interest in making some exchange. Negotiators of a wage contract or of an international treaty are engaged in this form of conflict. It is the essence of lawmaking. It was the form which even race conflict took when direct action in some communities led to negotiated settlements of grievances.

So far as community conflict is concerned, the manipulative form, or the mixed-motive game, is more important than the adjustive form, or the

[13] For example, in this situation, secrecy would not be important: $\begin{matrix} 4 & 8 \\ 6 & 12 \end{matrix}$ Ego will not select X because he gets more from Y no matter what Alter does; Alter will select *x* because he loses less, no matter what Ego does. The best they can do is *xY*.

[14] Schelling has suggested this terminology and greatly illuminated the social-psychological nature of the mixed-motive game.

zero-sum game. It is difficult, in fact, to find any conflicts which illustrate the zero-sum situation in pristine form. For if the conflict is as inexorable as the zero-sum form implies, the chances are that one or the other will be extruded from the community or withdraw from it.

In the zero-sum situation, interaction is at a minimum; each side tries to hide from the other. In mixed-motive situations interaction may be intense. Each illustrates a form of accommodating incompatible differences in goals or aims; but the nature of the accommodation differs greatly in the two forms.

> Hardly anything captures the spirit of the zero-sum game quite so much as the importance of "not being found out" and of employing a mode of decision that is proof against deductive anticipation by the other player. Hardly anything epitomizes the mixed-motive game so much as the advantage of being able to adopt a mode of behavior that the other party will take for granted.[15]

The way in which manipulative conflict operates will be clearer if we examine the nature of strategic moves.

Strategic Moves

In manipulative conflict, as we just noted, one party attempts to control—coerce or deter—an opponent by playing on his expectations; he himself behaves in such a way as to manipulate the motives of the other. Such forms of behavior have been called strategic moves.[16]

> A strategic move is one that influences the other person's choice, in a manner favorable to oneself, by affecting the other person's expectations of how oneself will behave. One constrains the partner's choice by constraining one's own behavior. The object is to set up for oneself and communicate persuasively to the other player a mode of behavior (including conditional responses to the other's behavior) that leaves the other a simple maximization problem whose solution for him is the optimum for oneself, and to destroy the other's ability to do the same.

Although not necessarily limited to human beings, strategy is a characteristically human technique; the use of verbal language enormously extends the repertory of strategic moves possible in any conflict situation and the existence of other institutions, including common collective expectations, further enriches the strategic moves available, making the use of force and violence a relatively decreasing recourse.

The essentially social or interactional nature of strategic moves is shown by the fact that basic to their effectiveness is a clearly communicated commitment to a certain course of action. If one can irrevocably commit oneself to a certain line of action and convince one's opponent that one is so committed, this may be enough to win, to force the opponent to do something he would much rather not do.

[15] Schelling, *op. cit.*, p. 160.
[16] *Ibid.*

"First move" is achieved if one enters the conflict situation with such a commitment. This is the strategy used whenever legislation or crescive rules fix prices, wages, or other objects, thus removing them from negotiation or bargaining. Before the practice of charging the same price for all comers was institutionalized, customers bargained with shopkeepers for goods. Today there is little of this. The shopkeeper has "first move." The customer can take it or leave it. To protect themselves still further, some retailers ask for protection of fixed prices. Minimum wage laws and labor contracts are other illustrations of "first move" strategy. They obviate bargaining. Segregation laws give the "first move" to white people. "I'd love to serve you in our dining room," the white proprietor may say to the Negro, "but my hands are tied; the law won't permit me to."

"Second move" is a special kind of commitment which takes the form of a threat or a promise. A strategic threat attempts to control the opponent's behavior by convincing him that unless he does what you want him to do *you* are committed to doing something that damages *both* parties.

> The threat differs from the ordinary commitment . . . in that it makes one's course of action *conditional* on what the other player does. While the commitment fixes one's course of action, the threat fixes a course of *re*action, of response to the other player. The commitment is a means of gaining *first move* in a game in which first move carries an advantage; the threat is a commitment to a strategy for *second move*. A threat can therefore be effective only if the game is one in which the first move is up to the other player or one can *force* the other player to move first.[17]

The threat is, in effect, a way of shouting "I mean it!" It is a way of communicating how much it means to the threatener to have the opponent act or not act in a certain way; it means so much that he is willing to punish himself. To be effective, however, the threat must be credible; it must be convincing. The union leader threatens a strike; the white community leaders threaten to close down its public schools; consumers threaten a boycott. Such threats are effective only if they include a commitment, a penalty for nonfulfillment of the threat.

Another name for threat is "promise"; both are "names for different aspects of the same tactic of selective and conditional self-commitment, which in certain simple instances can be identified in terms of the second party's interest."[18] "If you'll dismantle your desegregating apparatus we'll give you excellent schools." "If you'll stop supporting your union we'll give you better working conditions and wages than the union gets for you." The opposing party wants to be sure. "How do we know you'll carry out your promise?" If the promising party cannot convince his opponent, the promise has no effect in influencing his opponent's behavior. The promiser must

[17] *Ibid.*, p. 124.
[18] *Ibid.*, p. 134.

make his commitment ironclad. Enforcement must be provided for. Sometimes the opponent trusts the promising party because he knows that the promising party recognizes that if he reneges on his promise he will lose far more than he gains, that "cheating in a given instance is outweighed by the value of the tradition of trust that makes possible a long sequence of future agreement."[19] One instance of defaulting on a promise may make it forever impossible to achieve a working agreement. The desegregationists who, figuratively, "disarm" themselves only to find one delay after another in improving their schools, would be infinitely more demanding and aggressive in fighting for their goals. Promises may be said to be self-enforcing if the costs of reneging would be greater than of carrying out the promise. Sometimes promises are embedded in contracts which are enforceable in the courts. Promises to pay are enforced by demanding "security." The institution of hostages has been described as a technique for insuring the enforcement of promises.[20] Denial of enforcement of promises embedded in contracts robs the promise of its strategic significance; thus when the United States Supreme Court stated that promises of homeowners not to sell their property to Negroes could not be enforced in the courts, the restrictive covenants which kept homeowners from selling to Negroes lost much of their force.

Just as "first move" and "second move" (in the form of either threat or promise) depend upon firm and unalterable proof and communication of commitment to a certain course of action, there is another kind of strategic move which depends for its effectiveness on precisely the opposite kind of situation, a situation in which one no longer has any effective choice over his own behavior at all. This move has been called "relinquishing the initiative."[21] It is, in effect, a substitution of warning for threat. A warning conveys information. If you do this, then such-and-so will happen. Such-and-so is not under my control. I can't prevent it. If you bring it about I cannot be held responsible for the outcome. This strategy shifts the responsibility or blame to the opponent. Nonviolent resistance illustrates this kind of strategy.

After encouraging hostility and resistance to school desegregation, the mayor says, "The people are in an ugly mood; I can't be held responsible for what happens if you go ahead with your program."

Closely related to relinquishing the initiative is turning over one's initiative to some delegated agent. One use of this strategy is to "pass the buck." "Sorry, but I have no authority in the matter," says the bureaucrat, thus protecting himself from the irate public. The union member delegates to professional bargainers the fight with his employer; alone, he would hesitate to refuse to work overtime. Or the government, in effect,

19 *Ibid.*, p. 135.
20 *Ibid.*, pp. 135-136.
21 *Ibid.*, pp. 137-139.

assumes responsibility for protecting consumers and thus serves as their agent. They might not wish to prosecute; but the government agent is eager to do so.

Conflict As Power Relationships

The form which conflict takes is greatly influenced by the relative power of the parties involved. This does not mean that the party with greater physical power necessarily wins or has its way; the exact opposite may be true, as the great colonial powers have been learning so reluctantly in the twentieth century.[22] Strategic power depends on many other factors than sheer physical power.

Power may be thought of as a bank of chips of different kinds. Some are very much desired by almost everyone; others are shunned by almost everyone. They come in different denominations. Money is a close approximation to the first kind of chip in our society. Almost everyone wants it. But other kinds of chips stand for honor, reward, love, affection, fame, glory, or whatever else people want. Conversely, the other chips stand for disgrace, loss of face, loss of love, loss of loved ones, shame, humiliation, or whatever else people dread. A person who has a large stock of such chips can use them to motivate people to do things he wants them to do, often to do things they would not want to do if the alternatives were not even worse. He is in a position to make the alternatives worse.

We have all become familiar in moving pictures and television with the villain who tries to "get something" on the hero in order to control him. The underworld leader, for example, "has something" on a public official; he can use this to blackmail the official. The person who controls the chips can "turn the screw," "leave me no choice," "give no alternative."

Sometimes the chips are more positive. The manipulator still controls the alternatives, but now it is a case in which the manipulated person "can't afford not to" do what the manipulator wants him to do. Gifts and subsidies of one kind or another illustrate this kind of chip. The government subsidizes an industry or a school; the threat to withdraw the support becomes a strategic chip.

At a more refined level, strategic moves are likely to be veiled; they may be "understood" rather than be articulated. Again in moving pictures the hero may shout, "That's blackmail!" to which the polished villain shrugs his shoulders in disgust that his squeeze play should be so brutishly labeled.

There are some positions in any social structure where there is a great concentration of such chips. Top positions in most organizations contain many which pass as currency in the organization; strategic use of them coerces and deters members. Sometimes there is a duel between organiza-

[22] See *ibid.*, pp. 158-160 for an analysis of the paradoxes of power.

tions, each attempting to win over the other. The power chips that were effective within one organization may not be effective vis-à-vis an outside organization.

There are two quite divergent points of view with respect to the nature of power in our society. One sees many seats of power, often in conflict with one another. An interesting form of this view is represented by John Kenneth Galbraith, who developed the idea that whenever there is a too great concentration of original power in our society, the tendency has always been for it to give rise to so-called countervailing power to share it.[23] When management, for example, became too powerful in the nineteenth century, unions arose as a countervailing power. Whenever the concentration of power becomes too great—even in the church—countervailing forces are set into motion to limit it.

The other point of view emphasizes the tendency for all power centers to coalesce, so that the several power centers become a single power center. In our society, this point of view emphasizes, the economic, political, and military centers of power have, in effect, become one great reservoir of power capable of controlling all aspects of our society.[24]

The moves used in any particular conflict will depend upon the way the relationship between or among the parties is institutionalized, upon their relative strength, upon the way the relationship is structured, and upon the degree to which common interests as well as conflicting ones are present.

Institutions and Conflict

Institutions play an enormous part in conflict. For one thing, the alternative policies or actions available to the parties are determined by institutions. It would never be possible in the United States, for example, to embark upon a policy of extermination of Jews, a policy which was quite possible under Hitler in Germany. Some techniques are unthinkable in a given society because the mores forbid them.

Institutions also influence the strategies available to any particular party by defining the way the relationship between the parties is institutionalized. If, for example, one party is in a coalition with the government, this fact adds to its ability to use threats. For decades law was on the side of the white members of the community: laws and court decisions have now given Negroes bargaining power and thus altered the nature of race conflict.

Institutions supply the power to make commitments, a basic component in strategic moves, by standing ready to enforce promises and by making threats credible. Institutions also, it will be recalled, serve the

[23] John Kenneth Galbraith, *American Capitalism* (Boston: Houghton-Mifflin, 1952).
[24] C. Wright Mills, *The Power Elite* (New York: Oxford, 1956).

function of creating expectations. Where neither side has any idea what to expect from the other, where they cannot "read" one another, it is difficult to carry on a conflict on any other than a force basis.

Because of the ubiquity and pervasiveness of conflict and because the consequences may be so far-reaching, within any society conflict is regulated by numerous institutional norms, crescive and enacted. Even violence, which will be discussed later, is subject to institutional controls.

This discussion so far has viewed conflict abstractly, in a vacuum. Actually, of course, conflict in the community occurs in very specific situations and is enormously influenced by them. A specific conflict has a sort of natural history of its own; it changes as it proceeds.

We referred above to the applicability of the equations for contingent competition to a study of conflict also. If the subjective feelings—*g* and *h*—are hostile, then each side is, in effect, trying to outdo the other in hostile behavior. The hostility of one side stimulates more hostility in the other side in a snowballing effect. What began as a minor difference may balloon into a major cleavage.

One empirical study of a large number of cases of community conflict has shown that there are certain "dynamics of controversy" that show remarkable similarity in widely differing kinds of situations. There are, it appears, certain steps or stages that occur with almost monotonous regularity. These may be viewed as parts of the natural history of community conflict.

The Natural History of Community Conflict

There is, first of all, a threefold transformation in the original issue giving rise to the conflict: (1) it becomes more general and, in the process, it "uncovers the fundamental differences which set the stage for a precipitating incident in the first place";[25] (2) new and different issues, not related to the original issue, emerge, issues that had been latent before but, now that the conflict has become active, become manifest, and participants in the conflict invoke new issues in order to attract adherents and to win solidarity; and (3) disagreement turns into antagonism, so that the conflict maintains itself on the basis of hostility without regard to the original issues.[26] This threefold process has been schematized as follows:

[25] James S. Coleman, *Community Conflict* (New York: Free Press, 1957), p. 100.

[26] "The dynamics which account for the shift from disagreement to antagonism are two: 'involuntary,' and deliberate. Simmel explains the involuntary process by saying that it is 'expedient' and 'appropriate' to hate one's opponent just as it is 'appropriate' to like someone who agrees with you. But perhaps there is a stronger explanation: we associate with every person we know certain beliefs, interests, traits, attributes, and so forth. So long as we disagree with only one or a few of his beliefs, we are 'divided' in our feelings toward him. He is not wholly black or white in our eyes. But when we quarrel, the process of argument itself generates new issues; we disagree with more and more of our opponent's beliefs. Since these beliefs constitute *him* in our eyes, rather than isolated

Stage 1. There is a single issue.
Stage 2. It disrupts the equilibrium of community relations.
Stage 3. Previously suppressed issues are released.
Stage 4. More and more of participants' beliefs enter into the disagreement.
Stage 5. As a result the opponents look totally bad to one another.
Stage 6. Charges are made against opponents as persons.
Stage 7. The dispute becomes independent of the initial disagreement.[27]

Along with these changes in the issues there are concomitant changes in the social organization of the community also. There is a polarization of social relations as people tend to increase association with those on their side and cut out association with those on the opposing side. This polarization "tends to alter the social geography of the community to separate it into two clusters, breaking apart along the line of least attachment."[28] If there are no existing organizations to serve as nuclei for the two sides, such partisan organizations are formed. With the development of such organizations as nuclei, new leaders tend to take over the dispute. As the conflict continues, other community organizations tend to be drawn in, unless there are opposing views held by members which demand neutrality or unless their participation would endanger their position in the community. The momentum of the conflict leads to greatly increased need for news; the formal media of communication become inadequate to carry the load—and they are restrained by laws against slander and libel—so that word-of-mouth communication increases. Rumor, street-corner discussion, slanderous and libelous charges, hate-mongering abound and add to the intensity of the conflict.

Once a conflict starts rolling, mutual re-inforcement keeps it going.[29] But it does not always follow the same course. The actual course will depend on many factors which vary from one community to another, including: leadership, political structure, social structure, economic structure, and the part played by the mass media.

The influence of leaders is critical. It frequently happens that the responsible leaders of the community are immobilized by the emergence of new combat organizations with new leaders. These new leaders, spawned by the crisis, tend to be a special breed:

> Often they are men who have not been community leaders in the past, men who face none of the constraints of maintaining a previous community position and feel none of the cross-pressures felt by members of community organizations.

---

aspects of him, his image grows blacker. Our hostility is directed toward him personally. Thus the two processes—the first leading from a single issue to new and different ones, and the second leading from disagreement to direct antagonism—fit together perfectly and help carry the controversy along its course" *ibid.*, p. 11.

27 Based on Coleman's diagram, *ibid.*

28 *Ibid.*, p. 12.

29 The equations referred to in connection with contingent competition (Chapter 5) apply here. The more hostility one side shows the more the other side shows.

In addition, these leaders rarely have real identification with the community. In the literature they often emerge as marginal men who have never held a position of leadership before. A study of the fight against city-manager plans pictures the leaders of the opposition as men personally frustrated and maladjusted. The current desegregation fights have produced numerous such leaders, often young, one a former convict, usually from the outside. The new leaders, at any rate, are seldom moderates; the situation itself calls for extremists. And such men have not been conditioned, through experience in handling past community problems, to the prevailing norms concerning tactics of dispute. . . . The processes may be said to create a Gresham's Law of Conflict; the harmful and dangerous elements drive out those which would keep the conflict within bounds. Reckless, unrestrained leaders head the attack; combat organizations arise to replace the milder, more constrained pre-existing organizations; derogatory and scurrilous charges replace dispassionate issues; antagonism replaces disagreement, and a drive to ruin the opponent takes the place of the initial will to win. In other words, all the forces put into effect by the initiation of conflict act to drive out the conciliatory elements, replace them with those better equipped for combat.[30]

The political structure of the community is also important since it determines what tactics are available to the combatants. If there is a rigid dictatorial regime—and there are hundreds of American communities of this kind—which is unresponsive to the public, the form which conflict will take tends to be sporadic and irrational outbursts rather than organized opposition. If the regime indulges in some especially offensive act, or if the "climate of opinion" changes, dissatisfaction may find expression and leadership and attack it from the outside. In some political structures there are built-in provisions for the expression of dissent, so that "the system can drain off in small, everyday disputes the hostilities and dissatisfactions which otherwise accumulate and break out in intense controversy. Even in cases where dissatisfaction does reach large proportions, the system contains a means for redress within it."[31] The technique of "coöption" is available in some political structures; it gives the opposition apparent voice in policy. Whether this sharing of power is real or not, it often has the effect of breaking into the course of the conflict which divides the community into opposing camps.

The social structure, as well as the political structure, exerts a strong influence on community conflict. Four factors are involved; namely: (1) degree of identification of citizens with the community; (2) density of organizations and associations in the community; (3) distribution of participation among the citizens; and (4) the interlocking of organizational memberships.

Identification of citizens with the community has a twofold effect. It leads to a greater amount and intensity of controversy since the people are involved and want the community to develop along their line; but it also

[30] Coleman, *op. cit.*, pp. 12, 14.
[31] *Ibid.*, p. 16.

restrains the nature of the conflict since all parties have a common interest in keeping it within limits. Conversely, those who do not feel identified with the community really do not care that much and are therefore less likely to take part in conflict; but for the same reason, once they do take part they are more likely to overstep the bounds of legitimate methods, so that the conflict degenerates to antagonism.

Organizational density has both direct and indirect effects on conflict. Where there are a great many organizations, the pressure on individual members to become involved in any conflict is great. But where there are very few organizations, conflict may occur without involving the rest of the community. Indirectly the effect of organization density is to create identification with the community. Some organizations are more likely than others to be identified with the community. Churches, parent-teacher associations, civic luncheon clubs, and women's clubs show high identification with the community; veterans' groups, lodges, country clubs, and labor unions show less.[32] High organization density in a community tends to draw the community into controversy, but it also acts to regulate the controversy and contain it.[33]

The distribution of participation affects the nature and course of conflict because the lower socio-economic levels participate less in organizational activities and are therefore less likely to be drawn into controversies; but once they are drawn in they are more likely to pull it down to personal derogation and attack. Highly stratified communities tend, therefore, to have fewer people entering conflict situations, but when they do have conflicts the level at which it is carried on tends to be low.

Interlocking memberships in many organizations tends to weave community ties into a tight and homogeneous fabric. But if affiliations are limited to ethnic groups or class groups or religious groups, without interlocking memberships, cleavage lines are already present. Many kinds of communities have such separate, noninterlocking structures. New England towns with several "layers" of immigrant groups, service towns, resort towns are cases in point. An issue can easily split such communities along ethnic, class, or religious lines.

The social structure exerts its influence by determining how people will line up in a conflict. Thus even people who have no immediate stake in the issue tend to take sides with groups they identify with. Group discussions—to persuade or to re-inforce opinion—constitute a large part of community conflict. This kind of word-of-mouth communication becomes more important than the formal means of communication. For many people, and even, perhaps, for most, personal ties and group affiliations are more powerful than abstract issues in determining the position taken in a conflict. But the relative importance of issues and group ties in determin-

[32] *Ibid.*, p. 21.
[33] *Ibid.*

ing how people will line up varies from one community to another. The smaller the community the more likely it is that alignments in a conflict will be based on personal attachments and group affiliations. And within any one community the upper and middle classes seem to be more influenced by issues than are the lower classes. Sometimes strong action on the part of leaders or the authorities can have a profound impact on community conflict, either suppressing or at least drastically modifying it; conversely, absence of strong action can serve as an indication of permissiveness and greatly intensify the conflict.

The economic structure of a community affects both the kinds of issues which arise and the course which conflict will take. The manner in which it operates has been summarized as follows:

> It is useful to summarize these effects on the three economic variations noted: "service" towns in which townspeople derive their income from outsiders; "self-contained" towns, in which men both live and work; and economic "appendages," in which most men commute to work outside town.
>
> (a) In each of these, characteristic issues arise to provoke controversy. In economically self-contained towns, it is often issues of direct economic interest and of political control; in the others it is more often value differences deriving from differing backgrounds and experiences.
>
> (b) In the stratified, self-contained communities, participation in the controversy will ordinarily be restricted to the upper and middle strata, while in the one-class commuting towns it will be more evenly spread throughout the community.
>
> (c) When lower classes participate in controversy in stratified towns, the dispute is likely to get particularly acrimonious.
>
> (d) The voluntary aspect of relations among residents who need only to live together and not to work together—in new suburbia—tends to segregate the community into discrete value-homogeneous groups, and to create diverse consequences for controversy.[34]

The mass media may play an important part in community conflict. Sometimes a newspaper, for example, can inaugurate a crusade by a searing editorial; sometimes an exposé uncovers a situation which arouses the public and sets a conflict into motion. Newspapers have far less persuasive power than word-of-mouth communication, but they have powerful reinforcing effects. And combined with word-of-mouth communication the influence can be great. It has been pointed out that responsible national channels have had the effect of mitigating local community conflict by presenting it in perspective. A situation that looks world shattering seen close at hand looks quite different when seen at a distance. The behavior which seemed all right when "everyone" was doing it looks pretty awful when viewed from the vantage point of a national "generalized other."[35]

[34] *Ibid.*, p. 23.

[35] Sometimes outside media have precisely the opposite effect. If it looks as though the outside world is meddling in local affairs, the community may close ranks against the intruders. See *ibid.*, p. 25.

Part **IV**

Selecting and Ordering: Competition in the Community

IT IS A RATHER awesome thought that fundamentally the same process is at work distributing populations over a continent and members in the pews of churches. The working out of competitive processes in the allocation of rewards—whatever they may be—is one of the most fascinating aspects of community functioning. And the struggle to protect against the harsh results of competition is a perennial one. In Part IV only a small fraction of the ramifications of competitive behavior can be analyzed; nothing is said about competition among siblings in the family, among athletes on the field, among students in the classroom, among members of the club. But the principles are the same. Chapters 7-13 illustrate this kind of competition in selected areas of community life.

7

Competition among Communities

Competitive Forces Distribute Populations

If from a wide enough perspective of time and place, say from a perch on Mars, we could scrutinize the surface of the United States through a great telescope, we should find the population unevenly distributed, some areas empty, and others teeming with life. But whether sparse or dense, the population would show patterning. It would cluster. It would distribute itself around nuclei.

If we watched these communities over a long period of time we would see some growing at a rapid pace. Indeed, the current expression is "exploding" when referring to some of them. Contrariwise, we would note that some were shrinking; over a period of time some would even disappear.

Communities are not, then, distributed evenly. But neither are they distributed fortuitously. Competitive processes are at work distributing and redistributing people. Many factors, geographic, economic, and technological as well as sociological, are involved, both in the original location of communities and in their relative rates of growth or decline thereafter.

The Original Location of Communities

Communities arise at places where they can best perform certain functions. For the most part, at least in the past, the competitive tests have been those of economic efficiency, and the process has been autonomous. It was fairly easy to determine on economic grounds where communities could flourish and where they could not. And errors were, over a period of time, corrected autonomously. Sometimes, however, strategic or political suitability was the governing criterion. The process here would be one of judgmental competition. The Politburo decides to establish communities in Central Asia; the Brazilian government decides to build a brand new capital at Brasilia; our own government decided to set off the District of Columbia as the site of the capital. In the nineteenth century states decided where to establish college towns. (Often the criterion was inaccessibility to urban distractions) .

For the sake of simplicity, the factors that have determined the original location of communities are classified as: (1) geographic, (2) industrial or functional, (3) technological, and (4) strategic. It is, of course, highly artificial to separate these factors, inasmuch as they operate in an intimately related fashion. Geographic factors affect function, and technology can affect both; all may be involved in strategic considerations. But for purposes of discussion it will do no harm to consider them separately.

Wherever geographic conditions in American history created breaks in transportation and required reloading of cargoes—land to water, train to truck, wagon to pack animal—communities tended to spring up. If mountains, deserts, or swamps diverted transportation routes, communities arose. Mountain passes have also produced towns; rarely, however, large cities. Mountain barriers, blocking through transportation, have produced communities—Denver, for example. Sometimes the geographic factor which influenced the location of communities was centrality of location at intersections of transportation lines. Sometimes it was the presence of natural resources. Communities, then, have arisen when and where there was profitable work to be done.

Turning briefly to the economic or functional factors involved in the location of communities, we find that the "occupations" they pursue may be classified in three main categories: (1) trade, (2) transportation, and (3) industry. In addition, some students add higher education, public administration, military national defense, and entertainment and recreation.[1] Important structural differences, demographic and institutional, characterize these different kinds of communities, as it was noted in Chapter 3.

Communities which function as trade and social centers, especially in nonindustrialized areas, sometimes become religious and political centers also. They may range in size from tiny hamlets with only a store or two, through villages and towns, up to such great metropolitan areas as New York. In the United States, the trade center "is best represented by the numerous retail and wholesale trade centers of the agricultural Middle West, Southwest, and West. Such cities have imposing shopping centers or wholesale districts in proportion to their size; the stores are supported by the trade of the surrounding area. This contrasts with many cities of the industrial East, where the centers are so close together that each has little trade support beyond its own population."[2]

Transport centers are communities where cargoes must be unloaded and reloaded for further shipment. Usually repackaging, sorting, and storage services will also be performed. Sometimes transport centers are centrally located, but often they are gateways between quite different areas representing contrasting needs. Thus we have, in more than a merely figurative sense, "gateways" to the West at Kansas City, Omaha, and Minne-

[1] Otis Dudley Duncan and Albert J. Reiss, Jr., *Social Characteristics of Urban and Rural Communities, 1950* (New York: Wiley, 1956), Chapters 16-20.

[2] Chauncey D. Harris and Edward L. Ullman, "The Nature of Cities," *Annals Amer. Acad. Pol. & Soc. Sci.*, 242 (November, 1945), p. 9.

apolis-St. Paul; "gateways" to the South at New Orleans, Mobile, Savannah, Charleston, Norfolk, Baltimore, Washington, Cincinnati, and Louisville; and a "gateway" to the Southwest at St. Louis.

Some communities specialize in one kind of industrial job, such as mining, steel, manufacturing, amusement. Miami and Atlantic City specialize in recreation; Scranton and Wilkes-Barre, in mining; Pittsburgh and Detroit, in manufacturing. The kind of specialization will depend in large part on the available natural resources, including climate.

If there were no physiographic and geographic irregularities, such as those described above, central-place communities would tend to be evenly spaced at regular intervals, each serving its own little hinterland, and with no area lacking services.

Transport communities, under the same physiographic conditions, would tend to arrange themselves along waterfronts and transportation lines. Specialized-function communities would still distribute themselves according to the natural resources they exploited. In actuality, since most communities serve several economic functions, and since, regardless of these functions, physiographic irregularities influence their location, the distribution of communities becomes very complex.

The third influence which operates in the original location of communities—the technological—is closely interwined with both the geographic and the economic. Communities, we said, spring up wherever there is profitable work to be done. But the presence of profitable work is not something fixed once and for all. It depends on technology as much as on location and resources. When barges and ships are the chief means of transportation, communities spring up along waterways. Railroads add a new pattern, automobiles still another. There are thousands of villages and towns served only by highway and motor car. Before the automobile and the hard-surface road many of these communities could not have existed. And now that air transportation has arrived, it promises to open up new areas for community location. It is modern transportation that has made possible the modern "megolopolis."

Sometimes communities are established in certain locations not because of economic or geographic factors but because of strategic ones. Similarly the USSR establishes communities in Central Asia in part, it is alleged, to hold it against anticipated pressure from China.

If births exactly equalled deaths, if there were no gains in knowledge and hence changes in technology, if natural resources replenished themselves, if society, in brief, were static, the forces distributing population would tend to be primarily economic. There would still be sociological concomitants, but they would be relatively minor. Such stability has, of course, never obtained.

Communities, like individuals, have constantly to meet competitive tests. If they pass, they grow; if they cannot pass, they suffer the consequences. When they can no longer "earn their living," so to speak, they shrink; they may even die. Among the factors that influence their ability to compete are such things as exhaustion of natural resources, technological changes, and institutional changes.

The Unsuccessful

Soil erosion, exhaustion of some mineral resource such as gold or coal, or of some other resource such as timber, may make it impossible for a community to survive. The Dust Bowl is an example of a whole region which lost out when topsoil was destroyed by the plowing up of grasslands, leaving them to the mercy of wind and weather. In gold-mining regions there are scores of so-called ghost towns that illustrate the results of exhaustion of resources and ability to compete. Pennsylvania has towns suffering from the exhaustion of coal veins.

New inventions in technique, in transportation, in materials, may have profound effects on the competitive position of a community. Technological advance may mean retrogression rather than progress for communities. In 1940 mines in the Great Lakes region were still yielding about ninety percent of all the ore used in the United States; but improvements in techniques of extraction required only about half as many miners as in 1910 to produce half again as much ore.

Competitive failure of communities, whatever it may be due to, has tragic repercussions for the families living there, in the form of unemployment and poor schools, roads, and other facilities. There were at least 110—20 major and 90 minor—depressed areas, officially known as areas of chronic labor surplus in the United States in 1960, mainly in West Virginia, Pennsylvania, Kentucky, and New England.

That competitive failure would present numerous problems is understandable. But too great success is fraught with difficulties also. Communities are usually very pleased when their rates of growth are high. The problems associated with success seem less disturbing than those associated with failure. The experience of boom towns in defense centers during the 1940's, however, suggests that they can be very serious. There were no preparations for the swollen populations. War housing projects sprang up quickly to accommodate some of the families. But many more had to shift for themselves. Community facilities were simply nonexistent for them. The situation was one almost of chaos.

Intercommunity Competition for Industry

The following examples illustrate some of the important kinds of intercommunity competition in the past. New York, Portland, Boston, Philadelphia, Baltimore, and Norfolk, all having good harbors, were strong contenders for the shipping business to and from Europe. Before the Erie Canal and the railroads opened up the American hinterland, the race was nip and tuck. New York at length won out, because it had the easiest and most economical access to the continental hinterland through the Hudson and Mohawk valleys. The Erie Canal and then the New York Central Railroad continued to make possible the exploitation of this natural competitive advantage by offering cheap transportation connections with the rest of the state, the Great Lakes region, the Middle West, and the Northwest.

Cincinnati and Chicago at one time were in competition for the meat-packing business. While the Ohio River was a main transportation artery, Cincinnati was known as Porkopolis. When the railroads began to supplant river transportation, Chicago became the great meat-packing center. At present Omaha, Kansas City, and St. Louis are close competitors.

Other cities which have been in competition are Galveston and Houston, the latter winning out when a canal was built to the Gulf of Mexico. Fort Worth and Dallas have vied for economic dominance, Fort Worth representing the cattle industry and Dallas agriculture. With the passing of the open cattle range, Dallas moved ahead, for agriculture became relatively more important.

In the past, history, tradition, custom, freight rates, as well as geography and natural resources, gave communities of the North and Northeast a competitive advantage over those of the South and Southwest. In the 1940's, wartime expansion in manufacturing plants was based on such factors as newly developed resources, new industrial processes, new methods of transportation. These new factors favored the West, the Great Lakes area, and the South.[3] The harnessing of nuclear energy, it is believed, will have a profound influence on the competitive relationships among communities. Since power will be cheap and easily transmitted, such noneconomic factors as climate and scenic beauty may become important values.

When there is no fundamental economic or geographic advantage in one community as against another, the attraction of industry becomes a matter for contingent competition. Each community has to promise more than the others. Success under these conditions may mean that the competition has tested the publicity work of the local chamber of commerce rather than any characteristic of the community itself.

In recent years the function of competing for industry has become increasingly institutionalized. In some cases it is incorporated in the role of the governor. In some cases the function of competing for industry is assigned to a special governmental agency, the Pennsylvania Industrial Authority, for example. In some cases it is assumed by voluntary associations of local businessmen. However it is performed, it becomes increasingly intense.

[3] In the decade ending in 1970 it was estimated that the East's population would rise 11 percent, the West's 22 percent, and the Middle West's 10 percent. The South's population as a whole was expected to increase by only 8 percent, but Florida's by 25 percent. (*Newsweek*, Dec. 14, 1959, pp. 48-49).

PROBLEMS RAISED BY INTERCOMMUNITY COMPETITION FOR INDUSTRY

Intercommunity competition for industry raises the characteristic problems of competition everywhere—namely, the problem of cutthroat and fair methods, the problem of what should be tested, and the problem of the failures. In addition there is the problem of the braking effect it may have on community welfare.

When the advantage of one community over another is a natural one, we are inclined to accept the verdict of competition with good grace. Sometimes, however, the advantage is artificial, institutionally exploitative, as in the case of northern and northeastern cities which were formerly favored over southern communities by discriminatory railroad freight rates. Sometimes competition among communities has reached almost cutthroat intensity. Especially during the great depression of the 1930's there was keen competition for factories, mills, and other manufacturing plants. Communities vied with one another in their efforts to attract employers who would give their citizens jobs. They offered valuable incentives—tax concessions and, in some cases, free rent—to coax industries to their boundaries. Textile, garment, and hosiery mills from New England and Pennsylvania moved South, "lured by low wages, 'docile' and 'native white' labor, absence of unions, free rent, tax exemptions, and other baits from industry-hungry sections of the nation."[4]

When intercommunity competition becomes judgmental rather than autonomous, as, for example, in bidding for government contracts, it may become cutthroat by undue pressure on the decision-maker. Thus newspaper headlines report that "California fears industry pirates, fears New York is putting pressure on United States to lure back defense work," and the accompanying story refers to industrial "task forces," "strategy," "plots" to "lure" defense business back to New York.[5]

Even when intercommunity competition for industry is fair there is still the question as to whether it is testing the proper things. What was being tested in the race between New York and the other seaboard cities for shipping? Clearly, economy and efficiency in performing a vital function. The competition was fair because it tested what it was supposed to test. New York was the best harbor for transatlantic trade. But whether it was a good thing to permit such a piling up of population, to concentrate so many immigrants, or to encourage such complexity might well be questioned. It may be argued that it would have been better, and ultimately even more economical, to have distributed the shipping business more evenly among all the coastal harbors in order to avoid the growth of such a behemoth.

[4] Henry Hill Collins, Jr., *America's Own Refugees: Our 4,000,000 Homeless Migrants* (Princeton: Princeton University, 1941), p. 105.

[5] *New York Times*, May 17, 1959.

Some industrial leaders now think that perhaps other than strictly economic factors should be tested in intercommunity competition for industries. In the past, businessmen making up their minds as to where to locate new plants have looked for the following factors: a location as close as possible to raw materials and markets; good transportation; cheap power; and a buyer's labor market; that is, a community where more men were looking for jobs than there were jobs available, and a favorable political climate. At midcentury one industrialist proposed that in the future

> when we decide on location, let us demand a community which affords comfortable modern housing—not only for our factory but also for our people—and within the means their wage standard would provide. We should feel constrained to inquire into the liberality of the public school system with the same interest that we analyze the liberality of the local tax structure. We must recognize that the promise of a tax exemption might also well mean the exemption of our employees' children from the educational opportunities which make good citizens. When we look for plentiful power, we are bound to the corollary of inquiring into the recreational power and facilities of the community.[6]

In other words, he proposed that when communities competed for factories and plants, they be tested for their human values as well as for strictly economic advantages. The community that offered the best living conditions for workers should, in his opinion, win over the community that offered only economic advantages to the industry.

Such a change, has, indeed, taken place. Advertisements to attract industry now include school systems, churches, and recreational facilities in their bids for new industries, as well as labor supply and tax advantages. Thus when one industry announced that it had selected a certain community as the site of its new plant, it listed among the reasons "an adequate supply of skilled and semi-skilled personnel, attractive residential areas, an excellent public school system, a good network of state and county highways."[7]

To the extent that such intercommunity competition for industry has the effect of improving community facilities, it raises standards. But sometimes it can have precisely the opposite effect, acting as a brake on community welfare in the sense that whenever a reform measure is urged, such as minimum wage laws or improved factory laws, the stock reply can be that no community can enact such measures, for they would put its industries at a competitive disadvantage. We need not suppose that these objectors are insincere. Many industrialists doubtless might be willing to accept such reforms if they could do so and still compete successfully with industrialists in less progressive communities. In some instances, but not all, this prob-

[6] Charles Luckman, "A Capitalist Looks at the 'Labor Problem,'" *The Progressive*, Feb. 3, 1947, p. 4.

[7] *New York Times*, Jan. 12, 1959.

lem can be handled by federal legislation which covers all communities equally. But federal legislation cannot equalize every situation, and the fundamental problem still remains.

Competition for Personnel

Communities compete for industries to employ their citizens; but they are also in competition with one another for personnel to staff their service facilities. This situation is especially serious in the case of medical personnel and teachers.

There are not, for example, nearly enough doctors, dentists, nurses.[8] Moreover, the available ones gravitate to the larger cities where there are hospital, research, laboratory, and other facilities for adequate practice and where they can earn higher incomes. Rural areas sometimes lack the very minimum number of practitioners to maintain normal health. They cannot successfully compete with the larger and wealthier communities.

In evaluating this kind of competition we may grant that it is "fair," but still conclude that it tests the wrong things. Medical personnel ought to be distributed on the basis of need. Institutional devices are being worked out whereby young persons who wish to enter the medical or nursing profession will be granted generous scholarships if they promise to spend a certain number of years after graduation in rural areas. In other words, we cannot permit competition alone to distribute medical care among communities. If federal funds are necessary to supply poor communities with adequate medical care, such funds may be forthcoming.

A similarly tight situation exists in the case of teachers. The great increase in the school-age population in the 1940's and 1950's resulted in a marked shortage of teachers. During the war boom of the early 1940's, hundreds of schools and classrooms in poorer communities were closed because they could not pay enough to attract teachers. Competition was acute for teachers at all levels from grade school through college.

Although unfair competition was not a widespread problem, it was common enough in one state to lead to institutionalizing of the process by the setting up of a "no-raiding code" for school superintendents, specifying the conditions under which it was ethical to negotiate for teachers in other communities.[9]

[8] In 1950 there were 143.4 physicians for every 100,000 persons in the United States; a decade later there were 140.7; and it is anticipated that, at the current rate of training, it will be only 133 by 1975. "Just to keep up with our expected population growth, we would need to graduate 11,000 new physicians a year by 1975, to maintain our current physician-patient ratio. Currently we have 7,400 new physicians graduating each year. . . . To graduate 11,000 new physicians each year would require increasing the enrollments of our medical schools and starting at least twenty new medical schools" (*New York Times,* Nov. 8, 1959).

[9] *New York Times,* Jan. 24, 1959.

Here, as in the case of medical personnel, it is not considered good policy to allow ability to pay to be the sole criterion for distributing teaching services. The American ideal demands that communities have teachers whether they can afford them or not. An emergency solution has been to increase the supply of teachers by temporarily certifying persons ordinarily not qualified to teach. Married women whose children had grown up were encouraged to return to the classroom.

The feeling has become widespread that wherever necessary the federal government should help the poorer communities finance their educational systems. This policy runs counter to the tradition that education is a function of the local community. It happens, however, that the communities which have the largest number of children, those in the Southeast, are precisely those which have the smallest tax base and are therefore the least able to afford adequate educational facilities. Legislation has been proposed to provide federal funds for school buildings in local communities, thus freeing money for other educational needs.

Communities have similar problems with respect to personnel for nonhierarchical churches. It is difficult to get competent ministers for rural communities. Religious motivation may send zealous young men out to rural churches at small pay, but it is easy to become convinced that one can be of greater service in a city church at a good salary than in a poor rural church that pays little. Hierarchical denominations simply assign ministers to rural communities. Others may have to depend on increasing the attractions of such areas by scholarships and other inducements.

There is sometimes competition even for ordinary labor. During World War I agents canvassed the South for Negro workers, with the result that many Negroes went North, particularly to New York, Detroit, Chicago, and St. Louis.[10] Similar phenomena occurred during World War II, resulting in great movements of Negroes to the West Coast.

White skilled workers were competed for during World War II on an extensive scale and cities were accused of "pirating" labor. Communities with war plants could pay higher wages; they therefore attracted millions of workers from communities that had fewer defense industries, resulting in the changes described earlier in this chapter.

Competition for highly skilled and technical personnel continued after the war and became especially keen in the 1950's and 1960's. Community amenities became one of the major lures, especially of the newer industries. In brief, technical and professional workers were in a position to make communities bid up the price for their acceptance of jobs, and communities were meeting the demands.

[10] Sometimes this mass migration was opposed. In one community the departing Negroes were met at the railroad station by local white employers and prevented by intimidation from leaving (Thomas Sancton, "Gone to Chicago," *New Republic,* Nov. 12, 1945, p. 647). This behavior transformed the process from one of competition to one of conflict.

Implications

The complex and never-ending interplay of fundamental competitive forces distributing populations, channeling people into these communities and out of these, piling them into some areas, pulling them out of others, would be of little more importance sociologically than the great forces that produce the weather if it were not for the fact that they have widely ramifying consequences.

For one thing in a representative democracy they change the national political power structure. California, for example, gained seven representatives in Congress as a result of the 1960 census and seven more are anticipated in 1970. Another addition of six representatives in 1970 is expected for Arizona, Nevada, Washington, and Wyoming. National political campaigns must increasingly focus on voters in the West, which means candidates must cater to the wishes of people in these communities.

Equally significant is the effect of the South's success in attracting industry. Among the tests that southern communities have to pass in order to attract and keep industries are good race relations. "Business leaders know that closed schools and civil strife could pin-prick the big boom. In Little Rock, for example, not a single new industry has come in since the violence at Central High School."[11] As industrialization increases urban population at the expense of rural population, attitudes toward desegregation become less unyielding. The director of the Southern Regional Council has pointed out that "the traditional pattern of segregation was geared to the agrarian society. Basically, an urban culture is not congenial to traditional segregation as the South has known it."[12] And the editor of the *Atlanta Constitution* concludes that urbanization, not law nor public acceptance, was the greatest force at work in desegregation.[13]

[11] *Newsweek,* Dec. 14, 1959, p. 50.
[12] *Ibid.*
[13] *Ibid.*

8

Ecological Competition within Communities and Its Institutionalization

Institutional Framework in Cycle One

In Chapter 3 we referred briefly to the ecological structure of the community, that is, to its functional structure in terms of land use. This ecological structure, it was noted, is inextricably related to the demographic and institutional structure, both as cause and as effect. That is, the demographic structure and the institutional structure influence the ecological structure and it, in turn, reacts to influence them. A heavy concentration of ethnic or racial groups will reflect itself in the ecological structure; and so will customs and laws. But an existing ecological structure will itself have profound repercussions on the relationships among groups and hence, indirectly, also on the demographic structure. It will also have reverberations on institutional norms.

The ecological structure is the result of basic processes which allocate space to the different uses to which land can be put. These processes are competition, segregation, invasion, and succession.[1] In the so-called First Cycle[2] of development of American communities, that is, up to the middle of the twentieth century, the processes were primarily autonomous and the institutional framework was one of modified laissez-faire, with only relatively minor tinkering in the form of zoning regulations, or of "planning" which sought to impose other than strictly economic tests on the competitive process. It was not, however, until the beginning of the Second Cycle that the idea of radical rethinking of urban communities began to take hold.

To say that the institutional framework within which ecological proc-

[1] Other ecological processes, not pertinent here, include centralization, decentralization, and dominance. See Amos Hawley, *Human Ecology* (New York: Ronald, 1950); James A. Quinn, *Human Ecology* (Englewood Cliffs, N. J.: Prentice-Hall, 1950); D. J. Bogue, *The Structure of the Metropolitan Community: A Study of Dominance and Subdominance* (Ann Arbor: Michigan, 1949).

[2] Philip Hauser, interviewed in *U. S. News and World Report*, Nov. 28, 1958, p. 81.

esses operated in the First Cycle was one of laissez-faire does not mean that American communities permitted land to be allocated in an institutional vacuum. The settlers brought with them traditional ways of using land, imposing them on the competitive process. Thus, for example, the basic plan of the New England village came, according to one anthropologist, from the open-field village of the North European plain by way of the manorial village of the English Midlands.

By way of contrast, the distribution of land use of the southern community, according to the same analyst, was an American counterpart of the Iberian *municipio,* the French *commune,* or the German *Gemeinde;* it was a rural version of the baroque capital or city of palace and parade. It reflected and accommodated a two-class community.

> The distinctive community form of the South was and is the county. Dispersed a day's ride in and out around the county seat, that community assembled planter and field- or house-hand from the fat plantations, free white or Negro from the lean hills and swamps, for the pageantry and the drama of Saturdays around the courthouse, when the courthouse, the jail, the registry of deeds, and the courthouse square of shops and lawyers' row made a physical center of the far-flung community. . . . It is a mistake to treat this county and county seat for its separate parts and to try to find the community in the Old South at any other level. The poor white or Negro hamlets about a country church, set in hill or swamp retreat, the plantation, however large and proud and populous, the county seat as town . . . were and are none of them complete communities. The county itself was the unit of dispersal and assemblage, and it was a two-class community from its inception in the gathering-in of nobles into the king's palace and capital along with *noblesse de robe* and rich *bourgeois.* Formed from the coming together of landowner and *peón,* its pattern of dispersal was a double one, with estates covering the good land, and little men, now clients, now runaways, taking up the leavings in the bad.[3]

This type of land use spread all across the country to California.

The basic plan for allocating land use which characterizes the middle-western community, according to the same author, derives from West Britain, Scotland, and Scandinavia; it reflects a community resulting from the accretion of individual families rather than a planned settlement. "Their first communities were mere crossroads where scattered neighbors met. Their schools and churches and stores, like their camp meetings and their fairs, were set haphazardly in the open country or where roads met, with no ordered clustering and no fixed membership."[4] They were open-country neighborhoods.

The coming of industrialization in the nineteenth century created a characteristic pattern of relationships and the ecological structure of the

[3] Conrad M. Arensberg, "American Communities," in Morton H. Fried, ed., *Readings in Anthropology.* Vol. II. Cultural Anthropology (Crowell, 1959), p. 361. Original publication in *American Anthropologist,* 57 (1955), pp. 1143-1162.

[4] *Ibid.,* p. 365.

mill town or factory city reflected it. Play and park space disappeared; work and leisure were separated.

The major emphasis here is on the fact that although modern American cities tended to permit competitive processes to allocate land uses during Cycle One, these processes operated within a traditional framework. When industrialization introduced a new set of forces, the competitive process registered a new set of values. Economic efficiency was the value tested. The ecological structure of American cities thus expresses their values in the allocation of space. In Cycle Two values other than strict economic efficiency are increasingly taken into consideration and the competition tends to become judgmental rather than autonomous. The implementation of new values does not proceed without opposition; indeed some of the most basic values in American society are fought over in this area.

Competition, in brief, may be viewed as a process by which land use comes to respond to community values. The ecological processes have widely ramifying effects on the relationships among groups and classes, as well as themselves reflecting these relationships.

Ecological Processes in Cycle One

The ecological structures of communities vary widely. They vary according to the function served by the community, as suggested above; they vary according to the age of the community; and they vary according to the size of the community. In general, however, certain basic processes tend to operate, namely, competition, segregation, invasion, and succession.

SEGREGATION

In any community there may be many uses to which land can be put: it may be used for factories, mills, foundries; for wholesale warehouses or retail stores; for office buildings or banks; for theatres and amusement centers; for housing Negroes and foreigners or native-born whites, poor people or wealthy people. These several uses can be reduced to three main types: heavy industrial; business or commercial and light industrial; and residential.

Some of these uses of land profit from being in proximity to one another. Thus, for example, "retail districts benefit from grouping which increases the concentration of potential customers and makes possible comparison shopping. Financial and office-building districts depend upon facility of communication among offices."[5] High-grade residential use benefits from use for parks and boulevards.

Other combinations of land use, however, are detrimental to one another. "The antagonism between factory development and high-class

[5] Chauncey D. Harris and Edward L. Ullman, "The Nature of Cities," *Annals Amer. Acad. Pol. & Soc. Sci.*, 242 (November, 1945), p. 14.

residential development is well known. The heavy concentrations of pedestrians, automobiles, and streetcars in the retail district are antagonistic both to the railroad facilities and the street loading required in the wholesale district and to the rail facilities and space needed by large industrial districts, and vice versa."[6]

As a result of these congenial and antagonistic relationships in land use, there tends to develop a pattern of segregated land use—retail districts, wholesale districts, financial districts, residential districts, and so on. What is more to the point is that they are in competition with one another for desirable areas. For not all land uses are equally capable of paying for desirable sites. "Certain activities are unable to afford the high rents of the most desirable sites. . . . Examples are bulk wholesaling and storage activities requiring much room, or low-class housing unable to afford the luxury of high land with a view."[7] In the first cycle of community growth in the United States the allocation of land use rested basically on autonomous competition, and ability to pay was the value tested. The use that was most profitable won out.

In all American communities there resulted a definite segregation of land use, sometimes simple, sometimes complex. These segregations were sometimes spoken of as "natural areas." There was a business district, which was further segregated into a wholesale and warehouse area, into areas for retail stores, theatres and amusements, specialty shops, banks, and the like, according to the functional principles cited above. The physical structure of the community reflected this fairly stable segregation of land use.

INVASION

But the competitive process which sorted out these several natural areas, alloting space to the different functional uses was a continuing one. No segregation was fixed or final. Land which was desirable for industrial use at one stage of development later became undesirable. Areas which were desirable for residential purposes ceased to be so. There was a tendency for those who could afford it to move farther and farther away from the grime and dirt of the city, out into the suburbs. The mansions of the rich were deserted as the business district expanded. By what real estate men call the "trickling down" process, these houses in time were taken over by the poorest. Thus competition for the use of land was always blurring the original natural areas or segregation of land uses by a process known as invasion. Middle-class people invaded upper-class areas or Negroes invaded white areas. As a result, one group was displaced by another; a succession of groups moved through the same area.

[6] *Ibid.*
[7] *Ibid.*, p. 15.

SUCCESSION

In New York City in recent decades Harlem and the Bronx illustrate the process of succession of groups. Between the two world wars, "Harlem shifted from a moderately populated community of well-to-do, middle-class and working-class Jews, Italians, Irish, Germans and Greeks into a tightly packed, predominantly low-income region, inhabited largely by Negroes. . . ."[8] In the Bronx a similar process has taken place:

> Historically, the upper Bronx has been the top of an escalator on which successive waves of population rode from bargain-basement living in teeming lower Manhattan in quest of "a nicer neighborhood" and "a better life." First came the Irish and German, then Italian immigrants and Poles and Slavs and Jews, displacing and leap-frogging each other, hop-scotching from the lower East Side to Harlem to the lower Bronx to the upper Bronx. And the escalator kept moving, latterly bringing up Negroes and Puerto Ricans.[9]

Ecological Patterns in Cycle One

At least three types of community structure in the first cycle of development of American cities have been distinguished by students of community growth, namely: (1) the concentric-circle pattern, (2) the sector or axial pattern, and (3) the multiple-nuclear pattern.

The concentric-circle theory, developed by sociologists at the University of Chicago and based on studies of that city, asserted that communities tended to grow out from a center along radii, evolving five concentric circles around this center. The zones, out from the center were: (1) the central business district, "the focus of commercial, social, and civic life and of transportation. In it is the downtown retail district with its department stores, smart shops, office buildings, clubs, banks, hotels, theaters, museums, and organization headquarters. Encircling the downtown retail district is the wholesale business district."[10]

The second zone, which surrounded the first, was called the zone in transition. It was a "zone of residential deterioration. Business and light manufacturing encroached on residential areas, characterized particularly by rooming houses. In this zone were the principal slums, with their sub-

[8] Raymond Robinson, Jr., "Our Changing City: Harlem Now on the Upswing," *New York Times,* July 8, 1955. The phenomenon known as "tipping" in this invasion-succession process will be discussed in greater detail in a later chapter.

[9] Richard Amper, "Our Changing City: Conflicts in the Upper Bronx," *Ibid.,* July 15, 1955.

[10] Harris and Ullman, *op. cit.,* p. 12. A more detailed and technical description of the five areas may be found in Ernest W. Burgess, "The Growth of the City," in *The City,* edited by R. E. Park, E. W. Burgess, and R. D. McKenzie (Chicago: University of Chicago, 1925), pp. 47-62; also in "Urban Areas," in *Chicago, An Experiment in Social Science Research,* edited by T. V. Smith and L. D. White (Chicago: University of Chicago, 1929), pp. 113-138.

merged regions of poverty, degradation, and disease, and their underworlds of vice. In many American cities it had been inhabited largely by colonies of recent immigrants."[11] This was the area of the city where newcomers from rural areas also tended to live because rents were cheap. The landowners in this zone were holding their property in anticipation of increased value from higher-rent-paying land uses. The hope was that business would expand and invade the area, finally displacing the residential use entirely. In the past, while American cities were growing rapidly this was a fairly safe gamble. When Cycle One came to an end, however, at midcentury, holding for an anticipated rise in value was not so likely to be rewarded.

The community paid for such deteriorated areas not only in the high price for police, fire, and sanitary protection but also in the blighting effect such areas had on human personality. Extensive studies in Chicago showed that juvenile delinquency, gangsterism, vice, mental illness, physical illness—particularly contagious diseases—and family disorganization tended to characterize them. They did not constitute a suitable environment for human beings. In small communities the undesirable areas might be known as "the other side of the tracks."

The third zone which developed under the competitive conditions in Cycle One was one of independent workingmen's homes, inhabited by industrial workers who had escaped from the zone in transition but who wanted to live within easy access to their work. In many cities second-generation immigrants were important segments of the population in this area. This zone was usually thought of as lower middle class. It may have appeared bleak to outsiders, but it often signified an improvement for those who lived there and they took pride in it.

The fourth zone consisted of better residences, usually single-family houses, or of exclusive restricted districts, and also of high-class apartment buildings.

There was, finally, the commuters' zone. This included both suburban areas and satellite cities, as well as spotty developments of high-class residences along lines of rapid travel, primarily railroads. But it may also have included slums. Sometimes a so-called urban fringe was already present, neither part of the city nor yet suburban. It might contain heavy industry or residences of low quality.

This concentric-zone theory of city development did not apply without modification. It was supposed to represent what would have tended to be the typical situation if no interference were present, much as the law of falling bodies represents the rate at which bodies fall at sea level in a vacuum. Many factors served to distort the picture. The presence of water, hills, rivers, railroad tracks, arterial highways, or other natural or technological features may have distorted the pattern. Nevertheless, it was a useful concept in illustrating the basic structure of a community as determined

[11] Harris and Ullman, *op. cit.*, pp. 12-13.

by competition for the use of land when the quality being tested was primarily economic and the policy in force one of laissez-faire.

The sector theory of community structure, propounded by Homer Hoyt, was also based on competition. But it held that cities tended to grow along main transportation lines, or axes, or along lines of least resistance, forming a star-shaped pattern. The important feature was that growth along any one axis tended to consist of similar land uses.

> The entire city is considered as a circle and the various areas as sectors radiating out from the center of that circle; similar types of land use originate near the center of that circle and migrate outward toward the periphery. Thus a high-rent residential area in the eastern quadrant of the city would tend to migrate outward, keeping always in the eastern quadrant. A low-quality housing area, if located in the southern quadrant, would tend to extend outward to the very margin of the city in that sector. The migration of upper-class residential areas outward along established lines of travel is particularly pronounced on high ground, toward open country, to homes of community leaders, along lines of fastest transportation, and to existing nuclei of buildings or trading centers.[12]

A third, so-called multinuclear, theory described cities which consisted of six types of nuclei, namely: (1) the central business district, (2) the wholesale and light manufacturing district, (3) the heavy industry district, (4) the residential district, (5) minor nuclei such as parks, outlying and small industrial centers, and universities, and (6) suburban and satellite nuclei. (The satellite was farther away than the suburb and its residents practiced less commuting, although its economy was closely geared to that of the main center.) Certain activities required specialized facilities; thus, for example, retail activities must be accessible to the whole community, ports must, of course, be on water fronts, manufacturing must be near transportation facilities. This fact, together with the compatibility and incompatibility of different uses already commented on, and the fact that certain activities were unable to afford the high rents of the most desirable sites determined the relationships among the several nuclei.

What Values Were Being Tested?

What was this autonomous competition in Cycle One testing? What values did the resulting structures register? What policies guided it? Obviously it was testing ability to pay rent which, by implication, reflected economic productivity. If that was the value the community wished to register, the Cycle One competitive processes were fair, whatever the result.

Even in Cycle One, however, the necessity for some kind of control had

[12] Harris and Ullman, *op. cit.*, pp. 13-14. For a more technical statement, see Homer Hoyt, "City Growth and Mortgage Risk," *Insured Mortgage Portfolio,* Vol. 1, Nos. 6-10 (December, 1936-April, 1937), *passim;* and Homer Hoyt, *The Structure and Growth of Residential Neighborhoods in American Cities* (United States Federal Housing Administration, 1939), *passim.*

been recognized. Zoning restrictions were one of the first attempts made to regulate competition for the use of land. It was based, essentially, on a recognition of the different uses to which land could be put and the relationships among them. It had to begin with the structure as it was; it could not begin from scratch. But it did attempt to protect certain areas from the competition of more profitable uses. Commercial and industrial establishments were forbidden to invade residential areas, and so on. But often it became impossible to enforce the zoning regulations in the face of concerted opposition. It was, at best, a stopgap solution.

Increasingly, however, people began to question whether the values which competitive processes registered were really the values the community wanted registered. Water fronts illustrate the point. Europeans often commented on the fact that in so many American communities river, lake, and ocean fronts, which in such cities as Paris or London were reserved for nonindustrial uses that do not contaminate and destroy the beauty of the setting, were laced with railroad tracks and given over to heavy industry. So that what could have been the loveliest location, enjoyed by all, was shrouded in smoke and grime. Would the river land transformed into a public park be less productive? In Cycle One the answer was an unqualified Yes. But by midcentury many thoughtful people began to think it would not.

It began to be clear also that although competition was quite natural, it was not mechanical nor was it necessarily blind. It was a neutral engine that could be put to use for one purpose as well as for another. For a long time it had been assumed that this impersonal way of distributing land use through ecological processes, whatever they were testing, desirable or undesirable, was inevitable, "natural," inviolable. People may have deplored the results, but they took a shoulder-shrugging, laissez-faire attitude.

Increasingly, however, students of community life—planners, engineers, economists, sociologists, political scientists, and even the more advanced real estate specialists—came to see that the old way of deciding how land should be used—autonomous competition operating under a laissez-faire policy—was uneconomical on the basis of almost any standard of value. Slums and blighted areas cost more than they yielded in taxes. The smoke, grime, fumes, and other by-products of heavy industry cost citizens more in cleaning bills, ill health, and discomfort than the economy effected by the location of the factory. It was found that proper planning could house more people on less land and do it more healthfully and attractively than the old method.

By and large, then, those who went into the subject most completely opposed autonomous competition in assigning land to its several uses. True, there would always have to be some choice made among alternative uses, so that competition might be inevitable. But increasingly it was felt that it should be judgmental and designed to test other than merely economic values. Planning boards and authorities, on the basis of a consideration of many community values, tended to become the judges of land use.

The End of Cycle One

Whether or not this was a perfect solution to the problem was beside the point. By midcentury Cycle One had ground, or was in process of grinding, to a halt. The processes which characterized it had reduced it to an absurdity. Not only heavy industry, but also retail establishments—the so-called shopping centers—had leapfrogged out of the central business districts into low-rent areas outside of the city limits where parking facilities were available. Light industry, which now needed one-story, space-consuming areas, also with parking facilities, moved out. Drive-in movies sprang up in open fields. More to the point, residents were moving out of the cities into the suburbs. Indeed, the flight to the suburbs became almost a rout. Central cities could not compete with suburbs in holding people. It was estimated in 1959, for example, that by 1975 central cities would have 12,000,000 more people but the suburban ring would have 54,000,000 more. Of these, 32,000,000 would go to open country or unincorporated areas known as exurbia or interurbia; the other 21,000,000 would go into incorporated areas in the suburban ring.[13] For those who could afford it, as we noted in Chapter 2, suburban life seemed far more attractive than city life.[14]

The autonomous competitive processes of Cycle One—testing ability to pay, guided by laissez-faire policy—had been allowed to defeat their own purposes. The plight of American cities had become "the great unspoken, overlooked, underplayed problem of our time."[15]

The processes that produced this situation were not new; they were the same as those that had been operating for decades. Sociologists had been analyzing them for many years. What was new was automobile transportation on an unheard-of scale, making it possible to expand the suburban area in all directions, independently of railroad facilities. New also were the architectural requirements of factories, space-consuming both in layout and in parking needs. New also were machines and organizations that could build scores of houses quickly and cheaply.

As in the case of the national community the competitive processes which ceaselessly locate and relocate people in local communities would be of only incidental interest to sociologists if they did not reflect values and if they did not have profound effects on the relationships between and among groups of people. The flight of middle-class families from central cities to the suburbs deprived the cities of leadership; it left less privileged—not, of

[13] *New York Times,* Dec. 1, 1959.

[14] See William Dobriner, ed., *The Suburban Community* (New York: Putnam, 1958) for an excellent summary of sociological research in suburbs.

[15] Then Senator John Kennedy. *Ibid.*

course, innately inferior—people in its wake, poorer and hence less good customers, poorer sources of tax revenues, less able to meet the challenges posed by modern urban community living. It became clear, finally, that the autonomous competitive processes had almost destroyed the city as a functioning unit. Something had to be done if it were to be salvaged. Zoning, slum clearance, and housing projects were not enough. The concept of urban renewal or rehabilitation developed and became embodied in the Federal Housing Acts of 1949 and 1961.

Cycle Two: The Salvaging of Cities

The characteristic approach to community development in Cycle Two is one of salvaging the city, to redevelop it, to rehabilitate it, to try to win back people who can furnish leadership—as well, of course, as pay taxes—and to make the city functional once more by making traffic more efficient and parking space more available.

Such urban renewal implies a great deal more than a mere tinkering with existing patterns and the processes that produced them. It is not merely a negative undoing of past errors; it is, rather, a positive working toward new goals, the implementing of new values.

> Urban renewal . . . encompasses not just clearing away slums, but building something better in their place; not just ridding a city of slums but preventing their onset. Urban renewal embraces the act of continuously revitalizing the urban core; keeping cities, towns and neighborhoods fresh and growing, giving people better places to live, in areas adjacent and convenient of access to school, park, shops, church, health center or meeting hall.[16]

The process remains one of competition, but the values being tested have been expanded. In the first cycle, for example, the competitive tests were applied lot by lot. That is, each individual plot of land had to prove itself more profitable for one use rather than for another. But in the end this proved to be a wrong way to apply competitive tests. The sum of the individual "profits" added up to a loss for the whole community. It became evident that land use could not be allocated tiny parcel by tiny parcel; it had to be allocated in large units. It was found, for example, that when larger units were used more people could be housed in the same space, more comfortably, and with room to spare for yards, play areas, and lawns.

Even more radical is the proposal offered by some students to plan for deliberate diversity in neighborhoods, so that there will not be a segregation of low-income from high-income families. The feeling is that high-income families should not be shielded from contact with low-income families, and that low-income families should not be deprived of leadership from high-income families. It will doubtless be a long time before this set

[16] Thomas P. Coogan, "You—and Urban Renewal," in "Can We House Our Exploding Population?" in the *New York Times,* Oct. 11, 1959.

of values is reflected in the ecological structure of communities, if it ever is.

In addition to making cities more attractive in luring people back, other appeals are such things as freedom from the care of property, time saved in transportation, privacy, diversity, cultural opportunities—having them available seems to offer satisfaction whether or not they are taken advantage of—and more time with the family for the head.

One study of "returnees" from the suburbs found the largest number to consist of upper-income people whose children had grown up and married. But these were not the major sources to be tapped. People with long and irregular working hours, people with relatively short assignments in certain cities, say only two or three years, widows, divorcees, spinsters, bachelors, young unmarried people, childless couples, academic people—these were among the people it has been suggested cities should compete for. It is not supposed that the city can successfully compete with the suburbs for young middle-class families with children; but even for this class there may be more attraction when the cities have become rehabilitated.[17]

Urban Sprawl and Megolopolis

There is an old cliché to the effect that generals are always planning to fight the last war rather than the next one. While it is true that cities in Cycle Two are beginning to restructure and rehabilitate themselves to implement new values, larger units are developing which include areas even beyond the suburbs and they are being shaped as much without guidance as cities themselves were in Cycle One.

With modern transportation, suburban developments spring up anywhere and everywhere. The result has been called urban sprawl. There is no planned use of the land, its development being left almost completely in the hands of speculative builders. Again the sum of individual "profit" often adds up to community loss. It has been said that it takes five acres to do the work that one acre could do better and, in addition, the result of present trends is, aesthetically, a mess.[18]

Because of this uneconomic use of land, suburbs, or at least settlements and developments, tend to spread out until they meet. Thus metropolitan areas become great agglomerations to which the name megolopolis, or strip cities, has been given. Filling in the countryside would, it has been estimated, result by 1975 in a series of such megolopolises in different parts of the country. There would be a Great-Lakes-opolis around Chicago, stretching from Milwaukee at the north to Chicago to South Bend at the

17 The above discussion is based on William H. Whyte, Jr., "Are Cities Un-American?" in *The Exploding Metropolis, A Study of the Assault on Urbanism and How Our Cities Can Resist It,* by the editors of Fortune. Anchor (New York: Doubleday, 1958), pp. 1-18.

18 *Ibid.*, p. 116.

south. There would be a Gulf-opolis from Houston to Galveston to New Orleans, in addition to Tex-opolis extending from Fort Worth and Dallas to Houston and Galveston. There would be also Pacific-opolis (San Francisco to San Diego), Puget-opolis (Everett-Seattle-Tacoma down through Portland and Salem), Florid-opolis (Miami to Jacksonville, Fort Myers to Jacksonville), and Atlantic-opolis (Boston to Baltimore and Washington).[19]

Whatever the size and structure of communities may be in Cycle Two of American city development, they will certainly result from the operation of competitive processes, however institutionalized, and they will register the values the communities wish to have tested.

[19] Philip Hauser, interviewed in *U. S. News and World Report,* Nov. 28, 1958, p. 84.

9

The Institutionalization of Competition in the Market

Shreds and Patches

Nowhere does the shreds-and-patches nature of our society reveal itself more clearly than in the illogicalities and contradictions built into the competitive market. To the extent that the profit system operates according to theory, like a servomechanism, the market is a purely economic phenomenon which by means of autonomous and contingent competition registers community values. The earliest studies of economic phenomena were almost systems of logic, so autonomous was an unfettered market supposed to be.

But, as we shall presently see, the community is not always sure it wants market values more than it wants other values. It is therefore always changing the institutional setting in which market competition takes place, altering fundamental strategies, in order to make room for differing values. It cuts the system and patches it up. As a result the market is a sociological mechanism as much as it is a purely economic one and it attempts to implement other values in addition to purely economic ones.

Both autonomous and judgmental forms of competition can be reflected in the market. When the horseless carriage replaced the horse and buggy, or when gas and oil replaced coal, or when air travel replaced railroad travel, crescive competition was at work. One industry grows faster than another and finally may even replace it. It is now anticipated that the time will come when nuclear power "will become competitive" with conventional power. More immediate and more easily visible is the contingent form of competition in which competitors react to one another by lowering prices or conversely by raising their bids.

In a controlled economy or in a free economy under emergency circumstances, competition is likely to be judgmental in nature. That is, a board of planners decides among competing uses of the means of production which industries to encourage and which to discourage. They are allocated on the basis of some overall plan rather than on the basis of autonomous competition.[1]

The Economic Model

The original economic garment was extremely elegant; it was constructed on the Adam Smith model of free competition and free enterprise. The latter meant the absence of governmental regulation and was called laissez-faire. The argument was that governments did not have to regulate economic transactions because free competition coupled with free enterprise provided all the regulation that was needed. The economic system was a checks-and-balance one that operated automatically.

From the consumer's point of view this model would be ideal if it fit as it was supposed to. The consumer would be king. He would decide just what and how much should be produced at the price he was willing to pay. The price of goods would just cover the cost of production, including salaries of managers and replacement costs. But over and above these, plus rent (including the "rent" accruing to superior efficiency), wages, and interest, there would be no surplus. If prices fell below costs of production, then capital, labor, and raw materials would leave the industry, since no one is expected to produce at a loss. Less goods would be produced. If consumers wanted more they would have to pay more. The price would increase, and when prices rose above costs of production, then again capital, labor, and raw materials would rush into the business to take advantage of this fact. If now more was produced than was needed, businessmen would have to cut prices and hence profits. In this way prices and costs of production would tend to be equalized.

Theoretically it was a beautiful model, perfectly automatic. It has fascinated more than a few of the world's thinkers. No overall planning is required in the model. The whole thing works by itself. It seems democratic, impersonal, efficient. That was why its proponents were so insistent that the community keep its hands off the economic system (except, of course, in their own interests). No human brain, it was argued, could encompass the intricacies of this competitive system. Competition did better what human ingenuity could not do by itself, namely maximize productivity.

[1] A Soviet social scientist was once asked what the major research effort of his colleagues was. He replied that it was pricing. At what level should goods and services be priced in order to implement the goals of the total economy? The allocation of the factors of production was determined by judgmental competition. But even under these conditions, autonomous competition had to be resorted to from time to time to correct errors in judgment. If too much was made of something the consumer did not want, the goods would not be sold. The price had to be lowered. Aside from the major decision with respect to military goods and consumer goods, autonomous competition had to be used from time to time. The market behavior of the consumers constituted a sort of massive feed-back.

The model was elegant indeed. What then could be said against it? First of all it never really fit; in fact it was extremely uncomfortable. In the process of achieving one goal or value, it destroyed other goals or values. The normal outcome of competition is for one competitor to win out over the others. That, indeed, is one of the functions of competition—to select a winner. But winners imply losers and the losers did not relish the ruthlessness that eliminated them. The people who inhabit communities are not economic men. Very soon therefore the elegant model was being cut here, tucked in there, patched here and there.

A major criticism is that community values seem sometimes to conflict with purely market values, so that not all competition is acceptable in American communities. Specifically the major difficulties may be summarized under three headings: (1) the tendency toward monopoly, (2) the development of cutthroat methods, and (3) the deprivation of buyers who cannot successfully compete.

To cope with these three difficulties many laws have been passed, revised, altered by administrative rulings, and modified in practice as the community wrestles with the problem of how to institutionalize competition to maximize what are often conflicting values. A closer examination of these three difficulties will show how the tug and pull of clashing values reflect themselves in community policies.

What to Test?

Judged by the laws that have been passed to control competition, the community seems to want business competition to test quality, efficiency, and service. Back of the way it is institutionalized there is doubtless the picture of competitors that Adam Smith painted: a large number of small businessmen, none with any particular advantage or handicap. Our laws suggest that we do not want any businesses to become too large if—which is not always the case—this gives them an advantage over their competitors and leads to monopoly. Nor, on the other hand, do we want any competitors to use methods which others cannot also use, if such methods drive the others out of business.

If we think of competition along the continuum presented in Figure 6-1, ranging from elimination by cutthroat competition to assimilation (monopoly), we can picture the approved zone as one of equilibrium somewhere in the middle. There is an area, however nebulous, somewhere between cutthroat competition at one extreme and monopoly at the other, which we call fair competition because it seems to be here that competition tends to test the traits we want to test. We have created scores, even hundreds, of norms—legal, quasi-legal, administrative, and customary—which attempt to keep competition functioning within these limits.

This task is not always easy because of a fundamental inconsistency in our goals. The normal outcome of competition, as we have seen, is for one competitor to win out over the others. That, indeed, is one of the main functions of competition—to select a winner. But in the market that is not our goal. If one individual wins out over his competitors, he can crush all subsequent rivals and thus get a powerful stranglehold over the consumers. (The converse of this, in which one buyer corners the market, seems less likely to happen.)

Nor do we favor cutthroat methods. The usual result of such methods is to eliminate one or more of the competitors who cannot hold out, and thus to lead to monopoly. In reality the competitive continuum should be thought of as circular, since cutthroat competition is but a stone's throw from monopoly.

The point to emphasize, whether we look at the continuum as a straight line or as an open circle, is that competition is most likely to test the qualities we want tested—if we know what they are—when it is held to the zone of equilibrium. When conditions are the same for all, competition is fair in the sense that no party has special advantages. But if extraneous influences are at work—such as false advertising, adulteration, or misrepresentation, on the one hand, or secret agreements among competitors on the other—competition ceases to be fair. Something other than the traits we want tested tips the balance.

Two sets of rules have been developed, therefore, to institutionalize competition and to keep it fair. One consists of antimonopoly laws, to prevent competition from moving to the right in our continuum; the other consists of codes and laws regulating selling prices, to keep it from moving to the left. In the first class we have the conspiracy laws and the antitrust laws (first by the several states and then by the federal government, including the Sherman Act of 1890 and the Clayton Act of 1914) together with the court decisions which have interpreted them. Their purpose is to restrict business practices which lead to monopoly.

In the second class there are several kinds of rules. These are (1) laws whose ostensible purpose it is to keep competition fair, (2) out and out government price fixing, or at least established floors and ceilings to prices; and (3) codes of fair competition established by the Federal Trade Commission.

As a result of these two sets of rules for institutionalizing competition, it does not have much leeway. In spite of our apparent belief in the ideal of competition, in actual practice we are afraid of it. As long as it is weeding out others we may applaud. When it points in our direction we rush for protection.

Value Problems of Monopoly

One difficulty with business competition is that it does not work out as the theoretical model says it should. Uncontrolled competition may be perfectly natural among plants and animals—but not so among human beings. Sooner or later they learn to organize to overcome the rigors of its tests. Competition may, as the old cliché says, be the life of trade. But competition itself is hard to keep alive. Producers learn that they can do better by working together than by competing. (Consumers learn, too, but more slowly.)

Thus within a hundred years after Adam Smith's *Wealth of Nations* had entranced the intellectual world with its description of how a competitive system would maximize national wealth, the United States was plagued with monopolies—trusts, holding companies, giant mergers, and, later on, national and international cartels. Men shrewd enough to create huge industries were also shrewd enough to see that competition was not the life of trade for them. It kept prices, and therefore profits, down. Organization to prevent competition and to control the market was as natural as competition itself.

As the giant corporations expanded during the latter half of the nineteenth century they became more powerful than the local authorities. They spread over many states. They could not be controlled by the puny efforts of local communities or even of states. It took a powerful government to cope with them. When the monopolistic practices of these great corporations were revealed by the so-called muckrakers, the public was incensed and statutes were enacted to cope with them. The Sherman Act was meant to prevent practices which interfered with free competition and to encourage practices which fostered it. When this law proved too vague, it was reinforced by the Clayton Act, which definitely specified what was and what was not legal.

In spite of all this legislation, however, the long-time trend toward concentration has not been reversed. The reason is that we are faced with conflicting values. We want the advantages of competence and efficiency that go with size but we do not want the threat of consumer exploitation that goes with monopoly.

The conflict in values which confuses our policy with respect to competition is illustrated by post-war efforts to counter economic concentration. Because large firms were the only ones able to handle the contracts for military materiél, they had a great advantage in bidding. To even the score, legislation was passed permitting smaller firms to enter into agreements with one another, that is, to form "pools," under immunity from antimonopoly prosecution.[2] The problem that then presented itself to the

[2] The forms which such agreements take may be (1) "integration committees" which "call for the exchange of technical know-how, patents and patent rights and industrial experience between all contractor-members of the committees," (2) production committees which require when a firm is the sole source for a contracted product that supplemental sources be permitted to acquire technical indoctrination in the techniques of production and kept abreast of improvements and changes, and (3) production pools which "enable groups of small business concerns, unable to secure defense contracts individually, to pool their resources, and by their combined potential seek to obtain and

enforcing agencies was one of weighing two sets of values: (1) defense, which demanded anticompetitive activities and (2) competitive enterprise.

A similar conflict colors our policy with respect to monopoly in other areas. We have done relatively little to implement the ideal of free and fair competition. The antitrust division of the Department of Justice has nearly always been understaffed because appropriations for its work have been inadequate; often it was a case of the policeman simply looking the other way since he could do nothing about the law violation anyhow. There has been no consistent, overall governmental attack on the problem. It appears that we really do not want one.

Although the existence of monopoly does make it possible for prices to be kept high, many of the great evils anticipated from concentrated power have not materialized. There has been tremendous increase in productivity and a general lowering of prices. One reason why the evils of monopoly have not followed the trend toward concentration is, according to the so-called theory of countervailing power,[3] that brakes and controls have been built up by other special interest groups, which have insisted on sharing the original power. Thus labor has insisted on sharing the power which has inhered in large concentrations of economic power; so has agriculture. Where such countervailing power could not be achieved unaided, interest groups have not hesitated to call on the government to help them build it up. Thus the American economy might be viewed as a huge dialectic in operation. Great original power evolves but before it can become a real threat it generates its own brake in the form of countervailing power. By constantly checking the powers of certain groups, a kind of balance is achieved which prevents an exploitative situation from continuing forever. Control of great concentrations of power does not come, according to this theory, from competitors who prevent the rise of monopolistic organizations, as antimonopoly legislation implies, but rather from conflict groups which demand to share the power.

It would be a mistake, however, to conclude that the existence of antimonopoly legislation is not functional because it has not eliminated the concentration of economic power. Strategically it is like a first move; it is a potential threat, with an element of uncertainty.

Cutthroat Competition and Its Regulation

The function of the price mechanism, according to the theoretical model, is to serve as a guide to production. If too much of a certain kind of goods is being offered, the price goes down, warning producers to cut

---

perform defense contracts" (Report of the Attorney General Pursuant to Section 708 (e) of Public Law 774, 81st Congress, as Amended, Nov. 9, 1955, pp. 14-19). In addition, there were miscellaneous agreements which permitted cooperative activity from groups of competitors to deal with specific emergency problems, often of a nonmilitary nature.

[3] John Kenneth Galbraith, *American Capitalism* (Boston: Houghton-Mifflin, 1952).

down their operations. The price mechanism also serves the function, according to the theoretical model, of evaluating efficiency. The competent producer can sell at a lower price than others and gets the business; the producer who cannot meet this competitive test is supposed to be weeded out.

What actually happens, however, is quite different. Despite anti-conspiracy laws and without benefit of formal agreements, competitors play a "coordination game" so-called, and fall into a comfortable live-and-let-live pattern. They refrain from excessive price cutting in order to protect themselves against counter-price-cutting from competitors. In a massive way the price mechanism does reflect "supply" and "demand" but prices go up and down at about the same rate for most competitors. Prices tend to become stabilized by crescive institutional processes.

LEGISLATION

Sometimes, however, the coordinating game breaks down. During the great depression of the 1930's, for example, competitors became almost desperate. In their efforts to sell anything at all, they cut prices to unprofitable levels. To protect against such cutthroat competition, so-called "fair-trade" legislation was enacted to permit manufacturers to fix the prices at which their goods would be sold by retailers.[4] This effectively limited competition at the local level.

Another threat in the coordinating game is the entrance of a new competitor who does not behave in the expected or customary institutionalized manner. In the 1930's and 1940's the chain store introduced such competition, upsetting the old way of doing things. Again communities had to examine their values. Exactly what did they want to have tested by competition among retailers? If they wanted stores to serve as community centers, then the old kind of store was better than the new one. If they wanted efficient marketing services, regardless, then the chain was better. Apparently many communities wanted to protect their independent stores. Resentment on the part of independents stimulated antichain store laws by states.

In addition to state tax laws, federal legislation was also passed to institutionalize competition from chain stores. By the 1940's, however, this wave of antichain legislation had begun to subside and by the 1950's the chain store as such was no longer a threat; it had been assimilated. But a new threat in the form of the discount house had arisen. Advertising of brand products had reduced personal selling almost to a matter merely of exchanging the goods for money. The seller was immaterial to the buyer. He didn't care whether he bought his brand product from a lux-

[4] The story of this type of legislation is presented in Chapter 14 to illustrate buyer-seller conflict. The elimination of competition among sellers is to the disadvantage of buyers.

urious department store or from a stripped-down show room. He bought where he could get the product most cheaply. The result was a challenge to old ways of doing things and the innovation was resisted, as previous innovations had been before it. The pattern of development that a new type of retailer undergoes is so well known today that one writer has been able to formulate it succinctly:

> First, the new retailer appears on the scene; second, his operation receives public approval; third, his fellow-merchants cry that he is unfair; fourth, there is an attempt to wipe him out by legislation; and, finally, everyone learns to live with him.[5]

By the 1960's the distribution industry had learned to live with the discount house. There is no doubt, however, that future innovations which challenge institutionalized ways will be subjected to the same processes.

It is alleged of all the types of legislation here considered that although they have been held essential to preserve competition they actually violate the inner logic of competition, which aims to allocate rewards on the basis of relative efficiency in production and distribution. It transforms a competitive relationship into a conflict situation. It is, further, a double conflict. First it is a conflict between the innovator and those who seek protection against the new; in the other aspect it is a conflict between buyer and seller in which the seller, by asking for legislation which commits him to a given price, achieves "first move" against the buyer and is therefore protected against bargaining.

PRICE CONTROL

In addition to legislation which restricts competition in local markets, another kind of interference with free competition takes the form of direct control of prices in highly competitive industries with many small producers, such as bituminous coal or milk, in the name of protecting these small producers.

One system by which small producers are protected against competition is called parity. During the period 1909-1913 agricultural products exchanged for a larger volume of industrial goods than at any other period in our history. The ratio between agricultural and other goods which obtained in those years is called parity. It is taken as 100 percent. From time to time the federal government has guaranteed farm prices based on certain percentages of parity. During World War II, for example, farmers were guaranteed prices at 90 percent of parity until the end of 1948; this guarantee was later extended. A checks-and-balance system was instituted such that if prices fell below the guarantee, the government was obliged to buy up the product in order to sustain prices. This procedure was defended on

[5] R. E. Westervelt, "The Discount House Problem," *Journal of Retailing*, Summer, 1954, p. 69, quoted in Statement by Robert A. Bicks, First Assistant Antitrust Division, June 25, 1958.

the grounds that it stimulated production. It was predicated on the farmers' following governmental advice as to production. When farmers, thus protected, produced more than the market could absorb at the sustained price, the result was unmarketable surpluses.

The whole agricultural program originally embodied in the Agricultural Adjustment Act, and later in the Soil Conservation Act, which permits farmers to allot production quotas and to combine in other monopolistic ways, is designed to protect agriculture against cutthroat competition. A similar system in the bituminous coal industry was introduced by the Guffey Act of 1937. In all these instances, the federal government itself has attempted to limit competition.

This brief statement on the laws and methods for circumventing economic competition shows how, in spite of lip service to a free competitive system, businessmen, like others, are prone to run to the government for help when they feel that competition is contrary to their interests. For free competition is a severe taskmaster. If you cannot meet its tests, you ask to have the rigors softened.

CODES OF FAIR PRACTICES

Or, facing the constant temptation to cheat, you ask to have the field of competition well policed. Codes of fair practice sometimes are developed.

The discussion above dealt primarily with price competition. But there are other ways in which competition operates. One seller may attract customers by false advertising and misrepresentation. One producer may be able to undersell because he has adulterated his goods. Shoddy workmanship may be glossed over. Inasmuch as businessmen deprecate price competition and favor competition in quality, it becomes important that competition be practiced under rules which assure that quality actually will be the trait tested.

In addition, therefore, to the federal, state, and municipal laws for regulating competition, there are the so-called rules for fair competition set up by the Federal Trade Commission. Almost 200 industries have worked out such rules of self-regulation for themselves, rules as varied as the problems of the industries themselves. The object of these rules is, of course, to control competition and to see that it remains within the zone of fairness.

Competition among Buyers

Up to now we have been discussing competition among sellers only. This is the form which economists tend to emphasize most. But competition among buyers also has important repercussions in the community, and it is therefore of great interest to sociologists.

In an industrialized society more and more behavior is motivated by money. The person who offers more money gets the goods, no matter who he is; the person who offers less money does not get the goods, no matter how urgent his need. Ability to pay is therefore reflected in life chances.

Competition among buyers may be direct or indirect. An auction is archetypical of direct competition among buyers. It is contingent in form. That is, whatever one person bids leads to the raising of the price by another person. There need be no interaction among the bidders, although, to be sure, there may be. The theory is that the person who wants the object most will get it, assuming that all can afford the object.

But competition among buyers does not always take the pristine form of an auction. Sometimes the competition is indirect, taking the form of attracting goods and services into one set of channels rather than another.

DIRECT COMPETITION

When competition is permitted to operate freely, as at an auction, goods and services—assuming equal wants—go to those who can pay the most for them. The thing tested is ability to pay. The assumption is, in effect, that those who have the ability to pay have earned their right to the wanted economic goods and services. Their superior income means that they have contributed more than others and therefore deserve the goods and services their money can command. Usually we do not even question this; we take it for granted. Poor people eat cabbage and beans; rich people eat steak and asparagus tips.

During a major crisis, such as both world wars, for example, we become acutely aware of the problems involved in this method of distributing scarce goods and services. Since goods and services are hard to get, the competition among buyers tends to be severe. The injustice of the ability-to-pay criterion for distributing goods under competitive conditions in an emergency was illustrated in Florida during World War II. Living quarters were extremely scarce. Families of servicemen stationed there for only brief periods of time could not afford the competitive rates charged; civilians, on the other hand, flush with wartime prosperity, were spending money recklessly and thus bidding up the prices of everything, including housing. The dysfunctionality of competition under these conditions was also highlighted by the increased cost of the war effort because the government had to compete with makers of civilian goods for the factors of production.

The whole plan of distribution was therefore changed. Otherwise there would have been nothing for anyone but the rich, who would have bid prices up to fantastic heights. Government regulation stepped in, taking the form of rationing, so that no matter how much money one had, he could not buy more than his share. And in addition ceilings were put on the price of nonrationed goods to prevent competitive bidding, just as in the depression of the 1930's floors were put under prices to prevent destructive price cutting. Ability to pay was thus no longer being tested. Competition was suspended.

INDIRECT COMPETITION

Ordinarily rich and poor people are not buyers in the same markets. They do not therefore seem to be competing with one another, and the rich buyer seems to have no effect on the price the poor buyer must pay. But even if they are not in the same market and therefore not competing directly with one another, they are still in the same community and a more abstract kind of competition is involved. Production factors are attracted to making goods which rich people can pay for, leaving the poor buyer unsupplied. The operation of such processes may reflect good economic theory, but the sociological implications are invidious, that is, envy-breeding, and hence disturbing. The inability of poorer buyers to compete successfully in this abstract market may become a very sore spot in community relations.[6]

Individual versus Collective Consumer Goods

In an affluent society like that of the United States at midcentury, the great competition is not likely to be between luxury goods for the rich and basic necessities for the poor; there is enough productive capacity for both. The great competitive problem is more likely to be between individual and collective consumer goods, between more automobiles and more roads, between more gadgets and more schools, between more patios and more hospitals. It has been argued that the factors of production should be put to use more for urban redevelopment, road building, school construction, hospital construction, and other public or collectively consumed goods and less for more and more elaborate and luxurious individually or privately consumed goods. In the face of overcrowded and understaffed schools and hospitals, the question has been asked, "What do you mean, 'abundance'?"[7] And one economist has elaborated this thesis in great detail.[8]

Implicit in the autonomous competitive principle of allocating production factors is the theory that the welfare of everyone is maximized if consumers are allowed to channel the direction in which productive factors will be used. But during emergencies autonomous competitive processes are not, as we saw above, permitted to allocate them. Judgmental competition is substituted; boards and commissions decide among competing uses, and national safety and security are the tests applied. Implicit in judgmental competition in allocating the factors of production is the theory that the welfare of the state cannot be left to the whims of the individual in the market. If allowed to do so, he will always channel production in the direction of private consumer goods, even when military needs are great; he will, that is, choose butter rather than guns.

[6] St. Louis *Post Dispatch*, Oct. 20, 1946.

[7] Jessie Bernard, *Social Problems at Midcentury* (New York: Holt, Rinehart and Winston, 1957), Chapter 1.

[8] John Kenneth Galbraith, *The Affluent Society* (Boston: Houghton-Mifflin, 1958).

It is now being argued that even in nonemergency situations, permitting autonomous competition to allocate the factors of production results in starving community welfare needs and surfeiting individual consumer-goods markets. How to re-institutionalize the competition allocating factors of production, to change it from an autonomous to a judgmental form, is a major political issue.[9]

Evaluation of Economic Competition

The values of competition according to the theoretical model have already been commented upon. The difficulties may be summarized as fourfold.

It is difficult to keep competition operating as it is supposed to. Almost inevitably businessmen learn to cooperate to protect themselves against the rigors of competitive tests.

In a buyer's market competition almost inevitably becomes cutthroat. Price wars may end in the elimination of all but one or two powerful firms. Although the consumer may profit immediately, if the end result is a monopoly for one firm he has not gained in the long run. This anomalous situation has led to an outcry on the part of weaker competitors for laws to protect them against drastic price competition. Competition may be cutthroat in other ways than in price wars. Although the most efficient producer will be able to sell for the lowest price because his costs will be lowest, actually the most unscrupulous or dishonest producer may win by poor working conditions or marketing frauds. Competition often, therefore, may be a test of unscrupulousness. It may even be said that in a free contest, poor products and inferior working conditions, like cheap money, will tend to drive the good out of the market. Low standards will tend to drive out high standards. The dishonest competitor or the cheater tends to set the standard. Quality has to be protected when competition is uncontrolled and hence cutthroat. If not, what is being tested finally is not the product, but the degree of corruptibility of the producer. The codes of fair practices promulgated by the Federal Trade Commission are designed to restrain such competition.

Closely related to this difficulty is the fact that even with the best of intentions the producer may be obliged by the hard taskmaster, competition, to do things which harm his community. Here is a factory that pollutes the air with smoke and fumes. The outraged citizens have tried to make the factory install equipment that would eliminate the menace. But the factory manager replies that he cannot afford to install the necessary equipment if his competitors in other communities do not. If he is forced to add this to his cost of production, he cannot compete in the market. He will be forced out of business and the town will lose these jobs. Similar

[9] See *ibid.*

arguments are constantly raised against many kinds of local welfare laws, including labor legislation, minimum wage laws, or sanitary requirements.[10]

In a seller's market we find that under freely competitive circumstances those unable to pay high prices are deprived of essential goods and services. Among buyers, ability to pay is the only thing being tested. But no community can afford to overlook need in distributing at least some of its scarce goods and services—as in a choice between milk for slum children and ice cream for rich adults. Nor can a community permit competition among buyers to allocate the factors of production in an emergency, such as a war. And at least some students consider autonomous competition a dysfunctional way to allocate the factors of production as between public and private, that is, collectively and individually consumed goods.

[10] The usual solution to this difficulty is to make such laws national, thus eliminating the advantage which communities with lower standards have over those with higher ones. This illustrates the use of legislation as a coordinating strategy. Federal legislation to protect migrant workers was sought, for example, to prevent states without such legislation from an unfair competitive advantage. The governor of Pennsylvania argued that "the lack of federal legislation . . . is unfair to farmers in states that have laws to maintain high standards for itinerant workers. He said the farmers of those states, including New York, Pennsylvania, and New Jersey, had a 'direct economic self-interest in seeing similar decent standards established and enforced' in states where there were farmers with whom they competed" (*New York Times,* Dec. 13, 1959).

10

The Institutionalization of Competition in the Job Market

Competition Among the Sellers of Labor

Sellers in the labor market, as in any other market, seek protection against ruthless competition. And, like businessmen, they seek it not only through legislation but also through their own efforts. Both their aims and their methods are, in fact, very much like those of businessmen. They ask for price floors under the wares they sell—minimum wage laws—just as businessmen do. And they seek to limit the production of the goods they have to sell, their particular skills, in order to control the market. Efforts to escape competition are perfectly natural and therefore as much to be expected among workers as among businessmen.

It was not only businessmen, therefore, who long ago saw the handicaps of competition, for workers also soon learned the lesson. And trade unions have been as ingenious and frequently as successful as big business in restricting production of their goods, that is, their skills, by limiting the number of apprentices and of members, and in controlling the market by closed-union and closed-shop agreements.

From the worker's point of view a job is a fragile and often highly perishable commodity. It comes and goes in a way over which he has little control. Seasonal unemployment can be mastered because it can be predicted and anticipated by adjustments of one kind or another. But depressions wipe out jobs by the millions. Through no fault of his own the worker loses his job. So far there is no complete solution for the scarcity of jobs caused by depressions or recessions. Unemployment compensation is a poor substitute for a job. So is made work—jobs created simply to keep workers occupied. Most serious for those involved, perhaps, is the elimination of jobs resulting from new inventions which substitute machines for men—so-called technological unemployment.

It is illegal for businessmen to enter agreements to limit competition and businessmen must therefore pay lip service to the ideal of free competition. But there is no such restriction on labor. Labor is avowedly committed to opposing unregulated competition for jobs. It is, indeed, a basic principle of labor organization to do away with cutthroat competition for jobs, favors, or wage increases, and to substitute the union principles of seniority and solidarity.

How Competition is Institutionalized

Feeling, therefore, that they cannot afford the inevitable risks of exploitation when they bargain individually with employers, workers attempt to meet the problem of competition in several ways: (1) they form unions which substitute the principle of solidarity for cutthroat competition; (2) they attempt to substitute for competition segregation of the working population into noncompeting groups; (3) once unions are formed, they seek a monopoly in their particular markets by means of such devices as the union shop; (4) they may, in spite of the criticism which it arouses, attempt to substitute relative abundance of jobs for scarcity by sundry restrictive practices known as featherbedding or made work or by special legislation protecting them against competition, such as provisions in building codes which forbid prefabricated materials or plumbing laws which make it impossible for any but registered plumbers to work; and, finally, (5) they may attempt to mollify the rigors of competition by such protective legislation as child labor laws and minimum wage laws. In evaluating any of these practices we must remember that they stem from a conviction that there is a scarcity of jobs. If all workers were guaranteed an abundance of work as long as they live, they would feel less necessity to restrict the competition for jobs.

Substituting Solidarity for Competition: The Union

In order to protect themselves against the exploitation inherent in a buyer's labor market, as early as the eighteenth century workers began to form labor unions.

A good union attempts to substitute a cooperative spirit for competition among workers. Indeed, the creation of this psychological solidarity by an effective union constitutes one of its most important functions. Indoctrination in union principles often follows precisely the same pattern as in religion and politics. Unionism is, in fact, a kind of secular religion for many. Instead of viewing every other union bricklayer as a competitor and therefore an enemy, the good union man is taught that he must view every other bricklayer as his brother. Wage differentials on the basis of individual differences in ability are frowned upon. All union members doing the same kind of work, regardless of differences in ability, receive the same pay. The whole psychology of the worker must be oriented toward this point of view.

The notorious difficulty encountered in organizing professional workers stems in part from their highly competitive psychology. Their jobs are traditionally spheres of personal competition. Each wants to feel superior to his fellows. He would rather take his chance on winning a high rate of pay on the basis of individual merit or pull than join with others to bargain collectively. Such individualistic, competitive psychology is inimical to unionism; it is therefore opposed by organizers. On the other hand, it is encouraged by employers.

There are many people, proponents of incentive schemes and of scientific management, who stress that the elimination of competition among workers does an injustice to the superior worker. This is undoubtedly true. A superior worker may do much better by individual bargaining. Under many union contracts, promotions do not go to the best man. The best men are not the ones hired first and fired last. Hiring and firing must be done according to rules laid down by collective bargaining.

The union justifies its position on the grounds that if competition is permitted it quickly becomes cutthroat, every man becomes the enemy of every other and hostilities are generated which are demoralizing to the whole plant. The superior individual sets a pace which the average worker cannot equal. The hated speed-up results, by which the average worker must work at an unnatural pace. It may increase productivity momentarily, they argue, but it wears the worker out before his time. Production, the union contends, must therefore be keyed to what the average individual can do at his normal pace. Any competitive scheme which tries to increase his speed beyond normal limits is, the union argues, unfair.

The insistence of labor leaders on labor solidarity is intense precisely because there is so much natural competition among workers. It takes a great deal of indoctrinating to convince the top craftsmen that it is to their interest to unite with lesser craftsmen for higher wages. It is only when the top craftsmen see that with solidarity they get more than without it that they are willing to join with their fellows. A wage relatively higher than that of their fellow-workers becomes less appealing than a wage which is absolutely higher than the one they could get by individual bargaining.

Substituting Segregation for Competition

Another institutionalized substitute for competition is the segregation of workers into noncompeting groups. White workers inside and outside of unions have tried to protect themselves against competition from Negroes by designating certain jobs as Negro jobs, others as white jobs. Unskilled manual labor and certain of the personal-service and menial jobs have been traditionally assigned to Negroes. Ever since the abolition of slavery, skilled jobs have been taken as the prerogative of the white man, as have been the other high-status kinds of work.

Some unions, albeit a declining number, exclude Negroes from membership altogether, either through provisions in their constitutions or by means of special rituals. Other unions exclude Negroes through custom rather than by explicit rule. Still other unions require Negroes to have separate locals. There are, on the other hand, unions which explicitly forbid racial discrimination.

The American Federation of Labor was originally receptive toward Negroes; later it came to refuse membership to them or restricted their influence. Membership in the Congress for Industrial Organization, on the other hand, was always open to Negroes, as well as to women and to other minority groups (not excluding Communists). When the two organizations merged in 1955 the leaders declared the new organization would not tolerate any kind of discrimination. States that have laws against discriminatory hiring require unions to delete discriminatory rules in their charters.

But at the local level, despite policies determined by top leadership, some unions continue to keep Negroes segregated and hence noncompetitive.

Many unions, on the other hand, are beginning to recognize that in self-protection they cannot afford to discriminate. A large reservoir of unorganized labor—Negro, women, foreign-born—is a potent factor in the competition for jobs. White and Negro miners in Birmingham, Alabama, for example, found that they both lost by racial segregation. Segregation did not, actually, prevent competition but, in fact, aggravated it.

> Over the whole history of their separate competitive bargaining with industry and management, neither racial group achieved substantial economic improvements. In fact, the more intense the racial competition the weaker the wage structure became. It was not until the policy of racial segregation was made secondary to common economic improvement that gains for either were possible. There are now, despite the tradition of separation, over a hundred unsegregated unions in the area.[1]

This was an almost archetypical case of a mixed-motive game in which common interests were as important as conflicting ones.

Obtaining Monopoly

A union, like any association of businessmen, feels that in order to protect its market it must guard its members against competition from outsiders as well as from competition among themselves. This it has traditionally attempted to do by means of the so-called *closed shop,* which has taken many forms. Fundamentally it is a limitation on the right of an employer to hire anyone he chooses. Before the passage of the Taft-Hartley Act in 1947, there were several degrees of the closed shop, ranging from a

[1] Charles S. Johnson, *Patterns of Negro Segregation* (New York: Harper, 1943), p. 321.

provision which required all hiring to be done through the union halls, as in the maritime union on the West Coast, through the simple requirement —and this was the most common form—that employers hire only union members or persons willing to join the union as a condition of employment, to the loosest form, known as the union shop, in which the employer could hire anyone he chose provided the new employee joined the union after he got the job. Under the Taft-Hartley Act, the union shop remained but the closed shop was forbidden. This act also permitted states to pass so-called right-to-work laws which permitted men to secure and keep employment without joining unions.[2]

The closed shop grew up to prevent employers from exploiting the highly competitive labor market. It was an effort to give workers chips to use in bargaining with employers. For before unions had gained their present strength and legal protection, it was easy for employers to play one worker off against another in order to destroy the unions.

The competitive conditions which led to the agitation for the closed shop were described many years ago by the humorous character known as Mr. Dooley:

> "What's all this that's in the papers about the open shop?" asked Mr. Hennessey.
>
> "Why, don't ye know?" said Mr. Dooley. "Really, I'm surprised at yer ignorance, Hinnissey. What is th' open shop? Sure, 'tis where they kape the doors open to accommodate th' constant stream av min comin' t'take jobs cheaper than th' min what has th' jobs. 'Tis like this, Hinnissey: Suppose wan av these free-born citizens is workin' in an open shop f'r th' princely wage av wan large iron dollar a day av tin hours. Along comes anither son-av-a-gun and he sez t'th' boss, 'Oi think oi could handle th' job nicely f'r ninety cints.'
>
> " 'Shure,' sez th' boss, and th' wan dollar man gets out into th' cool wurruld t'exercise his inalienable roights as a free-born American citizen an' scab on some other poor devil. An' so it goes on, Hinnissey. An' who gits th' benefit? Thrue, it saves th' boss money, but he don't care no more f'r money thin he does f'r his right eye.
>
> "It's all principle wid him. He hates t'see min robbed av their indipindence. They must have their indipindence, regardless av anything else."
>
> "But," said Mr. Hennessey, "these open-shop min ye menshun say they are f'r unions if properly conducted."
>
> "Shure," said Mr. Dooley, "if properly conducted. An' there we are; an' how would they have thim conducted? No strikes, no rules, no contracts, no scales, hardly iny wages an' dam few members."[3]

Another monopolistic practice by which unions have attempted to prevent competition for jobs is known as the *closed union*. By making union membership difficult and expensive, by limiting the number of apprentices, thus creating a scarcity of skills and cutting down the number of workers

[2] Only seventeen states, and these mainly nonindustrial, have such right-to-work laws.

[3] Reproduced in Leo Huberman, *The Truth about Unions* (New York: Reynal and Hitchcock, 1946).

available, they seek control of their specific labor market. There are several ways of closing a union.

> The simplest and most common method of restricting membership is to close the union rolls and refuse cards to new applicants. In skilled crafts admittance to the union is regulated by aptitude tests and into the trade by entrance regulations. Often membership is restricted, by the constitution or tacit agreement, to sons or relatives of the members. Applicants are also kept out by excessive initiation fees . . . and by the issuance of "permit" or "privilege" cards to non-members at a weekly fee . . . thus enabling the union to assure as much steady work as possible to its regular members.[4]

The combination of a closed union and a closed shop had resulted in a monopoly as tight as any that business had ever achieved. The union decided who could become a member; and no one could work unless he belonged.

Most unions have preferred the advantages of large membership, more dues, and prestige based on numbers. But others, for reasons associated with their craft or industry, have chosen the closed union principle. The Taft-Hartley Act forbade the requirement of excessive or discriminatory fees as a prerequisite for membership, but it did not "impair the right of a labor organization to prescribe its own rules with respect to the acquisition or retention of membership." The closed union was thus still legal, although without the closed shop it lost some of its monopolistic force.

Like all attempts to achieve monopoly, the attempt of unions aroused resentment and hostility. A monopoly is a monopoly no matter who practices it. Workers excluded from jobs by monopolistic unions, as well as employers, spoke out against practices which, they felt, invaded their rights. Pleas were made for "the right of a person, if capable, to perform work in competition with any other qualified worker, without regard to his membership or non-membership in any organization, be it the Knights of Columbus, the Masons, the AFL, or CIO."[5] A number of states passed so-called right-to-work laws which made even the union shop illegal.

Substituting Abundance of Jobs for Scarcity

In addition to attempting to eliminate cutthroat competition and obtain monopoly control of the job market, unions also try to soften competition by increasing the supply of jobs available. This results in the creation of relative abundance, not by stimulating mass production but by stretching what work there is as far as possible. This enforcement of make-work rules is called featherbedding, and it has been classified into five kinds.

First there are restrictions on the use of new processes or inventions

[4] *Democracy in Trade Unions* (American Civil Liberties Union), March, 1946, pp. 7-8.

[5] Alphonse G. Eberle, legal staff, International Shoe Company, before the Missouri State Legislature in behalf of a bill to outlaw the closed shop, May 6, 1947.

which would eliminate workers. Second there are restrictions on the use of prefabricated products, especially in the building trades, thus requiring more work on the job at the site of building. A third kind of make-work rule requires the performance of unnecessary work. A fourth kind of rule requires the hiring of unnecessary men. A fifth kind is an elaboration of practices already referred to. We have pointed out how the superior worker's pace is held down, theoretically, to that of the average worker, in order to prevent unfair pace-setting. This shades very easily into rules which slow down even an average pace. Thus, for example, bricklayers who can lay 800 to 1,000 bricks a day without strain cut down their production to 400 to 600 a day by various rules, written or unwritten, and lathers who can put up 60 bundles a day set a limit of 30 to 35 bundles.

Not all featherbedding is embodied in union rules. Sometimes it takes the form of pressure on local authorities for municipal ordinances which make jobs, such as requirements that independent electrical contractors be called in to do routine building installations. Ingenious labor leaders can invent numerous ways to make laws operate in their favor, just as industrial leaders can.

Featherbedding produces public anger and resentment. Not only does it limit production but it is expensive to the consumer when costs are passed on to him. But workers ask, "Why should one group, labor, have to pay the entire cost of technological advance? We all profit by new inventions. Why should we not all share the cost?" Many union leaders recognize the harmful results of featherbedding, but they feel that they must protect their members from unemployment resulting from technological advances. They are, they say, ready to work with management to make industry more efficient, provided the savings which result are shared with the workers and a minimum of workers lose their jobs. The best way to get rid of featherbedding, it is argued, is to have a program of full employment or a guaranteed annual wage.

Competition among Unions

Although unions manage to substitute solidarity for competition within their own ranks and labor leaders aspire to achieve ultimate solidarity for labor as a whole, this ideal is far from realization. Competition for jobs is keen not only among individuals but also among unions themselves. This competition, especially characteristic of the building industry, affects community welfare in a very intimate way. When new materials, tools, and processes are introduced, new unions sometimes arise also and underbid long-established unions. Thus occur what are known as jurisdictional disputes.

The competition of unions in the form of the jurisdictional dispute is particularly baffling to the community because it leaves both employer and consumer defenseless. Even friends of labor condemn it. Here is a contractor sympathetic with the principle of union organization. He has contracts with all the crafts involved in his work. Everything goes well until one day the carpenters stop work. They are competing with laborers over the right to remove wood forms for the construction of concrete furnace pits. This work has always been done by laborers, but the carpenters want it now.

Such seemingly senseless activities alienate community sympathy. Is it simply a case of union stupidity? Not at all. It is part of the competitive struggle for jobs. Even when jobs are plentiful, fear haunts the workers that the condition is temporary. They feel they must establish their right to certain jobs even when they have plenty of work. They will not always have work. As we have said, a job is a fragile, perishable commodity, as far as the worker is concerned.

The American Federation of Labor tried for almost forty years to find a successful formula for solving this intense union competition for jobs. A building and construction trades department was set up to get rid of competition among the nineteen craft unions of the building industry. But the Federation itself had no power to solve the problem. The difficulties are tremendous. "The job is the source of one's livelihood. When it is encroached upon, especially by another group accepting work at a lower rate of pay, a strong reaction occurs."[6] The stakes are very high.

In 1961 the AFL-CIO set up machinery to handle jurisdictional disputes, which by then were threatening the integrity of the whole labor movement. It provided for compulsory arbitration of such disputes, with the decision binding on all parties. Whether or not this plan would succeed any better than earlier plans depended on the way it was administered and the willingness of unions to work to make it succeed.

It is extremely difficult to see what is being tested in this kind of competition. It is surely not skill. It seems to be entirely the will to win; the union with the strongest organization and the highest morale has the best chance.[7]

An abundance of jobs would greatly minimize jurisdictional disputes, but it would not get rid of them entirely, for unions may be imperialistic in the same way nations are. They may raid other unions in order to enlarge membership and hence power. An illustration of this kind of raiding of one union by another is offered by the teamsters union, which attempts to get many different crafts to affiliate with it. In one case, for example, it sought to get the butchers in cold storage plants to affiliate with it instead of with the butchers' union.

[6] Harry A. Millis and Royal E. Montgomery, *The Economics of Labor,* Vol. III, *Organized Labor* (New York: McGraw-Hill, 1945), p. 276.

[7] In many cases the jurisdictional dispute is not competition in the sense we have been discussing it, but conflict. Recognizing this, the American Federation of Labor set up a system of compulsory arbitration to decide which union gets which jobs. This might be viewed as judgmental competition, the arbitrator deciding which competitor wins.

This competition for power among unions sometimes leads to even more extreme behavior. John L. Lewis, the former head of the United Mine Workers, once went so far as to buy out a mine in which a rival union was strong, in order to kill the other union. In the 50's and 60's, the teamsters union engaged in similar activities.

Unfortunately even the merger of the Federation and the Congress did not end jurisdictional disputes among member unions. In fact, the inability of unions to agree on the affiliation of potential new members is one of the several reasons given for the recent lack of growth in union membership. In early 1960 the organizing staff had been cut to less than half its former strength because it was useless to organize new local unions when there was no agreement among the international unions as to which would get them. Interunion raids and counter-raids also increased.

So far our emphasis has been on the nonlegislative forms of institutionalization of competition in the job market. The ideal of labor solidarity, we have seen, is one of the most powerful. It is the union's task to keep its members thoroughly indoctrinated. Under such indoctrination in solidarity, union men will endure real sacrifice by not crossing a picket line, thus expressing in an effective way their support of fellow-workers. Contempt for "scabs," "strikebreakers," and others who refuse to abide by the rules of solidarity keeps many a worker from attempting to cross a picket line. The whole ideology of unionism constitutes a body of attitudes, ideals, unwritten rules, and other institutional norms, the main purpose of which is to prevent a competitive psychology from developing among workers.

In addition, there is a tremendous body of quasi-legal rules institutionalizing competition for jobs. There are thousands of contracts between unions and employers which serve as institutional limits to competition for jobs. Union-management contracts cover literally scores of issues and regulate competition for jobs by detailed provisions for seniority rights, promotion procedure, and the like.

Statutory Institutionalization of Competition in the Job Market

Added to these controls are many embodied in statutory law. Such legislation limiting competition for jobs has many aspects. Minimum wage and maximum hour laws, laws prohibiting the labor of children (which are not only humanitarian in origin but also economic in that they prevent the competition of cheap child labor from pulling down standards for adults), laws which specify the working conditions for women—all these have the effect of preventing cutthroat competition for jobs.

That there is great need for such institutional protection of unorganized workers against exploitative competition is illustrated by the low wages and poor working conditions of those who do not have it. Even with the Fair Labor Standards Act, many plants pay less than the minimum; violations of the law occur in a sizeable proportion of cases. Workers will underbid one another as long as there are employers willing to take advantage of their need.

The National Labor Relations Act, as amended by the Taft-Hartley Act of 1947 and the Landrum-Griffin Act of 1959, attempts to regulate the behavior of unions with respect to their control of competition for jobs. The closed shop, as we have pointed out, was forbidden, but the union shop was permitted. Without at least the latter, the unions could easily be destroyed. The closed shop has been under severe attack in state legislatures also. The Taft-Hartley Act made the jurisdictional dispute illegal; that is, it was declared to be an unfair labor practice to force or require "any employer to assign particular work to employees in a particular labor organization or in a particular trade, craft, or class rather than to employees in another labor organization or in another trade, craft, or class."

Still in the future is a permanent federal fair employment practices act which would render permanent the work of the Fair Employment Practices Commission set up by executive order during World War II to eliminate unfair discrimination because of race, color, creed, or sex. A number of states (19 as of 1961) and cities (26 as of 1954) have such legislation, however. The Ives-Quinn Law (1945) in New York, for example, attempts to make the competition for jobs scrupulously fair by setting up a commission empowered "to eliminate and prevent discrimination in employment because of race, creed, color, or national origin, either by employers, labor organizations, employment agencies or other persons, and to take other actions against discrimination because of race, creed, color or national origin, as herein provided."

The law does not hope to eliminate racial attitudes; it does hope to set up institutional controls to prevent the automatic exclusion of persons from employment simply because of color, creed, race, or national origin. The law also forbids closed unions. Practically all of the unions approached by the Commission promised to recommend to their next convention that discriminatory clauses in their constitutions be removed.

Also still in the future is legislation to soften the rigors of competition for jobs by increasing the supply—for example, proposals for the so-called guaranteed annual wage, whereby workers are assured of steady employment and do not, therefore, have to stretch their jobs by featherbedding or other restrictions. But a beginning has been made, albeit a very slow one. As long ago as 1946 an interim report on a study of the guaranteed annual wage was made at the President's request and the basis was laid for future legislative consideration. In the 1950's, without special legislation, provisions were incorporated in some labor contracts which specified that when workers were unemployed their employers would add to their benefits enough to bring total income up to a specified proportion of the normal wage. In 1961 Walter Reuther of the automobile workers' union was asking that his men be paid salaries rather than hourly wages.

Competition for Personnel

The continuing technological revolution which goes about destroying unskilled and semi-skilled jobs creates, at the same time, an almost insatiable demand for highly trained personnel. Thus we have the anomalous situation of millions of men unemployed while there are serious shortages of personnel in industry. While men in the lower stories of the industrial structure seek to protect themselves against the bitter competition for jobs, men at the higher levels are fiercely competed for. Modern technology is completely reconstructing the occupational structure of the community. Little by little it is erasing manual labor at the bottom; but at the same time it is creating new jobs at the top. There is need for personnel in an enormous number of new professions, professions never heard of a generation ago. There seems to be a shortage of such talented people as mathematicians, physicists, engineers of many kinds to staff them. There is a continuing need for a large number of administrators and executives, for the knack of getting things done remains a much-needed skill.

Despite the fact that higher ranks of workers are competed for by industries and by firms, within any one firm there may be extremely rugged competition among the workers, especially the so-called junior executives, for advancement. This competition is sometimes referred to as a "rat race," in which the competitive pace is extremely fast.

Competition among Independent Professionals

Among independent professional men competition is quite openly controlled in many communities by gentlemen's agreements with respect to fees, so that no doctor or lawyer underbids his colleagues. The members of local professional associations simply agree what shall be the minimum charge for office visits, home visits, inoculations, drawing up of wills, title search, and other standard services.

From this brief résumé of the way competitive behavior in the economic aspects of American community life is institutionalized, it will be readily noted that in spite of our exaltation of its virtues, we do not permit competition to function freely. We are afraid of it. It sacrifices values which we also treasure. We want sellers to compete when we are buyers; we want buyers to compete when we are sellers. But we want protection from our competitors when we are sellers and buyers ourselves. These general principles hold true in all kinds of markets.

11

The Way Competition for Room at the Top Is Institutionalized

The workers discussed in Chapter 10 were interested primarily in getting and keeping their jobs. We were not concerned there with efforts of workers to improve their relative position. Most workers are content to take their upward social mobility in the form of increased wages and fringe benefits won by their unions. They settle for the escalator ride that takes them up as the whole economy goes up. In time they acquire pleasant homes, equipped with electrical appliances, cars, and even boats and other prerequisites of the American standard of living. They may dream of a little business of their own, but they come in time to accept the limitations of their opportunities. Instead of becoming top men on the job, they may become top men in the volunteer fire department or in the union or in the lodge. They may become important in political party work. But they are not particularly interested in changing their occupations, life style, or social class. They may, however, wish more education, better jobs, and higher status for their children. All of which leads to the tremendously important problem of social mobility or, conversely, social stratification.

Horizontal and Vertical Mobility

In Chapter 8 we saw that in the past great competitive forces distributed people in different areas of the community primarily on the basis of their ability to pay for the use of land in the form of rent or taxes. Some areas were cleaner, prettier, or less crowded than others. In general the people in the same area had similar jobs, incomes, education, tastes, values; often they had the same ethnic background.

It is not difficult to distinguish such areas as middle- or lower- or upper-class neighborhoods. Whole groups have moved from lower- to higher-class neighborhoods, as we saw, and this has been the history of most American communities.[1] One group after another has ascended from lower-

[1] For an interesting account of these processes in New York City see Oscar Handlin, *The Newcomers* (Cambridge, Mass.: Harvard, 1959).

to higher-class neighborhoods. Such moves were, in fact, described as from "areas of first settlement" to "areas of second settlement." The "classification" of families in these geographic or horizontal terms is fairly simple and clear-cut. We can see that people are improving themselves, bettering their "class" position when they leave the poorer neighborhoods and move into cleaner, more attractive ones.

This chapter is concerned with class in a more abstract sense, with position in a vertical rather than in a horizontal spatial sense; that is, not geographic but "social" space, and not group but individual mobility.

Competition for places at the top is impeded by the fact that the competitors begin from different scratches, so that some have a head start over others. How to minimize these differences in life chances, if not wholly to eliminate them, is one of the most pressing problems of the present time when the search for talent is a fundamental preoccupation of both industry and government, and it is the major theme of this chapter.

Before continuing further along this line, however, it is essential to understand what is meant by "high" and "low" positions in the social sense, why we speak of social "climbing" or "upward" social mobility, why we speak of positions at the "top" or at the "bottom" of a social "ladder," and why we think in terms of social "stratification." What, in brief, constitutes "upness" and "downness" in a social sense?

Stratification As a Structural Fact

It is important to remember the distinction made in Chapter 3 between the structure of a community and the people who occupy it. The structure will be determined by such factors as size and industry. A mill town will have one kind of structure, an agricultural community, another.

But why are some positions in the structure considered "higher" than others? Positions that have the function of making decisions are "higher" in a structural sense than others, and the wider the area covered by the decision, that is, the more people affected by it, the "higher" the position. In general also positions that require more education are higher than those requiring less. Similarly positions requiring more skill are higher than those requiring less. Income and prestige may or may not be related to these structural positions, although usually they are.[2]

Some structures have more room at the "top" than do others. An industrialized economy requires relatively more people at the top than does an agricultural economy; that is, more decision makers, more educated people, more highly trained people. Concomitantly, positions formerly at the bottom tend to be eliminated entirely by mechanization and automation; the whole economy is thus upgraded. The net result is not

[2] Kingsley Davis and Wilbert Moore, "Some Principles of Stratification," *Amer. Soc. Rev.*, 10 (April, 1945), pp. 242-244.

entirely to erase differentials, for there still remain structural differences, but the trend is to attenuate the extremes.

The transition from primarily agricultural to primarily industrialized societies has the effect, therefore, of accelerating upward social mobility by making more room at the top. This trend has been documented for most western countries. A summary of the available data leads to the conclusion "that the social mobility of societies becomes relatively high once their industrialization, and hence their economic expansion, reaches a certain level."[3]

There are usually concomitants of position which become so closely associated with position that they sometimes confound the onlooker. Inherent in position, and not a mere concomitant, are privileges and prerogatives, as well as responsibilities. But such concomitants as insignia, badges, titles, awards, and prestige are also characteristic of high position.[4] These intrinsic and concomitant characteristics of high position make it much sought after by many persons.

These are all structural facts, independent of the people who actually man the structure. Stratification is an organizational or structural fact quite different from individual superiority and inferiority. It has nothing to do with the ideals of equality; it is not at all the same as the interpersonal relationship of ascendance and submission found even among lower animals. The number of positions at the top or bottom of an occupational structure is not determined by the number of able and of incompetent persons in the community, but rather by the nature of the underlying structure of the community.

"People and Places"

It is true, of course, that different communities tend to attract people with different interests, talents, and skills. In this sense the structure and the people who man it are not independent, but it is the structure that influences the people rather than the other way round. The concentration of talented people in and around New York City was not the cause of its structure; it was the structure which made room for the talented people. Conversely, the lack of talented people in a mountain mining community does not cause the small number of high positions, but rather the reverse.

There is, of course, further, an impact of position on personality, so that there is a relationship here also. Suppose two men equally capable of filling a certain position and then imagine only one of them selected—by chance, even—for filling it. Over a period of time he would become "superior" to the unselected man in many respects. He has access to more

[3] S. M. Lipset and Reinhard Bendix, *Social Mobility in Industrial Society* (University of California, 1960), p. 13.

[4] See Chapter 12 for a discussion of the invidious nature of high position.

information, he knows more about the community or organization; he is treated as a superior, he has a chance to meet more people, to learn more. In time he has become "better" than the man who was not selected, at least in these respects. There is, therefore, a reciprocal relationship between position and personality. Only certain people are willing to take positions of certain levels; only certain people are capable of filling them. Conversely, just as the position selects certain personalities, the position in turn influences the persons selected.

Filling the Positions in the Structure: Individual "Social Mobility"

In addition to the upward mobility of whole ethnic and racial groups and classes which has characterized industrial societies, there has been, in varying degrees, a parallel process of individual mobility. That is, while whole groups were rising on an escalator, individuals and families were running up the escalator stairs, outdistancing their fellows. It is this family aspect of the phenomenon of social mobility we wish to examine here.

What is the best way to institutionalize the allocation of positions in the community structure? Inheritance, nepotism, favoritism are among the possible answers. So is competition, testing merit.

A good testing process, one that would really sort people out—that is, "classify" them—on the basis of merit has been sought since the time of Plato. If we could sort out people accurately according to merit and award life's prizes accordingly, there would be at least a rational basis for assigning positions. Free competition is one way to do this. The idea is that if competition is allowed to operate autonomously over a long period of time without too many restrictions, a rough sorting out will take place. The people who reach the top will be those who belong there because of their natural superiority. Those at the bottom will be those who just did not have the ability to rise. All the babies born in the community in an ideal competitive set-up would begin at exactly the same point. There would be no handicaps, no special advantages. The same rules would apply to all. There would be no favoritism, no prejudice. Health care, nutrition, educational opportunity, access to jobs would be equalized. Under such ideal circumstances the best ones would probably win. Whenever we think of competition as a fair test we usually presuppose conditions of this kind.

But social competition is not free. We do not have a chaos of struggling individuals all starting from the same scratch. Babies are born into families and that means some will have a head start, regardless of their abilities. They will begin the race up the social ladder several rungs above others who are born into other families. This fact was, indeed, one of the arguments Socialists used to invoke in their indictment of the whole family system as a bourgeois institution for the perpetuation of property inequalities and, hence, inherently unfair. The competitive process which sorts people out is defective from the outset if it takes place in a family system, for "life chances"—hygienic, motivational, and educational—are determined by the family one happens to be born into.

Four "Models" of Styles of Living

In the middle of the nineteenth century a great French student of the family, Frédéric LePlay, pointed out that one could learn almost all there was to know about a family by studying how it spent its income. The allocation of money to the many competing demands made upon a family reflected its values. This may be an exaggeration, but style of life or consumption standards do give us insight into the life chances of the children involved.

Taking into account occupation, income, education, and residence, one can delineate at least six general styles of living. These have been characterized as lower-lower, upper-lower, lower-middle, upper-middle, lower-upper, and upper-upper. Only the first four will concern us here.

At the bottom are families often characterized as "ignorant," "shiftless," "riff-raff," "ne'er-do-wells." No one covets an invitation to dine with them; no one envies them; no one is proud to be seen with them. Few are interested in reading about them in the papers. They are the last hired, the first fired. They have few skills. They are known to social agencies even in times of prosperity, and their case histories are written in disparaging phrases. They are sometimes known as "multi-problem families," for pathologies of all kinds tend to have a high incidence among them. They scarcely belong to the social system at all; they are in but not of it. In rural communities they include the crop pickers and other migratory workers.

A second model includes people who manage to remain self-supporting except in hard times. They are wage-earning families in which more than one worker is often required to make ends meet at even a modest scale of living, so that the children may be taken out of school early and sent to work. These families live in the poorest areas, where the rents are cheapest, and their housing is usually substandard at best, unless subsidized. The simple problems of living are so engrossing that they have little time or energy for the amenities. If they have a roof over their heads, they are not worried at having no rug under their feet. So long as they have food on the table, they do not ask for a tablecloth. They are not worried about their children's personality problems, their emotional difficulties, their artistic or intellectual development. They are on rock bottom, so to speak, in personal and social relationships. They may work hard, but their life is often spoken of as a treadmill. It is almost impossible to get ahead. Their forms of self-expression are likely to be hearty rather than sophisticated. The work they do has little prestige. They read very little. They are therefore members of but a limited number of publics. Their vocabulary is limited.

In judging lapses from conventional sex patterns, they are likely to be tolerant. Because the conditions of their lives make individuality difficult to achieve, we sometimes speak of them as "the masses." Although aware that they are not as well off as others, they resent affronts to their self-respect. In rural communities, they are the poorest tenant farmers, never completely out of debt, moving frequently from farm to farm.

A third model consists of those who have time and energy for at least some of the amenities. In towns and smaller cities, rows of clean little bungalows and cottages with neat lawns and gardens, lovingly tended, are their homes. They are proud of their crisp curtains. If they cannot afford a rug, they at least have a linoleum covering on the living room floor. They may eat in the kitchen, but there will be a tablecloth, if only a plastic one. By careful allocation of funds, the thrifty ones manage in time to get most of the items of the so-called American standard of living—electric refrigerators, vacuum cleaners, sewing and washing machines, television sets, telephones, and other electrical appliances. They eat simple but substantial food. The women's magazines teach the housewives a good deal about nutrition and home decoration. These people read newspapers and popular magazines, but few books. Their homes are clean and well cared for. The work the wage-earner does is likely to be skilled; it may be clerical. These families want their children to have the advantages they themselves missed in childhood. They are usually supporters of the church, fairly strict in their moral beliefs. Modesty and propriety are valued. The subject of sex is likely to be taboo, and they lack an adequate vocabulary for discussing it. They have been described as "concerned with ethics, morals, talent and social serviceability. They have, as an ideal, primarily to gain an income, to become financially better off. Psychologically, they are a very secure group. They are comfortably aware of not being lower class and they have little contact with the upper class. Education, neat homes and personal cleanliness are matters of great importance" to them.[5] In rural communities these people are the substantial, successful family farmers, with large barns, comfortable homes, and the latest machinery.

A fourth model comprises most of the successful business and professional families—the doctors, lawyers, successful store owners, managers, bankers, clergy of the more prosperous churches. Their homes are likely to be large and well furnished. They have servants or at least some help in taking care of their homes and yards. They read books as well as newspapers and magazines; they belong, therefore, to many publics. They send their children to college. They may be careful in planning their expenditures, but they spend on a fairly generous level. They travel. They appreciate good music and enjoy the theater. They eat in the dining room, may use their sterling silver every day. Their food is attractive; they may play

[5] John Dollard, "Drinking Mores of Social Classes," in *Alcohol, Science, and Society* (New Haven, Conn.: Yale, 1945), p. 96.

at cooking exotic dishes. They belong to civic organizations and the country club. People like to be seen with them. Their comings and goings are news.

Almost all of the families in most communities—except the most complex—can be classified into one of these four models. In addition there is another style of living, often characterized as "Society," which performs an important function in some communities, but since it is not relevant for our discussion here, we defer discussion of it until later.

Social Position and Personality

The important fact to be emphasized here is that these different models or styles of living furnish quite different socializing media for children. They have different patterns of child-rearing practices, have different aspirations for their children, offer a different perspective on the total society, set different standards of behavior, and as a result produce different adult personalities.

The father, for example, in the lower-class family tends to be authoritarian when he is present, but he is not always present. The mother, therefore, although she is subordinate to her husband may nevertheless be the central focus of the family. Overt aggression is not only acceptable but even encouraged in the lower-class family. Deferred gratification is not taught to children: enjoy now while you have it, is the unstated motto.

Middle-class values reflect the so-called Protestant Ethic. This refers to a system of values which emphasizes self-discipline, deferred gratification, thrift, industriousness, conscientious effort. It creates ambitious people who work hard to "get ahead."

Class, then, as defined in style of living has an almost determinative influence on personality and therefore on chances of success in the competition of life.

Here, then, are two boys of equal talent. One even in the cradle is slated for a position at the top because his father is a leading industrialist. He will have the very best medical care; his diet will be carefully watched; his mother will be alert for incipient personality problems; he will be sent to the best schools where his individual needs will be catered to; he will feel at home with "the best" people. He will have self-confidence. He will finish college and there will be a job waiting for him in any one of several firms. The child born on the other side of the tracks will have to work hard to remain where he starts on the social ladder. He will be exposed to more infections. His teeth, tonsils, and adenoids will not receive the attention they need. He will be kept home from school whenever he is needed to help his father; school will seem a necessary—perhaps even an unnecessary—evil, unrelated to what goes on in the outside world. He may be glad to quit as soon as he can get a work permit. His father will get him a job in the mines; the foreman may even wink if he is below the legal working age. Even if the lower-class boy has the greater talent he must work harder, be better, in order to secure the rewards the favored boy achieves easily. The lower-class boy who continues his education does so often against great odds. It is much easier to accept the standards of our class than to try to rise above them.

Caste As a Barrier to Free Competition

In addition to class barriers to free social competition in American community life we have caste barriers. Caste is a system whereby one group is kept permanently in an inferior position. The essential characteristic of caste is that no one is permitted to rise from a lower to a higher caste, and intermarriage is prohibited between them. Theoretically if not always practically, caste divides a community into watertight compartments. It creates strong barriers between groups, strong patterns of cohesion within groups. It is also characteristic of true caste systems that they are hierarchical in nature. That is, certain castes have higher positions, as measured by privileges and rights, than others. And, finally, caste is hereditary.

The major caste cleavage in American communities is, of course, that between Negroes and whites. As such it differs from that of ancient China or of India in that it is vertical as well as horizontal. This is a complicating factor of great importance. Theoretically, one caste is supposed to be on a superior plane, which means that all white people would be superior to all Negroes. This is the doctrine supporting the policy of white supremacy. This ideology is not, of course, borne out by scientific findings. It is true that statistically the Negro can be shown as inferior to the white, just as, statistically, poor people are inferior to economically superior people. Some statistics show the average Negro as having a lower IQ than the average white person. Negro health is inferior. Negro life expectancy is lower. On the other hand, army tests during World War I showed that the IQ of northern Negroes was higher not only than that of southern Negroes but also than that of rural southern whites. In order to test whether this was a matter of selection—that is, whether it was because the superior Negroes went North—one psychologist went back to Alabama, South Carolina, and Tennessee to trace the school records of a group of Harlem Negro schoolchildren. He found that in the South they were in no way exceptional; they were just average, run-of-the-mill southern Negro children. Their superiority was due to the schooling they had received in northern cities. Furthermore, the longer they remained in the North, the higher their IQ became.[6] Data gathered in World War II also showed a direct relationship between Negro handicap and the community background of the indi-

[6] Otto Klineberg, *Negro Intelligence and Selective Migration* (New York: Columbia, 1935); *Race Differences* (New York: Harper, 1935). These studies are summarized in *Characteristics of the American Negro,* ed. Otto Klineberg (New York: Harper, 1944), pp. 44-46.

vidual.[7] The high venereal disease rate is, of course, social, not racial. The rachitic and other deficiency diseases are plainly acquired. Nor should we be deceived by averages. Many Negroes are superior to the average white person; indeed, some are superior to most white persons. The hurdles placed in the way of Negroes are higher than those which white persons have to overcome. Caste barriers to free social competition are more serious than class barriers.

Validity of Social Competition

Well, maybe most people belong where they are, say those who justify the status quo. After all, you can't keep a good man down. Of course some people have more than others. They deserve more. They are better people. To be sure, competition is a very rough and crude way to sort people out. There are many mistakes—talented people who never get a chance to receive the kind of training they require. And, of course, many inferior people are protected at the top. But by and large, and in the long run, in spite of minor injustices and errors, social competition, they say, does test basic fitness for the top positions.

People who agree with this point of view cite certain factual data to support their position. Numerous studies by psychologists, social workers, sociologists, and educationists show that in whatever way you look at the people at the bottom, they are, on the average, inferior to the people at the top. They tend to be smaller and lighter in physique. They are sick more often, more seriously, and for a longer time. Their average IQ is lower. They clutter up the courts more. The facts are unequivocal. And so, the apologists of the status quo conclude, as did the Social Darwinists of the nineteenth century, these people are at the bottom of the social ladder because they are inferior. They are, in fact, concrete proof of the efficacy of competition as a social testing device.

It looks different from the other end. What has she got that I haven't got, asks the girl from the mill as she studies the picture of a wealthy girl's $25,000 coming-out party. The mill girl sits eating a sandwich and coke for lunch at a drugstore counter, while the debutante is toasted in champagne at the Ritz. It would be hard to convince the mill girl that she is low on the social scale and the debutante high because of some benign process in the universe which sorts people out according to their just deserts.

Nor will the scientific facts actually bear out a verdict of success for the present family-bound method of allocating social position. The statistical inferiority of those in the lower positions is by no means demonstrably genetic. There are others who argue just as convincingly as the Social Darwinists that people are inferior because they are poor. They cite

[7] Eli Ginzburg and Douglas Bray, *The Uneducated* (New York: Columbia, 1953).

evidence to show that under proper circumstances children of the "inferior" classes blossom out and show all the earmarks of superior children.[8] By the time class influences have had a chance to set a personality in a characteristic mold, change may be difficult if not impossible. But there is a wealth of data to indicate that infants can be shaped into almost any class pattern. At any rate, such thinkers argue, enough mistakes are made by competition as it functions in most American communities to warrant calling it inadequate as a testing process.

The Great Value Conflict: Family versus Equality of Opportunity

It is impossible, then, to have equality of opportunity and the system of rearing children in families at the same time. Although both the ideal of equality of opportunity and the family system are values dear to American communities, there has never been in the United States any large-scale, serious consideration given to jettisoning the family system in order to equate opportunity—as there was, for example, in the USSR in the early years of the revolution and, more recently, in Communist China—but increasingly efforts are being made to minimize the inevitable differences which result from different family, and hence class, backgrounds. The goal is, as far as possible within the family system, to minimize the disparity in life chances between the more and the less privileged children. There are at least two institutionalized ways in which American communities attempt to render social competition more nearly fair, namely, education and welfare services, both public and private.

RENDERING SOCIAL COMPETITION FAIR: THE SCHOOL

The public school performs many functions, only one of which is purely intellectual. In addition to teaching the intellectual skills of reading, writing, and arithmetic, it attempts to inculcate civic and national ideals. It also assumes some of the responsibility for vocational preparation. Thrust upon it by the waves of immigrants has been the further function of acculturation, of taking whole generations of foreign-born parents and children and inducting them into the new world they found themselves confronted with.

Not all of these functions are compatible. Time spent teaching girls and boys how to brush their teeth, how to groom their hair and nails, how to choose their diet, skills which the middle-class child picks up at home without even being aware of it, cannot be used in teaching alegbra or modern physics. The controversy between those who defend the so-called "soft" subjects against the criticism of the advocates of the so-called "hard" subjects illustrates the complexities of the problems faced by the schools. If they are to equalize opportunity they must make up for a great many

[8] For a summary of the research data on this point, see Jessie Bernard, *American Family Behavior* (New York: Harper, 1942), Chapter 10.

nonintellectual deficiencies of the underprivileged child. The courses which attempt to do for the minority group or underprivileged child what the home and family do for the more privileged child can be held up for ridicule by those who want only academic subjects taught in the schools. But they are as important a contribution to implementation of the egalitarian ideal as any other offering of the school.

The present concern with equalizing opportunity is couched in terms of salvaging talent; it is motivated by the urgent need to cultivate ability wherever it is found. The feeling is that we cannot allow removable obstacles to stand in the way of locating and developing talent. A growing research literature documents the current thought in this area.[9]

It is estimated that about half of those in the top third or fourth of their high school class do not enter college and of those who do enter college a large proportion fail to graduate. Of those high school graduates in the top two percent as far as intelligence and grades are concerned, 38 percent do not graduate from college (as of 1953); of those in the top seven percent, 46 percent do not; of those in the top sixteen percent, 53 percent do not; and of those in the top twenty-seven percent, 58 percent do not complete college. The situation is not so bad now, but even as late as 1960 the loss between high school and college for the top tenth of high school graduates was estimated at anywhere between 28 and 45 percent.[10]

Increasingly schools have attempted to meet the challenge of locating and salvaging ability. Instead of tacitly accepting the class system as it reveals itself in the students as they come to school, schools have been experimenting with ways and means to encourage talent wherever it appears and to see that no hurdles stand in the way of its realization. The army originally accustomed us to this truly democratic principle. And the military service's principle of paying all those who want to be trained and who have the ability, regardless of their poverty or wealth, proved a good one to render competition fair. We need all the talent and ability we can train. As early as 1944 it was being urged that "some of the ills of the present are directly traceable to our failure to use trained people. Because of our status system we have maintained many people of inferior ability and training in responsible jobs who should have been eliminated to permit competent people to rise from lower levels to fill these higher places. We must spread our net wider to find people of talent wherever they exist and we must permit them to compete with everyone for the prized positions."[11] Since that time the competitive challenge of the USSR has accelerated the search for ways and means to find and develop talent.

Although economic factors are important in explaining the drop-out

[9] This literature is summarized and analyzed in Adam Yarmolinsky et al., *Recognition of Excellence, Working Papers of a Project of the Edgar Stern Family Fund April, 1960* (New York: Free Press, 1960).

[10] *Ibid.*, pp. 88-89.

[11] W. Lloyd Warner, Robert J. Havighurst, and Martin B. Loeb, *Who Shall Be Educated? The Challenge of Unequal Opportunities* (New York: Harper, 1944), p. 162.

rate of talented students, they are not necessarily the most important. Estimates in the 1940's and 1950's of the proportion of able high school graduates who did not go on to college because of lack of funds varied from one-third to one-half.[12] The loss due to economic reasons is probably still high, but decreasingly so. And the economic obstacles are among the easiest to remove. Liberal scholarship programs are increasingly available.

The school, however, can do relatively little about the class values which the child brings with him from his family. Scholarship funds do not markedly increase the proportion of high school graduates who enter college from different socio-economic groups.[13] Parental attitudes and values are more important than financial restrictions in keeping many talented young persons from college. Families in lower class positions do not set their sights high enough for their children. They do not have the perspective on the social system which shows the importance of education. The significance of family background as a motivating force in achievement was documented in a comparison of Italian and Jewish students in New Haven; the greater educational achievement of the latter was found to be related to family values.[14]

Nor can the schools do anything about the superior advantage of the more privileged child. The schools cannot prevent the more prosperous parents from giving their child every educational and vocational opportunity, no matter how mediocre his ability, nor should they. Conversely, the schools cannot furnish a family background which stimulates academic achievement, reading, and ambition. The school cannot make education as palatable to children, however bright, whose family, class, or caste background is not sympathetic or encouraging.

Nor can the school make the average poor child as attractive to his fellows as the average child of advantageous background. Class attitudes on the part of schoolmates are themselves important in driving away lower-class children from the schools—children whose clothing is shabby and whose personal habits are repellent. Such pupils are rejected by their classmates and fail to go on with their education because they find school unpleasant.[15]

The slum child is handicapped not only by his impoverished family background but also by the quality of the school he attends. The schools in slum areas are old, dilapidated, often rat-infested, poorly equipped; teachers avoid them when they can and those who cannot are often replaced by substitutes; standards of all kinds are low. There is little to stimulate or

[12] Adam Yarmolinsky *et al., op. cit.*, p. 91.

[13] *Ibid.*, p. 92.

[14] Fred Strodtbeck, "Family Interaction, Values and Achievement," in David McClelland, *Talent and Society* (Princeton, N. J.: Van Nostrand, 1958).

[15] August B. Hollingshead, *Elmtown's Youth: The Impact of Social Classes on Adolescents* (New York: Wiley, 1949), Chapters 6, 8, 9, and 13. See also R. J. Havighurst and Hilda Taba, *Adolescent Character and Personality* (New York: Wiley, 1949).

cultivate the interests of children in these dreary prison-like structures.[16]

Education has to overcome another kind of inequality in addition to those arising from class and caste. Some communities have a more educated population than others; some communities have more children to educate than others, and they are the poorer communities. There are, in other words, community inequalities as well as class and caste inequalities that have to be overcome if we wish equality of opportunity for all. Some children are denied opportunities simply because they are brought up in poor communities which cannot afford adequate schools. Mississippi, for example, spends far less than New York. It so happens that the states which have the largest number of children to educate are precisely those which have the least amount of taxes with which to support their schools. A child in these communities is thus at a disadvantage compared with a child in a community with fewer children to educate and a larger tax base upon which to finance its schools. The solution, if we wish to make educational opportunity equal to children in all communities, is some form of federal aid to local school systems. The school, then, seems to be drawing nearer to assuming a major burden in equalizing opportunity so that competition for positions at the top will test ability and not privilege or handicap. It is doubtful if it can ever completely eradicate the barriers that keep some children from maximizing their achievement; but it can work in this direction.

Despite these limitations the schools try to minimize the differences due to class background, especially by the introduction of counseling programs on an elaborate scale. In the past counseling tended to solidify class biases; counselors tended to guide children from lower-class backgrounds into lower-class vocations. More recently the best use of ability is coming to be the basic principle.

The importance of guidance cannot be denied. But there is one difficulty in it. A system of guidance would undoubtedly be able to single out the talented and the intelligent, but positions at the top do not necessarily go to the talented and the intelligent. Positions at the top go to people who have will to win, drive, ruthlessness, fighting personalities. The present autonomous competitive method of selecting lower-class people for top positions has at least the merit of testing this quality. It does not necessarily test talent or intelligence. It does test motivation or fighting ability.

A guidance system would tend to substitute judgmental for autonomous competition. It is a commonplace that the man who fights his way to the top can hire technical and professional brains. People with ability to fight their way to the top pay themselves well. Could a planned program for selecting lower-class people for top positions find tests for the fighting

[16] The relative inferiority of slum-area schools is documented by Patricia Cayo Sexton, *Education and Income: Inequality of Opportunity in Our Public Schools* (New York: Viking, 1961).

quality that would function better than the present criteria? It would have to, or fail; and the advantaged upper-class people would still retain their advantages. In other words, in order to give the privileged upper-class boy real competition, the guidance program would have to select boys with drive as well as ability.

An interesting illustration of the implications of substituting a judgmental form of competition for an autonomous one is afforded by the British system of selecting students for higher education. Ralph Turner contrasts "sponsored" with "contest" mobility, as follows:

> In England and the United States there appear to be different organizing folk norms, here termed sponsored mobility and contest mobility, respectively. Contest mobility is a system in which elite status is the prize in an open contest and is taken by the aspirants' own efforts. While the "contest" is governed by some rules of fair play, the contestants have wide latitude in the strategies they may employ. Since the "prize" of successful upward mobility is not in the hands of an established elite to give out, the latter cannot determine who shall attain it and who shall not. Under sponsored mobility elite recruits are chosen by the established elite or their agents, and elite status is *given* on the basis of some criterion of supposed merit and cannot be *taken* by any amount of effort or strategy. Upward mobility is like entry into a private club where each candidate must be "sponsored" by one or more of the members. Ultimately the members grant or deny upward mobility on the basis of whether they judge the candidate to have those qualities they wish to see in fellow members. . . .
>
> Contest mobility is like a sporting event in which many compete for a few recognized prizes. The contest is judged to be fair only if all the players compete on an equal footing. . . . Sponsored mobility, in contrast, rejects the pattern of the contest and favors a controlled selection process. . . . The governing objective of contest mobility is to give elite status to those who earn it, while the goal of sponsored mobility is to make the best use of the talents in society by sorting persons into their proper niches. In different societies the conditions of competitive struggle may reward quite different attributes, and sponsored mobility may select individuals on the basis of such diverse qualities as intelligence or visionary capability, but the difference in principle remains the same.[17]

Public Welfare and Social Work

A second institutionalized way of attempting to implement the egalitarian goals of our society is to set up voluntary or "private" social work agencies and public welfare programs of one kind or another.

Social work in its widespread ramifications has a double tie-up with the competitive process. One of these recognizes social competition and tries to render it fair by helping underprivileged individuals to overcome their handicaps; the other denies the validity of social competition and attempts to mitigate its results. In the first of these relations social work is creative;

[17] "Sponsored and Contest Mobility," *Amer. Soc. Rev.*, 25 (December, 1960), pp. 856-857.

in the second it is palliative. There are some people who feel that social workers should direct more of their efforts toward activities which equalize the opportunities and prevent the handicaps of the underprivileged, and less toward activities which merely console the failures. Both are considered essential in most communities.

In its relationships with children and families, social work attempts to minimize the handicaps of the underprivileged. Dietary, health, and recreational lacks are made up where possible so that the poor child will not be too far behind in the social race. Just how successful these efforts are is a moot question. There is a great deal of very searching criticism of much that the social worker does. But whether the work has been done well or poorly, the challenge remains. The egalitarian ideal requires that participants in the social race begin on as nearly an equal level as possible.

The standards set for this equalizing effort have been summarized as follows:

> 1. For each child a good home with the love and care of both parents.
> 2. A healthy start in life.
> 3. Schooling for every child to the maximum of his capacities and his powers.
> 4. Companionship with other children, free of humiliating barriers of race or class or creed.
> 5. An opportunity for self-expression and spiritual growth.
> 6. Full preparation for useful work in a trade, a business, or a profession.
> 7. A chance in adult life for a reasonable measure of security for self and his family, with ever broadening avenues for participation in the affairs of the neighborhood, the community, and the nation. . . .[18]

Viewed as an agency for equalizing opportunity, social work appears as one of the most challenging of professions and as one of the most important in a democracy.

The second tie-up of social work with social competition deals with the victims of social competition, those who, for one reason or another, have been outdistanced—the weak, the halt, the blind, the failures.[19] There is sometimes a good deal of resentment, expressed and unexpressed, at the good social worker's concern for people we sometimes label as shiftless, good-for-nothing, or worthless. Successful people often wish to have nothing to do with them. Since they have not made the grade, they should be eliminated from the race. The implication is, clearly, that social competition is just and fair and the winners should not be penalized for their victory by having to take care of the losers.

[18] Katharine F. Lentoot, in a speech reported in the press November 1, 1946. For a current statement of the goals of public and private social work and welfare activities, see Elizabeth Wickenden, "Frontiers in Voluntary Welfare Services," and Eveline M. Burns, "The Government's Role in Child and Family Welfare," in *The Nation's Children,* Vol. 3, Eli Ginzburg, ed. (New York: Columbia, 1960).

[19] See Jessie Bernard, *Social Problems at Midcentury* (New York: Holt, Rinehart and Winston, 1957) for a discussion of those who for one reason or another cannot perform their roles.

In sharp contrast to this Social Darwinian point of view is the democratic—and Christian—point of view which proclaims that every human being, regardless of his success or failure in the competition of life, has a worth and dignity which must be respected.

Whatever philosophy is accepted, each community is faced with the problem of what to do about those who are handicapped and those who have failed. The handicap may take such forms as physical and mental ill health (poorer in lower socio-economic classes), old age, blindness, deafness, physical infirmity, or mental deficiency. The failures are the demoralized, traumatized, disorganized people who were originally physically and mentally normal but who have failed to adjust successfully to the life of the community. They are sometimes spoken of as lazy, shiftless, good-for-nothing, "ornery," or just plain unambitious. What we really mean is that drive, incentive, motivation have been killed by constant failure. The reason is beside the point. The failure is what stands out. These failures are as much a part of the community as their more successful brothers. Social competition has tossed them to the bottom of the heap. But they were not killed in the process. Something has to be done about them.

Whose job is it to look after the failures? Historically and traditionally this has belonged to the local community, a responsibility fixed legally by the Elizabethan Poor Law of 1602. A very elaborate system developed to see to it that no individual obtained help in any community except his own and that no community was held responsible for any but its own citizens. So-called settlement laws fixed residence requirements for all who asked for help. Public assistance is still dependent upon a certain length of residence in the community, although welfare workers try to eliminate all residence requirements for public aid.

More recently, however, a different point of view has emerged. By 1933 the situation became so drastic that President Roosevelt set up national agencies to work with the states and with local communities, culminating in the establishment of the Social Security Board in 1935 to administer the national Social Security Act. This act recognized that the federal government as well as the local community share in the responsibility for caring for people who need help.

Although most social work has been public, that is, financed by taxation, private agencies have always been important. They, too, developed on the assumption that it was the responsibility of the local community to look after its own handicapped and failures, and private agencies in one community may send people back home rather than assume the financial burden of helping them where they are. It has been characteristic of American communities that private individuals, stung by needs of one kind or another, or driven by conscience or guilt-feeling, have organized to correct inequalities and injustices or to supply whatever it was that was missing. Thus in any large community one finds literally scores of private agencies—family agencies, health agencies, child welfare agencies—trying to fill in the gaps of our competitive institutions. Indeed, so great is the complexity of this web of private agencies that coordinating their activities has itself become a full-time job. With dozens of private agencies appealing to the public for funds there was much confusion, and even chicanery and fraud. Finally, several decades ago, the community chest idea was evolved. All agencies that come up to certain standards submit their budgets to one central organization which, in turn, conducts the annual fund-raising campaign to finance all the member agencies.

Comment

Our discussion in this chapter has accepted as given the American value of equal opportunity; it has not attempted to evaluate it as desirable or undesirable. Most people "believe" in it. But there are some people who at least raise the question of its rank in our scale of values. For example:

> . . . the evidence is far from clear that a classless society would be a good society. It may well be that the ideology of equalitarianism, with its components of ever-ready amiability, other-directedness, celebration of the common man, and gravity toward consensus, has much to do with the rampant invasion of privacy and erosion of individuality which have so often made it difficult to hold high the banner of intellectualism and cultural standards in our society. Further, social class has often been a bulwark against political power. Indeed, the historical evidence is clear that in the development of human civilization some astonishing outbursts of creativity have been closely associated with class societies.[20]

The answer to this line of argument would seem to be that it is not the existence of classes which the egalitarian ideal protests—they are structural facts—but the inequalities of opportunity which, unless institutional provision is made to prevent it, they render inevitable. The egalitarian ideal has for its goal a system of allocating positions in a social structure which minimizes the competitive handicaps which the family system fosters. Not equality in final position in the social structure, but equality in the starting point is the general aim.

The Upper Classes: "Society" As an Ethnic Group

We referred earlier to upper classes and they introduce a wholly different set of phenomena into the discussion. The upper-upper class, for example, is not merely the apex of a pyramid, access to which is governed by the same institutionalized rules as those governing access to lower levels; it is, rather, a tribal phenomenon and sociologically more like an ethnic group than a class. Admission is not by autonomous competition; one must

[20] Robert A. Nisbet, "The Decline and Fall of Social Class," *Pacific Soc. Rev.*, 2 (Spring, 1959), p. 11.

either be born into it or be admitted by judgmental competition. It is possible for a talented boy to rise from one rung of the social ladder to another by sheer talent and ability. But none of this will by itself gain him admission to the upper-upper class or Society. Status, in brief, up to the top level is achieveable; not so at the very top.

In a feudal society the Court and the nobility performed a set of functions that we may collectively label the glamor functions. They patronized the arts, they set aesthetic standards, they sometimes set patterns of heroic behavior.

A democratic society has no such traditional family-based aristocracy; the upper-upper class, or Society, is the nearest equivalent. It performs many of the same functions. It is, as we noted above, essentially tribal, that is, based on lineage or family. When a Society girl's engagement is announced her ancestors are part of the news. A major function of Society is to serve as a mating matrix, to display young women to eligible young men. "Family" means a great deal. The family of orientation remains stable even though the family of procreation may be very unstable. Much of the close-knittedness of these families is related to property interests. Indeed, as in feudal societies, it is the property which remains stable and the family members are appendages to the property.

As individuals the members of the upper-upper class, or Society, are often quite ordinary, untalented, and uninteresting; viewed out of their element there is little if anything distinctive about them. They have the advantage, however, of always choosing the stage where they will make their appearance and they choose usually to be seen only in their own element, where they are relaxed, at ease, and surrounded by the aura of elegance, itself often intimidating to those unaccustomed to it.

Within all social groups there is a constant competition for whatever it is that confers prestige.[21] Among the poor it may take the form of church activity or baking skill. Among middle-class families, entertaining.

Among families of the upper-upper class competition may take the form of elaborate entertaining, dress, domestic establishments—what Thorstein Veblen once called conspicuous consumption. Sometimes such expenditures become fantastic.

The existence of this anomalous—and anachronistic—closed, ethnically oriented, lineage-based group—in American communities influences the competitive race in an interesting way that will be analyzed in more detail later. At this point we merely point out that since a great deal of business is transacted over lunch at exclusive clubs and that people who are "in" have an advantage over those who are not, any barrier that excludes people constitutes a handicap for the outsider. Further, the man who lacks access to these exclusive organizations lacks an important ingredient for success in many positions which require him to mingle freely with stra-

[21] See Vance Packard, *The Staus Seekers* (New York: McKay, 1959).

tegically-placed people in the community. Much of the effectiveness of men in the power structure of a community results from the informal contacts they have with one another in these exclusive organizations. The person who is excluded is, therefore, kept from sharing in important decisions.[22] A second interesting sociological comment to make in this connection is that, like all such competitive spending or consumption, that of the upper-upper class, or Society, is invidious, designed, that is, to make fellow-competitors envious. But envy is a powerful and potentially dangerous force to play with. Expenditures must be great enough to impress peers, but not great enough to antagonize inferiors. To steer between this Scylla and Charybdis, relationships among members of the different classes have to be institutionalized in a very discreet way.

[22] The understanding which members of the upper-upper class or Society have among themselves is an interesting illustration of the way collective values operate. They play a "coordination game" with such success that to the struggling outsider it has all the earmarks of a conspiracy. The people on the inside are not conscious of any entity "Society"; they see their social circles and people who are congenial and those who are not. The unity and cohesiveness of Society is one of collective values, a "coordinating game," rather than one with self-conscious, articulated organization. This point emerges with clarity in Cleveland Amory's *Who Killed Society?* (New York: Harper, 1960).

12

Competition and the Biological Composition of the Community

The kinds of competitive forces we have been discussing so far have powerful impact on the structure of the community, but they do not affect the biological composition of the population. They distribute people hither and yon, regionally across the continent, locally throughout the urban area. They may change the age, sex, class, or race composition of particular parts of the community; but the total population is not changed. They operate on people already in existence.

But there are other kinds of competitive forces, quite different in nature, which affect the future composition of communities; they change the structure of the population of the future. These are the competitive forces which determine which group or class is going to survive, which is going to inherit the earth.

These competitive forces are autonomous. The entities involved are "in competition" with one another; they are not consciously or deliberately "competing" with one another. This competition takes the form of differential birth rates. It is to a brief consideration of these competitive forces we turn our attention here.

Competition for Survival

An aristocratic old dowager sits in her mansion on the Hill and shakes her head sorrowfully at this passing of her peers. The good old families, the best stock, the natural leaders are passing. What will the community do when they are all gone? The community is filling up with people who breed like flies. Look at the names in the city directory! Where are the good old families?

When aristocratic families bemoan the passing of their peers, they are describing a fundamental phase of crescive biological competition—the great race for survival, the "struggle for existence." The competitors are the living forms (from amoeba to man) which are seeking to maintain themselves. The object is simply survival.

What is being tested by this crescive competition? Is it fair? These are difficult questions. Actually the phrase "survival of the fittest" is meaningless as applied to human groups and classes. We cannot tell in advance what this struggle for existence is testing. Only after the test is over do we say that the survivors are the fittest. In other words, our definition of the fittest is arrived at retrospectively. The organism which survives is considered *ipso facto* the fittest, regardless of anything else. The competition is completely autonomous.

If we were to state in advance whom we considered the fittest, we should naturally say that the upper and middle classes were superior. They are superior according to most indexes—physique, IQ, and achievement. Surely they must be the fittest.

But who actually do survive among human beings? The fittest in the social or moral sense? Not necessarily. Those who survive are, other things being equal, those with the largest birth rate. The most prolific survive. It is curious that in many societies able, ambitious, energetic individuals rise from the ranks to the top of the social system and then proceed, so to speak, to sterilize themselves. They have comparatively few offspring and their families die out. Indeed, it is precisely this quality of ambition which serves as a brake on their reproduction, according to one of the leading students of the subject.[1]

The people who survive biologically are the "proletariat," or breeding classes, the term being originally derived from the Latin *proles*, or offspring. The fittest, in terms of actual survival, are the prolific breeders. And the same principles operate among races and ethnic groups as among classes.

Within the community this crescive competition for survival takes the form of differential birth rates. These differentials refer to race, to income, residence, occupation, and education. They refer also to religious groups, as it will be noted in a later chapter.

When we were discussing the ecological processes distributing people in cities we noted that those who could pay for the more attractive areas won out; this meant the white segment of the population. In that competitive situation it was the whites who won. But the influx of Negroes, and their higher reproductive rate, means that they have "won" in the sense that they outnumber whites in strategic areas of the city. Sheer numbers give them power.

Income is another factor in the differential birth rate. Women whose husbands had incomes between one and two thousand dollars had 2,889 babies per 1,000 in 1957; those with incomes of $7,000 or more had 2,160. The percent increase in number of births between 1952 and 1957 was 33.4 percent for the low-income set, but only 7.6 percent for the high-income set.

Although farm women have more babies than city or rural-nonfarm women, the relative increase in number of births per 1,000 women in urban

[1] Warren Thompson, *Population Problems* (New York: McGraw-Hill, 1942), pp. 205-207.

communities—26.3 percent between 1950 and 1959—is far greater than the rate of increase for farm women (10.2 percent), so that the differential between them is rapidly declining.

The occupation of the husband is also related to differentials in birth rate. The largest number of babies per 1,000 women were borne by the wives of farmers and farm managers and laborers; the smallest number by wives of sales personnel, and of professional and technical workers. But the rate of increase between 1952 and 1957 was in reverse order; those with the largest number of births were increasing at the lowest rate and those with the smallest number, at the highest rate. So here again the differential was declining.

The trend with respect to education has been so remarkable that it has been called a revolution. It is still true that the more educated a woman is the fewer the number of children she is likely to have; in 1957, for example, women with less than an eighth grade education averaged 2.346 children; those with a college degree or more, 1.046. But the rate of increase between 1950 and 1957 was only 19 percent for the least educated women; it was about 30 percent for the most educated.

It should be pointed out in connection with differential birth rates that a study made for the Milbank Memorial Fund by Clyde V. Kiser and P. K. Whelpton in Indianapolis in the early 1940's found that among populations which practiced birth control, the inverse differentials between income and birth rate noted above were reversed. That is, if only those who planned family size were considered, it was found that the larger the income the higher the birth rate. This finding has important implications for the future, suggesting as it does the reproduction pattern we may anticipate when all classes of the population plan the size of their families. This situation is, perhaps, still far from realization. The differentials presented above, though declining, are likely to continue, at least for the immediate future.

Whether or not inherent, hereditary superiority is assumed to characterize the middle and upper classes, and inherent, hereditary inferiority the lower classes, some of the thoughtful citizens in many American communities have come to the conclusion that uncontrolled competition for survival has harmful results. They urge, therefore, that birth control clinics be made available to poor people on the one hand, and that the economic costs of rearing children be minimized for all families by any one or any combination of several methods. One is government subsidy, that is, payment for each child beyond the second or third. Another is community services, subsidized housing, medical care, education, to lighten the load of child rearing for people judged superior who feel they cannot afford children. Another is the so-called family-wage system, under which wages are increased to takes care of additional children beyond a specific number. Another is greater tax exemptions for children. A program of sterilization of institutionalized mentally ill or defectives, whether their defect is hereditary or not, is carried out in 28 states. Advocates of sterilization point out that dependent families have birth rates as much as 50 percent higher than self-supporting families, that families contributing children to state homes for the feebleminded in one state multiply twice as rapidly as the rest of the population.[2] One does not have to assume that defects are hereditary to see the argument for such a program. Feebleminded parents may or may not transmit feeblemindedness to their children through their genes. But they handicap the children by the kind of home environment they offer them.

There is, however, another side to the story of differential birth rates. The lower birth rate among the upper classes, according to one school of thought, is not altogether a bad thing. The thinning of the ranks of old families at the top makes room for vigorous contestants working up from the bottom.

This point of view assumes that the number of places at the top is relatively fixed; we know that this is not true. An increasing number and proportion of people are needed at the top. Still the differential birth rates do open up more room at the top.

We may imagine the structure of the community as one in which, so to speak, families take turns at the best positions at the top.

Competition for Mates

The way mating is institutionalized will have a profound effect on the biological composition of the community in the future. Competition for mates among human beings is not nearly so simple as in the subhuman world where the process takes the form that Darwin described as sexual selection. The males with color or strength or song are the ones who win the mates and pass on their inheritance to succeeding generations.

Among human beings the competition for mates becomes extraordinarily complex, especially in American communities, where mating is left to the young people themselves. In cultures where marriages are arranged, competition takes on much the aspect of another business transaction. If there are two families after the same young man or woman, the bidder with the best prospects or largest dowry, other things being equal, will get the desired person for a spouse. (This fact has been adduced to explain the small size of families in such a country as France. A father with too many daughters to marry off will not be able to dower them well and they will therefore be handicapped in the competition for husbands. To avoid this difficulty he has few children.) We know, roughly, what is being tested under such circumstances. Usually it is economic and family suitability. But

2 *Human Sterilization Today* (Pasadena, Cal.: Human Betterment Foundation, n.d.), p. 2.

in the more or less hit-or-miss selection characteristic of American communities, it is not at all clear what is being tested.

Theoretically young people in American communities have a free choice of mates. Dating and courting proceed under a minimum of formal regulations. Actually, however, instead of a free choice there is great restriction in mate selection.

In the South, for example, there are enacted norms against interracial marriage. These laws are probably unconstitutional,[3] but they are not likely to be tested for constitutionality for many years.

In addition—and, of course, beyond the jurisdiction of any court—there are powerful crescive norms, especially religious taboos, which prevent free competition for mates. Catholics and Jews have especially strong restrictions on interfaith marriages. Ethnic groups, at least in the first and even second generations, impose restrictions on mate selection also. And there are, within all these restrictions, class barriers too. The cells are not completely airtight, of course, for there are cases of seepage or escape; but by and large there is a limited choice. As a result, the competition for mates takes place within a limited and circumscribed social field.

No court, as we noted above, can take cognizance of these "violations" of the individual's rights. But at least one sociologist has protested that the pressures which coerce the individual's choice of mates do violate democratic ideals. He chides family sociologists who justify endogamous taboos on the ground that, according to middle-class norms—of their own selection—marriages within religious, ethnic, racial, and class boundaries are more successful. He rejects their criteria of success[4] and he also rejects the restrictions on individual choice implicit in their counseling and educational materials:

> If we accept democratic values we must agree that the qualities of the individual outweigh the social class, family, economic status, religion, or race to which the individual belongs. Thus it is possible for the individual, with full awareness of the difficulties involved, to place himself in opposition to family, parents, church, state, and other institutional associations, and at the same time remain socially responsible. The emphasis on the individual at the expense of the class does not preclude the . . . [individual] from examining his mate-to-be with regard to the extent to which these social variables have affected his [or her] personality, since this would be an evaluation of personal qualities. But even here, the intelligent . . . [individual] would accept a much wider range of personal differences than the family sociologist, if he knew there were will and intelligence in addition to affection. . . . Stress on the individual as opposed to his family, class, religion, or

[3] An antimiscegenation law was declared contrary to the constitution of California in 1948. The court decided that such laws violated the individual's right to choose his own mate.

[4] William L. Kolb, "Family Sociology, Marriage Education, and the Romantic Complex: A Critique," *Social Forces*, 29 (October, 1950), p. 70.

race, is compatible with a broader conception of . . . man than that set out by the family sociologist.[5]

The individual, in brief, not his ethnic or class background should be the factor tested in the competition for mates.

Implicit in these strictures are such questions as these: instead of playing up the extra hazards involved in out-group marriages, should not our research and education be directed to ways of helping those who select mates outside of their in-groups to succeed in their venture? Should not counseling efforts be directed to showing how mixed marriages can overcome their difficulties rather than to discouraging them? Should we not be as indignant at the violation of individual choice in this area as we are at coercion in other areas of choice? The fact that the coercion is exercised by means of collective values—as described in Chapter 1—does not make them less, and it may even make them more, coercive than they would be if exercised through physical force.

Quite aside from the individual aspects of the problem, the way mating is institutionalized reflects some ideology about group relationships and, in addition, it leads to one or another actual pattern of group relationships. What do we have in mind as the "image" of the community? A "melting pot?" A triple melting pot? One, that is, for Jews, one for Catholics, one for Protestants? A "pluralistic" society, in which each group retains its identity? Do we want to use intermarriage as a method of homogenizing the community? Or do we want to forbid it in order to retain heterogeneity? Is the white southerner justified in his fears that desegregation will lead to interracial marriage, an "evil" to be avoided at all costs? Is it true that the Negro has an inherent appeal that has to be negated by severe proscriptive institutional norms? Is the Jew justified in his rejection of intermarriage? The Catholic? Do all these endogamous rules mitigate not only against democratic values for the individual as noted above, but also against the emergence of groupings of human beings more in line with spontaneous preferences? Just what kind of community do we want, anyway? These are among the many questions involved in the way competition for mates is institutionalized.

5 William L. Kolb, "Sociologically Established Family Norms and Democratic Values," *Social Forces,* 26 (May, 1948), pp. 451-456.

13

Competition in the Field of Religion

The Testing of Deity

If a religion is not exclusive—as Confucianism, for example, is not—there is no competition with other religions. Since one may accept any number there need be no competition for adherents. There are enough for all because professing one does not require the believers to reject the others. But most religions in American communities are exclusive. Adherence to one automatically means rejection of all the others. The conditions of competition exist.

Theoretically, however, no exclusive religion can admit open competition. There can be no testing of deity. Almost by definition, each such religion is the only true religion. This is a matter of faith, not subject to test.

In primitive communities there was less squeamishness about putting divinity to test. The Old Testament, for example, records at least one official contest between Baal and Jehovah. Missionaries still report similar experiences among their charges. "Will your God be able to make our crops grow better? Will He be able to protect us better against our enemies?" The object tested in this—contingent—competition of divinities is clear-cut, namely, service to human beings.

The Testing of Religions

To modern educated Americans the possibility of submitting deity to any such crass test would seem blasphemous. Actually, however, most religious denominations do compete among themselves. And, as we shall elaborate in Chapter 28, Christianity as a whole competes with other religions on the world stage. The religious groupings in American communities compete not for evidence of divine preference but for contributions, prestige, members, and, since in a democracy accession to power is by way of competition as well as of conflict, through them, for the control of secular institutions, whether they admit or recognize the process or not.

The Competitors

The chief competitors in this field are the several Protestant denominations among themselves and, most important, the Protestant churches and the Catholic church as a whole. There is little competition between any of these and Judaism, which long ago ceased to be a proselytizing religion. Catholics and Protestants compete for Jewish converts; the first maintaining three, the second, seventy centers in the United States for this purpose.

Another real competitor is what some church leaders call secularism, or "godlessness," referring to such nontheological religions as humanism as well as socialism, communism, fascism, and other isms. Some Catholic leaders, indeed, consider secularism a more serious competitor than Protestantism. And Protestant leaders place it in the same category.

Competition within the Protestant Church: What Is Being Tested?

At the end of the colonial period the denominations ranked numerically as follows: Congregationalists, Presbyterians, Baptists, Episcopalians, Lutherans, Reformed (Dutch and German), Quakers, the German Sectaries, and, last of all, the Methodists. By the middle of the nineteenth century, however, the Methodists ranked first, with a membership of one and a third millions, and the Baptists had climbed to second place with a membership of over eight hundred thousand. The Episcopalian and Congregational churches, which had been state churches in the colonial era, showed the least proportional gain. They were handicapped in their dealing with the West precisely because of the privileged position they had previously enjoyed and the consequent feeling of superiority it had given them. The German churches were handicapped because they used a foreign language and were thus restricted to their own nationals. The Presbyterians limited themselves to those of Scottish-Irish descent. This left the field of competition largely to the Methodists, the Baptists, and the Disciples of Christ, which became a separate church in 1830.

Not only methods but also doctrine was, perhaps, being tested. Presbyterian and Congregational Calvinism, with its aristocratic theology and its division of mankind into classes, did not appeal to the essentially classless society of the frontier. The teachings of the Methodists, Disciples, and Baptists, on the other hand, which emphasized individual responsibility and a democratic gospel of free grace, fitted more adequately into the pattern of frontier life.

Currently interdenominational competition seems to test something quite different. Skill in propaganda, industry, persistence, and determination on the part of church leaders is one thing being tested. Sometimes charm, personal power, or forcefulness on the minister's part, since we "catch" religion from powerful personalities. Sometimes esthetic considerations determine the outcome; sometimes dogmatism or social prestige—people often change their church as they climb the social ladder; sometimes willingness to assume paternalistic control; sometimes ability to satisfy inner needs; sometimes conformity to the demands of the time and place. Perhaps all of these are being tested.

The competition among Protestant churches for members may not differ fundamentally from that by which the political boss wins members for his party. In some communities, as one woman put it, newcomers are "rushed" by several churches when they move in. Wooing new members and keeping old ones satisfied lest they transfer their allegiance elsewhere takes much of a minister's time. The similarity to the techniques of a political boss is implied in the following complaint:

> Let any Protestant pastor examine his own routine with the purpose of appraising the quality of his daily labors in keeping his church going and building it up with new accessions to the membership. He will find that he has been engaged in making approaches and appeals that are dishearteningly superficial and trivial. He has not done this of his own accord or because he is unaware of the lack of depth and strength in his method; indeed, he often recoils from this cheapening of his vocation. And he would reproach himself but for one consideration: he *has* to do it! He is driven to it by the practical necessity that is forced upon him in the competitive struggle of local churches in his community.
>
> Vast numbers of Protestant Christians wait inertly to be coddled into a church when they have moved their residence into a new community. They lack religious spontaneity because their past relation to the church has been based, not upon profound feeling or conviction, but upon local attraction. This condition cannot be cured while such competitive Protestantism endures.[1]

It is interesting to extend our comparison with the work of the political boss. Both the Protestant minister and the boss must win followers by catering to human frailties. The big difference is that the political boss has no qualms about it. He does it with no feelings of guilt. The minister, on the other hand, feels that he ought to be appealing by means of principle, eternal verities, and theological truths. He feels shame and humiliation in appealing to human foibles. It is too much like a social club's bid for members. Mission churches and the Salvation Army have no such conflicts in their use of political methods. They feel they are not competing with other churches but with the Devil himself.

Many Protestant leaders now feel that whatever value there may once have been in this interdenominational competition, in modern American community life it is essentially wasteful. They point out that as a result of it many American communities are notoriously overchurched. The duplication of plant and administrative costs is a great drain on resources. In many

[1] C. C. Morrison, "Protestant Localism," *Christian Century*, 63 (Apr. 29, 1946), p. 687.

small communities two or three small churches struggle along with an inadequate program, competing one against another, rather than merging and using the same money more constructively.[2]

To prevent the worst evils of interchurch competition, Protestant denominations sometimes organize community councils. When a new real estate development or suburb is planned, a census is taken of religious preferences among the new residents, and the church with the largest following is given the field, thus obviating the danger of overchurching the area. Or so-called community churches are organized in which people of varied denominational backgrounds may participate.[3]

In spite of the unquestioned disadvantages of interchurch competition, however, there does remain the fact that it stimulates religious leaders to activity and prevents an authoritarian psychology from developing in them. The contrast with a noncompetitive situation is analogous to that between the politician and the bureaucrat. In an authoritarian situation there tends to be bureaucratic psychology; in a competitive one, the religious leader, like the politician, must constantly face his constituents. If his leadership is not satisfactory, he fails. This fact no doubt makes leadership much more difficult but it does test the mettle of the leader.

Competition between Protestantism and Catholicism

Perhaps the most important field of church competition today is that between Protestantism and Catholicism. The competition here is for the minds of men and thus, indirectly, for the control of institutions of power.

Until recently the United States was a missionary field for the Catholic church. That is, priests were sent from abroad to take care of Catholic parishes in American communities. Most Catholics were immigrants—Irish, German, Italian, Polish, Mexican, Puerto Ricans—and their priests were also foreigners. The Catholic church was too busy keeping its members in line and establishing itself in their communities during the transition from Old World to New World to devote itself seriously to converting others. Besides, proselytizing was difficult with foreign-born priests. Now that it is more secure, however, and has definitely established itself in American community life, the Catholic church has become aggressively evangelistic and seeks converts from other churches.

Protestants, who had assumed until recently that this was a Protestant country, discovered only yesterday that they had a very strong competitor in the Catholic church. They had been so involved in their interdenominational competition that they had not previously noted the new contender. Some Protestants, looking up from their interdenominational preoccupa-

[2] C. C. Morrison, "The Wasted Power of Protestantism," *ibid.* 63 (May 12, 1946), pp. 747, 749.

[3] William Whyte, Jr., *The Organization Man* (New York: Simon and Schuster, 1956).

tions, became alarmed at the prospect. Others welcomed the challenge. The test is clear-cut.

In the absence of outside competition, the Protestant church, according to some leaders, had become less and less militant and had wasted its energies in sectarian competition. It did not keep up with the changes which had come over American life. Although it was well equipped for the competition for members during the frontier period of American history, it had not adapted itself to the competition in an urbanized, industrialized community. The newly recognized challenge of Catholic competition, according to these same leaders, will force the Protestant churches to reconsider their programs. If Protestantism should catch up with the psychological changes of the present century, it would become a stronger competitive organization, they argue.

Competitive Techniques: "Propaganda"

The techniques used in this great competition are varied in nature. A principal one is propaganda, including appeals to individuals personally and appeals through advertisements, and bidding for "collectivities," or blocs. These techniques are as busily employed in religious as in political competition. Another technique of quite a different character is competitive breeding, or gaining new members by birth, which clearly resembles the social competition (for survival) described in an earlier chapter. This is crescive competition in archetypical form.

INDIVIDUALIZED PROPAGANDA

The term "propaganda" was used originally in connection with the Catholic church's propagation of its faith. It has acquired, however, a more or less sinister connotation, so that it is not used at the present time to describe the efforts of the Catholic church to win members. If we consider propaganda simply as an effort to spread a certain attitude or point of view, and if we forget its sinister connotations, we can evaluate it more objectively as a competitive technique.

Weekly instruction classes for non-Catholics and for poorly informed Catholics are held in many Catholic parishes; members of the parish are encouraged to invite non-Catholic friends; lecture and discussion series on the church's doctrines are held; premarital instruction for non-Catholics marrying Catholics is required. Where skillfully used, such techniques net many converts. Such individualized propaganda is used by Protestants as well. One enterprising Protestant policeman in New York, for example, organized a St. George Association to compete with the Holy Name Society and converted almost a hundred Catholics.[4]

[4] *Time,* July 1, 1946, pp. 86-88.

GENERALIZED PROPAGANDA: ADVERTISING

For at least a century missionary tracts and pamphlets have been widely used in winning converts. Recently, however, a new technique has been employed for this type of appeal. Instead of old-fashioned distribution of leaflets with consequent loss and waste, the ordinary channels of advertising are now used, notably the daily newspaper and weekly and monthly periodicals. The Religious Information Bureau of the Knights of Columbus has for many years been sponsoring a weekly advertisement "explaining the teachings of the Catholic Church . . . to acquaint our fellow-Americans with the doctrines of the Church established by Christ for the salvation of all men. . . ."

Among Protestant denominations, the Lutherans sometimes have availed themselves of this type of appeal, but only sporadically. They use billboards and streetcar and bus advertisements more consistently. The Christian Scientists use newspaper appeals regularly. Their advertisements are less elaborate and usually refer to public lectures rather than to pamphlets. More recently Protestants, Catholics, and Jews have all exploited television as a means of reaching the public. This kind of program would fall into the category which advertisers call institutional advertising; it is not designed to bring about an immediate "sale," but rather to create a favorable and sympathetic image of the sponsoring organization.

The ideological competition for adherents has been likened to economic competition. Justice Oliver Wendell Holmes was of the opinion that the theory of our Constitution was precisely that "the best test of truth is the power of the thought to get itself accepted in the competition of the free market" of ideas. The idea that there should be such competition for all shades of religious thought was novel when it was first embodied in the Constitution and early commentators watched the innovation with interest.

BIDDING FOR COLLECTIVITIES

Protestantism, with its evangelistic emphasis on the individual and on revivalism as a way of reaching him, has tended to act as though individual mentalities were still, as in the nineteenth century, the important target for competitive effort. The Catholic church, with a more urban background, has long recognized that a "collective mentality" now prevails; it therefore seeks to win such collectivities as "labor" and the "Negro."

Today Protestant churches, as well as the Catholic church, are making appeals to Negroes; the former to keep, the latter to win, their adherence. Hitherto the Negroes have been overwhelmingly Protestant, about 70 percent of them Baptist. But the Roman Catholic Church has many advantages in the contest for Negro members, especially freedom from the southern tradition of segregation. The Catholic press frequently deplores the treatment accorded Negroes in many American communities. Not to be outdone, Protestant leaders call for what amounts to a crusade against Jim Crowism in the church.

"Propaganda of the deed" in contrast to "propaganda of the word" is, of course, much harder. But even some churches in the South have tried to implement their ideals. The Catholic church has a remarkable record. In St. Louis, for example, while Washington University continued to exclude Negroes, St. Louis University, a Jesuit institution, opened its doors to them. The local archbishop threatened excommunication to laymen who opposed desegregation of a Catholic high school in that community. And even in the deep South, some Catholic schools integrated long before public schools.

Institutionalized Rules Regulating Religious Competition

Because it is so explosive in character and because religious freedom is still a precarious right, religious competition in American communities is regulated by a large number of institutional norms. There is, for example, the principle of religious freedom itself. This means that no one religious group is permitted to have an official monopoly. The first amendment to the Constitution specifies that "Congress shall make no law respecting an establishment of religion, or prohibiting the free exercise thereof." There is, therefore, no privileged religious group. The number of sects is not restricted. Competition is kept free.

Less official, but not less powerful, is the principle of tolerance. Each person may have his own religious conviction, no matter how far-fetched it may seem to others. How far this principle of tolerance can be safely carried is sometimes open to debate. But it remains, in spite of all-too-frequent violations, a fundamental American tenet.

There is, furthermore, a taboo against religious prejudice. To be accused of such a prejudice strikes at the roots of the self-respect of most Americans. No matter how prejudiced they may actually be, they vehemently deny that they are. Such prejudice is contrary to the professed ideals of Americanism. Among "well-bred" people there is a strict taboo against religious controversy. All such rules serve as institutional controls in the field of religious competition.

Whether or not these crescive and legislated norms are enough to render religious competition fair is moot. Catholics are not permitted to expose themselves to non-Catholic thought. And any form of censorship tends to give the censoring agency a monopoly. If the methods of religious competition were carefully guarded by rules such as those administered in the economic field by the Federal Trade Commission, the results might test definitely the kind of community life that Americans wanted.

One student of the subject has actually proposed such a code, which he calls "Rules of Fair Competition" (Leo Pfeffer, *Creeds in Competition,*

A Creative Force in American Culture [New York: Harper, 1958], pp. 160-163). It would condemn the use of force, of suppression, of government involvement, of ecclesiastical sanctions to affect government activity, of verbal blows, of chauvinism, and economic boycotts. The rule would be to keep the situation a competitive one rather than permit it to be transformed into a conflict situation.

It is precisely this problem of what should be the conditions of competition which constitutes a basic issue in the relations of religious, as well as of interest and racial, groups. Ecclesiastical organizations which are convinced of their rightness and their special charge from God to propagate their faith are not likely to take kindly to a program which asks them to permit error the right to compete with it. It takes an enormous confidence in man's ability to behave rationally, to accept Jefferson's and Holmes's principle of the marketplace of ideas.

Whether the appeal is made primarily to individuals or to blocs, whether it is made by face-to-face contact or by way of mass media, whether it is propaganda of the deed or of the word, whether it is fair or unfair, the competition so far discussed is contingent in nature.

In a quite different category is the crescive competition which, although autonomous in nature, is reflected in differential rates of growth based on differential birth rates rather than on differential rates of conversion. For by far the largest proportion of adherents to all established religious denominations are born into their church rather than converted into it.

Crescive Competition

The Catholic church has relied heavily on a high birth rate among its adherents as well as on a highly organized proselytizing system for increasing its membership. It has forbidden the use of contraception to its members; it has, furthermore, fought the legalization of contraceptive information for anyone because such information, once available, tended to lower the number of Catholic births.[5] One member of the Catholic church has expressed the competitive purpose of this ban as it looks to him as a layman as follows: "It is no doubt the hope of the clergy that the outlawing of birth control among Catholics will result in a relative increase in the Catholic population."[6] And a member of the hierarchy confirms this point of view.[7]

[5] It should be pointed out that the Catholic church opposes contraception for all, non-Catholics as well as Catholics, so that, theoretically, their position would have the effect of increasing the non-Catholic as well as the Catholic birth rate. Their power, however, is limited to the Catholic population. They seek, in effect, a coalition with the government on this issue.

[6] N. V. Fetterly, "The Catholic Church Needs—," *Forum*, April, 1940, p. 180.

[7] The late Cardinal O'Hara stated: "If they [those who have been urging birth control on the ground of a population explosion] do any research at all they must know that

How successful has competitive breeding been? Here are some indications. Although the Catholic birth rate falls, as does the non-Catholic birth rate, under such conditions as urban living, education, and high income, it remains nevertheless higher than the birth rate of non-Catholics under comparable conditions. As a result, Catholics do tend to outbreed non-Catholics. The most detailed data available on this point are, unfortunately, fairly old; they are contained in a survey made in Indianapolis in 1941.[8] It found that up to the age of about 27, Catholic and Protestant women of nonmixed marriages had had about the same number of children. The Catholic women, however, continued to have children over a longer period of time. Thus by the age of 40 to 45, when most families are completed, the Catholic women had borne 2.74 children on the average, while the Protestant women had borne 2.19. The fertility rate for Catholic marital unions was, therefore, about 25 percent higher than that for Protestant unions.

These figures become more significant when considered in the light of the number of babies required for replacement of the population. It is estimated that 100 Catholic unions would have to produce beween 255 and 295 births to replace the Catholic population. Protestant couples would require between 280 and 320. The reason Protestant couples would require more babies for replacement lies in the fact that more of such marriages are terminated by divorce and are therefore likely to be less fertile. The Protestant unions which remain intact must, as a result, make up for the deficit thus produced. It will be noted that the Catholic unions were just about meeting their reproductive quota, the figure 274 per 100 Catholic unions falling about halfway between the lower and upper replacement estimates for this group. Protestant couples, on the other hand, were anywhere from one third to one fifth short of the number of births needed to replace themselves. Thus Protestant churches in Indianapolis, and presumably also in other urban communities, were having to rely for maintenance of membership on newcomers from rural areas. Catholic churches, on the other hand, were probably producing their own replacements.

Since the above data were collected there has been a revolution in the birth rates of most of the constituent elements of our population. There has been an increase in the birth rates of Protestants as well as of Catholics and there is some evidence which suggests that perhaps the above differentials have been declining.

---

in this country only Catholics and Negroes show an extraordinary increase in births—the latter about 60 percent and the former 100 percent over the totals of, say, fifteen years ago. Are those who want to supplant divine wisdom by their own planning disturbed by this? Let them leave us to God. We ask no sympathy" (*New York Times,* Dec. 20, 1959).

[8] P. K. Whelpton and Clyde V. Kiser, "Social and Psychological Factors Affecting Fertility," *Milbank Memorial Fund Quarterly,* 21 (July, 1943), pp. 221-280. Oliver E. Baker, "The American Birth Rate and the Religious Factor," in *The Family Faces Forward* (Washington, D. C.: National Catholic Welfare Board, 1945), pp. 49-52, summarizes the Indianapolis data in a nontechnical manner.

In 1957, for example, the number of children ever born to Catholic women in the younger age brackets (15-44) was about the same as the number born to Protestant women. But the number of children ever born to older Catholic women (45 years old and over) was considerably larger than the number born to older Protestant women. For the younger women, the figures were 2,282 and 2,220 respectively; for the older women, 2,056 and 2,753. That is, the number born to younger Catholic women was only 2.8 percent greater than the number born to Protestant women; among the older women, the corresponding number born to Catholics was 11.0 percent greater than the number born to Protestants. These findings are similar in direction to those of the Indianapolis study; but whereas in the Indianapolis study the younger women were under 27, in the 1957 study women up to age 45 were considered in the younger group. What has happened, in effect, is that the Catholics' birth rate has not increased as rapidly as that of the Protestants so that the Protestant birth rate has almost caught up to that of the Catholics.[8] As a result the evidence suggests "a trend toward convergence of the fertility levels among women in the major religious groups."[9]

With respect to future trends, however, it is impossible to speak with certainty. Since differences in expected fertility are greatest among educated women, the convergence of fertility may be reversed as the educational differences between Catholic and Protestant women decline with the upgrading of the Catholic population.

One recent study of expected birth rates based on intensive interviews with 2,713 white wives aged 18 to 39 found that Catholic wives expected 3.4 children, Protestant wives only 2.9.[10] The differences between them were greatest at the college-educated level where the expectations were 3.9 and 2.7 respectively, as contrasted with 3.7 and 3.6 at the grade-school level. One interesting point was that the older Catholic women (35-39) reported wanting fewer children now (3.1) than when they were first married (3.5).

A second aspect in the breeding competition has to do with the children of mixed marriages. In order to secure permission to marry a Catholic, a non-Catholic must sign a document promising that "all children of either sex born of this marriage shall be baptized and educated in the faith and according to the teachings of the Roman Catholic Church." This requirement thus ensures the adherence not only of the children of Catholic marriages but also those of mixed marriages as well. Inasmuch as the

[8] The fertility of Catholic women, age for age, in 1957 was only 1 percent above that of the nation as a whole. See Donald J. Bogue, *The Population of the United States* (New York; Free Press, 1959), p. 696.

[9] Paul C. Glick, "Intermarriage and Fertility Patterns among Persons in the Major Religious Groups," paper read at the annual meetings of the American Sociological Association, Seattle, Washington, August, 1958.

[10] Ronald Freedman, P. K. Whelpton, and A. A. Campbell, *Family, Sterility, and Population Growth* (New York: McGraw-Hill, 1959). At the time of the interview the Catholic and Protestant wives had the same number of children. The reason the Catholic women did not have more children than the Protestant women was that, on the average, they married somewhat—1.5 years—later.

Catholic member to a mixed marriage seems more likely to be the wife,[11] and since mothers probably have a more intimate influence on the religious inclinations of their children, this requirement may be easily enforceable. The fertility of mixed marriages is, however, considerably lower than that of either Catholic or Protestant marriages, being approximately 10 percent less than that of Protestant unions.[12] Table XIII-1 summarizes some of these findings.

TABLE 13-1. NUMBER OF CHILDREN BORN PER 100 WIVES*

	Both parents Catholic	Both parents Protestant	Mixed Marriages
Education of wife			
One or more years college	139	99	89
One or more years high school	160	131	119
Grammar school only	217	211	182
Monthly rental value of dwelling unit (as of 1941)			
$60 and over	165	104	108
40-59	132	91	89
30-39	159	117	117
25-29	188	145	133
20-24	202	175	157
15-19	254	226	235
Under $15	245	282	185
Average for all above groups	173	149	132 (wife Catholic) 133 (wife Protestant)

* Kiser and Whelpton, "Social and Psychological Factors Affecting Fertility," *Milbank Memorial Fund Quarterly*, 21 (July, 1943), pp. 241, 253.

If success in religious competition depended solely on accessions through births, and if there were no defaults, the race would be won by the group that bred most rapidly, in this case the Catholic group. There are, however, other facts to be considered. Community background, for example. Most Catholics live in cities. Their birth rates tend to conform to the same pattern as that of other urban dwellers. That is, they tend to fall. Rural America is still Protestant to a large extent. Thus, although in any one community Catholics may tend to outbreed Protestants, in the country as a whole this is not likely for the present because of the greater urbanization of the Catholic population. There is a movement on the part of the National Catholic Rural Life Conference to meet this competitive handicap by strengthening rural parishes, by slowing down the cityward

[11] In the Indianapolis survey it was found that there were 32 percent fewer "husband Catholic, wife Protestant" marriages (975) than "husband Protestant, wife Catholic" marriages (1438). Whelpton and Kiser, *op. cit.*, pp. 226-227.

[12] *Ibid.*, p. 227.

movement of Catholic youth, by moving Catholic families from cities to living quarters more conducive to family life, and by making a concerted drive to win over unchurched rural people to Catholicism. The plan is "not anti-Protestant," but admittedly "it is a challenge to American Protestantism."[13] Race is also a factor. Negro fertility is higher than that of whites and most Negroes are still Protestant. Age at marriage is still another factor; Catholics tend to marry somewhat later than non-Catholics. Although religion per se does make a difference in birth rates, then, there are many other factors that influence them also and some of these work in one direction, some in another.

RESULTS

Who, in the face of these facts, is actually winning in this religious competition? The race is apparently very close.

With respect to secularism, over the period of American nationhood the number of church members has increased more rapidly than the population as a whole, the ratio increasing from 1 in 15 to nearly 2 in 3.

With respect to churches it is extremely difficult to evaluate the results of religious competition objectively, since some religious bodies count all baptized persons as members; others include all enrolled members; still others list as members only communicants.

Accession by conversion is relatively unimportant and so far as Protestantism and Catholicism are concerned they cancel one another out. A survey by the American Institute of Public Opinion in 1955, for example, reported 1,400,000 Catholics who had once been Protestants and the same number of Protestants who had once been Catholics.[14] But accession by births is relatively high in the Roman Catholic Church in spite of its urban membership, as we have noted above.

Bearing in mind the difficulties of defining membership, the situation is approximately as in Table 13-2.

TABLE 13-2. PERCENTAGE OF TOTAL POPULATION

	Protestant	Catholic
1920	—	17.0
1926	27.0	16.1
1930	—	16.4
1940	28.7	16.3
1950	33.8	18.3
1955	35.5	20.3
1958	35.5	22.8
1960	35.1	22.9

[13] *A Survey of Catholic Weakness,* with an introduction and a plan by Monsignor Ligutti (Des Moines, Iowa: National Catholic Rural Life Conference, 1948), p. 13. This pamphlet summarized the results of an extensive survey of Catholic population and institutions in rural areas.

[14] Public Opinion News Service, Mar. 20, 1955.

The rate of growth for the Catholic church, it will be noted, was relatively slow until 1940; since that time, and especially since 1950, it has been very rapid. And between 1958 and 1959 the rate of growth for the Catholic church—3.4 percent—was twice that for Protestant churches—1.7 percent.[15]

We have now reviewed the main problems which characterize competitive behavior in American community life. We have seen how pervasive competition is; how difficult it is to evaluate—that is, to balance its contributions against its costs—how complex its ramifications are; how inconsistent most of us are in our attitudes toward it; how hard it is in some areas of community life to keep people competing; how involved the problem is of determining what competition is testing, or even what we want it to test; and, finally, how puzzling the problems of fairness or validity in competition are. We have not been in a position to suggest here solutions to the problems raised; but with the perspectives here offered, it should be possible for the reader to evaluate the solutions presented—almost daily—in the halls of legislatures, in the press, and in other channels of public influence. We turn our attention now to a consideration of the equally pervasive and difficult problems associated with conflict, problems which are often even more fraught with emotion than are those of competition. Because of the difficulties inherent in an objective study of the sociology of conflict, this subject has only recently been thoroughly explored. Often the mere statement of the position of one side of a conflict is taken to mean favoring it, or opposing the other party to the conflict.[16] In fact, merely stating one side's position—however objectively—often does have exactly that effect, especially if the position of the opposite side is contrary to accepted patterns. In many areas of conflict we have been so reluctant to tackle the issues that until recently we scarcely even had a vocabulary with which to describe them objectively. The very words available for discussing them were fraught with emotion. We suggest these difficulties here so that the reader may be forewarned of some of the many pitfalls involved in any discussion of conflict.

[15] Reported in *World Almanac,* 1961, from *Yearbook of American Churches* for 1961, edited by Benson Y. Landis.

[16] See, for example, Robert K. Merton, "The Social Psychology of Housing," in *Current Trends in Social Psychology* (Pittsburgh: University of Pittsburgh, 1949), pp. 163-217.

Part V

The Accommodation of Differences: Conflict in the Community

The conditions under which competition shall take place, that is, the ways in which competition should be institutionalized constitute one of the basic issues in most conflicts in American communities. What this means in the market, in the labor market, in race relations, and in the relationships of different ethnic groups is illustrated in Chapters 14-19. Again, as in the case of competition, it is awesome to note the same fundamental processes at work in areas so different. It should be emphasized that the accommodation of differences which characterizes democratic regimes is not necessarily the same as that which characterizes other kinds of regimes. Democratic regimes try to avoid elimination as a way of dealing with differences; nor do they insist on assimilation. How they struggle in the accommodative range is the major consideration of Part V.

14

The Consumer's Conflict

The Idea of Exchange

The most primitive way to get something one wants is simply to take it. Animals and small children use this method and man may have done so also before he developed institutions. At some time in his development, however, the practice of giving something in exchange for taking things arose and became enforceable by collective sanctions. Trade became institutionalized to protect both parties to the exchange. Sometimes the exchange took the form of highly institutionalized gift-giving, but sometimes it took the form of bargaining.

The bargaining situation is archetypical of a mixed-motive conflict situation. Interests are in conflict to the extent that the seller wants to receive more and the buyer wants to pay less. But both want some exchange rather than no exchange at all. Theoretically both gain in a fair exchange.

The Market As a Scene of Interaction

If the market were only a place where goods changed hands, it would be a purely economic phenomenon. Actually it is much more than a place where goods are bought and sold. It is a place where people meet and gossip and enjoy themselves. It is a place where a great deal of other than purely economic interaction takes place. Travelers visit markets because they are the sites of the most intense interaction, as well as because they want to buy things. The fair, in fact, is as much fun as business.

Throughout history the market has been, and even today in many parts of the world still is, the scene of person-to-person haggling and bargaining. The processes may be institutionalized in different ways in different societies but the underlying interaction is the same. The seller is trying to get more, the buyer is trying to pay less. But vast changes in the institutional framework of exchange tend to change the process; it becomes transformed into an impersonal, almost mechanical, procedure, as we shall presently see. The parties to the conflict are no longer buyer and seller in face-to-face contact, but delegated agents of the buyer—federal agencies—and large corporations. The conflict takes on a quite different cast.

The issues change also. Even the perennial and timeless issues—price, quality, fraud, and deception—take on different forms. Instead of the simple, pressuring issue of how much will you give versus how much will you take, price becomes enormously complex. We noted in Chapter 5 that one of the basic issues in most conflicts in our society today is, What should be the conditions of competition. And so it is in the market: the buyer wants the sellers to compete freely; sellers want protection from competition. What should be the conditions of competition may become a schismatic issue.

Even quality as an issue becomes more serious. New foods, new drugs, new cosmetics may be poisonous. Fraud and deception change also, as psychologists learn how to use "hidden persuaders" to fool us.

The Issue of Intimidation

The bargaining model of conflict assumes that both buyer and seller want the transaction to occur; they have that much in common. But sometimes the conflict is between a would-be seller and a person who does not want to buy. It is not a case of bargaining but of manipulation or strategic control: the would-be seller wants his prospect to do something that he really does not want to do. He does not want the transaction to take place; he resists it.

There are laws protecting people against the grosser forms of intimidation and bullying in forcing payment of bills, but there are as yet no laws protecting them against the subtler forms of intimidation or bullying in sales practices. Perhaps there can be none. People may have to work out their own defenses.

Sometimes techniques are so wily that people are maneuvered into making purchases against their better judgment. Free samples create a feeling of indebtedness and make it difficult to refuse to buy. It has been pointed out that "salesmen, especially street 'stemmers,' know that if they take a line that will be discredited unless the reluctant customer buys, the customer may be trapped by considerateness and buy in order to save the face of the salesman and prevent what would ordinarily result in a scene."[1] A condescending saleswoman may make it virtually impossible for Molly Milquetoast to reject the dress far too expensive for her purse.

Indeed, so often does exchange take on the aspect of a battle that sellers even speak of "sales resistance." Perhaps the only protection for the individual is as thoroughgoing training in resisting pressure as the would-be seller receives in exerting it.

[1] Erving Goffman, "On Face-Work," *Psychiatry: Journal for the Study of Interpersonal Processes,* 18 (1955), p. 224.

Price Standardization As Strategic "First Move" and the Transformation of the Market

In the archetypical bargaining situation both parties want an exchange to take place. But each has some limit beyond which he will not go either in lowering the price or raising the offer. And each knows that there are such limits, and each knows that the other knows. They do not necessarily know the precise limits and they sometimes pretend to know less than they do. A solution often rests on "some voluntary but irreversible sacrifice of choice."[2] In the case of major interest to us here this irreversible "sacrifice" of freedom of choice may be imposed by law or it may be assumed voluntarily for strategic purposes. Such "sacrifices," however instituted, function, in effect, as "first moves." The seller wins if the law fixes a minimum price; the buyer wins if it fixes a ceiling price.

During a depression, for example, there are floors under prices; this "first move" protects the seller from pressures to lower his price. The seller can rightly point out that he cannot sell for less because he would be punished for so doing. During a war, on the other hand, the "first move" takes the form of ceilings on prices to protect the buyer. The buyer can now refuse to pay more because it would be illegal. In both of these cases "first move" is not a voluntary surrender of choice, but it is useful for one or the other party.

The advantage of "first move" can be achieved voluntarily also. The most interesting example of this is the so-called resale price maintenance legislation which blossomed in the 1930's under the name "fair trade." Amendments to the antitrust laws (the Miller-Tydings Act of 1937 and the McGuire Act of 1952) permitted brand manufacturers to fix the price at which their products could be sold by retailers. Toothpaste or vitamins or cosmetics made by any one company sold for the same price no matter where purchased. This was in effect a fixed price system and had the same effect as any fixed price. It obviated bargaining. "I'd like to sell you this for less," the retailer could say, even truthfully, "but if I did I'd lose my franchise."[3]

The custom of standard prices, however achieved, serving as, in effect, a strategy of first move has had as one of its consequences the elimination of bargaining. In the United States, and increasingly in other civilized

[2] Thomas C. Schelling, *The Strategy of Conflict* (Cambridge, Mass.: Harvard, 1960), p. 22.

[3] The purpose of such price fixing—essentially a depression-type move—was to protect retailers. It had the effect of raising prices for the consumer and penalizing the more efficient sellers who could have sold for less and still made a profit. After a rather uncertain constitutional history such resale-price maintenance legislation fell into obloquy. The new discount houses refused to comply with brand manufacturing price lists and enforcement was abandoned by some large manufacturers.

societies, the old-fashioned form of bargaining has ceased in most consumer markets so far as day-by-day buying is concerned.

To a large extent the actual seller becomes only an agent who has no freedom with respect to price. He might wish to lower the price for a favorite customer, he might say he wished to lower the price to just any customer, but he cannot be bargained with because he has no say in the matter.

The interplay between buyer and seller in a modern market tends to become quite impersonal. The true seller is no longer a specific store keeper with whom a customer may bargain nor is the buyer an individual customer. The seller is an advertising or marketing specialist or a merchandising expert. The buyer is not an individual but a statistical construct—"the consumer"—created by a polling or survey institute. Buyer-seller conflict, therefore, is not personal and face-to-face. It is, rather, impersonal and abstract. It is, even, in the case of the vending machine, mechanical.

The impersonal nature of the interaction between buyer and seller means, further, that the ordinary cues which people in face-to-face relations give one another have to be replaced by elaborate research on the part of the seller and by delayed "feedback" on the part of the buyer. Communication between them is vulnerable to distortion. The parties therefore act with only limited information. Sellers often have to wait, sometimes quite a while, for the feedback which tells them how "the consumer" is reacting. In the old market the seller could tell at once from the expression on her face what the housewife liked and did not like. It may take Madison Avenue weeks or months. Sometimes the sellers are very wide of the mark, as the story of compact cars illustrates. It took a long time—and the overt strategic "move" by buyers of buying large numbers of foreign small cars—before the automobile manufacturers got the message and began to supply what many consumers wanted.

The result of all these changes in the structuring of the market is that much of the conflict between buyer and seller is played out not in the market itself but in the political arena. Buyers and sellers confront one another not in the store or shop but before a legislative committee.[4] The issues are not price or quality or fraud per se but something more fundamental. They deal, rather, with the very structure of the marketing relationship. Whose side is the government to be on? How much deception and fraud is going to be tolerated? How much protection is the consumer

[4] One of the most interesting illustrations of the kind of buyer-seller interaction which characterizes modern markets is the story of the fight for and against the Office of Price Administration after World War II. See the first edition of this book, Chapter 14, for an account of this conflict. Every now and then consumers seem to find delight in direct action, as when, for example, subway riders in London staged a "sit-in" to protest against service curtailment (*New York Times*, Jan. 10, 1959). Sometimes they resort to vandalism to express the hostility against an opponent they cannot see or reach in any other way.

going to get against the depredations of the seller? The bargaining is political: What is the most the consumer can get in the way of legislation; what is the least the seller can have to concede?

The Issue of Abundance

It is to the interest of consumers to have abundance in the market so that sellers have to compete for their trade. It seems to be to the interest of sellers to have scarcity in the markets so that buyers have to compete for the goods and bid the price up. One of the expectable outcomes of competition, as we saw in Chapter 5, is some kind of cooperation among competitors, and one of the objectives of such cooperation is control of the market. How competition should be institutionalized is a major—and even schismatic—issue today. The implications for the competitors themselves were discussed in Chapter 9; but there are also implications for buyers. They are opposed to anything which restricts competition or makes for monopoly.

The Issue of Quality and Fraud: " . . . to the Great Deceit, Loss and Hindrance of the Common People"

We sometimes sentimentally bemuse ourselves with a nostalgic picture of "the good old days" when, presumably, there was less corruption, and less crime, less fraud and deception in the market than there is today. It has little basis in fact. The history of fraud and deception in the market is so long and so monotonously repetitive as almost to indicate a built-in or institutionalized structure.

One built-in structural situation which, despite centuries of legislation, seemed to render fraud inevitable was the common-law rule of "let the buyer beware" known as *caveat emptor*. The original function performed by this rule was to develop "the mercantile virtues; it made buyers and sellers sharp, cautious, and resourceful; it was 'a good old doctrine' for the encouragement of trade."[5] It stimulated trade when the seller was the dynamic factor and had to be encouraged. It institutionalized buyer-seller conflict in the seller's favor by depriving the buyer of threatening power.

The Heyday of *Caveat Emptor*

When the market was a local affair and the goods one had to buy were relatively few, so that one could be expected to be a fairly good judge of quality and value, *caveat emptor* made sense. For thousands of years there were, for example, only four fibers for weaving fabrics—silk, wool,

[5] Walton Hamilton, "Caveat Emptor," *Encyclopaedia of the Social Sciences,* Vol. 3, (New York: Macmillan, 1930), p. 280.

cotton, and flax. Most women could be expected to become passably good judges of quality in fabrics. There was not much variety in other goods either, so that marketing was fairly easy. It was harder to fool customers, and if one simply did not know his business as a buyer it seemed a due penality that he should suffer the consequences. *Caveat emptor* was a reasonable rule.

Some persons got a reputation as shrewd buyers or sellers; they were considered sharp in their practices, or good traders. The man who was fool enough to buy a pig in a poke had only himself to blame and a man who got cheated in a deal with a horse-trader was to blame for not knowing horseflesh.

Dealings with neighbors were protected by the mores and customs of the community, such as the practice of the baker's dozen or an extra item thrown in for good measure, a pound of liver, for example, thrown in for the cat with the meat order. When the man who butchered your beef sat with you in church on Sunday he was less likely to try to put anything over on you on Monday. But dealings with outsiders were governed by other rules. Trade with them was known to be a game of wits or even, among equally matched traders, a game of chance.[6]

But whatever function the doctrine of *caveat emptor* may have served in early market situations, its value was greatly diluted with the changes in the nature of the market referred to above. The variety of goods increased unbelievably. And when meat was butchered not in your own home town but in Chicago, you had no protection against unsanitary conditions, the use of diseased animals, the doctoring of inferior meat, and similar fraudulent practices. Old institutions had to be revised and new institutions had to be evolved. As a result, the courts did change the old *caveat emptor* rule, not in principle but in application, and legislatures did pass new laws for the protection of consumers.

Re-institutionalization of the Market: Consumer Protection

The parties in buyer-seller conflict now are (1) the fraudulent producers and/or sellers on one side and (2) a coalition of consumers (individuals or the government itself as a consumer), honest competitors, and some government agency, especially the Federal Trade Commission and the

[6] *Ibid.*, pp. 280, 282.

[7] Most of the early British legislation was designed for the protection of the consumer segment of the coalition, including the navy. It was not until 1781, according to Gustavus Myers, that the first law was passed which referred to the "fair trader" and recognized the damage done to him by fraudulent practices of a competitor (*America Strikes Back* [New York, Washburn, 1935], p. 14). In the United States, however, protection of competitors came before legal protection of consumers. For example, in a famous case of the Federal Trade Commission *v.* the Raladam Company, which made Marmola, an obesity cure extremely harmful to those who used it without medical supervision, the United States Supreme Court decided: "Findings, supported by evidence, warrant the conclusion that the preparation is one which cannot be used generally with safety to physical health except under medical direction and advice. If the necessity of protecting the public

Food and Drug Administration. The issue, whatever form it may take, is the practice of fraud both in production (quality of goods) and sale of goods (misrepresentation, false claims, deceptive packaging, labeling, or advertising).

In terms of strategy, changes in the common law as interpreted by the courts were in the direction of making promises on the part of the seller genuine commitments. This was done by means of two devices, namely the "warranty" and the concept of negligence. Originally a seller could be held only for an express guarantee made at the time of sale; if he specifically promised to deliver such and such, this was a legal commitment and non-fullfilment might be costly. Later on the concept of "implied warranty" developed and came to include any kind of representation of goods, labels, and even advertisements. And to increase the incentive of the seller to make good on any commitment, he could be punished for ignorance of his product. He had to know any defect in what he was selling; he could not claim ignorance.

The strategic difficulty in these approaches lies in the fact that they may be expensive to use. Although the buyer acquires an implicit strategic right to threaten the seller, the seller knows that he is not likely to use it. Sueing is expensive. The changes in the common law did not reduce the payoff for deceit enough to deter the seller. The costs when they did occur could be written off as a cost of doing business.

A second institutional change has taken the form of a spate of legislation designed to protect the buyer. As was to be expected, whenever legislation was proposed to curb the sellers, lobbies arose to kill it. In most states which had pure-food laws before 1906, these laws had been passed because farmers opposed the adulteration of butter, milk, and other foods by processors. Each state set up its own standards, a practice which resulted in such a complication of the market that producers who had first opposed federal legislation were finally won over to supporting it. If there had to be such laws they might as well be uniform. It was not, however, until the muckrakers had exposed conditions in the meat-packing industry, the fraud and deception in advertisements, and the actual health hazards in many foods, especially from the use of harmful preservatives and dyes, and not until the General Federation of Women's Clubs organized a crusade, that federal

against dangerously misleading advertisements . . . were all that is necessary to give the [Federal Trade] Commission jurisdiction, the order could not be successfully assailed. But this is not all . . . the unfair methods must be such as injuriously affect or tend thus to affect the business of . . . competitors . . . and it is against that condition of affairs, and not some other, that the Commission is authorized to protect the public." In other words, the function of the Commission was interpreted to protect the competitor part of the coalition but not the consumer part. This anomalous state of affairs was remedied in 1938 by passage of the Wheeler-Lea Act, which gave the Federal Trade Commission express power to act to protect the consumer part of the coalition as well as the competitor part. The Food and Drug Administration emphasizes the fact that law-abiding manufacturers and dealers, as well as consumers, need the protection of the law.

legislation—the Pure Food and Drug Act—was finally enacted in 1906. Other laws followed.[8]

Change soon renders old laws inadequate. New drugs enter the market. Cosmetics, furthermore, were not at all covered by the act of 1906; yet they became increasingly important as the century progressed. Starting in 1927, therefore, a new muckraking movement began, exposing the new evils and giving rise to a new consumers' movement of self-protection. A new federal Food, Drug, and Cosmetic Act was passed in 1938 which added protection to buyers chiefly by including new products, by improving labeling provisions, and by tightening the administration of the law.[9]

The continuing changes in products that characterize modern society led in 1954 to a federal law governing the use of insecticides and pesticides and in 1958 to the so-called food additives amendment for the control of chemicals added to foods.

This large and growing body of statutory law represents a reversal from the theory of the common-law *caveat emptor* rule. The consumer now turns over to the government the task of protecting him. The fight is no longer between buyer and seller in a face-to-face bargaining situation but rather between a government agency and the representative of the seller, itself often the legal staff of a giant corporation. The issues[10] are likely to be pressuring: how much can we do and get away with it? How much restriction can we pin on and make it stick? In strategic terms this new trend may be viewed as a strategy of delegation. The government is, in effect, the citizen's agent. The defect in this strategy lies in the fact that the agencies serving as the citizen's delegated agents—the Federal Trade Commission and the Food and Drug Administration—are understaffed

[8] A federal meat inspection act was passed in 1906; a legal standard for butter was enacted in 1923. Formulation of reasonable standards for canned goods was authorized by the McNary-Mapes amendment to the Pure Food and Drug Act in 1930. Voluntary inspection for canned goods by the Food and Drug Administration—expenses to be borne by packers—was provided in 1934. Other consumer-protecting acts were: Wool Labeling Act (1940), Oleomargarine Act (1950), Fur Products Labeling Act (1951), Flammable Fabrics Act (1953). Inspection of poultry by the Department of Agriculture became compulsory in 1959. In addition to such federal legislation there are numerous state and municipal rules relating to intrastate goods and to such local products as milk and bakery goods, and to the local selling of foods in eating places. Without such local protection food manufacturers have been known to produce goods that were adulterated or of low quality for sale in their own communities and a quite different, superior line to sell outside their state.

[9] Under the new law, the use of injurious substances in cosmetics was forbidden. Dyes used in foods, drugs, and cosmetics had to be certified. Labels on food, drugs, and cosmetics had to give adequate information and avoid false or misleading statements. Fraud did not have to be proved in order to prove a selling method illegal. The Food and Drug Administration could now halt injurious practices immediately by injunction. This power greatly facilitated enforcement and gave added protection to consumers. Formerly it had taken so long to bring sellers to justice that many people could be injured before the dangerous practice was stopped.

[10] The Federal Trade Commission deals with antimonopoly issues and deceptive practice issues. The Food and Drug Administration deals with issues of quality, but also with deceptive practices.

and underfinanced, so that regardless of incentive they cannot always really commit themselves by threats. The adulterating producer or the deceiving seller can therefore be conceived of as in a game against "nature" in which he can compute the chances of his being caught, knowing that they are less than certainty; the payoff for continuing his violations of the law may therefore still be considerable.

Recognizing that not all the responsibility for carrying on the fight can be delegated to governmental agencies, the Federal Trade Commission has attempted to return to the consumer the part that he can deal with. It believes that "a combination of hard-hitting enforcement plus the encouragement of public skepticism toward spurious bargaining will go far toward achieving an honest market-place."[11]

The "Enemy"

Since both common law and statutory law have repudiated the old *caveat emptor* rule we can no longer explain or interpret the continuing of fraudulent practices in terms of the protection if not actual encouragement it provided for them. But it takes a long time for a new point of view to be completely institutionalized. There is still no strong public sanction against the perpetrator of fraud or adulteration. There may even be sympathy for him and public indignation against the agency prosecuting him. A modern market is so complex, so abstract, and so involved that it is difficult to see the adulterating producer or the deceptive advertiser as criminal. One criminologist has coined the term "white collar crime" to cover violations of the kinds of laws we have been discussing here and others like them. The question has been raised, are the men who violate these laws "really" criminals? They are, it is argued, often just ordinary businessmen. They are not like ordinary criminals. This criminologist replies that their behavior fills all the criteria of crime and he therefore labels them as criminals.[12]

The Seller as Victim

We must not suppose, of course, that the seller is always the victor and always wrong in the great buyer-seller conflict, or that the buyer is always the innocent lamb and always right. The customer is no more always right than the seller is always wrong. There are always chiselers among buyers too. The woman who falsifies the age of her child on the bus, train, or plane in order not to have to pay full fare; the woman who buys a garment, wears it, and then returns it; the man who buys goods on credit and never pays for them—these are among the customers who are not always right. If it is true that in a sellers' market producers do not hesitate to exact the

[11] William M. Blair, "F.T.C.'s New Goal: Make Buyer Aware," *New York Times*, Dec. 6, 1959.

[12] E. H. Sutherland, *White Collar Crime* (New York: Holt, Rinehart and Winston, 1949).

last drop of blood from their victims; if the black marketer has no mercy on his victims; if, to the buyer's protests the cynical seller replies that he does not have to buy, that there are others who will if he does not, we must not forget that in a buyers' market the consumer pays back in kind. It is now his turn to call the tune; and if the producer complains that he cannot stay in business at these prices, the buyer coldly says, "So what?" Bankruptcies do not move him.

During a depression when there is a buyers' market, the methods used by buyers to evade paying the going price are often as exploitative as those used by black marketers during a sellers' market. In the 1930's, instead of price ceilings there were price floors, to protect sellers against the temptation to lower quality and wages in the competitive struggle and against bargaining pressures from buyers. The methods used by buyers to violate these regulations were very similar, indeed identical—but in reverse—to those of the black market of the 1940's. Buyers can be as exploitative as sellers. But it is easier for sellers to organize and take advantage of buyers than the reverse because there are, in most markets, more buyers than sellers and because it is more difficult to make buyers see their common interests.

Assimilating Buyer-Seller Interests

We have concentrated our attention so far on the buyer-seller conflict and the rules which institutionalize it (federal, state, and local legislation in particular). We have seen that the characteristic model for this conflict is the mixed-motive game, in which the parties have both common and conflicting interests, rather than the zero-sum game.

Another level of solution—assimilation of interests of buyers and sellers—is the aim of some people. Such a solution is, in effect, a special kind of coalition in which differences disappear entirely. The popular term for this solution is consumers' cooperation. In a consumers' cooperative a new principle is introduced. Groups of buyers band together for self-protection. Buyers and sellers are thus the same people, so that there can be no conflict of interest.

The principles of consumers' cooperatives are simple. They constitute, in a sense, a social and economic philosophical system. Consumers' cooperation is institutionalized on the basis of certain principles. There is, first of all, the principle of "brotherhood." This means that membership is open to everyone, without regard to class, color, creed, or residence. There are no restrictive clauses. The larger the membership the greater the benefits to each member.

A second principle is that of economic democracy, meaning that each member has one vote, no matter how many shares of stock he owns. A cooperative considers the person to be the most important value and gives each member equal voting power no matter what the amount of his wealth.

A third institutionalizing principle is that there shall be no speculation in cooperatives' stocks; thus interest is limited to 4 or 6 percent. A fourth principle states that business is run for service rather than for profit, so that whatever earnings are left after returns on stock have been made are refunded to members on the basis of patronage. The more one buys the greater his refunds.

In addition, there are other principles and practices which institutionalize cooperatives. The most interesting, from the sociological point of view, are: constant education of members, and political and religious neutrality. These are essential to keep morale high and to prevent disruptive conflicts. Constant group study and discussion of the principles of cooperation develop cohesion and make for solidarity. Without close contact on the part of the members, cooperatives lose their vitality.

The consumers' cooperative movement has not made as much headway in the United States as it has in some other countries. For one thing, while cooperatives were new, small, and experimental they could not afford to hire efficient managers at the salaries private business could afford to pay. But more important, the conditions necessary for successful cooperative effort do not prevail in most American communities. To facilitate the basic principle of brotherhood, the groups which organize cooperatives should be homogeneous, stable, conscious of common interests, and willing to devote some thought to the enterprise. In urban communities these conditions are not likely to prevail. In some rural communities, especially among groups which have a common ethnic background, they do obtain; and cooperatives have been successful there. There are, nevertheless, substantial consumer cooperatives in many American communities. Cooperatives are, in fact, successful enough to have incurred the enmity of certain businessmen, who attack them through efforts to have them more heavily taxed—a point which illustrates the perennial and inevitable problem of conflict: no sooner is one conflict solved than another arises.

Consumers' cooperatives have much more than economic motivation, as will be noted from the institutionalizing principles listed above. They are almost religious in flavor and there are great evangelical zeal and social idealism among their leaders. They seek to combine social responsibility with self-interest. Like other evangelistic groups, consumers' cooperatives are confident that they ride the wave of the future and that their opponents must perish. Though they denigrate conflict as a principle, they are nevertheless at war with selfish interests and think in terms of victory and defeat.[13]

[13] "It is because cooperation is in line with social advance that it is destined to grow and expand among all classes of people, urban as well as rural. Selfish interests can never succeed for long when opposed to social interests. . . . Scientific discovery has made possible an abundance of the necessaries of life to a degree never before known or even dreamed of. Those who oppose the onward sweep of democracy in its fullest sense are doomed to defeat" (Joe Gilbert, "Co-ops Grow Because They're in Line with Social Advance," *Midland Cooperator,* Oct. 10, 1945, p. 2).

15

Labor-Management Conflict

Parties and Coalitions: The Class Conflict Image

Although the concept of class implies, as we have seen, a good deal more than merely economic position, when we speak of "the class struggle" or "class conflict" we refer specifically to economic classes, to "labor" and "management" (formerly "capital"). Karl Marx, father of so-called scientific socialism (in contrast to romantic and utopian socialism, which preceded it), interpreted all history in terms of class struggle. The class which controlled the prevailing means of production, according to him, controlled the government; its ideology dominated all cultural life and all institutions. Historically, he said, the last great class struggle was between a landed aristocracy, which represented an economy based primarily on agriculture, and a rising class of bourgeois merchants, financiers, and manufacturers, which had been brought into being originally by the commercial revolution of the fourteenth and fifteenth centuries and was augmented by the industrial revolution of the eighteenth and nineteenth centuries. The political crisis which marked the final triumph of the bourgeoisie over the landed nobility was the French Revolution. From that point on, the bourgeoisie rather than the landed nobility was the decisive factor in government and culture. The next great class conflict, the conflict of the nineteenth and twentieth centuries—according to followers of Marx—was between the now dominant bourgeois class and the rising proletariat, or urban working class. Ultimately, according to Marx, the bourgeois class would be overthrown; its defeat would be followed immediately by a dictatorship of the proletariat and ultimately by a classless society. According to the Marxists, then, the parties to economic conflict are the property-owning class or their representatives on the one hand and the nonowning class on the other. They deny the existence of a disinterested public. It is a myth.

The Marxists' conception of a two-party class conflict is much too simplistic to describe the industrial conflicts of a modern society. Conflict between management and labor, or employer-employee conflict, does exist but it cannot be described or explained or interpreted in terms of bourgeoisie and proletariat locked in mortal combat for power.

Parties and Coalitions: Labor-Management Conflict

Rather than all-encompassing classes such as bourgeoisie and proletariat, the parties in any one case of industrial conflict are, on the one hand, either the organized or the unorganized workers in a small, insignificant local store or factory, or a great nation-wide union; and, on the other hand, either a small individual owner of a single local business or a huge national corporation.

Both tend to seek coalitions with the public or with the government. A specific labor-management conflict often lines up a community according to assumed class interests. The business and professional families tend to align themselves on the side of management; manual workers on the side of labor. (Farmers usually side with management.)

If the public does not originally take sides, both parties make every effort to prove that the interests of the public lie on their side. "Labor feels that its interests are the community's interests. What is good for labor—most of the people—must be good for the community. Promote the welfare of the workers and you promote the general welfare.[1] During any serious conflict, both sides compete for the public's support.

Issues: Schisms and Pressures

The issues in the Marxist conceptionalization of class conflict are schismatic in nature. They deal with the control of government. They are designed to widen, if not actually to create, cleavages in the community.

But the avowed goals sought in industrial conflict in American communities have not been control of the government. The American labor movement during most of its history has, in fact, though it has sought to influence government, fought shy of political control of government. The ostensible issues have centered rather about recognition of unions and wages, hours, and working conditions.

The nonpolitical nature of industrial conflict does not mean that there have not been schismatic issues. The recognition of unions was originally a schismatic issue. The most violent strikes in our history had to do with the rights of workers to organize. The resultant breach in the community became very deep, tearing the community wide open. On the national level they verged on civil war or revolution. Union recognition was such a schismatic issue because it involved a reinstitutionalization of the whole relationship between worker and employer.

It has always seemed to be to the interest of management to keep complete control of all working conditions, including hiring, firing, and disci-

[1] Leo Huberman, *The Truth about Unions* (New York: Harcourt, Brace & World, 1946), p. 81.

pline, as well as physical plant set-up. It has seemed to be to the interest of labor to have some say in the conditions of hiring, firing, discipline, security, job tenure, and the like. Management, concentrated on filling contract obligations to customers, hates to be blocked by demands of labor which seem to interfere with its freedom of action. Management would like to be able to treat its labor force as it treats its physical plant: as a means of production, flexible, pliant, and docile. Labor wants to be treated as an end in itself as well as a factor of production. It wants to be felt in the policies of management. This position was anathema to the great industrialists of the nineteenth and early twentieth century; that was why they fought unions so bitterly. Actually, a series of studies of the causes of industrial peace found that it was not to the interest of management to try to destroy unions; strong, stable, and responsible unions were a help rather than a hindrance to good management.[2]

Once unions are recognized, the issues tend to be pressuring-resisting in nature. One great labor leader, Samuel Gompers, when asked, What does labor want? replied succinctly, "More." The unions push for more—wages, fringe benefits, leisure, control—and management resists. It has seemed to be to the interest of management to make as much profit as possible for stockholders; it has seemed to be to the interest of labor to make as high wages as possible. "Capital wants to continue to take for itself the lion's share of the money spoils of production, while labor wants to secure for itself a more favorable division of those spoils."[3]

This conception of the conflicting interests between employers and employees is very old. Everyone who has ever hired a worker is familiar with it. The slave and his master were parties to it. Adam Smith pointed out as early as 1776 that "the workmen desire to get as much, the masters to give as little as possible."[4] In addition, it has seemed to be to the interest of the employer to work his men as long and as hard as possible. Moreover, according to the labor point of view,

> the capitalists are interested in keeping expenses down, in making profits; the workers are interested in higher wages, shorter hours, better working conditions, security. What the workers want costs money—and the capitalists are not willing to dig into their profits to pay that cost.[5]

As a matter of fact, the definitions of the interests of management and labor as sketched above are increasingly felt to be inaccurate, as some econ-

[2] George Golden and Virginia D. Parker, ed., *The Causes of Industrial Peace* (New York: Harper, 1949).

[3] Leo Huberman, "Historical and Economic Backgrounds of Current Conflict Situation," in *Industrial Conflict, A Psychological Interpretation,* ed. George W. Hartmann and Theodore M. Newcomb, for the Society for the Psychological Study of Social Issues (New York: Holt, Rinehart and Winston, 1939), p. 27.

[4] *Inquiry into the Nature and Causes of the Wealth of Nations,* edited with an Introduction by E. Cannon (London: Methuen, 1904), Vol. I, p. 68.

[5] Leo Huberman, "Historical and Economic Backgrounds of Current Conflict Situation," *op. cit.,* p. 27.

omists and indeed even some leading industrialists now recognize. Not the zero-sum model but the mixed-motive model is felt to be the most suitable one. If wages are low, there is no market for the products of mass-production industries.[6] If everyone restricts production, less is produced and everyone has less. High wages and abundant production are to everyone's interest in the long run.

SPECIFIC ISSUES

On the surface, the specific issues between the buyers and sellers of labor are fairly concrete. An analysis of the causes of strikes between 1881 and 1943, for example, showed wages to be by far the major issue, rarely accounting for less than 40 percent of all industrial disputes in any given year. Working conditions were rarely the cause of strikes before 1942, but in 1943 almost a third of all strikes centered about them. Hours were the source of friction in about one-fifth of the disputes in 1943.[7] In the 50's wages as an issue took the form of so-called fringe benefits such as pensions, paid vacations, insurance benefits, and the like. These issues are of the pressuring type; the unions push for more and management resists.

Recognition of the union and other issues involving unions were the foci of conflict in more than half of all strikes in the period of 1936-1939. Union recognition is closely tied up with that most basic of all community issues, namely, what should be the conditions of competition? How should competition be institutionalized? As we saw in Chapter 10, unions are bitterly opposed to competition. Everything workers do to eliminate competition can become an issue. The representative of management, on the other hand, wants workers to be competitive; he wants them to be competing for jobs in the first place and for advancement thereafter. He wants them to be trying to out-do one another. Competition on the part of the workers gives him more chips in the game.

This is a battle for control and power. What are the strategic limits beyond which management cannot retreat? Before which labor cannot afford to stop pressing? At what point does the surrender of managerial power reduce the payoff for both parties? These are some of the problems reflected in the issue of work rules. It is not a new issue, but the accelerating pace of automation is rendering it acute. How much veto power should the union have over management in the introduction of new techniques? What should the procedure be in the introduction of new techniques? How should workers be protected when new techniques eliminate their jobs? All other issues fade in significance compared to this, as illustrated by the great steel strike in 1959.

6 *Ibid.*

7 Harry A. Millis and Royal E. Montgomery, *The Economics of Labor, Organized Labor,* Vol. III (New York: McGraw-Hill, 1945), pp. 699-702.

Conflicting Images

Such categories as "union recognition," "hours," and "working conditions," are useful for statistical compilations. They do not, however, give much insight into the specific behavior of men and women in the local plant. The following statements show how the situation in the local plant looks, first to management, and then to labor.

First, the employer's version:

In assigning men, keeping down absences and tardiness, discouraging delinquencies, encouraging good workmanship and greater productivity, promoting men, preventing strikes, keeping peace between the union and employees who are not members or who do not pay dues, settling grievances, keeping order, the Company has put foremen there to further the Company's interest in producing goods of high quality in great volume and at low cost. . . . The employees often mistakenly think they are working too hard, or they are lazy. They wish to work irregularly, when they find it convenient or only when they need the money. They like to visit in the plant, pick their own jobs and their own hours. They like to do their work some other way than the way that is most efficient, that makes for the best output, or that is safest. In all these things and many others they are opposing interests of the Company. . . . The conflict of interest does not arise between the Company and every employee, but it arises often . . . and the possibility of conflict is always there. . . .

There are other areas of conflict in which the interest of the rank and file union is peculiar to itself. It opposes the introduction of machines and methods that decrease manpower and, accordingly, the number of its members and potential members. It teaches its members to look to it, not to the Company, for betterment of their lot. It seeks to sign up members, collect dues and carry on other union activities in the plant and interrupt people at their work for these purposes. Its officials seek to take advantage of the bargaining procedure provided by the contract. It goes to extreme lengths to foster ill will in employees toward the Company, publishing all sorts of scurrility notwithstanding its admissions that the Company is fair. . . . These conflicts, which the union and its officials enter into on behalf of employees or on their own behalf, give rise to thousands of grievances. . . . They sometimes result in strikes and stoppages. . . .[8]

Now the worker's definition of the situation:

Suppose the worker finds that the room he's working in is badly ventilated. The window at the far end works O.K. but the one just behind his machine won't open. He tugs at it with all his might—no use, he can't budge it. He gets hotter and hotter, until he feels he can't stand it any longer. He goes to the foreman and asks for a screw driver and a hammer to open the window. The foreman says, "Listen, Bud, you're paid for tending that machine, not for opening windows. Now scram, and don't let me catch you away from that machine until the whistle blows."

[8] *Shall the Rank and File Boss the Plants?* Pamphlet (Detroit: Chrysler Corp., 1946), pp. 37-39.

The foreman is a dictator. There's no doubt about that. In the locker room after 6 P.M. when he's putting on his street clothes, the worker hears some of the other men complaining, "What a bastard! I asked him to have the light fixed over my machine so I could see better. He said if I was getting so old I couldn't see, I'd better quit."

"He told me," says another, "that I was through on Saturday. Been working here 12 years, now I've got to look for another job. He's been after me for a long time. Today when I told him to stop swearing at me, he blew up. Said he wouldn't take any back talk and to get the hell out."

The rules and regulations within the factory are set by the employer. And so long as each worker tries to improve conditions, by himself, he won't get anywhere. The Supreme Court made that clear a long time ago. In 1898 the Court held that "the proprietors of these establishments and their operatives (workers) do not stand upon an equality . . . the proprietors lay down the rules and the laborers are practically constrained to obey them.[9]

The employer, or his representative, the foreman, is not necessarily a villain. It is simply that the man who assumes responsibility for production involving the work of other men has, to paraphrase Francis Bacon, given himself as a hostage to Fortune. He has to be ransomed by those who do the work. He has orders to fill, contractual obligations to live up to. He has the engineering point of view. Efficiency is his goal. Management stands, therefore, for discipline, machines, and technology. Life in an industrialized community calls for an extraordinary amount of discipline of human nature by clocks, machines, technology, bureaucratic organization, regimentation. It allows for little spontaneity. It mechanizes our lives. We stand for it only because modern technologies turn out so many goods that we want. Management is identified with this disciplinary phase of production.

Labor, on the other hand, represents the human side of production. It sees men and women who have families, personalities, human weaknesses, and foibles. The man loitering at the window or taking time off to smoke is violating the rules laid down for efficient production. To the union this is no heinous crime. Workers are not simply means to an end, as they are for management, but feel that they are ends in themselves. Production, they argue, should be keyed to what the average man can do at his normal speed.[10] Labor does not want to see human beings crushed by too rigorous discipline either by machines or by foremen. Labor wants leeway for the human frailties that two hundred years of machine production have not

[9] Huberman, *The Truth about Unions*, pp. 2-3.

[10] Students can appreciate this point of view. Suppose they worked as hard every day as they do just before examination time. Cramming and all-night study represent the same kind of thing as the speed-up. But why should students work at that pace? The frayed nerves of examination time correspond to the frayed nerves of men who are worked at a speed too high for the average worker. We pace learning for the average rate of speed of the average student. Workers ask that production be paced in the same way. This, it should be noted, is not the same problem as that of artificially restricted productivity discussed in Chapter 10.

eliminated—resentment against monotony and against being "pushed around," desire for recognition, longing for security.

The employer, as disciplinarian, might put the situation this way: "Men are naturally lazy. You have to scare them to keep them working. You have to have the right to fire them to get any work out of them. You have to force efficiency on them." The union leader might put it this way: "Workers are human beings. You can't work them too hard. They can't do their best work if they are scared to death about losing their jobs. They don't want to be pushed around. Living is more important than making profit."

The issues between management and labor are not, then, merely economic in the superficial sense. They go deeper; they have roots that go to the core of human nature. The conflict between management and labor reflects a basic conflict within each one of us. We have all felt it within our own personalities. We might reduce its dimensions by decentralizing industry, but we can never eliminate it. For even if the employer and the employee are one and the same person, the conflict persists within that one person. It is a conflict between his desire for the goods he must work to produce and his desire to relax and take things easy.

The Institutional Background

The nature of labor-management conflict depends, as in all cases of conflict, on the way the relationship is institutionalized. Our concern here, of course, is with the conflicts resulting from the way it was institutionalized in the West. At the beginning of modern industrialization it was institutionalized on the basis of the common law doctrine of master and servant, of conspiracy. Both crescive norms—customs, mores, collective attitudes and beliefs—and enacted norms—statutory law—were on the side of the employers. They condemned attempts of workers first to organize and then to gain their ends by the most effective means in their reach, namely picketing, strikes, boycotts. Even the workers themselves, except when they had been indoctrinated by organizers, tended to accept the general point of view that all rights were on the side of the boss. These institutional patterns thus defined the role of the employer as one of great power and that of the employee as one of subservience and obedience. And the courts which interpreted the norms were also on the side of the employer.

The function of this mode of institutionalizing employer-employee relationships was similar to that of the *caveat emptor* rule referred to in Chapter 14. Just as *caveat emptor* so served the function of stimulating trade by siding with the seller of goods, so the master-servant and conspiracy doctrines served the function of stimulating entrepreneurship in the early years of industrialization by assuring docile labor, by siding with the buyers of labor. The capital for financing the first stages of industrialization was, so to speak, taken out of the hides of the workers.

Thus for over a century industrial conflict was umpired by a set of institutional rules which gave all the advantages to one side and penalized the other. Slight modifications were made in these rules until World War I, when the principles of labor organization and collective bargaining were definitely recognized and in many cases made compulsory. These principles were later made permanent, expanded, and implemented in three basic statutes which revised the relationship between management and labor, transferring more power to the latter and vastly enlarging its strategic armory. The three statutes were the Norris-LaGuardia Act (1932), the Fair Labor Standards Act (1938), and especially the National Labor Relations Act (1935).

Concomitantly with these changes in enacted institutional rules there went changes in crescive consensual norms also, that is, in public assessment of what was right and wrong in employer-employee relationships. As industrialization proceeded it generated capital at an accelerating rate, so that it no longer had to be taken out of the hide of the workers. Indeed, as productivity increased, institutional means had to be devised to get it distributed for consumption.[11] The function of consumption became as important as that of production.

The changes which the three sets of statutes made in the relationship between management and labor were reflected in the relative strategic resources, and hence power, they had vis-a-vis one another.

The Fair Labor Standards Act—sometimes known as the Wages and Hour Act—like any price-fixing rule, utilized the strategy of first-move. It was intended to help workers in interstate commerce, who did not have the protection of unions, to execute the first-move strategy for them by contract. It placed a floor on wages and a ceiling on hours, with time and a half for overtime. In addition, many state laws have been passed aiming at the same ends and often modeled after the national act.

Before such legislation, the employer had the strategic advantage of first move; he could set wages and the workers had to accept them. After such legislation, the government set a minimum level which transferred first move to the workers, and the employer had to accept it.

There are, of course, defects in this strategy. As in the case of other first-move approaches, the commitment of the labor sellers' delegated agent —the law enforcing officer—is not always firm. His incentive may not be strong enough to make him enforce the commitment. And it may be to the employer's advantage to pay him for not enforcing the commitment. "Corruption" may be built into the situation.

The Norris-LaGuardia Act deprived management of one of its most potent weapons, the injunction and the threat of injunctions. An injunction is an order issued by a court telling someone to stop doing something.

[11] See Jessie Bernard, *Social Problems at Midcentury* (New York: Holt, Rinehart and Winston, 1957), Chapter 1 for some of the implications of this change.

It is a useful weapon. It can prevent great public injury. But as used in industrial conflict it had stopped labor dead in its tracks. For whenever workers had threatened to strike or had actually called a strike, when they merely picketed, or, in fact, did anything at all—legal or illegal—that their employers did not like, the employers could go to court and get a restraining order. And if they did not obey the court order they were cited for contempt of court, which meant that they were liable for fines or imprisonment or both.

From the early 1890's on, the injunction had been used in most of the big strikes. It had tended to demoralize strikers, to restrict picketing, and to stop publication and distribution of "unfair lists." It had brought labor leaders into court and wasted their time in legal battles, to the detriment of their leadership activities. It had cost unions a good deal of money for legal counsel. It had made policemen more severe in handling local strikes. The injunction had also been used to enforce the so-called "yellow-dog" contracts—that is, contracts forced upon employees when they were hired, in which they had had to promise not to join any union while they worked for this employer.[12]

Labor leaders tried to get laws limiting the use of injunctions and thought they had succeeded when the Clayton Act was passed in 1914. But the courts, until the 1930's more hostile to labor than legislatures, which have to be responsive and responsible to their constituents, interpreted away the protection against injunctions which that act had set up. Labor leaders continued their fight; and finally, in 1932, they succeeded in getting federal legislation which was effective—the Norris-LaGuardia Act.

There is a great strategic loss to management and corresponding strategic gain to labor from the reduction of the injunction and hence the strategic threat of invoking it.

The National Labor Relations Act handicapped and reduced employers' antiunion activities. Employers were obliged by that act to bargain collectively: that is, to recognize unions.[13] It also specified what constituted unfair labor practices on the part of an employer.[14] In 1947, as a result of

[12] The use of the injunction in this connection was confirmed in the so-called Hitchman case. The Hitchman Coal & Coke Company of West Virginia had imposed a promise on its employees, when they were rehired after an unsuccessful strike, never to join a union. When organizers came into the area trying to get men to promise to join the union, the Hitchman Coal & Coke Company went to the courts and asked for an injunction, saying that the organizers were inducing breach of contract. The Supreme Court in 1917 upheld the injunction.

[13] Section 7 stated that "employees shall have the right to self-organization, to form, join, or assist labor organizations, to bargain collectively through representatives of their own choosing, and to engage in concerted activities, for the purpose of collective bargaining or other mutual aid or protection."

[14] Section 8 specified the unfair labor practices to be: "(1) To interfere with, restrain, or coerce employees in the exercise of the rights guaranteed in Section 7; (2) to dominate or interfere with the formation or administration of any labor organization or contribute financial or other support to it . . .; (3) By discrimination in regard to hire or tenure of employment or any term or condition of employment to encourage or dis-

the first decade of experience with the new law, it was modified substantially. One of the most plausible-sounding attacks that had been made on the law was that it was unequal and one-sided, favoring labor, and that it should be amended to restrict labor as it restricted management. Since the National Labor Relations Act had been intended in the first place to equalize the bargaining position of labor, bringing it up to the level of management, labor felt that this attack on it was scarcely valid. But the Taft-Hartley Act (1947) did require labor to bargain collectively; it could not resort to first-move strategy in arriving at contracts.

Strategically, the end result of collective bargaining is a contract which constitutes a first move in the sense that it fixes the conditions of work, just as legislation does for unorganized workers, so that the specific buyers and sellers of labor are no longer vulnerable to individual bargaining techniques. The union also employs the strategy of delegated bargaining. The union agent is not employed by the firms he is bargaining with; he is therefore independent of them and immune to personal threats; his job does not depend on their good will. Being able to speak for a large number of workers, he has the enormous power of the threat at his disposal. The net effect is a complete restructuring of the relations between employer and employee.

There were, as in the case of legislation to protect consumers, strategic defects in the above legislation. There was great temptation for leaders to enter coalitions with employers against workers. In 1959 the Griffin-Landrum Act was passed to help meet this contingency, to offer workers protection against their leaders as well as against their employers.[15]

Withdrawal from Community As a Method for Dealing with Issues

At the lowest level on the conflict continuum—the destruction of community—is the technique of moving a factory or plant from a community in which it has labor troubles. The conflict is ended by destroying the relationship. This has been the situation in a number of cases—not all, of course—in which factories have moved from New England to the South. This maneuver has, however, been declared an unfair act and companies that engage in it are obliged to pay their former workers for damages. The Meilman case illustrates how this avenue of escape is closed to employers:

---

courage membership in any labor organization . . .; (4) to discharge or otherwise discriminate against an employee because he has filed charges or given testimony under this act; (5) to refuse to bargain collectively with the representatives of his employees."

[15] This act includes a "bill of rights" guaranteeing freedom of expression to union members even when these views are contrary to those of their leaders. Secret elections are provided for as well as protection for opposition candidates. Union funds may not be used to advance the candidacy of any individual. Deals between employers and union officials are forbidden. Union trials are regulated. The rights of disgruntled members are protected. Felons are excluded from union office for at least five years after leaving jail. In addition to these intraunion matters, the act also limits secondary boycotts and restricts picketing for organizational purposes.

A "runaway" clothing manufacturer, under court orders to pay a union $204,861 in damages for moving his plant to Mississippi, has closed his operations there and resumed business in New York. . . .

The conflict between the union and Mr. Meilman developed after he had surreptitiously shifted all his equipment and unfinished garments from the factory . . . to a new plant in Coffeeville, Miss. The Southern factory had been built for him with a $360,000 issue of community bonds.

. . . the arbitrator upheld a union complaint that the transfer violated the union's contract with Mr. Meilman. He directed the manufacturer to "cease and desist" from operating a factory anywhere outside of New York, to reopen his plant here and to pay the union damages for the wage loss suffered by its members. . . .

The union made no secret of its belief that the outcome of the case would discourage other manufacturers from suspending their operations here and seeking lower labor costs in the South.[16]

Manipulative Techniques

Sometimes the battle can be won by threats rather than actual withdrawal. In one southern community a union was defeated by threatening to close down the plant:

A calculated campaign to thwart a victory for union representation has paid off for the Deering, Milliken textile chain, owners of the Darlington Manufacturing Co. Workers in the Darlington mill voted September 6 for representation by the Textile Works Union. Almost immediately, Roger Milliken, head of the firm, ordered a stockholders meeting for October 17 where he will recommend liquidation of the mill. The reign of terror had its expected effect: workers are now petitioning the NLRB to void the election and withhold certification so they can hold their jobs. "We only hope we can persuade management to keep the mill open," says a leader in the movement to cancel the election. . . .[17]

Similarly, "a 'successful' employees' strike," it has been suggested, "is . . . one that never takes place."[18] Both management and labor attempt to get what they want by indirect or strategic rather than by direct means.

At a very low level, the worker can be controlled by threats of firing, of downgrading, of demotion, of wage-reduction. The workers, on their part, fight back by shirking on the job, by slow-downs, tardiness, absenteeism, material wastage, or anything else they can get away with. The strategic model which explains their behavior is that of extortion. They are saying, in effect: "It will improve your payoff if you give us more because we can destroy more in materials than the cost of giving us higher wages." With the advent of powerful unions, this state of affairs has become less common even in plants where there are no unions. The fear of having unions come

[16] A. H. Raskin, "'Runaway' Plant Returns to City," *New York Times*, Oct. 20, 1960.

[17] *Durham Labor Journal*, Oct. 17, 1956.

[18] Thomas C. Schelling, *The Strategy of Conflict* (Cambridge, Mass.: Harvard, 1960), p. 6.

in to organize their workers tends to modify the attitude of employers so that, apart from small and out-of-the-way plants, excessive exploitation is not so common as formerly except in industries which employ women and children and other minority groups. Improved working conditions and personnel management are, in fact, among the most powerful weapons used by management to fight unions.

Collective Bargaining

When there is a recognized union among the workers the opposing parties are more nearly equal and the outstanding technique of conflict is collective bargaining. The collective bargain itself is a printed book of rules which tells just what rights and duties each party to the contract has. These rules regulate the behavior of all the individuals in the industrial unit covered by it. It does not, of course, eliminate the conflict; it simply keeps it under control, institutionalizes it. The rules, further, must be applied and there are numerous occasions in which the rules have to be interpreted.

Since this agreement on the rules of the conflict is so important a document, it is necessary that it embody the best each side can get. Obviously an employer cannot sit down and bargain with all his employees—there may be five or ten thousand in his firm. The employees therefore select representatives to bargain for them. The employer may bargain himself, with the help of his own research and statistical experts, superintendents, foremen, and any other qualified assistants; or he may designate his personnel manager or some vice president to represent him.

The collective bargaining situation usually conforms to the mixed-motive strategic model. Both sides usually wish to avoid a strike if possible; they have this much in common. They therefore have some incentive to find a point both can accept.

If the meeting is the first that has ever been attempted, the union representatives come prepared with a list of the conditions they want embodied in the contract. These may deal with wages, holidays, vacations, rest periods, grievance procedure, the check-off, group insurance, pensions, retirement, hiring procedure, firing procedure, seniority, promotions, rest rooms—in fact, with anything or everything that seems important in that plant or industry. There is often a great advantage for one party or the other in having a number of issues involved. Not only can a concession on one issue be traded for a concession on another issue, but if properly managed, one party may be able to win on both issues.[19]

Once the demands have been studied, the employer and his staff attempt to show that they are wholly unreasonable, completely out of bounds. Some of the demands can be met, with modifications—but not the wage demands. If the firm attempted to comply with them it would go

[19] Schelling, *op. cit.*, pp. 31, 51 ff.

bankrupt within a year, its credit would be impaired, it would lose out with its competitors. The union representative, of course, has expected precisely this reaction. He, too, has facts and figures. He argues that the cost would be nowhere near $320,698; it would more likely be $150,000, an amount which could easily be paid out of profits, as reported in the company's last brochure for stockholders. The fight is on.

If the ground has been well laid it is possible for the union agent to convince the company that he has strong and insistent support from the union, that even if he were willing to settle for less his men would not, that he really cannot make any concessions. His would constitute first-move strategy and the company would have to accept the demand or face a strike. Contrariwise, in a different social and economic and political atmosphere the company might convince the union agent that it could not make any concessions, that if it did the stockholders would fire them, or creditors force bankruptcy, or what-have-you. If so, then the company would have the advantage of first-move strategy and win.

Sometimes the union gets most of what it asks for; sometimes it has to settle for far less. The same is true for management. If the employer has a lot of orders to fill, if the union is strong and likely to go out on strike to get what it wants, he may be willing to make many concessions he would not make if he could help it. Similarly the union representative may settle for a good deal less than he asks for if there is a considerable amount of unemployment, if the union is not financially strong enough to support a long strike, or if business is poor so that the employer is not hard pressed for workers.

A promise not to strike—that is, the so-called no-strike agreement—is especially important to the employer, for then he can go ahead and plan his production without fear of losing time because of strikes. He is often willing, therefore, to "pay" quite a bit in the way of concessions for such a promise. Similarly job security is especially important to the worker. Promises of job security are not quite as enforceable as promises not to strike; they can be violated by degrees and there may be incentive to violate them.

Neither side in collective bargaining is usually completely satisfied with the results, although they both usually pose for the press as completely happy about them. If one side is completely satisfied it would probably mean that the other side had been defeated. Ordinarily each side concedes something it would have liked to get, but gains other things it considers more important.

This bargaining process is considered by some people to be the best way to carry on the conflict between management and labor. It is a nonviolent way to fight out issues. For the most part it is highly successful. It does not, however, always succeed or run smoothly. If the opposing demands cannot be compromised or resolved, the conference may break up. This in turn may lead to a strike or lockout. Because the consequences of failure in the bargaining process are so serious for both sides, several techniques have been worked out to avoid it wherever possible. Among these are conciliation-mediation and arbitration.

CONCILIATION AND MEDIATION

If common interests—avoidance of a strike—predominate over conflicting interests so that both sides are trying hard to avoid a showdown in the form of open warfare, they may attempt a conciliation before matters get entirely out of hand. If they cannot do this by themselves—if, for example, a further concession by one side will be interpreted as weakness by the other and therefore only lead to demands for further concessions—they may be willing to accept the services of a disinterested outside mediator. He first secures permission from both sides, to be sure that his good offices are acceptable. Or perhaps they may themselves call him in. He talks to each group separately in order to familiarize himself with the situation. He does not meet them both at the same time until he feels he has worked out a satisfactory accommodation which both sides will accept. Each side, talking to him in confidence, lets him know just how far they are willing to go in making concessions rather than go to war. It is this readiness of both sides to talk to him freely which constitutes his greatest strategic usefulness.

The mediator himself is simply interested in seeing how he can coordinate the goals of both sides and at the same time save face for both parties. If either or both sides are adamant, the mediator withdraws and admits failure. The conflict may proceed to open warfare; or, if the parties are willing, it may be submitted to arbitration.

The mediation of labor disputes is a highly specialized profession. A conciliation service within the federal government furnishes help where it is needed; but it is greatly understaffed. Because of the size of the problem, regional and even community conciliation services have come into being since 1946. Great flexibility of approach is necessary. In Detroit, for example, where violence, fierce competition, and disorganization are characteristic, both management and labor tend to be hard-boiled and truculent. Gentle methods of conciliation or mediation do not have much chance in such an atmosphere. Collective bargaining becomes a bludgeoning rather than a strategic process and the contract which results may be one not of good will but of suspicion and distrust.

In view of the relative recency of mediation and conciliation in collective bargaining we should not despair of achieving successful ways for implementing it. New social inventions are always being made; some may be very successful.

ARBITRATION

In addition to conciliation as a solution to labor-management conflict there is the approach of arbitration. Arbitration is basically very different from conciliation. It is a judicial process. The arbitrator does not listen to each side separately, as does the mediator. There is, rather, an open hearing at which both sides present their case, with rebuttals, before a judge. He hands down a decision stating which side is right and which side is wrong. Presumably both sides to the arbitration have agreed to abide by the decision handed down. In order to be effective, therefore, arbitration must be in the hands of a man or men in whom both sides have complete confidence. Often the arbitration is done by a board composed of three members, one selected by each side and the third selected by the other two.

Arbitration may be viewed also as a form of judgmental competition. Each side competes in its efforts to convince the judge of the rightness of its case. The judge, for his part, must, on the basis of very complex criteria, decide which side has more validity.

Arbitration may precede or follow a strike. That is, it may be tried even after a strike has been called. Though both management and labor favor voluntary arbitration, both are opposed to compulsory arbitration. They want to settle their difficulties voluntarily.

In 1946 the director of conciliation of the federal government published a statement of policy recommended by a labor-management advisory committee. It included suggestions for: (1) a panel of men of national repute in labor relations to serve as special conciliators in major disputes; (2) a tripartite panel system, consisting of representatives of labor and of industry, to serve with federal conciliators in especially difficult cases; (3) provisions for voluntary arbitration in all collective agreements; and (4) in cases of national importance, emergency boards of inquiry, set up with the consent of both parties to conduct hearings and publish their findings.

Within a decade even these suggestions were inadequate. New concepts of collective bargaining were being called for. The idea was then gaining currency that just as bloody strikes gave way to collective bargaining, so must collective bargaining as practiced at the time give way to new and more efficient methods of dealing with labor-management relationships. Timing, as we noted above, is of great strategic importance, favoring one side or the other according to the prevailing social atmosphere. The sporadic timing of bargaining is viewed by some observers as anachronistic. There should be an on-going process available for dealing with industrial problems at all times. There should be no dead-line, as there so often now is, putting extreme pressure on the negotiators.

The successful solution of these problems, it is argued, has not only domestic importance but international implications as well. Unless or until management and labor learn to fight out their differences in a civilized manner, our whole economic system will fall into disrepute and we will be at a competitive disadvantage in appealing for the allegiance of nations trying to make up their minds between capitalism and communism.

Coalescing Interests of Labor and Management

The basic conflict of interests may be minimized and all but eliminated and the common interests enlarged if the worker feels he has a vital share in the success of the business. The techniques of conflict at this coalescent level become persuasion and education. Enlightened employers and labor leaders attempt to teach their colleagues and confrères that common interests can be cultivated and divergent interests accommodated constructively. The union tries to prove to its members that efficient production—management's interest—will not work them out of a job. Advanced managers try to convince boards of directors that high wages and low prices are the best policies to pursue in the long run. Economists try to teach both.[20]

Among the methods that have been proposed to render the interests of buyers and sellers of labor consonant, if not identical, are profit-sharing and the guaranteed annual wage.

In the past profit-sharing was frowned upon by leaders of organized labor; it was looked upon as a method of fighting unions—as, indeed, it sometimes is.[21] Or it was viewed with misgivings because of fear that if men worked hard and earned a large share of the profit, the rate of pay would be reduced so that they would simply be working harder for the same amount of pay, even if part of their pay was now called "profit." Profit-sharing has, however, been accepted by some unions and is now an approved method of coalescing the interests of management and labor. It is incorporated into the contracts of some labor agreements. Union leaders find that there is no necessary incompatibility between a strong union and profit-sharing plans. Profit-sharing gives the worker a personal interest in the company; he feels identified with it. He feels less resentment against the discipline inherent in mechanized industry when he has a stake in the output.

Another approach to the coalescence of interests of management and labor is the guaranteed annual wage. This system, successful in such widely different industries as the Hormel Packing Plant at Austin, Minnesota, the Nunn-Bush Shoe Company of Cleveland, and the Procter and Gamble Soap Company of Cincinnati, works on the principle of eliminating or at least minimizing unemployment. It guarantees workers 48 or 50 or 52 paychecks a year. The workers are not, therefore, opposed to efficiency techniques

[20] Edwin G. Nourse, a member of the first Economic Advisory Council set up under the Full Employment Act of 1946, has long since been propounding the point of view that "business and labor leaders must realize that they have common interests, and enter into an amicable partnership. . . . It is a mistake to deal with them as if their interests were opposed. . . . The best system is one of high wages, with prices constantly lowered through steadily improving efficiency—an efficiency that will make possible a lasting mass production of goods." That this overstates the identity of interests between management and labor is probably true; but that it is a useful reminder that there are common as well as conflicting interests is also true.

[21] As, for example, in the Avondale textile mills of Alabama.

which increase production and lower costs, as they might be if they felt such devices would rob them of their jobs. This system thus lowers costs of production for the manufacturers themselves. Both sides gain.[22]

Sometimes the coalescence of interests between management and labor takes the interesting form of union assistance to management. It sometimes happens, notably in the needle trades industries, that the entrepreneur is a less talented and intelligent man than the labor leader with whom he has to deal. In order to make the business successful enough to meet their demands, union leaders may help promote efficiency by suggestions that increase production. Instances are on record in which the unions have even come to the rescue of their employers, lending them money, or even—and this verges very close to assimilation—buying large blocs of stock in the company. It is to the interest of such unions to see that the employers are prosperous enough to guarantee jobs to workers.

It is not necessarily to the interest of the community to have labor and management identify their interests. It may, indeed, be detrimental to the community as a whole. For it sometimes happens that they combine against the consumer or against competitors, much to the consumer's harm. Many of the restrictions imposed by unions on their members are actually for the benefit of their employers. Some, in fact, were established by management itself in order to minimize competition and to prohibit technological improvements. The union merely enforces them. Four kinds of such devices have been distinguished by which labor and management, acting jointly, exploit the public.[23]

First of all, some contracts between union and management fix prices directly. This is the case with barbers, beauty shop operators, wholesale bread delivery men in the East, milk distributors, and in some instances in the construction industry. Such price-fixing—the first-move strategy—is no more palatable to the consumer when it is done in cooperation with unions than when it is done by the businessmen by themselves.

In some industries prices are to all intents and purposes fixed by a device known as the bid depository. All bids for a particular construction job are submitted to a central authority consisting of representatives of both unions and construction companies. This central authority goes over the bids, throws out the exceptionally high and low ones, averages the rest, adding overhead and expenses. The bids are then submitted. The main purpose seems to be to prevent competition among the bidders and to restrict competition among the workers. Unions refuse to work for contractors who are not members of the depository association.

[22] The guaranteed annual wage, like some other kinds of regulations, tends also to increase the efficiency of the plant. It demands better planning and organization of production. Thus it does not necessarily throw an additional burden on the consumer in the form of higher prices. At least these results have been reported by firms that have tried it, such as Procter and Gamble. The stabilizing effect has also been reported by the Hormel Packing Plant in Austin, Minnesota.

[23] Robert Littler, *Make-Work Rules and Collective Bargaining's Future* (San Francisco: The San Francisco Industrial Relations Conference, 1945), pp. 6-9.

Another technique used by labor and management to the detriment of the community is the setting up of rules and practices which restrict the number of competitors in a field and thus prevent the establishment of new enterprises. This practice has been found in the plumbing and tile contracting industries; in the heating, woodworking, and fur industries in the East; in milk distribution in New York, Chicago, and Seattle; and in poultry distribution in New York.[24]

A fourth method by which management and labor form coalitions which connive against the community as a whole involves the erection of a figurative wall around a local industry in order to prevent competition from other firms outside the community. It is, in effect, a tariff barrier.[25]

In 1945 the Supreme Court declared in the Allen-Bradley case that this kind of agreement was a conspiracy in violation of the Sherman Act and therefore illegal.

Some labor leaders are sensitive to criticism which alleges this kind of connivance.[26] And yet it is generally felt that some way must be found by which the conflicting interests of labor and management can be accommodated without at the same time tempting them into a coalition against the public.

There is an even more sinister form which coalescence may take. This is the coalition between labor leaders and management against the rank-and-file membership. It sometimes happens that labor leaders sell out to management—for a consideration. They make deals. They use their power to control workers as an asset to be used for their own benefit rather than for that of their workers. It was to prohibit this kind of coalition or deal that the Landrum-Griffin Act was passed in 1959.

Farmer-Labor Conflict

The parties in the conflict we have so far been discussing are labor and management. There is another related cleavage which deserves at least passing mention, although it is usually too abstract to reveal itself concretely in

[24] The Association of Service Station Owners in Minneapolis in 1944 went so far as to transform itself into a local of the teamsters' union with the avowed purpose of limiting the number of service stations and to fix the prices of the products they sold.

[25] In New York, for example, union members were not permitted to install any electrical fixtures or equipment manufactured outside the city if similar fixtures or equipment were manufactured by any firms within the city. The building trades and other industries in Chicago, New Orleans, Seattle, and San Francisco have also indulged in this kind of labor-management restraint of trade.

[26] Thus, when labor and management signed a labor-management charter that was hailed as a historic step in the improvement of labor-management relations and the secretary of the so-called People's Lobby wanted to know whether the Department of Justice had approved this conspiracy against consumers, Philip Murray, then president of the CIO, replied warmly that there was absolutely nothing collusive in the agreement. In 1946, moreover, when Walter Reuther was leading a strike of automobile workers for increased pay, he publicly opposed passing the cost of the pay increase on to the consumer. He wanted it to be known that his union would not conspire with automobile manufacturers against the public.

community life. This is the conflict of interests between farmers and urban industrial workers.

Many farmers, simply because they are themselves managers, share management's image of the relationship between management and labor. The resulting attitude has tended to be hostile.[27] Nor has this hostility of farmers toward unions been lessened by efforts of labor organizers to include agricultural workers in union contracts. Union leaders have come to see that agricultural workers in large factory-farms need the protection of unions as much as city workers do. They have therefore attempted to organize cotton pickers, orange and berry pickers, and other workers on factory-farms. Some of the most violent labor conflicts have been those in the factory-farm areas of California and Arizona.

In addition, even when he is not a large-scale employer himself, the farmer as buyer of industrial goods feels he has a stake in the conflict of management and workers in urban industries. He tends to resent high wages paid to industrial workers on the grounds that they increase the prices he must pay for manufactured goods. He is likely, therefore, to be antiunion on two counts.

Although industrial workers, on their side, resent having to pay artificially high prices for food and clothes as a result of governmental programs for the support of farm prices, labor leaders do not make the mistake of attacking such programs. Nor do they lobby for the abandonment of the principle of parity, which intrinsically favors the farmer.[28] Indeed, they cannot logically make such an attack, inasmuch as they also seek government protection for the prices of their product, that is, wages.

Their approach is to try to win over farmers to a pro-labor point of view by convincing them that high wages, far from being inimical to the best interests of farmers, are entirely to their benefit. When industrial wages are high, they argue, city workers can buy what the farmer produces, and at good prices. When wages are low the farmer cannot sell his produce.

[27] The American Farm Bureau Federation states, for example, "The concentration of economic power in labor unions permits resort to measures which, if used by other economic groups, would result in drastic antitrust action. Such economic power has been used to increase wage rates in excess of the national gain in productivity, thus denying consumers the benefits of improved technology, and contributing to inflationary trends. . . ." (*New York Times,* Dec. 18, 1959).

[28] The principle of parity guarantees the farmer a certain price in terms of the buying power of agricultural products in 1909-1913. In those years agricultural products exchanged for more industrial goods than at any other time in our history. The converse of this statement is, of course, also true. That is, in the period of 1909-1913, industrial goods exchanged for less agricultural products than at any other time in our history.

16

Negro-White Conflict

A Changing Status Quo

Any particular status quo is an accommodation of conflicting groups. The particular position which any group occupies at any given time reflects the best it can do under the given circumstances, including ignorance and weakness. Any change, presumably, would be worse for one or both. They are, figuratively speaking, locked into a relationship which, under the given conditions, neither can change. But there is a constant jockeying back and forth, probing, even feinting. And there is no necessary reversion to any given accommodation. It is not a checks-and-balance type of system. The ignorant may become enlightened, the weak may become stronger, the strong may become weaker. When such changes occur a new "strategic game" emerges and a new status quo may result.

In any particular status quo it is likely that some groups profit more than others or even profit at the expense of others. Some groups therefore want to preserve the status quo; but others want to change it. In general, conservative people who profit from the status quo line up to resist the pressures of innovating groups; it is not that they want to gain anything. They want to preserve what they have. Any change they interpret as loss to them.

Although any particular status quo or accommodation of incompatible differences may be as good a one as possible under the given circumstances, it is never static; there is always a great deal of interaction going on. And there are some periods when such interaction becomes particularly intense; an accumulation of efforts leads to almost cataclysmic changes. We are now in such an accelerated period of change with respect to race relations.

The Parties

Negroes are not all alike. It is as erroneous to speak of "the Negro" as it is to speak of "the white man." Negroes are not more alike than white people. We have at one end of the scale gifted and cultured individuals such as Marian Anderson; at the other, the isolated rural southern type which is retarded almost to the point of feeblemindedness. When the educated northerner speaks of Negroes he is often speaking of cultivated men and women of his own standing. The southerner is often talking about a type which may lack most of the restraints that education imposes. Upper-class Negroes avoid contacts with white people in order to protect themselves from insult and humiliation. Most white people, therefore, form their opinion of Negroes on the basis of observation of lower-class Negroes who may jostle them on subways or shirk on the job.

When we speak of race conflict we cannot therefore lump Negroes all together into a homogeneous mass. Neither can the whites be so lumped. There are Negroes who do not line up with their fellows on racial issues. Some Negroes identify themselves with the white race. Others exploit fellow-Negroes as mercilessly as do whites. They are not interested in the Negro's battle. They profit from his plight. Some are "Uncle Toms"—that is, Negroes who fawn on white people. And, conversely, some of the most ardent advocates of Negro rights are white men and women. They fight the Negro's battle more valiantly than do many Negroes themselves.

The parties to race conflict are not, therefore, a monolithic and homogeneous group called "Negro" on one side and a similarly monolithic and homogeneous group called "white" on the other. Much conflict with respect to race is between northern white liberals and southern white conservatives, with Negroes primarily interested bystanders. There is conflict among Negro groups also, not necessarily with respect to goals but with respect to means of achieving them. There is conflict between educated white southerners and uneducated white southerners. Indeed, the parties are so variegated as almost to defy clear-cut delineation. But however the parties line up, all attempt sooner or later to win over the government into a coalition. The government itself, therefore, is one of the most important parties in race conflict.

The Issues

When the parties involved in a conflict are clearly discernible on the basis of such ascriptive traits as race and sex, the issues between them are very likely to be schismatic in nature. In race conflict, as also in ethnic-group conflict, the basic issue, whatever specific focus it may center about—jobs, schooling, housing, transportation, recreation—is schismatic in nature, namely, What should be the conditions of competition? How should the allocation of goods and services be institutionalized? Should the allocation of privileges and rewards be on a competitive basis? Or should one or the other of the alternatives to competition be used? And if the allocation should be on the basis of competition, what should be the criteria of success? What should be the ground rules? These are the kinds of questions which are likely to tear communities apart. Those who want a noncompetitive answer—segregation—line up against those who want a competitive answer. And the intensity of the interaction is high.

Even if desegregation is accepted as a solution, pressuring issues arise. Negroes press for greater degrees of desegregation; whites resist as best they can. But, even more anomalous, desegregation comes to involve a quite noncompetitive answer to the questions of race relations. The concept of the so-called "benign quota" emerges, to be discussed in somewhat more detail below.

Schismatic Solutions

Schismatic solutions to race conflict have a long history, ranging in form all the way from colonization plans for deporting Negroes "back" to Africa to the "tipping" phenomena shown in modern cities in which white families flee central areas as Negro families enter them.

It is true that the proportion of the population in the South which is Negro is declining as Negroes migrate to other parts of the country. But no one seriously argues that all Negroes will soon, if ever, depart; most of them are just as attached to their homes as are their white counterparts. Nor would the white population necessarily want them to depart. The truth of the matter is that the Negroes are an integral part of American society; they cannot be deported; they cannot be wiped out; they cannot be wished out of existence. They cannot even be gerrymandered out of a community.

Schismatic solutions in the past have usually taken the form of removing the Negro from the community situation. But sometimes they take the form of removing the whites from the situation. In the 1950's and 1960's the so-called Black Muslims were also agitating for a separate Negro state. Sometimes the withdrawal of the white families in an area is not the result of policy or plan; it is not conspiratorial. No one decides it should occur. It is, rather, the result of tacit or implicit coordination.

> When whites and Negroes see that an area will "inevitably" become occupied exclusively by Negroes, the "inevitability" is a feature of convergent expectations. What is most directly perceived as inevitable is not the final result but the *expectation* of it, which, in turn, makes the result inevitable. Everyone expects everyone else to expect everyone else to expect the result; and everyone is powerless to deny it. There is no stable focal point except at the extremes. Nobody can expect the tacit process to stop at 10, 30, or 60 percent; no *particular* percentage commands agreement or provides a rallying point. If tradition suggests 100 percent, tradition could be contradicted only by explicit agreement; if coordination has to be tacit, compromise may be impossible. People are at the mercy of a faulty communication system that makes it easy to "agree" (tacitly) to move but impossible to agree to stay. Quota systems in housing developments, schools, and so forth, can be viewed as efforts to substitute an explicit game with communication and enforcement for a tacit game that has an undesirably extreme "solution."[1]

[1] Thomas C. Schelling, *The Strategy of Conflict* (Cambridge, Mass.: Harvard, 1960), p. 91. See also M. Grodzins, "Metropolitan Segregation," *Scientific American*, 197 (October, 1957), pp. 33-41.

It should be noted that this withdrawal is based on expectations; it has traditional roots. It is not based on inherent hostilities. We shall have more to say about the substitution of quotas for competition presently.

Schismatic solutions may succeed in small patches here and there and even in whole communities occasionally. But, as we noted above, they do not constitute a feasible solution for most communities and certainly not for the country as a whole.

Accommodational Solutions

The term integration has been used by many people to refer to the process of desegregation. Others make a distinction between the two processes; they argue that desegregation merely removes handicaps in the competitive process, so that race in and of itself is no longer a factor but that integration refers to a situation in which Negroes and whites are no longer separated by prejudices, hostilities, false stereotypes, conflicting images, or definitions of the situation. They see desegregation as only a first step; integration may or may not result. Sociologically speaking, however, there has—once he had been introduced—never been a time when the Negro was not integrated into American society. He was, indeed, so integral a part of the southern economy under slavery that efforts to remove him met with belligerent defense, as evidenced by the famous Dred Scott decision. It was the intensity of his integration that made slavery such an issue.

It is, then, sociologically misleading to picture the Negro as ever not integrated into American society. It belongs to him as intimately as to anyone else. There have, of course, been different forms of integration, namely, the slavery form, the segregation form, and—hopefully—the egalitarian form, now in process.

INTEGRATION: SLAVERY MODEL

Slavery made possible a very intimate form of integration. Some Negroes lived in white households as nursemaids and servants; as confidantes of their mistresses they might share the most intimate secrets of the household. That there were both black and white branches of many old southern families was a generally accepted fact.

This close integration was possible only because the institutions of slavery forbade any possibility of competition between the races. Where such competition might occur, as among the poor white families and Negroes, other institutional structures were erected which minimized the hazard, such as assigning certain jobs to whites and others to Negroes on the basis of custom and tradition.

The Civil War destroyed the old integration based on slavery and for a generation afterward the South wrestled with the problem of devising new ways to institutionalize race relations. Disintegration of one accommodation had occurred and a different form of living together had to be worked out. The answer finally arrived at was that of segregation, the so-called "separate but equal" system. A set of roles was defined for Negroes vis-à-vis the whites and the whole apparatus of crescive and enacted institutions was set to work to operate it.[2]

INTEGRATION: THE SEGREGATION MODEL

Segregation is, in a way, a modified form of the getting-rid-of-one-party solution to conflict. It is an attempt to both expel and retain one of the parties. It creates sociological and social-psychological distance while at the same time retaining physical proximity.

Segregation was actually a step in disintegrating the old relationship between the races. From the perspective of the second half of the twentieth century segregation appears to be unfair, exploitative, and wholly contrary to American ideals. It served in its time, however, as a transition from one form of integration—the exploitative form of slavery—to another one—the equalitarian one now in process of being worked out. As it finally crystallized, the segregation model for race relations called for separate facilities for Negroes in schools, transportation, recreational facilities, housing, shopping, churches, hospitals, and, in fact, in all consumer as well as in productive activities.

In its original form, developed in an agrarian society, segregation was a feasible accommodation. The Negroes, many of them ex-slaves, most of them uneducated, all of them defined as inferior, expected very little and, in fact, hardly even knew what there was to want in the way of rights and privileges. They worked in the fields, on the levees, on the roads. Segregation seemed like a stable and enduring setup—despite its allegedly temporary nature[3]—a status-organized society with power in the hands of families who owned the land. As long as the Negro knew his place in this structure, relationships could be cordial, even warm.

But the twentieth century could not be held back. The South wanted to industrialize. It wanted to cease being, in effect, a colonial dependency of the North. It began to compete aggressively for new industries.

Nothing illustrates more dramatically the nature of a community as a social system than the results of this industrialization. Change in one aspect necessitated change in other aspects. Business boomed, payrolls swelled, but things were no longer the same. Unions came. Political elections were less predictable. Little by little the old accommodation between the races was eroded. A larger and larger proportion of the population went to the cities. The old personal relationship between worker and employer gave way to the more formal contractual type of relationship. Concomitantly with the rise of industry there was a transfer of power from the landed

[2] For a detailed description of these roles, see the first edition of this book, pp. 343-347.

[3] Robert B. Johnson, "Changing Status of the Negro in American Life," *Journal of Intergroup Relations,* 1 (Spring, 1960), p. 57.

families to the industrial leaders, often to financiers and even to absentee corporations. As a result, "both the mood and the manner of control . . . [lost] the quality of intimacy and paternalism and . . . [became] rationalistic and impersonal."[4] Another result was greater centralization. The chain store, the branch bank, the regional office of the large corporation looked to New York or Chicago or Philadelphia. Public welfare activities were controlled by state offices and increasingly federal programs of all kinds ramified throughout the local community structure, nibbling away at its autonomy. Industrialization also changed the political complexion of the South; it weakened the one-party system and stimulated the development of the Republican party to reflect the interests of the new classes coming to power.

These changes, among others, redefined the role relationships of rural workers, of urban workers, of middle-class professional workers. Small-farm owners, tenants, and sharecroppers were no longer continuously in debt to the credit-extending merchant or the plantation store; instead they were mortgaged to a finance company for appliances, automobiles, or equipment. In a pinch they could always go to work in a neighboring industrial plant. The city worker could join a labor union. He also bought on credit what he needed for a comfortable level of living; he might even send his children to college.

The old professional classes who had been, in effect, the deferential servants of the old families were now independent of them, with medical and legal practices that freed them from dependence. In brief, "whether farmer, industrial worker, middle-class person, or minority-group member, the new individual in the South is growing independent, mass-minded, and capable of direct social action on a wide range of fronts."[5] He is increasingly American rather than southern in outlook.

The segregation model of race relations which had been a moderately successful fit for the status-organized agricultural economy of the nineteenth century was not nearly so suitable for this new industrialized society. To millions of southerners, Negro and white, however, it seemed the only model; it seemed natural; it seemed right. It was not only "the" southern way of life but, indeed, the only southern way of life. The changes they saw, or which were reported to them, seemed outrageous. The United States was seceding from the South. Despite their anguished protests, however, a new integration was in process of working itself out. It differed from both the slavery and the segregation model in that for the first time it called for the elimination of all competitive handicaps based on race.

INTEGRATION: THE EQUALITARIAN MODEL

The equalitarian model of integration means such things as these: (1) in the economic field, employment, upgrading, and wage policies

[4] Joseph S. Himes, "Changing Social Roles in the New South," *Southwestern Social Science Quarterly*, December, 1956, p. 236.

[5] *Ibid.*, p. 239.

which know no color bar or differential; union membership open without reference to race or color; (2) in the political field, opportunity and encouragement to register, vote, run for office, and serve when elected, regardless of color; (3) in housing, the freedom to occupy a home within one's means, and to feel welcome in the community without reference to color; (4) in educational and cultural services, no separation of pupils and patrons on the basis of color, the employment and promotion of teachers and staff persons on the basis of merit without reference to color, the designing of curriculum and teaching to include the fully rounded experience of the entire human race; (5) in all public facilities, such as restaurants, hotels, trains, and buses, freedom of access by patrons regardless of color; (6) in churches, and religious life, an open welcome to all persons of whatever color, both as ministers and as officials and as worshipers; (7) in "social" life, freedom to form one's own friendships and to carry on one's own social life without pressures of any kind based on color or the lack of it; (8) in home life, including marriage and homemaking, the same freedom of choice to act with a high indifference to color.[6] Many other items could be added to this list. These are enough to illustrate the meaning of the integrationist point of view. The integrationist, believing that caste must be eradicated, wishes to build a society in which color of skin has no more significance than blood type.

The first step that had to be taken in working toward this equalitarian model of integration was to undo the segregation model. Laws, customs, mores, and the whole institutional apparatus which buttressed the segregation model had to be dismantled. So far as the legal support for segregation was concerned a series of 38 Supreme Court decisions and a spate of legislation and executive orders in the first half of the century breached the barriers in transportation,[7] housing,[8] education,[9] recreation,[10] job opportunities,[11] and voting.[12]

But despite all these legal and administrative rulings, discrimination

[6] Buell G. Gallagher, *Color and Conscience* (New York: Harper), p. 174.

[7] In 1946 the Supreme Court declared segregation unconstitutional in interstate travel; in 1956, the Interstate Commerce Commission declared segregation in intrastate trolleys and buses unlawful.

[8] In 1948 the Supreme Court declared that so-called restrictive covenants which bound owners not to sell or rent to Negroes or other ethnic groups were not enforceable in the courts.

[9] In 1950 the Supreme Court declared that Negroes could not be refused admission to institutions of higher learning and in 1954 it declared that segregation in lower schools on the basis of race was unconstitutional.

[10] In 1953 the Supreme Court held that Negroes could not be refused service in restaurants and hotels. In 1959, golf facilities were opened to Negroes.

[11] During World War II a Federal Fair Employment Practices Commission was established by executive order to prevent discrimination in hiring practices. Both President Eisenhower and President Kennedy issued executive orders to prevent discrimination against Negroes by all firms under contract to the government.

[12] In 1944 the Supreme Court declared the so-called white primary unconstitutional. In 1957 a Civil Rights Act was passed which gave the federal government power to take the initiative in communities where Negroes were denied suffrage.

remains. (Fig. 16-1). It is implemented by crescive rather than by enacted norms. But this does not make it less real. As an accommodation it is, however, on the defensive; it is on the way out.

Techniques and Strategies

The techniques and strategies used in Negro-white conflict have varied according to the way the relationships between the races have been institutionalized. The institutional definition of their respective roles and statuses determines what is available to them in the way of threats, promises, commitments, and so forth. The slave could not use the same strategies as the freedman; the Negro who lives in a community that has no fair employment practices law does not have the same armory of strategies as the Negro who lives in a community that does. The institutional framework determines the nature of coalitions, especially which side the government and the courts will be on. By determining expectations, as well as making commitments possible, it determines the availability of strategies.

In general, the techniques and strategies available to Negroes may be subsumed under three categories: (1) direct action, violent or nonviolent; (2) legal force invoked by courts on the basis of legislation; and (3) persuasion, "conversion," or winning over the "hearts" or minds of opponents. The three are not mutually exclusive in the sense that the use of one precludes the use of another. But in any one "play of the game" they may be viewed as alternative choices and any "mixes" as separate strategies. We shall discuss them as though they were separate.

THE STRATEGIC ASPECTS OF DIRECT ACTION

Direct action may be either violent or nonviolent. Because violence is in-and-of-itself a phenomenon of major significance and because it has more than strategic significance, it is discussed in greater detail in Chapter 26. Our concern here is therefore limited to nonviolent direct action.

On the part of the Negro direct action in the past has been an almost intuitive strategy. It was either deterrent or retaliatory in nature. Sabotage and/or inefficiency were common; in terms of strategy they fit the extortion model. The use of the automobile as a strategic threat was also intuitive. It illustrates the use of action rather than words in conflict and is almost a classic model of control by means of the deterrent threat. It has been described as follows:

> Those who can afford to own an automobile have a way of expressing their hostility toward whites in a more or less indirect manner. A furnace worker in Texas said of his own experience, "I drive in a way that makes it look like I'll run over them if they walk in front of me when I have the right. I act like I don't see

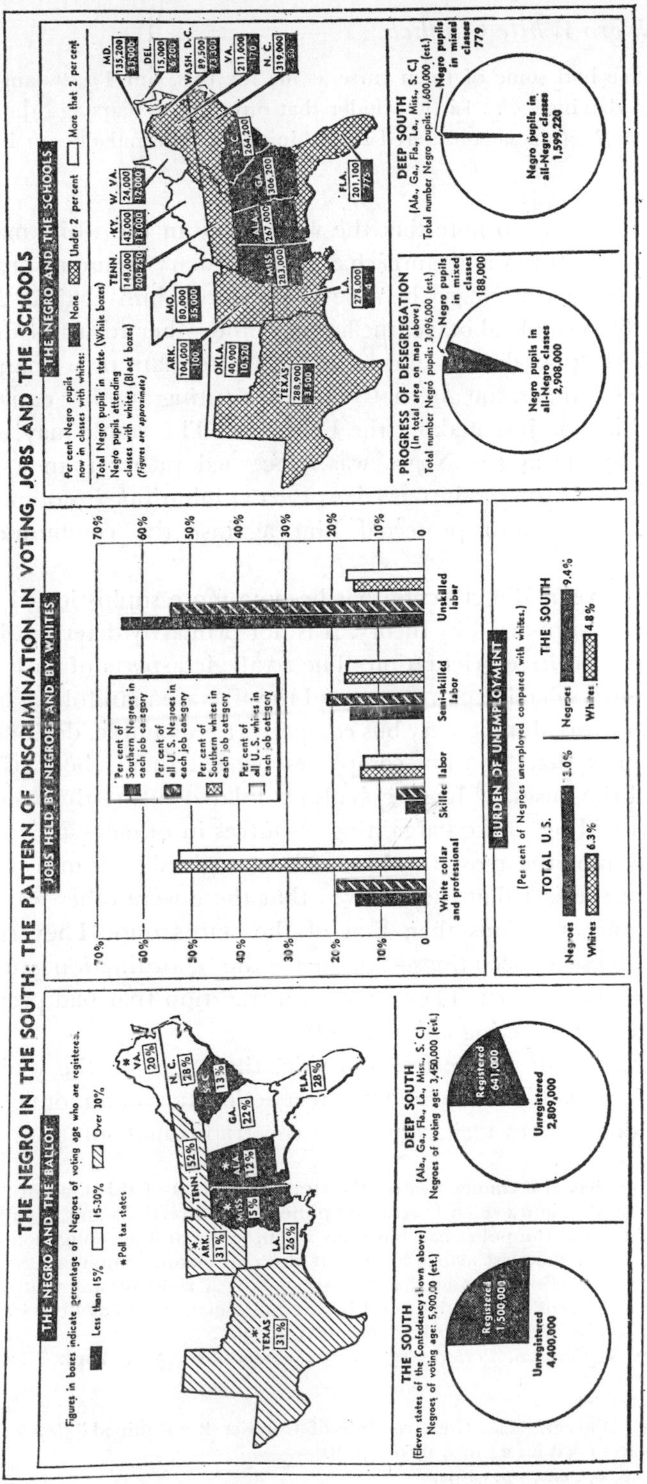

FIG. 16-1. (Reprinted from the *New York Times,* May 28, 1961.)

them.[13] I have had some of them curse at me for this, but I just laugh at them and keep on driving." . . . Little wonder that only a few years ago the possession of a car by a Negro was considered something of a criminal offense in the deep South.[14]

It is interesting to note that the very image in the white man's mind of the Negro as stupid and unreachable by ordinary communication was a strategic asset to the Negro because it protected him against the consequences of his use of sabotage, inefficiency, and other forms of deterrence. He could just "play dumb" and leave the white man, or woman, helpless with frustrated anger, the alternative of substituting another equally dumb Negro for him, or just making the best of it. The result may have been a stand-off so far as the Negro was concerned rather than a net gain, but it protected him against even worse exploitation. Ignorance, or the appearance of it, also protected him against the communication of threats.[15]

In recent years direct action has become more sophisticated, more organized, better supported by theory. It is not primarily deterrent in nature. It has a more positive orientation. The strategic aspects of such tactics as sit-ins, boycotts, selective patronage, and the like are manifold. The boycott by Negroes of the Montgomery bus company, for example, demonstrated to the community that "the bus companies needed them about as badly as they needed the buses."[16] Its success also validated future threats of similar tactics, thus adding to the bargaining resources in other tests.

But perhaps the most fundamental strategic significance of all such tactics lay in the fact that they showed that there were other ways to institutionalize race relations than that of the status quo. They challenged collective values—expectations—and hence the "coordination game" which underlay the old pattern. They attacked a tradition that had prevailed because it had no competing alternative.[17]

The boycott, the sit-in, the freedom ride, the kneel in, the wade in, the picket line, and similar nonviolent direct-action tactics announce that the Negro no longer gives tacit consent to the traditional solution; they also

[13] Schelling has also commented on the strategic aspects of this kind of "blindness." "If the motorist sees, and evidently sees, the policeman's directions and ignores them, he is insubordinate; and the policeman has both an incentive and an obligation to give the man a ticket. If the motorist avoids looking at the policeman, cannot see the directions, and ignores the directions that he does not see, taking a right of way that he does not deserve, he may be considered only stupid by the policeman, who has little incentive and no obligation to give the man a ticket" (*op. cit.*, p. 149).

[14] Charles S. Johnson, *Patterns of Negro Segregation* (New York: Harper, 1943), pp. 303-304.

[15] *Ibid., passim.*

[16] Dan W. Dodson, "The Creative Role of Conflict Reexamined," *Journal of Intergroup Relations*, 1 (Winter, 1959-1960), p. 8.

[17] Schelling, *op. cit.*, pp. 91-92.

destroy the victory-by-default[18] of the status quo by offering the possibility of alternative solutions; everyone can no longer act on the expectation that "everyone" else will behave in a certain way. They arouse awareness of situations that have always been taken for granted. They take old ways out of the realm of inviolability and force the white man to examine their bases.[19] They protect individual violators or nonconformists to old norms from the "pain of conspicuousness" since the pain is shared by many and thus greatly diluted.

Equally important is the fact that participation in well-organized and responsibly led direct action has an exhilarating effect on those involved. After the Montgomery bus boycott, for example, a profound change was reported in the self-feeling of the Negroes:

> There was a new dignity among the Negroes. You could sense it before you had been in the community an hour. They walked a little straighter, and carried themselves with more self-assurance. They knew a little better their stake in citizenship, for they had been confronted with paying for their freedom.[20]

The new self-image which the Negro is little by little developing itself has enormous strategic significance. In the past when insults, humiliation, jeers, rejection, and degradation had made pride impossible and self-hatred common, treatment as inferiors had made Negroes accept collective values and hence themselves as inferiors. Even when, as among professional people, there was a façade of equality, the Negro knew his place; he was deferential; he kowtowed to the white man. When both Negroes and whites shared this common image, it was impossible for the Negro to look the white man straight in the eye; his eye faltered because he knew that the white man knew that he knew that he expected to be treated as an inferior. Collective values were enormously coercive. But young Negroes today do not share those collective values and that common image; they cannot be intimidated because the white man's weapon—knowledge that the Negro knew he expected to be treated as an inferior—has been blunted. It comes as a shock to some white persons that young Negroes do not share their expectancies and hence cannot be coerced by collective values. One white southerner, returning after many years to the community of his birth,

[18] The purely traditional nature of a specific "solution" is illustrated by the very matter-of-fact acceptance of bus desegregation in Montgomery, once it had been achieved. "To an outsider, it would be hard to imagine that there had been so much controversy over a situation which, when changed, was accepted with so little difficulty" (Dodson, *loc. cit*).

[19] Direct action is sometimes confused with conflict itself. This is a fallacy. The people who select direct action as a tactic do not create the conflict; they only prosecute it. They raise the issues; they demand the confrontation; they inaugurate new accommodations; they precipitate crises. But the conflict was there long before they undertook direct action. The fallacy of confounding conflict with particular strategies or tactics is illustrated in a paper by Dodson, *op. cit.*, pp. 5-12.

[20] Dodson, *op. cit.*, p. 8.

commented on this fact. "They now look you straight in the eye" was his surprised reaction.

THE STRATEGIC ASPECTS OF LEGISLATION AND LEGAL FORCE

It is sometimes argued that race relations cannot be changed by law; only by changes in the hearts of people. In reply, it is argued that it is true that attitudes cannot be legislated; but, it is insisted, behavior can. One cannot forbid a man to hate another; but one can forbid him to act in a discriminatory manner. It is argued, further, that legislation itself has an educational effect. In addition it demonstrates a commitment. To the argument sometimes made that conditions in the South are no worse actually than in the North since even without legislated segregation there is, nevertheless, segregation by custom, it is pointed out by Negroes that it does make a difference to know that in the North the government is on their side, that they have its power behind their efforts to change conditions.

What the law does, in terms of strategy, is twofold: it creates a coalition of the government with the Negro and in the process it delegates to the government agency the enforcement of threats;[21] but even more important it gives the minority group bargaining capital. Contrariwise it diminishes bargaining capital for the whites. The payoff, for example, for carrying out massive retaliation, for closing schools, is rendered so costly for whites as well as for Negroes, that there is enormous incentive not to have to do it. Some things come to be seen as worse than desegregation or, conversely, desegregation comes to be seen as the lesser of two evils. Or, short of that, vast improvement in segregated schools at costs that would once have seemed prohibitive seems cheap at any price.

CHANGING HEARTS AND MINDS: "CONVERSION" AND PERSUASION

As institutionalized by leaders such as Martin Luther King, Jr., nonviolent direct action performs a coalescing function. It is based on Christian ideology and seeks to win the "hearts" of opponents by love. By reassuring them that direct action is based not on hatred, hostility, or resentment, that it is not retaliatory or punitive, that it does not seek to destroy, King seeks to "convert" them to a new point of view, a new image, a new definition of the situation. This is not a zero-sum game, he says in effect. We do not aim to destroy or even to hurt you. We can all gain.

[21] Even with the government on their side, Negroes often hesitate to invoke its support. "A fact often overlooked in the complex business of school desegregation is the reluctance of most Negroes to press for it. It takes great courage to become a plaintiff in a desegregation case. The prospect of cross-examination in court is frightening and Negro parents are understandably reluctant to expose their children to embarrassment and threats of violence. Of those who do go to court, some withdraw before the case goes to trial and others hesitate to appeal if the lower court rules against them. Even if there is no threat of violence the plaintiff often fears he may lose his job or face other economic reprisals if he presses his case" (G. W. Foster, Jr., "1960: Turning Point for Desegregation?" *Saturday Review*, Dec. 17, 1960, p. 52).

Much of the conflict between those hostile to desegregation and those who are for it takes the form of debate and seeks to persuade or convince. We are talking now of sincere and high-minded people, people even of good will, people who are convinced of the evidence they bring to bear in the controversy. We are not talking of hate-mongers, the ignorant, the "certain element," but rather of sober and responsible leaders.

Among the most emotion-fraught issues in this great debate is that of racial inferiority. Insistence on white supremacy is based on a belief in white superiority.

The question of race superiority or inferiority is by no means the simple matter which disinterested science makes it appear to be. Anthropologically and psychologically it is not demonstrable that Negroes are racially inferior to whites. The quality of the Negro's personality is intimately associated with the kind of community he lives in. But having recognized these irrefutable scientific facts we are, nevertheless, confronted with the equally irrefutable fact that statistically—*not,* we emphasize, racially or innately—Negroes are inferior. Because of their history, their community backgrounds, their culturally underprivileged status, they average lower on IQ tests; they show very high tuberculosis and venereal disease rates; their longevity is lower than that of whites; they suffer from deficiency diseases more often; they suffer more emotional traumata. They must split their personalities, developing one for the white world and one for their own. Their moral standards are less rigorous than those of whites, except in the case of middle- and upper-class Negroes, whose moral standards are, if anything, higher.

When, therefore, the segregationist expresses his belief in Negro inferiority and wishes to regulate race relations on the basis of this conviction, he has in mind a type which is statistically very important. To white citizens in a community in which more than half of the population is made up of ignorant, perhaps resentful or sullen, benighted Negroes, it does little good to preach the scientific facts about race. These whites are, as the saying goes, confronted with a fact, not a theory.

Older people are impervious to evidence, but there is reason to believe that little by little scientific findings about race are beginning to make their imprint on the minds of younger southerners. Young people educated in the better universities of the South show surprisingly liberal attitudes toward the Negro. For collective attitudes do change if not as a result of debate at least as a result of education.

A second great issue in the debate on race conflict is derivative. It takes the form of states' rights. The argument states that the relations of the races is a matter for the state to decide, especially in connection with education. In some cases this is a genuine concern lest the federal government take over too many local matters. In other cases, however, the use of this issue is an excellent example of community dissociation. Its proponents do not see the inconsistency of their upholding states' rights on constitutional grounds at the same time denying constitutional rights to Negroes. They argue, in effect, that the state has the right to violate Negro constitutional rights, and that the federal government cannot protect Negroes against such violation by the state.

The strategic aspects of debate on this issue are of exceptional interest. Ever since the publication in 1947 of *The American Dilemma* by the Swedish observer Gunnar Myrdal, it has been common to point out the conflict between the American ideal and the actual practices of race relations in this country. The ideal of equality of opportunity has been contrasted with the practice of exploitative control; and so on. It has seemed that the ideals have been so completely ignored as to be functionless.

In the great moral debate between Negroes and discriminatory whites, Negroes have not hesitated to use this powerful paradox. Negro leaders have kept before the public the conflict between ideals and practices. They have used literally scores of ways of doing this; picketing, for example, and letters to the editor reminding white people that "the privileges to go to any university or theater, qualify for any job and join any union, to eat at any place, stop at any hotel, are privileges that belong to the former enemies of democracy," but not to Negroes.[22]

But the true strategic significance of ideals in this aspect of the conflict lies in the commitments they imply for serious, responsible people. No more than the most benighted rabble-rousing member of a white citizens' council did such people want desegregation. If it had been possible—as it had been for decades—to avoid a confrontation between ideals and practices, they would almost certainly have continued to do so. But where such a confrontation was inevitable and the alternatives were open aligning with the rabble-rousers and advocates of violence to uphold old practices on one side and acceptance of at least token integration on the other, the compelling force of ideals came into play. They could not join a coalition with the white citizens' councils. In a showdown, they were compelled to behave according to accepted ideals or suffer intolerable loss of face.

Assimilation

It will be noted that King's program is one for winning over the hearts of the whites; it is not aimed at racial amalgamation. For racial amalgamation as a policy or as a goal or as a solution to conflict has little enthusiastic support from either Negroes or whites. Although it is waved as a red rag before the eyes of those who urge race equality—with the fighting words, "Would you want your daughter to marry a nigger?"—it is not advocated as a policy by any serious student of the subject at the present time.

Still, there is perhaps no issue more emotional than this one of racial

[22] *St. Louis Post-Dispatch,* Dec. 23, 1946.

intermixture. To be sure, for many decades there was no concern at all if white men had Negro children. The right of white men to have access to Negro women was accepted as a matter of course. But there is nothing that whips up uncontrollable rage in white southerners more than the idea of a Negro having access to white women. And the great fear of many segregationists is that unless racial barriers are meticulously enforced, the natural attraction between the races will lead to a race of mongrels. Racial intermarriage will be the natural corollary of free contacts between the races. The recorded data are not copious but they do not support this fear.

In 1939 only eight out of every 10,000 marriages was interracial. Whether the husband or the wife was white varied from one place to another; in some places it was more likely to be the groom, in other places, the bride. Overall, the proportion in which the man was the white partner was 51 percent (583 cases). But in some cities and states the reverse was true. This geographic variation was due largely to the relative infrequency of mixed marriages, so that a few cases can change the picture drastically. There is no clear-cut tendency either way.[23]

A more recent study based on Detroit over a period of 60 years found a decrease from a rate of 31.6 per 10,000 Negroes eligible to marry in 1900 to 2.2 in 1956; the authors examined other data and concluded that the rate of intermarriage was decreasing everywhere.[24] Evidence of this nature is not, of course, convincing to fearful segregationists.

Despite the decline in interracial intermarriage it would be irresponsible to slough off the possibilities that it may occur. It is interesting that a church group should be among the first openly to face and discuss this problem and its implications. The February, 1960, issue of a church publication, *Social Progress,* was devoted to a symposium on racial intermarriage.[25] The editors asked 20 persons—both Negro and white—to reply to an imaginary letter that asked:

> Isn't it true that if this movement toward desegregation continues unabated in our country there will be a large number of mixed marriages at best and illegitimate interracial liaisons at worst? Be honest now, would you want your daughter to marry a Negro (or a white man, as the case may be)?

The respondents included pastors, theologians from both South and North, housewives, and professional workers in the United Presbyterian Church. In general the replies stated that the choice of a mate was highly personal, that if the daughter found a congenial mate who happened also to be Negro they would point out all the hazards to such a marriage, but they

[23] Paul H. Jacobson, *American Marriage and Divorce* (New York: Holt, Rinehart and Winston, 1959), pp. 62-63.

[24] Albert J. Mayer and Sue M. Smock, in a study reported at the 1960 meetings of the Population Association of America.

[25] This is a publication of the Department of Social Education and Action of the Board of Christian Education of The United Presbyterian Church in the United States of America.

would make no effort to stop it. The men from the South—Tennessee and Virginia—placed more emphasis on the current social difficulties, but they did not oppose the idea for the future when or if customs had changed. All felt that if or when such a marriage did occur, it should be helped to succeed rather than hindered by the behavior of others. The general consensus was that although they did not feel intermarriage should be either encouraged or discouraged as a matter of principle, it should be entered into only with great preparation and that it should have the support of the family and the church. There is no reason to suppose, it should be added, that the offspring of such unions will be inferior.

A Re-examination of the Basic Issue

The basic issue in inter-racial relationships, it was pointed out, is equality of competitive conditions. We now know enough about the processes involved that some people are beginning to wonder. It sometimes happens that when the conditions of competition are open and equal, segregation results. In housing, for example, the phenomena of tipping referred to above result in competitive success for the Negro but in a segregated situation. The concept of "benign" quotas is developing as a solution. Quotas of any kind violate the principle of competition. Those who accept them argue that if a choice has to be made between free competition and desegregation the latter is more important. Thus one real estate developer specifies that only a certain proportion of all the new houses in his projects may be sold to Negroes, the proportion varying according to the ratio in the community. It has been argued that a similar principle should be applied even to public schools on the theory that it is not good for either race when Negroes predominate.

With respect to job opportunities it is now felt by some that a conscious and deliberate effort should be made to recruit Negroes for higher-level jobs, jobs for which they are prevented by tradition from aspiring.

In brief, the principle of free competition, which has been a guide-line in much of our thinking with respect to race relations, is now coming under re-examination. When there must be a choice between it and desegregation, there are some who argue that desegregation is the more important value.[26]

[26] With respect to residential desegregation some Negro leaders are opposed to it on the ground that diffusing Negroes over a wider area would water down their political power which often rests on their concentration in segregated areas.

17

Denominational Conflict

Historical Setting

Two generations ago many American communities, especially those on the eastern seaboard, were in the throes of attempting to absorb European immigrants at the rate, in some years, of about a million a year. The problems engendered by this process were enormous. There were problems of housing, problems of furnishing schools, of teaching the newcomers the American language. There were problems of protecting them against industrial exploitation. There were problems of protecting American political institutions from the unscrupulous exploitation by politicians of blocs of foreign-born voters.

With the damming up of the flood of immigration in the 1920's, a breathing spell was granted. With no new influx to face each year, communities began to take stock of just what the situation was. Now the emphasis was no longer on immigration problems as such. The problems were those of minority groups in general. Thus a generation ago the attention of students of community life turned to the problems that arose not from "masses"[1] of unassimilated immigrants but from the presence in the community of widely differing cultural groups.

At the present time the issues have fallen into sharper focus. Second- and third-generation Americans speak the American language, dress like everyone else, eat the same foods, get the same protection of the same unions. The problems that beset the community at the present time are not, therefore, likely to focus on the more superficial differences since, with the exception of Mexican-Americans and Puerto Ricans, these superficial differences have all but disappeared.

The residual differences that remain, however, are fundamental; they are closely associated with religious differences. After 1880 the complexion of immigration changed. Most now came from the south and the east of Europe and they were predominantly Catholic, as were the more than a million Mexicans. In addition there were some four million Jews. The differences in value and orientation springing from differences in religion

[1] They never had been "masses"; they only looked that way. Actually they were members of structured groups from the beginning.

were far too profound to suffer the erosion that differences in language, dress, style of living, and other more superficial differences underwent.

The Concept of "Majority Group"

The concept of minority group implies the existence of its complement, the majority group. There have been some who have denied that the majority group in American communities has a distinctive culture. Because so many foreign groups have contributed to our culture, it is sometimes argued, we have a mosaic or conglomerate of many cultures rather than a distinctively native culture. As a matter of fact, whether one likes it or not, the American culture is a distinctive entity. It was created originally by English-speaking men and women who brought their own legal, religious, and political patterns with them; and it has been molded by a distinctive set of historical forces. It is true that there were Dutch, French, Jews, and Catholics among the early colonists. But the culture which finally prevailed was neither Dutch, French, Jewish, nor Catholic. Many groups have contributed to the American culture, but it remains essentially a modification of an Anglo-Saxon culture. That is, it retains the common law, the jury system, traditional rights guaranteed by great English documents and institutions from Magna Charta down, a parliamentary form of government, and a traditional veneration for—and for a long time a colonial attitude toward—the literature of England. On this base, the American frontier operated to produce a characteristic American culture.

To say this is in no way to imply that it is superior to other cultures. It is conceivable that the Dutch, the French, or the Spanish could have set the basic pattern for American institutions (as, indeed, the Spanish did in the other Americas) . But it is simply a matter of fact and record that here they did not. Great individuals of many cultural backgrounds, Irish, Jewish, German, Polish, French, Italian have contributed to the American culture. But they did not change the basic pattern of our institutions. The contributions were assimilated, but they did not transform the American culture into an Irish, Jewish, Polish, French, or Italian culture. There are pockets in which foreign cultures have been predominant, into which the American culture came as an invader—Louisiana and the Spanish Southwest, for example. But even here the invading American culture finally took over.

After more than a century and a half of British colonial status, the United States fixed and set its basic pattern of culture, so to speak, in the Constitution. We have already commented on the essential nature of the values of American culture, the insistent emphasis on freedom and equality.

Three Historical Tests of American Values

The values, ideals, and beliefs of the "majority group" have been subjected to innumerable tests, strains, stresses, tensions, and assaults during the last century and a half. The first major test was the slavery issue. We have already seen the results of that test.

A second test began in the 1840's when the eastern seaboard cities were in process of being swamped by impoverished immigrants from Ireland. This was an extraordinarily severe test, for it introduced differences which challenged one of the very fundamentals of the recently formulated American tenet—religious liberty. The new principles thus put to test showed strain and tension, but they survived. In spite of a series of "American" political parties demanding such laws as one requiring twenty years' residence before naturalization, and opposing candidates for public office if they owed allegiance "to any foreign prince or potentate," the principles stood firm. There were no changes in the fundamental law of the land. The hated immigrants—hated because they were considered to be ignorant and superstitious, and especially because they were competitors for jobs—were not ejected; they were not persecuted politically; they were not deprived of their rights. Indeed, within a generation they were well on their way to control of the political machinery of the communities where they were concentrated. Historically we have been so impressed by the revulsion of feeling against the Irish immigrants that we have overlooked the much more impressive fact that in spite of this revulsion, in spite of the individual, personal, and even organized reaction against the foreigners, the basic institutions of freedom and equality stood fast. When the immigrants and their children had taken over many of the American cultural patterns, they found their place in the social structure without legal or political barriers.

In the last quarter of the nineteenth century the third test of American institutions proved increasingly severe. The Irish test had been more or less localized—primarily in Massachusetts, specifically perhaps in Boston and a few other northern seaboard towns. Probably American institutions had been able to pass this test for that very reason—the great mass of Americans, especially those in the West, were untouched. After about 1880, the flow of immigrants with conflicting culture patterns began to enlarge to overwhelming dimensions, as noted above.

The problems of cultural assimilation became peculiarly complex in part because of the nature of American ideals and in part because of the nature of immigration and the minority groups themselves. During World War I the so-called "hyphenated Americans" caused a good deal of concern. It began to be clear that assimilation, which had been taken for granted, had not, as a matter of fact, really occurred. Instead of a melting pot, the war revealed numerous separate cultural groups, trying, not always successfully, to live together.

A hastily devised program of Americanization was inaugurated, in which students trained in social work or cultural anthropology taught English to foreigners. The result was not very successful. Assimilation was found to be a far more difficult problem than had been anticipated. The difficulty lay in the complexity of the process itself. The assumption of superiority in the whole concept of "Americanizing" foreigners rankled with some. Some even argued that we had no right to "Americanize" immigrants; that the American culture was really a fusion of many cultures rather than a distinct culture itself. This view, of course, presupposed no incompatibility in the cultures; it held that differences were all integrative, or at least not too divisive, rather than in conflict.

The minority groups themselves were ambivalent in their attitude toward the majority, or native, culture. On the one hand, they loved it because it gave them opportunities to live a free kind of life. The first generation often had to pay the price of strangeness and newness in the form of poverty and exploitation. But there were no legal or political barriers to rising on the social ladder. Their children and grandchildren did rise.[2] These opportunities they loved. But they also resented the people who represented this native culture. These, except for individuals such as Jane Addams and Graham Taylor and other devoted social workers, teachers, and reformers who identified themselves with the immigrant and fought his battles, seemed cold, distant, aloof, condescending, self-consciously superior. There were great class barriers.

As in the second test, so in this third test, the native group, in spite of its frequently snobbish treatment of the foreigners did, nevertheless, cling to the fundamental ideals of freedom and equality. Members of the majority group might take advantage of the foreigner's inexperience and ignorance to exploit him industrially, but it was never possible legally to deprive him of the suffrage or to deny him free education or to prevent him from rising politically or even socially. In other words, whatever their personal reaction might be to foreigners, institutionally the native group remained loyal to the principles of American community life.

The Contemporary Test

In the second half of the twentieth century the test of American values takes on a somewhat different aspect. The erosion of the status differentials between the majority and the several minority groups redresses the balance of power. The majority group can no longer take its predominance for granted. As seen through Catholic eyes, the situation is something like this:

> The Protestant . . . has seen the ancient strongholds in New England and the Middle Atlantic States lost to him. Boston, Providence, New Haven, New York, Philadelphia, and Pittsburgh today have anything but a Protestant color. The rural areas are still in large part Protestant but the country as a whole is every day becoming more urban, and it is in the cities that the Catholics have their strength. This has produced a change and this change has frightened the Protestant.

[2] Samuel Lubell has analyzed the political implications of this ascent in his illuminating book, *The Future of American Politics* (New York: Harper, 1952).

> The change was like the experience of an adult who is accustomed to ruling a group of children. He takes it for granted that he will command and that the children will obey. But the children grow up and the adult with a shock realizes that his once obedient charges are no longer children and they will not obey. In fact he does not even dare to command. He must now come to terms with people whom he still considers his inferiors, and there is resentment and a feeling that things are not right. What is more, the situation now demands that he adjust to changes which he can only deplore. He can fight a rear-guard action but he knows that in the long run this is meaningless. He can cheerfully make the best of it, but this is no easy task. . . . The coming of age of the American Catholic community does not mean that the Catholics are "taking over." But their maturity does mean that the Protestants are no longer in charge. To the Protestant who was in charge for over a century, this new situation is itself distressing.[3]

The contemporary test of American values is no longer a test only of the majority group; it is as much a test of American Catholic values. "Freedom and equality" are extremely difficult to define in the field of religion. Is it possible for American values to assimilate Catholic values, or, rather, perhaps, the reverse? This is the form which the test takes today.

Conflict within Protestantism

What, specifically, are some of the differences which inhere in groups with differing church affiliations? Among Protestant churches in America there were, in colonial times, two distinct wings, left and right. Luther, Zwingli, Calvin, and Cranmer were conservative; their followers were upper-middle-class people; they founded state churches with official confessions of faith and elaborate forms of ecclesiastical polity.[4] The union of church and state was accepted as a matter of course. This pattern was taken over by the colonists in all the colonies except Rhode Island and the three Quaker colonies—New Jersey, Pennsylvania, and Delaware.

The other wing in the Protestant tradition was quite different. It appealed to lower-class people, rejected man-made creeds, and considered the Bible to be the sole authority on faith and practice. But, most important, the followers of this tradition insisted on freedom of conscience, fought all official church-state relationships, held that religion was essentially a personal matter, and demanded that the state have no control at all over ecclesiastical affairs. Between 1660 and the American Revolution, these two points of view were in conflict in American communities. By the time the Constitution was written the second had triumphed completely.

This process was accelerated by (1) the immigration of dissenting groups from Europe in the seventeenth and eighteenth centuries which

[3] Gustave Weigel, S.J., in *An American Dialogue* (New York: Doubleday, 1960), pp. 164-165.

[4] This discussion follows William Warren Sweet, "The Protestant Churches," *Annals Amer. Acad. Pol. & Soc. Sci.*, 256 (March, 1948), pp. 43 ff.

joined and hence strengthened the second group; (2) the great revival movement of the eighteenth century, with its emphasis on inner experience and equality of all men in the sight of God, which won over the frontier population; (3) the influence of pioneering conditions which emphasized equalitarianism rather than ecclesiastical authoritarianism; and, finally, (4) the influence of John Locke's theory that religion is a personal matter, that the church is a voluntary society, and that church and state should be completely separated, which added to the weight of the left wing's influence.

The victory of this point of view culminated in the guarantees of religious freedom finally incorporated into the new state constitutions and also into the national Constitution. The separation of church and state was exalted as a principle as well as an expedient practice.

The process whereby the left wing of Protestantism, with its essentially individualistic emphasis, gradually came to prevail has been called the Americanization of Christianity.[5] American Christianity came thereby to reflect the conditions of American community life. It emphasized in church organization the same principles as those political doctrines emphasized in governmental organization. They were mirror images of one another. "The left-wing emphasis on religion as a way of life rather than the emphasis on creed became and remains the common man's pattern of Christianity in America."[6]

Protestantism as it has developed along these lines in the United States has been especially prone to conflict. The issues have tended to be schismatic in nature—differences in fundamental doctrine and creed, or in ecclesiastical organization, or in forms of worship. Or varying degrees of orthodoxy may have been involved. The issue may have been quite nonreligious or nonecclesiastical. The Civil War, for example, split up the great denominations on the issue of slavery and it has taken years to reweave them into a single fabric. In many of the great denominational organizations even today there are cleavages between the fundamentalists and the modernists, the orthodox and the liberal. Here the issues are matters of basic orientation. In local churches, however, sometimes there is no issue at all but simply personality clashes, "fights," rather than either games or debates. One study of closed churches in Pennsylvania, for example, found that 12.7 percent had been closed because of personal conflict within the congregation.[7]

A characteristic pattern of religious behavior in American community life has been sectarian schisms in which dissident groups have split off from major groups with which they disagreed. Often the seceding group or sect has opposed the worldliness of the parent body or its lack of warmth. In order to prevent conflict with a world with which they disagree so strongly

[5] William Warren Sweet, *op. cit.*, p. 44.
[6] *Ibid.*
[7] Theodore Schiefele, MA thesis, The University State University, 1948.

some religious sects have—with varying degrees of success—created their own isolated community life, as, for example, the Mormons, the Mennonites, the Amish, the Dunkers, the House of David, and the Positivists.

But inevitably the outer world encroaches upon the isolation of such sects and the conflict inherent in their differences becomes open and patent. The younger members bring home new ideas from school; the older generation strives vainly to counteract the attractions of the outer world. Sometimes the conflict may be fought out in the courts, as in the instance of a farmer who was "mitred" or ostracized because he bought an automobile, forbidden by his sect. He took his case to the courts and the courts decided in his favor. The conflict between the Mormon practice of polygamy and the laws of the secular community were also fought out in the political arena. The fight of the isolated religious community against the outer world seems ultimately to be doomed to failure, especially in the face of the increasing ease of communication characteristic of life in American communities today.

Even within homogeneous denominations conflicts arise. Each denomination sets up its own requirements for membership. This may lead to conflicts which to the outsider have little meaning.

As a result of the kinds of schismatic conflict we have been describing there are, in the opinion of some students of the subject, too many struggling little churches in many communities competing among themselves, hugging their differences, weakening rather than strengthening their programs. Vested interests rather than principle often prevent mergers or church unions among compatible denominations. There is, however, a strong movement among the larger Protestant denominations toward an ultimate accommodation at the assimilation level, that is, union.

There are conflicts not only among and within the several Protestant denominations, sects, and churches but also between churchgoers and nonchurchgoers dealing with such issues as drinking, dancing, card playing—even smoking. These are of declining significance in most communities.

Conflict within Catholicism[8]

A process similar to what we have called the Americanization of Christianity in Protestantism took place in the Catholic church as well. As a result the American Catholic church today is quite a different organization, regulated by a quite different institutional pattern, than, say, the Spanish Catholic church or, for that matter, the French Catholic church or the Polish or even the Irish. For although the papal hierarchy has won the battles, the American laity has won the campaign.

In the absence of a powerful hierarchy some local Catholic congrega-

[8] For an illuminating discussion of some of the conflicts which rage within the Catholic church throughout the world, see Lord Acton's analysis of the Vatican Council which pronounced the pope infallible, in his *Essays on Freedom and Power,* edited by Gertrude Himmelfarb (Boston: Beacon Press, 1948), pp. 298-356.

tions at the beginning of the nineteenth century claimed control of their property and the right to elect their pastors and even their bishops. This decentralizing trend culminated in the 1820's in "the most serious crisis in the whole history of American Catholicism, an attempt to set up an Independent Catholic church of America, free of all reference to Rome."[9] This crisis was weathered, but it was followed by a period of intermittent schism, during which eloquent and persuasive priests sometimes acquired large personal followings, ran afoul of the bishop's authority, and even kicked over the traces. This kind of reaction would seem to be a natural congregational accommodation of any religious body, given the individualistic conditions of life in America. But although the laity lost this battle, they have won many since that time, not with respect to formal control of property but with respect to informal control over their leaders. Congregations find ways of making it known to bishops when a local priest is a *persona non grata* and there are not many bishops who wilfully ignore this "feedback," especially in well-educated congregations.

In teaching as well as in organization an "Americanizing" accommodation tended to occur. One American bishop spoke against the promulgation of the doctrine of papal infallibility and one even voted against it. High-ranking officials in America insisted on having as bishops men who understood and sympathized with the American temper and they spoke favorably of the prevailing religious freedom in America. The trend toward a liberal point of view was officially stopped by an apostolic letter from Pope Leo XIII in 1899 in which he warned the faithful against certain beliefs which have, since that time, come to be known as the heresy of Americanism. "Americanism" refers, it is important to emphasize, not to American political principles or institutions, but to an attitude of mind willing to modify Catholic teachings in order to win converts. Since that time the American hierarchy has hewn close to the official papal line. Flexibility and adaptability have, nevertheless, gone hand in hand with doctrinal firmness. And in general political points of view, the distance traversed has been great. This will become clearer when we discuss four different kinds of conflict within Catholicism in America, namely: (1) conflicts in ideologies within the church, (2) conflicting political and social points of view among members of the hierarchy, (3) ethnic cleavages, and (4) conflicts between laity and hierarchy.

IDEOLOGICAL CONFLICT WITHIN THE CHURCH: RELATIONS OF CHURCH AND STATE

The ideological conflicts within the Catholic church are deeper than those which disturb Protestantism. For the universal Roman Catholic Church must find formulas for community life which will be equally acceptable to such diverse countries as the United States, Italy, Hungary,

[9] Willard L. Sperry, *Religion in America* (New York: Macmillan, 1946), p. 207.

Argentina, Germany, Spain, and Paraguay. Its principles must be both American and universal: a difficult order.

The dilemma is especially difficult in the area of church-state relationships. The church feels it must formulate its principles on this issue in such a way as to justify a demand for a privileged position for itself where this is possible, as in Spain or Argentina, yet at the same time so as not to condemn the practice of equal tolerance of all religions in such countries as the United States, where it is still a minority organization.

The term "separation of church and state" means different things in different contexts. The converse term, "union of church and state" may refer to complete subjection of temporal affairs to church control, as in the Middle Ages; it may mean an equilibrium in which each keeps within its own orbit but in case of conflict of jurisdiction the church takes precedence; it may mean such an equilibrium in which the church has a privileged position although other religions are permitted; or it may mean only tax support for church activities. Separation of church and state may mean the forbidding of Bible reading in public schools or forbidding the use of tax monies for church activities. The precise line separating church and state is not easy to draw.

For our purposes at this point the major concern is the ideological position with respect to religious tolerance. The Catholic church has a particularly difficult adjustment to make in America on this issue, for it professes loyalty to two conflicting ideologies, one American and one traditional Catholic. The fundamental distinguishing characteristic of American Christianity has been its insistence on the separation of church and state and this principle remains one of the most distinctive traits of American culture as far as organized religion is concerned. In the past the Catholic ideal was a situation in which the Catholic church had a privileged position, but in which as a concession to circumstances, where such a condition was impossible, toleration of all religious faiths (with some reservations), would be acceptable as a substitute.

Specifically the Catholic position has been, as the right wing of Protestantism once agreed, that:

> . . . a commonwealth that is to endure can be erected only on a theistic basis . . . a well-ordered commonwealth can no more recognize the maxim of unlimited and unbridled religious freedom than it can adopt the suicidal principle of irreligion. . . . Christian public law erects a third barrier to complete religious freedom in forbidding that the principle of the separation of Church and State be raised to the true ideal of the State and regarded as fundamentally the best form of the State.[10]

Separation of church and state was, according to this position, only the lesser of two evils; that is, it was not a matter of principle but only an expedient, and better than a warring union. The analogy was used that if

[10] *Ibid.*

husband and wife could not live together amicably a separation was legitimate; but this separation was not to be considered the normal condition. The situation in the United States, though successful, was not ideal. Tolerance of non-Catholic faiths was justified ethically only when it avoided evil or achieved some good. But when circumstances made it no longer necessary, it should be replaced with a more normal condition.

This accommodation of the conflict has not satisfied all Catholics (and it has frightened most Protestants). There has, therefore, been in process a continuing re-examination of the relationship between church and state by Catholic scholars, European as well as American.[11] As a result a new position has been emerging which (1) makes religious tolerance not a mere matter of expedience, to be discarded as soon as possible, but a matter of positive principle; (2) distinguishes between error, without rights, and persons in error, who do have rights; and (3) "explicitly repudiates intolerance, since the latter is a usurping by men of a judgment which can properly be made only by God."[12] The new scholars wish to distinguish between what is essential to Catholicism and practices which are not, including the Inquisition. And their position "stresses that Roman Catholic statements which appear to contradict the principle of religious liberty must be judged and interpreted in the light of their historical context, and not treated in isolation from the specific situation to which they were speaking."[13]

For the most part ideological conflict among scholars within the Catholic church takes the form of debate, each side attempting to persuade the other of its correctness. But it is, of course, possible for it to take other forms. Books may be censored or forbidden publication by withholding the imprimatur or withdrawing them from circulation. If the offending position continues to be promulgated, the author may be disciplined and in extreme cases, excommunicated.

CONFLICTING POLICIES AMONG MEMBERS OF THE HIERARCHY

Members of the hierarchy differ greatly in political and social as well as in ideological, if not in doctrinal, matters. A great many priests, for example, believe strongly in an authoritarian and even a fascistic state, whereas others are strong supporters of political democracy and a few have even been founders or promoters of crackpot reform schemes. Leaders may be more different from one another than each is from a non-Catholic of the same ethnic group and class. In one community the bishop may cooperate wholeheartedly with non-Catholic denominations; in another, he may forbid such cooperation.

[11] The views of some of the participants in this process—Father John Courtney Murray, S.J., Father Léonard, Father Max Pribilla, S.J., and Professor Étienne Gilson—are summarized by Robert McAfee Brown in *An American Dialogue* (New York: Doubleday, 1960), pp. 64-73.

[12] *Ibid.*, p. 73.

[13] *Ibid.*, p. 74.

So long as the priest remains loyal to the church the form of any conflict he engages in is likely to take the mixed-motive form, for he will have more in common with his adversaries than in conflict with them.

ETHNIC CLEAVAGES

In many communities there has also been conflict among the several ethnic groups in the church. In some instances the conflict reached the point of secession, as when, in 1897, a Polish-Catholic group in Scranton, Pennsylvania, withdrew and, in 1904, established the Polish National Catholic Church. The cultural differences were often more powerful than the religious similarities. In the Southwest even today the impression is that there are two Catholic churches operating, one closer to the Mexican pattern than to that of the United States.[14]

For a long time the hierarchy in the United States was dominated by the Irish and there was some feeling of resentment about this on the part of other ethnic groups. It was felt that they had imposed an Irish rather than a strictly Catholic position on the church and the relative absence of sophisticated scholarship, it was alleged, reflected this Irish influence. Whatever truth there may have been to this complaint, in recent years German, Italian, and Polish leadership has come to share power with the Irish leadership and ethnic differences become of relatively minor significance.

CONFLICT BETWEEN LAITY AND HIERARCHY

As irreconcilable in principle as are separation or union of church and state are the American emphasis on individualism and the emphasis by the hierarchy on authority. This conflict, indeed, is far more serious from the hierarchy's point of view than is that between hierarchical and American traditional principles on the separation of church and state. For Catholic laymen become imbued with American notions of individualism and are thus rendered more difficult to control and hold in line in political and social, if not in religious, matters.

We have already traced some of the organizational and administrative problems which have plagued the church historically in their dealings with the laity in America, and at this point we elaborate the discussion, this time in the area not of organization but of conformity. During the first half of the present century one of the most striking conflicts was between the immigrant and the Old World priest. As we saw in Chapter 13 most priests were, until fairly recently, foreign-born. Many, if not most, of these priests associated the imported Old World ways of life with the interests of the church. They therefore fought vigorously to keep their congregations from adopting American customs. They deliberately tried to perpetuate Polish, German, or Czech mores and languages because they feared that in losing these mores and languages their parishioners would also lose their Catho-

[14] Ruth D. Tuck, *Not with the Fist* (New York: Harcourt, Brace & World, 1946), p. 153.

licism. Nor were they entirely wrong. Many thousands of Catholics did abandon their old religion as they took on the ways of the majority. This process still goes on, and so to an ever-diminishing degree does the effort of "foreign-minded" priests to oppose any yielding to American ways.

A great deal of the power and authority of the priests among immigrant groups lay in the fact that they were educated, perhaps the only educated members of the immigrant community. That their intellectual orientation was foreign did not diminish their influence although among the native-born children of immigrants it may have made for a good deal of conflict. The lower clergy do not, in theory, have power to dictate to their congregations on anything outside the realm of faith and morals. They can and many do, however, try to attach all sorts of social and political ideas to matters of faith. A great many of their flock follow obediently, a fact which gives them great actual if not theoretical power in the political life of communities where Catholics are numerous. Such power is possible only when the laity does not know the limits of the priest's authority.

As laymen become more educated and more aware of the limits of hierarchical control, a re-alignment of power relationships takes place. Devout but educated Catholics know where they are free to make their own decisions and where they must bow to hierarchical decision.

Many Catholics do not follow obediently. Indeed, anticlericalism has, historically, been more common among Catholics than among non-Catholics. Protestants have been fighting hierarchical pretensions for only about four and a half centuries; Catholic laymen—including kings—have been fighting them for many more centuries.

Many laymen rebel against some of the social and political teachings of their church. For example, some Catholics object to the hierarchy's position with respect to political tolerance,[15] contraception,[16] and even to

[15] "The plain inference" from the position taken by Catholic leaders, complains one Catholic, "is that our Constitution is a temporary makeshift and that Catholics are to look forward to the time when they will have the strength to bring about the constitutional changes necessary to put our civil institutions in line with papal teachings. Catholics are thus placed in the uncomfortable position of sharing with communists a tacit opposition to the principles of our democracy" (N. V. Fetterly, "The Catholic Church Needs——." *Forum,* April, 1940, p. 181). A Catholic lay organization advertises in the national press and implicitly, though not explicitly, denies that Catholics do not believe in religious freedom for all or oppose separation of church and state.

[16] Many Catholics believe in the right to have contraceptive information disseminated to married people. National polls as long ago as 1938 and again in 1943 show that most of the Catholic women questioned—51 and 69 percent respectively—favored this policy. Even in Connecticut, where strong pressure from Catholic leaders has prevented legislation in this direction, 54.9 percent of the Catholic women who voted were in favor of it. The editor of *Commonweal,* a liberal Catholic periodical, has stated that "other citizens cannot expect Catholics to change either their beliefs or their practices . . . but neither can Catholics expect to control the beliefs and practices of others. . . . There are many sound and compelling reasons why Catholics should not generally strive for legislation and directives which clash with the beliefs of a large portion of the society." And in June,

parochial schools. And even among laymen who accept the parochial school there are some who reject the attempts of Catholic leaders to secure public tax support for it.

Sometimes, also, Catholic laymen begin to chafe under the restrictions of censorship; they do not honor the recommendations and boycotts of the Legion of Decency. And labor leaders who may be devoutly Catholic in their religious beliefs reject suggestions from the hierarchy that they organize independent Catholic trade unions. In the past these quarrels sometimes reflected a differing degree of Americanization between laity and clergy, as we saw above. But sometimes they presage a new orientation in which the laymen are ahead of their religious leaders.

So serious does the hierarchy view this growing tendency of Catholic laymen to assert their independence in political and social matters that a set of basic principles was set forth in 1960 to guide Catholics:

> An unhealthy anticlerical theory . . . has, in many minds, beclouded the basic principles of Christian doctrine on the structure of the Church, on her mission and her teaching authority. There is a tendency to separate the Catholic from the ecclesiastical hierarchy, narrowing the liaison between them to the sacred ministry alone, and proclaiming the full independence of the believer in the civil field.
>
> Hence the absurd dichotomy of conscience as between citizen and believer, as if the Catholic religion were only a special and occasional phase in the life of the soul, and not the powerful idea that involves and gives direction to man's whole existence.
>
> Therefore it is useful and necessary to recall these basic principles:
>
> 1. The Church, established by Jesus Christ as a perfect society with its hierarchy, has full powers of true jurisdiction over all the faithful, and therefore has the duty and the right to guide, direct and correct them on the level of ideas and on the level of action, in conformity with the dictates of the Gospel and insofar as is necessary to achieve the final end of man, which is eternal life.
>
> For this purpose, the Church sets forth a truth to believe, a law to obey, and offers Divine Grace for the exercise of all the virtues, individual, domestic and social. The Catholic can never overlook the teaching and the instruction of the Church; in every field of his life he must base his private and public behavior on the guidance and instruction of the hierarchy.
>
> 2. The political-social problem cannot be separated from religion. . . . The Church cannot be agnostic. . . . It is her duty and her right to intervene, even in this field, to enlighten and aid consciences. . . .

1958, another Catholic magazine stated that a "Catholic can justifiably favor repeal of the Connecticut and Massachusetts anti-contraceptive laws or breathe happily if they are declared unconstitutional." By their actions as well as by their statements, Catholics assert their independence. Thus one survey reported that almost a third of Catholic married women under 40 used contraceptives not acceptable to the Church, and half of those married at least ten years have used such methods. In June, 1960, the National Catholic Family Life Conference published a study which showed that Catholic married couples used contraception to about the same extent as non-Catholics. (Reported in *Redbook,* November, 1960, p. 78.) The Catholic birth rate falls as rapidly as that of non-Catholics under similar circumstances (S. A. Stouffer, "Trends in the Fertility of Catholics and non-Catholics," *Amer. Jour. Sociol.* [September, 1935], pp. 43-66) .

3. On the political ground, the problem of collaboration with those who do not admit religious principles may arise. In that case, it is up to the ecclesiastical authority, and not to the choice of the individual Catholic, to decide on the moral lawfulness of such collaboration, and a conflict between that decision and the opinion of the faithful is unthinkable in a truly Christian conscience. In any event, such a conflict must be resolved in obedience to the Church as custodian of the truth.

4. The irreducible antithesis between the Marxist system and Catholic doctrine is self-evident. . . .[17]

The shock with which this editorial was greeted in the United States showed at once how far the hierarchy was from the American Catholic. The day after the editorial appeared, "a high Vatican source" was quoted as saying that "the warning would not equally apply to countries like the United States, in which religion is not threatened."[18] The American Catholic continued to assert his independence.[19]

The accommodation of these conflicts illustrates the process whereby each party to a conflict molds and shapes the other. We are usually so impressed by the influence which the Catholic hierarchy exerts on its followers that we forget the almost equally important, if slower, influence which the latter exert on the church. The flexibility which has made it possible for the institutional framework of the Catholic church to withstand the vicissitudes of two thousand years of history stem from its long experience in meeting not only attacks from without but also modifications from within. It is this necessity for reinterpreting positions in order to prevent loss of allegiance of followers which, perhaps as much as anything else, keeps the Catholic church from hardening into a fatal rigidity. The process may be, as some laymen think, glacier-slow; and the churchmen themselves may, on the whole, be well behind the times in their social ideas, but the reciprocity exists nonetheless.

Two recent historical events highlight the processes we have been delineating. John F. Kennedy, as knowledgeable a Catholic as one could find, has consistently drawn a line between areas in which he is subjected to church control and areas in which he is not. Thus, for example, he accepted without question hierarchical banning of his participation in a ceremony as the representative of the Catholic church:

I was invited by the Reverend Dr. Poling to attend the dinner in connection with the financial drive to build the Chapel of the Four Chaplains. I was happy to accept. A few days before the event, I learned . . . that I was to be the spokesman for the Catholic faith. I was not being invited as a former member of the

[17] Editorial in *L'Osservatore Romano,* unofficial Vatican City newspaper, May 17, 1960. Present reference from *U. S. News and World Report,* May 30, 1960, p. 73.

[18] *Ibid.,* p. 74.

[19] Then Senator John F. Kennedy's press secretary made the following statement: "Senator Kennedy has repeatedly stated his support of the principle of separation of church and state as provided for in the United States Constitution. He has stated that this support is not subject to change under any condition."

armed forces or as a member of Congress or as an individual, but as an official representative of a religious organization. I further learned that the memorial was to be located in the sanctuary of a church of a different faith. This is against the precepts of the Catholic church. Because of the fact that the Archdiocese of Philadelphia was unable to support the drive . . . I felt I had not credentials to attend in the capacity in which I had been asked.[20]

Mr. Kennedy, then Senator, also consistently opposed legislation granting tax monies for support of parochial schools:

There can be no question of Federal funds used for support of parochial or private schools. It's unconstitutional under the First Amendment as interpreted by the Supreme Court. I'm opposed to the Federal Government's extending support to sustain any church or its schools.[21]

Mr. Kennedy repudiated without equivocation hierarchical pressures on his decisions: in his address accepting the presidential nomination he stated that his decisions on every public policy would be his own "as an American, a Democrat and a free man."

The other recent event dealing with conflict between church and laity was the attempt by the hierarchy in Puerto Rico to influence voters against Luis Muñoz Marin. Its ignominious failure only revealed how badly in need of modernization the church was.

The form which conflict between hierarchy and laity takes in the local community varies. It may be a simple fight—"dog fights" some have been called—between a dogmatic or authoritarian or over-worked or idealistic priest or prelate and a rebellious congregation. It may take the form of a legal battle, as when parents in one parish organized to fight desegregation of parochial schools. It rarely takes the form of debate. Sometimes it takes the form of simply rejecting church positions, as in the case of Kennedy and Muñoz-Marin. On the part of the church there is always the weapon of excommunication. In one urban parish the bishop did threaten excommunication of a whole community to quell an uprising against his order that Negro children be admitted to the local parochial high schools. From a larger perspective the conflict may be viewed as a tacit game in which any concessions made by the church are tactfully hidden by face-saving techniques.[22]

We are not, of course, here concerned with whether this principle of pliability and adaptability in the Catholic church is good or bad, divine or secular, right or wrong, admirable or censurable. We merely point out that

[20] *New York Times,* Sept. 9, 1960.

[21] *Ibid.*

[22] For an acute analysis of face-saving see Erving Goffman, "On Face-Work," *Psychiatry: Journal for the Study of Interpersonal Processes,* 18 (1955), p. 224. One insightful layman made the comment that he hoped non-Catholics would be tactful enough to permit the church to change its position quietly, without gloating observers to make the process humiliating.

as in all organization where community must be maintained, there is a mutual and reciprocal relationship between leader and follower, a give-and-take which keeps them within hailing distance of one another.

Conflict between Catholics and Non-Catholics

FORMS

The conflict between Catholics and non-Catholics may take on any of several forms. We shall refer in Chapter 26 to the violence which has from time to time characterized Catholic–non-Catholic relationships. Such conflict is rare at the present time, or if it occurs it may take the form of vandalism or, in the South, Klan attacks when racial issues are hot. Hostility, resentment, fear, prejudice are still widespread in many communities, sometimes as accompaniments or as consequences of community issues, but sometimes primarily as legacies of a remote past in communities where there are few, if any, Catholics at all.[23]

Our concern here is primarily with the forms of conflict in which there are issues. It is not always easy, however, to distinguish between conflicts in which there are genuine issues and those in which there are not. Non-Catholics, for example, may attack the Catholic attitude toward sex, toward the use of amulets, toward science, or toward certain forms of worship, and a score of other matters which are not, as a matter of fact, genuine issues inasmuch as such attitudes on the part of the Catholic do not in any way prevent the non-Catholic from holding quite opposite points of view. That is, there is no issue so long as one group does not attempt to impose its attitudes on the other. Such conflicts are the result of misunderstanding and may be amenable to peaceful solutions. They are the areas where most success can be achieved in community projects for improving interfaith relationships. Enlightened non-Catholics and Catholics understand what is inherent and essential and what is not inherent and essential in their respective faiths and are therefore less likely to be victimized by misunderstanding. They are more likely to see the common core than the tangential differences in their faiths.

[23] Much of the prejudice and hostility between Catholics and non-Catholics has traditionally been a matter of class differences. The membership of the Catholic church, has been predominantly lower class. More than half of all Catholics are urban blue-collar workers. Fewer than half have completed high school, and only seven percent are college graduates. This class picture reflects the presence of a large number of in-migrants, especially, in recent years, of Puerto Ricans. In class composition Catholics have resembled Baptists more than any other Protestant denomination, but they have been less nativist in background. They have sometimes been discriminated against socially, barred from clubs and societies. In the thinking of many non-Catholics they were "ignorant," "priest-ridden," "superstitious," "bigoted." They were "shanty Irish," "wops," "dagoes," "hunkies"—in brief, "foreigners." The class and ethnic nature of much of this thinking is indicated by the fact that such discrimination against educated native-born Catholics has declined toward the vanishing point.

But to emphasize this important fact does not mean to deny that there do exist, especially in matters of policy, genuine issues. These differences in policy are not necessarily inherent and essential to the faiths of the parties involved. Usually they are not. That is, such conflicting policies could in many instances change without affecting the core of theological dogma or creed. Ordinarily they are policies with respect to quite secular relationships. The changing position with respect to church-state relationships which we traced above illustrates the point. The American Catholic church has lost none of its theological orthodoxy by coming around to the American position with respect to church-state relationships. It is extremely important to distinguish between matters which are intrinsically matters of faith and dogma—which can never be issues in a society which guarantees religious freedom—and derivative matters which may have traditional tie-ups with faith and dogma but which are not essential to them. People may remain devout and loyal Catholics and at the same time disagree with their Church on many nonreligious issues. John F. Kennedy, as we saw above, is an outstanding example.

There is, of course, a difference between conflict between Catholic laymen and their church and conflict between non-Catholics and the church. The strategic armory of the church vis-à-vis the non-Catholic lacks such disciplinary techniques as threats of excommunication in extreme cases or deprivation of church privileges in less extreme cases. But the issues are often the same.

PARTIES

It will readily be appreciated from our discussion of intra-Catholic conflict that the Catholic party in Catholic–non-Catholic conflict is not an undifferentiated, homogeneous, single-minded body. There are Catholics of many kinds of ethnic backgrounds as we have seen. There are liberal, broadminded, tolerant Catholics, and there are ignorant, narrow-minded, and bigoted Catholics. In brief, we can no more lump all Catholics together than we can the non-Catholics. The issues we shall emphasize are for the most part those between the Catholic hierarchy—or "the Catholic church"—and non-Catholics, remembering always that they are often identical with the issues which exist between the hierarchy and the Catholic laity.

We should also point out that Catholic–non-Catholic relations vary widely from community to community. In the South, Catholics may be victims of aggression on the part of members of the Ku Klux Klan; in communities in the North and East, on the other hand, Catholic prelates may attempt to extend their power into control of matters that concern non-Catholics as well as Catholics and it is the non-Catholic who feels himself to be the victim of aggression.

ISSUES

The issues that divide Catholics and non-Catholics—whether schismatic in nature or pressuring—are social and moral and, since so many moral issues in our society tend to be fought out in the political arena, also political, especially with respect to the use of public or tax moneys. These issues may be classified substantively as (1) those dealing with marriage, the family, and elementary education; (2) those dealing with moral values; and (3) those arising in connection with attempts at cooperative community activities.

The "Battle for the Babies"

INTERMARRIAGE

Both Catholics and non-Catholics deplore marriages between their respective adherents for many reasons, especially because of the extra hazards involved; for marriages in which the partners have differing cultural backgrounds have less chance for success than more homogamous marriages.

The major difficulty arises because of the requirement of the Catholic church that the non-Catholic member of a mixed marriage sign a written promise to rear within the church all the children born to the union.[24] Two separate "games" are involved here. In the first the church has first-move strategy; it is committed to a position and the laymen can take it or leave it. If they do not take it they have only the alternative of not getting married at all or of not having their marriage recognized by the church as valid. In the second game, however, the church is at a disadvantage because although it can extract a commitment in the form of a promise to rear children in the church, it cannot enforce fulfillment.

Although many non-Catholic denominations resent the insistence of the Catholic church on this promise with respect to the children, for the most part this issue is fought out verbally rather than in terms of specific countermeasures. It should also be pointed out in this connection that many Catholics select an alternative course, they leave the Church to marry non-Catholics, a matter of some concern to Catholic leaders. The intermarriage issue, however, while intense, does not usually reverberate widely in the community. Another aspect of the issue, however, does have wide reverberations at the local, state, and even national and international level. It is contraception.

CONTRACEPTION

The Catholic church is opposed on moral grounds to the use of contraception. It exerts its influence wherever possible to prevent the dissemina-

[24] Canon 1062 of Catholic church law also states that "the Catholic spouse is obliged to prudently take care of the conversion of his [or her] non-Catholic spouse." Often the birth of the first child leads to conversion to Catholicism.

tion of contraceptive information, using both nonpolitical and political methods to fight it.

Nonpolitical pressure may take the form of requiring non-Catholic doctors connected with Catholic hospitals to sign promises that they will not give contraceptive information to patients either inside the hospital or outside the hospital in private practice. In this "game," the church has more chips than in the one referred to above. It can enforce fulfillment on pain of being removed from the hospital staff in case of nonfulfillment. Removal from hospital staffs is so serious to doctors that the mere threat of it gives enormous coercive power to the church. In New York City Catholic doctors even in public hospitals were forbidden to give contraceptive information as late as 1958, when this ban was removed. There is also some feeling among non-Catholics about censorship of radio, television, and the press with regard even to discussion of this topic.

The conflict moves into the political field when efforts are made to prevent the above restrictive practices by law or by court order. Thus in Maryland, Louisiana, and Kentucky suits were instituted in 1960 to bar the transfer of public land and funds to build Roman Catholic hospitals on the grounds that public moneys should not be used to subsidize hospitals that discriminated against doctors who wished to prescribe and patients who wished to receive contraceptive information.[25] This strategy would give the hospitals the alternatives of surrendering their control over the private practice of physicians or loss of public support.[26]

Another approach through the courts was made in 1959 when three women from Connecticut brought suit in the Supreme Court against the Connecticut state ban on contraceptive information on the ground that this law violated the Fourteenth Amendment. They argued that prohibition of contraceptive advice unreasonably threatened their lives and liberty and thus denied them due process. In 1961 the Court decided against them on the grounds that the law was not enforced anyway.

[25] Glenn L. Archer, executive director of Protestants and Other Americans United for Separation of Church and State, stated that "the chief moral issue in this case is freedom for birth control. The Catholic Bishops have declared against that freedom and have ordained for all their hospitals a code of sectarian medicine which excludes this and other desirable and legitimate features of medical practice. We do not believe that public funds should be used to support such a discriminatory code" (*New York Times,* Jan. 5, 1960). Similarly the Committee on Church and State of the American Humanist Association stated that under the Hill-Burton Act, $168,000,000 had been distributed to Roman Catholic hospitals; this money had been paid in taxes by non-Catholics as well as by Catholics. They should not be ignored. "Where Federal tax funds are used there should be no sectarian limitations of any sort upon the medical freedom of patient and physician" (*New York Times,* Dec. 27, 1959). This, incidentally, is an illustration of how the granting of funds can become a strategic chip; threats to withdraw them can become coercive.

[26] Since this is a mixed-motive game in which it is to the interest of all concerned to see that the hospital functions at optimum efficiency, it is likely that concessions can be worked out—with adequate face-saving provisions—as they were in the New York City situation, where policy was modified.

The church's position on contraception became an issue in the national community also when the question of helping underdeveloped areas of the world solve their population problems was raised in 1959. At that time the bishops of the United States issued a statement opposing the inclusion of contraceptive information in any program of assistance. Leaders of Protestant and Jewish organizations entered the fray on the opposite side. The issue, it should be pointed out, was never whether or not contraception should be forced on any country or made a condition of assistance but rather whether or not requests for help in a contraceptive program already a matter of policy should be granted to any country which asked for it. The form of conflict at this level was largely that of debate.

The Catholic church, it should be pointed out, views contraception not only as a matter of vital importance to Catholics but also as one which affects the general welfare of all. No one can deny them the right to try to persuade others to accept their principles. In the debate form of conflict there may even be an advantage. But coercion is something else again. Whether the church has the legal right to impose its views on non-Catholics is another matter entirely.

ELEMENTARY EDUCATION

The third front in the "battle for the babies" is the elementary school. It has two aspects. One is the attack on the public school system by the Catholic church and the other is the attack on the use of tax moneys for children in parochial schools by non-Catholics.

The Catholic church has never granted that education is a state function. It has always believed that elementary education is essentially and basically a church function. The hierarchy—and even some, though not, of course, all the laity—are therefore opposed in principle to the traditional nonreligious public school system. They consider it "bad in principle and bad in its ultimate consequences."[27] Some identify it with paganism, with totalitarianism.

Some believe that "the Catholic and non-Catholic school systems are absolutely irreconcilable."[28] "The Pope does not approve of our public school system; no Catholic could approve a system where religious instruction is barred."[29] The lack of religious instruction in American public schools has been called a tragedy by the Vatican.[30]

Some members of the hierarchy have gone beyond opposition in principle; they have advocated direct action in the form of sabotage by protesting against the use of tax moneys for the support of public schools.

[27] Paul L. Blakely, S.J., *May an American Oppose the Public School?* (American Press, 1937).

[28] Editorial in *America,* Oct. 3, 1925.

[29] Father W. J. McGucken, S.J., *The Catholic Way in Education* (Bruce Publishing, 1934), p. 98.

[30] *L'Osservatore Romano,* reported in the *New York Times,* Dec. 15, 1954.

"Our first duty to the public school is not to pay taxes for its maintenance. We pay this tax under protest; not because we admit an obligation in justice. Justice cannot oblige the support of a system which we are forbidden in conscience to use or a system which we conscientiously hold to be bad in ultimate consequences."[31] The withdrawal of support of public schools can be effected of course only where a majority of the taxpayers are Catholic. Such a case occurred in a New England community when non-Catholics proposed at a town meeting that the local public high school be enlarged, that a gymnasium be added, and that other improvements be made. A solid bloc of Catholic voters rejected the proposition; they did not wish to have public tax money spent on the public school which they did not patronize.

Despite this official Catholic opposition to the principle of public school education, Catholics do become members of public school boards, public school superintendents, and public school teachers in many communities. The influence exerted by such strategically placed individuals may become an issue, especially if it seems to non-Catholics to be blatantly denominational.

The church proclaims the right and duty to supervise all schools, public as well as private, with respect to religious teaching.[32] Where Catholic officials exercise this self-appointed function with tact, or where there is consensus with respect to what constitutes faith and good morals, no issue may ever arise in the community. Where this supervision is performed tactlessly, however, the conflict may become warm.

In contrast to the Catholic principle that the church has the right to supervise the religious instruction of all students, is the American principle, espoused both by Catholics and by non-Catholics, that only the academic program of the parochial schools, not their religious program, is subject to supervision by public educational agencies.

The second aspect of the elementary school front in the "battle for the babies" is that of the parochial school. It is not the existence of the parochial school that is at issue, for although most non-Catholics probably subscribe to the American belief in the public school, especially those who look to common experiences in the public school as a great unifying force in American life, they have never denied that the Catholic church has a right

[31] Paul L. Blakely, *op. cit.* See also Bishop J. F. Noll, *Our National Enemy No. 1—Education without Religion* (Fort Wayne, 1925).

[32] Canon 1381: "The religious teaching of youth in any schools is subject to the authority and inspection of the Church. The local ordinaries have the right and duty to watch that nothing is taught contrary to faith and good morals in any of the schools of the territory. They, moreover, have the right to approve the books of Christian doctrine and the teachers of religion, and to demand, for the safeguarding of religion and morals, the removal of teachers and books." Canon 1382 continues: "Ordinaries have the right, either in person or through others, to visit in reference to religious and moral instruction, any schools, oratories, summer schools, etc., and from this visitation the schools conducted by a religious community are not excepted unless it is a school exclusively for the professed members of an exempt order."

to establish its own school system. They are not opposed in principle to the parochial school, as the Catholic church is to the public school.

The issue with respect to parochial schools arises rather in connection with the uses of tax moneys for their support. The Catholic church exerts political pressure to obtain public funds to help support its parochial school program. The issue becomes particularly salient for the church because of the increasing difficulty of recruiting members of the teaching orders and the consequent necessity to compete with public schools for lay teachers, thus enormously increasing the burden on the church and its members. Catholic leaders argue that Catholics are doubly taxed since they help support the public schools with their taxes and they must also support their own parochial schools. Furthermore, they argue, they are educating a large proportion of the children of the community. Hence these Catholics ask that they receive a share of public funds, "just enough tax funds to make the Catholic schools an integral part of American education."

Non-Catholics—as well as many Catholics who fear the consequences in the form of control—are opposed to the use of public tax moneys for parochial schools. The theory has been suggested that whatever sums are supplied by public taxes for parochial schools would release that much money for the religious activities of the Catholic church and thus would constitute subsidy of a church, contrary to the Constitution.

Although the Constitution forbids the levying of taxes for the support of sectarian schools, many states have laws which permit, or at least do not forbid, the use of tax money for services to children who attend parochial schools. Such services may include transportation to and from school (18 states), health services, school lunches, and even the furnishing of non-religious school supplies (5 states).

Difficulties arise in the interpretation of the word "services." How much does it include? Catholic leaders have interpreted it to include even aid in the construction of parochial school buildings;[33] non-Catholics have argued that this was stretching the meaning unreasonably.[34] This issue has arisen regularly since 1948 whenever federal aid to education is under consideration.[35]

Communities themselves vary greatly in their interpretation of what is permissible and what is not. History, ethnic composition, court decisions, and the skill and power of lobbies have created a very complex pattern in which a practice may be legal in one community but not in another.

[33] Editorial in *The Catholic World,* April, 1955: ". . . in the matter of erecting new school buildings," American children "are entitled to benefits of public welfare legislation regardless of race, creed or color."

[34] Glenn L. Archer, executive director of Protestants and Other Americans United for Separation of Church and State: ". . . if even the erection of school buildings can be termed a 'welfare' service rather than an 'educational' aid, then there are no limits to the extent of the support which the Government will be expected to grant the religious schools" (*New York Times,* Nov. 22, 1955).

[35] Bills proposed for federal aid to education sometimes specifically forbid federal money to be alloted to parochial schools; some specifically permit it; others leave to the state the decision on how federal funds should be used.

The application of laws governing the use of public tax moneys for school purposes is a vexatious problem for both Catholics and non-Catholics in many communities. In one Ohio community in 1947 a school board, consisting mainly of Catholics, incorporated a parochial school into the public school system, paying the local archdiocese a rental fee and placing the nuns on the public payroll. A local court took over the school district's affairs and terminated the contract. It was unconstitutional.

In 1961 tax support for the parochial school became a national issue of peculiar intensity. The influence of the Catholic hierarchy was exerted in such a way that no help for any schools was possible if it was not also made available to parochial schools. In order to solve this deadlock, it was proposed that federal funds be made available for the teaching of only the secular subjects in parochial schools. Even this amount of help would greatly relieve the load on parochial schools, which, in the absence of enough teaching nuns, were finding it increasingly difficult to compete with public schools in securing teachers. Opponents were not slow to point out the anomalies and inconsistencies in this proposal; if some subjects were to be secularized, why not send the children to public schools for them and retain the parochial school for only religious subjects. It was, precisely, to suffuse all education with a religious spirit that the parochial school aspired. The solution was still not in sight.

Moral and Cultural Issues

Differing moral codes do not necessarily involve conflict. It is possible for groups to observe different moral prescriptions without in any way interfering with the moral observances of others. But in practice there are often many community ramifications of moral standards; and when these become political also, involving coercion, conflict does occur. Moral issues are especially likely to engender emotion because they deal with fundamental values, but so long as they remain in debate form, each trying to persuade the other of its correctness, the repercussions are not likely to be serious.

When, however, coercion is exerted, either political or nonpolitical, the aspect changes. Some moral issues do become political. The Catholic church, for example, forbids divorce to its members. There is no issue on this rule. But the Catholic church in some communities prevents any activity which might lead to the modernizing of divorce procedures for anyone. The outstanding illustration is New York, where the only ground for divorce is adultery. Even the setting up of a commission to study the question of modernizing the law was successfully fought by Catholics until 1956. The use of their power by the Catholic blocs to prevent such reforms becomes a bitter issue, especially when it is held that "it is naïve to believe that present laws are discouraging broken families."[36] Indeed, it has been found that

[36] *New York Times,* March 30, 1955.

the proportion of white women ever married, excluding widowed women, who are reported as living apart from their husbands was a third higher in New York than in the whole country.[37] No one argues that the Catholic church does not have the right to forbid divorce to its own members on moral grounds; it is argued only that it does not have the right to coerce non-Catholics in the matter of divorce.

Other moral issues may also become political and hence involve coercion. Thus just as the position of the Catholic church on contraception and divorce may become an issue, so the position of many Protestant denominations on gambling and drinking may also. But now the positions are reversed: it is the Protestant groups that wish to forbid to everyone activities they consider wrong or immoral. The Catholic church does not believe that gambling is immoral;[38] many Protestant churches do.[39] The issue is especially warm with respect to bingo.[40]

Even—or perhaps especially—when the coercion is not political, the "game" becomes very warm, as in the case of censorship. In the course of protecting its own membership the Catholic hierarchy often attempts to censor and control the behavior of non-Catholics also. The major strategies used are threats of boycott which are often so effective that merely blacklisting a book or program is enough to secure compliance with its wishes.

Motion pictures,[41] books, plays, radio and television programs, and periodical literature have all been subjected to Catholic censorship. So serious is the result for Catholic–non-Catholic relationships that, despite a call by Pope Pius XII upon Catholics to extend their censorship to include radio and television, one Jesuit scholar, Father John Courtney Murray, has argued that imprudent censorship by groups of Catholics may be dangerous since it tends to identify the church as a power association, an identification which he considers injurious, arousing hatred for the church.

In addition, the Catholic hierarchy has opposed programs for sex education in the school. The Catholic War Veterans blocked the continuation of the distribution by the army of matchbooks containing information about venereal disease.

[37] Paul H. Jacobson, *American Marriage and Divorce* (New York: Holt, Rinehart and Winston, 1959), p. 117.

[38] Associated Press release, Nov. 28, 1946; *New York Times,* Jan. 2, 1955; *The Catholic Lawyer,* Vol. 1, 1955.

[39] *New York Times,* Jan. 17, 1955.

[40] *New York Times,* Sept. 24, 1955. Bingo was legalized in New Jersey in 1954 and in New York in 1958.

[41] For example, the Catholic League of Decency condemned the motion picture *Baby Doll;* Cardinal Spellman appealed for a boycott; it was not permitted in Gary, Indiana; newspapers refused advertising for it. "Faced with this, exhibitors in many cases did not show the movie, thus depriving members of other faiths, and the non-religious, of their right to see it" (Richard Schickel, "Catholic, Protestant, Jew," *Look,* Sept. 30, 1958, p. 106).

The Price of Cooperation

In some communities Catholics give the least enthusiastic support to efforts to promote fellowship among Protestants, Catholics, and Jews. Although such efforts may be encouraged in some dioceses, they are discouraged in others, so that, as the editor of a Catholic weekly observed, "a depressing attitude of doubt, hesitation, [and] embarrassment" results.[42] When the National Conference of Christians and Jews published a religious book list to acquaint members of different faiths with the principles of each one, Catholics were forbidden to read those which explained and defended Protestantism and Judaism.[43] "Debate," in other words, is forbidden. The Catholic is not to be exposed to a favorable image of non-Catholics.

Sometimes non-Catholics complain that the price placed by the church on Catholic cooperation in community enterprises is high, especially where it has good bargaining power. In 1955 Catholics boycotted the Community Chest in Princeton until the Planned Parenthood group withdrew. In another community a staff member of an agency working on slum clearance was asked to serve on the executive board of a Committee to Safeguard Religious Freedom, a committee formed to fight the use of school "released time" for religious instruction. When the local bishop heard of the staff member's affiliation with the committee, he said he would have to withdraw his support, which had been extraordinarily effective, from the slum-clearance organization unless the staff member withdrew his membership from the committee.

When the issue moves into the political arena, the situation becomes anomalous. The characteristic level of accommodation for political conflict is that of equilibrium, involving compromise, give and take, logrolling, and "deals." In brief, bargaining in the game theory sense. But this is not possible when religious convictions are involved. It is impossible to compromise with evil. Thus when non-Catholics in one state asked for a conference with a local Catholic bishop in the hope of working out an accommodation with respect to contraceptive legislation, usually a routine procedure in ordinary political conflict, the church prelate refused, replying that Catholic opposition to contraception was a matter of principle upon which there could be no compromise, so that there was no point in holding a conference. In another community, when non-Catholics continued to agitate for the legalization of contraceptive information, a Catholic bishop criticized them, saying that the issue of contraception was a closed matter.

There is, of course, nothing unusual in the exertion of pressure by Catholic leaders in behalf of their convictions. Like all groups they drive the best bargain they can. The point here is simply that the price they demand may be so high as to create resentment among those who have to pay it. Or they may refuse to bargain at all.

[42] Michael Williams, "Views and Reviews," *Commonweal,* 36 (Aug. 21, 1942), p. 42.
[43] *American Ecclesiastical Review,* September, 1946.

18

Jews and Non-Jews

The Jews, it will be remembered from Chapter 1, constitute one of the most unusual examples of a people who have maintained community in the collective value sense even in the absence of territoriality. They have retained their identity in the most diverse community settings.

But within these diverse settings they have, actually, always maintained spatial communities also. Indeed, it is impossible to live according to Jewish norms outside of a community. We speak, therefore, of the Jewish community of Paris or London or Warsaw or St. Louis or Atlanta or Buenos Aires or Cairo.

We spoke also in Chapter 1 of the generations of people who sweep through communities, occupy them for a while, and then pass on. In the case of ethnic groups in American communities this sweep of generations is especially interesting because of the very rapid transformations that take place from one generation to the next, as children move away from their parents into the surrounding world. Thus a Jewish community inhabited by an immigrant generation is not at all the same as a Jewish community inhabited by a third generation. And the objects of non-Jewish hostility in 1900 are not the same as the objects of hostility two generations later. Both Jew and non-Jews have changed and both live in a world totally different from that of their forebears.[1]

Nowhere is it more important to emphasize the cultural nature of a conflict than in the case of conflict between Jews and non-Jews. Not all cultural differences produce conflict and where they do not, it is senseless to demand change. For differences are frequently piquant, enriching. It is important also to remember that culture conflict is not personal. Individual Jews and non-Jews, as people, often like one another very much. It is not a clash of personalities; even high-ranking Nazis often had "pet" Jews. The conflict is one of values as expressed in customs, mores, and other cultural norms, not of individuals. The application of these principles will become clearer as we proceed with our analysis.

[1] For a thorough analysis of intergenerational changes in a Jewish community, see Judith Kramer and Seymour Leventman, *Children of the Gilded Ghetto* (New Haven: Yale, 1961).

Effect of Class Differences

The cultural conflict between Jews and non-Jews is complicated by another kind of conflict: one involving class differences. Socially, that is, class-wise, the Jews resemble such religious bodies as Presbyterians and the traditionally aristocratic denominations such as Episcopalians and Congregationalists which are middle- and upper-class groups. The proportion of Jews listed as upper class in a 1945-1946 survey by the American Institute of Public Opinion was 22 percent, compared with an identical figure for Presbyterians, and with 24 percent for Episcopalians and Congregationalists—in contrast to 8 and 9 percent respectively for Baptists and Catholics. Jews, furthermore, were also found to be an educated group, about two-thirds having had at least a high school education and over 16 percent being college graduates. Here, again, they resembled Presbyterians (63 percent of whom had at least a high school education and 22 percent being college graduates), Episcopalians (65 and 22 percent), and Congregationalists (71 and 21 percent). Occupational structures showed the same resemblance—36 percent among Jews being in business and professional occupations, as compared with 31, 32, and 33 percent among Presbyterians, Episcopalians, and Congregationalists respectively, and as contrasted with 12 and 14 percent for Baptists and Catholics.

Recalling our discussion of class in Chapter 11, we note that access to upper-class status demands a proper class lineage. Most Jews do not have that. They are still usually only two or three generations removed from immigrant status. Thus a good deal of what passes for anti-Semitism, especially in the higher social realms, is simply an exaggerated and magnified version of an identical exclusivist behavior pattern toward non-Jews.

The specific focus of conflict between Jews and non-Jews varies from class to class, in some cases being primarily economic, that is, buyer-seller, in other cases social or class conflict, and in still others, political. Each has to be analyzed separately. "Anti-Semitism" and its converse, "antigentilism," are blanket terms which are meaningless unless broken down into their specific constituent phases or aspects.

Anti-Semitism and anti-gentilism are correlated phenomena. Both Jew and non-Jew consider themselves to be victims, each of the other. It is usually difficult in any conflict to determine who is the aggressor, who has the grievance, who is victim. Jews often interpret the behavior of non-Jews as an aggression—often gratuitous—against themselves. They look upon themselves as going peacefully about their business, injuring no one, and then, for reasons quite beyond their own control, being victimized and persecuted by the outside world in one form or another. Non-Jews, on their side, insist that what the Jew labels as persecution or discrimination in the non-Jews is often merely a defense against Jewish aggressions.[2] Thus each group has a picture of itself as being victimized by the other. Neither views itself in the role of the aggressor. If we think of the entire population of the country, it may seem slightly ridiculous for the majority group to feel itself victimized by so small a minority group. But we are speaking of local community behavior here; and in specific communities where the number of Jews is large, even though their proportion is small, non-Jews sometimes express concern at the possibility of Jewish aggression. Since it is practically impossible to divest ourselves of our own group's point of view, the Jew's definition of the situation seems to the non-Jew myopic, one-sided, prejudiced. He thinks the Jew never sees how the situation may look from the angle of the non-Jew. If, the non-Jew continues, the Jew could see that the non-Jew feels more defensive than aggressive, it would be better for the Jew's own mental health.[3] Such reasoning, naturally, makes little sense to the Jew, whose experience as a member of a minority renders it difficult for him even to imagine the possibility of such fears on the part of the dominant group. He does not picture himself as powerful; quite the contrary, he pictures himself as insecure, threatened. That he should appear to be a threat to the majority seems incredible to him.

Parties

Although in common speech we have no difficulty in understanding what we mean when we talk about Jews, scientific literature is full of arguments, discussions, and debate with respect to the nature of the group called Jews. Jews themselves are not in agreement as to their status. Are they a race? Hardly. There are many races among Jews; not only are there Nordic, Alpine, Dinaric, and Mediterranean types among white Jews but there are also Negro Jews and Chinese Jews and Yemenite Jews. Are they a religious sect? It would be hard to find any religious group where religious belief is less standardized. A great many Jews profess no religion at all, even in Israel. Reform Jews are probably nearer to Unitarians in creed than they are to orthodox Jews. Almost the only thing that Jews have in common religiously is their rejection of Jesus as the Messiah or Christ. But even this does not solve the problem. For even when Jews become Christians they are still often spoken of as Jews. Are they a nationality? If all the Jews in the world were assembled in one locality we would find them as diverse as the nations of the world from which they came.

Nor is the other party to the conflict here considered a clear-cut entity —any more than are the Jews themselves. The people with whom Jews are

[2] For a strong statement of this position, see George A. Lundberg, "Some Neglected Aspects of the 'Minorities' Problem," *Modern Age,* Summer, 1958, pp. 285-297 and *Pluralism, Integration and Assimilation* (American Council for Judaism, 1957).

[3] George Lundberg labels the Jew's wish to abolish discrimination against him while at the same time he retains his own separatism as psychopathic (*Modern Age,* p. 289).

in conflict are not, as some Jews imply, "Christians." Indeed, those Christians who follow Jesus' teachings are the least likely of all to show hostility or discrimination toward Jews. The Jew is wont to view the world as divided into Jews and Christians—his own in-group and then a homogeneous out-group which he labels Christian. There are, of course, millions of non-Jews in American communities who are no more Christians than Jews are Jewish, so far as religious beliefs or formal church affiliations are concerned. To speak of the conflict as one between Jews and Christians is to imply that it is religious, which in the ordinary sense it is not; or, where it is, is so only incidentally to a more fundamental cultural conflict.

In some phases of the conflict Jews are in conflict with upper-class people intent upon keeping those without proper class lineage out, or with climbers on their way up who cannot afford to take chances by associating with people who do not have the "right" kind of background. In other phases, Jews are in conflict with buyers who fight back against what they consider exploitation. The situation in Harlem is an illustration of this. The non-Jews, then, in the Jew–non-Jew conflict are as varied as are the Jews themselves.

Trends and Extent of Discrimination

Before proceeding, it is well to point out that anti-Semitism as an official governmental or public policy of discrimination against Jews has never prevailed in American community life.

The amount of hostility toward Jews varies from time to time and place to place. One student places the peak of intensity in the late 1930's, reaching a high point at the time of Pearl Harbor. Thereafter it dropped sharply.

Even in the early 1940's, not all non-Jews felt hostility toward Jews. One student of the subject estimated in 1944 that from 5 to 10 percent of the people in American communities were violently anti-Semitic, and that about 45 percent were mildly so, leaving almost half who were not anti-Semitic at all.[4]

The general picture, so far as spatial distribution is concerned, as revealed by polls has indicated that anti-Semitism is strongest in the Northeast and Middle West, where the concentration of Jews is greatest; and weakest in the South and West. It appears to be stronger in urban than rural populations, especially in large cities. It seems to be stronger in upper-income brackets than in lower-income brackets, and stronger among whites than among Negroes.

The relationship to education was equivocal. The better educated people are less likely to harbor stereotyped conceptions about minority groups than less educated people; but they are more likely to reject social

[4] G. W. Allport, "Bigot in Our Midst," *Commonweal*, Oct. 6, 1944, pp. 582-586.

contacts beyond casual meetings. Education was found in one study to be more effective among persons of lower socio-economic status than among those of higher; indeed "in some cases its effect is so strong on these individuals as to make them less prejudiced than the educated of the upper status group."[5] The same student continues: "when anti-Semitism in American society has risen or fallen the changes have been sharpest among educated people."[6]

Issues

ECONOMIC

An old, but now vastly mitigated, issue in the relations between Jews and non-Jews lay in the economic realm. A good deal of the resentment against Jews in the past was really but another aspect of economic conflict in general, such as already described in Chapter 14. By historical accident rather than choice Jews had been traditionally sellers and money-lenders. They were often landlords. And, as we have seen, no matter who fulfills these economic functions, conflict of interests results and often leads to hostility. Lenders, landlords—sellers in general—are in conflict with borrowers, tenants—buyers in general. It was an unfortunate fact that Jews had become identified with conflict-laden occupations. Sellers are likely, as we have seen, to be exploitative unless they are restrained. If sellers belong to the same cultural group as buyers, there are cultural restraints imposed on their predatory tendencies. The usual in-group controls will soften the rigors of the conflict. But if sellers belong to a different cultural group, they are not subjected to such restraints. Then the sky is the limit; anything goes. Primitive people felt no compunction about exploiting members of other groups. The white men felt no compunction about exploiting the Indians or, indeed, natives anywhere. Jews as sellers behaved like sellers everywhere. As a result they were accused of sharp practices in business. When they replied that other people were equally guilty of sharp practices, non-Jews felt that this *ad hominem* argument was somewhat beside the point, since a larger proportion of Jews than of other peoples were sellers.

A non-Jewish buyer who felt that he had been intimidated, bullied, or bamboozled into buying inferior goods at a high price might have two different reactions, depending on the seller. If the seller was a non-Jew, the buyer would be infuriated at sellers in general. If the seller was a Jew, the buyer might forget about his conflict with sellers in general and vent his anger upon Jews in particular as sellers. It would be small compensation to know that some of the most enlightened selling practices had been Jewish inventions too, the one-price system, for example.

[5] Charles Herbert Stemberg, quoted in the *New York Times,* Apr. 29, 1961.
[6] *Ibid.*

Many non-Jews resented the concentration of Jews in certain business and professional occupations, many of which they considered "parasitic," and they attributed to the Jews strategic and disproportionate power with respect to the press, recreation, and the movies. Between one-third and two-fifths (35 to 40 percent) of Jews in the 1940's, and therefore of first and second generation Jews, were in commerce and trade, as contrasted with 13.8 percent of the general population; one-tenth to one-eighth (10 to 12 percent) were in the professions, compared with 6.8 percent. Even within these occupations there was concentration. In trade, it was retail trade, especially food, clothing, furniture, and drugs. In manufacturing, Jews were primarily in the light industries producing consumer goods, especially clothing, headwear, furs, printing, and foods. Among the professions, Jews have been outstanding in law, medicine, pharmacy, and dentistry.

This occupational picture reflected not only the vestigial tradition which first and second generation Jews brought with them from Europe but it also reflected the attitudes of the outside world. In the late 1930's, for example, one study found as many as 95 percent of job orders in employment agencies were closed to Jews.[7] But times and generations changed. The need for talented personnel, the opening up of new professions, the improved education of third-generation Jews—88.2 percent with college education as compared to 20.3 percent in second-generation Jews in one community—and the impact of fair-employment-practices legislation transformed the picture.

Discrimination against Jews declined to such an extent that in 1956 one study reported that only 22 percent of private employers in major industries in the San Francisco Bay area admitted such practices.[9] Consumer-goods industries, dealing with the public directly, appear more ready than producers-goods industries to eliminate discrimination. Most discriminatory are white-collar, clerical, and administrative positions.

The justification for rejecting Jews for executive positions was spelled out by one industrialist as follows:

> It is important for our business that our plant managers maintain a certain status in their communities. They must join the country club and the leading city club. Today, that's where the big deals are discussed and made. They must be socially acceptable to the banking and business leaders of the town. They must be able to maintain a free and easy association with the people who count. If we promote Jewish personnel into key, sensitive positions, we run a risk of social non-acceptability. We avoid this by picking someone else.[10]

The implications of this point of view will be examined in the discussion of discrimination in social life.

[7] Benjamin R. Epstein, *Anti-Semitism in the United States: A Current Appraisal* (Anti-Defamation League of B'nai Brith, n.d.), p. 6.

[8] Kramer and Leventman, *op. cit.*, p. 130.

[9] Epstein, *loc. cit.*

[10] *Ibid.*, pp. 3-4.

The battle is not over, but the enormous progress made between the second and the third generations suggests that the fourth generation, and the generations they are surrounded by, will look back and wonder what all the shouting was about.

EDUCATION

A second focal point of conflict between Jews and non-Jews centers about the admission of Jews to institutions of higher learning. The issue is, in allocating the limited resources of higher education, what method should be used? If competition is used, what should be tested? If a substitute for competition is used, what principle should be applied?

Unlike the example of Catholics, there is little conflict between Jews and non-Jews at the elementary or even the secondary level. Jews do have their religious schools, to be sure—250 all-day Hebrew schools with 50,000 pupils[11]—but they do not in any way compete with the public elementary schools. Nor do Jews ask for public support for their schools or attempt to control the public schools.

The real issue arises at the college and university level. There are not enough facilities in certain institutions to accommodate all who wish to take advantage of them. This is especially true in the prestige colleges and in professional schools. The question then arises, How should the scarce facilities be allocated among applicants? The problem is not so likely to arise in publicly supported institutions, where such an issue cannot legitimately arise: the criterion for admission is ability.

In the past Jews protested that colleges and universities imposed quotas on them; admissions were, so to speak, rationed. Although unofficial in the sense that this practice was not part of the written charter or official by-laws of the several colleges and universities, it was nevertheless an established fact.

But here again a revolution has taken place. The new emphasis on talent and ability made other criteria for selection obsolete. The results showed themselves in a drastic increase in the proportion of Jewish students at the prestige colleges. Between 1945 and 1955, for example, enrollment of Jews at Ivy League colleges rose from 15 to 22.9 percent and at the prestige women's colleges, from 10.4 to 15.8 percent.[12] The proportion of Jewish young people of college age who are attending college is estimated to be 62 percent, contrasted with about 27 percent for non-Jewish young people. The drop in applicants to medical schools has had a mitigating effect on discriminatory practices here also.

POLITICAL

In 1947 and 1948 a new issue in Jew–non-Jew conflict was the Jews' attitude toward the establishment of a Jewish state in Palestine: that is,

[11] *New York Times,* May 8, 1961.
[12] *New York Times,* Nov. 12, 1956.

Zionism. Candidates for office kept bidding up the price of the Jewish vote until all candidates had virtually to demand a national Jewish state in Palestine if they wished to secure votes in key districts, notably in New York. The result was a series of commitments culminating in pressure on the United Nations to vote a partition of Palestine in 1947 and to assign certain areas to the Jews as an independent national state. In succeeding months, the United States changed its official policy with respect to Zionism. The military necessity for keeping Arabian oil available was advanced as the reason for refusing to antagonize Arabian leaders by implementing the decision of the United Nations.

Ever since the beginning of its existence, then, Israel has posed problems for American policy. Thus, for example, when Saudi Arabia refused to admit American citizens of Jewish faith—even to man an air base—the United States government was put in a delicate position. All policy in the Middle East is complicated by the fact that no position can be taken which antagonizes a large voting bloc. During the presidential election of 1960, Republicans quoted an editorial from an Israeli newspaper which "pointed up the fact that there were 2,000,000 Jewish votes in the United States and that for the sake of Israel they should be cast for Vice President Nixon."[13] It looks to the man on the street as though Jews were divided in their loyalties, as though they were putting the welfare of Israel above that of their own country.

It should be pointed out that not all Jews are Zionists; many are indifferent; some are even ardently anti-Zionists. In fact, Zionism is more of an issue within the Jewish community than it is with outsiders.

SOCIAL LIFE

As it has already been suggested, the social life of Jews is complicated by the anomalous class structure of their community. Jews who, on the basis of their class status, occupation, and education, might be expected to associate with upper-class non-Jews are, in fact, excluded from such association because they do not have the proper lineage. They do not "belong." Jews have risen on the social ladder much more rapidly than other immigrant groups because they came at a time when the general trend in this country was toward urbanization and industrialization, in both of which the Jews had had more experience than other immigrant groups. They have made spectacular progress up the social ladder, but the fact remains that they do not have "family" in the sense necessary for upper-class acceptance.

Feeling superior to the non-Jews with lower class status than their own and with less intellectual and artistic interests than their own, these Jews are thrown back upon themselves. They create their own upper class. They, too, in time come to demand "family"; but the lineage need not, of course,

[13] *Ibid.*, Oct. 14, 1960.

be of such long standing as in the case of non-Jews. The discrimination which these upper-class Jews experience is cultural, mainly in the sense of a class culture rather than in the sense of ethnic or religious cultural differences as between Jews and non-Jews. In time, they gain acceptance in the upper regions.[14]

One by one the bastions of discrimination crumble; new times, new practices. New York has been in this, as in other areas, a pace-setter. In 1952 its antidiscrimination law was extended to include places of public accommodation, resort, and amusement. Thereafter hotels and resorts were not permitted to advertise themselves as "Christians only" or as not allowing Jews. And even private clubs, if they solicited conventions, have been held to be bound by anti-discriminatory laws.

By 1959 a great decline in social discrimination was reported in residence, fraternities, and city social clubs. A study of housing showed, for example, "a gradual decrease in the number of exclusionary residential areas in most communities, throughout the country."[15] National fraternities had been abolishing barriers at an accelerating rate so that within five years only two out of sixty-one still retained restrictions against Jews, as compared with twenty-five about fifteen years earlier.

The social club is a very special kind of issue. And here the most subtle sociological forces are at work. They ramify widely, however, and exert an influence in many areas of group life. The justification given for exclusion of Jews from the social club is usually based on social grounds. It is argued, for example, that pleasant social intercourse presupposes the consensus that results from similarity of background. There must be consensus with respect to values. There must be similarity of moral and social backgrounds. The same things must be taken for granted; the same taboos must be observed; the same values must be respected. The norms regulating behavior, in brief, must be congruent. Differences may not represent inferiorities, but they may represent friction. Easy and relaxed social contacts are impossible where codes of behavior differ too much. The behavior which is objected to in a group may not be immoral; it may not be wrong; it may not be inferior. But if it is different, that is enough to throw a monkey wrench into the delicate machinery of personal relationships.

These subtleties of human contacts were cogently stated by a perceptive Jew:

> The members of any group are usually at ease among themselves. They can afford to deal with one another on the plane of habit. But let an outsider appear among them and they become wary. They watch themselves, they calculate their behavior; in sum, they are "self-conscious." They keep asking themselves whether they can properly say this before the stranger, or do that. Sooner or later the necessity for self-scrutiny and deliberation becomes a nuisance. They end by wish-

14 Cleveland Amory, *Who Killed Society?* (New York: Harper, 1960), Chapter 8.
15 John Slawson, quoted in the *New York Times*, Oct. 31, 1959.

ing that the intruder would get himself off. But suppose he does not oblige them by doing so? An active resentment may be engendered. Hence it comes to pass that Gentiles would often prefer to do without the company of a quite unexceptionable Jew. He puts them too painfully on the *qui vive*. The process, needless to say, works in reverse also. Jews who are altogether comfortable with one another may turn awkward as soon as a Gentile pops up in their midst, and may sigh with relief once he is gone.[16]

Since this is unquestionably so, the argument of the non-Jew concludes, and since it is our own private social life, we have a right to run it to suit ourselves. We have no desire to practice official or political or economic anti-Semitism. We simply wish to have our own social life uncomplicated by unnecessary frictions.

If social clubs, particularly so-called city clubs or town clubs, were simply that—social clubs—the argument would be plausible and irrefutable. For no one should be forced to associate with people he is uncomfortable with in his private life. But, Jews argue, these clubs are not just private social clubs. They have ceased to be primarily social organizations. They are instruments in the hands of power groups and are used to retain exclusive control of community structures. The "impersonal hotel-like atmosphere" of these clubs "completely belies the premise of congeniality and cameraderie" of its members.[17] *Business Week* concluded a study with the statement that the private social club had become the "business man's castle."[18]

It is argued that the social club has become a place where important business is transacted and that anyone who is excluded is thereby cut off from participation in important decisions. The work of researchers on the community power structure, to be presented in Chapter 22, is invoked to show how much policy-making is done at informal social gatherings, private clubs, and after-business-hours associations. When Jews are excluded they are cut off from participation in decisions. The main purpose of the exclusionary practices, it is alleged, is precisely to exclude in order not to have to share power.[19]

It is argued, further, that such exclusion ramifies. The company that did not hire Jews at the executive level because they could not perform their roles adequately unless they had access to the proper social clubs has already been mentioned. Exclusion therefore spreads from the club to the job.

It is not, therefore, just a frivolous desire for social "status" or a callous desire to intrude where they are not wanted that leads Jews to

[16] Rabbi Milton Steinberg, *A Partisan Guide to the Jewish Problem* (New York: Bobbs-Merrill, 1945), p. 51.

[17] Carey McWilliams, quoted in N. C. Belth, *The Private Club and the Power Structure* (Anti-Discrimination League, n.d.), p. 7.

[18] Belth, *op. cit.*, p. 7.

[19] *Ibid.*

raise the issue of discrimination in city clubs. It was particularly significant that "New York's most successful social clubs of the 1960's . . . all have Jewish members. So, too, do the extraordinarily successful college clubs."[20] Modern Americans, face-to-face with third generation other Americans found them no threat at all. The dire predictions that presage the demise of any status quo did not materialize. All that happened was the emergence of another status quo, and it was just as comfortable as the old.

Old people, it has been reported, tend to be more exclusionary than younger persons.[21] It is the undergraduate members of the fraternity who want the Jews—and Negroes—in their organization; it is the alumni who object. Women were also found to be more reluctant to give up exclusionary practices than men.

What social discrimination remains, according to the same report, persists "more out of cultural lag and habit rather than antagonism. . . . Vituperative, hostile language . . . against other groups is rare today in private social circles as contrasted with ten years ago."[22]

There is an intrinsic inconsistency between the goal of free and unfettered social contacts, however, and another goal of the Jewish community, namely that of retaining its ethnic identity which, at least in the past, has proscribed intermarriage. For social life implies that social distance is slight. Antipathy to intermarriage increases social distance. Indeed, when instruments for the measurement of social distance are devised, willingness to permit marriage constitutes one of the best indexes of absence of social distance. If, it is argued, a majority of Jews—even, as we shall see, in the third generation—maintain an "exomagous taboo," as it has been called, then free and unrestricted social life between them and non-Jews becomes difficult to maintain. A wall, real though invisible, is erected between the Jews and the outsiders. College fraternities and sororities provide a complex example. At the present time, these organizations in coeducational institutions are, whatever their ostensible and publicized purposes, in large part dating and courting agencies. The presence of barriers in these college organizations makes it impossible for Jews and non-Jews to participate freely in an intimate social life which is conducive to marriage. In the case of Negroes, "social equality," as we have seen, is proscribed by whites because it might lead to intermarriage; the prevalent Jewish opposition to intermarriage automatically proscribes "social equality." The reaction of friendly non-Jews to this opposition to intermarriage is that it represents what seems to them a wholly unnecessary barrier to cultural unity.

INTERMARRIAGE

Intermarriage does not become an issue between those who oppose it. Nor between those who are indifferent about it; these people accept it or

[20] Amory, *op. cit.*, p. 226.
[21] Slawson, *loc. cit.*
[22] *Ibid.*

ignore it; they do not care. Intermarriage becomes an issue in two kinds of situations: (1) between non-Jews who object to intermarriage and those Jews who would be willing to adopt a policy of intermarriage but are prevented from so doing by the attitudes of some non-Jews; and, conversely, (2) between friendly non-Jews who have no feeling against intermarriage and those Jews who oppose it strongly.

(1) Among non-Jews, opposition to intermarriage probably springs from many sources. In the case of Catholics there is a strong religious motivation. We have seen how strong is Catholic opposition to intermarriage, even with Protestant Christians. It is even stronger in the case of Jews. It requires much determination on the part of the contracting parties to enter marriage under such discouraging and inauspicious circumstances.

Among upper-class non-Jews there is likely to be opposition to intermarriage on a class basis. Where status is important, marriage to a person without the proper family background or lineage is not countenanced. The opposition may conceivably be as strong to a non-Jew as to a Jew lacking the proper credentials. Such outsiders do not "fit in" to the class pattern. There are, of course, exceptions: occasionally an upper-class family is willing to accept a social "inferior" if he happens to be extraordinarily famous, wealthy, or distinguished.

In the past there were doubtless also many non-Jews who opposed intermarriage because Jews seemed to them different, queer, and strange. They, like Jews, feared the extra hazards involved in such marriages. If they were religious, they dreaded the problems the Jew's religious difference would raise; if they were not, they might still dread the conflicts in mores and general point of view, especially within the immediate family and social circles. These sources of objection, like so many others, become attenuated with respect to third-generation Jews.

(2) The attitude of many if not most Jews with respect to intermarriage has traditionally been no less strict than that of Catholics. If a rabbi marries the Jew and non-Jew, he may even, like the Catholic priest, ask for a formal promise that the home be a Jewish home and the children reared as Jews, although there is no ecclesiastical requirement in this respect as in the case of Catholics. In the first generation a child who married outside the fold was mourned as dead; there was scarcely a more lamentable catastrophe that could happen to such a family. Even among the more liberal Jews, intermarriage may be frowned upon. Thus a Reform rabbi in one community was forced to resign when his son married a non-Jew. And this resistance to intermarriage is one value which persists even into the third generation.

Despite increasing contacts with the outside world, for example, in the third generation in-group tendencies persist:

Nowhere are the in-group pressures stronger than in the area of marriage choices. Although two thirds of the sample once dated gentile girls, 87 per cent preferred to marry a Jewish wife, either because of family pressures (52 per cent) or because they felt there would be fewer marital problems (48 per cent). (Of those married, 93 per cent actually have Jewish wives). Few offer any clearly formulated reasons for their decided preference for religious endogamy. This is simply the way things have always been, as far as they are concerned.

I was brought up that way in my environment. It's just not kosher to marry a gentile and I never thought differently.

I have irrational feelings about intermarriage. It's just not done. I almost married a superior type of non-Jewish nurse myself, but I decided against it and I'm not sure why. Maybe because it's too good for the *goyim* (having a Jewish husband, that is).

Their ambivalence is projected into the future; sixty-nine per cent disapprove of intermarriage for their children as well. Some are indifferent or don't know how they would react to such a hypothetical situation. Only 10 per cent would actually give the intermarriage their parental blessings, or at least accept it, although none of the others anticipate sitting in mourning for the intermarried offspring as the orthodox first generation did. Most of those who object to the prospect of intermarriage suspect they would accept it after it was a *fait accompli.*[23] Whatever the reason for the resistance, if not active opposition, to intermarriage even in the third generation, it has, as in the case of Catholics, the effect of arousing resentment on the part of outsiders who themselves feel no hostility toward Jews. It seems to them more blatantly discriminatory against non-Jews than that of non-Jews toward them. Indeed, one third-generation Jewish informant stated that he was "much more bothered by the Jews' antigentile behavior. They're more discriminating than gentiles."[24]

Levels of Accommodation

So much, then, for a summary statement of the chief foci of Jew–non-Jew conflict in American community life. What point on the accommodation scale should we aim at in working out a *modus vivendi?* Since the conflict cannot be dealt with by removing either of the parties from the scene, this mode of dealing with conflict may be ignored here.

Accommodation on a manipulative and even bargaining level has been characteristic of Jew–non-Jew relationships in many lands for many centuries. If a king coveted a beautiful Jewish woman for his queen, as Ahashueris did, this might give Jews bargaining chips. So also might their financial prowess. Individual Jews, in turn, often exploited individual buyers and borrowers for their own ends also. This level of accommodation was one of the best ways to engender hatreds and hostilities on all sides. Most American communities deplore such relationships. Certainly no one would consider them a desirable goal.

[23] Kramer and Leventman, *op. cit.,* pp. 180-181.
[24] *Ibid.,* p. 180.

An accommodation at the level of tolerance called cultural pluralism or cultural heterogeneity rather than cultural unity or homogeneity is advocated by some Jews and non-Jews. They suggest that American communities ought to encourage cultural variety rather than insist on cultural similarity. We ought, they feel, to love rather than hate one another for our differences. Some Jews believe it is "Israel's mission" to stand for this principle of dealing with minorities throughout the world. Cultural pluralism implies more than tolerance; it implies a cooperative relationship. Proponents of this point of view advocate cooperation between Jews and non-Jews in a great many phases of community life. And, indeed, Jews do enter freely into the National Conference of Christians and Jews and community chests receive their wholehearted support. There is, it is argued, room for a great deal of cooperation against common enemies—lack of housing, job insecurity, inadequate health facilities, to name but a few—to demand the cooperative assault of all groups. Cultural pluralists feel that the existence of strong structured ethnic sub-communities is the best guarantee of such cooperative effort.

This is, however, a radically different picture of America from that which has traditionally characterized our thinking. We have, consciously or unconsciously, been thinking in terms of a melting pot; we have cherished the idea that at some time or other we would be able to fuse minority groups into a common American culture. We have thought of the Balkanization of our community life as somehow or other a temporary makeshift until something better could be worked out. The idea of deliberately perpetuating differences for their own sake comes as something of a shock. Many non-Jews resent

> a philosophy which postulates the permanence and perpetuation of cultural pluralism. . . . They recognize the importance of allowing for time to remove the difficulties, but they resent the conscious effort to maintain and perpetuate walls when nature is doing its best to eliminate them. . . . The presence of a minority does, moreover, complicate . . . the life of the majority. It does constitute an "imperium in imperio"; it must be dealt with often as a separate entity through its leaders; by reason of its cohesion and clannishness and its location at strategic centers it may exercise a control out of all proportion to its actual numbers or even its actual contribution to the well-being of society; it does prevent the full and efficient functioning of many social institutions; it raises barriers such as intermarriage to normal social life.[25]

This point of view, expressed a generation ago, continued; it is still argued that there must be a *community* before difference can be welcomed or even admitted at all. Community does not consist of a set of distinctive enclaves, self-contained, self-fulfilling. If that is what the ambiguous expression "cultural pluralism" means, then "it must be rejected as a ground

[25] C. E. Silcox and G. M. Fisher, *Catholics, Jews and Protestants* (New York: Harper, 1934), p. 353.

of any rights whatever. . . . We conclude that for the development of community relations between Jews and non-Jews separate organizations for causes that Jews share with others should be discouraged wherever an inclusive organization is or can be made reasonably available for the same objective."[26]

The third mode of accommodating differences, assimilation, is not an issue between Jews and non-Jews, but it is a major problem within the Jewish community itself, as we shall presently note.

Intra-Jewish Conflict

As in the case of Catholics, the cleavages within the Jewish community are as great, if not greater—because so much more immediate—than those between Jews and non-Jews; and the issues are often the same within the community as those between it and the outside world.

For despite, and, indeed, even because of, the success of Jews in achieving a national homeland in Israel and in "selling" the idea of a pluralistic society at home, Jews are in a crisis of self-identity. Both in Israel and in the United States the differences within the Jewish fold which until now have been overshadowed by the presence of common enemies are coming into clearer focus. The differences strike at the very roots of group relationships.

We noted in the case of Catholics that in the third generation people learn to be Catholic in an American way. In the first and second generation the ethnic matrix of their religion is still so powerful that jettisoning any part of it seems to imperil all parts. But after a while it becomes clear that one can be Catholic in the American language, so to speak. One does not have to speak a foreign tongue or eat certain foods or court a mate in the Polish or Italian or German or Irish manner in order to be a Catholic. The ethnic adhesions of Catholicism tend to be snipped away.[27]

A similar process occurs among Jews, but the problem is far more complicated. The religion of Judaism has become so completely tied in with ethnic patterns that it seems impossible to be Jews in any but an ethnic manner. Thus when Arnold Toynbee suggested that Jews abandon the ethnic, and to him irrelevant, restrictions of their religion, thus breaking down barriers between Jews and non-Jews and making Judaism the spiritual possession of the whole human race,[28] he was attacked by leading rabbis as advocating ethnic suicide.[29]

[26] Robert M. MacIver, quoted by George Lundberg in *Pluralism, Integration and Assimilation,* p. 12.

[27] This process has been analyzed by Will Herberg in *Protestant, Catholic, Jew* Anchor (New York: Doubleday, 1960).

[28] In a talk before the American Council for Judaism, reported in *New York Times,* May 7, 1961.

[29] Reverend Doctor David J. Seligson, reported in *New York Times,* May 14, 1961.

The establishment of the state of Israel has made it even more difficult to achieve identity, for it does indeed interject nationality into the situation. And Zionism itself becomes an issue among American Jews. The American Council for Judaism, formed in 1943, has consistently defined Judaism as a strictly religious phenomenon; it has rejected out of hand all ethnic and national qualifications. It opposed Zionism from the beginning and continues to do so. The Council holds that "nationality and religion are separate and distinct; and that our nationality is American, our religion Judaism; that we do not accept, for ourselves, any concept of Jews as a separate national group."[30]

Among Zionists themselves the most disconcerting developments were occurring in Israel. Here, indeed, the ethnic adhesions of Judaism were being stripped away; the Israeli government was, in fact, according to some of the more conservative, "persecuting" the Jews; fist fights occurred at a rally of protesting Zionists in New York. American Jews were exhorted to use their influence with the Israeli government to make them permit religious freedom.

More serious, as a challenge to identity, many of the younger Israelis were not at all religious. They were not Jews in a religious sense at all. If Zionism in the sense of a national homeland for Jews—prayed for daily for milennia—resulted in actual fact in a homeland for Israelis who were not at all Jewish, in the old ethnic sense, where did this leave American Jews?

If the withdrawal of the hostile pressures from the outside world in the form of anti-Semitism had had the effect of diluting or even destroying the religious identity of young Israelis,[31] a similar set of forces was eroding ethnicity in American communities also. The third generation, without in any sense making an issue of it, was nevertheless moving in the direction

[30] *New York Times*, Mar. 21, 1955.

[31] One function of the Eichmann trial was to teach young Israelis, who had themselves never experienced it, the nature of anti-Semitism and thus to strengthen ethnic bonds. "The trial was intended partly as an invocation to young Israelis to look back to their heritage of suffering and study the history of an anti-Semitism they never experienced themselves. It was a way for the adults to impress upon the children that they belonged to a nation of Jews, invisibly tied to the Jewish people all over the world. 'How can I explain it to my child?' an Israeli asked the other day. 'How can I make him understand that when I was a child in school in Austria I got pushed around because I was a Jew? In Israel everybody is a Jew. So who is going to push my boy around because he is a Jew?' The soliloquy was one of only mock despair. But the fact is that the younger generation is growing up in Israel without 'feeling' Jewish. The youngsters feel like ordinary people in an ordinary state and most parents here have discovered to their surprise that at some stage they must explain to their children that not all people in the world are Jews. This is what the old Zionists wanted. They wanted a state where the Jews could be free from prejudice and persecution. But they had not foreseen that in such a state Jews would not feel especially Jewish" (Lawrence Fellows, "Israelis Hope Eichmann's Trial Will Awaken Young to Heritage," *New York Times,* June 25, 1961). Actually it was the political, not religious, hostility of the surrounding—also Semitic—Arab world which kept Israeli morale at high pitch; and the integrating bonds were nationalistic, not religious, in nature.

of assimilation. Despite warnings from leaders that there was a "rising tide of assimilation" leading to a decline of Jewish cultural life[32] and that "assimilation was the greatest peril to Jewish survival"[33] third generation Jews showed "some ambivalence . . . as to the allegiance they owe to the Jewish community and its institutions."[34] Half of the informants in one study felt they should belong to Jewish organizations. Comments of those who felt they should retain affiliations with the Jewish community and its organizations took this form:

A lawyer has obligations to his community. B'nai B'rith does community work. These Jewish philanthropies also provide contacts for me.

I'm still Jewish in the eyes of others, therefore I remain Jewish and owe some obligation to the Jewish community, even if I've neglected it in the past.[35]

Comments of those who objected to exclusive participation in the Jewish community, the "rebels against the institutionalized pressures for in-group behavior who deny any common interests with members of organizations whose only reason for existence is their 'Jewishness,' " were of the following cast:

I join organizations on the basis of common interests, not to play cards or bowl. I have no common interests with these people.

I have no particular interest in Jewish organizations which operate only in terms of fund-raising.

I don't feel strongly affiliated with Jewish affairs and social activities. Cultural interests are important to me and these are not the basis of these Jewish organizations.

I don't feel clannish or insecure and afraid to get out of the ghetto. I'm proud of our heritage, but I don't believe in ghettos and organizations only for Jews.[36]

This part of the third generation rejects the very idea of a Jewish community:

I don't think there's a place today for a 100 per cent Jewish community. . . .

Jews are too tight a social group here. They don't try to integrate and they create problems for themselves. They're prejudiced themselves.[37]

Assimilation in a new form appears to be in process, not as a group policy, as it was among some nineteenth-century Germans, nor, painfully, indi-

[32] *New York Times,* Nov. 30, 1959.
[33] *Ibid.,* June 11, 1961.
[34] Kramer and Leventman, *op. cit.,* p. 184. Compare with Herberg's evaluation of third generation attitudes.
[35] *Ibid.,* p. 184.
[36] *Ibid.,* p. 185.
[37] *Ibid.,* p. 186.

vidual by individual,[38] but in an almost imperceptible withdrawal of support from community agencies and a rejection of self-exclusion.

> Respondents who have become sophisticated in the ways of a gentile world . . . do not yet speak for all of the third generation, but they are a vocal minority wary of any social characteristics that distinguish Jew from gentile, particularly those that might impede the development of peer relations. . . . Above all, these respondents are disturbed by discriminatory practices on the part of the Jews that contribute to their own social segregation. Exclusion is bad enough; self-exclusion is intolerable.[39]

The success of the American assignment in community living has made it possible for Jews to decide whether or not they wish to remain Jews. It is possible for them to wish to cease to be Jews without feeling they must remain Jews as a matter of loyalty to an attacked group; there is no shame associated with the desire not to be affiliated with the Jewish community. Ceasing to be a Jew does not take the form of renunciation; it is not a negative attitude but a positive one, one of acceptance. Assimilation in this sense is not forced on anyone, any more than segregation is. If reluctant, resentful Jews pass out of the fold, it means that those who remain are willing, cheerful, voluntary Jews, a selected group with high morale. Having made a choice, they are willing to pay the asking price for differences. Assimilation in this form does not take the humiliating form of a superior group's forcing the capitulation or surrender of an inferior group, nor the almost equally humiliating form of "missionary" work, of attempting a conversion. This is not the old "melting pot" in action, to be sure, but it is not a mosaic either.

Success in achieving group goals, a national home land and the breakdown of barriers in the case of Jews, can have the most surprising—and unanticipated—results.

[38] For an account of this process, see Anonymous, "I Was a Jew," *Forum*, January, 1940, pp. 8-11.

[39] *Ibid.*, p. 187.

19

Other Minority-Group Conflict

The basic pattern of all minority-group situations with respect to the majority group is similar. The fundamental issue is, what should be the conditions of competition? How should competition for jobs, for housing, for facilities of all kinds be institutionalized? Should there be competition in the first place? Or should some alternative to competition be substituted? If there should be competition, should some individuals be handicapped? others privileged? Or should we aim at equality of opportunity?

The details may vary, but the general pattern is similar. The conflict between Americans of Oriental or Mexican origin or descent and native white Americans is, for example, both racial and cultural. Like the Negro, the Japanese, the Chinese, and the Mexican American bear on their bodies the signs of nonwhiteness. They belong to marked peoples. To this extent we may speak of "race conflict." But unlike the Negro, these Americans have recognized, literate cultures behind them. They cannot be dismissed as culturally inferior; nor can any ideology of white supremacy be forced upon them. That most terrible weapon in race conflict, the denial of self-respect, the foisting of negative self-images, is not available in this conflict. Americans of Oriental or Mexican descent can be exploited, but they cannot be culturally browbeaten. Having a literate culture behind one is a powerful, almost an unbeatable, defense weapon in culture conflict. The Jews illustrate this fact better, perhaps, than any other group. But so do the Chinese, the Japanese, and the Mexican Americans. Unlike the Negro, too, the Americans of Chinese, Japanese, or Mexican nativity or ancestry speak a foreign language. This fact may seem very simple, but it is not. A foreign language, even a foreign accent, may not only act as a barrier to communication but also as an excuse to perpetuate separation by segregating Spanish-speaking children, for example, in schools of their own. Again unlike the Negro, Americans of Chinese, Japanese, and Mexican origin or ancestry have a different religion from that of most white Americans. In the case of the Mexican Americans, to be sure, it is a Christian religion, but it is often a different kind of Christianity from that which other Americans practice.[1] And, finally, the Chinese and Japanese Americans are very few in number; and even the number of Mexican Americans is far less than that of Negroes. But they are concentrated, so that for specific communities they constitute very sizable segments of the population.

There is one minority group that is, however, quite unique in its relationships with the majority group, namely the American Indians. Theirs is the only case in American history in which the elimination of one of the parties to a conflict was legal policy. In the case of no other group were reservations set aside for exclusive occupancy. In the case of no other group were formal treaties drawn up specifying the rights and obligations of each. It is true that religious groups have voluntarily withdrawn from the outside world; but they retained at least some contact with it. And there was no governmental policy involved. The American Indian was not at all integrated into the larger society.

Chinese Americans

The builders of American transcontinental railroads found it to their interest to have the cheap labor of Chinese coolies during the middle years of the nineteenth century. Chinese labor was also useful in the lumber camps and mines. It was to the interests of the Chinese themselves to come to the United States, even at the low wages offered, because the Opium War with England and the Taiping Rebellion had aggravated the chronic poverty and hardship at home. There was at that time, then, no conflict of interests.

But when the pressing need for cheap labor passed in the 1870's, it was no longer to the interest of native Americans to have the Chinese workers here, constituting a reservoir of labor against which to compete. Strong agitation arose to put a stop to Chinese immigration, resulting in 1882 in the first Chinese Exclusion Act, a law barring Chinese laborers from entrance into the United States for ten years. Nor were they permitted to become American citizens, a fact which deprived them of certain rights. In 1904, all Chinese except visiting students and professors were banned from entrance into this country. In 1917, and again in 1924, the restrictions were tightened so that Chinese could not enter even as part of another nation's quota. Although an unknown number were smuggled in after 1904, the number of Chinese in this country in 1950 was only 117,629, or 0.1 percent of the total population. In 1943, chiefly as a morale measure during the war, the Exclusion Act was repealed and Chinese were finally permitted to enter on a quota basis—105 could enter annually. In 1949 Orientals were permitted to become citizens.

The original conflict was handled, then, by eliminating, to all intents

[1] Ruth D. Tuck, *Not with the Fist* (New York: Harcourt, Brace & World, 1946), p. 97.

and purposes, one party to the conflict. Because the Chinese have ceased to be a serious competitive threat to native workers and because they are clever enough to resist the more blatant forms of exploitation, the level of accommodation is likely to be one of tolerance, or even cooperation. Traces of exploitation still remain, however, in the now outmoded restrictive covenants; in segregation into certain occupations such as hand laundries, restaurants, and merchandising in their own communities, which are noncompetitive with whites. But laws against intermarriage—in communities where it would make any difference, at least—and exclusion from citizenship no longer exist.

The Chinese in the United States are highly urbanized, 93 percent being urban dwellers in 1950. Most of them (54.3 percent in 1950) are in the Pacific region and (20.6 percent) in New York, largely in San Francisco and New York City.

Japanese Americans

The Japanese began to come to the United States in the 1880's, after the passage of the Chinese Exclusion Act of 1882. Unlike the docile Chinese coolies, the Japanese came with cultural pride and ambition; and they had great ability; they were successful. They had a knack for farming. They worked hard, lived simply. They set a competitive pace which native Americans found difficult to maintain. The conflict which resulted was bitter. The Japanese were forbidden by law from owning land. They, like the Chinese, were forbidden from becoming citizens. Finally, in 1907, they were forbidden, by the so-called gentlemen's agreement, or unofficial treaty between Japan and the United States, from even coming to the United States at all.

In 1950 there were only 141,768 Japanese in the United States, only 0.1 percent of the total population. For most communities they constitute no problem at all, since all but about ten percent are concentrated in the Pacific, East North Central, and West South Central Regions. Even this level of concentration is a reduction from prewar levels. Events of the 1940's, to be noted presently, had the effect by 1950 of reducing the proportion of Japanese in the Pacific region from 2.3 percent to 1.7 percent, while increasing the proportion in the Middle Atlantic and East North Central regions from 0.1 percent to 0.2 percent and in the East South Central region from zero to 0.1 percent.

Before World War II there was strong hostility against many of the Japanese, especially because of their success. The problems of the American-born Japanese, or Nisei, who constitute an increasing proportion of all Japanese, were especially acute. They knew no life except that of the American communities where they had been born and reared. They felt like other Americans, read American books, went to American schools, dressed, played, and worked like Americans, but they were anchored in a Japanese culture by their strong family ties. Nor were they allowed to participate freely in American life. They were truly marginal or bicultural in many cases. None of their problems was, however, especially different, except in degree, from similar problems of other children of immigrants. The war, however, brought into the open the hostilities and aggressions which in peacetime had lurked behind a semblance of friendliness.

In 1942, therefore, something happened which was unique in American history. This was the wholesale transplanting of 110,000 Japanese—only one-third of whom were foreign-born and two-thirds of whom were native-born American citizens—from their homes on the Pacific Coast to ten relocation centers or concentration camps east of the coastal mountains. This was justified at the time as a necessary measure of military security. Actually there was no proof of such necessity. The underlying pressures for the evacuation came from interest groups which wished protection against Japanese competition, both crescive and economic. Citizens in California communities feared they would be outbred:

> The principal complaint of the Native Sons of the [Golden West] has been that Japanese, by reason of an abnormal birth rate, would crowd the white population out of California. The virtues of the state as a "white man's paradise" have been extolled, and it had been charged that the Japanese goverment sent women to California to "live with Jap-men for the sole purpose of breeding . . . children" in order "to gain control of this State. . . . Unless routed now, within the next fifty years they will have control, if not possession, of California!"[2]

The fear of economic competition developed in whatever group the Japanese happened to be competing with, first among laborers, later among farmers. In 1906 a Congressman expressed the difficulties of workers competing with the Japanese as follows:

> As is well known, no white man can compete with the Japanese laborers. They are satisfied to be housed in such cramped and squalid quarters as few white men . . . could live in, and the food that keeps them in condition would be too cheap and poor to satisfy the most common labor in this country. . . . The Japanese has the science of living at a minimum reduced to the finest point of any nationality that I know of in the world.[3]

His conclusion was that the government should enter a coalition with American workers to "assist him to maintain every equitable right and protect him from every enemy who would destroy his home and his American standard of living." And in 1909 the plight of the farmer competing with the Japanese was stated as "we need enough Japanese as workers to keep some lines in our agriculture going; it is hard to see how a ruinous

[2] Morton Grodzins, *Americans Betrayed* (Chicago: University of Chicago, 1949), pp. 6-7. Copyright 1949 by the University of Chicago.

[3] *Ibid.*, p. 9.

slump could be avoided without them. But we do not wish too many of them, nor do we wish them to buy up and lease up all the good things of the State and paint the future for Americans on this coast dark brown."[4]

The relocation policy was not, it has been alleged, a matter of military necessity but a camouflage seized upon by interested persons who wished, at one strike, to get rid of competitors and to take advantage of forced sales of businesses, homes, and other properties. It was, according to this view, an attempt to solve a community conflict by getting rid of one party to the conflict as "honorably" as possible, that is, on the pretext of military necessity.

Whether or not this analysis was correct, the Supreme Court declared that Japanese Americans of unquestioned loyalty could not be detained in the relocation centers. In January 1945 the relocation order was revoked and by the end of that year all the relocation centers were closed. While the evacuation order was in force, the policy of the War Relocation Administration was, so far as possible, to resettle the loyal Japanese Americans in communities away from the Pacific Coast. In this the authorities were successful to a large degree—some 53,000 having settled east of the Sierra Nevadas. Most observers agreed that this scattering of Japanese Americans into communities where there was no tradition of hostility was a good thing. It helped to decrease friction; it gave both Japanese Americans and other Americans a new perspective on the problems involved. By separating the native Japanese Americans from their Japanese parents, it cut them off from cultural forces which had tended to prevent complete acceptance of American culture.

But the problems of the 50,000 Japanese Americans who went back to their old homes on the Pacific Coast and of the communities to which they returned remained acute. Indeed, the conflict which had existed for many years was then resumed. Fear was expressed that return of the Japanese would provoke another wave of anti-Japanese hatred like that of 1942, and, indeed, in May and June 1945 there was a wave of terrorism in California, as well as boycotts, job discrimination, denial of business and professional licenses, extortionate insurance premiums, and legal barriers. With the return of more nearly normal conditions, with the prosperity which softened the conditions of competition for everyone (except buyers), and with the public condemnation which such behavior aroused, hostility and violence subsided.

One of the most interesting aftermaths of the crisis in the conflict between Japanese Americans and white Americans was the method which the Japanese Americans used to fight back. The state of California had sought to have property owned by the Japanese returned to the state on the ground that it was illegal for Japanese to own property under the Alien Land Act of California. The Japanese Americans now challenged the

[4] *Ibid.*

legality of this action, since the property had been held by American citizens and was therefore not subject to the terms of the Alien Land Act. In 1948, Congress passed a bill authorizing the Attorney General to settle claims up to $2500 for losses by Japanese Americans evacuated from the West Coast during the war.

Even more far-reaching was the fact that Japanese Americans filed with the federal courts several suits challenging the constitutionality of the section of the Federal Nationality Act, which limited the privilege of naturalization to members of the white race only. Using the Fifteenth Amendment as their basis of argument, they claimed that such provisions were unconstitutional. They pointed out that they were nationals, not aliens. A movement developed in Congress to make it possible for Japanese still classified as aliens to acquire citizenship. In 1949, Congress finally passed a law permitting Orientals to become citizens.

It would hardly be worth reporting this brief episode in American history and the relationships between 110,000 Japanese Americans and others if it did not have significant sociological overtones. It revealed how extremely difficult the American ideals of community life are to implement in fact; it revealed how easy it is to fall into the fallacy of racism; but it revealed also the strategic power of ideals. Policies changed under the pitiless scrutiny of the public and of the court. In a showdown it is impossible officially to violate the professed values of the community.

Mexican Americans

Although there are Mexican Americans in many communities throughout the country, especially in the industrial cities of the Middle West and East, they are for the most part concentrated in the Southwest and in California. Many have lived for centuries in small American villages, little different today from those of a hundred years ago.

Attitudes toward Mexican Americans vary from community to community. Where they are not numerous, they are treated like other immigrants; perhaps they have more glamor than some. In other communities their status is about as low as that of the Negro.

Because in the past most statistics have lumped Mexicans with the white races and because records of immigration from Mexico have been faulty or even nonexistent, and because there have been many cases of illegal entry of Mexicans, we have very little reliable information about the numbers of Americans of Mexican origin or descent in our country.

As in the case of so many immigrant groups, it was to the interests of their employers as well as to their own interests that they come. They were needed as laborers. They were eagerly sought out and recruited in their native villages and in market towns. They were called in, literally, by agents of developing industries—railroads, mines, citrus farms, sugar-beet plantations, winter-vegetable ranches, and cotton plantations. And they were glad to come to jobs that paid so well. The conflict arose when they remained and had, somehow or other, to be accommodated to as neighbors and fellow-citizens—as Americans.

For it was one thing to call them in to work and quite another thing to house them, educate their children, and live with them. Here the issues were essentially similar to those in Negro-white relations—jobs, housing, recreational and social facilities, schooling. The Mexicans were imported, frankly, to do the dirty work of railroad maintenance and factory-farm agriculture. But when their children aspired to higher jobs they found themselves blocked by the older traditions of occupational specialization. "We don't hire Mexicans for the office—go down to the sacking department." "The board doesn't want a Mexican teacher." As a result, the Mexican Americans were poor, often unemployed. The demand for labor during the war, however, meant new opportunities; pay was good. But even under these circumstances, opportunities for advancement were not good for Mexican Americans.

Like the Negro, the Mexican American in business or in a profession depends largely on his own people for patronage.

> If he (or she) is hired as a teacher, it is for a "Mexican" school. If he operates a store, it is for Mexican Americans; if a newspaper, it is for them, too. Social workers carry Mexican case-loads; doctors and lawyers find their most dependable source of income among their own group. . . . Carried to excess . . . this process bottles up and frustrates good talent. A subtle form of segregation, it is perhaps more injurious than all the rest, because it closes—or limits sharply—the way out at the top of the semi-caste.[5]

It is discouraging to young Mexican Americans and it deprives the community at large of the skills and talents of a sizable segment of the population. In brief, as in the case of other racial minorities, especially the Negroes, the basic issue as far as jobs are concerned is simply that of equal opportunity, removal of competitive barriers, so that all may reach as high a level as their talents permit.

The housing of Mexican Americans, like that of Negroes, is the worst in the community. They live in *colonias,* or segregated areas, in the poorest part of town. It is often argued, by those who wish to assuage their consciences, that Mexican Americans prefer to live that way, with their own communal life. The efforts of those who can afford it to move away belie the accuracy of this assertion. But although restrictive covenants do not usually bar Mexican Americans from good neighborhoods, other pressures do. In the absence of antidiscrimination laws landlords do not rent to Mexican Americans; or owners refuse to sell.

> Some families of "high type" pseudo-Mexican or Spanish origin, have always lived outside the *colonia;* this group usually includes the consular officials and their

[5] Tuck, *op. cit.,* pp. 181-182.

families. Once a Mexican American family is settled in a neighborhood, there is little friction. Sometimes there is active good will and friendliness, if the neighbors happen to be Catholic also. The friction arises when another family of Mexican extraction tries to move into the same general neighborhood. "We don't want any more Mexicans on this street," is the slogan, applicable no matter how "high-type" and "Spanish" the invaders may be. If a number of families of Mexican extraction begin to move into a neighborhood, it may suddenly develop that there are no houses for sale for miles around. Owners have just changed their minds about selling, say the agents, and what can one do? Thus, without recourse to anything so crude as a restrictive covenant, a quota system is actually set up for movement away from the *colonia*.[6]

Since the areas where Mexican Americans are concentrated are less likely than others to have antidiscrimination legislation, they do not have the protection of enacted norms on their side.

In many communities the recreational and social facilities for Mexican Americans are often inferior to those of other Americans. Like Negroes they may find it difficult to secure service in eating places. It is, however, becoming illegal to display signs such as "White trade only."

The education of Mexican American children is often complicated by the fact that their native tongue is Spanish. This was formerly the excuse offered for segregating them into separate schools. In the late 1940's, however, this practice was declared unconstitutional in California. Nevertheless, since Mexican Americans live in segregated *colonias* they are likely to attend essentially segregated schools. Teachers prefer not to teach in these schools, usually the oldest and poorest equipped. The bright Mexican American child is often discouraged from carrying his education beyond the elementary level both by his own family and by teachers and counselors. Why complete your education, the family would argue, when you can only do manual labor anyway? Or teachers themselves would argue that it would be a disservice to stimulate a bright boy or girl to continue his or her education in view of the difficulties of placement. Thus a vicious circle was completed. When accused of discriminatory practices, employers claimed that they could not find adequately trained Mexican Americans for jobs; precisely this attitude, in turn, discouraged the Mexican Americans from training for better jobs.

The issues discussed above are, it will be noted, precisely the same as those in Negro-white conflict. The Mexican American does not, however, have certain other issues which the Negro has. He is not disenfranchised; he can vote if he wants to, and his vote is carefully watched. There are no legal caste barriers; the Mexican American is usually classed with the white race, at least legally. He can intermarry if he wishes to. He has a cultural background which protects him from self-contempt. He has race pride, which is something the Negro is only now, slowly and painfully, achieving.

As in the case of other minority groups, there is conflict within the

[6] *Ibid.*, pp. 201-202.

Mexican American community also. There is, as with other immigrant groups, intergenerational conflict. There are also exploiting leaders who take advantage of the ignorance of the immigrants. There is, finally, often a conflict between Mexican religious practices and American ways or between Mexican Catholicism and Protestantism. Although the parish priest may have little following in most matters, especially where the Mexican American has some knowledge and experience, in new areas his word is accepted. Thus, if he is opposed to public housing, unionization, day nurseries, and antivenereal-disease publicity, his parishioners will follow him. Often he is opposed to things which would be to the advantage of his flock and help them assimilate the American culture.

The techniques used in the conflict between Mexican Americans and other Americans range all the way from open violence, to subtle playing upon race pride at a more exploitative level. Thus, although there may be no legal barriers against housing in good areas or against patronage of good shops and eating places, Mexican Americans can be effectively barred by having it implied that they are pushing in where they are not wanted. Proud and sensitive, they often respond to this type of attack by withdrawing from even an honest demand for basic rights. Or the hope is held out that for the "better type" Mexican American there is a chance for complete acceptance if he cuts himself off from his group; or the more Machiavellian technique of playing the Mexican American off against the Negro is used. The Mexican American is told he is better off than the Negro, so what is he complaining about? Divide and conquer is still a powerful device in any conflict.

On their part, Mexican Americans, long docile and exploitable, are learning to fight back. They are beginning to organize civic leagues, defense committees, Mexican American movements, and similar groups to fight for their rights. They are beginning to take their cases to the courts, particularly the federal courts. Their leaders are beginning to see the power inherent in the ballot, and although there is as yet no strong Mexican American voting bloc, the creation of such a bloc is not far in the offing. The experience of Mexican Americans in the armed forces was stimulating to many of them. They were dispersed into communities that did not share the Southwest's attitude toward them; some broke the caste barriers and married whiter Americans. The kind of exploitation their home communities practiced seemed wholly incompatible with the ideals they were told they fought for. For some Mexican Americans there has been complete assimilation. Most hope to achieve an accommodation which will preserve for them "the best of both ways," that is, Mexican and American.

The account so far is not very different from the standard pattern of relationships between racial groups in American communities. Substitute Negro, Jew, Japanese, Chinese—the story is monotonously the same. But just as there is great similarity, so in each case there is also something unique. In the case of the Mexican Americans it is the interesting and peculiar institution of imported-deported workers. The purpose of the innovation, instituted during World War II, was to furnish American industry with Mexican workers when needed but to repatriate them when they were no longer needed. The worker was not left stranded, as he was after World War I, and the community was relieved of the necessity of having to care for him. The plan was carried out by the United States government and was intended to benefit both worker and industrialist. The United States government entered into agreements with the Mexican government whereby workers were brought in especially for work on the railroads and in agriculture, chiefly in California and Texas. The Mexican government recruited the workers and in this country the Federal Security Administration was entrusted with their care. The contributions of these workers to the winning of the war was freely acknowledged but, once their contribution was made, they were not permitted to remain in the United States. The contract under which they came required that they be returned to Mexico.

In 1948, the Mexican government took advantage of this new device and used it as a powerful strategic weapon against exploitation of its nationals in this country. Aiming where it hurt most, at the community's pocketbook, it produced a phenomenal response. By augmenting the power of Mexicans, it raised the level of accommodation for all Mexican Americans. It gave them bargaining power. The Mexican government revoked the alien-labor agreement, thus cutting off the chief transient-labor supply for the cotton fields of Texas. Without this labor, harvesting of cotton was well-nigh impossible. The Texas Cotton Ginners' Association therefore went to the Mexican government to seek a new agreement. The Mexican government pointed out the educational, social, and economic discrimination which Mexicans faced in Texas. Under such conditions the Mexican government did not wish to sponsor an alien-labor pact.

The cotton ginners realized the price they would have to pay for imported labor would have to include a modification if not reversal of the community policy of discrimination. The so-called Stilley Plan was evolved, whereby the ginners agreed to apply pressure to schools and industrial and agricultural centers where discrimination was practiced. They sponsored meetings "to explain to farmers, businessmen, peace officers and others that for the well-being of the community discriminatory practices against Mexicans must cease. Local groups . . . set up boards or committees to investigate discrimination and to work with the ginners' association, the Texas Good Neighbor Commission and the Mexican consul."[7] Anything that improved the lot of the imported Mexican worker would, ipso facto, also improve the lot of the Mexican American.

[7] John E. King, "Texas Fights Bias to Insure Supply of Mexican Labor," *New York Times*, July 4, 1948.

The importation of Mexican workers was opposed by religious groups for humanitarian reasons and by competing domestic workers for self-interest reasons. The peak of importation in California was reached in 1956 and declined to 73,700 in 1960. The feeling was general that although the *bracero* must continue to be used, greater effort should be made to recruit domestic workers first. The major interest here is the use made of the social device of importing workers by the Mexican government in improving the lot of its nationals and thereby also of Mexican Americans in American communities, a novel and unique kind of bargaining in the history of intergroup relations in this country.

The American Indian

Indian-white relations, as noted above, are and have been unique. Until the frontier came to an end, the relations had been those of aggression and resistance. By the late 1880's the result was that all the Indians were settled on reservations and a new pattern of relationships was established. Well, not established, really. For policies have changed so often and so drastically that Indians have become confused, uncertain exactly where they stood.

In 1887 the Dawes Act allotted reservation land to individual tribal members, remaining lands to be sold. Title to the land allotted to individuals would be held by the United States for 25 years. This looked like a feasible solution, especially since the Indian population was declining, but at the end of the century the number of Indians began to increase. There was an estimated million Indians in the area of the United States when the white man discovered the continent. This number was down to 25,731 in 1870. It increased, slowly at first, but almost quadrupled between 1880 and 1890. In 1950 it was up to 343,410.[8]

In the face of this increase, the allotted land proved to be wholly inadequate; in some cases allotments were divided and subdivided to such an extent that heirs held less than four acres. Some Indians lost their holdings to white men. By the 1920's it became evident that the paternalistic policy had not succeeded in overcoming the Indian's poverty or his apathy.

Citizenship was granted in 1924, and the Indian Reorganization Act of 1934 embodied a new approach to Indian-white relations. Tribes were now permitted to organize and operate their own enterprises. More land was bought and added to Indians' holdings. Serious mistakes were made by tribes and their leaders, but in 1948 the Hoover Commission reported that "tribally owned and controlled economic enterprises are playing a significant part today in the improvement of Indian life. There are tribal (or

[8] Donald J. Bogue, *The Population of the United States* (New York: Free Press, 1959), p. 123.

village) loan funds, herds, forests, range lands, sawmills, fisheries, canneries, stores, marketing cooperatives, and other enterprises."[9]

From the human point of view, as well as the anthropological, there are many interesting aspects of the story of the Indian. But from the sociological point of view it is especially interesting because it illustrates a pattern of relationship without parallel or precedent. Unlike the Negro, the Indian was never integrated into our society; he remained a foreign enclave. This kind of relationship was not consonant with our ideals and in the 1950's the so-called policy of termination was inaugurated. The idea was that the government would end the reservation status of Indians and encourage them to enter the outside world and assimilate. Some tribes welcomed this policy; the Klamath Indians in Oregon, for example, accepted their checks in July, 1961, and began to take part in community affairs in nearby towns.[10] Even termination, fair as it seemed, was not the solution for all tribes. Many Indians who left their tribal homes did succeed in the outer world; some became judges, some sheep herders. Indian blood was a source of pride for many prominent people, from a vice president of the United States to a popular humorist. Some became millionaires from oil on their land—But these were exceptions. The outer world was often a demoralizing factor. Unprepared, unskilled, without sufficient guidance and help, many "terminated" Indians sank into poverty worse than that of the reservation.

Opposition to termination developed also because many Indians felt that it was a scheme on the part of unscrupulous white men to deprive them of their land. They wished to have it modified. In its place they wanted the same kind of help as that accorded other underdeveloped areas in the world by the government. And, indeed, reservations were more like underdeveloped areas than they were like integral parts of the United States.

But the American pattern of intergroup relations was beginning to emerge. In 1943, for example, the National Congress of American Indians was formed, and annual meetings were held thereafter. They hoped to become a pressure group comparable to the American Legion or the National Association of Manufacturers. In 1959 the keynote of their meetings was "Register—Inform Yourself—Vote—Participate in the Political Party of Your Choice."[11] In 1961 the convention drew up a set of requests to be presented to the President. Whatever else the organization achieved, it welded all the diverse tribes into a single group, it taught them to state their problems, and it gave them increasing confidence in their dealings with whites. It would only be a matter of time until they learned how to

[9] Quoted by John C. Ewers in "Happy Hunting Ground for Historians," *Saturday Review*, May 6, 1961, p. 51.

[10] *New York Times*, July 2, 1961.

[11] *New York Times*, Dec. 13, 1959.

carry on conflict in the white man's way, how to exert pressure where it counted, how to exploit the white man's professed ideals, how to affect the alternatives open to the white man in a way that helped them. When they have learned this art so that they count political rather than, as their ancestors did, military coups, they will be well on their way to being Americanized Americans.

In the meanwhile, Indians who seek to take advantage of the termination policy and to enter the outside world will need all the good will and help they can get; the vulnerability of atomized individuals, deprived of group and cultural support, has been documented again and again. Most immigrant groups protected their members for at least two generations. The existence of an ethnic community helped the transition from one culture to another. But such ethnic communities were possible because the immigrant's culture and the American one had at least some roots in common. But how, one wonders, can even a third generation learn how to be Indian in an "American" way?

The Puerto Ricans

Compared with the American Indian, the Puerto Rican represents an almost classic illustration of the course of intergroup relations in American communities. Like other immigrant groups, they came to supply the work needed at the lowest industrial levels; like other groups, they began with great handicaps, suffered discrimination, even exploitation. Like other groups they seemed to the established community hopeless prospects for Americanization; like other groups they learned how to use American institutions. Like other groups they will ultimately find a place in the variegated mosaic of American community life.

There are some variations on the classic theme. A certain indeterminate proportion of Puerto Ricans—officially stated to be seven percent—are Negro. This fact acts as a deterrent on their learning to speak the American language, for as long as they speak Spanish they are not considered the same as native Negroes. Unlike earlier ethnic groups, furthermore, they have not concentrated in isolated neighborhoods, so that "in Manhattan there is scarcely a major residence district, with the exception of the middle East Side, that has not felt the impact."[12]

New York City has been an "area of first settlement" for most Puerto Ricans; most not only entered the country in New York City but also remained there. But an increasing number use New York only as, in effect, a transitional phase and then fan out to other cities. Thus Chicago and Philadelphia were among the cities to which an increasing number went, and in Chicago where, according to a Catholic priest, of all foreign-language groups, they integrated fastest, they adjusted "without strife."[13]

[12] Harry L. Shapiro, in the *New York Times,* May 9, 1957.
[13] *New York Times,* June 4, 1961.

In New York, the Puerto Ricans learned little by little how to use the laws at their disposal to fight the battles of discrimination. In 1953 there were only four cases before the state commission against discrimination; in the first three quarters of 1956, there were 155.[14] The weapons were there; it was a matter of learning how to use them. They were learning.

Full Circle

In view of the history of ethnic- and racial-group relations in American communities, it is interesting to note that in the 1950's many southern mountain people—so-called hillbillies—came out of the hills and entered the cities. Of purest old American racial stock, they fell into precisely the same pattern as the early foreign-born groups had. They were no different, sociologically speaking, than nineteenth century immigrants from abroad. And the second- and third-generation Americans viewed them with about the same mixture of shock, disapproval, and annoyance as that with which the old-line American families had viewed their own grandparents; all of which goes to prove that it is less the blood that runs in one's veins than the paths in the social structure in which one's life course runs that makes the difference in intergroup relationships.

It will be noted that in our discussion of minority groups we have resorted very sparingly to the concept of race or religious prejudice. The term "prejudice" is, upon analysis, almost meaningless. It hardly explains anything at all. We cannot really understand group relations if we think in terms of irrational "prejudice." If group hostilities were a matter of mere prejudice they would be more amenable to therapeutic action. But group hostilities are not mere subjective biases. Concepts of "scapegoats," "stereotypes," and the like may be useful in explaining individual phenomena; but they are hardly sufficient to explain phenomena of the magnitude and significance of group hostilities. Gratuitous hatreds are not the common rule. Group hostilities arise because of conflict, not vice versa. Where there are genuine incompatibilities among groups the conditions for conflict exist, and under such circumstances hostilities are likely to be engendered. Where there are security and abundance in American community life, the conditions of conflict are mitigated; where there are insecurity and scarcity, these conditions are aggravated.

We should also point out, finally, that there is so much conflict in American community life in part because of the very ideals, creeds, beliefs, and other facets of the American pattern which characterize it. If we did not have the egalitarian ideal, if we accepted a caste theory of living, if we did not base our creed on freedom, there might be much less conflict. We would then simply keep certain groups in their place, isolated from streams of thought which might be subversive. Many societies have lived peacefully

[14] *New York Times,* Dec. 4, 1956.

and harmoniously on such a basis. But we take the children of immigrants and of Negroes, send them to school, indoctrinate them with ideals of freedom and equality of opportunity, expose them to ideas which stimulate thinking about their own lot, give them "bargaining chips," and inevitably they come to challenge their exploited position. They come to want to share fully in American life. The more Americanized they become, the more they insist upon their rights, even if they have to fight for them.

In a very real and profound sense, the spectacle of Japanese, Mexican Americans, Negroes, Puerto Ricans—even American Indians—fighting back through the courts, the press, and the ballot is a stimulating, even exhilarating, one; the success of their efforts is a measure of the success of the dominant culture in American community life. No matter what individual members of the majority group may do or say that is contrary to American ideals, the ideals themselves seem to have a dynamic vitality and force of their own; they create a kind of personality in the second or third generation which demands their implementation. However much the dominant group may resent having to surrender its privileged position in the competition of life, as minority groups come to demand a fairer chance, the seeming failure of the majority group in being able to hold on to its favored position is in reality a resounding success. The success of the minority group is, in a fundamental way, the success of the majority group.

Part **VI**

The Process of Institutionalization of Enacted Norms

THE PROCESSES which give rise to crescive institutions such as custom, mores, convention, and tradition are difficult to determine. But the processes which give rise to enacted institutions have been studied and reported on from many angles. The actual method by which laws are enacted in any particular society or community is itself a matter of institutional arrangements. They may be promulgated by a ruler or they may be hammered out by a legislative body.

Many models may be devised also for institutionalizing access to positions where law is enacted. A strong man may fight his way to a position where his word takes on the force of law. In another situation intrigue, guile, and craft—the manipulation of incentives—may be the road to positions where law is made. Or men may inherit such positions, as in hereditary monarchies.

In the West a characteristic set of institutions, both crescive and enacted, has evolved which assigns the lawmaking function to a body of elected representatives of the people and access to this body is competitive. In American communities this involves competing for votes in an election.

Legislation itself also involves conflict. Conflicting groups must find ways of accommodating their differences and the battleground may be inside the legislative chamber or outside and, since law must be interpreted, also in the courts.

Throughout our discussion of conflict we have noted that the form which any conflict takes in any area—consumer, industrial, race, religious—is profoundly influenced by the way the relationships among the groups involved are institutionalized. Do customs and traditions and laws favor one against another? And we saw that a large part of conflict consists of efforts to get the government into a coalition with one's own side; this involves getting legislation which commits the government. For this reason control of the lawmaking process is basic. It is essential that norms be enacted to institutionalize relationships in your favor. The struggle to get control of the legislative process is political conflict, and access to positions of control involves political competition. It is to a consideration of these processes that Part VI is devoted.

20

Political Conflict and Competition: The Institutionalization of Community Behavior by Legislation

Consent and Resistance

Political power is only one kind of power; but it is crucial. All other concentrations of power—religious, labor, industrial—sooner or later must reckon with political power. Sooner or later access to legitimate force must be sought. The exercise of all kinds of power may, and indeed has, therefore, come under the scrutiny of those who wield political power.

It is sometimes said that all government rests on the consent of the governed, that unless people are willing to accept it, it fails.[1] Public opinion is said to be the basis of all government. Such conclusions are ex post facto. They define their conclusions in terms of what happens. Although it is not necessarily true that governments rest on the consent of the people, it is true that all governments must base their strategy on the possible reactions of the people to whatever they do.

Where there is no institutionalized "feedback" system, as there is in a democratic state, the people may have to rely on a tacit-game strategy to protect themselves. The people may not deliberately or consciously revolt or reject; but if millions of people feel themselves to be too misused, the chances are that there will be a feedback, even if it is not deliberate, or conscious, or purposive. Common interests or grievances emerge and then people discover them. Thus a great resistance movement may exist a long time before it is discovered even by the people who are resisting. In totalitarian states, for example, millions of individual peasant families may resist the pressures put upon them, not deliberately, not necessarily with

[1] A distinction is made by political sociologists between consent and legitimacy. People may consider as legitimate even a government to which they do not consent. "Legitimacy, in and of itself, may be associated with many forms of political organization, including oppressive ones." (Seymour M. Lipset, *Political Man* [New York: Free Press, p. 77]) .

malice aforethought, but with a kind of automatic sabotage. They give a minimum of time and attention—and even this perfunctorily—to their obligations to the commune or collective and a maximum of loving care to their private plots. We need imagine no vindictive or hostile motivation. The cadre member who supervises the operation may seem to them as impersonal as a mountain, just something to be reckoned with. We need posit no rebellion or revolutionary sentiments; nor any conscious organization—just, family by family, an inarticulate resistance to the work on the commune or collective. So long as this resistance is not discovered by the resisters, so long as it is not organized, it can be dealt with case by case by the commissar. One function of informers, aside from the information they report, is the prevention of the discovery of mass resistance by the resisters themselves. Barriers are placed in the way of communication so that each resister feels isolated and powerless. Once communication becomes open and free, people feel more secure in their resistance, organization becomes more feasible, and resistance more strategic. Skilled leaders learn to read signals, to sense when the people are uneasy, disturbed, tense, filled with malaise, and accommodate their behavior to them before it is too late.

It is because of the importance of communication and publics in control that one of the most critical tests of any regime is the amount of freedom it permits to the communication media. Where there is freedom there will be many and varied publics. Dissatisfaction easily reflects itself in the formation of protesting publics. People quickly discover that their private dissatisfactions are common, that there is, indeed, a public with the same dissatisfactions. It is easier to organize these dissatisfied publics into action groups. A regime which is designed to make provision for such protesting groups can afford to permit, even encourage, them. But a regime not designed to cope with dissenting groups cannot afford to permit protesting publics to emerge in the first place. That is why censorship and control of the mass media are among the critical characteristics of nondemocratic regimes. The channels to men's minds are important; they have to be guarded assiduously. Freedom of the press, of speech, from censorship, these are the central keys to the dialogue of power; they are essential to permit feedback.

In a democratic regime feedback and resistance are not left to chance. Clear-cut provision is made for them in the institutional structure of the community. Effort is made to ventilate grievances. There is a great dialogue between the public and persons occupying positions of power. All major legislation is preceded by weeks, months, or even years of debate between and among representatives of differing points of view. Television, radio, the press are all recruited to carry on this vital function, to extend and amplify the day-by-day debate in tavern, bus, club, and home. Everyone is encouraged to have his say. The theory is that this is the way a consensus is reached.

In addition it is expected that interest groups will organize not only to participate in the great public debate but also to persuade or bargain with those in positions of power.

Legislation As an Institutionalizing Process

As the existence of legislation institutionalizing all kinds of competitive and conflict relationships, summarized in Parts IV and V, indicate, they have become a matter of governmental policy, hence political. The goal sought by the parties to the conflict is access to legitimate power to enforce their will on their adversaries. They want to make the rules which institutionalize the relationships. They want to control the lawmaking, the law-interpreting, and the law-enforcement processes. Political conflict, therefore, centers about legislative bodies, municipal, state, and national, and about courts of law and about administrative boards and commissions as well as in the mass media.

In a sense this chapter is a continuation of the discussion begun in Chapter 4 on the nature of institutions. In Chapter 4 we were concerned chiefly with crescive institutions, those that grew up and were then discovered. By way of contrast we referred to institutions which arise as the result of decisions, which are enacted. Legislation is the process which gives rise to legal institutions, to the thousands of statutes which thereafter determine—with what success we will presently note—the relationships between and among groups, systems, and structures.

The Strategic Functions of Legislation

The ostensible function of legislation is to control or regulate behavior. The strategic function, that is the way it operates as a strategic force, is manifold. For one thing, it signals that the government—with its access to the legitimate use of force—is on one side in a conflict situation, buyers or sellers, labor or management, Negroes or whites, and so on, rather than on the other side. This is extremely important. We have seen time and again that the strategies available to any party in a conflict situation depend in large measure on how the relationships are institutionalized. A strike, for example, is one thing if the law is on management's side, quite another if it is on labor's. A sit-in, similarly, is one thing if the courts are on the Negro's side; it is another if they are on the other side. Legislation also creates commitments. It enforces promises in the way of contracts. It makes threats credible. It is often a "first move." Legislation, in brief, gives strategic "chips" to one side or another in a conflict situation.

Parties and Issues

Because any conflict may become political, the parties to political conflict may be groups of any kind—religious, professional, property-owning, citizens', industrial, sectional, racial, ethnic, veterans'—in fact, any type of group at all. Since almost any kind of conflict in our day is likely sooner or later to come within the purview of government, practically any conflict may become political in nature.

For the same reasons, the issues in political conflict, schismatic or pressuring, are as variegated as the groups involved. They may be economic in nature—consumers versus producers, buyers versus sellers, management versus labor, rural versus urban, one industry versus another, one section against another. The use of tax monies is likely to be the general form any number of specific issues may take.

At the local level, municipal or private ownership of public utilities such as gas, electricity, and transportation may be an issue. Public or private housing plans or slum clearance and urban renewal constitute another economic issue at the local level. Local option with respect to the prohibition of the liquor traffic may be a local issue. Control of gambling, prostitution, and commercialized amusements is another. As regulation of race and industrial relations becomes a municipal function, policies in these fields are also formulated as a result of political conflict. Control of the school system is another. Rat control, rubbish and garbage collection, vaccination, traffic and parking, milk and food inspection, water fluoridation, —in fact, anything that communities do or should do through their governments may become issues in local political conflict.

The characteristic level of accommodation in political conflict is the equilibrium level, and bargaining is the characteristic form. If one side is attempting to get rid of the other by means of violence, political conflict becomes revolution or rebellion and is of relatively short duration. If one side is definitely superordinate, the subordinate group is not likely to have much to say about policy.

Because of the variegated nature of both parties and issues in political conflict, we shall simplify our presentation by dealing specifically with only two aspects of political conflict, namely, the making of laws and the interpretation and enforcement of laws, particularly those relating to civil liberties.

There are two battlegrounds in the conflict which produces law: one is outside the legislative halls and one is inside. On the outside interested groups and their professional representatives or lobbyists exert tremendous pressure either directly on the lawmakers or indirectly through the lawmakers' constituents. Inside the legislative chamber, the lawmakers confront one another. The techniques used outside include participation in the great dialogue referred to above: advertising, propaganda, letters to the editor, public or even mass meetings, letters (open and private) to officials, public hearings, and direct action, so-called, such as picketing and even, sometimes, violence; they include also the more professional form of lobbying. Inside techniques include such practices as parliamentary strategy, filibustering, committee assignments, manipulations of rules, riders, and amendments. Only lobbying and parliamentary techniques will be discussed here.

Political Conflict outside the Legislative Chambers: Exerting Pressure

Although legislators are presumably selected on the basis of issues, during the term of their office numerous new issues arise and the people who voted for them find it necessary to keep them posted on their own wishes with respect to these new issues whenever their own interests are involved. Sometimes it is the citizens themselves, acting directly in their own organizations or even individually, who put pressure on government officials. This is the simplest and most direct way to exert influence. There is nothing sinister about it. We know who is trying to bring pressure to bear on policy-making officers.

Sometimes, however, it is not citizens themselves but professional lobbyists, hired by special interests, who fight for control of the policy-making machinery. In ways that are sometimes devious and doubtful, they exert pressure where it will count most in the lawmaking or policy-making process. They operate at all levels of government, municipal, state, and national. They represent special interest groups in legislatures. The lobby today is considered by some students to be more important than the political party itself.

PRESSURE AT THE LOCAL LEVEL

At the local level the pressure of interested groups is likely to find fairly direct expression. It is nearer to the citizen; he is inclined to take a more active role. Thus, when a certain area is to be rezoned, interested property-owners protest at an outdoor meeting. When a local Committee for a Fair Employment Practices Ordinance wishes to get a proposition submitted to the voters in a primary, its members picket the local board of aldermen until they get what they want. When white citizens wish to protest the designation of a playground as a Negro playground, they hold mass meetings, burn fiery crosses, and write letters to the editors of local newspapers. Examples such as these could be multiplied endlessly. Sometimes dramatic, sometimes not, the conflict for the control of policy goes on day in and day out in every community. The lobbying is likely to be more spontaneous, less permanently organized, nearer to those whose interests are involved than is pressure at higher levels. Perhaps the only serious criticism to make is that too few citizens participate in this form of pressure exertion.

PRESSURE AT THE STATE AND NATIONAL LEVELS

The exertion of pressure on state or federal legislators is not likely to take so personal, face-to-face a form as it does in the case of interested groups and their representatives on the local level. But it may do so. More commonly pressure is exerted by telegram or mail. Or personal delegations may present the case of interested groups for them. Or groups may pass resolutions for the benefit of legislators, to remind them of what their constituents are thinking.

Perhaps the most powerful form of pressure is the use of threats of reprisals at the polls. This use of the ballot as a threat in political conflict has been very effective among Negroes and also among ethnic and labor groups. Racial and ethnic groups, labor and industrial groups keep a record of the votes of all legislators on bills they are interested in and do not hesitate to use such records during political campaigns. Such threats are the opposite side of the coin of promises during a campaign.

At one point in the legislative process provision is made for all interested groups to present their case directly to the legislators themselves. Congressional committees dealing with especially controversial issues often hold open hearings, at which anyone is entitled to speak. Since the recommendations of committees are usually accepted by the larger body, it is extremely important to convince the committee members of one's own point of view. Congressional hearings are often the arena for fundamental conflicts.

More usual, however, is the exertion of pressure through paid lobbyists. Great economic interests keep well-paid men on the job all the time to see that laws favoring them are passed and laws opposing them are not passed. Thus silver-mining, meat-packing, food-processing, motion-pictures, railroads, banking, unions—the list could be greatly extended—illustrate interest groups fighting political battles by means of lobbies.

The National Catholic Welfare Conference, the Congregationalists, two Presbyterian bodies, the Northern Baptist Convention, the Friends Committee on National Legislation, the Christian Amendment Movement, the YWCA, the WCTU, the Militant Church Movement, the American Jewish Committee, the American Jewish Congress, and so forth are among religious organizations with representatives, each with from one to three lobbyists. Citizens' groups, consumers, and welfare interests also may have lobbies exerting pressure for their interests.

Although only about 800 lobbyists are officially registered as such, it is estimated that more than twice that number of persons are actually involved in such activities. There were, in fact, almost 150 registered lobbyists representing 102 organizations trying to influence farm legislation in one year. The specific techniques used in exerting pressure vary with the lobby. Sometimes they are based on facts and figures to prove the benefit of their program. Sometimes there is, in effect, a bargaining situation. Open bribery is not common, although the line between gifts and bribery is often difficult to draw. Entertaining is a common form, or rather occasion, for exerting influence; but for the most part lobbying is a fairly prosaic job.

A composite picture of a "typical" lobbyist has been sketched as follows:

> The full-time professional for a well-heeled lobby is in his mature middle years. If he is the head man, he earns as much as a Congressman: $22,500. His assistants match pay with a Congressman's assistants at about $18,000. He lives in a house costing $30,000 to $40,000, and sends his children to good schools.
>
> He favors a pipe, wears plain, good, ready-made clothes and puts something on his hair to keep it groomed. He can run a big office and a big staff with skill, and operate on a formal budget. He is a master of his special subject matter, and can exercise or direct modern techniques of research and analysis in his field.
>
> If he is a union lobbyist, he is probably an intellectual; otherwise, he takes his coloration from the practical affairs of his clients. He probably has law, economics or public relations somewhere in his background.
>
> He may have been a legislator himself. . . . He certainly knows as many Congressmen as possible, and understands politics in detail, at least as far down as Congressional districts.
>
> He has little time for back-slapping. He lives in staff conferences, communications and expositions to clients. When a lobbyist is not home at night, he is likely to be not in a saloon or night club, but at his office.[2]

The table of organization of a lobby includes the lobbyist himself, a supporting staff of lawyers, researchers, editors, and writers; policy groups; and, if necessary, regional, state, county, and local units. The lobbyist sends information down through this structure and receives it in return.

Lobbying is a competitive process in the case of uncommitted legislators. Representatives of both sides of a conflict compete to convince them of the superiority of their own point of view. John Nance Garner is quoted as saying that when a hard decision has to be made "the best thing is to find a lobby for and a lobby against, and between them you'll find the truth."[3]

There is, of course, nothing inherently wrong about lobbies or the exertion of political pressure. There is nothing to prevent disinterested citizens as well as special interest groups from forming lobbies. Indeed, there are some students of the subject who argue that lobbies correspond more nearly to the facts of modern political life than legislatures selected on a regional or geographic basis. They would go so far as to substitute functional representation, that is, representation selected by special interest groups, for geographic representation. They would have laws made by men representing different professions, industries, and occupations rather than by men representing different districts or states.

Although such a scheme may have much to recommend it in theory, actually the present method of "representation by lobbyists" poses a serious problem in a democracy. The difficulty is that lobbying is an expensive occupation; it costs a great deal of money. Salaries for lobbyists may range

[2] Frederic W. Collins, "Another Potomac Army: The Lobbyists," *New York Times Magazine,* Apr. 23, 1961, p. 99.

[3] *Ibid.,* p. 101.

up to $65,000 or more. In view of the benefits derived from the services of these men, such salaries are not at all exorbitant. But the average citizens' group cannot afford to spend even this much on lobbying. And some interest groups, such as children, sick people, and underprivileged groups in general, can afford no hearing at all. The lobby, therefore, is a well-to-do or rich organization's weapon in political conflict and it can be used to the detriment of the public. The crippling of public welfare programs by predatory pressure groups has, in the opinion of some students of the subject, sufficiently militated against the general well-being of the community to raise serious doubt as to the unrestricted right of individuals to create such irresponsible groups with power to intimidate government officials and endanger the common good.[4]

The need to institutionalize, that is, subject this kind of behavior to control, was officially recognized in the 1940's and resulted in the Federal Regulation of Lobbying Act, sometimes called the La Follette Act, of 1946. It requires all lobbyists to register with Congress, which is a first step in regulating this powerful form of political conflict.

Political Conflict within Legislative Assemblies

One of the great achievements of Western society—how great we can only appreciate when we see how difficult it is for other societies to achieve —is the so-called parliamentary system of government. The conditions for the achievement of this substitution of talk for violence are not common throughout the world. The very idea of a parliament strikes those unaccustomed to it as somehow or other absurd.[5] Conversely, to those accustomed to the idea of government by talk or debate, the "strong man" or "führer" principle is anathema. Except in nations in the British and Scandinavian tradition, there is a constant tendency for the strong-man principle to take over and subvert the parliamentary principle.

Since this verbal form of political conflict is likely to arouse a good deal of emotion, even, despite everything to prevent it, violence, it has become important to keep it strictly under control. The institutionalization of political conflict in parliamentary bodies is, therefore, extremely tight. The whole tradition of parliamentary debate, with its customs, mores, conventions, and rules of procedure—as codified, for example, in Roberts' *Rules of Order*—is designed to keep political conflict in deliberative bodies from degenerating into violence. Even under the best circumstances, violence may occur, but it is kept at a minimum by the strict adherence to

[4] George B. Galloway, *Congress at the Crossroads* (New York: Crowell, 1946).

[5] Totalitarian leaders have only contempt for parliamentary forms. Khrushchev, returning after participating in the fifteenth Assembly of the United Nations noted with a sneer that the United Nations could only talk. Both the League of Nations and the United Nations have been criticized as only glorified debating societies. Hitler found the British system, which paid a "loyal opposition," inconceivable.

parliamentary rules and conventions. People may speak only when recognized by the chairman; nothing can be discussed unless at least two people, the mover and the seconder of a motion, want to discuss it; order is a first consideration and anyone can rise to a point of order at any time; the group cannot be forced to talk if they do not want to, so a motion to adjourn takes precedence over everything else. In addition, to prevent the discussion from deteriorating into a personal battle, personalities are kept to a minimum: "The previous speaker" is referred to rather than "John Doe"; "his facts are at error," instead of "he's a liar."

Parliamentary debate is a combination of competition and conflict. It presupposes adversaries; but it also presupposes a body of reasonable and rational listeners who can be swayed by logic and by facts. The adversaries are not necessarily trying to change one another; but both are competing for the listeners.

Every great parliamentary body develops its own corpus of rules, in addition to the bedrock of traditional rules of order. And within the framework of parliamentary law numerous fighting tactics may be used. Skill in the use of parliamentary methods is a prime essential for success in political conflict. A clever parliamentarian can out-maneuver his opponents even when he represents only a minority faction. A good strategist can wage successful battles against any bill he wishes to kill.

Debate is, however, only one form which political conflict in legislative bodies may take. Equally characteristic is the process which goes under the name of logrolling, a process which has been called "the most characteristic legislative process."[6] It is common to speak of logrolling as somehow or other malodorous; the term is one of opprobrium.

It is trading. Logrolling fits well into the bargaining model of conflict. How much does the representative of one interest have to concede in order to secure the support of the representative of some other interest? The number and the value of the "chips" any specific interest has at its disposal will depend on the way the rules are set up. The most unlikely coalitions—since politics makes strange bedfellows—may result when two groups with conflicting interests in one area combine to oppose a third group against whom they have common interests.

Despite the apparent or seeming absurdities and inconsistencies of the American system, absurdities and inconsistencies which observers are not slow to comment on, it has the improbable characteristic of success. Somehow or other it manages to work. Fundamental to the successful operation of the parliamentary system as it works in the United States is the common interest of all conflicting groups to avoid a stalemate. The legislative "game" is therefore a mixed-motive game. Each interest group wishes to wring as many concessions as possible from its opponent and make as few

[6] A. F. Bentley, *The Process of Government* (Chicago: University of Chicago, 1908), p. 370.

as it can get away with; but accepting less than one would want or conceding more than would want is better than a stalemate. And, as political behavior is institutionalized in this country, there is great stability and there is always tomorrow—or, at least, the next election.

In addition to parliamentary debate and logrolling, there are other ways of fighting bills. One is to assign them to unsympathetic committees which will report them out unfavorably. Another way to kill an act if one cannot prevent its passage is to nullify it by seeing to it that the persons chosen to administer it will administer it the way its opponents want it administered. And if this tactic is unsuccessful, one can kill a law by refusing to give the administrative agency adequate funds to function properly. Starving popular legislation financially is simpler than running the risk of opposition to repeal.

The Fight in the Courts

In discussing the processes of institutionalization in Chapter 4 we noted that sometimes there is some difference of opinion about what exactly the norm is. In such cases there must be a judge or interpreter who can authoritatively state what it is. The function is, in effect, one of lawmaking. In a primitive society this function may be performed by a learned elder who presumably remembers all the precedents. In our society it is highly institutionalized in a complex court system. Thus it is not only outside and inside of legislative bodies that political conflict is waged in American communities but also before the courts as well. For it is a truism that merely getting a law on the books is no guarantee that it will function as planned. It may be administered in such a way as to nullify completely the will of the people and their representatives.[7]

As many kinds of conflict can come before the courts as there are kinds of legislation to be interpreted. Consumers and producers, buyers and sellers, management and labor, believers and nonbelievers, in fact, just about any interest may be the parties involved in the conflict.

We use for illustration here one of the most important kinds of political battles waged in the courts, those, namely, which deal with the protection of civil rights. It is usually a battle between some minority group—Negroes, various religious sects, conscientious objectors, even Communists—and those who control power. It is one of the most civilized forms of

[7] When the Clayton Act was passed in 1914, for example, labor leaders felt that at last they had secured adequate protection against the use of the injunction by employers as a weapon against unions. But the courts interpreted this provision completely out of existence and labor was left as vulnerable as before. It was not until the Norris-LaGuardia Act was passed in 1932 that the use of the injunction was finally limited in any really effective way. Another illustration was the Federal Trade Commission Act. The courts held that the Federal Trade Commission, set up in 1914, could protect not the public but only competitors. Not until the passage of the Wheeler-Lea Act of 1938 was this defect remedied.

political conflict. Very often it is in behalf of people we consider wrong. It is a fight for the right of people to differ from those in power.

As an example of political conflict waged through the courts the National Association for the Advancement of Colored People is outstanding. Today it is predominantly a Negro organization. It has won all but two or three of the cases it has taken to the Supreme Court. In 1944 it won the so-called Texas primary case, in which the Supreme Court declared that inasmuch as political parties were state-controlled organizations performing essentially a governmental function in running primary elections, they had no right to exclude qualified voters because they were Negroes. This was truly revolutionary in spite of the many devices contrived by southern states to circumvent it. In 1946 the Court declared racial segregation on interstate (but not intrastate) buses to be illegal on the grounds that it interfered with interstate commerce. In 1954 came the historic decision which declared segregation in schools on the basis of race to be unconstitutional. This series of decisions has had the effect of setting in motion a fundamental re-institutionalization of race relations.

Before we leave the institutionalizing function of the court, especially with respect to conflict, a word about a basic conflict in which the parties may be, in effect, the present generation against past generations.

In our society, for example, there has been fixed within our Constitution a set of principles guaranteeing such civil rights as freedom of speech, of the press, of assembly, and the like. And the courts are solemnly bound to protect them.

But suppose that at any given moment of history the public changes its mind. It raises the issue of granting civil rights to, let us say, members of the Communist party. And suppose the opinion of the public which prevails is that they should not have their civil rights protected. And the public becomes a pressure group, lobbying for restrictive legislation.

Should the public of any particular moment of history be permitted to change the constitutional principles on which the government is based? In a moment of fear or panic should the rights embodied in the Constitution be abrogated? To those who have studied the long hard road by which such rights have been finally achieved, the answer is a ringing No. Yet if public opinion were measured in terms of the sum of individual opinions, the answer might be Yes!

Political conflict, it should be pointed out, wherever it takes place, is a very rough-and-tumble affair. Not everyone has a stomach for it. Highly trained technical persons, scientists, and others accustomed to the discipline of science are not likely to be good at it. Reformers who expect the weight of their arguments or sheer logic to win their battles for them are bound to be disappointed. No matter how good one's arguments are, one still has to fight. Facts and even science are not self-enforcing. Anyone who wishes to take part in political conflict cannot afford to rest his case on its merits.

The right will not automatically prevail. He has to be willing to enter the ring with everything he has. He must expect rough treatment. He is certainly going to get it. Strategy is no less important here than in any other area of conflict.

Political Competition[8]

So far we have assumed as given the people who occupy positions of power in government. As pointed out in the introduction to Part VI, these positions may be filled in a variety of ways. In our society it is usually by means of some kind of competitive process.

Competition is probably the most prevalent method in communities, primitive or modern, for determining political leaders. This competition is of two kinds. One is a kind of "merit" system; this characterizes intraparty leadership, to be discussed below. The other is electioneering and campaigning. Whether or not this is a merit system is a moot question.

The Values Registered in Political Competition

What is being tested by political competition? Theoretically the candidate's fitness for office. Actually what is usually being tested is ability to win votes, and this may depend on something as extraneous to merit as good looks, or as ability to raise and spend money strategically. What the competition for political office tests, in other words, is not necessarily competence or ability to make good decisions, but simply ability to win elections. They may or may not be related talents.

Some people, in fact, argue that the relationship between them may be inverse, that the worst, not the best, man wins. They find political competition as it is carried on in many communities discouraging, even frightening. Their fear stems

> not so much from contempt for *demos* as . . . from distrust of the operation of the political mechanism by which certain types of persons come to positions of influence or power and the sort of programs and procedures that will be selected under majority rule. Basic here is . . . their conviction that under a democratic system of political life "the worst get on top."[9]

A somewhat different point of view was expressed by one sociologist who suggested that although *demos* or the common man might lack competence in deciding complex and technical economic and political issues, his judgment about human nature was nevertheless likely to be trust-

[8] For a resumé of research on the voting aspect of political competition see Eugene Burdick and Arthur J. Brodbeck, *American Voting Behavior* (New York: Free Press, 1959).

[9] E. G. Nourse, "Serfdom, Utopia, a Democratic Opportunity?" *Public Administration Review,* 6 (Spring, 1946), p. 179.

worthy.[10] The electorate, therefore, studies the man as a human being under all the seemingly irrelevant activities of a campaign. If they trust him as a man they will turn over to him the important decision-making and legislating jobs of their community.

Even so, no one is under the illusion that the best man always, or even nearly always, wins. But there is this to be said. Perhaps the man who knows how to be elected is also the man who knows how the people want him to decide on issues. His judgment may not be correct; but it may reflect that of the people who vote for him. If this is true, then the competition for office registers the values—good or bad—of the electorate.[11]

A team of researchers set themselves the question: "When does the political competition of an election produce a 'process of consent' which contributes to effective representative government? When does it constitute [instead] a 'process of manipulation' "?[12] They assumed three conditions to be necessary:

> One, a democratic election requires competition between opposing candidates which pervades the entire constituency. The electorate derives power from its ability to choose between at least two competitively oriented candidates, either of whom is believed to have a reasonable chance to win.
>
> Two, a democratic election requires both parties to engage in a balance of efforts to maintain established voting blocs, to recruit independent voters, and to gain converts from the opposition parties. The intent to appeal to these three groups is a fundamental factor that works to limit the scope and curb the intensity of campaign competition.
>
> Three, a democratic election requires both parties to be vigorously engaged in an effort to win the current election; but, win or lose, both parties must also be seeking to enhance their chance of success in the next and subsequent elections. The process of political competition thus involves short- and long-run considerations.[13]

On the basis of these assumptions they set up five criteria which must be

[10] C. H. Cooley, *Social Organization* (New York: Scribner, 1910), pp. 143-144.

[11] In Communist communities, where the succession of power has not been solved, the competition for power takes on a different aspect and registers different values and tests different qualities. It is not competition for the votes of an electorate but competition for the support of coalitions in the Praesidium or in the party. Joseph Alsop has contrasted this kind of political competition with that in the West, as follows: ". . . a Soviet leader needs the very greatest ability in order to survive indefinitely in the cruel competition of the Kremlin. . . . Leaders of the free societies are not required to pass such terrible tests. The free leaders can reach and remain on the pinnacle of power, without being cold, hard, calculating, ruthless, and sometimes even without possessing conspicuous ability and intellectual capacity. Without mentioning Americans, Stanley Baldwin and Neville Chamberlain are proof enough that the free societies' system of choosing their leaders can sometimes be very risky indeed. The counterweight is the free peoples themselves, whose courage and common sense will eventually rebel against weak leadership. . . ." (Column, "Matter of Fact," Jan. 19, 1959).

[12] Morris Janowitz and Dwaine Marvick, "Competitive Pressure and Democratic Consent," *Public Opinion Quarterly*, Vol. 19 (Winter, 1955-1956), pp. 382-383.

[13] *Ibid.*, p. 383.

met in order for political competition to be a process of consent rather than one of manipulation. The quality of an election depends, then, upon (1) the degree to which it produces a high level—but not necessarily one-hundred-percent—of citizen participation among all—not merely higher—social-economic groups; (2) the extent to which citizen participation is based on a belief in the importance of the democratic process itself as well as on self-interest, on confidence in their ability to influence it; (3) the extent to which the competition stimulates effective political deliberation on both the issues and the candidates and creates a meaningful basis on which citizens can make their voting decisions on ideological as well as on personal bases; (4) the extent to which limitations operate to preclude either side from monopolizing or even exercising pervasive influence by means of the mass media; and (5) the extent to which the influence exercised by interpersonal pressures (to be discussed in Chapter 21) operates substantially independently of the influence exercised by the mass media.[14]

The Institutionalization of Political Competition: Enacted Norms

Because the stakes—control of policy and of power—are so high in political competition there is tremendous temptation to cheat. In order to keep political competition from descending to cutthroat competition there are stringent election laws in all states.

The maximum amount of money which individuals or corporations are permitted to contribute to political campaign funds for federal elections is limited by the Hatch Act ($5,000 for individuals, none at all for corporations), although anyone determined to violate this law can usually find a way. The author of this act himself points out that "all the laws, both state and federal . . . have not succeeded in their purpose of curtailing and controlling excessive contributions and expenditures."[15] He suggests that a law requiring advance publicity on all campaign spending be substituted for the present federal law, but it is doubtful if any law could catch all violators.

The "lug" or assessment on officeholders is forbidden by federal law and also by many state laws, though here again violation is easy; the contribution is called "voluntary." How "voluntary" it is, the officeholder may soon learn when he chooses not to pay. Contributions and expenditures must be made public, either before or after the election. Federal law and the laws of most states forbid campaign contributions by corporations. The Smith-Connally Act of 1945 forbids unions to contribute to campaigns for national offices.

The uses to which campaign funds may be put are regulated by law. There are numerous laws prescribing the conduct of voters at polling

[14] *Ibid.*, pp. 384-400.

[15] Quoted in the daily press, Dec. 11, 1946.

places. Sample ballots and instructions must be posted. Private booths for the voter must be provided. Almost every detail, in brief, of the process of political competition is regulated by law in order to keep it as fair as possible.

The Institutionalization of Political Competition: Crescive Norms

In addition to the numerous laws which regulate the competition for political office there are many customary, traditional, attitudinal, and other unwritten rules which govern this kind of community behavior. In Chapter 21 we shall illustrate how custom has modified the Constitution with respect to the residential requirements of congressional representatives. In a similar way the constitutional requirements for President, age thirty-five, native birth, have been added to by custom and tradition until now we know that only certain kinds of men have any chance at all for the office.[16] We have here a highly institutionalized way to violate enacted laws.

One of the most important of the unwritten rules institutionalizing political competition in American communities is one that prescribes that there be two, but only two, major parties competing for office.

Alternatives to the two-party system are, at one extreme, the one-party system of totalitarian states and at the other extreme, numerous parties such as in the Fourth Republic of France.[17] The difficulty of the first is that there is not enough competition. It is monopolistic. In the traditional South where there was to all intents and purposes only one party, the real competition came in the primaries. But it was nevertheless a disadvantage for it to have only one party. It was discounted by the national offices of both major parties.

The drawbacks to the second alternative—many parties—is that it is difficult to secure majority control and responsibility; there must usually be a coalition of parties to muster a working majority. In our two-party system the coalitions are within the party.

The several competing factions within parties must run their race within the party before they face the public. Within both major parties, therefore, reactionaries and progressives compete for control. Indeed, com-

[16] See, for example, Sidney Hyman, "Nine Tests for the Presidential Hopeful," *New York Times Magazine*, Jan. 4, 1959, pp. 11 ff.

[17] There is another alternative to the two-party system—namely, any one of several forms of proportional representation: limited voting, cumulative voting, list systems, or the best known, the single transferable vote or so-called Hare system. According to the latter, the voter is presented with a list of candidates without party labels. He specifies his preference by marking them 1, 2, 3, and so on. The candidates receiving the largest number of votes are elected, whatever their party affiliations or their residential distribution. It is especially urged for municipal elections where party labels have little significance. The idea is that candidates with enough supporters, even if they do not live in the same wards, will be elected. Although it is claimed that the plan eliminates the need for primary elections and ward politics, insuring fairness for all groups, it has not achieved widespread popularity.

petition inside the party is often more persistent and more continuous than between parties.[18]

There is competition not only among groups and factions within the party but also among individuals, from precinct captains up to the city, state, or national bosses. A man holds his position only so long as he can control votes, and no longer. The only question asked of a party leader, whatever his rank, is, Can he swing the election? If he can, he remains leader. If not, he goes. The stakes are too high. Parties cannot carry dead timber. It is in this sense that political competition within parties is quite fair. It tests strictly what it sets out to test—vote-getting ability.

Bidding for Collectivities

One result of the two-party system is that any group which wishes to make its will felt must work through the regular parties; there is no adequate provision for incorporating their program in strong independent parties. Labor, for example, has never formed a political party of its own (except in New York), but has worked on the principle enunciated by Samuel Gompers, first president of the American Federation of Labor, of rewarding its friends and punishing its enemies at the polls. It has made both parties compete for its political support. Each party has, in effect, bid up the price for labor's vote by outdoing the other in campaign promises.

Not only labor but also other blocs of voters have made the most of the two-party competition. Thus minority groups—Jews, Catholics, Negroes, Poles, Germans, Italians—have also put a price on their votes. Each party, therefore, has had to bid against the other in promises. Bloc voting made it easier for machines to become powerful in urban communities; they could get votes wholesale by simply making deals with leaders of minority groups.

There is some question at the present time whether there are any longer such solid ethnic blocs of voters. As third and fourth generations of ethnic groups come of voting age they are less and less likely to vote on the basis of ethnicity as advised by their ward bosses. There is even some question as to the validity of such concepts as the women's vote or the farmer's vote or even a labor vote. The 1960 presidential election revealed evidence of a Catholic vote, but one not nearly as clear-cut as had been supposed. Studies of the way people make up their mind to vote demonstrate that they are indeed greatly influenced by certain individuals in their environ-

[18] We spoke in Chapter 6 of the neutralization of conflict as a result of the many issues which align people. They are together on one issue, in conflict on another. Such multi-group interests have been analyzed as a basic condition of democracy. "A stable democracy requires a situation in which all the major political parties include supporters from many segments of the population. A system in which the support of different parties corresponds too closely to basic social divisions cannot continue on a democratic basis, for it reflects a state of conflict so intense and clear-cut as to rule out compromise" (Lipset, *op. cit.*, p. 31).

ment, but these influential individuals are not necessarily political bosses. They may be professional persons or even fellow-workers. The phenomena associated with such influential individuals are broader than political competition and they will therefore be discussed in greater detail in Chapter 21.

The Object Competed for: The Voter

Our adherence to the two-party system raises some practical problems for the conscientious citizen as well as for blocs. Must he, for example, be an active member in one or the other major party? If so, does he owe allegiance to the party above everything else? What if he disapproves of his party's candidate? Should he always vote a straight ticket? Is it even necessary to be a party member? What if he cannot accept either party? Both major political parties are such congeries of disparate principles and blocs that the sincere voter is honestly baffled. He sees the importance and necessity of parties—but just what is his own duty with regard to them?

There are, as usual, several points of view on such problems. One view states that since parties are the dynamos that make our government work, it is the duty of every person to join a party. If he cannot accept everything his party stands for, he must try to change it. But even if he fails, he must stick by his party. It is, furthermore, his duty to vote a straight party ticket. Otherwise there is likely to be a deadlock. That is, if you vote for a Democrat for governor, but give him a Republican legislature, you are simply courting a stalemate. (Actually, of course, parties do not always line up strictly on issues. A Republican may give better support to a Democratic governor than some of his own party members.) For many people the man is more important than his party and they vote a split ticket, for some Republicans and some Democrats.

Another point of view holds that although the two parties perform a major governmental service, the independent voter is also performing an important function. If everyone were a member of a party and always voted a straight ticket, there would scarcely be any need for an election. We would know in advance how the balloting would run. The thing that really renders an election competitive is the independent voter. He does not care for party labels. He is the one who can demand concessions. He is the one both parties must bid for. It is up to the independent voter to make the bids run high. It is up to him to wring from the parties concessions, progressive planks, new ideas. He is as indispensable as the party hacks.

Despite the unwritten rule that there be only two basic parties, sometimes a third party solves the independent's problem. The new party, fresh, without an accumulation of mistakes, can often make a very attractive bid to disinterested voters. Because the party is new in a highly competitive field, it must offer more to voters than the older parties do. The older parties fight it tooth and nail, putting all kinds of obstructions in its path. They must reluctantly match its bids. The independent voter is in an especially strategic position when there are third parties in the field.

Sometimes the two major parties establish what is in effect a third party within their own organizations; they set up units to work for their candidates outside of the regular party organization, so that voters who like their candidates but not the party may register their position.

Every voter, then, whether he is a party member or an independent performs a function in the competitive process. Whether he works through the regular party organization or through civic organizations, he can put the competitors through their paces, demanding as much as possible from them. He often demands a high return for his vote.

Financing Political Competition

Political competition is expensive. On the basis of a study made by Senator Gore of campaign expenditures in 1956, it has been estimated that congressional and presidential campaigns in 1960 cost $100,000,000.

The financing of political campaigns is one of the most vexing problems in a democratic community. It is by no means solved. At the present time voluntary contributions from party members or interested persons—"Jackson Day Dinners" at $100 a plate, "Lincoln Day Dinners" at similar prices, the "lug" referred to above, contributions by candidates and their friends, by businessmen, and by corporations (in some states only) —are the major sources of revenue of political parties. There were 3,000,000 small givers in 1952 and 8,000,000 in 1956.

Legislation to help solve the problems of financing political competition has been proposed on several occasions, varying from contributions from the federal government—since running an election is a basic function that has to be performed—to allowing contributions to be deducted from income for tax purposes. Only the last has a good chance for success.

The Influence of Technological Changes on Political Competition

Political competition used to be a face-to-face relationship. The candidate met the voters directly. Torchlight parades and rallies aroused emotional response; but reasoned debate was also important. The advent of the railroad meant that candidates could "whistle stop" through their areas and meet more people to present their arguments to. It was not until 1924 that the radio came in to supplement the face-to-face appeal; and not until 1952 that television entered the scene.[19] Each innovation had profound effects on the way the competitive process was carried on and even on the qualities tested.

Oratory was once a major talent required of candidates.

The use of television has made appearance as well as voice a matter of

[19] Ithiel De Sola Pool, "TV: A New Dimension in Politics," in Burdick and Brodbeck, *American Voting Behavior* (New York: Free Press, 1959), pp. 236-261.

great concern and the habit of associating television with amusement rather than with learning makes it necessary for the candidates to compete not only with one another but also with popular television programs. The comprehensive audience available has changed strategy. It aims to win over people who have not voted before rather than independents or converts. In 1952, for example, this led the Republicans to pitch their television campaign to women, since they were more likely than men to have been nonvoters.[20]

One great campaigner, Senator Douglas, is of the opinion that the mass media should never take the place of face-to-face campaigning.

> There are writers who argue that . . . face-to-face meetings . . . should be largely cast aside and one should turn instead to other media. . . . The advertising and public relations men are the expositors of the theory that they can "sell" a candidate or a party in the same way they can sell soap or a beauty lotion. There is, of course, a great deal of truth in this last contention and advertising men are playing an increasing part in political campaigns.
>
> But reliance on such methods at the expense of political argument is unfortunate and not in the public interest. In the first place, such methods seek to exploit the emotional and nonrational and what the mass-motivation group labels "subliminal" factors, rather than the conscious and rational. . . .
>
> The second objection to the mass-communication techniques is that their sheer cost makes them available only to those candidates and parties which have large funds. . . .[21]

Technology, then, has changed the specific techniques used in political competition, but the underlying sociological nature of the process remains much the same. Television makes it possible for the electorate to examine candidates more minutely, under more circumstances, and closer up; but the electorate still wishes to see them in action. It still wants to see how they handle themselves under differing conditions. It still wants to see what manner of men they are rather than wanting to know precisely where they stand on issues.

Today the same audience hears the same candidates dozens of times. They probably get to know the men more intimately but the issues more superficially.

[20] Sidney Hyman, "What Trendex for Lincoln?" *New York Times Magazine,* Jan. 17, 1961, p. 33.

[21] Paul H. Douglas, "Is Campaign Oratory a Waste of Breath?" *Ibid.,* Oct. 19, 1958, p. 72.

21

How Successful Are Enacted Norms?

"There Ought to Be a Law?"

Efforts to institutionalize behavior by means of enacted norms—legislation—are as natural and pervasive as any other kind of community behavior. Confronted with a major problem one of the first reactions of many people is likely to be, "There ought to be a law." It seems so logical. If there is something we don't like we should legislate it out of existence or, contrariwise, if there is something we want, we should legislate it into existence. It is almost a belief in magic on the part of some.

Others oppose efforts to control behavior by law. They believe that the best government is the one that governs least. They dislike "tinkering" with a system. They feel it does more harm than good. Or they think it oppresses individuals. Institutionalization by means of enacted norms, in brief, is a controversial issue.

It has, however, become a pressuring issue. Proponents of legislative control push for more, opponents resist and concede ground inch by inch. It is generally conceded that in a complex society many things have to be controlled by legislation; but the precise limits are not agreed upon.

The alternatives to such controls are not, as advocates of laissez-faire believe, an absence of controls and a free play of impersonal beneficent social forces. The alternatives are, rather, either control by custom, tradition, mores, and other crescive controls; or manipulative control by powerful personalities, and more likely the latter than the former. All community behavior is controlled. The questions are simply, By whom? How much? For what ends?

Covert versus Overt Behavior

Many crescive norms operate in the field of inner behavior. But it is generally conceded in American communities that legislation has no business here. Freedom to think and believe what we please is a fundamental right guaranteed by the Constitution. But freedom to act is conceded to be subject to legislative controls:

> No law should require men to change their attitudes, but most laws require something that is contrary to the attitudes of some groups of men, whether large or small. No law should punish men for their beliefs or attempt to suppress these beliefs, but many laws are necessary or desirable that require behavior contrary to what some men approve or believe to be the right course. The whole sphere of opinion must be held inviolate by law, if the primary condition of democracy is to be fulfilled. But it does not follow that the behavior prompted by opinion or belief should not be regulated for the public good. The distinction is elementary. In a democracy we do not punish a man because he is opposed to income taxes, or to free school education, or to vaccination, or to minimum wages, but the laws of a democracy insist that he obey the laws that make provisions for these things.[1]

The distinction is, of course, more easily conceived than implemented in practice. The man who is forced to have his child vaccinated, an overt act, can claim that his religious freedom is being violated. There is not the same neat cleavage in fact as the one so logical on paper. Still the fundamental principle seems right.

Enacted Norms as "Educational" Forces

There are many who argue that the institutionalization of behavior can best be achieved not by means of force—which law is—but by means of education and persuasion, by the use of rational or even emotional appeals, or by voluntary organization. There is, of course, no inconsistency between these two approaches to control, as the illustration of the antidiscrimination laws to be referred to presently shows.

In fact, law itself, it has been pointed out, is a great educational force. Not only does the law coerce or deter overt behavior but also it affects attitudes, even prejudices.

And, perhaps most important of all, the mere fact that a law is passed shows which side official standards are allied with. It shows whose coalition the government is in. This may itself have "educational" effects for many in the community, especially for those who have no deep prejudices one way or the other.

Criteria for Evaluating Success of Institutionalization by Means of Enacted Norms

In evaluating the success of enacted norms at least two sets of criteria or standards may be applied. One can, for example, approach the problem in terms of the degree to which enacted norms achieve their stated goals:

[1] Robert M. MacIver, in Foreword to Morroe Berger, *Equality by Statute, Legal Controls over Group Discrimination* (New York: Columbia University, 1952), p. viii.

how successful are they in doing what they set out to do? A second criterion is in terms of the amount of control of behavior achieved; and here at least two models must be considered, one assuming merely lack of support from crescive norms and the other, active opposition from them. The two criteria are not, of course, independent or mutually exclusive. The first may include the second; that is, the purpose of enacted norms may be precisely to change crescive norms. In such cases the two criteria might be identical. Sometimes, however, a norm might be quite successful in achieving a high degree of conformity and changing crescive norms but not in achieving its purpose. A housing law, for example, might change customary housing practices, as planned, and be adhered to by most people—thus being successful according to the second criterion—but still not get rid of the slums, the stated purpose. For one reason or another the law was not properly designed to achieve its goal. It is to highlight this important point that the two criteria are distinguished.

THE ACHIEVEMENT OF LEGISLATIVE GOALS

The first criterion for evaluating the success of enacted norms has to do with the relative degree of achievement of their stated goals assuming consensus. The purpose of legislation, usually stated in the preamble of the act, is to institutionalize behavior along certain specified lines in order to achieve a specified goal. We have referred to numerous such acts throughout our discussions in this book. How successful are these efforts? How well are the purposes achieved? We are assuming that there is consensus, no opposition, organized or unorganized, in order to simplify the problem. And still the answer to the question just stated is, we do not know with complete certainty.

Even when there is no opposition we cannot always tell in advance what is going to be the total effect of any law, court decision, or administrative ruling. What we do is pass a law and then watch to see what the results will be. Legislators admit that they do not know what the results will be of acts which they sponsor. We may know quite well what we want to happen. It does not always coincide with what does happen.

Herbert Spencer exposed our ignorance with respect to the effects of legislation as long ago as 1873. He presented a graphic analogy to drive his point home:

> You see that this wrought-iron plate is not quite flat; it sticks up a little here toward the left—"cockles," as we say. How shall we flatten it? Obviously, you reply, by hitting down on the part that is prominent. Well, here is a hammer, and I give the plate a blow as you advise. Harder, you say. Still no effect. Another stroke? Well, there is one, and another, and another. The prominence remains, you see; the evil is as great as ever—greater, indeed. But this is not all. Look at the warp which the plate has got near the opposite edge. Where it was flat before it is now curved. A pretty bungle we have made of it. Instead of curing the original defect,

we have produced a second. Had we asked an artisan practiced in "planishing," as it is called, he would have told us that no good was to be done, but only mischief, by hitting down on the projecting part. He would have taught us how to give variously directed and specially adjusted blows with a hammer elsewhere: so attacking the evil not by direct but by indirect actions. The required process is less simple than you thought. Even a sheet of metal is not to be successfully dealt with after those commonsense methods in which you have so much confidence. What, then, shall we say about society? "Do you think I am easier to be played on than a pipe?" asks Hamlet. Is humanity more readily straightened than iron plate?[2]

To this day we have not learned enough about how purposive legislative controls operate to draw up laws that will give us precisely what we want without producing evils as bad as those we are trying to eliminate. The precise nature of the "variously directed and specially adjusted blows" is not altogether clear.

For as yet laws have very unexpected and unanticipated consequences. A state passes a law providing a pension for its elderly citizens; presently its whole tax structure is thrown out of balance, so that health services, schools, highway construction, and other services suffer. An income tax law is passed to obtain revenue and it turns out to be one of the strongest weapons against racketeers and criminals who are too big for local law enforcement officers to handle. It also changes the whole structure of philanthropic giving, enormously stimulating foundations of one kind or another. It transforms business entertaining by means of the expense account and affects standards of living. Enacted norms achieve something, but whether it is the goal aimed at is another question.

So far we have been assuming no opposition to the enacted norm; but this is rarely the case. Opposition may come from conflicting crescive norms —customs, mores, conventions—or from actively organized groups. In either case deflection from the stated aim of the legislation is increased.

THE DEGREE OF CONTROL ACHIEVED

Our second criterion for measuring the success of enacted norms has to do with the extent of control achieved in terms of the amount of conformity produced. As a scientific or engineering term, control implies at least three characteristics. When we have control of an object, (1) we have eliminated or at least minimized the operation of chance, (2) we get precisely what we have aimed at, and (3) the controlled object can be manipulated at will. Control in this sense is typical of the laboratory; it may be well-nigh absolute. In engineering practice outside the laboratory control is not likely to be so complete, but it must approach certainty within specified limits. Obviously the concept of control as applied to human behavior in the hurly-burly of community life is not the same as this labora-

[2] *The Study of Sociology* (New York: Appleton, 1896), pp. 270-271.

tory or engineering concept. For a number of reasons, to be discussed in more detail later, there are always cases that fall outside the limits of the standards set. We are interested here in the extra-individual forces involved, more especially in the effect of the presence or absence of crescive norms.

That crescive norms have enormous influence on enacted norms has long been recognized. The Roman adage, "Custom tempers the rigors of the law," expresses an important sociological fact. Crescive norms, customs, traditions, mores, conventions, may actually reshape enacted norms.

In at least one case, for example, custom has created a situation which, if attempted by legislation, might actually be declared unconstitutional. Federal statutes require states to divide themselves into as many congressional districts as they are entitled to in terms of representatives. Each such district is then to elect its own representative. The Constitution does not state that the representative must be a resident of the community he represents. But custom does. If a statute should attempt to require representatives to be residents of the communities they represent, "it would probably be held unconstitutional as an attempt to add to the qualifications prescribed by the fundamental law for the office. But a custom, rooted in local pride and sectionalism, is practically as effective as a constitutional provision would be in assuring that no district is represented by a non-resident."[3]

A similar situation exists with respect to the qualifications for the president of the United States. There are no constitutional requirements with respect to race, religion, or sex; yet custom bars Negroes, Jews, and women from the office. There is, again, no provision for parties in our Constitution, yet we know that actually parties furnish the dynamo which makes the legal framework function. Presidents are nominated by party conventions, not by presidential electors. The whole complex system of mores, customs, conventions, and other crescive norms which implement the segregation model of race relations violates the Constitution as well as the separate "and equal" laws on the statute books.

Until fairly recently enacted norms and crescive norms coincided quite well. Criminal acts were also regarded as immoral, although immoral acts were not always considered criminal. This was true because both the crescive norms, mores, for example, and enacted norms, legislation, were clearly for the protection of what was generally considered by everyone to be the fundamental welfare of the community. Everyone could see why it was illegal as well as immoral to kill within the we-group of the community, or to destroy common property. More recently, however, there is an increasing cleavage between what is immoral and what is criminal. New laws are created much faster than new mores to support them. Thus there is relatively little moral stigma attached to a good deal of modern law violation. The old types of crime, or law violation, were both immoral and

[3] Harvey Walker, *Law Making in the United States* (New York: Ronald, 1934), p. 107.

illegal; modern law violation is illegal but not necessarily immoral, that is, condemned by the mores. Among many people there is no feeling that violating the income tax laws or the antitrust laws or wages-and-hours laws is immoral. In other words, we have not developed moral attitudes about such modern forms of law violation.

This divorce of the law from the mores in modern communities is important in our understanding of how enacted norms operate. Since so many modern laws do not have the support of the mores, there is no revulsion in the community against violations, and therefore enforcement and control are difficult. A man convicted of violating antitrust laws suffers little if any moral stigma. His job may be waiting for him when he leaves jail—if, indeed, he is even sent to jail. He is not considered a bad man, certainly not a criminal.

Many modern laws are difficult to enforce because it is difficult to convince people that they are necessary for the welfare of the community. To understand the welfare needs of a small, simply organized community is relatively easy. To understand the welfare needs of a complex, derivatively organized community is a job for experts. During World War II, for example, the economist could see why black markets were ruinous. The individual housewife who patronized them saw only that they had what she wanted and was willing to pay for. She could not see the wider implications of her act.

People injured by the violation of many modern laws are often affected only indirectly. Sometimes it is even difficult to prove to them that they are affected at all. They do not see how the violation of the law injures them, any more than they see how it injures the community as a whole. It seems to them far-fetched to believe that their tax bills are higher and that commodity prices are higher because of law violation. They are not ready to help in catching the criminal. They leave it all to the law-enforcing agents. The man who swindles the government out of millions of dollars on a contract may be a model of personal moral behavior, so that rather than help to convict him, his community may elect him to office. It is difficult for us to realize the criminal nature of much law violation which is not covered by the mores. Yet it is precisely this new kind of law violation which is most likely to disrupt the life of the community.

Sometimes it is not a matter of simply the absence of support from crescive norms; sometimes enacted norms are actively opposed by crescive norms. How much control can be achieved under these circumstances? The question usually arises in connection with reforms of one kind or another. We may cite cases from history for either side of the question. Sometimes legislated reforms are undoubtedly successful. The upheavals produced by the Russian revolution (s), especially in the 1930's, and by the Nazis in Germany in the 1930's and 1940's, point in this direction.[4] Sometimes,

[4] Despite his successes, Hitler disclaimed credit for the changes he brought about; the changes his laws produced were actually shaped by the people themselves, not by the

however, they are costly failures. Why? Some students will glibly say that no reform can be successfully legislated that goes contrary to the spirit of the time or the current social forces or the mores. This, however, is a tautology, like the phrase "survival of the fittest." Just as we define fitness in terms of survival—those who survive being by that very fact labeled fittest—so if a reform fails, we "explain" the failure in terms of the reform's being contrary to prevailing mores. On the other hand, when reforms do succeed, in spite of the mores, we "explain" them as in line with the spirit of the times. Experiments in controlled or planned change are numerous in history; but unfortunately they are not scientific experiments, so that we know little actually about the effects of various techniques or the conditions of their success or failure. In the absence of such scientific experiments in the field of reform by means of legislation, much of the discussion of the subject is blind, often opinionated and prejudiced.

A Case in Point: Antidiscrimination Laws

One of the most spectacular attempts to secure change by means of enacted norms by law, by court decision, by administrative ruling—in the face of opposing customs, mores, and conventions—is in the area of race relations. This is an attempted reform which involves both controverting established mores and innovating unfamiliar patterns of relationships. How successful has it been?

One of the first steps was the 1945 Ives-Quinn Act in New York, designed to prohibit discrimination in hiring, firing, conditions of work, application forms, employment agencies, membership in labor unions, and upgrading. The law stated the rationale of its goal in these words:

> . . . practices of discrimination against any of its inhabitants because of race, creed, color or national origin are a matter of state concern, . . . such discrimination threatens not only the rights and privileges of its inhabitants but menaces the institutions and foundation of a free democratic state.

The hue and cry which arose when this law was proposed and then enacted was tremendous: you can't legislate that sort of thing; it will do more harm than good; you can't change human nature; it will ruin plant morale, other workers will leave, factories will leave the state; you can't enforce that kind of law. . . .

> It is doubtful whether any legislative measure purely local in its application . . . [had ever] been the subject of so much editorial comment in the nation's press,

---

enacted norms per se, he said. He saw himself as essentially a servant of the popular will. He is quoted as saying: "There is no such thing as unlimited power, and I should never dream of pretending to it myself. The word dictatorship is misleading; there is no such thing as dictatorship in the accepted sense. Even the most extreme autocrat is compelled to correct his absolute will by existing conditions. Considered soberly, there are only various means of giving shape to the public will" (From Hermann Rauschning, *The Voice of Destruction* [New York: Putnam, 1939], pp. 198-199).

or . . . inspired so much discussion as . . . this attempt to eliminate . . . racial, religious and national discrimination in the State of New York.[5]

None of the predicted dire calamities occurred.

An examination of the cases dealt with during the first critical year suggests why. They were handled without ever descending lower in the accommodation or conflict continuum than conciliation. Although the law had sharp teeth, not one of the almost 500 cases had to be fought out in court. Every one was settled by conference. The commission made it clear that it was not out to pillory any particular person or firm, that what they wanted was not only compliance with the law but also willingness to comply. It was "debate" in the image-changing sense. They made every effort to enlist the cooperation of employers. The success of their policy was attested by the fact that almost two thousand employers voluntarily asked the commission to look over their employment practices and let them know if they had complied with the law.

Since this first law, other states and local communities have also set up fair employment practices commissions with no less success.

The Supreme Court school desegregation decision of 1954 was an attempt to bring about reform by means of another kind of enacted norm, namely court decision. And there has been an extensive research literature interpreting the relative success of this attempt in different communities. When it has all been winnowed the conclusion seems to be: enacted norms do change behavior. They may not change beliefs, attitudes, or feelings, at least, not immediately; for such changes, "debate" or conversion or brainwashing or other methods of changing images are necessary. But for changing behavior itself, law may succeed:

> . . . it has been argued by many writers that law can control only the external actions of persons—it can make us act in certain ways, but it cannot make us act from certain motives. Where law requires for compliance a particular attitude and inclination or taste, it is not the appropriate means for control. This view has been put forward by political thinkers at least as far back as Aristotle. In a democracy, where public opinion must be considered, such limitations upon law operate with added strength.[6]

This does not mean that just passing a law or enacting a norm is in and of itself enough to produce the change. The new behavior still has to be institutionalized in the sense of gaining consent if not active approval.

What Kind of Control? The Special Case of the Commercialized Vices

With the exception of the military and similar hierarchical organizations, all we usually expect of enacted norms is that they influence behavior

[5] *Annual Report of the New York State Commission against Discrimination,* 1945-1946, p. 1. For a detailed history and analysis of the Ives-Quinn Act, see Berger, *op. cit.,* Chap. 4.

[6] Berger, *op. cit.,* p. 171.

in a given direction. We do not always eliminate chance. We do not necessarily get exactly what we aim at; nor can the situation be manipulated at will. In this sense social control by means of enacted norms is far from scientific. It is true that if one has a monopoly on access to the minds of a people and also of force—as totalitarian states do—the approach to complete control is closer than it is in nontotalitarian states.

If we say that perfect control has been achieved when there is no nonconformity at all to the rules, then it is certainly very rare. Where it is approximated it is with regard to norms which are not only enacted but also crescive in nature, that is, to norms which have many kinds of sanctions to shore them up. All American communities probably have perfect control, in this sense, of cannibalism, for example, or nudism or incest or slavery. But in most aspects of community life, control is far from perfect and with respect to enacted norms, certainly limited.

There are three areas in which this limited success is a perennial problem, namely the commercialized vices, so-called: the liquor traffic, commercialized prostitution, and commercialized gambling. The issue with respect to them usually shapes up as follows: (1) shall we prohibit them? or shall we regulate them by licensing and taxing? or (3) shall we just let them go on? All three policies have been tried out at some time or other in American communities. The third, the laissez-faire policy of the so-called "wide open town," is rarely advocated openly any more, at least not officially. The issue usually resolves itself, therefore, into a choice between prohibition and some form of municipal regulation and control through licensing.

Prohibition of the liquor traffic is the enacted norm in only one state, Mississippi. Other states have varying regulations. But legalization of the liquor traffic does not mean that the rules which regulate it are not constantly being violated. It is estimated that there is as much illegal liquor in the market as legal.

Prostitution has not been officially sanctioned in American communities except for four years between 1870 and 1874 in St. Louis and in Reno before 1942. With these exceptions it has always been against the law. It has, however, been under police regulation almost always and in most communities. In 1961 there were people openly advocating a return to official recognition of prostitution—in Philadelphia, for example—but the trend throughout the world seemed to be in the direction of prohibition.

At midcentury the most troubling situation was that with respect to commercialized gambling. Gambling was said to be the largest single industry in the country; allegedly $47,000,000,000 was spent on it annually.[7] Legislative policy with respect to gambling has varied from time to time and from place to place. At the present time the mood seems to be in the direction of nibbling away at some of the restrictions. No one proposes that

[7] Daniel P. Monyhan, "The Private Government of Crime," *The Reporter,* July 6, 1961, p. 14.

the numbers racket or policy be legalized; but legalizing off-track betting has many advocates. In the 1950's several states legalized bingo.

As in the case of the liquor traffic, legalizing gambling does not eliminate violation of the law. It is difficult to get honest people to man the gambling industry; legal or not, it remains in the hands of people with less than remarkable scruples. In 1957 New York legalized bingo on a local option basis beginning in 1958. Three years later an investigating commission opened hearings on abuses in the operation of the law.

> . . . The Commission of Investigation has summed up ways in which bingo played for charitable or religious fund-raising has gone astray contrary to public interest: commercial operators have been able to pervert the law to their private gain; every regulatory provision in law has been violated; revenues that should have gone to charitable purposes have been mis-appropriated in substantial amounts; otherwise decent citizens have been duped or persuaded to commit fraudulent acts; some public officials charged with supervision have been corrupted; bingo halls controlled by commercial renters have mushroomed, and the rent roll of these operators generally equals and in many cases exceeds the profits of the charitable organizations themselves. . . . If bingo playing cannot be kept clean, then the people of the state made a mistake in authorizing it.[8]

Laws against commercialized gambling are among those—like laws against black marketing, for example—which are difficult to explain or interpret to the community. It is hard to convince people who believe that "gambling never hurt anybody," of its widely-ramifying effect on the economy of the community.[9] They belong also to the category of laws

[8] *New York Times*, May 6, 1961.

[9] It should be made clear that we are talking about the commercialized aspects of gambling, the economic and political, not the personal, moral aspects. One may, without any inconsistency, enjoy a private poker game and yet be opposed to commercialized gambling. The opposition to gambling is not from holier-than-thou busybodies attempting to interfere in the private lives of other people, forbidding them to spend their money as they will. Such a picture almost invariably arouses indignation at the bluenoses who persecute others who do not follow their puritanical moral precepts. The true picture is this: one group of businessmen arrays itself against another because the conditions of competition are against the goods and services it has to sell. People will spend money on gambling and pay cash but will not pay the butcher, the baker, and the grocer. It is self-interest, not moral idealism, that prompts a community to attempt to control commercialized gambling. Where gambling is viewed complacently by other businesses it is likely to be communities which cater to a transient population, as in Nevada, so that the gambling losses are at the expense of outsiders. As a leader in a move to clean up gambling in New Albany, Indiana, said: "In Jeffersonville, a few miles up the river, the gamblers are smart and don't bleed the local residents. They make their profit on out-of-towners" (*St. Louis Post Dispatch*, Sept. 8, 1946). Conversely, when Congressman Adam Clayton Powell attacked the policy situation in Harlem it was not on moral grounds but on the grounds that it was white runners who were pauperizing the Negro community and taking money out of it rather than Negro runners who would keep the money in the community. He read into the Congressional Record the statement; "$50,000,000 a year to support Italian and Jewish policy bankers" (Daniel P. Monyhan, *op. cit.*, p. 17). For a vivid and colorful account of the history of gambling in this country see Herbert Asbury, *Sucker's Progress: An Informal History of Gambling in America from the Colonies to*

which do not have the support of the mores of some groups and, in some cases, the actual opposition of the mores. For all these reasons they are far from successful in achieving their goal and the amount of nonconformity is high. The special nature of the laws we have been discussing here is analyzed in greater detail in Chapter 27, dealing with parallel dissociation in the community.

The American Tradition of Civil Disobedience

No discussion of the success of enacted norms in American communities would be complete without some consideration of the tradition of civil disobedience. The whole idea that the individual should scrutinize every law passed by a legislature and himself decide on its merits in terms of higher standards is one that is completely foreign to totalitarian communities, yet it is one that democratic regimes have to cope with.

There have been very great advocates of civil disobedience in American history. Henry David Thoreau, went to jail for refusal to pay his taxes. He then wrote his great essay "On the Duty of Civil Disobedience" (1849) which expresses a characteristic attitude toward nonconformity in most American communities:

> Must the citizen ever for a moment, or in the least degree, resign his conscience to the legislator? Why has every man a conscience, then? I think that we should be men first, and subjects afterward. It is not desirable to cultivate a respect for the law, so much as for the right. The only obligation which I have a right to assume is to do at any time what I think right. . . .

This point of view is sometimes called one of "the higher law." Its poignance and cogency are usually lost on those who favor the laws involved. But they become particularly cutting when the opposite point of view, that every law must be strictly obeyed, is invoked by an Adolf Eichmann to justify the slaughter of six million human beings. It is then that the "inconsistencies" and "contradictions" of democratic regimes, which so baffle totalitarians, come to be seen as well worth their price.

Canfield (New York: Dodd-Mead, 1938). For a lurid journalistic account of the industry at midcentury see Fred J. Cook, *A Two-Dollar Bet Means Murder* (New York: Dial, 1961). See also, of course, the report of the famous Kefauver committee.

22

Influence and Power in Community Life

The Dialogue of Decision: The Individual's Role

It is inherent that the final decision in a complex situation must be the responsibility of those who occupy top positions in organizations. But such decisions are not made in a social vacuum. The "public" is always there in the form of the "generalized other." It contributes feedback, as we noted in Chapter 20. It participates, to use a currently fashionable figure of speech, in the great dialogue of decision. The "consent of the governed"—or the lack of it—is, as we saw, a very real phenomenon that cannot be ignored.

Our concern here is the mechanism by which individuals participate in this great process. How do they leave an impress on community?

History may or may not be but the elongated shadow of great men, as the Emersonians used to claim. But community life clearly reflects the personalities of outstanding individuals. For the perceptive student of community life the way personality functions in the drama is itself important. Thus people with social imagination see communities not as physical structures alone. Back of all the buildings, back of all the programs, they see personalities—competing, fighting, organizing.

The intuitive stranger who wants to understand the community asks less about the buildings and the programs than he does about the people who originated them, fought for or against them, who are competing for control of them, and who are organized to maintain or to wreck them.

We shall begin our discussion of the influence of personality on community life with a kind which is highly personal; and we shall end it with the anonymous role of the individual in associations which seek to influence community life. Finally we shall add a word about the fact, distressing to many persons, that because so many people find even this small degree of participation in community life more than they can manage, we appear to some observers to be becoming in many respects a congeries of collectivities or "masses," the policies of which are determined by powerful leaders rather than by actively participating individuals.

THE INFLUENCE OF "STARS"

To illustrate how an individual may exert influence on a community the case of Louise DeKoven Bowen, of Chicago, is offered here. Her ability to influence community life came from her great wealth. She had enough money, prestige, and social position to indulge generously in the luxury of social welfare. At sixteen she was already interested in the problems of juvenile delinquency and established, in the basement billiard room of her father's lake shore mansion, the first boys' club in Chicago. She fought for the first antisweatshop laws ever enacted in the West. She fought political bosses and politicians until she saw the first juvenile court in the world established in Chicago. She contributed generously to Hull House and insisted that her friends do likewise. During a great strike she helped raise money for the strikers' children. She crossed swords with the formidable United States Steel Corporation for the abolition of the twelve-hour-day. She was a large stockholder in the Pullman Company but fought it tooth and nail for the removal of industrial hazards. She studied labor laws and fought for better laws to govern the wages and hours of women. It has been said of her that her "fingerprints are on the cornerstone of every important organization in Chicago."[1]

Mrs. Bowen's power to influence community life came from her wealth. Prototypes could be found in most other communities. These are the "stars," the "heroes," the people whose position and resources put them in a category by themselves. In smaller communities the "stars" might be inspired schoolteachers, nurses, doctors, ministers, priests, social workers.

Sometimes the "villains" also exert great influence, for slums, brothels, gambling joints, and taverns have personalities behind them as well as settlement houses, clinics, art museums, and recreational programs. Although there is scarcely a single community in America that does not have its hall of fame, many also have their halls of infamy. Chicago reflects Al Capone as well as Jane Addams. The influence of personality on community may be nefarious as well as constructive.

We have been considering so far the "stars," so to speak, of community life, the prima donnas and those who perform the "hero" role. Every community probably has its roster of such outstanding personalities. They are the "name" people of whom everyone thinks when there is a big job to be done. And their contribution to community life is undeniable. But there are not many of them. And it is perhaps just as well that such outstanding personalities are not commoner than they are. The "star" who dazzles everyone may not be as useful as the less glamorous leader who gets everyone

[1] Virginia Irwin, "She Made Chicago a Better City," *St. Louis Post-Dispatch,* Aug. 25, 1946.

interested in working for the project. A little bit of such personality impress on a community goes a long way. It adds glamor, so to speak, to community life. A community that does not have such personalities is poorer, perhaps, for the lack. But a little bit of such influence is enough. There is no reason to encourage it.

The Concept of Interpersonal Influence

The impetus for the scientific study of patterns of influence in the community came originally from a desire to learn how people decided to vote as they did[2] and also from the need of the mass media to determine how to aim their appeals.[3] On the basis of research on these problems the concept of "the influentials" was developed. Influentials, located by asking informants who were the people they would go to for advice or help, are individuals to whom other people listen or turn to for help or advice regarding such personal decisions as choice of job, educational plans, selection of books, plays, or furniture.[4]

Influentials have been classified as "localites" and as "cosmopolitans." The localites were found by one researcher to be more firmly rooted in the community, usually having been born and reared in it; they rarely even considered leaving it. The opposite tended to be true of cosmopolitans. The localites were interested in establishing frequent contacts with many people; the consmopolitans were more selective. The localite tended to belong to associations which emphasized making contacts, for establishing personal ties (secret societies, fraternal organizations, service clubs) ; the cosmopolitan tended to belong to associations which fostered the exercise of special skills and knowledge (professional societies, hobby groups). Localites tended to hold political offices (commissioner, mayor) ; cosmopolitans held positions requiring special skills or knowledge (health, housing, education boards) . The influence exerted by localites rested on an elaborate network of personal relationships built up over a long period of time; the influence exerted by the cosmopolitan was a result of previous achievements and previously acquired skills, rather than on a long record of personal contacts in the community. The localite had a following because he understood; the cosmopolitan because he knew.

The influential has an interesting role, one that he sometimes performs almost without knowing how or why. He or she is sometimes called a "natural leader." Often without office or special position, he or she determines the success or failure of some community program. Theoretically interpersonal influence was found to take many forms and to use many techniques.

[2] Lazarsfeld, Berelson, and Gaudet, *The People's Choice* (New York: Columbia University, 1944, 1948) .

[3] Robert Merton, "Patterns of Influence: Local and Cosmopolitan Influentials," *Social Theory and Social Structure* (New York: Free Press, 1957) , pp. 387-420.

[4] *Ibid.*, p. 390.

It could be highly active, purposive or passive, and even unwitting, as suggested by the schema in Table 22-1 offered by Merton.

TABLE 22-1. FORMS AND TECHNIQUES OF INTERPERSONAL INFLUENCE[5]

Forms	Techniques
Coercion	Force, violence
Domination	Commands, but with no threat of force
Manipulation	Influencer's objective kept hidden
Giving advice	Opinions, recommendations, but not commands
Exchange	Mutual modification of a situation
Clarification	Specifying alternative lines of action
Serving as prototype of imitation	Unwitting or unknown modification of behavior or attitudes of others

The county agent who is trying to introduce a new plan finds that if he can get the influential to accept it, the others will be more likely to accept it also.

The function of the influential may be that of serving as a focus in a "coordinating" game. The people follow him because he is the one they can all agree on even without consultation. It is a case of "everyone turns to him because everyone expects everyone to turn to him."

The people we are here discussing influence others in a personal way; they are not, characteristically, persons who use the mass media. Not one of the influentials located in studies of two communities, one in the North and one in the South, was the editor of a local newspaper.[6] The nature of the influence exerted by means of a newspaper is not the same as that exerted by the influentials. The editor is not sought out for advice.

Influentials are sometimes further classified into "top influentials" and "key influentials." "Key influentials" are, in a sense, the elite among the influentials; they are sociometric leaders.

> The initiation and sanction of policy tends to be centered about them so that they may greatly influence the values which dominate in decision-making. The key influentials are . . . persons . . . most often chosen by the top influentials as the 10 leaders they would want if they were responsible for a major project before the community and were seeking leaders nearly everyone would accept.[7]

Although key influentials participate very actively in community affairs, they may receive less publicity than other top influentials. This is explained by the fact that much of their activity is behind-the-scene policy-making and also by the social convention that key influentials do not seek publicity.

The "stars," "heroes," and influentials so far discussed may constitute

[5] *Ibid.*, pp. 387-420.

[6] *Ibid.*, p. 415.

[7] William H. Form and Delbert C. Miller, *Industry, Labor, and Community* (New York: Harper, 1960), p. 591.

a diverse and nonhomogeneous set of people. Some have wide areas of influence, some narrow. Some have specialized fields of influence, some generalized. The name of Mrs. Yale Jones on the letterhead of a committee working to establish a concert series will exert a great deal of influence in behalf of its sponsors; her name on a committee to attract industry to the community will be meaningless.

We have been emphasizing the individuals with influence. But even among influentials relationships become structured. The individuals who exert influence are not separate and unrelated, acting without reference to one another. There is organization, however informal, among them. The nature of this structured relationship is a matter of some importance.

The Community Power Structure: Relationships Among Influentials

On the basis of a detailed study of almost 40 communities, including great metropolises as well as smaller towns, one student of community life was able to delineate the system of relationships which he found among these influentials and he called it the community power structure.[8] It consisted of a number of persons who were in positions to make decisions and who had the resources, contacts, and skills to get them carried out. This structure was hierarchical in shape, and graded with respect to power. There were a relatively small number at the top; more just below them; and others fanning out from them.

In Detroit, for example, the men on the top rung of this power structure were found to be men who were directors and managers of great industries or banks. Some were more important than others. They differed in interests, age, and approachability. Some had achieved their position by working their way up; others had inherited their positions. They were alike in that they depended on one another rather than on superiors in formulating judgments and opinions; in fact, they had no superiors.

These men knew one another well; they shared membership in at least one club; they called on one another in making or implementing plans requiring top-level decision. Most of the preliminary work was done at lower levels; but for large projects the actual initiation was a function, often primarily symbolic, of the top persons. In addition to the contribution of prestige and symbolic guarantees, such men were often in a position to contribute money also.

In a smaller community, of about half a million, called Regional City, the top forty persons included directors in great commercial, financial, and industrial enterprises, professional persons, government personnel, labor leaders, and leisure personnel (including one woman who contributed

[8] Floyd Hunter, *Community Power Structure: A Study of Decision Makers* (Chapel Hill, N. C.: University of North Carolina, 1953); Floyd Hunter, *Top Leadership U.S.A.* (Chapel Hill, N. C.: University of North Carolina, 1959).

handsomely to charitable causes but who spent little time in the city). These people, as we noted in Chapter 3, tended to live in an area of the city which was removed from poorer parts, a fact which had the effect of isolating them from the problems of the average citizen.

Persuasion, intimidation, coercion, and even physical force, were at the disposal of these persons. Because resentment is aroused when such exercise of power is exposed, the exertion of power was often kept hidden. But hostility was found in the understructure toward upper leaders, revealed in the use of such derogatory terms as: bigwig, big wheel, high mogul, high-muckedy-muck, and so forth. Other derogatory terms were applied to persons who were working too hard to win approval of the top men: fireball, hot-shot, stoolie.

The positions occupied by these influential men reveals the relative power distribution among the several functional institutional agencies of the community. This distribution has been visualized in Figures 22-1–22-4 for 1900, 1960, and 2000. Figure 22-1 illustrates the pre-eminent position of business—relatively free from government regulation—in community life in 1900. Sixty years later, as suggested by Figure 22-2, government institutions had almost caught up with business institutions as countervailing concentrations of power and three new concentrations had arisen, two of them—military and labor—to almost challenging proportions. Figure 22-3 suggests a *possible*—however improbable—power structuring in A.D. 2000, in which the military has been replaced by ethics and business, the state and labor relegated to relatively low levels. An alternative, as shown in Figure 22-4, could, of course, be one in which the military, business, and state institutions—under the compulsions generated by the threat of war—accumulated practically all of the power, reducing the others to insignificance as countervailing concentrations of power. These relative power relationships are presented by Form and Miller not as statistically based history or as firm predictions for the future but rather as graphic ways of viewing fairly abstract and complex power relationships.

Other students of the relationships among influentials distinguish at least four types of structure among influentials:

> At one extreme is the exclusive elite type, made up of a few elites who have more or less inherited their positions for life. They are a relatively small cohesive and exclusive group who make unilateral decisions for the community. . . . In extreme cases, where the top influentials are a very small and highly integrated clique, they are also the key influentials.
>
> At the other extreme is the democratic type. There is no limitation on the number of the top influentials, for members tend to change with the type and seriousness of the issue or project. Here the top influentials constitute a highly individuated and temporary social system of associational representatives who have little independent and enduring power . . .
>
> The two middle types, the fluid influentials and the core elite, . . . differ primarily in the size of the elite core and the ease of access into it . . . Both . . . have

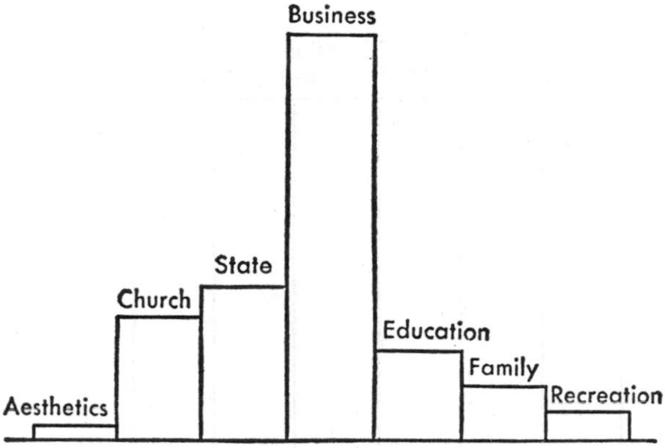

FIG. 22-1. A suggested ranking of American institutions by power and influence in 1900. (Reprinted from Delbert C. Miller and William H. Form, *Industrial Sociology*, Harper, 1951.)

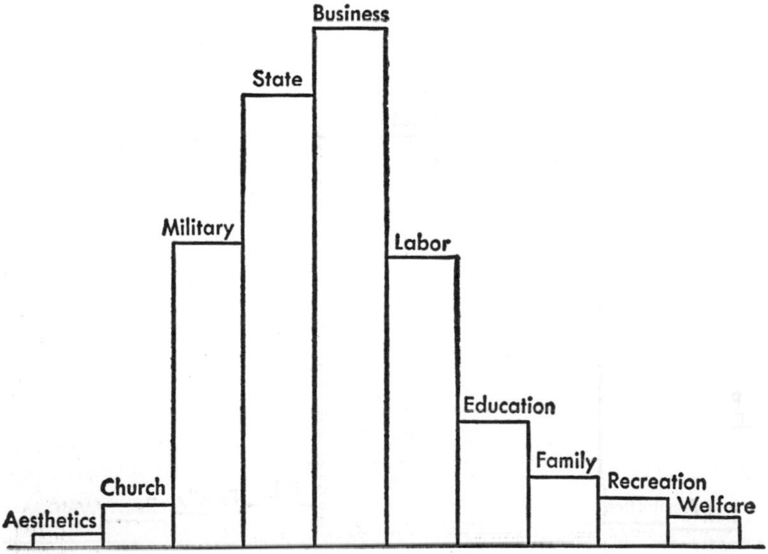

FIG. 22-2. The power structuring of American institutions in 1960. (Reprinted from Delbert C. Miller and William H. Form, *Industrial Sociology*, Harper, 1951.)

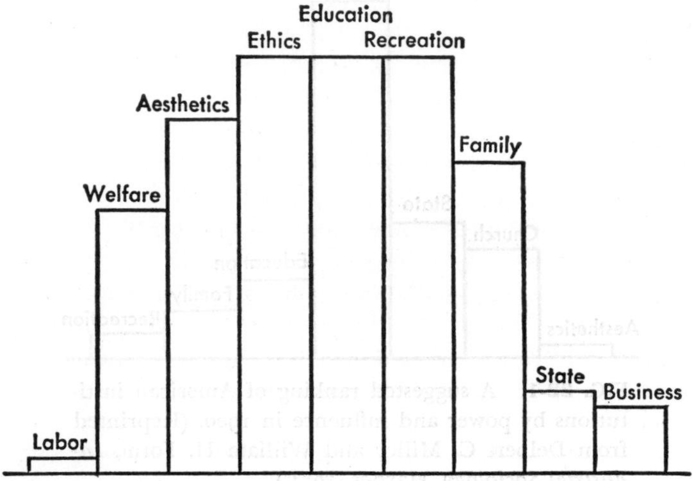

FIG. 22-3. A possible power structuring of American institutions in AD 2000—option A. (Reprinted from Delbert C. Miller and William H. Form, *Industrial Sociology,* Harper, 1951.)

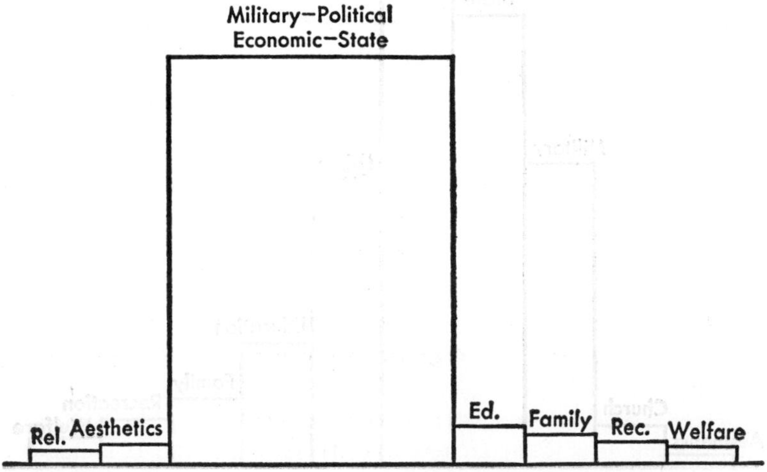

FIG. 22-4. A possible power structuring of American institutions in AD 2000—option B (Reprinted from Delbert C. Miller and William H. Form, *Industrial Sociology,* Harper, 1951.)

some degree of fluidity in their internal organization. . . . Some degree of mobility in and out of the top influentials is also found in both types of structure.[9]

The exclusive type of structure characterizes one-industry towns with dominant families, communities with a cohesive ruling aristocracy, and communities dominated by a strong economic-political clique. The democratic type of structure tends to characterize new communities in process of developing top influentials or older communities in which power is fairly evenly distributed among highly organized major groups. The intermediate types are the commonest in Western society and tend to prevail where the above conditions do not exist.

On the national scale, another student has analyzed the nature of the relationships among what he calls the power elite.[10] He sees it as a product of the concentration of the decision function in fewer and fewer positions as the size of organizational units in our society has grown. He sees power, further, concentrated in the hands of those who implement three great institutions, namely the state, the military, and the economy; or, rather, in the political economy and the military. The men who occupy the top decision-making positions in these great structures constitute, he believes, *the* power elite. The decisions they make—or even the decisions they do not make or shy away from making—affect the lives of millions of people everywhere. They constitute a de facto "ruling class."

The Nature of the Power Elite As a Structure

There are differences of opinion with respect to the nature of this power elite. Some people argue that these men in decision-making positions do not constitute a single unit, with "consciousness of kind," that they are not a well-knit, cohesive group but rather that there are many elites, many persons occupying decision-making positions, and that they do not add up to a single power elite, that there is therefore no "ruling class," but that there are many centers of decision that contribute to shaping the direction of events.[11] We have already referred to the theory of countervailing power which states that whenever too much power becomes concentrated in any group or institution, forces are generated which produce other groups to share in the original power.[12]

C. Wright Mills argues that neither conception of the nature of the power elite, that it is a single, solidary structure or that it is made up of many elites, some even countervailing one another, is alone adequate; both are necessary. Basically men have power because they occupy certain key

[9] Form and Miller, *op. cit.*, pp. 446-447.

[10] C. Wright Mills, *The Power Elite* (New York: Oxford, 1956).

[11] For a succinct summary of the critiques of Mills's point of view by Robert S. Lynd, Paul M. Sweezy, Fred Rodell, Daniel Bell, and Dennis W. Brogan, see Form and Miller, *op. cit.*, pp. 518-519.

[12] John Kenneth Galbraith, *American Capitalism* (Boston: Houghton-Mifflin, 1952).

positions, positions that have many "power chips." But these key positions are themselves interrelated and this fact itself makes for solidarity. ". . . if these hierarchies . . . have many interconnections and points of coinciding interest [as they do in America today] then their elites tend to form a coherent kind of grouping."[13] The coordination of the hierarchies may not be willful at first, but in time the decision makers "come to see that these several interests could be realized more easily if they worked together, in informal as well as in more formal ways, and accordingly they have done so."[14]

But in addition to structural and coordinating factors which tend to produce unity among members of the power elites are two others, namely psychological and social factors. The men who achieve decision-making positions tend to have similar backgrounds and education, they have a similar style of living, they share "old school ties," they "understand" one another. And, finally, they associate together in clubs and share a common social life. As a result, they are influenced by the same collective values. They can coordinate their behavior even without communication; they know what they can expect others to do. All of these kinds of factors operate, says Mills, to unify the members who occupy decision-making positions into a single power elite, regardless of the specific area in which their position is located.

Mills makes it clear, however, that he does not attribute to these men any conspiracy. They need not themselves even be aware that they constitute a power elite. They may, in complete sincerity, reject the idea that they do. The picture is not that of a clique of power-hungry men usurping the decision-making positions; it is rather that of men who, by one means or another, have come to occupy such positions and then find common interests, common styles of living, common associates. The unity of the power elite is not necessarily in the minds of the men themselves; it is in the interrelated nature of the structures they control and the observer may see it much more clearly than do the occupants themselves.

Influence through Voluntary Associations

Most people, by the very nature of social structure, are not in a position to stamp their die—good or bad—on community life as individuals. They may not, of course, even want to. For those who do wish to have some say in community life, however, the channel through which their influence must flow is an association of some kind or other.

Alexis de Tocqueville was the first commentator to note the importance of the function performed by voluntary associations in a democracy. He saw them as imposing a brake on the tendency for power to become concentrated in centralized governments.

[13] *Op. cit.*, p. 19.
[14] *Ibid.*, p. 20.

> Involvement in . . . [local self-government and voluntary associations] seemed to him a condition for the stability of the democratic system. By disseminating ideas and creating consensus among their members, they become the basis for conflict between one organization and another. And, in the process of doing so, they also limit the central power, create new and autonomous centers of power to compete with it, and help to train potential opposition leaders in political skills.[15]

Specifically, voluntary associations "are a source of new opinions; they can be the means of communicating ideas, particularly opposition ideas, to a large section of the citizenry; they train men in political skills and so help to increase the level of interest and participation in politics."[16]

Voluntary associations can often do what no individual could possibly do. They have a snowball effect. They create a social atmosphere or climate conducive to their cause. They create, that is, a favorable "public opinion." They constitute, in effect, a kind of feedback so that those in a position to make decisions know what to expect. Voluntary associations carry on a dialogue with those in power.

The top officers in voluntary associations may have a considerable stack of "power chips" and those of some associations may be members of the community power elite. And the organizations themselves may be important elements in the so-called "community power complex," or structure of power among groups, as distinguished from the structure of power among individuals.[17] But the rank-and-file membership who drive and motivate voluntary associations belong in a category of community participation far below the "stars," "heroes," "influentials," and power elites. They are just hard-working, conscientious, civic-minded citizens who leave their comfortable fireside chairs or favorite television programs on cold, rainy nights to attend dull committee meetings, council meetings, agency meetings, and board meetings of all kinds.

The support of civic voluntary associations (as distinguished from interest groups) is contributed by individuals who have vision or fervor or just social conscience. No one who has participated in such associations has any illusions about the difficulties involved. Each step of the way involves hours of tedious, grueling, boring detail. People who are willing to undertake such labors are not numerous in any American community. The actual percentage of members in associations who perform actively is remarkably small.

In fact, the studies made so far of degree of participation in associations have revealed a decided lack of interest on the part of most members. Using as a criterion of participation any one of the following activities: (1) joining in discussions of policies, (2) serving on a committee, or (3) carrying out an assignment of any kind, one set of studies showed that even in a

[15] Seymour Martin Lipset, *Political Man* (New York: Free Press, 1960), p. 27.
[16] *Ibid.*, p. 67.
[17] Form and Miller, *op. cit.*, p. 443.

powerful political machine, the proportion of members participating ran to about only one fourth of one percent; in a section of a powerful union, considered an active, aggressive organization, it was just one percent; in church and parish activities (outside of Sunday attendance), less than one-half of one percent; in a powerful reform organization, five to six percent.[18]

Even lower on the participation continuum which we have been analyzing is mere membership in associations, with or without active participation in their programs. There is a popular stereotype of the typical American as a chronic joiner. It is certainly true that there are more associations of one kind or another in American communities than anywhere else, yet actual membership is not nearly so widespread as we have thought. Poor people, for example, do not belong to many associations. One study of voluntary associations among urban dwellers found that

> ". . . sixty percent of working class and 53 percent of white collar men . . . did not have a single organized group affiliation with the exception, perhaps, of a Church. . . . The figures for the women are even more striking: 88 percent of labor and 63 percent of white collar women were without any affiliations. Indeed, in all occupational classes, male or female, earning under $3,000 [as of 1934-1935] and other than professional, that is, in the bulk of the City's population, the unaffiliated persons constituted a majority. Conversely, it is only when we reach the business classes earning $3,000 and the professional classes that the majority is found to be organized. . . . Non-membership in . . . associations . . . no doubt implies that sections of our population are cut off from channels of power, information, growth, and a sense of participation in purposive social action."[19]

This general picture is as likely to be true for rural as for urban communities. A study of 25 young married couples in a rural community in central New York found, for example, that degree of participation depended upon such factors as economic status, education, participation experience, degree of occupational and residential mobility, psychological attitudes toward the stranger, and degree of family adjustment.[20]

In general, then, the poor, the uneducated, the minority group member, the mobile, the timid, or the person with a heavy load of personal or family maladjustment is not likely to have either the desire or the facility for contributing to community decisions or for impressing his will on the community either directly or through an association. That is a luxury reserved for the well-to-do, the educated, the majority-group member, the stable, the self-assured, and the person free from emotional load. The privilege of sharing in community decisions, of leaving an impress on com-

[18] Saul Alinsky, *Reveille for Radicals* (Chicago: University of Chicago, 1946), pp. 199-200.

[19] Mirra Komarovsky, "The Voluntary Associations of Urban Dwellers," *Amer. Soc. Rev.*, 11 (December, 1946), pp. 687, 698.

[20] W. M. Smith, Jr., *The Social Participation of Rural Young Married Couples* (Ithaca, N. Y.: Cornell University Agricultural Experimental Station, Bul. 812, 1944).

munity life is, it appears, an upper-class prerogative for the most part. And only a small number of even this class care to take advantage of it. On the side of the "masses" the proportion who may aspire to the privilege of participating in the great dialogue between decision-makers and public, of contributing to the "feedback" is almost infinitesimal.

American and European Participation

This pattern of community life is, we are told, characteristically American. One European student has commented on the contrast which he found between class leadership on the one hand and mass passivity on the other in American community life. He explained the passivity of the lower income groups in terms of what he called cultural fragmentation.

> They have been split in national, linguistic, and religious sub-groups, which has hampered class solidarity and prevented effective mass organization. Folk movements require close understanding among the individuals in the group, a deep feeling of common loyalty, and even a preparedness to share in collective sacrifices for a distant common goal. Only on a basis of psychological identification with the interest group is it possible to ask the individual to renounce his own short-range interests for the group's long-range ones. The immigrants have felt social distance to other lower class persons with different cultural origin. Also because they have difficulty in communicating with other Americans, immigrants have had to have leaders for this purpose.[21]

A second reason he found for mass passivity was that leaders have been sucked up out of the lower classes by free opportunities to rise.

> Cultural fragmentation, the division of interest of the lower classes, and their loss of leaders, thus stamped the masses with inertia. They are accustomed to being static and receptive. They are not daring, but long for security. They do not know how to cooperate and how to pool risks and sacrifices for a common goal. They do not meet much. They do not organize. They do not speak for themselves: they are the listeners in America.[22]

This pattern of outstanding and powerful leaders and passive followers was found, this same writer reported, not only in political life but also in the field of labor, of higher education, and of business. "Even in small groups—civic committees, research projects, or Sunday schools—the same pattern prevails: the leaders run the show, the masses are passive except for an occasional election."[23]

This picture of ourselves as being passively pushed around is jolting. We picture ourselves as members of a democratic society in which we are all entitled to share in the formation of policy. In addition to the reasons we have already presented for the lack of active participation in community

[21] Gunnar Myrdal, *An American Dilemma* (New York: Harper, 1944), pp. 713-714.
[22] *Ibid.*
[23] *Ibid.*, p. 719.

affairs, cultural fragmentation, division of interest, and loss of leadership by upward mobility, there are others. Many Americans are, so to speak, rootless and do not live in the communities in which they were born. Modern communities are lacking in close kinship ties. They are overwhelming. Residents seem to despair of making themselves felt. They are apathetic, sometimes cynical. In addition, an active interest in community welfare may call forth ridicule and contempt from others. One of the hazards which organized activity for community welfare faces is rooted deep in the psychology of American community life. If a person fights for his own selfish interests, even if we disagree with him, we understand him. We see why he fights. He has, so to speak, in a roundabout way, our moral support. But if a person has no immediate stake involved and still fights, he becomes a target for such epithets as "reformer," "do-gooder," "uplifter," "busybody," "crank." Many people simply cannot understand disinterested service to the community. They are suspicious of it. There must be something in it for these queer people. Otherwise why would they be poking their noses into other people's business? Naturally, then, if one is to be rewarded for his efforts by becoming the butt of jokes, he would do better to save his energies in the first place.

Even if the welfare activity is closely tied up with one's own interests, this fact is not always obvious. Because modern communities are so complex, it is often difficult to make people see their true interests. The busy housewife, absorbed in her home and family duties, finds it hard to see that commercialized gambling has anything to do with her. The harassed businessman, immersed in the affairs of his factory, feels that he cannot be bothered with slum clearance projects. It is only a very skilled leader who can dramatize community problems so that everyone can see how near home they really strike.

Direct Action

Sometimes those who feel themselves excluded from the great dialogue with the decision-makers, who feel they are not contributing to the feedback, resort to direct action. Direct action may be violent or nonviolent. The function of such direct action is to force those in positions of power to pay attention to persons who have no other access to channels of communication. The great decisions about the use of nuclear weapons are made by a small group of men in positions of power. Another small group of men sail a small ship, The Golden Rule, to the testing area to communicate to the decision-makers that they too want a say in these decisions. The use of nonviolent direct action as a contribution to the great dialogues of our day is also illustrated by the Montgomery bus strike of 1955, the sit-ins of Negro students in 1959, the Freedom Riders of 1961, the marches, the vigils, the street meetings of Friends.

Influence through Trained Professionals

Perhaps the lowest level of personal participation in community life, for those who really wish to take part in the dialogues with power, is simply one of supporting associations which work for their ideals: civic groups, crime commissions, citizens' committees, and the like. The creation of a solid foundation of moral support for the more aggressive activity of these associations is, of course, a contribution of no little importance. Without such support, the associations can achieve little.

Sometimes the most effective way that disinterested citizens who wish to contribute to community welfare can make themselves felt is to hire paid professional leaders to organize and run their civic groups for them. At one time the advice to idealistic young people who wished to influence community life was to get into political organizations, to get elected to precinct committees or central committees. They found, however, that this almost never happened. The boss saw to that. They were frozen out. They gave up. They were no match for the professional politicians. Political parties have ceased to serve as a channel for making a contribution to community welfare, if, indeed, they ever did serve this purpose at all. If the citizen wishes to make a constructive contribution to community welfare he must set up permanent, nonpartisan civic organizations to formulate programs of municipal reconstruction.

Other kinds of organizations that are set up to exert influence are social planning agencies, community councils, and professional social work organizations of a dozen different kinds. The only way left to many citizens who wish to participate in community decisions is—to write a check. They can do little more than hire someone else to stand for their principles for them. It takes training, professional skill, time, and energy to make oneself felt in community life. It is more than the average citizen can contribute.

The citizen is not, of course, thereby left free to go his way without another thought, once he has written his check. He still has to read, keep informed, know what is going on, and be prepared to offer the indispensable moral support without which no community program can succeed.

Part VII

Disorganization and Dissociation

SINCE ORGANIZATION itself is such a complex phenomenon it is understandable that disorganization should also be. In Part VII we shall approach it from several points of view. First of all, from the functional point of view. We shall view disorganization as the result of a breakdown in some subsystem in the community. Since a community depends on the adequate functioning of its several subsystems, when one or more is not performing, disorganization results (Ch. 23). We shall then examine disorganization as a group phenomenon; this is schismatic disorganization, resulting when for whatever reason the groups that constitute the community fall apart, balkanizing the community and making integrated behavior difficult (Ch. 24). The third approach to disorganization is in terms of the nonconforming behavior of individuals (Ch. 25).

Since violence is likely to create disorder and hence to disorganize a community, at least temporarily, and because violence is itself an important phenomenon in any event, Chapter 26 is devoted to a discussion of this interesting kind of behavior.

Finally, in Chapter 27 the phenomenon which we have labeled community dissociation is dealt with. Here we find communities dealing with incompatible differences in a peculiar sort of way; they find ways to institutionalize violations of their own norms, either by themselves (façade dissociation) or by others (parallel dissociation). It is often the only alternative to disorganization.

23

Functional Community Disorganization: The Breakdown in Subsystems

The Breakdown in Subsystems

If a community is viewed as a system of subsystems, each contributing to the whole in specialized services, it can readily be seen how a malfunctioning or breakdown in any one or more of the subsystems may have a greater or lesser disorganizing effect on the total community. The breakdown might occur in any subsystem. It might occur in the legal or court system resulting in so many cases choking the docket that justice is interminably delayed; it might occur in the market, so flooded with counterfeit money that trade is cut off, or so fearful of inflation that everyone wishes to trade money for almost anything else; it might occur in the political system, so inefficient that there is no police protection. Wherever it occurs, a breakdown in any part of the total system has repercussions in other parts. Community disorganization in this functional sense may be conceived of as a state in which one or more of the subsystems, for whatever reason, is not contributing its expected service to the community. It is, of course, a matter of degree, ranging from an almost imperceptible malfunctioning of one subsystem to a total breakdown of all subsystems, as in a disaster.

The conditions which give rise to large-scale community disorganization in this functional sense may be classified as natural disasters, such as floods, storms, earthquakes, and the like or as man-made "disasters," such as strikes, booms, depressions, and wars.

Natural Disasters

When the last glaciers melted they let loose great masses of water. As a result much folklore to this day is haunted by stories of disastrous floods. Earthquakes and fires have leveled many communities. The remains of Sodom and Gomorrah are being sought today in the Dead Sea, victims, presumably of earthquakes. Such great disasters have challenged theologians as well as philosophers and scientists. They have also been subject matter for literary works. How do human beings react in the presence of great disaster?

Despite the long history of natural disasters and the human preoccupation with them, it is only recently—stimulated especially by the requirements of civil defense—that systematic research has been undertaken on the effects of these great disorganizing phenomena.

A disaster has been defined as follows:

> Disaster means the impinging upon a structured community of an external force capable of destroying human life or its resources for survival, on a scale wide enough to excite public alarm, to disrupt normal patterns of behavior, and to impair or overload any of the central services necessary to the conduct of normal affairs or to the prevention or alleviation of suffering and loss. Usually, the term disaster refers to an episode with tragic consequences to a substantial portion of the population.[1] [At least five families must be involved according to Red Cross standards.]

Disasters include hurricanes, tornadoes, and other windstorms; other storms (snow, hail, dust, electrical) ; floods; explosions; fires; wrecks; and such other disasters as earthquakes, landslides, drought, structural collapse, and epidemics. Tornadoes are the worst disasters so far as fatalities and injured persons are concerned, as well as number of homes destroyed; but floods are the worst in terms of number of homes damaged and families suffering. Fatalities and injuries are most numerous in disasters occuring in March and September; the number of families involved is greatest in August.[2] Epidemics are usually seasonal and with modern medical and public health programs are usually held below disaster levels. In the fourteenth century, the Black Death has been credited with serving as a major force breaking down the feudal system; epidemics today never reach these proportions.

Efforts to deal with disaster take several forms. Expectably, there is a spate of legislation ranging from the so-called Swamp Acts of 1849 and 1850 to deal with floods to the Flood Control Act of 1936, an act to make surplus property available for the alleviation of damage caused by disaster in 1947, a Federal Disaster Act in 1950, and a Federal Flood Insurance Act in 1956. (In 1961 an act was passed for dealing with another kind of "disaster," namely chronic depression.) In addition to legislation there are organizations which specialize in disaster relief such as the Red Cross and the Salvation Army; even the armed forces may be called in if necessary.

Both the military and the civilian defense organizations are interested to know how people behave under the stresses of disasters and how best to

[1] John Walker Powell, "An Introduction to the Natural History of Disaster," unpublished report of the Psychiatric Institute, University of Maryland, 1954. Present citation, Hoyt Lemons, "Physical Characteristics of Disaster: Historical and Statistical Review," *Annals Amer. Acad. Pol. Soc. Sci.*, 309 (January, 1957) , p. 2.

[2] *Ibid.*, pp. 11ff.

deal with them. A distinction is made between behavior in the pre-impact phase, the impact phase, and the post-impact phase. If the pre-impact phase is short and there are useful things to do, people respond fairly well, especially if they have been prepared. If the pre-impact phase drags on and there is nothing left to do, they often become demoralized. The longer people have to wait the greater the tension that results. If it is a recurrent type of disaster so that people know in general what to expect and what to do there is less disorganization, as shown by a comparison of the matter-of-fact reaction of an experienced Kansas farmer to a tornado with the confused reaction of people in Worcester, Massachusetts, unaccustomed to tornados.

The impact phase may be short. Some people become galvanized and behave heroically; others may become more remote and "frozen," with glassy eyes. Some behave in a seemingly pointless manner. Relatively few, if any, are panic-stricken. What looks like confused behavior may actually be quite rational; it only looks disorganized to the observer.

> To an outside observer the initial behavior of persons in a disaster-struck area is likely to appear completely irrational, chaotic, and confused. In the physical devastation surrounding him, the observer sees what appears to be aimless, random, uncontrolled, or conflicting activity on the part of the survivors. People are running or driving vehicles in opposite directions, often-times passing each other without acknowledgment or seeming awareness. Some persons are moving out of the impact area, many others are moving into it. Others are "standing around," apparently just looking or talking with each other. Here and there small groups of people are digging in debris, comforting the injured, or attempting to retrieve their scattered belongings. Behavior is so heterogeneous that it defies description in terms of a few simple categories.[3]

It is this lack of uniformity in action that often leads the outside observer to the erroneous conclusion that the population has "panicked." What the outside observer is witnessing is not panic, but social disorganization—uncoordinated activity on a general, community level.

Panic or Disorganization?

The "panic myth" is itself an extremely interesting sociological phenomenon. One psychoanalytic observer believes that "the image of panic as an animal-like stampede in which wildly excited people crush each other to death" has a terrible fascination for people and that "the readiness to anticipate panic is more related to the haunting quality of this image than to observations of how people actually behave in danger situations."[4]

This analyst distinguishes six meanings which have been attached to the term panic: (1) intense subjective terror, with or without cause; (2)

[3] Charles E. Fritz and Harry B. Williams, "The Human Being in Disasters: A Research Perspective," *Annals Amer. Acad. Pol. & Soc. Sci.*, 309 (January, 1957), p. 45.

[4] Martha Wolfenstein, *Disaster, A Psychological Essay* (New York: Free Press, 1957), p. 85.

nonuseful or self-destructive behavior resulting from extreme alarm; (3) contagion alarm; (4) flight of a group from a danger which seems impossible to combat; (5) a group situation in which each individual's concern for himself prevents concern for others; and (6) a group situation in which individuals injure one another in efforts to flee. Each of these may occur separately or together. She concluded that "the definition of panic as irrational and anti-social mass flight [that is, as including items 2, 4, and 6] should not lead us to infer that every instance of precipitate group flight [4] is unuseful [2] or involves mutual damage among the fugitives [6]." The specific studies which have been made of community reactions to disaster in this country and of the reactions to bombings in other countries tend to confirm this conclusion.

There are, to be sure, circumstances, such as fires in which exits are blocked, for example, in which the conditions for panic prevail and panic does occur. But panic circumstances do not seem to characterize the kinds of disasters which are more likely to occur in communities today.

A sociologist studying panic, defining it as dysfunctional or maladaptive behavior, found only one-fifth of his informants describing their own behavior as dysfunctional. Women aged 25 to 40 seemed most susceptible. They were more active than others and much of even their behavior was functional. The chief distinguishing characteristic of those who were susceptible to dysfunctional behavior was that they were either alone or separated from their families at the time of impact. He concluded that although people under the stress of disaster might show some symptoms of panic or shock, they were not wholly stripped of their social and institutional patterns of behavior.[5]

The essence of institutionalized behavior, as we have pointed out on several occasions, is its expectedness. Interdependent decisions are made on the basis of expected behavior on the part of others. But when disaster strikes a community, the conditions necessary for such concerted and coordinated activity are destroyed; people don't know what to expect. Their behavior tends to become individualized and, without the props of expected behavior from others, perhaps sometimes even uncontrolled. Nevertheless, "panic . . . [though] frequently anticipated, . . . [is a] rarely occurring reaction to disaster."[6]

The Post-Impact Phase

One of the most interesting phenomena associated with disaster is the emergence of increased social solidarity, a breakdown of previous barriers.

> The net result of most disasters is a dramatic increase in social solidarity among the affected populace during the emergency and immediate post-emergency

[5] William Form, *et al., Community in Disaster* (New York: Harper, 1958).
[6] Wolfenstein, *loc. cit.*

periods. The sharing of a common threat to survival and the common suffering produced by the disaster tend to produce a breakdown of pre-existing social distinctions and a great outpouring of love, generosity, and altruism. During the first few days or weeks following a major community-wide disaster, persons tend to act toward one another spontaneously, sympathetically, and sentimentally, on the basis of common human needs rather than in terms of predisaster differences in social and economic status. This solidarity is of major significance in facilitating both personal and social recuperation. It helps persons to overcome the shock of severe personal injuries, losses, and deprivations and motivates volunteer participation in the numerous rescue, relief, and restoration tasks.[7]

In time, of course, this new-found social solidarity fades out and is replaced by traditional cleavages.

The re-establishing of order, reuniting families, making provisions for the homeless, setting up first-aid and hospital facilities, feeding the people are no longer in and of themselves difficult tasks. Long experience has taught the most effective ways and standardized policies and procedures for performing these functions. But organizational difficulties are more problematical. Whose responsibility is it to do what? The in-group, who are first to begin rescue operations, develop strong feelings of euphoria and pride.

If the actions of the outsiders do not coincide with the new sentiments and emergency norms that have arisen among the affected populace, the outsiders tend to be criticized and resented. . . . Many of the problems of disaster management result from the temporary lack of "fit" between the conceptions of need of the victim population and of the organizations attempting to administer to this population. As a consequence of these different conceptions, the activities of the organization and the needs of the clients get out of phase, incompatibility and even conflict may result. From an organizational viewpoint, solutions to this problem lie primarily in developing greater sensitivity to the prevailing climate of opinion among the victim population and greater capacity to make rapid adjustments to local situations.[8]

The natural disasters we have been considering so far destroy the physical structure of the community and the havoc wrought is observable for all to see. But economic, social, and political forces may be just as disorganizing to a community as physical forces, if not more so, but the havoc they wreak is not always so clearly discernible. A strike, boom conditions, a long depression, or war can be more disorganizing than even a fire or flood. The machinery of community life stalls; the ordinary expectations which keep community life operating smoothly break down.

Man-made Disasters

Selected for illustration here are the disorganizing effects of a strike, too-rapid growth, a long period of depression, and war.

[7] Fritz and Williams, *op. cit.*, p. 48.
[8] *Ibid.*, p. 49.

STRIKES

Violence seems to be declining in strikes at the present time. To that extent communities are less likely to be disorganized than they were in the past when a strike could amount almost to civil war. But the development of three kinds of strike, even when they are not violent, has rendered communities more susceptible to disorganization than before. The three types are industry-wide strikes, strikes in public utilities, and sympathetic strikes, that is, strikes in which workers in many branches of work walk out to help fellow-workers win a strike.

There was a time when communities need not be seriously disorganized by strikes. When both unions and industries were small and local in extent a community might tolerate a strike and take it in its stride. The rest of the community could go right on, even though it might limp a little. The strike might be very inconvenient, but not really disorganizing. Nowadays, however, when both unions and industries are gargantuan, even national in scope, a strike can virtually paralyze not only the local community but the national—even international—community as well. In 1946, for example, the entire nation suffered serious dislocation because of industry-wide coal strikes. The strikes themselves were quite peaceful, but stoppage of mining gradually produced stoppages in steel, automobiles, and in the scores of other industries which depended on iron and steel. Because the economic system is, indeed, a system in which all parts are functionally related to one another, it was like a kind of creeping paralysis which affected the remotest communities. It even reached European communities, which were deprived of American coal shipments.

Strikes in public utilities can produce acute disorganization. Twice in 1946 the experience of Pittsburgh illustrated how critical such a strike could become. In February the electric-power workers went out on strike with the following results:

> Public schools were closed. Downtown department stores and many other businesses closed their doors. Elevator service was suspended in skyscrapers. Half of the large business buildings and some hotels were without heat in the dead of winter. Streetcars suspended operation. At the Children's Hospital, which has no emergency electric power facilities, volunteers were called for to be ready to hand-pump an iron lung to keep a 16-year-old boy alive. If it had not been for the existing steel strike, steel mills would have had to close.[9]

Although newspapers are not usually classified as public utilities, they do "transport" news and thus serve almost as vital a function as transportation facilities themselves. The great dependence of communities on these carriers of information is illustrated by the disorganization which set in at Springfield, Massachusetts, when its chief newspaper was closed by a strike:

> The community chest drive fell below its quota for the first time in history,

[9] *St. Louis Post-Dispatch,* Sept. 11, 1946.

missing it by 20 per cent. Always before the newspaper had gotten behind the movement and it had never failed.

Florists report their business off 50 per cent. People don't know their friends have died or are ill, so they send no flowers.

The "Ice Capades," an annual sell-out, played to almost empty houses, even though promoters hired criers to stand on the street corners and shout about it.

People didn't learn who won local elections for weeks, and many of them still are not certain that the information they have gained by word of mouth is correct.

Dogs are lost, and found, and there is no way to notify the public or the owner. The dog pounds are crowded with the largest canine population in history.

Moviegoers don't know what is showing at the picture houses, and the telephone system is clogged nightly by people calling the theaters to find out. Attendance is off.[10]

Strikes are disorganizing to communities nowadays, then, not so much because they are necessarily violent—violence in the old sense having all but disappeared—but because they are so wide in scope, both geographically and occupationally, and because they may occur in such vital industries as public utilities. It was for this reason that they were restricted by the Taft-Hartley Act of 1947.

BOOM TOWNS

There seems to be a limit to the rate of growth to which communities can successfully adjust themselves. If it is too rapid, they break down under the load. A great influx of people stalls the machinery of community life. Schools, transportation, elementary sanitation, housing, recreational facilities, police protection, and religious accommodations are all inadequate. People may have to live like animals. The usual community amenities are not available. Family life is put under severe strain; race relations become tense; people become more easy prey to hate-mongering. Consensus may break down.

During the war millions of people poured into defense centers. There were no preparations for them. Housing projects sprang up quickly to accommodate some of them. But many more had to shift for themselves. Community facilities were simply nonexistent for them. The result of the tremendous social upheaval was almost traumatic. Sex mores were among the casualties; family stability was another:

Thousands of men and women have been housed in the most deplorable conditions of overcrowding. Absent husbands and long working hours have created serious dislocations in family life. Families and parts of families have been uprooted from familiar customs and thrust into exciting boom towns often with

[10] "What Does It Mean to a Town?" *The Daily Advertiser*, Aurora, Mo., Dec. 2, 1946.

more money than they know how to manage. Home supervision has been slackened as all of the responsible heads of the family have gone to work in the local shipyard or aircraft factory.[11]

Communities are self-pacing organisms. They require time to assimilate new members. Even if proper physical equipment had been available, the psychological and sociological processes of assimilating newcomers in huge quantities is difficult. People have to feel one another out, so to speak. They have to explore one another with their social antennae. Differences have to be perceived and accommodated. Relationships have to be created. These are not processes that can be hurried. Great urban centers throughout the world today are suffering from attempts to ingest millions of newcomers from rural areas. Communities, it appears, can tolerate only so much strain and no more.

LONG DEPRESSIONS

When a natural catastrophe strikes a community the impact is spectacular, quick, and immediate. Legislation has been passed and organizations formed to come to the rescue. But when depression hits an area the impact is not spectacular; it is slow and takes time to make itself felt. As a result, although there have been chronically depressed communities in New England and in hard-coal mining areas and in cut-over timber areas for decades, it was not until 1961 that federal legislation was passed designed specifically to help them.

Without jobs, people cannot pay taxes. Some communities go bankrupt. Essential services are curtailed. Streets deteriorate. Schools suffer. Parks and playgrounds are neglected. Buildings are not kept in good repair. A generally down-at-the-heel appearance characterizes the whole community.

If panic is a characteristic, though not usual, accompaniment of natural disaster, so anomia is a characteristic accompaniment of long depressions. Anomia refers to despair, hopelessness, discouragement, personal disorganization, demoralization, disheartenment. With respect to its incidence among individuals, it has been found to occur when they are denied access to the means for achieving their life goals.[12] It is inversely related to the economic status of the neighborhood where people live, as well as to occupation, income, and education, and to amount of informal and formal group participation.

More interesting for our purposes here, however, is the fact that anomia may characterize whole communities also. It is the subjective counterpart to the breakdown of normative systems. Long endured it may destroy whole

[11] *Challenge to Community Action* (Washington, D. C.: Federal Security Agency, 1945), pp. 46-47.

[12] Robert Merton, *Social Theory and Social Structure* (New York: Free Press, 1958), Chapter 4.

generations, even rendering them incapable of helping themselves when help is offered. A case in point is Coal Town:

> . . . the vast majority of these people . . . have grown up amidst patterns of violence, fear, cynicism, and hopelessness. In this regard it is well to point out that an entire generation has been reared in an environment where they have never known their fathers to have steady work and where unemployment was the rule rather than the exception. Further, they have little faith in the motives of others and lack the capacity to identify consistently, be it with other persons or with things abstract such as community growth. Life in the community has fostered skepticism to the point where their confidence in any new enterprise or scheme can readily be undermined and destroyed; and while such an attitude is understandable in view of their experiences, it constitutes a formidable barrier to their acceptance of new things. The capacity for these people to change, to visualize new alternatives, is limited. For the native population, social change is reminiscent of the introduction of coal mining and brings back memories of the native-immigrant conflict. Equally significant is the notion that social change . . . means accepting things that are different. Differences, be they matters of food, language, or work, have now become identified with frustration. Thus social change and personal disorganization have become linked in the thinking of these people. Attempts to bring about changes have produced inner conflicts for many already weary of a life of frustration. Many have simply withdrawn from the conflict and remain inert.[13]

Thermonuclear War

All natural and man-made catastrophies pale into insignificance compared with the man-made disaster of war. And the destruction wrought by wars in the past pales into insignificance compared with the destruction possible in thermonuclear war. There is little if any relevant empirical research on the effects of thermonuclear war on the scale possible today. The discussion here is based on so-called Systems Analysis of the best estimates available. It presents what is probable as well as what is possible. It is taken from a book "dedicated to the goal of anticipating, avoiding, and alleviating crises."[14] Much of the book is devoted to military and economic problems. For our purposes here, however, the discussion of the sociological problems related to recuperation after a thermonuclear war is most pertinent. The author believes that we have fooled ourselves by speaking of "total annihilation," "mutual suicide," "the end of the human species," and similar forebodings. Even thermonuclear war, he argues, does not mean total annihilation. It is his purpose to analyze what it does mean.

That there would be unheard of dislocations in community life is, of course, expectable. Three kinds of calamities may produce them: (1) radio-

[13] Herman R. Lantz, *People of Coal Town* (New York: Columbia University, 1958), p. 209.

[14] Herman Kahn, *On Thermonuclear War* (Princeton: Princeton University, 1960), p. x.

active fallout which would threaten health and longevity as well as the heredity of the future; (2) widespread destruction of the physical plant of our society; and (3) high casualty rates.

RADIOACTIVE FALLOUT

One of the effects of radiation on human beings is the production of genetic mutations, most of them defects. The estimated genetic consequences of world-wide radiation doses approaching the limits established by the National Academy of Sciences (10 roentgens), would be as shown in Table 23-1.

TABLE 23-1. TOTAL INCREASE AND PERCENT INCREASE IN SPECIFIED CONSEQUENCES WITH WORLD-WIDE DOSES OF RADIATION APPROACHING 10 ROENTGENS*

Type of Damage	*First Generation* Total Increase	Percent Increase	*Later Generation* Total Increase	Percent Increase
Major Defects	1,000,000	0.04	10,000,000	0.4
Minor Defects	10,000,000	0.4	200,000,000	6
Early Mortality	2,500,000	0.08	40,000,000	1.3
Decreased Fertility	5,000,000	0.17	100,000,000	3.3

* Herman Kahn, *On Thermonuclear War* (Princeton: Princeton University, 1960), p. 44.

The figures are astronomical. Even for the United States alone the figures are enormous: 65,000 defective children in the first generation and 650,000 in every succeeding generation when new levels of stability are reached.

WIDESPREAD DESTRUCTION

Kahn divides the United States into two basic communities or "nations," A and B. A consists of the 50 to 100 largest cities and B of the rural areas, towns, and small cities. The relationship between them he compares to that between a mother country and colony; A supplies managerial and technical services, B, basic raw materials. But A is far more dependent on B for survival than B on A. In a thermonuclear war, A would be the major target. It contains most of the wealth of the United States. Most of it would be destroyed.

HIGH CASUALTY RATES

Estimates of casualties from a surprise attack on the United States run around 50 to 80 million (35), from a fourth to two-fifths of the total population.

What would be the effects of such catastrophes? On the basis of seven assumptions, (1) that we have not lost the war, (2) that society has begun to function again, (3) that economic activities are started, (4) that bottlenecks are cleared, (5) that "bourgeois" virtues survive, (6) that workable postwar standards are adopted, and (7) that neglected effects are unimportant, Kahn believes recuperation would be possible.

One of the above assumptions is of special relevance here, namely the fifth. Kahn believes it is justified on the following grounds:

> The fifth optimistic element in our calculation was the assumption that people would be willing to work at reconstructing the country and would have a productivity at this task about equal to that of their prewar work. To many this seems like a rather bold assumption. They ask, "Would not the shock of the catastrophe so derange people that every man's hand would be against every other man's?"
>
> This seems entirely wrong. Man never lives in a Hobbesian state of nature. There is always a society of some type. However, this fear is proper if it is stated more cautiously. There would be the possibilities of demogoguery, or sectionalism, or banditry. Some people would not be willing to work hard for the rewards available to them. Possibly the good "bourgeois" virtues so essential to a modern business society would disappear, and many people would become unambitious, irresponsible, dishonest, or lazy. The destitute survivors might war with the less destitute ones.
>
> I do not believe that any of these events would necessarily occur, especially if we have made preparations to preserve our society and to alleviate the strains that would inevitably occur. . . .
>
> It is my belief that if the government has made at least moderate prewar preparations, so that most people whose lives have been saved will give some credit to the government's foresight, then people will probably rally round, especially if the government has the organization, equipment, and manuals that it needs for recuperation and survival activities, and (most important of all) if the over-all plan for recuperation looks sensible and practical. It would not surprise me if the overwhelming majority of the survivors devoted themselves with a somewhat fanatic intensity to the task of rebuilding what was destroyed. . . .
>
> Of course, if there is a fantastic disparity between the government's preparations and the problems to be solved, then none of this would hold. Quite the contrary. There would probably be a complete rejection of the prewar government, and possibly the prewar ideals and institutions as well.[15]

What the precise nature of the breakdown in community structures would be cannot be foretold. The experience of the South after the Civil War is not pertinent nor is that of Europe after the two world wars nor even that of Hiroshima or Nagasaki. In all of these cases there were other resources available for reconstruction. What "nation B" could or would do without the leadership, talent, experience, and stimulation of "nation A" is anyone's guess.

[15] *Op. cit.*, pp. 89-90, 92.

24

Schismatic Community Disorganization: The Breakdown of Group Relationships

The Nature of Social Ties in a Pluralistic Society

"Blut and Bod"—kinship and territorial bonds—are very primitive ways in which groups relate to one another. Within these major ties there may be many others—age, sex, occupational—which tie people together. But kinship and local bonds are basic to the others. Tribal loyalties take precedence over others. As we saw in Chapter 2, however, industrialization demands new kinds of relationships. The difficulty involved in making a transition from tribal to political ties is tragically illustrated in the problems accompanying the independence of the Congo in 1960.

Ethnic and racial ties are the modern counterpart of kinship bonds. They seem to make the same kind of claim on people's loyalties. A common language, a common dietary, a common neighborhood, common experience with outsiders, a common history make people feel more comfortable with one another, more at ease. They understand one another. They "read" one another; they get one another's messages. They feel they can count on one another for support. They constitute an in-group; everyone else is in an out-group.

The bonds that hold people together also separate them from others. Invisible lines are drawn to protect the boundaries between them and outsiders. Ghettos, Little Italys, Irish Channels, Black Belts, Chinatowns in American cities reflect this ethnic and racial separatism. Such separatism is at its peak during the lifetime of the first generation; it becomes attenuated in the second and third generations,[1] but it remains a potentially divisive force even then.

Sometimes the divisive forces were deliberately used by employers at the turn of the century. Signs in factories were posted in half a dozen languages and men were discouraged from learning English, which would

[1] Judith Kramer and Seymour Levantman, *Children of the Gilded Ghetto* (New Haven: Yale, 1961).

serve as a communicating medium. As long as the men could not communicate with one another they could not unite in unions.

During World War I, however, it was found that group separatisms interfered with the successful prosecution of the war. So-called hyphenated Americans retained their old loyalties; they were Americans only in the sense that they lived in America. Ethnically they remained German or Italian or Polish or Irish. An effort was deliberately planned to "Americanize" them.

It soon became evident that the problem was far more profound than had been anticipated. Precisely what was meant by "Americanize"? Did Americanization involve destruction of old ethnic relationships? ethnic customs? traditions? Was the old idea of America as a "melting pot" in which all kinds of ethnic groups were melted down into a homogeneous new type the goal?

Gradually the concept of a so-called pluralistic society emerged to take the place of the melting-pot idea. Not a homogenized community but one in which differences which were not compatible were accommodated and differences which were compatible were at least permitted if not actively encouraged. The presence of compatible differences was to be welcomed; they made life more colorful, more varied, more interesting

The demands of a pluralistic society are new; they are difficult to meet. They are especially difficult if they are made under the conditions specified in American society, namely freedom and equality. Groups are to live together amicably on a basis of freedom and equality without demanding complete uniformity. This is, in a way, a revolutionary demand to make of human beings.

Differing groups can accommodate themselves nicely on an exploitative basis; that is, on a basis of subordination of one to the other. This has been done successfully many times in human history as the story of colonial empires illustrates. But the American assignment is much harder, for it asks that community life rest not on a basis of exploitation but on a basis of equality. Whether or not this is even possible is still debated by many. We are committed, nevertheless, to making the attempt. And a new profession—specialists in intergroup relations—has developed to implement the goals of a pluralistic society.

We do not, as a matter of fact, know exactly what the relationship between groups in a pluralistic society should be. We are only groping our way. We are sure in general that discrimination against any group in transportation, schooling, public accommodations, job opportunities, voting, and the like is either against the Constitution or contrary to specific statutes. The application of these norms to specific cases in the process of administering them raises countless questions, however.

People with an "exclusive" mentality show great concern about the trends in group relations. Little by little the areas which are public and hence ruled by antidiscrimination norms become larger and encroach farther and farther into purely private areas where they are, presumably, not applicable. Even fraternities and social clubs become subject to non-discriminatory norms.

Separatists ask where will it all end? Even laws forbidding interracial marriages are probably unconstitutional, although they are not likely to be tested in the Supreme Court for a long time. But in California they have been declared contrary to the California constitution on the grounds that they deprive people of the right to select their own mates.

It is, as we saw in Chapter 21, sometimes argued, with truth, that although it is possible to legislate against overt discrimination it is not possible to legislate against hostile feelings or prejudices. This is true, but the time may come when the only place it will be permissible to express hatred will be in the privacy of one's own closet! Certainly the mongering of hate will sooner or later come under interdiction.

Hate-mongering and Its Effects

Hate mongering is not an individual phenomenon; it is organized. It is practiced especially by extreme rightists with a fascist slant. A preliminary report by the Committee on Un-American Activities in 1954 was called *Neo-Fascist and Hate Groups*. It found that:

> The hate group appeals to the unwary by a cynical use of concepts having a deep emotional appeal to the majority of decent citizens—love of God, country, home; or antipathy to communism. Amid protestations of patriotism and religious devotion, these groups propagate hoaxes and smears aimed at setting creed against creed and race against race. They use the divisive tactics of the Communists whom they allegedly deplore. Depending upon the type of audience to be reached, this propaganda is couched in language ranging from violent vituperation to subtle innuendos.[2]

Hate-mongering is not the same as conflict. It has already been pointed out that there are civilized ways of carrying on conflict. The civilized way is to keep attention concentrated on the issues involved, not to descend to personalities. In political conflict we have evolved the elaborate machinery of parliamentary debate in order to prevent conflict from degenerating into a mere fight. Responsible religious leaders, likewise, carry on their conflicts on a plane which emphasizes the issues, not the personalities of their opponents. Conflict conducted in this way need not disorganize the community at all.

Hate-mongering, however, is highly disorganizing. It violates all the canons of civilized conflict. It descends to personalities. It inflames the emotions. It beclouds rather than clarifies issues. It destroys consensus. It rips

[2] p. 2. There were 400 to 500 anti-Semitic groups in the United States before World War II; by 1960 there were only about sixty.

groups apart. It hits below the belt. It breaks down community. It is, therefore, a particularly virulent form of social disorganization.

The difference between normal conflict and hate-mongering may be simply illustrated. One may say in all sincerity, without hatred, malice, or hostility, "I fear the growing political power of the Catholic church because I think it is opposed on principle to many of the civil liberties upon which community life in our society is based. I fear that if the Catholic church secured control of our government our civil rights would be reduced, as I believe they have been reduced in other countries where it is in control." This, right or wrong, is a legitimate statement of an issue. It is nonemotional; it can be argued. Facts can be marshaled pro and con. There are no personalities involved. The focus of attention is on an objective issue—civil liberties. In hate-mongering, on the other hand, the smear technique is used. The hate-monger does not attempt to use verifiable facts or rational arguments. He calls names, appeals to fears, plays on unexpressed aggressions, and uses emotion instead of facts to make his point.[3]

For example:

> The Roman Catholic Church . . . is not Christian; it is anti-Christian. It is not of God; it is of the devil. It is not of heaven; it is of Hell. Call it "Christian?" Never. . . . I repeat, there is no language too strong to exaggerate the evil of this thing, and when you admit for a moment that the Roman Catholic Church is a Christian institution, you have surrendered the field. It is not![4]

This kind of behavior is a far cry from a candid and above-the-belt discussion of true issues. It violates the American code against attacks on the religious beliefs of people. It is destructive not only because it is divisive but also because it tends to obscure issues rather than to clarify them.

Peddling hate against Jews follows a similar pattern:

> Jews are . . . a curse, a reproach . . . very evil . . . false religionists, evolutionists, atheists, broken cisterns . . . anti-Christ, killers of the prophets, murderers of Christ, children of the devil, serpents, vipers, contrary to all men. . . .

> I am NOT against Jews because they are Jews; but because it is the Zionist Jews who supported the Jew-Bolshevik Revolution in Russia; it is the Jews who rule Russia today, as Communists; it was the Jews who were about to overthrow Germany, which is why Hitler overthrew them. It is Jews who are largely in control of our Government today.

> Until people understand how money is manipulated by the international Jew bankers, we will always have poverty and wars. . . .

[3] The psychology of the individual bigot or hate-monger has been subjected to careful scientific scrutiny, and a large bibliography is available on the subject. See, for example, David Krech and Richard S. Crutchfield, *Theory and Problems of Social Psychology* (New York: McGraw-Hill, 1948), pp. 443-498.

[4] These statements were assembled by John Roy Carlson in *The Plotters* (New York: Dutton, 1946), pp. 85, 89, 95.

Human nature being what it is, it is not strange that the Germans decided against the Jews and in favor of Hitler. . . . Hitler put it up to the Germans to decide between Jewish ownership and domination of the country or domination and ownership by the ninety-nine percent German population.[5]

Again, this kind of hate-mongering befuddles the real issues. If the presence of Jews in a community does complicate its life, we can face the problem openly. There is no other way to work out an accommodation. Hate-mongering does not promote the ideals of America. It runs counter to them.

Negroes, labor, Communists, Mexicans, Japanese, all have been victimized by hate-mongering. It is to the community's interest to see that this kind of behavior is restrained and limited if not stamped out. Where there are real issues they can be fought out in the open according to the rules of fair play.

Because of its fruits—often bitter violence—hate-mongering revolts most honest and sincere believers in the American ideal. As a result, for fear of being bracketed with hate-mongers and bigots, they recoil from even honest conflict. Do they honestly and sincerely oppose the Supreme Court decision permitting state funds to be used to transport students to parochial schools? Or efforts to take Bible reading out of the classroom? They hesitate to say so for fear of being branded as bigots. The field of religious conflict is therefore left wide open for the true bigots.

Difficulties arise in attempting to control hate-mongering because such control may violate the rights of free speech. Libel and slander laws protect specific individuals; but they do not protect whole groups. In general, the mails may not be used for materials that might incite to violence; but anyone is permitted to say anything he pleases in a meeting so long as what he says does not lead to violence. If a known hate-monger is speaking there will usually be a large police force present to see that rioting does not occur.

Envy and Its Uses

If the victims of hate-mongering are likely to be ethnic and racial groups, the victims of envy are likely to be the rich, the powerful, the "wellborn." No one envies the Jews, Catholics, Mexicans, Puerto-Ricans or other victims of hate-mongering. The man who practices it has contempt for his victims; he does not share their values; he does not want to be like them.

Envy, on the other hand, is experienced by people who share the values of those they envy. It is thus related to competition for, as we saw in Chapter 5, competitors want the same things; they live in the same world of collective values. The French word *ressentiment* has been used to refer to the phenomenon we are here discussing. It has three components, namely:

[5] *Ibid.*, pp. 101, 110, 126, 152-153, 170, 174, 179, 184, 270, *passim.*

(1) diffuse feelings of hate, envy, and hostility; (2) feelings of being powerless or of inability to express these feelings actively against those who provoke them; and (3) a continuing re-experiencing of this impotent hostility.[6]

Ressentiment is distinguished from rebellion despite the fact that both involve "dissociation between culturally prescribed aspirations and socially structured avenues for realizing these aspirations,"[7] in that *resentment* accepts the values aspired for, but rebellion does not. Rebellion seeks to change values.

The essential point distinguishing *ressentiment* from rebellion is that the former does not involve a genuine change in values. *Ressentiment* involves a sour-grapes pattern which asserts merely that desired but unattainable objectives do not actually embody the prized values—after all, the fox in the fable does not say that he abandons all taste for sweet grapes; he says only that these particular grapes are not sweet. Rebellion, on the other hand, involves a genuine transvaluation, where the direct or vicarious experience of frustration leads to full denunciation of previously prized values—the rebellious fox simply renounces the prevailing taste for sweet grapes. In *ressentiment,* one condemns what one secretly craves; in rebellion, one condemns the craving itself.[8]

The target of rebellion is an institutional structure which makes for injustice; the object of *ressentiment* is the wealthy class; the rebellion is designed, let us say, to equalize opportunities; the goal of *ressentiment* is to share or appropriate the values its victim feels deprived of. "But though the two are distinct, organized rebellion may draw upon a vast reservoir of the resentful and discontented as institutional dislocations become acute."[9] It is for this reason that the nature and uses of *ressentiment* are of significance in community life.

The incidence of *ressentiment* is related to the social structure in which it occurs. Where social distance is great and rigidly institutionalized, it is not likely to occur. The German sociologist Max Scheler has specified the conditions under which it arises and the classes most vulnerable to it, as follows:

Oppressed social classes constitute an especially fertile soil for the growth of ressentiment, provided there is not felt to be too great a distance between the oppressed and those who oppress them. The slave with a slave's heart, the servile footman, the child who is slapped feel no resentment, neither do the members of the lower castes in India. But the combination of economic and social inequality with political and legal equality which is characteristic of modern European societies is especially apt to evoke the resentment of the lower classes. . . . The older

[6] Robert K. Merton, *Social Theory and Social Structure* (New York: Free Press, 1958), p. 156.

[7] *Ibid.*, p. 134.

[8] *Ibid.*, p. 156.

[9] *Ibid.*

generation is always prone to resentment when it feels incapable to cope any more with the younger, and the same is true of women. . . .[10]

Another sociologist, Max Weber, concluded that a disinterested tendency to inflict punishment, very much a component of *ressentiment,* is likely to be especially strong in the lower middle classes. These are the people who have tried very hard to achieve generally accepted values but who have, for one reason or another, failed. They are therefore susceptible to the blandishments of anyone who promises to "soak the rich" or to bring down the mighty or to dispossess the privileged.

Theoretically the structure of American communities should create a great deal of *ressentiment* for there is that "combination of economic and social inequality with political and legal equality which is characteristic of modern European societies" referred to above, as conducive to its rise. Yet it is relatively rare.

Why, despite the egalitarianism which should stimulate *ressentiment,* is it so relatively rare in American communities? For one thing, the relative abundance which characterizes them has meant that improving the lot of the poor did not have to be at the expense of despoiling the rich.[11] It was not a zero-sum game. The pie could be enlarged. In addition, there has been a nice balance worked out between public and concealed display among the wealthy. From time immemorial people have depended on lavish expenditures for prestige. Kings and potentates, nobility and clergy, prelates and emperors have used display to bolster their prestige and positions. But in a democratic community the display—which, as Thorstein Veblen said, is intrinsically and inherently invidious, that is, designed to produce envy—must not be so great as to produce resentment among the less privileged. Rich people may dazzle the public, but not to the extent of creating class hatreds. Most of the expenditures must, therefore, be kept within their own precincts. When they leak out, widespread bitterness may result, as revealed in letters-to-the-editors columns every day. When a coming-out party costing a quarter of a million dollars is reported in the newspapers, all the efforts of skilled public relations counselors are called upon to neutralize the effect. A noblesse oblige norm has been evolved so that the wealthy feel they must tie in their public displays with charitable purposes.

Even more important, perhaps, is the way egalitarianism is institutionalized:

American institutions make people feel themselves to be the equal of anyone and everyone. This feeling is fostered, at least in part, by the fact that as a member of an audience or public, as consumer or as voter, as target for advertising or propaganda, the American is accustomed to being constantly catered to, coaxed, cajoled,

[10] Svend Ranulf, *Moral Indignation and Middle Class Psychology, A Sociological Study* (Levin & Munksgaard-Ejnar Munksgaard, 1938) p. 200, from Max Scheler, *Vom Umsturz der Wertex* (Leipzig, 1923), pp. 59 ff., 80 ff., 83.

[11] Jessie Bernard, *Social Problems at Midcentury* (New York: Holt, Rinehart and Winston, 1957), Chapter 1.

wooed, courted, and competed for. He has something, a consumer dollar and a vote, which powerful interest groups want. They must win him over; therefore he is made to feel important. A sure-fire campaigning technique is the so-called folksy touch; the great must appear to be humble and no better than anyone else. Public-relations counsels make their clients . . . appear just like anyone else.

As a corollary of the equality ideal there have arisen conventions so strict as to amount almost to mores. No one in public life is permitted to "look down" on his inferiors. Even the social worker must deal with her clients as a friend, certainly not condescendingly or patronizingly as a superior. Anyone may be contemptuous or act superior to his equals, but no one may similarly treat his inferiors. The wealthy may not publicly condescend to the poor; the powerful may not "push people around." Power must be exercised with humility, even apologetically. Hauteur provokes guffaws rather than obeisance. The professor has no special privileges; the boss stands in line in the cafeteria. The fiction must be maintained that all persons actually are equal. Children must be "consulted" in making rules for their discipline; workers must "participate" in decision-making; all must share in policy determination. A great scandal was precipitated at mid-century when a Cabinet member spoke contemptuously of the unemployed. There is a great cult of the underdog.[12]

The success of these institutional norms and the social structure in which they operate is great enough to protect most Americans from *ressentiment,* much to the disconcertion of would-be rabble-rousers.

Relatively rare as it is, even *ressentiment* or envy or a "disinterested tendency to inflict punishment" does nevertheless exist and from time to time it is exploited by leaders. The most spectacular illustration was the career of Huey Long of Louisiana. His success was a complex phenomenon, demanding a consideration of many factors for complete explanation. For one thing, his opponents included some of the most corrupt and exploitative politicians in the state's history. But in addition, according to one analyst

After two hundred years, the people of Louisiana—heir to the yearnings and frustrations of the Populists, the Whiskey Rebels, the Know-Nothings, the Free Silverites, of all the have-nots of capitalism—were ready and waiting for a messiah who would translate their needs into accomplishments. Theirs was the ground swell of the little people, a people undisturbed by his tactics as long as they got the roads, the free bridges, the hospitals, the free school books, the public works; as long as the men whom Long pilloried and broke and banished were identified with the leaders of the past, bumbling representatives of an indifferent, negative ruling class. . . . Huey Long was in the image of these little people. He talked their language. He had lived their lives. He had taken them up to the mountaintop and shown them the world which the meek would inherit.[13]

[12] Jessie Bernard, "The United States" in Arnold Rose, ed., *The Institutions of Advanced Societies* (Minneapolis: University of Minnesota, 1958), p. 599. Copyright by the University of Minnesota.

[13] Hodding Carter, "Huey Long: American Dictator," in *The Aspirin Age,* 1919-1941, ed. Isabel Leighton (New York: Simon & Schuster, 1949), pp. 354, 360.

Despite the institutional provisions for preventing *ressentiment,* in brief, it can happen here.

The Uses of Fear

It may be gratutitous to try to separate hate and fear; fear may be at the base of a good deal of hate. But it is useful to make a distinction because the schismatic processes are somewhat different in the two emotions. The hate-mongering described above was a group phenomenon and had groups as its victims. The fear under discussion here operates on individuals, causing them to withdraw; it isolates them; it atomizes.

Fear is not "mongered," as hate and envy are. It can, however, be just as disruptive of social ties. In fact, the use of informers by totalitarian states and by those in charge of prisoners-of-war camps was refined almost to a routine technique for precisely this purpose. Situations were created in which people began to suspect one another. In order to organize the new régime, the Nazis, for example, found it necessary to destroy old kinship and friendship ties and allegiances and to transfer them to the state. Children were taught to inform on their parents, friend on friend, worker on worker, wife on husband. A major contribution of informers, as a matter of fact, is less the specific information they monger than the fear and suspicion they seed throughout the community. As a result communities become atomized. There is a minimum of communication.

Fortunately the use of fear for such intimidatory purposes has not happened often in American communities. But it can happen and on occasion it has. The most spectacular recent case was that of McCarthyism, so-called, or Communist "witch-hunting" in the early 1950's. It disorganized by rendering people fearful of one another, distrustful, afraid to do or say things that might be interpreted as subversive or "Un-American" or unpatriotic or disloyal. For people were accused of subversive activity without proper legal protection. They were, in effect, held to be guilty without trial. They lost their jobs. They were shunned by neighbors. Even if they had the opportunity, which not all of them did, to prove themselves innocent by a court, the shadow remained over their reputations. The result was fear and malaise, especially among those of a liberal persuasion and also among so-called intellectuals.

Because of the relative infrequency of the kind of schismatic fear under consideration here, it has not been well researched. But there is one study of the disorganizing effect on college and university faculties in the witch-hunting years which is pertinent and relevant to our discussion here.[14] Apprehension was felt by these professors and precautions were taken which were in the direction of withdrawing from community ties:

[14] Paul F. Lazarsfeld and Wagner Thielens, Jr., *The Academic Mind, Social Scientists in a Time of Crisis* (New York: Free Press, 1958).

> The apprehension felt by teachers at the time of our study . . . sometimes found outward expression in acts of caution and withdrawal. . . . While as a group, even our most apprehensive respondents cannot be described as paralyzed with fear, the evidence indicates that the difficult years did place a noticeable damper on the activities and opinions of a sizeable minority.[15]

The malaise among these men made them fearful of one another:

> The recent growth of distrust and suspicion between respondents and their colleagues . . . was described by a respondent: "In faculty discussion, in our department at least, there is fear of one another and a consequent hesitating to speak out on issues". . . . An atmosphere of restraint and distrust is . . . suggested.[16]

In addition, a sizable proportion—28 percent—had no confidence that their colleagues would support them if they got into trouble.

The case of the professors and the disorganizing effect of fear on their community is not one of major proportions. But it is extremely illuminating. It illustrates how fear can destroy the fabric of interrelationships, built on confidence in one's fellows, which is basic to community life.

[15] *Ibid.*, p. 192.
[16] *Ibid.*, pp. 230-231.

25

Normative Community Disorganization: Individual Nonconformity

Community Disorganization as Individual Nonconformity

Because organization depends so fundamentally on expectedness of behavior, anything which destroys this expectedness will be disorganizing, mildly or drastically. So long as people are conforming to community norms we know what to expect of them and can plan our own behavior confidently. It is when we don't know what to expect that normal functioning is disorganized. Like other forms of disorganization, normative disorganization is a matter of degree.

Socialization is the process by which community norms are inculcated into the individual so that he does conform to them. In Chapter 4 it was pointed out that there was practically no kind of behavior an individual is capable of which did not come under the shaping power of institutions or norms. Chapters 7-24 considered more massive group behavior, competitive, conflicting, disorganized. At this point we turn to the individual again, noting first how he is socialized, but emphasizing also his rebellion against the imposition of norms on his behavior. As long as he conforms to the norms which define his several roles, there is no disorganization—but sometimes he cannot or will not.[1] When this happens, there is, to greater or lesser extent, normative disorganization.

In Chapter 4 we noted that institutional controls are imposed on even the autonomic functions of the human body. Home and community, especially church and school, are especially charged with seeing to it that the accepted institutional norms of the community are translated into personal behavior. Sometimes they perform this function unwittingly, but whether they know what they are doing or not, it is being done.

[1] See Jessie Bernard, *Social Problems at Midcentury* (New York: Holt, Rinehart and Winston, 1957) for a detailed discussion of disorganization in terms of role impairment.

Socialization: The Family's Part

The infant is trained very young in the proper and improper way to deal with such autonomic functions as defecation, urination, and other body functions. He is taught how to control the expression of feelings and emotions also, to keep them within conventional limits. His relationships with others are similarly patterned. Institutional patterns in all these levels are, figuratively speaking, siphoned from the community into the child. At first, of course, this is done through the family. We begin almost as soon as a baby is born to inculcate into him the institutional norms—for physiological, emotional, and social behavior—of his community. A two-year-old is, in fact, more of a martinet than his parents in enforcing the rules he knows. Property mores ("mustn't touch!") are bred into him before he can walk or talk. Conventional and moral attitudes become second nature to him. He comes in time "naturally" to conform. Language, personal hygiene, food habits, manners, etiquette, and attitudes toward sex, cleanliness, race, age, and property are patterned in him according to the canons of his community.

Producing conformity to norms of this type is called socialization, whether the norms are those we approve of or not. That is, a child can be socialized into a "contraculture" as well as into the official culture. He can learn to steal as naturally as he can learn to be honest. The processes are the same whatever the norms may be.[2]

To one who has had the care of children in their earliest years, the most interesting question is not: "How are nonconformists made?" but rather, "How are socialized human beings made?" One need not go into the theological subtleties of original sin to perceive that little children are unsocialized. We are not born knowing the rules nor do we obey them instinctively. It takes years of daily, almost hourly, training to transform the unsocialized infant into the conforming adult.

Sample questions of a four-year-old illustrate one aspect of this continuous process by which the child imbibes from his family the norms of his community: "Will people laugh at me if I go outdoors without a shirt?" "You mustn't talk about——outside the family, must you?" "If I find a dog who doesn't have a name on him, that won't be stealing, will it?" The answers to these and the countless other questions which the child asks constitute his socialization diet; and they are as important for his social development as bread, butter, and milk are for his physical development. The family's role in socialization is fairly obvious.

[2] William Whyte's *Street Corner Society* (Chicago: University of Chicago, 1952) and Albert Cohen's *Delinquent Boys* (New York: Free Press, 1955) describe the processes by which boys and young men are socialized into the "contraculture."

THE COMMUNITY AND THE SOCIALIZING PROCESS

The community is as much responsible for this socialization as is the family. A let-up any place along the line, in the family or in the community, may have irrevocable consequences.

The role of the community in the socialization process is, then, extremely important. Once beyond the toddling stage, a child may spend many hours away from parental supervision. But the socialization process still goes on. The child is imbibing attitudes all the time. The child who is exposed to gambling on street corners, to taverns and saloons, and to streetwalkers gets an entirely different socialization diet from the one who lives in a community that protects him from exposure to such influences. Motion pictures, radio and television programs, and comic books all play their part in forming his personality.

Often the lessons which the home tries to inculcate are completely nullified by the lessons which the community teaches. Sometimes parents feel helpless in the face of community influences on their children. They find it almost impossible to contend successfully with commercialized amusements and exploitative purveyors of the vices. Sometimes, of course, the parents are themselves the product of such socialization diets and think nothing of it.

Even where families feel competent, the community must supplement the work of parents in socializing children. Modern urban living increases not only the opportunities for cultural improvement but also those for demoralization. Delinquency is a problem not for families only; it is a problem for the community as well.

SOCIALIZING THE ADULT

So far we have been discussing the influence of the home and community in socializing children primarily. But the socializing influence of the community on personality continues long after the family has done its job; for the socializing process is never complete. It continues for life. In fact, conformity to community standards, explicit and implicit, is so well maintained that ordinarily the existence of community rules is more apparent in the breach than in the practice. We usually do not become conscious of them until they are violated. Policemen, detectives, newspapermen, and others who are interested in deviant behavior are probably more conscious of them than most of us are. But all of us, when we see people loitering about, or prowling in strange places, or behaving "suspiciously"—which means, after all, acting contrary to institutional expectations—feel that something is wrong. The scaffolding which conformity to expected norms offers our lives then becomes dimly apparent to us.

As a matter of fact, we are always checking our behavior by the way we observe people about us in our community reacting to what we do.

They thus help us to conform. They keep us socialized. Some people are very accurate in judging how others are evaluating them. We say they are sensitive; they have insight or role-taking ability; they are empathic. Others, at the opposite extreme, seem quite oblivious of the way their behavior affects people about them. For some reason or other they are, we say, obtuse, lacking in insight. In its pathological stage, such lack of insight is termed insanity. The insane person is queer because he does not conform to the expectations of those about him and seems to be impervious to the thousand and one little devices we usually use to warn people when they are violating community expectations.

The community, then, shares with the family the function of socializing its members, and it continues in this role of socializer even after the family has ceased so to function, long into adulthood; indeed its influence is felt as long as we are sensitive to what other people think.

There is also nonconformity, also ubiquitous and perennial. We do have rebels, innovators, criminals, and other violators of norms. And we have to explain nonconformity as well as conformity, disorganization as well as organization.

At this point we turn to a kind of conflict which involves the individual as such as he confronts the social world. There are many ways of viewing this conflict. The protagonists are, variously, the "individual," "human nature," "the conformist," "the nonconformist," "the rebel," or "the dissenter" on one side and "society," "the social order," "the normative system," "the status quo," "organization," "bureaucracy," "institutions," or "the establishment" on the other. Different people see different aspects of this conflict and define the protagonists differently. Some, for example, see the individual as the "good guy" and the social order as the enemy, a point of view to be documented below. Others, conversely, see the social order as the "good guy" engaged in a constant war with resisting and recalcitrant "human nature." Thus for some observers, "conformity" means coercion; for others, decent—that is, conventional, moral, law-abiding—behavior. For some, "nonconformist" means a bold innovator; for others, a criminal. Imbedded in these several points of view lies the age-old philosophical controversy about individual freedom, but we shall not attempt to examine the issues here. We turn, rather, to several ways in which the existence of nonconformity, however evaluated, has been explained.

Three Models of Nonconformity

(1) "HUMAN NATURE" VERSUS THE "SOCIAL ORDER"

Several kinds of models or conceptualizations have been promulgated to explain or interpret nonconformity or the failure of institutional norms to hold behavior in line. The most general statement may be formulated as follows: the *extent or degree* of nonconformity is some function of the nature of "human nature" and the nature of the normative system. The *kind or form* of nonconformity is some function of the individual's personality and his position in the social structure.

One model for explaining or interpreting nonconformity may be called the classic model in which "human nature" is somehow or other emphasized or given great weight. Examples are the Christian model, the Freudian model, and the Durkheim model. A second kind of model may be called structural in that emphasis is placed on the structure of the community; it has been set forth for urban communities by Robert Merton and for peasant communities by George M. Foster. A third kind of model, the so-called J-curve, explains nonconformity as a complex resultant of both human nature and norms.

THE CHRISTIAN VERSION

The characteristic element in the Christian version of the classic model is a conceptualization of human nature as unruly, undisciplined, and filled with impulses and drives that are a constant threat to the social order. The concept of innate human depravity or original sin embodies the major premise of this model. Social life is a continuing battle between the social order, or normative system, and human passions. Revolt and rebellion against restraints are viewed as almost the natural state of man. It is only by dint of constant effort that the lid is kept on. Crime, disorder, rebelliousness do not have to be explained; they are natural. Order is what needs explanation.

THE FREUDIAN VERSION

Freud rediscovered the great Christian epic. His version is somewhat different in terminology but basically he also finds man at war with civilization. He sees man's instinctual drives as thwarted; he sees enormous aggressions seeking expression. He sees civilization imposing ever more deprivations.

> . . . this tendency to aggression . . . is the factor that disturbs our relations with our neighbours and makes it necessary for culture to institute its high demands. Civilized society is perpetually menaced with disintegration through this primary hostility of men towards one another. . . . Culture has to call up every possible reinforcement in order to erect barriers against the aggressive instincts of men and hold their manifestations in check.[3]

As in the Christian version of this model, disorder would be the natural state of man; it is civilization, order, that has to be explained. Freud explains it in terms of the development of conscience and the sense of guilt with the accompanying and all-pervasive anxiety which, he alleges, accompanies civilization.

[3] *Civilization and Its Discontents,* Anchor (New York: Doubleday, 1958), pp. 61-62.

THE DURKHEIM VERSION

A great French sociologist, Émile Durkheim, also pictured the social order in a way that resembled that of Freud, and, indeed, that of the Christian fathers. He is most famous for his emphasis on the objective nature of the social order. He played up the fact that the social constraints that operated on man had an independent existence of their own, independent of the psychology of individual men. But in order to magnify the importance of these social constraints he had to play up also their subjects or, even, adversaries. He therefore pictured man as possessing infinite, insatiable needs, so that, in order to make social life possible at all, "the passions must first be limited . . . by some force exterior to him."[4] Durkheim differed from Freud in emphasizing the socially induced rather than the inherited needs of man. If for any reason the social order fails to hold men's passions in check, they rise beyond the level of possible fulfillment and "de-regulation or anomie"[5] results.

> At the very moment when traditional rules have lost their authority, the richer prize offered these appetites stimulates them and makes them more exigent and impatient of control. The state of deregulation or anomy is thus further heightened by passions being less disciplined precisely when they need more disciplining.[6]

When, according to Durkheim, does the collective order thus break down? Under sudden depression, sudden prosperity, and rapid technological change. Sudden depression, for example, results in

> something like a declassification . . . which suddenly casts certain individuals into a lower state than their previous ones. Then they must reduce their requirements, restrain their needs, learn greater self-control. . . . But society cannot adjust them

[4] *Suicide,* translated by George Simpson and J. A. Spaulding (New York: Free Press, 1951), p. 248.

[5] Anomie should be distinguished from anomia, discussed in Chapter 23. Anomie refers to a condition of normlessness in the outside world, anomia refers to the subjective accompaniment of such a condition. Anarchy—absence of governmental norms—is a special case of anomie—absence of any kind of norms. The term has been variously translated as normlessness or deregulation. There is a difference. Normlessness might refer to a situation in which norms had not yet developed to regulate a new condition; deregulation refers to a breakdown in a normative system that once did function. The lack of regulation that characterized nineteenth-century capitalism would be an example of normlessness; the breakdown of the Roman Empire in the sixth to the tenth century, of deregulation. A perhaps somewhat exaggerated picture was painted by the sociologist W. G. Sumner as follows: "The Latin world was disintegrated to its first elements between the sixth century and the tenth. Such a dissolution of society abolished the inherited mores with all their restraints and inhibitions, and left society to the control of fierce barbaric, that is physical forces. . . . Passion, sensuality, ferocity, superstitious ignorance, and fear characterized the age. . . . Every sentiment was extravagant. Men were under some mighty gregarious instinct which drove them to act in masses, and they passed from one great passion or enthusiastic impulse to another at very short intervals. The passions of hatred and revenge were manifested, upon occasion, to the extremity of fiendishness. . . . What was lacking was discipline. There was no authority or doctrine which could set limits to private passion. Life was held cheap. The gallows and the pit were in use all the time. The most marked product of invention was instruments of torture. . . ." (*Folkways,* [Boston: Ginn, 1906], p. 211-212).

[6] Durkheim, *op. cit,* p. 253.

instantaneously to this new life and teach them to practice the increased self-repression to which they are unaccustomed. So they are not adjusted to the condition forced on them, and its very prospect is intolerable; hence the suffering which detaches them from a reduced existence even before they have made trial of it.[7]

Rapid prosperity has the same effect by heightening aspirations beyond the possibility of fullfilment, thus putting a strain on the regulatory apparatus of the society. Writing of conditions in the late nineteenth century, Durkheim felt that "the sphere of trade and industry . . . is actually in a chronic state" of anomie. Since the producer of goods "may assume to have almost the entire world as his customer, how could passions accept their former confinement in the face of such limitless prospects?"[8] He felt that

> such is the source of excitement predominating in this part of society . . . [that] the state of crisis and anomy are constant and, so to speak, normal. From top to bottom of the ladder, greed is aroused without knowing where to find ultimate foothold. Nothing can calm it, since its goal is far beyond all it can attain. . . . It is everlastingly repeated that it is man's nature to be eternally dissatisfied, constantly to advance, without relief or rest, toward an indefinite goal.[9]

Against such exigent drives, according to Durkheim, the regulatory norms tended to break down.

Rapid technological change—a revolution every three years, for example—has the same kind of effect. Even when spaced over a long period of time, technological changes are likely to render old norms nonfunctional. We noted the effects on personality in Chapter 2.

Both Freud and Durkheim made man's drives, inherited or socially inbred, a basic theoretical factor in explaining or interpreting the breakdown of normative structures. Neither is complete in the sense that it explains or interprets all kinds of violation of norms. They do, however, fit some forms. Social disorder as manifested in violence of all kinds, mobs, lynchings, riots, pogroms (Chapter 26), may involve some elements of the Freudian model, although even here it must be supplemented. The eruption of violence in a community may sometimes be pictured, roughly, as the triumph of shackled emotions over civilized restraints but, as we shall see, institutional factors must also be invoked. Durkheim's model fits more accurately the situation that exists in a transitional period, between the obsolescence of one set of norms and the development of another. The nineteenth century, which was in the throes of learning how to operate an industrialized society, or transitional societies today in the process of industrialization, may fit Durkheim's model best.

The Christian fathers, Freud, and Durkheim are strange bedfellows. But they do have in common a conceptualization of normative breakdown which specifies an on-going battle between human depravity, human in-

[7] *Ibid.*
[8] *Ibid.*
[9] *Ibid.*

stincts or libido, or acquired social drives on one side and restraining forces however conceived, the Church in the case of the Christian fathers, civilization in the case of Freud, and societal norms in the case of Durkheim, on the other.

(2) KINDS OF NONCONFORMITY: MERTON'S MEANS-GOAL PARADIGM

Nonconformity may take different forms. The model here presented to explain them moves away from the point of view which attributes great importance to "human nature" and seeks to locate the causes of nonconformity in the social order itself. The most famous exponent of this point of view is Robert Merton. He takes over Durkheim's terminology but he defines anomie as "an acute disjunction between cultural norms and goals and the socially structured capacities of members of the group to act in accord with them."[10] He is particularly concerned with the situation in which there is great emphasis on certain goals, say wealth or success, but differential access on the part of the population to legitimate means for achieving them.

Merton distinguishes five forms of adaptation to this disjunction between cultural goals and institutionalized means for their achievement, namely: conformity, innovation, ritualism, retreatism, and rebellion. Innovation results when one accepts the goals but rejects the institutionalized means; ritualism results when one rejects the goals but accepts the institutionalized means; retreatism results when one rejects both; and rebellion results when one substitutes new values for prevailing values. Thus:

Mode of Adaptation	Culture Goals	Institutionalized Means
Conformity	Acceptance	Acceptance
Innovation	Acceptance	Rejection
Ritualism	Rejection	Acceptance
Retreatism	Rejection	Rejection
Rebellion	Substitution of new values	Substitution of new values

Innovation can be illustrated by the behavior of the great industrial "robber barons" of the nineteenth century who accepted the cultural goals of success but found institutional means too restrictive and who resorted to extra-legal means. Actually, however, it is those in the lower levels of the social structure who are most likely to be cut off from legitimate institutional means for success and who therefore seek success by other means, as Al Capone did. ". . . when poverty and associated disadvantages in competing for the culture values approved for all members of the society are linked with a cultural emphasis on pecuniary success as a dominant goal, high rates of criminal behavior are the normal outcome."[11]

[10] *Social Theory and Social Structure* (New York: Free Press, 1957), p. 162.
[11] *Ibid.*, p. 147.

Ritualism results when one must scale down his aspirations but when he nevertheless continues to abide by institutional norms. These are the people who are "in a rut," who are not trying to keep up with the Joneses, who over-conform to the rules, who are bureaucratic "virtuosos." Merton believes this kind of deviance is most expectable in lower-middle class families. "For it is in the lower middle class that parents typically exert continuous pressure upon children to abide by the moral mandates of the society, and where the social climb upward is less likely to meet with success than among the upper middle class."[12]

Retreatism is the least common adjustment to the disjunction between culture goals and institutional means; those who use it are in but not of their society; they are, says Merton, the true aliens. "Not sharing the common frame of values, they can be included as members of the society (in distinction from the population) only in a fictional sense."[13] The retreatist is condemned by the conventional world. It cannot accept his repudiation of their cherished values. He is viewed as a nonproductive liability. "In contrast to the innovator who is at least 'smart' and actively striving, he sees no value in the success-goal which the culture prizes so highly; in contrast to the ritualist who conforms at least to the mores, he pays scant attention to the institutional practices."[14] His deviance is privatized, not collective. He may seek the company of others in his same condition; they may even develop a kind of "code"[15]—indeed, Skid Row seems to have one—but for the most part "their adaptations are largely private and isolated rather than unified under the aegis of a new cultural code."[16] They do not believe in any common values, there is no collective pattern here. Their "code" is primarily a set of individual habits. They are, even when huddled together, only a lonely crowd. In this respect they differ radically from the rebellion form of deviant behavior.

Rebellion implies the withdrawing of allegiance from the prevailing social structure and transferring it to new groups; the rejection of old myths and the acceptance of new ones. The new myth pictures a social structure that would not frustrate the deserving as the present one does; the conservative myth states that these frustrations are in the nature of things and occur in any system. Rebellion is likely to occur in rising rather than in the depressed classes of a society.

Merton's analysis at bottom rests on a theory of competition. "When . . . the cultural emphasis shifts from the satisfactions deriving from competition itself to almost exclusive concern with the outcome, the resultant

[12] *Ibid.*, p. 151.
[13] *Ibid.*, p. 153.
[14] *Ibid.*, p. 154.
[15] Peterson and Maxwell, "The Skid Row 'Wino'," *Social Problems*, 5 (Spring, 1958), pp. 308-316.
[16] Merton, *op. cit.*, p. 155.

stress makes for the breakdown of the regulatory structure."[17] It adds to the first model the variable of position in the social structure, or class, or status, as part of the explanatory picture. Lowered access to institutional channels for success is one of the penalties of low status.

(3) DEGREES OF NONCONFORMITY: ALLPORT'S J-CURVE

When chance alone determines the distribution of phenomena the result is described by the so-called normal curve. In the field of natural phenomena it has been found again and again that this is the usual way for data to distribute themselves. This familiar symmetrical or bell-shaped curve, illustrated in Figure 25-1, may be described as follows. Most traits

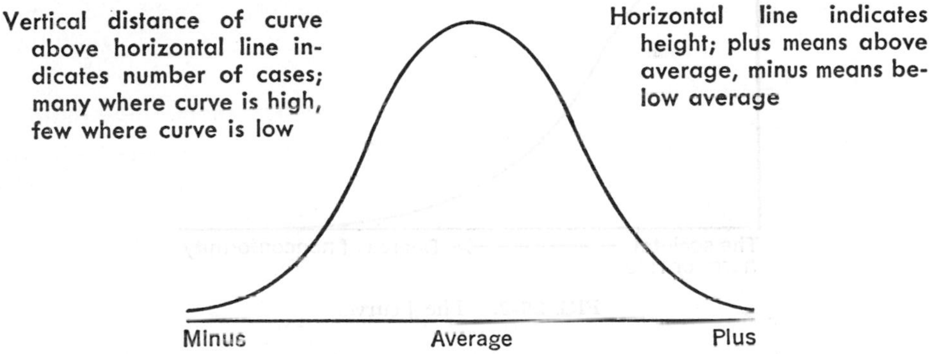
Vertical distance of curve above horizontal line indicates number of cases; many where curve is high, few where curve is low
Horizontal line indicates height; plus means above average, minus means below average
Minus
Average
Plus

FIG. 25-1. The so-called normal curve.

(in the realm of biology, for example, height, weight, and stature of organisms of a specified type) tend to cluster about an average. That is, most of the organisms are average or very near to the average in the trait measured. This is shown in the curve by the fact that it is highest at the average. Now the farther one gets from the average on either side the fewer cases there are. Extremely tall or extremely short persons are few in number.

In order to get this symmetrical curve, however, there must be no bias in the data which may pull them out of shape. In the realm of community life, however, we do not leave things to chance. We introduce norms of all kinds, as we saw in Chapter 4. Our behavior is regulated by literally scores of such norms. For community behavior, therefore, the symmetrical curve is rare. We cannot expect it to follow a chance curve when it is pulled in certain prescribed directions by societal norms or institutions.

A quite different type of distribution is therefore to be expected for community behavior. The curve describing it will have properties which mark it off sharply from that of "natural" or noncommunity behavior. Empirical studies of many different kinds of behavior have revealed the

[17] *Ibid.*, p. 157.

characteristic curve for nonconforming behavior to be the so-called J-curve,[18] illustrated in Figure 25-2. The horizontal line indicates the degree of nonconformity, that is, how far from the norm the particular behavior lies. The vertical line indicates the number of cases in which this behavior occurs. Where the curve is high there are many cases; where it is low, few cases. Because the curve has a long tail to the left we say it is negatively skewed in the direction of nonconformity.

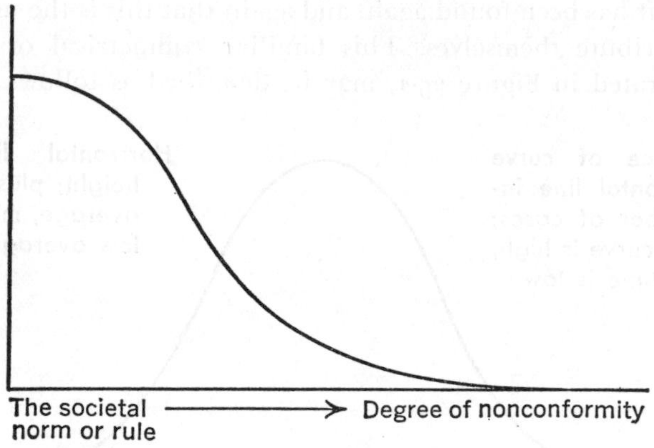

FIG. 25-2. The J-curve.

What the curve means is simply this: most people tend to obey the rules of their community fairly well; but not everyone does. The more serious the violation of the rule, however, the fewer the number of people who are guilty of it. These few people may be pretty bad—or pretty good—and that is why they attract attention. They are the criminals—and the reformers and leaders—and they stand out.

The J-curve has been found in many aspects of community life, including education, political life, and economic life.[19] Even the distribution of criminal behavior of a fairly serious nature has been found to conform to this curve in a general way.[20] Moral and domestic behavior of a nonconforming nature has also been found to show this kind of distribution.[21]

[18] Pioneering work in this field was done by F. H. Allport and his students. See Paul Achilles (ed.), *Psychology at Work* (New York: McGraw-Hill, 1932), Chapter 8; "Individuals and Their Human Environment," *Proc. Assn. for Research in Nervous and Emotional Disease,* xiv (December, 1933); "The J-curve Hypothesis of Conforming Behavior," *Jour. Social Psychology,* 5 (May, 1934), pp. 141-183; "Rule and Custom as Individual Variations of Behavior upon a Continuum of Conformity," *Amer. Jour. Sociol.,* 44 (May, 1939), pp. 897-921. A number of studies by Allport and his students are summarized in Donald Katz and R. L. Schank, *Social Psychology* (New York: Wiley, 1938), Chapter 3.

[19] See Katz and Schanck, *op. cit.*

[20] Jessie Bernard, *American Community Behavior* (New York: Holt, Rinehart and Winston, 1949), footnote 9, p. 467.

[21] Jessie Bernard, *American Family Behavior* (New York: Harper, 1942), Chapter 6.

We shall, however, use only one kind of behavior, obedience to traffic regulations, to illustrate the curve because it is simple, easy to measure, and quite characteristic.

Where there is no traffic rule and no policeman, the behavior of motorists at street intersections has been shown to follow the characteristic normal curve. LaPierre, for example, found that one hundred drivers approaching an unguarded street crossing in a residential area behaved as follows: 1 percent stopped, 21 percent slowed up considerably, 65 percent slowed up a little, 12 percent went on as before, and 1 percent speeded up a little.[22] Plotted, this gives something approaching a symmetrical curve. Previous experience of the drivers, driving habits, age, sex, urgency of reaching their destination, driving skill, condition of the car, and a score of other factors probably influenced the shape of this curve, canceling one another to result in the symmetrical curve.

Quite a different situation was found when there was a traffic ordinance involved. Now most of the chance factors were eliminated and behavior showed the J-curve distribution. The reactions of 2144 motorists to traffic stop signs on busy streets in three cities were studied. Three-fourths of the drivers conformed completely to the prescribed norm. About one-fifth slowed down; about two percent showed some recognition of the sign by slowing down slightly but not stopping. And, finally, about half of one-percent disregarded the sign completely.[23]

This was by no means the whole story. When there was a conformity-producing agent present, in this case a policeman, there was a tendency for more people to conform completely. There remained the confirmed nonconformists; in fact, the presence of the policeman seemed to act as a challenge to increase the number of extreme nonconformists. His presence had little effect in reducing the number of minimum conformists. It seemed to influence most those who were least marked in their nonconformity.[24] Obedience to ordinances regulating parking-time limits has also been shown to display this characteristic type of curve.

The J-curve merely describes. It has been explained in terms of five kinds of factors: (1) the presence of a clearly defined objective (in the case of law the purpose for which it is passed); (2) conformity-producing agencies (policemen, courts, jails, etc.); (3) individual differences which make conformity easier for some persons than for others; (4) common biological reactions; and (5) residual chance factors.[25] To this should be added (6) the relative difficulty of the norm and (7) the presence or absence of competing norms.

[22] R. T. LaPiere and P. R. Farnsworth, *Social Psychology* (New York: McGraw-Hill, 1936), p. 400.

[23] The traffic studies are cited by Allport in *Psychology at Work,* pp. 228 ff.

[24] *Ibid.,* p. 234.

[25] Floyd H. Allport, "The J-curve Hypothesis of Conformity Behavior," *ibid.,* pp. 141-183.

For simplicity's sake we may reduce these factors to two: (1) the presence of conformity-producing agencies, such as family, church, school, police, courts, gossip, "talk," suggestion, imitation, press, and all the other agencies whose job it is to see that we conform to the rules of our community and (2) the difficulty under given circumstances for human beings of the norm itself. (This factor covers Merton's conceptualization of deviant behavior. Conformity to institutional norms is more difficult for persons placed in levels of the social structure which make access to institutional means for achieving cultural goals difficult.) In effect we are back to our original two variables, "human nature" and the social order. We may think of the conformity curve as the result of these two vectors, pulling in opposite directions. Behavior tends to bunch at or near the norm because of the presence of the conformity-producing agencies at work pulling it in the direction of conformity. It does not bunch up completely, however, because the individual is not always amenable to control. That is, the norms are often too difficult or too contrary to human wishes and impulses.

The *shape* of the curve, then, may be said to be the result of these two sets of forces pulling against one another. When they are exactly equal we get a symmetrical curve, because they cancel one another and chance factors alone determine the shape of the curve. If conformity-producing agencies are weak or lax, the curve may also be pulled out of its J-curve and approximate a chance distribution, provided the norm is fairly difficult. On the other hand, if conformity-producing agencies are strong, they will tend to pull behavior toward the norm, even if the norm is difficult. When the norm is easy and the conformity-producing agencies strong, we get the maximum amount of conformity. If the norm is easy, conformity may tend to be great in spite of lax enforcement.

In actual life situations the conformity continuum is to be thought of as a very unstable thing, ready to be pulled in one direction or the other according as the conformity-producing agencies tighten or loosen their control, or as the norm becomes easy or difficult under the given circumstances.

The *extent* of nonconformity cannot be explained without taking into account the attitude of the community toward it. For the community attitude will affect the amount of pressure exerted to secure conformity as well as the form it will take.

Community Attitudes toward Nonconformity

Implicit in most theories attempting to explain conformity is the factor of community attitude towards it. The assumption is that there are conformity-producing agencies and that conformity is desirable. And a factor that cannot be ignored in explaining nonconformity is precisely this community ambiance. How much nonconformity will it permit? How is it evaluated? Is there a tradition of encouragement or of suppression of nonconformity? The answer to such questions will make a difference.

Totalitarian states tend to find nonconformity dangerous; they seek to standardize and homogenize their members. Communities in a democratic regime, on the other hand, exalt freedom.

In the United States, for example, there has been a long tradition of nonconformity, sometimes called lawlessness, which can be traced back to the Declaration of Independence itself, as well as to Plymouth Colony, and the Boston Tea Party. It has been an important ingredient in the ideal of rugged individualism. It has produced great inventive genius as well, of course, as criminals. Originality and experimentation flourish in an atmosphere that permits nonconformity; so also does crime.

We may think of community attitudes toward nonconformity as ranging along a continuum from one of (1) encouragement and stimulation (as in the field of invention), through one of (2) simple approval, to one of (3) mere tolerance, thence on to (4) disapproval, and, finally, to (5) active discouragement and punishment. The last-named attitude might be viewed as conformism, a set of values that will not tolerate any deviation from the norm.

On such a continuum American communities have tended to lean toward the approval side of the scale, as the historical incidents mentioned above illustrate. Americans still tend to resent too many rules and regulations—"red tape," as they are called. "Rugged individualism" in the nineteenth-century sense, may no longer be possible, but the ideal of individuality remains one of the basic values of American society. And although this often leads to nonconformity and even to criminality—and handicaps us in fighting crime—we are loathe to modify it. The nonconformist has, therefore, been tolerated and often actually approved, encouraged, and even exalted.

Earlier in this chapter it was pointed out that there are two ways of defining the relationship between the individual and the social order. There is, it was noted, one point of view which emphasizes the social order as the hero and the nonconformist as, in effect, the villain. At this point is presented the other point of view in which the roles are reversed. Now it is the state or the organization or the institution or the status quo in general which is the villain and the individual who can stand up against it—the innovator or the spontaneous person or even the rebel—who is the hero. Conformity is now interpreted as submission to coercion, to conformism. The problem is now not disorganization but too much pressure from organization. It is this status-quo-as-villain point of view which has tended to characterize American community life, as a long tradition of apologists for nonconformity illustrates.

Individual Attitudes Toward Nonconformity

Status-quo-as-Villain. "Man is born free and is everywhere in chains," said Jean-Jacques Rousseau. Heaven lies about us in our infancy, said the poet Wordsworth, but the prison bars begin to close in about us as we grow up. Man is naturally good but he is corrupted by the society that surrounds him. A cognate conception of the relationship between "human nature" and the social order was part of the Marxist theory of society. It held, for example, that crime was entirely the result of poverty and the economic institutions that made it inevitable. Marx did pay his respects to the human-nature factor but he believed that socialism would create a new kind of human nature by its new regime and crime would disappear. The USSR still speaks of the New Soviet Man it is creating and characterizes its deviants as relics of the capitalist past. The philosophical anarchists also shared the belief that the causes of disorganization were to be sought not in human nature but in the social order. They viewed human nature as essentially good. We are born good but are corrupted by a bad social order. Get rid of restraints and give human nature a chance to express itself and you will get rid of disorganization.

In American history there has been a long line of great apologists for nonconformity. Theodore Parker preached the doctrine of civil disobedience which was the rationale for Abolitionists in the nineteenth century, as it was, indeed, for the opponents of the Eighteenth Amendment in the twentieth century. Henry David Thoreau was another great exponent of civil disobedience, teacher of Gandhi—and, through him, of present-day Negro leaders.

Institutions-as-Villain. Allport has been the most articulate expounder of the point of view that the mere existence of so many institutions is disruptive of personality.

> . . . many of our dilemmas result, not from some flaw in the working of institutions, some technical error which industrial, legal, or educational experts can remedy, but from the nature of these institutions themselves, and from the conflict between the attempt to direct life from the standpoint of a perfectly organized social system on the one hand and the personalities of individuals upon the other. If this is true, our problems will never be solved until we can work out some harmony between these two points of view.[26]

The basic problem, according to this interpretation, is how to protect human beings from too much institutional pressure, how to release them from too much regimentation, how to keep them free, rather than how to protect institutions or the social order from the depredations of the nonconformist. The piling up of laws, of prescriptions, of moral injunctions has, he thinks, a crushing effect on personality. Modern community life is too complex;

[26] *Psychology at Work,* p. 252.

we cannot solve our problems by adding to the complexity. We must, rather, attempt to solve them by simplifying our lives. He contrasts the distribution of natural human traits (the normal curve) with the distribution of institutionalized behavior (the J-curve) and concludes that the discrepancy between them means that human nature is being violated. There is not enough room for spontaneity. There are too many rules.

Bureaucracy-as-Villain. Some observers see in the increasing tendency toward regimentation and bureaucracy the emergence of a so-called "organization man"[27] who not only does not rebel but who actually enjoys his gilded shackles. The bureaucratization of society has a standardizing and homogenizing effect on people not necessarily because such bureaucracies are harshly coercive but rather, in many cases, because they are benignly so. Such observers deplore the resulting inhibition of great experimenters, daring inventors, and bold nonconformists. They sense a hostility in the common people toward the great, successful leader. They fear a cutting down of the gifted individual to the level of the average man. They see rules of all kinds stifling men.

The above points of view are quite in line with the tradition of rugged individualism which has characterized American community life. But another line of thought has engaged the attention of observers of the current scene in recent years. It might be called "conformism," a set of values demanding a high degree of conformity, regardless of spontaneous impulses. Conformism in this sense of insistence on conformity has been found to be associated with the so-called authoritarian personality. Social psychologists have found that some people feel extremely insecure in the complexities of modern community living. They are disturbed by spontaneity and therefore become rigid, unable to permit nonconformity either in themselves or in others. They tend to demand of both themselves and others strict adherence to their own norms and to reject the norms and values of others. Such overconformity is itself a kind of deviance, as we shall see; and the too-strict rule-enforcer may be a very disorganizing force in the community. But the authoritarian personality is not concerned so much with the stability of the community as he is in his own stability.

Trends and Costs: The Function of Disorganization as Individual Nonconformity

Whichever model one invokes to explain or interpret nonconformity, it is safe to say that nonconformity will never cease to exist—nonconformity to law as well as to custom, mores, and convention. Almost any social system would be free from nonconformity if everyone worked to make it so. But some people do not. People violate the rules. They commit crimes. Nor does it help to show exactly how they got the way they are. If the conditions which make for these disturbing personalities persist, these

[27] William Whyte, Jr., *The Organization Man* (New York: Simon & Schuster, 1956).

personalities will also. The fact that we know the conditions that make for nonconformity does not mean that we can eliminate them. Perhaps the conditions which make for "virtuous" people cannot, by the very nature of social structures, be generalized to cover everyone.[28]

There are great costs involved in a permissive attitude toward nonconformity. The lack of "order" or disorganization that Khrushchev commented on is one. Still most people feel it is worth the cost. For the same tolerance of nonconformity which leads to crime also leads to innovation, to creativity, to inventiveness.

Even more to the point, perhaps, is the fact that a democratic regime depends on the individual who is willing to shake his fist at the status quo. The price we pay for consensus may sometimes be too high. The man who is willing to challenge it is performing an indispensable function. The price we pay for creative direct action may be destructive direct action, but it is a price that, apparently, has to be paid.

[28] Albert Cohen in the book cited above elaborates this thesis in some detail.

26

Social Disorder: Violence

Ubiquity of Violence

America has been called a lawless and violent nation. Indeed, vivid evidence for such a statement is not difficult to find, ranging from rioting to vigilantism to gang warfare. But it is doubtful if there is anything peculiarly American about violence. Violence has been a folk preoccupation from time immemorial; folk tales are full of it, from Snow White to Little Red Riding Hood. The Old Testament is replete with blood-curdling massacres, and classical history has its share of war, rapine, and pillage also, including the implacable Cato's "Carthage must be destroyed." The violence of the Cossacks has become legendary; pogroms, beating of serfs, and conspiratorial attacks were common in Russia. Sicily has been and even to this day still is characterized by individual and collective violence. The French have torn up the streets and manned the barricades on many occasions. Great exaltation of militarism characterized the Junker class of Germany for decades. Bull fights are the favorite amusement for millions in countries with a Spanish tradition. Massacres and revolutions and armed rebellions and hangings and plots and counterplots, raids, riots, feuds, conquests, concentration camps, lynchings, assassinations, terrorism, guillotining and other forms of violence mark the history of most nations. So far as violence in political succession is concerned, indeed, America ranks among the least violent nations of the world.

The Functions of Violence

Although it makes little difference to the victim of violence what function it is performing, it does make a difference to the community in deciding what, if anything, should be done about it. The victim is just as injured if the perpetrator attacked him out of hatred as if he did it without emotion in order to take his wallet. The result is the same in either case. Confusion in analysis and understanding, however, results from not clearly distinguishing the quite different functions being performed in the two kinds of cases. War, for example, or rioting, is one thing if it is interpreted as an expression of hostility, as the result of negative stereotypes, as the concomitant of hatred, as a mechanism for reducing tensions, and quite another if it is viewed as a means to an end, as a way of achieving some goal. Policies or programs for dealing with violence will be quite different if violence is viewed as emotional than they will be if it is viewed as rational.

Sociologically speaking, violence may be either "hot," that is, a way of reducing tensions or "cold," a means to an end. You may kill a man because you hate him, can tolerate him no longer; he has shamed you, injured you. Killing him releases your tensions. Or you may kill him because he stands in the way of your inheriting a million dollars. You may strike a man because he has insulted you or because you want his wallet. And the law will take cognizance of the difference. A mob may "explode" into a riot because hatred has been welling up in the community toward a Negro accused of rape; or rioting may be used by students to oust a government leader.

"HOT" VIOLENCE

"Hot" violence conforms to the model of conflict which Rapoport calls a "fight."[1] It falls into the category which, in Chapter 6, we called social-psychological in nature, in which there was no issue necessarily involved. As an emotional phenomenon, violence is the expression of powerful accumulations of hostility and hatred, envy and resentment, fear and insecurity; it is cathartic, a way to get rid of tensions. This fact is sometimes used to explain and interpret wars. It is alleged that men welcome war which gives them a chance to kill with impunity, which releases them from dull routine, which frees them from frustrations. Similarly racial violence and violence against ethnic groups and industrial violence are sometimes explained as emotional outbursts. Violence of this kind fits the model of society described by Freud of a suppressed "human nature" kicking over the traces in a kind of moral holiday, taking revenge, in effect, against the restraints of moral, customary, conventional, and even legal norms. It is a social-psychological phenomenon of awesome proportions.[2]

"COLD" VIOLENCE

History is filled with the use of violence as a technique for achieving ends. Torture and persecutions have been widely used to secure confessions, to deter, to punish. Persecutions of minority groups were often a means of winning popularity by rulers.[3] In personal relations, the dictum "spare the rod and spoil the child" regulated parent-child relations until well into the

[1] Anatol Rapoport, *Fights, Games, and Debates* (Ann Arbor, Mich.: University of Michigan, 1960).

[2] Violence is also a symptom in certain kinds of mental illness in which it becomes compulsive. Violence is sometimes "displaced," that is, turned inward toward oneself rather than directed outward toward an enemy. Suicide and self-mutilation, self-punishment are interpreted in these terms by some students.

[3] W. G. Sumner, *Folkways* (Boston: Ginn, 1906), p. 246.

twentieth century. The efficacy of whipping as a method of teaching was taken for granted.

Violence in cases such as the above is sometimes decided upon quite rationally. It is planned and weighed against alternatives. There need be little if any emotion attached to it, no personal hostility or hatred. The whipping parent may say, in all truthfulness, that it hurts him more than it does the child.

Violence may, indeed, be quite impersonal. Modern wars, for example, are becoming increasingly violent and increasingly impersonal. Men fly over cities and destroy them with no feeling of hatred toward their victims. Indeed, whipping up hatred for an enemy is often a major enterprise during a war. The resistance worker assigned to kill a certain strategically placed enemy had to be cool in order to be efficient. The professional killers employed by the underworld to get rid of opponents need have no personal antipathy toward the men they line up and machine-gun with military precision.

In all these cases violence is used deliberately, according to plan, as part of a decision. On the part of those who make the decision to use it as a means to an end, it is rational. Here, for example, is Karl Marx' advice on the art of insurrection:

> Firstly, never play with insurrection unless you are fully prepared to face the consequences of your play. Insurrection is a calculus with very indefinite magnitudes, the value of which may change every day; the forces opposed to you have all the advantage of organization, discipline, and habitual authority; unless you bring strong odds against them you are defeated and ruined. Secondly, the insurrectionary career once entered upon, act with the greatest determination, and on the offensive. The defensive is the death of every armed rising; it is lost before it measures itself with its enemies. Surprise your antagonists while their forces are scattering, prepare new successes, however small, but daily; keep up the moral ascendency which the first successful rising has given to you; rally those vacillating elements to your side which always follow the strongest impulse, and which always look out for the safer side; force your enemies to a retreat before they can collect their strength against you.[4]

No catharsis here, no explosion of hatred but rather "a calculus with very indefinite magnitude."

The distinction between cold and hot violence, that is, between violence as a means to an end and violence as an expression of emotion, is often blurred by the fact that although those who decide on violence may do so on coldly rational grounds, those who implement it are not likely to remain coldly rational. For them it is usually very emotion-fraught. For them it is not a means to an end, not a technique; it is an end in itself, a release, a catharsis, a form, even, of ecstasy. Hostilities long held in check

[4] *Revolution,* etc., pp. 161-162. Present citation from Barnes-Becker, *Social Thought from Lore to Science* (Boston: Heath, 1938), p. 646.

are allowed expression. Frustrations which have become intolerable are freed from control. In face-to-face situations violence almost inevitably turns hot.

Those who use violence as a means to an end may take advantage of this fact. Strike breakers used to be hired to create violence, their employers knowing that it would become hot and thus justify calling in the militia since the state would almost certainly enter a coalition with them against the strikers. Communities are incited to riot in order to justify a turnover in power. Soviet agents, it is alleged, stir up violence in order to discredit a status quo.

Another danger inherent in the use of violence as a deliberate technique is the high probability that, once started, it will tend to become an end in itself. It brutalizes those who become accustomed to it. The parent who is accustomed to beating the child for his mistakes comes in time to beat the child to vent his own frustrations.

THE NEW YORK DRAFT RIOTS: A CASE IN POINT

On a collective level, violence easily gets out of bounds. The so-called Draft Riots in New York City during the Civil War illustrate this danger. Hostility planned against conscription turned into race riots and class warfare. Here is Carl Sandburg's account:

> During the three days of July 13, 14, 15, mobs or crowds in New York City met by prearrangement, with a specific design as to what points they would attack and carry, drove out the U.S. provost marshal from his office, . . . wrecked the wheel or revolving drum from which the names of drafted men were drawn, tore to pieces the books and papers, poured turpentine on the floor, set the building on fire, fought off police and firemen, and the draft office and six adjoining buildings burned. . . .[5]

So far, so good. This was "a healthy Democratic opposition to the draft." But, once started, the mobs could not be held in check:

> They [not only] wrecked and burned the U.S. draft office . . . , [but they also] looted stores nearby, and burned twelve buildings; they smashed windows and doors and sacked the home of Republican Mayor Opdyke and burned at midnight the home of U.S. Postmaster Abram Wakeman, first stripping the premises of furniture and clothing; they burned a ferry house, hotels, drugstores, clothing stores, factories, saloons where they were refused free liquor, police stations, a Methodist church, a Protestant mission, the Colored Orphan Asylum. . . .
>
> Besides the many mobs carrying banners inscribed "No Draft" and "No $300 Arrangements with Us," there had been many other mobs with varied and mixed motives. Class war was the cry behind the big placards of one division: "The Poor Man's Blood for the Rich Man's Money." Eagerness for loot lay back of the stripping of houses of jewelry, plate, furniture, rugs, clothes. . . . In thousands of boys the savage was unleashed; they robbed houses and set them on fire. . . .

[5] Carl Sandburg, *Abraham Lincoln* (New York: Harcourt, Brace & World, 1954). All quotations from Laurel edition, pp. 364, ff.

The lesson is that violence is a dangerous technique to resort to. Its history shows that it is extremely difficult to hold within bounds. And a violent mob can be as destructive as an earthquake, a flood, or a volcanic eruption.

The Institutionalization of Violence

Because of the destructiveness of violence and because it is so difficult to control or hold in check once it is unleashed, even cold violence is everywhere subjected to institutional controls. The state is usually the only agency which is permitted the legitimate use of violence. And even here it is controlled by restrictions. It is to be used defensively and as a last resort. If a policeman is known to use his club too indiscriminately he will be criticized in the press. Tear bombs or water hoses rather than gunshot are used to disperse mobs. Even the legitimate use of violence is hedged in with precautions lest it get out of control.

If private individuals wish to carry guns they must get permission to do so. They may not wear concealed dangerous weapons. Violence is permitted only in self-defense and the user must prove that it was in self-defense. Crimes of violence are more likely than other crimes to be sought out and punished. Even in its milder forms, such as physical punishment in the family, violence, though permitted, is legally restricted to limited forms.

Despite the saying that all is fair in love and war, men have struggled for millennia to find ways of subjecting even war to international law.

Although hot violence may be viewed as an expression of "human nature"—as, indeed, all behavior is—not only law but custom, mores, and convention also influence its expression. There are numerous crescive norms which regulate its use, as well as enacted ones.

The norms regulating the use of violence vary from one historical period to another, they vary by class, by region, by nationality, by culture. The norms influence the form which violence takes and also the victims against which it is used.

There are class norms regulating the form which violence may take. The duel, for instance, was an upper-class form of violence, as highly stylized by custom and convention as a ballet. The street brawl, conversely, is a lower-class form of violence, as is also the fist fight, although the latter has been known to occur even on the floor of the august Senate.

The use of poisons and acids, especially throwing acids in the face of opponents, has been very largely an Italian practice. Czarist Russia went in for riots in the form of pogroms against Jews; in this country, however, violence against Jews is likely to take the form of throwing things at them or bombs at their property.

Regional differences in norms regulating violence also occur. Lynching, forbidden by law, was sanctioned by custom for many years in the

South, just as vigilantism had been in the old West. Like duels, the procedures were highly stylized; everyone knew just what to expect.

The form which violence takes is also influenced by the values expressed in the norms of the community. Thus the Comanche Indians cultivated warriors whose status in the community depended on successful aggression against outsiders. The Plains Indians counted coups; often status depended on the number of scalps one could boast. A similar situation existed among the head-hunting Dyaks of Borneo. Race riots in the North are not the same as those in the South. Violence against Negroes in this country, further, is governed by different norms from those regulating violence against, let us say, Jews.

Community forces channel the expression of "human nature," so that it becomes violent in one community but not in another. One permits violence; another does not. Human nature is the same in St. Louis, for example, as in Detroit; but St. Louis did not suffer race riots as Detroit did in the 1940's. Human nature is the same in Virginia as in Arkansas; but Virginia did not explode into violence as did Arkansas in the 1950's.

In brief, violence is such a dangerous phenomenon, so likely to spread, so contagious, so likely to become emotion-fraught that even its legitimate use must be minimized and constantly hedged in with controlling norms. Even when it occurs outside of the law it is likely to follow patterns established by custom and convention.

Violence and Strategy

In a certain sense violence is a substitute for strategy, or vice versa. It might even be said that resort to violence is an admission of strategic failure. The good strategist attempts to secure his goals without violence. Strategy attempts to get the opponent to do what one wants him to do by "reading his mind" and behaving in such a way that he will make up his mind to do what one wants him to do.

Violence in its most primitive form reduces the opponent to a thing or to a symbol. He is ignored as a human being. He is moved about and operated upon without regard to his own motivations. He is, literally, violated. In its most refined form—torture, for example—it does take account of motivation but on a fairly mechanical level. The human body is viewed as a mechanism that gives way under certain conditions, the problem is to find the conditions.

Animals, as we saw in Chapter 6, may be said to use a primitive kind of strategy when they bare their teeth, bark ominously, or growl. But they fall back on violence when their small stock of strategic moves is exhausted. The same may be said of many human beings. War, Clauswitz said, is the continuation of diplomacy.

Violence is often used at the bottom of the conflict continuum to damage or to get rid of one party to the conflict. Conflict is dealt with by destroying the enemy. Blood baths, purges, liquidations, massacres, reigns of terror, take the place of strategic interaction.

But sometimes violence, and not merely the threat of violence, is used strategically. Or violence is used to validate a future threat. Negroes, for example, may be subjected to physical violence almost at random, not for anything they themselves have done and not necessarily to satisfy aggressions in the white perpetrators, but primarily to create fear in the minds of other Negroes so that in the future it can be used to control them. Whenever the threat of violence is being used as a strategic deterrent, as in the case of capital punishment, an occasional display of violence may be required to prevent the attrition of the threat's potential.

Since in most modern societies there is an onus associated with the aggressive use of violence, strategy is sometimes used to provoke an opponent to violence, to hang the incubus of aggression on him, or, preferably, to force him to concede to one's own wishes as the only alternative to such aggression. The *agent provacateur* leaves his opponent only the choice of giving in or of striking him and the payoff for the first is better than for the second. The strike leader arouses strong emotions in his followers and then tells his opposite number across the bargaining table that if his men don't get what they demand he can't assume responsibility for the consequences, thus shifting to his opponent the responsibility for any violence that ensues.[6]

By and large, however, violence and strategy tend to be poles apart in their operation and to win one's point by strategy is usually considered better than having to resort to violence.

Individual and Collective Violence

Only a word or two will be devoted here to the discussion of individual, unorganized, noncollective violence. It takes the form of street brawls, private fist fights, assault and battery, armed holdups, and murder. Their occurrence is fairly regular, almost predictable. The techniques of violence used may change, but not necessarily the result.

Statistical correlations have been found between homicide and aggravated assault on the one hand and the business cycle on the other; they go down in times of depression and up in times of prosperity. Homicide and aggravated assault are more likely to occur among Negroes than among whites. Crimes of violence are more common in the South than in the North, for both Negroes and whites. They are more common in rural than in urban communities. Homicide rates tend to be high in certain parts of the city, namely the slum areas. Violent crimes are committed by fairly

[6] This is the strategic move called relinquishing the initiative. See Thomas C. Schelling, *The Strategy of Conflict* (Cambridge, Mass.: Harvard, 1960), pp. 137-139.

young people, between 20 and 39, for the most part. Almost five times more murders are committed by those between 25 and 29 than by persons 50 to 54, and the ratio is twenty times greater for the 25 to 29 men than for those 65 and over. This decline occurs later for Negroes and foreign-born persons.

According to the records, males are arrested for assault eight times more frequently than women, and for murder, seven times more frequently. Women exceed men in violence only with respect to inflicting fatal injuries on infants less than one year of age. All records are defective, of course, including those the above comparisons are based on. But there is one sociologist who believes that the records of female murder are especially defective. He claims that a great many murders are committed by women by nonviolent means, such as poison, which appear on the record as natural deaths; their victims are likely to be members of their own families, husbands or children.[7] Assault by women tends to take the form of throwing disfiguring acid.

Interesting and even fascinating as the phenomena of individual violence may be, we shall not pursue them further here. Our concern here is with collective forms which, if they are sanctioned at all, are, with the exception of war and revolution, sanctioned by implicit rather than by explicit or official institutional norms. The remainder of this chapter deals, therefore, with race relations, religious group relations, industrial relations, and gang relations. In addition a description is presented of violence as a way of life in a small coal mining community.

Race Violence[8]

The initial relationship between whites and Negroes was one characterized by violence; and thus it has continued. The slave trader had to kidnap the Negroes, chain them in shackles, and forcibly control them with the whip until he could bring them to market. Since the physical odds were so heavily against them, resistance on the part of Negroes was often turned in upon themselves and took the form of suicide and infanticide. They could not succeed against the stronger whites, but they could take out their frustrations in aggressions against themselves.[9]

[7] Otto Pollak, *The Criminality of Women* (Philadelphia: University of Pennsylvania, 1950).

[8] The discussion of Negro-white violence here leans heavily on the work of Allen D. Grimshaw's two reported studies, namely, "Lawlessness and Violence in America and Their Special Manifestations in Changing Negro-White Relationships," *Journal of Negro History*, 44 (January, 1959), pp. 52-72, and "Urban Racial Violence in the United States: Changing Ecological Considerations," *Amer. Jour. Sociol.*, 66 (September, 1960), pp. 109-119.

[9] Some of the violence characteristic of Negroes today has also been traced to this displaced reaction. "The high degree of intra-Negro quarreling, crime, and homicide, revealed by statistics and observation, can be directly correlated with a Negro's frustration in being unable to vent his hostility on the whites. . . . The substitution of Negro for

But even under slavery there were insurrections and rebellions, some of them almost successful. As noted in Chapter 16, it took about three years to domesticate a Negro and make him a profitable slave. Not all of them took meekly to their new status. Assaults and homicide occurred. There were instances of brutal treatment of slaves although as the institution matured, especially after the slave trade was abolished, brutality was not typical. It was not to the interest of the owner to mistreat a slave.

In New York in 1712 and again in 1741 there were slave plots of some size; both Negroes and whites were killed. In the early nineteenth century there was a "near obsession . . . over the possibilities of slave revolts" among the whites and in many cases this anxiety was well founded. There were planned rebellions or insurrections which aimed to exterminate all classes of whites except those who had been friendly. "The characteristics of the rebels varied. Some were relatively new arrivals still imbued with the militance of their African tribal heritage, others were longer sojourners in this country who had become literate, acculturated and too familiar with ideas of equality which were meant only for their white masters."[10]

It was not until the period of Civil War and Reconstruction (1861-1877) that the pattern of racial violence became one of rioting. These riots were presumably based in large part on fear that Negroes would take jobs away from white, especially, at that time, from Irish, workers. The rioting in New York, described above, was the bloodiest in American history.

In the South, night-riding organizations, so-called, sprang up after the Civil War with the main purpose of terrorizing Negroes. The late nineteenth and early twentieth century might be called the heyday of the lynching. Riots continued, to be sure, but they were not nearly so characteristic as lynchings. They have, however, outlasted lynchings.

Southern-styled riots in the past differed from northern-style riots in that violence was one-sided and usually sparked by charges of Negro assaults upon white women. Northern-style riots are characterized by resistance on the part of Negroes to the accommodative pattern, particularly in housing, the labor market, public facilities, especially transportation. In the North, furthermore, organized as well as unorganized members of both races engage in occasional pitched battles, and there is widespread occurrence of attacks on isolated individuals by roaming gangs of either race. The police are likely to be more nearly neutral in the North.

Since World War II there have been no major riots, but there have been a large number of disturbances that might well have become riots if

---

white is encouraged by the culture pattern of white official and unofficial leniency toward intra-Negro crime. Courts, more particularly southern ones, are mild in their view of intra-Negro offenses, and the prevailing white attitude is one of indulgence toward those intra-Negro crimes which do not infringe on white privileges." Hortense Powdermaker, "The Channeling of Negro Aggression by the Cultural Process," *Amer. Jour. Sociol.* 48 [May, 1943], pp. 750-758.

[10] Grimshaw, *op. cit.*, p. 58.

police protection had not been adequate. Both northern and southern cities have been the scenes of such disturbances. Bad as they were, they were but pale echoes of earlier violence. The tempering of violence, reducing it from riots to "disturbances" has been attributed not to a lowering of tensions between the races but rather to the fact that the police and law enforcement officers have not been in the coalition against the Negroes but have, rather, attempted to enforce order impartially.

An analysis in 1960 of three "disturbances"—in Chattanooga, Montgomery, and Little Rock—concluded that whereas in the past the police had, in effect, done the bidding of the white mob, a reversal had now occurred. "Now, to maintain law and order he [the police officer] must protect the nonviolent Negroes from the whites. And he must do it quickly."[11]

Ecological Factors in Racial Violence

We have had occasion to note that the physical structure of a community may have profound influence on the relationships among the groups who live in it. So, also, does its ecological structure.

A detailed study of the incidence and forms of interracial violence in urban communities has shown that, through World War II, ecological factors were of major importance. In Negro residential areas with few if any business establishments, for example, neither rioting nor individual assault was likely to occur, either because there was a lower population density and hence less likelihood of large gatherings or because there was less opportunity for looting or because there was more police protection in such relatively higher social and economic status areas.

When violence occurred in white higher-class residential areas, it was found to take the form of assault on Negro servants going home or coming to work, but by outsiders, not residents of the area. In areas characterized by great hostility to Negroes and hence not contested by them, there was likely to be little violence, mainly because Negroes remained away from them; but along the boundaries between such areas and Negro areas, violence was likely to occur. In so-called contested areas, the pattern was one of fairly high incidence of violence when there were no actual riots in process but of little if any violence during actual rioting, and when violence did occur it was usually not the work of local residents but of outsiders. In areas where Negroes and whites have lived together for some period of time, violence, if or when it occurred, tended to result from invaders from the outside and not from the explosion of local tensions.

In white-dominated central business districts the form which violence has taken has been that of physical assault by white mobs on individual Negroes or small groups of Negroes. Looting of white property has not been

[11] George McMillan, *Racial Violence and Law Enforcement* (Southern Regional Council, 1960). Reported in the *New York Times*, Nov. 21, 1960.

characteristic, although there has been destruction of property as incidental to assault on Negroes.

It has been primarily in Negro slum areas served by white businesses that riots have tended to concentrate. Three forms have been distinguished: (1) mass racial war in which whole areas have been destroyed and Negroes shot down in large numbers; (2) looting and destruction of property but the actual clashes being between the resident population and the police rather than between races; and (3) in addition to property damage and looting and clashes with the police, violence between Negroes and cruising bands of whites or between Negroes and whites who just happened to be in the area.

The research we have been citing here reported two types of location to be of special significance; transfer points of public transportation lines and government buildings; the first, because they focus crowds, and the second because they tend to be refuges for Negroes.

Since World War II the pattern of interracial violence has changed somewhat. "Disturbances" rather than riots have been characteristic. They tend to occur in residential areas where Negroes are first moving in, at schools, and at eating places. The participants are usually transients at the site of conflict, usually from areas of militant anti-Negro prejudice. And local municipal officials and police forces have tended to be impartial rather than in coalition with the whites.[12]

Participation and Leadership: The Violent Ones

In some cases violence is a symptom of a pathology; mentally ill patients sometimes become violent. There is also an emotional disturbance known as sadism that takes the form of enjoying sexual cruelty, and, by extension, all kinds of cruelty. But the participants in interracial violence are probably not to be explained in these terms. For the most part they (known as "a certain element" by nonviolent members of the community) come from lower socio-economic classes in which violence is an acceptable, indeed honored, form of behavior.[13] Often their violence has a defiant character; the perpetrators—often rural, with a rural background—feel that there is implicit value support for what they do. They are usually uneducated, isolated from the main currents of contemporary society as channeled through the mass media, especially the written word, and hence they have little conception of how their behavior looks to others. The self they see reflected from their fellows produces no feeling of shame or guilt.

The white leadership in interracial violence is somewhat more sophisticated. Its members know that the middle and upper classes reject violence and they therefore publicly protest against it; all the while they know how

[12] Grimshaw, *op. cit.*, p. 119.

[13] See section following on "Violence As a Way of Life."

to stimulate and use it."[14] Care is usually taken not openly to advocate hitting or striking Negroes, although violence in the form of shaking and kicking is permitted. There may have been a time when violence was accepted by responsible members of the community, it is sometimes said that the original Ku Klux Klan was composed of solid citizens. At the present time, however, the leaders in violence are extremists and usually an embarrassment to other whites.

John Kasper illustrates the nature of white leadership. He is quoted in a newspaper report of a National States Rights party in Louisville in 1958 as saying: "I used to think all our problems would be solved if every nigger would kill a kike. That is what I was doing working with them in New York. But I find that I overestimated the nigger mind."[15] His rejection of violence was not on the grounds that it was contrary to civilized principles but because he did not "think we can win that way. When we had our meeting in Nashville . . . we had a crowd of about 10,000 people and they were ready to go. If I had said, 'Come on, let's go clean out nigger town,' they'd have gone. It would have been one of the biggest mass murders in history. But we didn't do that. We just wanted to do things the legal way."[16]

In this connection it is well to point out the strategic value of ideal norms. There were a great many white southerners who were as opposed to desegregation as John Kasper and other extremists were, as anxious as they to keep Negroes in their place. But they could not publicly express such sentiments nor countenance violence. They had professed democratic ideals so vehemently and so long that they could not now betray them and ally themselves with the extremists. They would lose face if they lined up with the Kaspers, the Klans, and the white citizens' councils.[17]

Reference has already been made to the displaced hostility among Negroes and the consequent high incidence of violence among them. Not all hostility takes this displaced form; sometimes it is expressed directly on white persons. So-called "mean niggers" have arisen in many communities and although they may have suffered the consequences of their aggression,

[14] The leaders in the January, 1961, rioting at the University of Georgia, kept in the background themselves while manipulating the students. ". . . the leaders of the violent faction took little part in the violence. Few if any threw giant firecrackers at University officials, but two of them are said to have supplied some of the rioters who did. While these leaders did not provide the bricks that shattered the dormitory windows, they did provide the inspiration. . . . Those student leaders apparently received advice from outsiders with more than passing knowledge of other riots. . . . Other students have been told by the leaders of telephone calls of encouragement and advice from several of the militant white supremacists on the state's political third string. Young and politically ambitious, the youths have accepted the counsel of those whom they would emulate" (Claude Sitton, "Anatomy of a Campus Riot: Segregationists Prove Their Skill at Playing on Confusion," *New York Times*, Jan. 15, 1961).

[15] Drew Pearson, "Hate Groups Anti-Everything," column, Dec. 4, 1958.

[16] *Ibid.*

[17] The related situation has frequently been commented on, namely one in which the antisegregation southerner was kept silent because of the difficulty in establishing the identity of other antisegregationists. This situation is discussed in Schelling, *op. cit.*, pp. 139 ff.

they served to limit the aggression of white persons against other Negroes.

Unlike the Negroes in the past, those who now take part in "disturbances" are young, well-educated, usually college students, who invite white persons to knock the chip from their shoulders but who are trained to react without violence. They are well dressed. They are well disciplined. And part of their effectiveness results from the contrast between them and the white hoodlums who are trapped into violence.

A conclusion that seems to be justified, if past trends continue, is that violence as an emotional outburst, as an expression of hostility and aggression, as a nonrational explosion of hatred is on the wane in race relations. It has fallen into the hands of persons of low prestige, of low socio-economic status, or of an authoritarian caste of mind. As the level of education among both Negroes and whites rises, as it inevitably will, violence may be expected to decline. The rabble-rousers can intimidate a community for a while but they cannot long maintain leadership in communities of educated people exposed to the printed page.

Violence against Religious Groups

In the three decades before the Civil War, violence against Catholics, especially Irish Catholics, was not uncommon. Street fights and personal assault sometimes eventuated in major riots. Much of this violence was an expression of nativism, so called, expressed in the "Know-Nothing" movement, itself a kind of shock reaction to the great influx of Irish immigrants. But even today vandalism in the form of desecration of religious buildings occurs from time to time.

Violence against Jews has taken many forms, differing from one society to another, and ranging from merely "spitting on my Jewish gabardine," in the case of Shylock, to the systematic extermination of six million persons in the gas chambers of the Nazis. In American communities it rarely takes the form of mob rioting, as in the case of Negroes or as it took in the Russian pogrom. Nor does it take the form of cold, bureaucratically efficient elimination. Except when it is part of a more complex situation, as in the case of the great Harlem riot of 1943, it is likely to take the form either of personal assault or of throwing things—stones or bombs—or vandalism, ranging in seriousness from broken windows to destroyed buildings. Temples and synagogues were bombed in Atlanta, Peoria, Nashville, and Jacksonville in 1958; attempts were made at Charlotte, Gastonia, N. C., and Birmingham. In 1959 there was a wave of desecration of altars and cemeteries by vandals.

The reference by Kasper to Jews, quoted above, was not fortuitous; for it has been found that violence against Jews is associated with racism in almost any form. And the epidemics of violence in the 1950's was attributed by some to the general violence stimulated by the Supreme Court decision on desegregation. It was, they pointed out, part and parcel of the "outbreak of lawlessness in the South since the United States Supreme Court's racial desegregation decisions. The two are interrelated and any effort to meet the problem of anti-Semitism without attacking the underlying lawlessness that gives rise to it will necessarily be futile. . . . This is the crucial fact: lawlessness is the inevitable consequence of disrespect for law."[18]

Not too much is known about those who perpetrate such violence. A study of vandals in New York found them to be younger than other delinquents and almost always male. Relatively more whites than Negroes were found among them than among other delinquents. They were mostly from slum areas. This study contradicted the opinion of some that vandalism was more common among middle-class than among lower-class children. The author of the study concluded that "correcting slum conditions that breed the hostilities, rather than fining parents or relying on psychiatric care, should be the principal means of checking vandalism. If the causes of problems like vandalism are more social than personal, as the data seem to indicate, it is naïve to expect psychiatrists to solve them."[19]

With respect to those who engage in bombing and dynamiting, there is not even this much research. They are certainly disaffected and hostile, if not pathological, personalities, with an erroneous assessment of the amount of implicit support they have from the community, and their violence is probably hot rather than cold. Those who are arrested tend to show strong Nazi, or at least rascist, leanings, according to a report in the *Atlantic Monthly* (March, 1960, p. 4).

Industrial Violence

Although violence in the labor movement has subsided since unions achieved legal sanction in the 1930's, wherever there is a strike and a picket line the danger of violence is great.

The history of strikes in American communities has had all the earmarks of actual warfare. Strikes have come perilously close to revolutions. (Communists, when they had charge of strikes, used to steer them in this direction.) They have represented class warfare in a very dramatic and often violent form. A good deal of blood has been shed in strikes. As recently as 1936, efforts to organize unions in the Ford plants, in the steel industry, and in the rubber industry were accompanied by great violence.

Strikes were most likely to involve violence when the issue was the schismatic one of union recognition. Employers fought unions with every weapon in a well-stocked arsenal, including machine guns, tear gas, and grenades, as well as with propaganda, spying, and court orders.

[18] American Jewish Congress, "Bombings and Hate Sheets," (pamphlet), December, 1958, p. 7.

[19] John M. Martin, quoted in *The New York Times,* Dec. 16, 1959.

One historian has singled out the year 1877 as "the year of violence."[20] In that year, after four years of depression, the militia had to be called out time and again to maintain order in the Pennsylvania mining areas; lynch law was almost supplanting the courts in the South and West and in the summer, rioting from coast to coast accompanied a nation-wide railroad strike. The workers were protesting a cut in wages (while dividends remained untouched), and "thousands of the disgruntled—coal miners, stevedores, farmers and the unemployed—joined in the demonstrations. State militias waveringly resisted and Federal troops were summoned. During the short period of the strike, thousands were killed or injured; disorder richocheted across American cities. . . . A general social convulsion seemed to be in the making."[21] Violence on this scale seemed to be required to reorient industrial leaders and make possible "the modern American system of capitalism by compromise."[22]

Violence was especially likely to occur if strikebreakers were used. The strikebreaker was trained in strong-arm methods and violence and he often terrorized the whole community; he usually had a criminal record. The Byrnes Act of 1936, based on findings of the LaFollette Committee, forbade the transportation of persons across state lines for strikebreaking purposes.

Since the passage of the National Labor Relations Act in 1935 there has been less incentive to the use of violence. It is illegal to attempt to destroy unions. The great battles against unions are not, therefore, now fought by thugs and strong-arm men as in the past but, for the most part, by clever lawyers and lobbyists. Incidents do continue to occur, of course, but the Wagner Act has done much to tame industrial warfare.

Gang Violence

The violence engaged in by the underworld has quite a different pattern from that, let us say, of the Indian or of the Nazi or the Russian *mujik*. It shows, allegedly, the Mafia pattern developed in Sicily. The use of disfiguring and blinding acid, for example, is said to trace back to the conspiratorial tactics of the Mafia. Violence is a means to an end, as well as an end in itself. Machine guns, bludgeons, knives, bombs, abductions, "taking for a ride," are among the techniques used. Murder is a professional activity. Members of the underworld are often more frightened of one another than they are of the police. One former gang member lived safely within prison walls for some fourteen years only to be shot dead within two weeks after his release.

Because the problem of the succession of power has not been solved in

[20] Robert V. Bruce, *1877: Year of Violence* (New York: Bobbs-Merrill, 1959).
[21] Eric F. Goldman, reviewing Bruce's book, *New York Times*, Dec. 13, 1959, p. 24.
[22] *Ibid.*

the underworld, leadership is often achieved by violence, as it was often in the case of feudal chieftains. The top men fight it out and the survivor takes over the power. Without access to the courts to solve their conflicts, violence often remains the only alternative.

Gangs of younger men and even of boys have fought in city streets for at least a century. They fight ostensibly to protect their "turf" against invasion. They fight for prestige. They fight for their honor. They fight to be doing something. They fight because they have few and limited alternatives. They fight because they are frustrated. They fight because violence is part of slum culture. It is valued and rewarded.[23] They use home-made bombs, shotguns, knives, clubs, lead pipes, anything they can get hold of, in their so-called rumbles. Most gang members finally outgrow their violence, but violence is never far from the surface in the slums.

Gang violence is seasonal; it tends to rise in the warm months when there is more street life. Violence in the schools is cyclical, rising and falling, according to some rhythm not yet fully understood.[24]

Attempts to institutionalize street gang violence take the form of increased police surveillance, increased lighting, and, more especially, of adult supervision. Specially trained social workers are assigned to win the confidence of gangs and to try to channel their activities into equally satisfying but nonviolent forms of aggression. Their success, while not total, is impressive.

Violence As a Way of Life: A Community Case Study

Television has accustomed us to the prevalence of violence in the old West. Guns were part of conventional garb. Justice did not wait for the courts. Violence has characterized many kinds of communities. The story which follows of Coal Town, incorporated in 1914, illustrates long-continued community disorder characterized by violence.[25] All the forms of violence described above occurred there. The people of Coal Town fought for fun, for money, for revenge, for anything. Everyone carried guns. The dead were found in the wells, in the woods, even on the streets. No one seemed to mind enough to do anything about it. No one was arrested, let alone tried. The women were afraid to go out in the streets; even many of the men found it safer to stay home. Hold-ups, arson. . . . Think nothing of it.

The people of Coal Town were proud of their violence; it was a prized community value:

[23] Rocky Graziano, for example, "was the toughest kid on the East Side and 'the sworn enemy of the human race.' . . . Beating up other kids and snatching their dimes or candy or skates were easy. Soon Rocky had a reputation as a thief and a street fighter and the leader of his own gang. He was proud of that reputation. . . . 'A guy who fights is a guy with friends.' Rocky always fought. Fighting meant prestige and eventually it meant money" (*New York Times,* Mar. 21, 1955).

[24] *New York Times,* Sept. 26, 1958.

[25] Herman R. Lantz, *People of Coal Town* (New York: Columbia University, 1958).

> Violence was usually met with violence. So pronounced was the tendency that over the years it spread to all ethnic groups and became a well-ingrained pattern imbued with much pride and satisfaction. . . . There was and is considerable pride in the violence which characterized Coal Town for so many years.[26]

When the interviewers in this study noted that interview material indicated a good deal more violence than was reported in official records, "informants became annoyed at the inference and reacted as though we were denying them a valuable chapter in their community history."[27]

Violence permeated all aspects of life in the community, from the courts down to the family:

> A lack of political order and maturity characterized the county during the nineteenth century. Differences were often settled outside the legal framework and were characterized by violence. When court was in session the room was crowded with adults desiring to be entertained. . . . An autobiography reveals: "During the trial, the opposing attorneys became involved in an exchange of hot words. One of the attorneys drew a pistol from his holster and fired at the opposing attorney. He failed to hit the attorney, however, and outsiders intervened to stop the fight." The failure of institutions to deal with violations against person and property often left popular justice as almost the sole preserver of public peace. Citizens were frequently terrified by gangs of horse thieves, robbers, murderers, and counterfeiters. . . .
>
> Patterns of violence found their expression in family feuding, in father-son relationships, in the development of mother-centered patterns, and in certain pranks which followed the wedding ceremony. . . . The patterns of feuding, fighting, and drinking often made the life and behavior of the male unpredictable and tenuous. At times serious injury and death followed the carousing activities of the male.[28]

Violence, continues the author, was so highly valued that to depend on the law was viewed as a sign of weakness. Thus one informant, a merchant, reported:

> The group considered the most violent person the best. This is what the group believed. If the differences is [sic] a great amount of violence, they will be held up by the group, if not, they are held in contempt. The most preferred companion was one who could give and take violence. If he could give and take he was held in esteem and with less contempt regardless of what position they were supposed to maintain in the community. That was both in action and words. If attacked, he had to fight. If he would not resist, he might as well forget about it. He would fit alright if he defended himself with violence. . . .[29]

Industrial violence also characterized Coal Town:

> From the first, violence was associated with mining in Coal Town. Either mining management was in conflict with labor when it wished to organize; or

[26] *Ibid.*, p. 94.
[27] *Ibid.*
[28] *Ibid.*, pp. 17-20.
[29] *Ibid.*, p. 261.

miners of different unions were in conflict with one another. The fact that the community was beset by violent strikes helped matters little. During the period 1908 to 1925 at least five major strikes occurred, each associated with marked violence.[30]

Ethnic-group violence was also part of the picture:

Although the immigrant felt that virtually all natives were prejudiced toward him, physical violence as a manifestation of prejudice was experienced most frequently in relation to the miner from the South, with whom he was in economic competition. An immigrant miner's son: "Those blamed poor white trash from the South used to make it tough on us. I've heard my dad tell many a time how they used to push him off the sidewalk . . . , call him a dago or a garlic snapper, even spit on him. There wasn't anything he could do, he just had to take it and go ahead, or get mobbed."[31]

Political Violence

A discussion of violence in the field of political behavior has been conspicuously absent in this chapter. So far as American communities are concerned this is wholly justified. However much violence may have characterized race and ethnic-group relations, or industrial relations, it has not been characteristic of political life. It is true that there used to be a certain amount of slugging on election day, and there have been instances of recourse to violence from time to time; but in view of the fact that there are, in addition to the federal and state governments, 155,000 units of local government in the United States, one cannot but admire the smoothness with which political succession is handled.

Although, therefore, there is little to say about the use of violence for political ends in American community life, the matter is of major concern in other parts of the world and warrants at least a cursory overview here. It is almost customary in states that have not solved the problems of political succession to resort to violence. Such resort to violence is almost an unfailing test of political maturity. A major distinguishing characteristic between Communistic states and many Latin American states on the one hand and those with long parliamentary traditions on the other is precisely that the former rely on a strong man or a military junta or a military coup to accomplish the succession and to re-establish order.

Violence tends to be used in mass social reform movements where it serves several functions. First, it dramatizes issues and appeals to persons who are not amenable to rational argument.[32] One student of the subject, in fact—Georges Sorel—believed that the only practical justification for

[30] *Ibid.*, pp. 115, 116-117.

[31] *Ibid.*, p. 72.

[32] The discussion here leans on Sidney Hook's article on violence in the *Encyclopaedia of the Social Sciences,* Vol. 15, pp. 265-267.

"the poetic cult of violence" was to dramatize conflicts of ethical values. Violence may also be the only way to win concessions from a well-intrenched power. The capacity to threaten violence may be the best strategy to secure wanted reforms from resisting governments. The use of violence is limited by fear of reprisals; it may be suicidal if used prematurely or if it is not properly timed.

Karl Marx was the great codifier of the principles of violence. He deplored individual use of violence as irresponsible petty bourgeois anarchism or downright police provocation; he advocated, rather, a disciplined and organized form of violence that followed rather than preceded the long process of organization of labor.

> The objective presupposition of any violent action is a revolutionary situation defined as one in which there is chaos in economic life and in which the traditional psychology of all classes is demoralized. Revolutionary action is not begun unless there is reason to believe that a majority of the population stands behind the representative councils of the workers and the producers in whose name power is taken. The amount of violence which must be employed is a function of the intensity of resistance which is encountered. For Marxism the moral and social justification of the use of violence consists in the fact that it is a measure of defense on the part of the majority of the community against the horrors of war, poverty and political repression and aims to establish the political conditions under which the transition from a profit to a use economy may be effected.[33]

Until the middle of the twentieth century violence was assumed by Soviet Communists to be an indispensable technique for achieving the overthrow of governments anywhere. In the 1950's, however, Khrushchev introduced a revision into Communist doctrine. The ultimate triumph of communism could come by means of competitive coexistence, in which the intrinsic superiority of communism would win over effete capitalistic regimes. Competition was to be substituted for violent conflict.[34]

Evaluation of Violence

Evaluation of violence may be in terms of the functions it performs. For those who are concerned with violence as the expression of frustrations, the problem takes the form of substituting less destructive ways of achieving the same end. For those who see violence as the result of fears and prejudices, programs for allaying fears and overcoming prejudices seem to be the answer. Or changing the social structure which gives rise to the emotions which seek violent expression.

Evaluations of violence as a means to an end may be in terms of effectiveness or correctness. Is violence the best way to achieve this particular goal? Or are there better alternatives? This is the level on which respon-

[33] *Ibid.*, p. 266.
[34] Subversion and revolution were still acceptable however.

sible people evaluate war or capital punishment or calling out the militia.

Evaluations are also made in terms of ethical standards. Here the question asked is not, is violence the correct way of achieving this goal, but rather, is violence the right way, in the sense of ethically best, way of achieving this goal? At the present time the trend in thinking appears to be against violence on both technical and ethical grounds among civilized nations; it continues in many parts of the world, not because it is considered ethically right but because it is the only resource available in an impoverished institutional framework.

Functional Alternatives for Violence: Direct Action

The underdog is greatly hampered in the strategic use of violence. The legitimate uses of violence are reserved for the status quo. If the underdog resorts to violence it is in the form of uprisings—of peasants, of Negroes, of slaves, of workers—and, as Marx pointed out, they are usually doomed to failure. Such violence is usually a spontaneous revulsion against intolerable circumstances rather than a studied strategic move.

As Georges Sorel pointed out, the function of violence is often dramatic, a kind of communication, to show the world the exact situation. It is a way of crying out, or shouting that something is wrong. Since there are no institutional channels for making their grievances known, underdogs may have to resort to violence, if only as a symbol.

Recently there have been people who have asked whether there were not nonviolent ways of accomplishing the same end. The use of nonviolent direct action has resulted.

Nonviolent direct action serves several functions. In the first place, like violence, it dramatizes the one-sidedness of an accommodation to a conflict which the world has become so accustomed to that it no longer sees. We have already commented on the fact that it is almost impossible to behave contrary to the system, contrary to the institutionalized expectations of others, or, in a bureaucracy, almost impossible to behave contrary to the bureaucratic structure. No matter how much Tolstoi wished to improve the lot of his serfs, for example, it could hardly be done one by one; the system demanded certain kinds of behavior. No matter how much individuals might wish to desegregate, they could not do it in the face of a social system which demanded it. And so on. A functioning system has its built-in coercions. Direct action is deliberately designed to disorganize such a system.

Sorel and those who believed in direct action to disorganize or break the coercion of any status quo or "coordination game" felt that only violence could do this. They felt that violence dramatized the inequities of any status quo and forced people to become aware of them. It thus broke into the functioning of the system and raised questions. It was, in this sense, symbolic. Sabotage, for example, did not really change a system, but it protested the system and made people examine it.

It has occurred to more sophisticated thinkers that the disorganizing and dramatizing incident did not have to be violent. It could be equally effective if it were nonviolent. Since its main function was symbolic anyway, the symbolism could be nonviolent as well as violent.

Originally nonviolent direct action was largely individual; Thoreau is the great example here. He believed that any government that permitted slavery was wrong and he would resist it by not paying taxes for its support. Gandhi learned the principle of nonviolent resistance from Thoreau but he organized it; he made it a corporate rather than an individual phenomenon.

In the United States the use of nonviolence as a conflict technique has become extended and refined. It has taken the form of walks, vigils, boycotts, sit-ins, freedom rides, wade-ins, kneel-ins. Its potency has scarcely been tapped.

In Chapter 25 we referred to the function performed by the nonconformist willing to shake his fist at the status quo. Now we see that he does not have to use hate and violence; he can disorganize a community in a spirit of love even more effectively. His crime, committed without hate, may land him in the same jail as that holding the nonconformist who commits his crime in anger or resentment; but the resulting disorganization is creative in one case, destructive in the other.

27

Community Dissociation

Conflicting Values

In Chapter 4 we referred to three areas of institutionalization which were to concern us in this book. In Part Four we examined how competition is institutionalized and in Part Five how conflict is institutionalized, both crescively and legislatively. At this point the paradoxical processes by which the third one, violation of institutional norms, is itself institutionalized are the focus of our attention. The function of this institutionalization of the violation of norms is that of accommodating conflicts which cannot be dealt with in the usual ways since they reflect conflicts within the members of the community themselves. They want incompatible things. They want, for example, many governmental services but they also want taxes to be low. They want to have good, honest government; but they also want to have their traffic tickets fixed. They want to exploit minority groups; but they also want to preserve the ideals of democracy. They want to have laws on the statute books enforcing sobriety, virtue, and high moral standards; they also want to indulge their carnal appetites. This kind of internal conflict reflects itself in the community. The conflicting parties cannot be separated spatially or geographically; they cannot be assimilated. The accommodation is achieved by a set of devices which make it possible to permit violation of institutional norms without admitting it. People legislate many ideals into laws and then make provision for violations. As in the case of individual dissociation, the basis for community dissociation is some kind of conflict which the community cannot reconcile. It therefore either develops ways to permit violations or it splits off the conflicting patterns and lets them go their own way.

How Violation of Norms is Institutionalized

There are several ways of institutionalizing nonconformity or violation of norms. There is (1) explicit *legal* provision for violation—individual and/or collective—of societal norms. There may be not legal but (2) *conventional or customary* provision for nonconformity which is not openly espoused but which operates consensually behind a façade. Finally, there may be (3) *tacit permission* to violate the legal and moral norms, sometimes bought and sold, especially in relation to the underworld.[1]

LEGAL PROVISION FOR NONCONFORMITY

Laws often make specific provision for individual or group nonconformity. Exceptions and exemptions are written into laws which provide explicit and accepted nonconformity to the general rule. Hardship cases or unusual cases, for example, may be granted permission to violate the norms. This is all above-board; the violation of the norms or nonconformity to them is institutionalized in a way that is in no sense itself illegal. Sometimes, to be sure, tricks or devices are used, such as turning back the clock or legal fictions or technicalities or re-interpretation or casuistry. A very fine line sometimes separates this kind of permitted or sanctioned violation from the third kind to be discussed below. But in its archetypical form it is often a necessary accommodation to the complexities of any living society.

CONVENTIONAL AND CUSTOMARY PROVISION FOR NONCONFORMITY

Conventions, as we have already pointed out, also belong to this category of above-board or sanctioned violation of professed norms, but they, too, merge imperceptibly into the doubtful area between accepted and tolerated. The mores state that one should always tell the truth; but convention provides for certain exceptions to this rule. It would, for example, be considered wrong in the sense of improper to tell a hostess her party was boring. We are required to say we are sorry when we are not. Conventions of academic freedom permit the discussion of topics in the classroom that the mores would forbid in other circumstances. Convention even permits rather gross violation of the mores. Thus if pictures of nudes are labeled as art, they are permitted.

Farther in the direction of unsanctioned behavior which is nevertheless protected by convention is violation of sex mores. The basic institutionalizing norms for permitting it might be summarized as: "keep your nonconformity as quiet as you can; don't openly flaunt the mores or the law; don't force us to take cognizance of your violations; don't be flagrant about

[1] Our major concern at this point is not with the way the nonconforming behavior is itself organized or institutionalized. It is rather in the way in which provision is made for violation of norms. A resistance movement is a collective way to violate the laws of a hated status quo; but it is not permitted by those in power. Gandhi perfected passive resistance and it was used successfully by his followers; but it was not permitted by the British. Soviet satellites, especially Poland, it is reported, have evolved collective patterns of nonconformity to Communist norms. But these are not accepted by the Communist party. One of the functions of cliques of workers in industry is to organize—informally and sometimes only implicitly—violation of management rules; but such nonconformity is not permitted by management. Crime is one of the most highly organized activities in American communities; but it is not openly approved. In brief, our focus of interest here is not the way the nonconforming behavior itself is organized but rather the institutionalized ways in which it is permitted, tolerated, or actually prescribed.

them; show a decent respect for the conventions of our society." So long as these rules are obeyed, individual nonconformity is permitted. The legal and moral proscription of adultery is a universal; the law makes no provision for exceptions or exemptions. A large amount of violation goes on—Kinsey reported between 35 and 50 percent of his cases—and provided it is not flagrant it is accepted by general consensus. People either pretend they do not know about it or they act as though it did not exist. If gossips ferret out violations and attempt to bring sanctions against them, the community may punish them for their pains. Here, again, the distinction between conventionally sanctioned violation of the norms and unsanctioned violation becomes very fine, as periodic exposés of scandals in government, in television, and in schools indicate.

THE SALE OF PERMISSION TO VIOLATE THE NORMS

Now we proceed somewhat farther in exploring permitted or tolerated violation of norms into an area in which the process is not legal nor conventional or customary and often not even explicit. In both of the situations described above, the function of permitted nonconformity was often really to permit us to be better than the law or the mores. In the situation here discussed it often has the effect of permitting us to be worse than the law or the mores permit. The phemonena here referred to have even been labelled as "contraculture"; they contradict the professed norms of the community. Permission to violate the law may become a marketable commodity. Payment is offered or exacted. Blackmail and/or bribery are, in effect, licenses or franchise fees for such nonconformity. The asking price for tolerance or permission is bargained out. This nonconformity may be collective rather than individual; it may be highly organized. It may constitute, in fact, a set of illegal institutions and organizations parallel with that of the conventional world. We are referring, of course, to the underworld.

Community Dissociation

The existence of the last two forms of institutionalized nonconformity to professed norms is here referred to as community dissociation.[2] This term provides a conceptual tool for use in perceiving and describing an important aspect of community structure.[3] The term is taken by analogy from

[2] The term "dissociation" has been used by Robert Merton to refer to a situation in which cultural aspirations are frustrated by the absence of institutional means for reaching them. The dissociation referred to is between means and ends. See *Social Theory and Social Structure* (New York: Free Press, 1957), p. 134. Merton uses the term "institutionalized evasion" for the phenomena here labeled dissociation (pp. 318, 343, 344, 345).

[3] Our culture has been called schizoid because of its many internal inconsistencies. See Read Bain, "Our Schizoid Culture," *Sociology and Social Research*, 19 (January, 1935), pp. 266-276.

the study of abnormal individual behavior. Students of such behavior have familiarized us with a type of split in personality which reveals itself in the form of two or even more distinct integrations of behavior within the same body. One may be conventional, respectable, circumspect; the other, often just the opposite. Usually the conventional personality does not know or recognize the nonconforming personality, but the latter often knows the conventional one. A common explanation for this phenomenon is that all the impulses to which the socialized personality refuses to give expression organize themselves surreptitiously, so to speak, and thus outwit the socialized personality. A harmless form is the dream; but these impulses may even integrate themselves strongly enough to take possession of the body. In this case we have multiple personalities alternating in possession of the body, or the suppressed personality may exist along with the acknowledged personality. Basic to this phenomenon is some kind of conflict which the personality cannot reconcile.

The existence of community dissociation, like that of personal dissociation, also results from conflict of one kind or another. Certain kinds of behavior are so incompatible with the professed ideals, values, and standards of the community that it is futile even to try to accommodate them. We have within ourselves conflicting values and goals. We "believe in" certain values but find it impossible to implement them. Or there is a conflict between the values of one segment of the community and those of another. The result is analogous to personality dissociation. The concept of community dissociation is admittedly an analogy, but the similarity of the two sets of phenomena is so striking that the term seems warranted. Communities, like individuals, may have "split personalities."

We distinguish two general forms of community dissociation, namely: façade dissociation and parallel dissociation. Façade dissociation refers to the situation when the members of the community profess one set of ideals and then behave according to a radically different code. Parallel dissociation refers to the existence of an underworld which exists parallel to the conventional world, of a "contraculture" which operates with the tacit but unacknowledged permission of the respectable segments of the population.

FAÇADE DISSOCIATION: IMAGE VERSUS REALITY

Before presenting illustrative cases it is important to emphasize that façade dissociation is not the same as hypocrisy.

Hypocrisy is an individual matter; façade dissociation is a collective phenomenon. In this sense it may be coercive, so that individuals who see through the inconsistencies or who comment on them may be made to feel alienated and isolated.

A sociological researcher is called into a hospital, say, and is shown the organizational chart with its clear and orderly map of status positions.

This is the theoretical structure of the hospital, the façade. He is not deceived. He goes about the building and observes and interviews; he studies reports and files. He returns and presents the operating map of the organization as contrasted with the theoretical one. Theoretically the nurses are subordinate to the doctors; actually they may be making the vital decisions. The research sociologist goes into an industrial plant, or university, or government agency, school, court, parish, any institutionalized situation, and he finds this discrepancy between the theory or image or façade and the functional performance of actual people. There is no question of hypocrisy here; everyone believes the organizational chart but so does everyone believe in the contradictory crescive norms which structure their relationships. As its name implies, façade dissociation refers to the existence of a public, official, avowed, openly espoused set of norms of behavior and the unofficial, but actual, norms which in fact regulate behavior. The façade represents an ideal, it stands for the image the community wishes to project of itself.

When we have only the official documents of a community to study, as in the case of vanished societies, we have no way of knowing how it actually operated, unless there are also tales or dramas or epics to supplement the documents. The life of the people may have been very much like the façade presented by the official documents; but the likelihood is that it was different.[4]

Illustrations from several functional areas of community life may clarify the nature of façade dissociation.

Façade Dissociation in Economic Institutions. In the field of eco-

[4] Façade dissociation is not, of course, limited to American communities. There is a similar split between theory and practice among Communists. Soviet social scientists announce that they have abolished exploitative classes and, along with them, the bourgeois evils that accompanied them. When asked about crime or delinquency or alcoholism they reply indignantly, "Why do you always probe our weak spots?" A continuing battle, further, is waged in the party against what is called indulgence toward dissipation in everyday life. "A most important integral part," said *Pravda* in 1955, of all Party activity should be the "struggle for 'strict observance of the norms of Communist ethics' " (*New York Times,* Apr. 8, 1955). Communist publications called for "most severe public condemnation of those who preach Communist morality in their official capacities but practice immorality in their private lives." *Pravda* said that "certain workers presume that it is possible to separate their professional activities from their private life, from their behavior in everyday life. That is not true." Five years later, Communists were still complaining that "instead of being dedicated warriors for communism, large numbers of Soviet citizens exhibit what seems to the true believer to be horrifying signs of ideological sickness. An uncomfortably large number of citizens get drunk from time to time. Others steal government property or commit other crimes. Still others put their own interests first and try to get paid as much as possible while doing as little work as possible. . . . The disillusionment with Communist ideology . . . appears to have produced among an important section of the Soviet population a sort of 'me first' attitude, a frame of mind leading to actions quite different from those implied by the stereotype of the ardent, self-sacrificing builder of communism that Soviet propaganda poses as the ideal type of Soviet citizen" (Harry Schwartz, "Russia: Switch in the Party Line," *New York Times,* Jan. 17, 1960).

nomic behavior, façade dissociation is illustrated by the contrast between theory and practice with respect to free competition. We profess to believe in the ideals of free competition and then proceed to violate the rules by handicapping opponents or by making agreements not to compete. We never really wish to have competition put rigorously into practice. We do not appropriate enough money to enforce the antimonopoly laws. We add amendments to these laws which nullify their intent. We permit trade agreements which restrict competition. All the legislation restricting free competition which we discussed in Chapter 9 illustrates a mild form of economic dissociation. We profess the ideal of free opportunity for individual ability, yet we permit unions to bar membership, so that some aspirants to their skills may not learn them. We permit some businesses to become so large that new firms find it impossible to get a start in competition with them. We proclaim a belief in laissez-faire, but we run to the government for protection whenever the going becomes rough. We never allow the "laws" of economic life to run their course; we are afraid of their drastic consequences. We believe equally strongly in a free individual enterprise system and in a regulating and protecting one. We are not here discussing differing interest groups in the community but rather the same groups accepting diametrically opposing points of view, and expressing shock and indignation if anyone points out to them the inconsistencies in their norms.

Façade Dissociation in Family Institutions. In the area of family behavior a similar conflict between theory and practice exists. When students are asked to list a dozen mores of our society they find no difficulty with, let us say, the tabu against cannibalism or against nudism. But how about sex relations outside of marriage, they ask. The law presents a clear-cut ideal with respect to this matter. It is that there shall be no sex relations outside of marriage. But how about the mores? Are extra-marital sex relations proscribed by them? If so, why are they so common and unpunished? Why does one study report that "85 percent of the total male population has premarital intercourse . . . , nearly 70 percent has extramarital intercourse, 37 percent has some homosexual experience. . . . The persons involved in these activities, taken as a whole, constitute more than 95 percent of the total male population."[5] If asked whether they "believed" in the sexual mores of our society most of these men would doubtless say they did. Still they also "believed" in violating them.

Motion pictures, television programs, popular fiction, drama, and other art forms make violations of the mores glamorous. Children soon learn that it is not infraction of the rule that is important; it is being caught that is bad. So long as lip service is paid to the professed moral ideal, actual practice is not important. If people are discreet, so that the community is not obliged to take cognizance of their nonconformity behavior, it is permitted.

[5] Kinsey, Pomeroy, and Gebhardt, *Sexual Life of the Human Male* (Philadelphia: Saunders, 1948), pp. 384-393.

Divorce legislation is another example of community dissociation in the area of family institutions. Societies have wanted to keep marriages stable but they have also wanted to provide escapes from marriage; and this has been true for centuries.

> That dissatisfaction with divorce laws and their administration is chronic is shown by the incessant criticism that has been voiced throughout the ages and by the gap between law and practice. Perhaps this is inevitable because of popular ambivalence towards the social institutions of marriage and divorce, the common desire to have one's spiritual cake and to eat it too, to profess high ideals but to seek personal gratification. If in reality we as a people are primarily committed to the pursuit of individual freedom and happiness, the sanctity of marriage most surely will be impaired whether our law on the statute books recognizes that fact or not.[6]

Pre-Communist China offers another illustration. When students of the Chinese family asked informants about family relations in China in the 1940's, they received answers that described the traditional Chinese gentry. Asked if their own families were like that, they replied, Why, no.[7] Their image of the Chinese family in no way corresponded to the actual Chinese family.

Dissociation in Intergroup Relations. We have already pointed out how actual practice with respect to minority groups violates the professed American ideal in many cases. People profess a belief in equality of opportunity and then deny educational and job opportunities to minority groups; they profess a belief in the Constitution and proceed to deny civil rights to nonconformists; they profess a belief in religious tolerance and then proceed to indulge in bigotry and hate-mongering.

Our professed or official institutions forbid discrimination on the basis of religious affiliation. Yet we know that such discrimination does exist in many communities. Certain schools and colleges have their quotas of Jews, Catholics, or Protestants beyond which admission is not permitted. Newspaper advertisements in communities that do not forbid such practices specify that applicants for jobs must be white Protestant, or at least Christian. Clubs, resorts, and hotels develop their own devices for keeping out unwanted groups. Such forms of discrimination have no overt, official, legal sanction; yet they are as clear-cut as any institution. The unwritten rules to which people conform are in direct contradiction to the ideals which they, in all sincerity, profess and they are oblivious to the conflict.

The traditional accommodation of the races in the South is a commonly cited example. It has been a permitted, even enforced, violation of the law. Behind a legal façade of equality, custom has not only tolerated, permitted, but actually prescribed inequality. The law prescribes separate but equal facilities for Negroes; separate they always were, but rarely were

[6] Henry H. Foster, Jr., "Spadework for a Model Divorce Code," n.d. (mimeographed).
[7] This illustration was supplied by Marion Levy.

they equal. The Constitution forbids deprivation of suffrage rights on the basis of race, color, or previous condition of servitude; violation of this law has been so firmly institutionalized in the mores and in custom that new civil rights legislation was required to make it possible for many Negroes to vote. Two well-integrated systems, in brief, have operated in the community—one an affirmed belief in the Constitution and one a well institutionalized system of threats and intimidation—and no one seemed to feel that there was any contradiction here.

The conflict between the two contradictory sets of norms, both equally accepted, has been highlighted in the case of a Southwestern community with the pseudonym of Descanso, as follows:

> There are no signs in Descano which say, "The State has a penalty for speaking broken English" or "By decree, preferential hiring will be given to native sons" or "By civic ordinance, all persons of Mexican descent, with certain exceptions, will be housed west of the railroad tracks." Descanso's best instincts would be outraged by such tactics. . . . But Descanso, having accomplished practically the same ends by indirection, considers its methods, not regimentation, but "common sense." Its practices toward its Mexican groups actually constitute a large unwritten body of law. This law, in effect, says: "Those of different culture and/or race, particularly if they lack economic power, are to be treated by standards inferior to those prevailing for residents of the United States at large." In carrying out the unwritten law, Descanso found it necessary to abridge a constitutional amendment, certain sections of the civil code of the state, as well as a civic ordinance or two of its own. The unwritten law, or any intimations of it, never stood a chance of getting on a statute book. Public opinion would not have stood for seeing it in black and white, for Descanso's assertion that it wants to be fair is not an idle one. If the cards had been laid on the table, in the form of crystallization of practice into law, Descanso would have been sickened by the sight of the marked deck it was dealing.[8]

The same might be said of any other minority group. The actual rules which govern the practice of the majority group do not correspond with the written rules. But the people are oblivious to this. As the author of the foregoing quotation points out, they would be horrified at the thought of putting the actual rules into writing. So long as they do not have to verbalize them they can dissociate the two conflicting patterns and accept both.

Shame, Guilt, and Community Dissociation

No one feels moral qualms about telling the hostess that her party was delightful, no matter how boring it really was; nor does any one feel qualms about the other white lies he tells to protect people's feelings. This guilt-

[8] Ruth D. Tuck, *Not with the Fist: Mexican-Americans in a Southwest City* (Harcourt, Brace & World, 1946), pp. 90-91.

lessness and lack of shame are characteristic of community dissociation when it is functioning well. Indeed, it is precisely to protect those who are involved from guilt and shame that dissociation—individual or community—exists; this is the function it performs.

Social psychologists make a distinction between shame and guilt. People who violate norms they have assimilated, norms they have "internalized," norms they believe in, are likely to feel guilt. This is a self-generated reaction. It can occur even if no one knows about their violation. The violation is almost self-punishing. Shame, on the other hand, is generated by the reaction of others to us. If we are found out in our violation of the norms of our community we feel ashamed. Shame and guilt may, of course, occur in the same person; but they need not. An alienated person might feel shame on being exposed in his nonconformity; but he might feel no guilt at all, just as a culture-comfortable person might feel guilt even if the violation was never exposed to the public. It is this distinction which lies back of the cynical cliché: it isn't the violation that's bad but being caught. It is this distinction which also makes it difficult to enforce community norms on the alienated; since they are not likely to feel guilt, they are more likely to yield to the temptation of nonconformity.

For decades no one felt either guilt or shame with respect to the exploitation of Negroes. It was not until the conflict between their professed belief in constitutional rights and the deprivation of rights of Negroes was forced upon them that some individuals began to experience guilt. And it was only those who were exposed to national mass media and who could therefore see their community as it looked to the outside world who developed any sense of shame about the conflict. For most people, however, the dissociation continued; of course they believed in the Constitution but—

The acceptance of the principle of the prohibition of sale of alcoholic beverages sometimes goes along with acceptance of the principle of the right to purchase alcoholic beverages; of course they believe in prohibiting the sale of alcoholic beverages but—Or gambling: of course it's wrong but—

Naïve, Cynical, and Sophisticated Definitions of the Situation

Some people take the façade of their community or society as the basic reality; they will admit that there are some people who do not live up to it, but such exceptions are few and far apart. This might be called the naïve image of the community. Some people, conversely, see the violations as the basic reality; they view the façade as window dressing, not the real facts of life in the community. This might be called the cynical image of the community. There are others, finally, who are knowledgeable about both the façade and the behavior behind it; theirs might be called the sophisticated image of the community.

The kind of literature that the local chamber of commerce publishes and the kind of material that goes into high school civics texts illustrates the image or definition of the situation which accepts the façade as the basic reality. The work of muckrakers, who investigate violations of all kinds of laws, of certain novelists and reporters, illustrates the second kind of image, the cynical one. The scientific researcher who studies all aspects of community structure, façade as well as the behavior behind it—one of the functions of such research is precisely to determine what goes on behind the façade—illustrates the third definition of the situation.

Parallel Dissociation

When sociologists began to study how societies actually functioned rather than how they are theoretically set up to function, they found not only such disparities between theory and practice, image and reality, façade and actuality as those referred to above as façade dissociation, but also a set of phenomena, related but not identical, which we have labelled "parallel dissociation." That is, parallel with an avowed policy which forbade gambling and prostitution, for example, they found well-established, institutionalized, though not openly recognized, systems of permitting these activities. Parallel with an avowed policy of prohibiting the sale of alcoholic beverages they found well-institutionalized systems of permitting such sale. Parallel with the official institutions they found a "contraculture" operating to outwit them. They found institutionalized ways of permitting forbidden or prohibited behavior.

Façade and parallel dissociation are not wholly separate and unrelated phenomena, but they are different enough to warrant a distinction. In façade dissociation it is the same people who set up the norms and also violate them. The conflict is between the norms they profess and the norms which actually regulate their behavior, or it is a conflict between norms, both of which they accept. It is an accommodation of conflicts within the people themselves. In parallel dissociation the conflict is between the norms of the respectable community and the norms of the underworld; it is between two different systems. It is a way of permitting conflicting systems to live together by a kind of institutionalized isolation or insulation. The respectable segment of the community does not have to take note of the contraculture.[9]

Parallel Dissociation As an Alternative to Community Disorganization

We are accustomed to thinking of crime or law violation as a disorganizing process. To be sure, Durkheim spoke of the integrating effect of crime; it united the group against a common enemy. Crime, however, is

[9] In terms of strategy, looking the other way is a method of shutting off communication. See Thomas C. Schelling, *The Strategy of Conflict* (Cambridge, Mass.: Harvard, 1960), pp. 26, 35-39, and especially p. 149.

usually viewed in its disorganizing aspects rather than the reverse. Yet Lincoln Steffens once said that sometimes crime is the only way to make a system work. Without it the system would collapse. Parallel dissociation is sometimes the only feasible alternative to community disorganization. If a thoroughgoing attempt were made strictly to enforce every statute on the books the result would be chaotic. It would, in the first place, demand greatly enlarged police forces. Courts, overburdened even now with their present loads, would stagger under the new demands. And, finally, jails and prisons would overflow. One judge, in fact, who was opposed to the gambling laws he was required to enforce, used strict enforcement as a form of direct action to dramatize the problems.[10]

The institutionalized pattern is, therefore, in a sense a bargain which may never be put on paper or even into words, completely tacit or implicit, which takes the form of an understanding that if the underworld will be discreet the police will look the other way. There need be no bribery involved, no corruption. It is a "gentleman's agreement."

The situation may, and in large cities usually does, become one of bribery. In most large cities payment is enacted for looking the other way. The payment is viewed as, in effect, a license fee.

Whether paid for or not, however, it is always understood that if the public is aroused, if violence breaks out, if publicity is generated, then the permission is withdrawn. Arrests must be made.[11]

In our society the contraculture is viewed as an underworld; the laws it violates are also mores of the respectable world. But in the USSR the contraculture is "capitalistic"; the laws it violates are not backed up by the mores of the rest of the society. It is easier, therefore, for us to view community dissociation there without involvement.

Until the decentralization of industry was begun in the USSR, every industry was run by a ministry in Moscow. The head of the steel industry, for example, was responsible for every plant everywhere in the union. He had to meet certain production quotas. Often the vagaries of planning put him at the mercy of other industries for procurement. In order to protect himself against bottlenecks that would slow down his own production, he tended to build up vertical integrations, mining his own coal, supplying his own specialized machinery, transportation, and other services regardless of what other ministries were doing.

The whole system would have collapsed of its own weight if it had

[10] Judge John Martin Murtagh, "Gambling and Political Corruption," *Atlantic Monthly,* November, 1960, pp. 49-53.

[11] In January 1960, Adam Clayton Powell, Jr., Negro Congressman from Harlem, complained that white men ran the numbers racket; the police denied knowledge of the situation. Yet as soon as Powell made his accusations, the police closed every gambling spot and arrested over 100 people. "One of the unanswered questions that I would like to pose," said Powell, "is how is it possible for the Police Department to say that they do not know the numbers operators yet, on a thirty-six-hour warning from this pulpit, were able to close down every place in this area and arrest over 100 people?" (*New York Times,* Jan. 11, 1960).

not been for the emergence of the "Fixer" who, by circumventing the official system, made it work. The Fixer was the man who arranged deals which violated the whole legal substructure of industrial organization as set up by the central planners but did get things done.[12] And the industrialists, when faced with the impossibility of achieving their objectives under rulings from Moscow, welcomed the services of the Fixer. The ways of procurement which they developed were contrary to law but they were efficient.[13] Everyone knew that laws of all kinds were being violated. The violation was sanctioned by custom. Even the Moscow ministeries winked at it "for without these informal arrangements production would have stopped or been slowed down while the various factories waited for the slow, creaking, ponderous machinery of the central bureaucracy to get to work."[14] It was the Fixer, specialist in *blat,* who made the cumbersome production system work. If it had not been for him, industrialists could not have committed the violations of the law that made possible achieving their production goals. If they had not used the services of the Fixer, who found buyers for sellers and sellers for buyers, the system would have collapsed. This kind of crime not only paid the individuals involved in it; it paid the whole system by making it work. It prevented complete disorganization.

American businessmen sometimes justify their own shady practices

[12] ". . . The main task of the Fixer was to ensure the smooth delivery of raw materials, building materials, special machinery, vital components, and so on; and his ways were often devious. If a bicycle factory in Novgorod found its production, its Plan, threatened for want of inner tubes, the Fixer would know where to get those inner tubes without red tape. The proper channel would be for the factory director to request his trust to indent for the tubes through the Moscow Ministry, which would then contact the relevant tire trust—and so on. The Fixer would cut across all that. He might arrange a straight barter deal with an individual tire factory, so many inner tubes in return for so many finished bicycles for the use of the tire-factory workers. But that depended on the director of the tire factory being in need of bicycles, which he probably was not. So the Fixer, in contact with fellow-Fixers, would discover that bicycles were badly needed by a cement works in the next town. . . . The bicycle factory had no interest in cement; but a neighbouring electric-cable factory was screaming for cement to complete a new range of buildings. Without the Fixers this would not seem to help very much. But it would take no time at all for an accomplished Fixer to discover that electric cable was just what the tire factory needed most in the world, and in that case nothing could be easier. The bicycles would go to the cement works; the cement would go to the cable factory; the cable would go to the tire factory; the tire factory would pay in tires—which would go direct to the bicycle factory (Edward Cruikshank, *Khrushchev's Russia* [Baltimore: Penguin, 1959], p. 75).

[13] The Fixer was a specialist in *Blat,* which is more than bribery; it is a pattern of living. "To have blat means that you are in a position to give favours in return for favours received. In bad times, and in its crudest form, it may mean that you are well in with the storeman on a nearby collective, who will let you have two hundredweight of potatoes (earmarked for delivery to the State) in return for a word in the ear of some State or Party official; and with these potatoes you can feed yourself and buy all manner of badly needed things. On a much higher level it may mean that you can get a doctor to sign a certificate saying that you need a month's free holiday in the Crimea. What do you do in return? Not necessarily anything: the doctor simply feels that you are a useful person to be friendly with because you have a cousin in good standing in the Moscow Soviet" (*Ibid.*, p. 72).

[14] *Ibid.*

with the argument that there is so much legislative restriction on their activities they could not operate if they did not ignore some of it. We know that no political campaign could be waged if the candidates obeyed to the letter the laws restricting expenditures. In brief, violating the law is alleged by some to be the only way a system can be made to work.

Our concern here, however, is not with law violation as a method of making a system work but with the way organized law violation is institutionalized in the underworld, with the way the relations between the underworld and the respectable world are conducted.

Parallel Dissociation: The Underworld[15]

Parallel dissociation is, in effect, a corollary to façade dissociation. It serves a similar function. In the conflict continuum we noted that if or when the conflict between or among the parties is so deep and so irreconcilable that no common elements can be found, community is dissolved either by the withdrawal of one party or by the elimination of one party. The conflict is dealt with by eliminating one or the other of the parties.

But such elimination of one or the other party may in certain cases take a unique and peculiar form. Instead of deporting or exiling or ejecting or in other ways getting rid of the opposing party, a community may simply declare it illegal, contrary to law, abolished. This declaration serves the function of formally getting rid of the opposing party. It is no longer in the community. There is no official recognition of it. The conflict has been dealt with by getting rid of one of the parties by, in effect, wishing it out of existence.

Actually the opposing party remains in the community, despite its formal and official nonexistence. But it is kept hidden from the respectable party.

HOW RELATIONS BETWEEN COMMUNITY AND UNDERWORLD ARE INSTITUTIONALIZED

The function of conducting relations between the respectable community and the underworld is performed by politicians and police. The upper echelons on both sides are like a state department that conducts negotiations with foreign powers. They have a common meeting ground in the political arena. Sometimes the representatives of the outer world may decide on a policy of war; the orders go down the line and the power of the community is exerted against the underworld; in some communities it may even mean getting rid of the underworld. But usually the policy makers decide on peaceful coexistence. So long as the underworld remains

[15] The term "parallel dissociation" is limited to the underworld to distinguish it from ordinary conflicts among ethnic and racial groups. It is not the same as "cultural parallelism" sometimes advocated for ethnic-group relationships or "racial parallelism" sometimes advocated for race relationships.

orderly, inconspicuous, and does nothing to outrage the outer world, it will not be molested. Orders go down the line and police officers no longer see violations of the law.

The modern underworld could not exist without political protection. The underworld therefore makes it a point to control as nearly as possible the sources of legitimate power. Since the politicians who decide on the policy to be pursued by the outer world vis-à-vis the underworld in any community are of such critical importance, it is toward the control of these men that underworld leaders address their major efforts. They purchase their franchises to violate legal norms from them. They start at the beginning. They make large contributions to election campaigns. It has been estimated, in fact, that organized crime pays for 15 percent of all campaign expenditures at state and local levels, roughly ten times the amount contributed by organized labor.[16] One underworld official is quoted as saying, "Show me a punk who wants to run for office, and I'll show you a man who can be had."[17] Such payments—and those to police officers, to be noted below—are viewed by the underworld as a normal expense of doing business. If the underworld could not exist without the protection of the politician, so, conversely, it might be said that the politician in many cases could not exist without the support of the underworld.

Once in office, a powerful strategy of control by the underworld is blackmail. It takes only one mistake, fixing one case, for example, to give the underworld a weapon against an official. Fear of exposure then cements the alliance with the underworld; and the more fixes engaged in, the firmer the cement becomes. "It is axiomatic in the underworld that once a public official allows a case to be fixed, thereafter the underworld owns him."[18]

The marginal men who patrol the border between the outer world and the underworld are the police officers; they are, literally, right on the firing line. But they are only the bottom men in the power structure. The policeman and the man who sells numbers or operates the bookie joint or operates the gambling parlor are relatively minor figures in determining the relations between the outer world and the underworld. Both are, in effect, employees or dependents of more powerful figures higher up. Both are taken care of by the higher echelons of the underworld. The little men of the underworld receive the protection of their employers, who pay their fines as part of the cost of doing business. But the policemen, it has been estimated, receive more money from criminals than they do from the taxpayers.

Aside from the temptations to which his position subjects him, the police officer is in a particularly vulnerable position. Even with the best

[16] Daniel P. Monyhan, "The Private Government of Crime," *The Reporter,* July 6, 1961, p. 18.

[17] *Ibid.*

[18] Kefauver Committee Report on Organized Crime, 1944, p. 163. For an explanation of this in terms of strategy, see Schelling, *op. cit.,* p. 13.

intentions in the world he may find himself punished if he carries out his duties when this is against the policy decided upon by those higher in the power structure. Although men create systems, a specific individual man may find himself trapped by it, powerless to act contrary to it, as we noted in Chapter 3. In addition to the whole question of payment for looking the other way, the police officer is subject to a set of subtler hazards and dilemmas peculiar to his role.

HAZARDS AND DILEMMAS OF THE POLICE OFFICER'S ROLE

It often happens that both the police officer and his opposite number in the underworld come from the same general background, that his personal sympathies are with his opposite number whom he has known from childhood. It may even happen that one son in a family becomes a police officer and another an employee of the underworld. Roger the Terribly Touhy, the notorious Chicago gangster, was a police officer's son.

Even in a well-intentioned police force, therefore, the well-intentioned police officer may find himself caught in a dilemma. Both the outer world and the underworld compete for his allegiance. He has to decide between doing his duty according to the official definition of his role and accepting pay for not doing his duty as so defined. He must weigh the odds between being caught and not being caught; or even without pay, between performing his role one way or performing it another way.

Paradoxically, too, he may be more effective in achieving order by laxity in law enforcement than by rigor. If, for example, he conceives his role to be that of keeping order on his beat, he may decide that developing close ties with the people he deals with enhances his potential as a mediator so that he can settle difficulties on a personal basis and not have to make arrests.[19] If the outer world defines his role as a strict enforcer of the law, without fear or favor, then good strategy demands that he should not identify with the people on his beat; if he does, he will not be able to act against them as the law demands.[20] As a matter of fact, the policeman is likely to conceive his role to be that of regulating illegal activities rather than as that of enforcing the law, and to act accordingly. Under these circumstances it has been said that the remarkable thing is not that so many police officers throw their lot in with the underworld but that so many do not.

The relationship between the police department and the underworld fits the specification of bargaining in a mixed-motive game. They have a common interest in maintaining order, in keeping down violence, in not arousing public opinion, in remaining inconspicuous. But they also have conflicting interests: the underworld wants as much protection as it can

[19] This discussion of the underworld is based on William Foote Whyte's perceptive analysis in *Street Corner Society* (Chicago: University of Chicago, 1943), pp. 136-139.

[20] For a discussion of the strategic aspects of police-public relations see Schelling, *op. cit.*, pp. 146-147.

get for as little as it can pay; the police department wants to minimize the hazards of protection for as large payments as it can get. To make this statement does not imply that there is a wilful conspiracy between the police department and the underworld to agree on a common policy. "The relations between them are established not in the mass but between individuals of both groups, and the actions on both sides become a matter of habit and custom just as they do between other people and other groups."[21] The situation may be an institutionalized tacit game.[22]

[21] William Foote Whyte, *op. cit.*, p. 139.

[22] "In times of crisis it becomes difficult for the policeman to play his dual role. An outbreak of violence arouses the 'good people' to make demands for law enforcement which must be carried out to a certain extent, even when they disturb police-racketeer relations [conflicting interest]. Therefore, it is in the interest of the departments to help maintain a peaceful racket organization. Since competition in illegal activities leads to violence, it is also in the interest of the department to cooperate with the racket organization in eliminating competition [common interest]. By regulating the racket and keeping the peace, the officer can satisfy the demands for law enforcement with a number of token arrests and be free to make his adjustment to the local situation" (*ibid.*, pp. 138-139).

Part VIII

The World Community

28

The Area of Interdependent Decision Grows

There was a time when African tribes could decimate one another and there was not a ripple in the diplomatic circles of the great capitals of the world. Riots could occur in Russia and American policy was not involved. Revolution succeeded revolution in South American countries without reverberating throughout the world. No more.

The world has become a community not only because all peoples have many common interests but also because major decisions in all great nations are interdependent. The success or failure of policies, the wisdom or folly of actions, depend not only on conditions and circumstances we can control but also on conditions and circumstances we cannot control, on conditions and circumstances, in fact, which are controlled by others.

So far we have spoken primarily of the local and national community because that is the closest to our everyday lives and the processes at work there are more easily illustrated by events that strike home to all of us. But it does not take much imagination to see that the same fundamental processes are at work in the world community also. The nature of community processes is basically the same, although the larger scale and greater complexity of the world stage may obscure this fact. But competition and conflict are as real at the international level as they are at home. And attempts to institutionalize them as urgent, if less successful. A brief survey of the salient facts should convince us of this general truth.

Economic Competition

Just as communities in the United States compete for industries, so also in the second half of the twentieth century do communities in Europe compete for American industries. Thus Frankfurt, in an advertisement, sounds very much like any American community when it states:

> Despite its tremendous growth, Frankfurt is looking for still more industry. We have the space for it. We have all the necessary resources, like sufficient

power, a reservoir of skilled and semi-skilled labor. And we offer the fullest co-operation not only of the Frankfurt financial community but of the Frankfurt municipal authorities. Particularly, we are interested in talking with American business officials thinking of establishing European manufacturing facilities, or expanding their existing European facilities.[1]

And Holland makes its bid with such inducements as desirable industrial sites, economic and political stability, transferability of profits, low production costs, easy access to raw materials, easy access to markets, and freedom of operation, and duty-free access to European markets.[2] Cologne and Lübeck were also bidding for industries. In fact, the success of European communities in attracting American plants was becoming a matter of concern to many Americans by the 1960's.

Aside from communities, the economic competitors in the world community are the industries in the several industrialized nations. The objects they compete for are markets, both for acquiring raw materials and for selling their finished products. The usual continuum, ranging from cutthroat competition at one extreme to monopoly at the other, can be found on the international level as well as at home.

Cutthroat competition in international economic life sometimes takes the form of "dumping," that is, of selling products in a foreign market below cost in order to keep the home market up, or to undersell a competitor, or to forestall competition. Or it may take the form of an export subsidy by the government to enable sellers to dispose of their wares abroad at an unprofitable price. It may take the form of a tariff so high that foreign goods cannot enter the country, thus eliminating competition. It may take the form of lowering the value of the country's currency, which is, in effect, a form of price-cutting in foreign markets.

At home we have a Federal Trade Commission to pass on the fairness or the unfairness of competition in the market. In the international community there is no such umpire. The nearest approach is the International Monetary Fund, the member nations of which promise as a condition of membership not to engage in currency manipulation, that is, general price-cutting. In 1948, for example, 53 nations in an effort to institutionalize international competition drew up a code of fair international competition to be administered by the International Trade Organization under the general auspices of the United Nations. Among the practices proscribed was the use of quotas, subsidies, and discriminatory tariffs.

At the other extreme from cutthroat competition, there is in the international community the same tendency for competition to end in monopoly as there is at home. The result in the past was the international cartel. A cartel is an international agreement among big industrialists for the purpose of "regulating" or "organizing" or controlling the market in some

[1] *New York Times,* Jan. 13, 1959.
[2] *Ibid.*

particular product—rubber, industrial diamonds, chemicals, tin, electrical goods, optical goods, pharmaceutical products, or chocolate, for example—in order to stabilize it. The cartel assigned production quotas, restricted production, and divided the world market. In the past, British firms were usually given the British Empire, United States firms were given North and South America, and German firms were given European markets. The results of cartels were the same as the results of monopoly anywhere—scarcity, high prices, lowered standards of living for consumers.

Many European governments approve, indeed, foster, cartels. Many of the former colonial nations which depend on the sale of raw materials find themselves at the mercy of the vagaries of the international market for their product and they feel strongly the need for some form of organization, whatever it be called, which would do what cartels have done, namely stabilize the market.

The United States has opposed cartels. We have traditionally believed in free competition, whether or not we have been consistent in our actual behavior. But in the international community there are many complications which render the problem extraordinarily difficult, including the powerful monopoly exercised by the USSR, transforming competition to conflict.

What the most rational alternatives are to economic competition in the world community is not altogether clear. Equal access to raw materials and systems of priorities and of rationing have been proposed; just how they would be implemented is not certain. The Food and Agriculture Organization of the United Nations once worked on plans for distributing wheat and other agricultural products among the peoples of the world on a rational rather than on a blindly competitive basis; little ever came of them. The use of force—war—as a substitute for competition is, of course, the least rational of all.

The development of the so-called free market area of Europe, or the Inner Six, or the European Economic Community is a new attempt to institutionalize economic competition rationally. Within this community free competition is to be encouraged. But between this community and the rest of the world tariff barriers will continue.

Ethnic and Racial Competition

In the nineteenth century population theorists, influenced by Malthus, concentrated their interests on the problems of overpopulation. The great bugbear then was fear that population would tend to outstrip food supply. With the spread of the knowledge and practice of contraception, however, there was added to the original negative or preventative controls—celibacy and delayed marriage primarily—an effective method of controlling births; and the birth rate throughout the industrialized countries of the world, where records are available, tended to decline. The norms which had hitherto been taken for granted underwent transformation. When the death rate had been very high, the biblical injunction to multiply and cover the earth had been the chief rule with respect to reproduction. With the introduction of knowledge and devices of contraception, however, this old rule was abandoned. The size of families in industrialized countries, especially in western and northern Europe and the United States, declined markedly. The so-called small-family system was inaugurated. The rule now was to have only as many children as one could raise at the standard of living to which one was accustomed. The rate of population increase declined.

The alarmists then went to work to try to raise the birth rate. Biological competition, which had always been crescive in nature, now became contingent, a matter for government regulation. Laws and schemes to increase the birth rate became common practice in western and northern Europe. In general, these plans were of two kinds. One kind attempted direct help to families in the form of subsidies, privileges, or honors. Germany, Italy, and France used these methods. In Sweden, on the other hand, the method was indirect, in the form of community services to all families to help defray the expense of raising families; no means tests were required.

The reason for such emphasis on increasing the birth rate was the feeling that national survival, if not dominance, depended on a large population. Germany, for example, was frightened at the high birth rate of the Poles, Slavs, and Italians and felt that she had to outbreed them:

> In the course of its history every nation has passed through wars and economic catastrophes and still survived; but decline in fertility strikes at the very marrow of a nation's being. A dwindling posterity suggests the writing on the wall asking us: What of the future? The question includes the political one: What will happen if the neighboring nations remain immune from the disease of a declining fertility and continue to increase in numbers? Thus, for instance, though Italy has only 40,000,000 inhabitants, in round figures, the annual number of births exceeds the number in Germany. And in Poland, which has only 32,000,000, the annual number of births is equal to the German number. Among the Slav nations, and especially in the Ukraine, the birth rates are still higher.[3]

To counteract this seeming threat, the Germans had a well-worked-out scheme for outbreeding other peoples; it was planned that in less than two generations the result would be nearly 200,000,000 members of the *Herrenvolk,* or master race.[4] The Japanese government in 1920 had set a population goal of one hundred million by 1960 in order to maintain its leadership in the Far East.

France, one of the first nations to feel the results of failure in biological competition, feared that she would finally be blotted out as other nations

[3] Rudolf Frercks, *Germany's Population Policy* (1938).
[4] Max Mandellaub, "How Many Germans?" *The Nation,* Mar. 31, 1945, p. 362.

outbred her. Her birth rate had been falling most sharply and for the longest period among European nations. Efforts to increase the birth rate had been unsuccessful. The goal in 1946 was 12,000,000 babies in a decade. It was reported unofficially that Frenchmen were being encouraged to take hormone injections to increase fertility.[5] One leader proposed in 1947 that France be given a share of Germans to make up her own population deficit. The contrast between a population density of 196 per square kilometer in Germany and a density of only 75 in France seemed a threat to peace. Somehow or other, according to this view, other nations would also have to meet this competitive challenge in the field of population.

Great Britain, too, felt compelled to engage in the competition for more population. Winston Churchill, in a broadcast in March 1942, pointed out that "one of the most somber anxieties which beset those who look ahead is a dwindling birth rate in 30 years. . . . If this country is to keep its high place in the leadership of the world and to survive as a great power that can hold its own against external pressure, our people must be encouraged by every means to have larger families."[6]

Russia, which, after the Communist Revolution had instituted a very libertarian policy with respect to the family—in line with Marxian doctrine that the family was primarily a bourgeois property institution—later reversed this policy. She inaugurated instead a very strict, almost puritanical policy in order, it is alleged, to stimulate population growth. She began to give medals to prolific mothers, as well as bonuses that rose with each additional child, and to tax unmarried men heavily.

Most of the highly industrialized nations of the world, then, since they had declining birth rates, looked with fear—and some even with terror—at a future in which they would be swamped by more fertile people. "The fight with arms yields merely temporary decisions. The birth rate decides the fate of nations for a long time ahead."[7]

Americans never took kindly to the idea of a race for numbers. There was never a popular clamor for population increase. Even from a military standpoint sheer numbers were no particular asset. Modern wars were fought by scientists, technicians, and engineers. A smaller, well-fed, well-cared-for, well-trained population was at an advantage over a larger, hungry, poorly cared for, inadequately trained population.

The competition among the several nations of the Caucasian race is matched in seriousness by that among the major races of the world. During the last three centuries the white race has outbred all other races. This was the natural concomitant of industrialization. The introduction of power machinery increases wealth; medical science is stimulated as a result; the

[5] Guy Irving Burch, "The World Has Too Many People," *The American Magazine*, May, 1946, pp. 38-39.

[6] *Reader's Digest*, October, 1943, pp. 115-117.

[7] Hans Hertel, quoted by Mandellaub, *op. cit.*

death rate declines faster than the birth rate; and there is a great spurt in population growth. This time of population growth following industrialization has been called the swarming period. It results not from an increased birth rate but from a rapidly declining death rate. The last three centuries have been the swarming period for the white races and they became the largest single race in the world—over 1000 million. Negroes constitute a smaller proportion of the world's population today (about one-fifteenth) than they did three centuries ago (one-fifth) ; the same is true of the Mongolians.

In the 1950's the situation was changing. Modern medicine and sanitation were reducing the death rates in underdeveloped areas very rapidly; but birth rates remained high. The result was an unheard of rate of population increase. The checks that had been able to operate when the West industrialized did not operate.

In 1957 China became interested in population controls. An editorial in a party newspaper, *People's Daily,* reported that health department workers had been instructed in August, 1953, to give birth control information to the public. No one was to be forced to limit family size, but it was "suggested that Chinese should change their custom of early marriage and that propaganda should be directed toward encouraging youths not to marry until they were 25. Contraceptives should be sold at cheap prices and all methods of birth control should be investigated and those that are safe should be widely practiced. . . ."[8] Soon after this, however, there was a complete reversal in policy. Population control was abandoned. And Mao-Tse Tung was alleged to have said that if a nuclear war came and destroyed more than half of all the people in China there would still be three hundred million left. The implication was that a large population was wanted not necessarily for aggressive warfare but in order to have enough to spare in case of nuclear war.

Japan and India made and continue to make population control a part of national policy. Japan succeeded, but the problem in India was more difficult because the people were less educated and industrially more retarded.

When the United States was asked for help by underdeveloped areas in controlling population growth it was argued by some that to offer such help would be interpreted as an inverse kind of competitive technique. Instead of racing to outbreed the darker races, the white race was, in effect, trying to achieve the same end by slowing down their rate of increase.

In speaking of this ethnic and racial competition in the world community can one apply any criteria of "fairness"? What, first, is it testing? Do we have here a case of Darwinian "natural selection"? or Spencerian "survival of the fittest"? Was the white race fittest to survive during the last three centuries and has it now become effete and therefore no longer

[8] Reported in the *New York Times,* Mar. 6, 1957.

fittest? Are the swarming Asiatics now the fittest to survive because of their rapid increase? Such questions are meaningless. The rapid increase of the white race in the last three centuries tested only their superiority in science, wealth, medical care, and sanitation, that is, cultural and technological superiority. In that sense the competition was "fair." But any race may borrow and assimilate these cultural assets. When it does, and lowers its death rates, shall we then speak of it as fittest to survive?

Obviously the whole framework of evaluation is too narrow for the problem as thus stated. It may not seem fair to us to have the Asiatics outbreeding the white races; but as they become industrialized, that will be the result. As population theorists have been telling us for a long time, and as sociologists have been supplementing their statements, the white race is going to have to face the fact of swarming Orientals and somehow or other arrive at a rational solution to the division of the world's area and resources.

Religious Competition

On the world stage, religious competition has been intimately related to political forces. In the past this was reflected in the fact that "the type of Christianity prevailing in any region . . . tended to reflect that of the western nation . . . there dominant."[9] Thus Protestant missions prevailed in British possessions, Roman Catholic missions were dominant in French, Belgian, and Portuguese areas. The relative strength of Roman Catholicism in the Dutch East Indies varied with its strength in Holland. Since the United States had no colonial empire, its missionary activities were influenced by American business spheres of influence; they were especially strong in China, Korea, and Japan.

Whatever there was of modern medicine and sanitation in most underdeveloped nations when they achieved political independence was likely to have been the result of missionary effort. "Schools for the blind, leper asylums, famine relief, public health education, western forms of athletics, agricultural improvement, action against slavery, the abolition of the opium traffic . . ." have been missionary projects.[10] In some countries the only college-educated people were those educated in schools founded and operated by missionaries.

World War II had a devastating effect on the physical equipment of many missionary churches, especially in the Orient. But it had an even more profound effect on the peoples toward whom missionary efforts had been directed. Nationalism, which came with almost explosive force with the attenuation of colonialism, became accentuated and it has now become a

[9] K. S. Latourette, "Missions," *Encyclopaedia of the Social Sciences* (New York: Macmillan, 1933), Vol. 10, p. 536.

[10] Latourette, *loc. cit.*

strong competitor of Christianity. In Egypt, for example, nationalism has meant greater emphasis on Islam, resulting in restrictions on Christians and especially on Christian conversion. Communism, although to a lesser extent than nationalism, has also become a competitor.

Political forces are more powerful than ever in religious competition. Islam, which for centuries had not been a proselytizing religion, has re-entered the competitive race as part of the anticolonial movement.

> A resurgence of zeal for conversion to Islam of the colored races has accompanied the winning of political independence and the strong ties of national sentiment. With government according to the principles of Mohammed becoming practical politics, a new vitality is being infused into what is held out to be the Black Man's religion. In this the hand of Cairo exerts strong political pressure.[11]

If the success of Islam were at the expense of native African religions only, most Western observers would feel a gain had been won. Actually, however, Islam competes not only with native religions but also with Christianity. And it has an advantage in this competition. Catholic missionaries are quoted as saying, for example, that it is closer to the African villages, finds compromise with fetishism easier, does not have to quarrel with polygamy, and is not handicapped by being identified as the white man's religion.[12] No race bias goes with it. In fact its antiracism is one of its strong "selling points" and it goes well as part of the repudiation of departing colonial masters.

It is difficult to state exactly what values are being registered by religious competition. In underdeveloped areas the native is very practical. He asks: Can your God serve me better than my own? If the missionary brings science with him, he can demonstrate very objectively the superiority of his God. And that is why modern missionaries leaned so heavily on medical and agricultural science for converting natives. More recently, however, science, technology, education, hospitals, sanitation, and other humanitarian projects have become governmental activities. The missionary is left only with his God; and many anticolonial leaders reject the racism of so many of His followers.

An interesting if not important aspect of religious competition in our day is the success in the West of Zen Buddhism which appears to attract many who find solace in its message.

In 1960 the United Nations attempted to institutionalize this religious competition by proposing a 16-point code of rules to guide governments in the eradication of religious discrimination. Among many other items included was one calling for "freedom to disseminate a religion or belief, provided it does not impair the rights of other religions or beliefs" and another calling for "freedom to maintain or change religion."[13]

[11] The ecclesiastical correspondent of the London *Daily Telegraph,* quoted by James Reston, *New York Times,* Mar. 26, 1960.

[12] *New York Times,* Feb. 5, 1961.

[13] *New York Times,* Jan. 9, 1960.

Political Competition

Nowhere are the principles of competition more useful in attempting to explain or interpret behavior than in the area of political competition in the world community today. To the man-on-the-street and letter-to-the-editor-writer the use of human resources to explore space when there are so many more immediate uses for them seems quite nonrational. Why try to reach the moon when there is still so much to be done on our own earth, they ask.[14] Despite President Eisenhower's insistence for many years that we were not in a race with the Soviet Union, we were, or found ourselves, in such a race. And the values being registered by that competition covered everything from ability shown in Olympic games to dancing skill. On the part of the United States, it was often defensive competition; we engaged in it because we were, in effect, forced to by the Soviet challenge.

When Nikita Khrushchev suggested that competitive coexistence be substituted for war between the Communist and the Western world[15] almost every aspect of national life became competitive, whether we wanted it to or not. It was said that whatever we wanted to do in the United States came to be justified on grounds that we had to outdo the Russians. We spoke of the "race" in technology, space, productivity, rate of economic growth (Fig. 28-1), number of engineers and scientists—in almost everything, in fact. The scorekeepers were the "uncommitted" nations.

Except in the United Nations, which we are disregarding at this point, there is no formal or institutionalized election in international political competition. The competition is not for office. It is, however, like all political competition, competition for control of policy. It does not take the shape of an avowed campaign, but it has all the earmarks of a campaign.

The Communist bloc, led by the USSR, and the West, led by the United States, are competing for the "votes" of other nations. Or, as we sometimes say, two ideologies are competing for the allegiance of men everywhere. Specifically the two parties are trying to "sell" their social and political and economic philosophies. Competitive coexistence refers to this process of winning support or allegiance.

[14] The reluctant nature of United States participation in the scientific "race" with the USSR was illustrated by the concern shown by scientists over the direction it took. They asked, in effect, "in the rush to engage in an item-by-item scientific race with the Soviet Union, have some costly prestige projects been undertaken that will take away dollars from other more important areas of research?" And is it wise for competing uses for our resources to be decided upon by criteria imposed by this race? "What worries many scientific advisors within the Government is that the nation may be dragged piecemeal into such an expensive program with no clear national decision that reaching the moon is more important than other scientific and educational programs on earth: (John W. Finney, "Changes Weighed in Science Policy," *New York Times*, Jan. 29, 1961).

[15] In March, 1959, he said: "We believe in our social system, and we prove and will prove our belief not by means of war, but by peaceful competition, by developing cultural and economic contacts with others. We will fight for our ideas not by means of war, but by struggling for man's mind. And man's mind can be conquered only if man himself understands which idea is better."

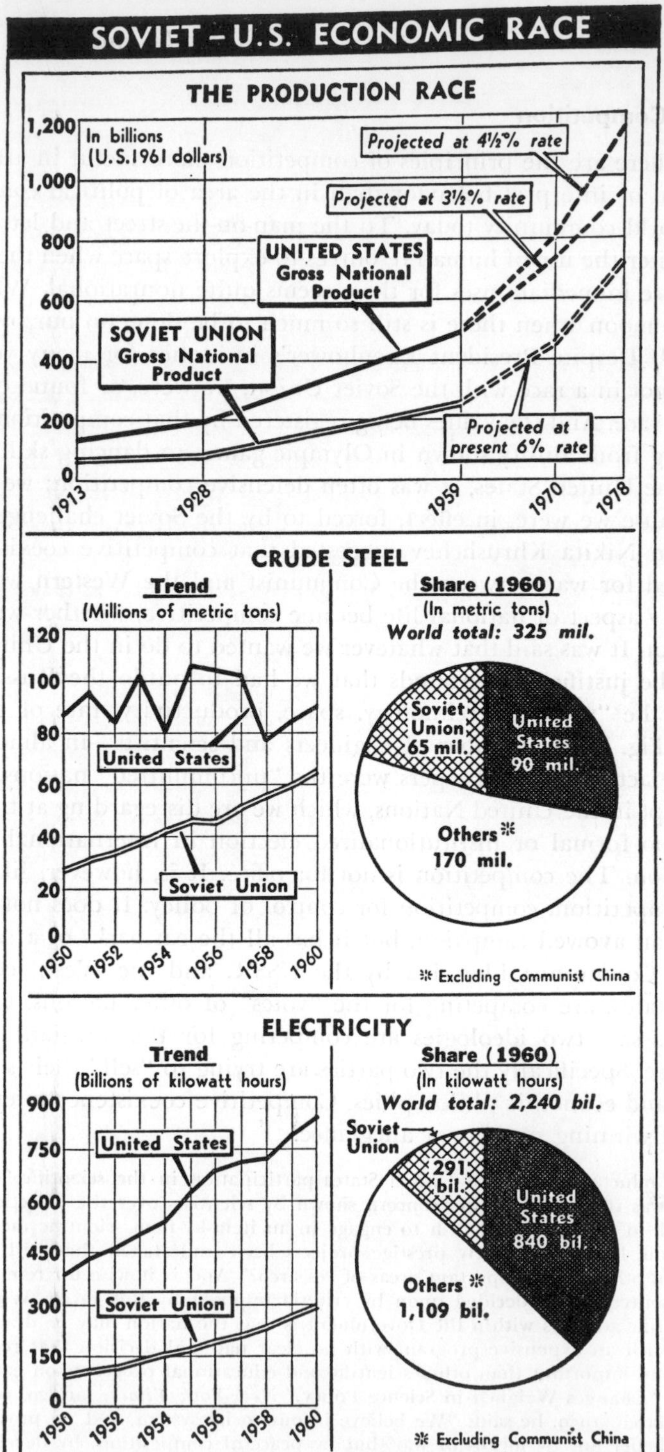

FIG. 28-1. Top chart based on figures used by President Kennedy, in a news conference June 28, 1961. Lower charts drawn from U. N. data. (Reprinted from the *New York Times,* July 2, 1961.)

In addition to the standard techniques of verbal propaganda, propaganda of action was also invoked. Khrushchev made industrial productivity a major criterion of a political system, claiming that the Soviet system was so superior it would ultimately and inevitably bury the capitalistic system without having to fight it. He thus laid down the challenge which became an issue in the United States. It had long been pointed out that the successful functioning of our own system was the most powerful competitive technique in our repertoire. It had been argued that if we can manage our own economy without too much overt hostility, offer good wages, produce enough for high consumption, and offer political equality and social welfare, this would be incontrovertible evidence that democratic capitalism was better than communistic or totalitarian processes. Khrushchev managed, nevertheless, to change the values registered by competition from actual levels of functioning to relative rate of growth. And here, for many reasons not germane here, the USSR was ahead.

Nonpolitical assistance to underdeveloped areas has also been used in this political competition. The side that offers more gets the "vote." For example, "the Soviet Union and the United States are competing over which can offer the handsomest subsidy to the tin mines in Bolivia."[16]

During the 1940's and the 1950's the peoples of the world found it to their advantage to exploit this market for their "vote" to the limit; they forced the contenders to up their bids. There was almost a race to see which country, the USSR or the United States, could build more dams, steel mills, irrigation ditches, or send more engineers, technicians, and medical supplies. In his inauguration address in 1961, however, President Kennedy announced that help from the United States would be offered not because it was being offered by the USSR but because it was right. The United States was not going to ask that nations be on our side; it was going to ask only that they be on their own side. He announced that American foreign policy would be determined not by defensive competitive reaction to Soviet challenges but on the basis of what was right on grounds of human welfare. In strategic terms he was substituting a higher imputation for a bargain.

Whatever might occur in the competition for the votes of uncommitted nations on the diplomatic level, in cultural and scientific achievements the competition continues. Not only the exploration of space, but also the peaceful uses of atomic power have political coloring as each competitor seeks to outdo the other in impressing the world. There has developed a prototype of the "moral equivalent" of war which the psychologist William James had called for early in the century.

What values are really being registered? If it is really testing the ability of two contrasting systems to achieve a just social order with a minimum of human sacrifice, it is a worthwhile effort. It would be fine if we could

[16] Peter Bart, "U.S. and Soviet Battle over Bolivia's Tin," *New York Times*, Jan. 22, 1961.

actually test the superiority of one or the other system in a scientific fashion. This is, of course, impossible. It is not a purely intellectual or objective race. We cannot imagine ourselves conceding that we are wrong, no matter how convincing the performance of our opponents may be; nor can we imagine the USSR conceding itself wrong.

Is this competition fair? At home there is a Federal Trade Commission to decide when advertising is false or misleading. Is it fair, for example, for the USSR to keep harping on race relations in the United States? On economic inequalities? On our failures in minority-group relations? On the frivolity of so many motion pictures? On strikes? Should they not, instead, emphasize our successes as much as our failures? And conversely, is it fair for us to emphasize the relatively lower standard of living of the USSR? Their lack of civil liberties? The lack of glamor in everyday life? Is this cutthroat competition? Is the censorship exercised by the State in the USSR a monopolistic practice and hence unfair? Even applying the concept of "fairness" to political propaganda on the world stage seems absurd.

Political-Economic Conflict

Economic conflict in the sense of buyers and sellers bargaining with one another over prices does occur in the world community, whether in terms of ordinary money-mediated trade or in terms of barter. But the relationship between economic and political conflict is very close and it is almost impossible to disentangle them.

There has been a change in the relationship, however, in recent decades. Whereas formerly political conflict was incidental to economic conflict, in the world today the reverse may be true; economic conflict may be incidental to political conflict.

POLITICAL CONFLICT AS AN ASPECT OF ECONOMIC CONFLICT

The conflicts between or among the "haves" vis-à-vis the "have-nots" were primarily economic, but they depended on political support. The great powers fought among themselves for colonial empires, but for the most part they did not rely on economic forces to decide the issue. If they did, the form the economic struggle took may have involved political weapons such as sieges or blockades or cutting off of supplies.

As among individuals, the simplest form of economic conflict occurred in a pretrading or premarket situation, as when one group owned or controlled something—land, harbors, mines, oil wells, transportation systems, or routes—which another group wanted and therefore attempted to appropriate by force and, if necessary, even by violence. There was no show of trade. Sometimes there was a rudimentary form of trade, as when the English and Dutch traded baubles or whisky for land in America. The old saying was that trade followed the flag. Often, however, it was just the reverse: the flag followed trade. In the case of the British Empire, for example, the characteristic pattern was for traders to set up businesses all over the world and then, in order to assure themselves of favorable government and protection, to call upon the Crown to protect them and to take over the local government if necessary. If force, violence, even warfare ensued, these were considered part of the price that had to be paid.

Colonial empires represented the exploitative level of international economic conflict. The industrially advanced country annexed the industrially undeveloped country and established a trade relationship favorable to its own economy. Manufactured products went from mother country to colony; raw materials went the other way. In order to protect the market for industrial goods, the colonial country might be punished for developing itself along industrial lines. Americans are familiar with this pattern from their own history. The American Revolution was in part a rebellion against it. A modern counterpart of colonial imperialism is the method employed by the USSR whereby satellite nations are incorporated into its economy on an exploitative basis.

The old colonial relationships have all but disappeared, and where they have not, they are in process of dissolution. In some instances the former colonies choose independence; in others they remain within a "commonwealth" or "community" and the relationship is transformed into a mixed-motive game in which the advantages of remaining together influence the strategies used.[17]

ECONOMIC CONFLICT AS AN ASPECT OF POLITICAL CONFLICT

Economic conflict as a technique of political conflict was first perfected by German cartels.

In the 1950's the USSR also used international markets as part of political conflict. Dumping, undercutting, and manipulation were allegedly used to disorganize the economies of opponents. One of the last pronouncements of Stalin welcomed the destruction of a single world market and the evolution of two parallel world markets, one Communist and one non-Communist. Such a system, he thought, would render the Communist

[17] The case of Great Britain is illustrative: "Britain has done well by its former empire. In the past five years British aid to Commonwealth countries has exceeded $3 billion. Of the new capital invested since 1947 . . . 70 percent [has come] from Britain. But outside of Canada and Australia, this great area . . . is poor. It must have industries. It needs 650 million jobs; they are the precious metals of today. And industries mean competition. The full weight of this low-wage competition is likely to fall on Britain because, under the system of Commonwealth preferences, the entry of goods is restricted almost as little as the entry of people. What this means can be seen most clearly, and poignantly, in Lancashire. In face of unrestricted imports of cheap cloth from India, Pakistan, and Hong Kong, cotton mills have been closing every week in Lancashire—ninety during 1955, ninety-six in 1956, sixty in 1957, and five or six every month during 1958. Whole towns are now temporarily on the dole. India and Pakistan are voluntarily restricting their exports of cloth to Britain. . . ." (Report on London, *Atlantic Monthly,* January, 1959, p. 6).

world independent of imports from the non-Communist world but permit it to invade the free world market for its own purposes.

Soviet foreign trade was a state monopoly and could maneuver like any monopoly. James Reston quoted a "high official of the United States Government" as saying: "They control all of their foreign trade. They can use it as a political instrument regardless of cost. They can take losses to drive competition out of a given market precisely as large producers once were able to do to eliminate small competitors in this country."[18] In 1958 headlines began to point out that the Soviets were snapping up Uruguayan wool, flooding the world aluminum, tin, and platinum markets, and underselling the West in the oil market. Khrushchev had threatened to bury the West. This was one way of doing it.

The United States also used trade politically; it did not permit the sale of strategic materials to the USSR.

Economic conflict on the world stage has become so much a part of political conflict, that is of the cold war, that the idea of permitting economic forces to operate freely no longer prevails.

Race and Culture Conflict

Race and ethnic conflict on the world stage in our day has taken an unexpectedly brutal turn. In Germany, for example, race conflict became an accepted part of the national ideology and was carried out in systematic fashion. It took the form of genocide, so-called, that is, of exterminating whole peoples. Alfred Rosenberg, the official anthropologist of the Nazi party, pointed out that "history and the mission of the future no longer mean the struggle of class against class, the struggle of church dogma against dogma, but the clash between blood and blood, race and race, people and people." Marshal von Rundstedt, speaking before the Reich War Academy in Berlin in 1943, sketched the proper policy for Germany to pursue: "One of the great mistakes of 1918," he said, "was to spare the civil life of the enemy countries, for it is necessary for us Germans to be always at least double the numbers of the peoples of the contiguous countries. We are therefore obliged to destroy at least a third of their inhabitants."[19] He proposed organized underfeeding as a better method than machine guns for this purpose. But that is only one of the weapons in the arsenal of genocide. That these ideas were not mere fantasies is attested by the fact that an estimated 6 million Jews were systematically destroyed in gas chambers. As applied to occupied peoples genocide took the form of reducing the birth rate by keeping the sexes separated, chronic undernourishment, specific vitamin deficiencies.

[18] "Trade Policy Quandary," *New York Times,* Dec. 2, 1958.

[19] Raphael Lemkin, "Genocide—A Modern Crime," *Free World,* April, 1945, pp. 39-43.

Sometimes the objective is not to destroy the people as physical beings but to destroy them as bearers of culture. To do this one does just the opposite of what one does when one wishes to keep a system functioning well. Thus, for example, one weakens the cohesion of the several parts of the community "by dividing them into more or less self-contained and hermetically enclosed zones . . . to prevent communication and mutual assistance by the national groups involved."[20] Primary education is encouraged because it can be used as a channel of indoctrination of the young; and the acquisition of certain skills is permitted because they are useful. But liberal arts training is forbidden, "since that might stimulate independent national thinking." Religious sanctions must be thoroughly wrecked.

Short of thus exterminating peoples, one may simply subordinate and exploit them. Slavery was once an acceptable method of doing this; caste was another. Both are on their way out. Increasingly the darker races are rebelling against their status as exploited peoples. And increasingly they have the support of world opinion. The *apartheid* accommodation of race relations in South Africa—which seeks physical as well as social separation—is on the defensive. Other ways of accommodating the races of the world are in process of development.

Political Conflict: War and Deterrence

Nations remain in a ceaseless struggle to impose their own wills upon the world. Who is going to determine policy? Who is going to make the important decisions? Who is going to make the choices? Who is going to call the tune? The answers lie in the outcome of the struggle for power. We speak of "power politics." The expression is redundant. All politics is power politics. Whether a nation wishes to play this game or not, it is forced to do so if for no other reason than self-defense. For the equilibrium among nations is never perfect or complete. It is constantly being challenged. Now one nation runs the show; now another. There is always a runner-up ready to step in when the old champion shows signs of slipping.

The issues in political conflict in the international community are protean, as in the case of political conflict in the local community. The issue may be economic; it may be ethnic; it may be religious; it may, in fact, be anything at all. But whatever the issue is, the conflict itself is essentially political—that is, a conflict of wills as to who is to determine policy with respect to the specific issue involved, who is to control whom.

The stages in the accommodation continuum for political conflict in the international community range all the way from open warfare to complete union. At this point our attention is turned to the lower end of the continuum, to war and to deterrence.

[20] *Ibid.*

War, as Clauswitz is quoted as saying, is the continuation of politics with other means. In terms of game concepts, war may be viewed as both a strategy and as an outcome. It may, that is, be viewed as one of several alternative choices open to the players—nations—or it may be viewed as the result to be expected if one player selects A and the other player selects B. Any nation can have war if it wants war; the choice of war is made under conditions of certainty. But if war is viewed as an outcome, then choices are made under conditions of uncertainty. One choice will deter the enemy; another would not. The problems are quite different.

War as a strategy is selected, when it is, as the preferred means of gaining an end. It is weighed on a scale of values. At one extreme is the pacifist position; it places war at the very bottom of any ordering of alternatives; it is the least preferred: nothing is worse. It holds that the very values one may wish to protect by means of war—democracy, let us say, or free enterprise, or individual civil rights, or any other—are sacrificed in the process of waging war. At this evaluation level, war would never be chosen.

At the other extreme there have been those who glorified war. In contrast to the fundamental pacifism of Americans was the German ideal of war and militarism. It came to most Americans with something of a shock to find German writers who justified war as "a necessary phenomenon in the nationalist tradition"; who agreed with von Moltke "that permanent peace is a 'dream—and not a pretty one at that.' Only a nation that has preserved its will to wage war deserves to continue its existence. . . . Future wars will always find their moral justification before a 'superhuman tribunal' which alone is qualified to judge it."[21] Or another writer who urged the necessity of the "voluntary participation of a heroic nation united" in what he called " 'German Socialism,' conditioned and morally mobilized for the accomplishment of the only possible goal: permanent struggle, i.e., war." War to such men is at the top of a rational scale of values. It would be selected in preference to almost any alternative.[22]

Between the two extremes of pacifism and aggressive militarism lie attitudes toward war which assign to it differing values. Some people consider war bad but the lesser of two evils. They hate both. But war should be chosen, they argue, if the choice is, let us say, between submission to a

[21] J. Binder, *Die sittliche Berechtigung des Krieges und die Idee des ewigen Friedens* (Berlin: Junker und Duennhaupt, 1930). Present citation from *German Psychological Warfare,* edited by Ladislas Farago, p. 64 (Copyright, 1941, 1942, by the Committee on National Morale, Courtesy of G. P. Putnam's Sons).

[22] The apologia for war of this school of thought has some basis in fact. It is true that war does tend to unify a nation and to make warring factions recognize their basic community of interests. And wars have been used for just such purposes. It is true, too, that wars speed technological advance. Inventions are stimulated which would take years to perfect without the urgency of war. On the other hand, theoretical science suffers. It has been estimated that the taking away of young scientists from their laboratories in World War II set us back many years in basic theoretical research. The apologists for war point to the many and indubitable achievements made possible by war; they do not feel that the price is too high.

hated aggressor and taking up arms against him. Often, they feel, it is Patrick Henry's choice between liberty and death.

In the 1950's, with the improvement of military destructive power, the evaluation of war as a strategic alternative underwent a change. Only China among the great powers favored war unequivocally as a means to an end. The position of the USSR was based on a distinction among kinds of wars. On January 6, 1961, Khrushchev defined the so-called doctrine of three wars. These were: (1) atomic and hydrogen "world wars;" (2) limited or local war, and (3) wars of national liberation. He ruled out the first two as too destructive and therefore not a rational alternative. But wars of national liberation were not only permissible; they were inevitable and necessary and these he would support wherever they occurred. Most other nations judged war too expensive in every way. Thus although people continued to think about war, it became "unthinkable." The problem came to be not one of choosing between war and some other way of achieving a goal—with the certain knowledge that whatever one chose one would get—but rather one of deterring an opponent from going to war or from provoking one into war, in a situation not of certainty but of interdependent decision.

Deterrence problems are problems of choice among alternatives which must be made to avoid war as an outcome. Not war itself, but the ability to manipulate and maneuver, brinkmanship, is among the strategic alternatives. International relations, often referred to as a great chess game, have become a huge mixed-motive game. Both sides have a common interest in avoiding war; both sides have conflicting interests, or think they have.

Three kinds of deterrence have been distinguished in terms of the acts which are deterred. One is deterrence by automatic retaliation of a direct attack; one is deterrence by means of strategic threats of any provocative act that might require retaliation; and one is graduated deterrence, or tit for tat, which keeps the enemy from engaging in any act which could be responded to by limited actions, not necessarily involving total war, but serious enough to make aggression unprofitable.[23]

Political Conflict: Subversion

War is not, then, the preferred means to political power in the world today. Achieving the control of governments by subversion is a more desired method. There is, thus, as a consequence not only an ideological competition between the Soviet bloc and the West for the adherence of people all over the world but also active attempts to gain control of the governments of nations everywhere. Even, according to Khrushchev's doctrine of the three wars, fomenting and supporting revolutions if necessary.

[23] Herman Kahn, *On Thermonuclear War* (Princeton: Princeton University, 1960), p. 126.

The several branches of the Communist party in nations throughout the world are organized precisely for this kind of political conflict.

The United States, of course, also attempts to influence or control the legitimate governments of other countries. Thus the conflict between the great powers of the world may take the form of civil wars in Korea or Laos or Cuba or the Congo or where-have-you. The old colonial pattern gives way to a new one. But whereas the old conflict was between the colonial power and the colony, the new conflict is between two great powers, with control of the former colony as the stake.

Alternative Ways to Perform the Functions of War: "The Peace Game"

Quite aside from the glorification of war which militarists used to indulge in, there has been sober recognition by social scientists of the functions which war has performed in the world community. And if it is true that war, at least thermonuclear war, can no longer be depended on to perform these functions, then it becomes necessary to devise new institutions to perform them. We are not here speaking of William James's moral equivalent for war which was to be primarily psychological. We are speaking rather of effective ways to perform two quite contradictory functions, one of order and one of change. Wars have protected the territorial integrity of nations and thus maintained order; but they have also provided for the revision of national boundaries, for the creation of new nations and thus allowed for change. Wars have reallocated natural resources. Wars have even been resorted to to decide great moral issues. Wars have also determined or ratified the power relationships among nations, although in this day and age even fairly small nations can achieve thermonuclear bombs and thus wield at least extortionate power far beyond their resources.

Some of the new institutions required to carry out the functions performed by war will be purely domestic—using our productive resources for civilian rather than military purposes, providing careers for military men, providing employment for all now engaged in military production. Some will have to be world-wide. International courts have been instituted. The United Nations has been established. But we are a long way from acceptable institutions that can deal with all the problems and solve them as definitively as war can.

Competitive coexistence appears to be the immediate form which the substitute for war will take.

Organization in the World Community

In the remote past, when tribes or nations were small, they did not collide with one another very much. But even then there had to be rules to guide them when they did. At one time it was usual to try to exterminate one's enemies. Later on the rule was that one enslaved them. A rather important rule was that although one might raid another people and kill them, one did not take their land. The land belonged to the people in a mystic and inviolable way. The whole business of intergroup conflict early developed mitigating codes of behavior: safe-conducts for ambassadors, treaty-making rituals, places where war was not permitted, times when it was not permitted, rules about hostages, prisoners, and arms. Trade relations as well as military conduct were subject to rule. To keep trade from erupting into war there was the custom of silent trade. One group, as we saw earlier, left its goods at a specified place and retired. Its customers came, looked over the wares, and then left their own goods in payment. The whole business of trade became subject to rules of the market. In brief, international law is very old indeed. The moment isolation ceases, organization begins. Sharing a common world renders this inevitable.

The earliest international law was doubtless very informal, based on custom, mores, and tradition. There may have been peace conferences, intertribal councils, treaties, and alliances, but they were not expressed in written charters or constitutions. There were rules about how to fight and how to trade, but there was little if any administrative machinery to enforce them. The rise of great empires imposed a more rigorous kind of international organization upon peoples, with administrative systems to enforce it. The Catholic church set up an international organization that functioned with admirable efficiency in the trying period during which Europe was trying to reorganize itself locally under the feudal system after the collapse of the Roman Empire.

Modern international law, that is, the true law of nations rather than imperial or colonial law, was first formulated by the Dutch jurist Hugo Grotius in the seventeenth century. The main form which international law took in the nineteenth century was that of treaties of one kind and another, international conventions, and agreements. The Hague Tribunal, or International Court, was set up to adjudicate cases arising out of alleged violations of this international law.

The spectacular failures of world organization have tended to blind us to the very substantial amount of success it has achieved. When nations have felt their interests to be in common, as in fighting such common enemies as the traffic in women and children or the drug traffic, they have worked together to safeguard them.

The League of Nations did not prevent World War II, but it did offer a tremendous amount of international cooperation in fields where nations had a common interest, such as labor, health, and migration. The United Nations did not prevent aggression in Korea; it was impotent to help the Hungarians against Soviet suppression. It has, nevertheless, served an indispensable organizing function.

The developments in Western Europe in the late 1950's and 60's illustrate some of the basic sociological principles of organization on the world stage. The threat from communism led, soon after World War II, to the banding together for mutual protection of members of the so-called Atlantic community, in the coalition called the North Atlantic Treaty Organization. This was at first a purely military alliance. In addition, there evolved the European Economic Community, consisting of the so-called inner six nations which were pledged to integrate their economic systems and constitute a great free-trade area. This was soon countered by the organization under the leadership of England of the so-called outer seven into the European Free Trade Association. And, finally, early in 1960 plans were under way by the above thirteen nations and the U.S. and Canada to organize a still broader Organization for Economic Cooperation and Development.[24] The purpose of the new organization included accommodation of conflicts between the several sub-systems, but also the mitigation of wasteful competition among donor nations in extending economic aid to underdeveloped areas.

The advent of nuclear bombs has had a revolutionary effect on the relationships among nations. Not only did it stimulate cooperation in the form of Euratom or the European Nuclear Organization but the enormous destructive power which they make possible has forced a revaluation of the nature of war itself. Everyone has a common interest in seeing that no one has occasion to resort to its use.

Reprise

We began the study of the principles and problems of community life in American communities with the basic problem of how, within the restraints imposed by democratic values, do they institutionalize disintegrating forces and maintain community. How do they deal with differences? Without insisting on uniformity, why do they not fly apart at the seams?

American communities, it appears, are systems of change. The checks which operate in them do not restore them to a past status quo but always to a new and different one. No process is permitted to operate unchallenged. Men scrutinize their operation carefully and when the results are not to their liking they protest; consistency is not a god to be worshipped. Competition is not permitted to run its logical course; when the shoe pinches it is kicked off and a new one is fitted. A powerful set of institutions—legal and moral—has taught American communities how to deal with incompatible differences; conflict is viewed as a nonzero-sum game. It is institutionalized in a way to make it a source of strength rather than of weakness. Too great concentrations of power are thus avoided—there is always a countervailing power to share it—and the individual is protected

[24] Henry Giniger in the *New York Times,* Jan. 14, 1960. The Charter was ratified by the Senate in March, 1961.

from too great coercion. In the great duel between the individual and government, the edge is given to the individual; the price, a high crime rate, is not considered too high for the value received. These solutions to schismatic forces seem adequate to keep American communities from falling apart. When they are not enough, they dissociate incompatible differences from their professed values and proceed calmly as though they did not exist. Lumbering, slow, inconsistent, quite lacking in the apparent order of totalitarian communities, they have their own improbable stability; no group ever wins completely, or, if it does, remains the winner forever. The people who inhabit American communities are not Utopists; they are not fanatics. They do not look forward to the time when their communities will be perfect; they are satisfied if they can solve the parking problem or get several new plants to settle there. Cleavages there are, to be sure, and often violent ones. Sometimes they cut communities into shreds. But they heal. No one looks for inevitable progress; all that can be expected is that the crescive norms—the traditions of democratic community life—will be adequate to meet the new problems as they arise.

Index

n indicates footnote * indicates diagram